KOREA

Seoul Selection Guides: KOREA

Written by Robert Koehler
Photographs by Ryu Seung-hoo, Robert Koehler & Korea Tourism Organization

First edition published in Mar. 2012.

Published by Seoul Selection
B1 Korean Publishers Association Bldg., 105-2 Sagan-dong
Jongno-gu, Seoul 110-190, Korea
Tel: 82-2-734-9567
Fax: 82-2-734-9562
E-mail: publisher@seoulselection.com
Website: www.seoulselection.com

ISBN: 978-89-91913-99-8   13980   ·

Printed in the Republic of Korea

Printed by Leeffect Prepress & Print
Tel: 82-2-332-3584

Additional Photo credits
  Brenda Paik Sunoo: 648
  Derek Winchester: 65, 422, 425
  Image Today: 247, 312, 313, 619, 622, 624, 670
  Yonhap Photo: 15, 16, 19, 35, 37, 41, 51, 192, 194, 203, 208, 218, 237, 240, 241,
  254, 255, 259, 261, 262, 265, 283, 284, 319, 335, 371, 374, 406, 417, 420, 421,
  445, 447–452, 516, 517, 527, 528, 575, 584, 600, 605, 608, 620

This book is published under the sponsorship of Korea Tourism Organization.

SEOUL SELECTION GUIDES

K O R E A

WRITTEN BY ROBERT KOEHLER

TABLE OF CONTENTS

History & Culture

INTRODUCTION

Korea—Land of Contrasts

Korea is a land of dramatic contrasts. Boasting some 5,000 years of history, it is a country with one foot firmly planted in the past, but at the same time one dashing headlong into the future. In Korea, ancient temples and historic palaces coexist side-by-side with glittering skylines of glass and steel. In the countryside, high-speed trains blaze past tranquil pastoral landscapes little changed for centuries. One night you can be partying the night away at one of Asia's hottest clubs, and the next meditating at a serene Buddhist monastery on a remote mountainside. Even from the cacophony of downtown Seoul, verdant forests and pleasant hillside trails are never more than an hour away.

Long overlooked by international travelers in favor of its larger, better-known neighbors, Korea is finally coming into its own as a tourist destination. And it's about time. With exciting cities, a rich and ancient culture and splendid natural scenery, Korea's got something for everyone.

No country—let alone one like Korea—can be fairly reduced to a guidebook, no matter how many pages. Korea must be experienced to be properly understood. What this guidebook seeks to do, however, is point the visitor in the proper direction.

How to Use This Book

For practical purposes, this guidebook is divided into two parts:

Part One

This section introduces Korea province-by-province, exploring the wealth of history, culture and entertainment to be found within. General tourist information is interspersed with helpful and informative tips about local culture and history in order to enrich your experience. Each chapter is concluded with information on recommended restaurants in the area.

Part Two

This part provides basic information that visitors must know, including customs procedures, visa information, hotel information and the like. For the convenience of the user, information has been arranged in a logical manner so that you can find what you want to know quickly. A small section on the Korean language has been included, too—it won't make you fluent, but it will help you get around.

Features

This guide contains a number of special features that aim to enrich your travel experience, including a section on history, maps, tips and notes on Korean culture.

Korea's Best 8

Don't know where to begin? Too busy to fumble through the pages? Our opening "Korea's Best 8" lists will put you on the right track.

Itineraries

Here are some itineraries to get you started. We've organized our itineraries by theme—urban tours, history & culture, etc.—with three, five and seven-day options available.

History of Korea

We've managed to pack 5,000 years of Korean history into 10 concise pages. While you'll learn a lot about Korea's past while you're on the road, it helps to know a little bit before going in.

Maps

Lots of useful maps to give you an idea of where you've got to go. You can pick up more detailed local maps, too, at Tourism Information Centers found at many train stations, bus terminals and popular tourist destinations throughout Korea.

Travel Tips

These notes give you helpful advice on tourist destinations and tour options. They also include "Off the Beaten Track" destinations, including some of Korea's hidden gems.

History and Culture

These notes provide details and helpful historical and cultural background information on places, individuals and stories related to the city. Wondering who King Sejong the Great was? Haven't a clue about the Baekje Kingdom? Don't worry—we'll tell you all about them. You can read these while you're out and about or at your own leisure.

MAP OF KOREA

Goseong

Cheorwon
The DMZ
Hwacheon
Sokcho
Seoraksan
National Park
Yangyang

Gangwon-do

Chuncheon

Gapyeong

Paju
Namyangju
Hongcheon
Odaesan
National Park
Gangneung
Jeongdongjin

Ganghwa-do Island

Incheon

Seoul
Yangsu-ri
Gyeonggi-do

Hoengseong

Donghae

Suwon
Yeoju
Wonju
Pyeongchang
Jeongseon
Samcheok

Hwaseong
Yongin
Icheon
Chiaksan
National Park
Yeongwol
Taebaek

Chungju
Danyang
Sobaeksan
National Park
Uljin

Dangjin
Chungcheongbuk-do
Woraksan
National Park
Yeongju

Taean Haean
National Park
Seosan
Cheonan
Cheongju
Yecheon
Mungyeong
Andong

Hongseong
Songnisan
National Park
Sangju
Juwangsan
National Park
Yeongdeok

Chungcheongnam-do

Gongju
Gyeryongsan
National Park
Buyeo
Daejeon
Gimcheon
Gyeongsangbuk-do

Boryeong

Geumsan
Muju
Pohang

Gunsan
Jeonju
Deogyusan
National Park
Daegu
Gyeongju

Byeonsanbando
National Park
Jeollabuk-do
Gayasan
National Park
Cheongdo

Naejangsan
National Park
Hapcheon
Miryang
Ulsan

Gochang
Namwon
Gyeongsangnam-do
Yangsan

Damyang
Jirisan
National Park
Jinju
Gimhae
Busan

Gwangju
Hadong
Jinhae

Suncheon
Goseong
Geoje-do

Jeollanam-do
Namhae
Tongyeong

Mokpo
Wolchulsan
National Park
Boseong
Yeosu
Hallyeo Maritime
National Park

Heuksando
Haenam
Goheung
Dadohae Maritime
National Park

Jindo
Wando

Jeju-do

Yellow Sea

East Sea

South Sea

Ulleungdo

Dokdo

KOREA IN STATISTICS

- **Location** Northeast Asia, between latitudes 33° and 39°N, and longitudes 124° and 130°E
- **Area** 100,033km² (109th in the world)
- **Population** 48,580,293 (2010)
- **Population Density** 485.6/km²
- **Male/Female Ratio** 98.7 males for every 100 females (2010)
- **Life Expectancy** Male: 76.12 years, female: 82.7 years (2012 est.)
- **Urbanization** 83% of total population (2010)
- **GDP** US$1,014.3 billion (15th in the world)
- **GDP Per Capita (PPP)** $31,700 (2011 est.)
- **Average Marrying Age** 31.6 for men and 28.7 for women (2009)
- **Mean Temperatures** 22.5 to 25 °C (Jul), −5 to −2.5 °C (Jan)
- **Foreign Population** 918,917 (2010)
- **Exports** US$558.8 billion (2011 est.)
- **Chief Exports** Semiconductors, wireless telecommunications equipment, motor vehicles, computers, steel, ships, petrochemicals
- **Chief Export Partners** China 27.9%, US 10.2%, Japan 5.8% (2010)
- **Imports** US$525.2 billion (2011 est.)
- **Chief Import Partners** China 17.9%, Japan 16.2%, US 10.1%, Saudi Arabia 5.2%, Australia 4.9% (2010)
- **Chief Imports** Machinery, electronics and electronic equipment, oil, steel, transport equipment, organic chemicals, plastics
- **Crime Rate** 1,836,496 cases in 2007

<Sources: Statistics Korea, CIA World Factbook>

Scenic Spots

1

1 JEONGDONGJIN (See p264)
This railway station-on-the-sea boasts Korea's most romantic sunrises.

2 NAMHANSANSEONG FORTRESS (See p210)
The views from this historic hilltop fortress south of Seoul are inspiring

3 SOSWAEWON GARDEN (See p456)
Rock, wood and bamboo form a sublime harmony in this amazing garden

4 BUSEOKSA TEMPLE (See p561)
The sunset at one of Korea's most historic monasteries is a spiritual experience.

2

3

4

5

6

7

8

1
1 SEOUL'S JOSEON PALACES (See p50)
How many cities in the world can boast five royal palaces?

2 GYEONGJU (See p531)
The Silla Kingdom's ancient capital is an outdoor museum.

3 SUWON HWASEONG FORTRESS (See p202)
Suwon's old city walls utilize modern construction techniques and represent the height of the Joseon Renaissance.

4 GONGJU & BUYEO (See p359, 369)
The temples and tombs of these two towns testify to the greatness of the Baekje Kingdom.

5 **INCHEON** (See p171)

Korea's biggest "treaty port" is home to a fascinating and exotic architectural heritage.

6 **DMZ** (See p192)

The truce village of Panmunjeom and the inter-Korean DMZ are living history.

7 **ANDONG HAHOE VILLAGE** (See p554)

A visit to this beautiful oxbow village is like stepping back in time.

8 **HAEINSA TEMPLE** (See p546)

This spectacular monastery is home to Tripitaka Koreana, a 13th century wood-block print of the Buddhist cannon.

1 JUSANJI RESERVOIR (See p570)
When the lake steams in early morning, it's a mysterious but entrancing landscape.

2 JIRISAN NATIONAL PARK (See p618)
This giant mountain park offers some of Korea's best hiking.

3 UPO WETLANDS (See p631)
Korea's largest inland swamp is an ecological paradise.

4 ULLEUNGDO ISLAND (See p572)
The volcanic island of Ulleungdo boasts of Korea's most unique landscape.

5 JEJUDO ISLAND (See p628)
Recently designated a wonder of nature, the volcanic island of Jejudo is a nature lover's paradise.

6 SEORAKSAN NATIONAL PARK (See p239)
The craggy peaks of Mt. Seoraksan present Korea's most dramatic mountain scenery, especially in autumn.

7 DADOHAE MARITIME NATIONAL PARK (See p483)
The countless islands of this park off Korea's southwest coast require weeks to explore fully.

8 SUNCHEONMAN BAY (See p496)
The sunsets over this beautiful stretch of coastal wetland are well worth the visit.

Things to Do

1 **SKIING** (See p278, 285)
Korea is fast becoming one of Asia's top ski destinations.

2 **TEMPLESTAY** (See p688, 733)
Reconnect with your spiritual side at one of Korea's beautiful Buddhist monasteries.

3 **HONGDAE CLUBS** (See p114)
Some of Seoul's finest nightlife can be found in the indie music and dance clubs near Hongik University.

4 **NON-VERBAL PERFORMANCES** (See p75, 78)
Energetic shows like "Nanta" and "Jump" transcend the language barrier.

5 DONGGANG RIVER RAFTING (See p282)
The wilds of Gangwon-do are best experienced from the white waters of the Donggang River.

6 BORYEONG MUD FESTIVAL (See p380)
Get dirty at Korea's biggest summer festival.

7 SKYJUMP IN DAEGU (See p516)
Combine bungee jumping with BASE jumping, and this is what you get. One of only four in the world.

8 SURF THE SEAS OFF BUSAN (See p583)
Enjoy a bit of yachting, surfing or swimming off the Korean Riviera.

1

1 PALACE CUISINE (See p690)
Eat like a king and experience the height of Korean cuisine.

2 JEONJU BIBIMBAP (See p405)
Korea's signature dish is best tried in its spiritual homeland.

3 TRADITIONAL WINES AND LIQUORS (See p700)
Koreans love to drink, and you'll find plenty of places to sample the local firewater.

4 JAGALCHI FISH MARKET (See p586)
Korea's most famous seafood market must be experienced to be believed.

2

3

5 NAMDO CUISINE (See p693)

In the Korean southwest, the food comes cheap, plentiful and good.

6 SUWON GALBI (See p203)

Meat eaters will like the city of Suwon and its famous barbecued short ribs.

7 STREETFOOD (See p699)

Walk along the streets and you'll find stalls selling some very tasty eats.

8 JEJUDO FOOD (See p693)

Not surprisingly, the island of Jejudo produces a rich variety of seafood.

ITINERARIES

The Korea Experience

(Almost) all trips to Korea begin with Seoul (p43), and it's worth spending a couple of days in the dynamic political, cultural and economic heart of the country, exploring its **historic palaces**, taking in the sights, enjoying the **nightlife** and gaining an appreciation for the dramatic contrast between old and new of today's Korea.

While in Seoul, be sure to take a day trip to the surreal "truce village" of **Panmunjeom** at the Korean Demilitarized Zone (DMZ), the dividing line between North and South Korea and the world's last remaining Cold War frontier. Time permitting, make another day trip to the **historic walled city** of Suwon, whose 18th century fortifications mark the pinnacle of Joseon Dynasty science and engineering.

When you're done with the Seoul area, take the scenic train trip to the East Sea town of Gangneung, passing through the rugged mountains of central Korea. From Gangneung, take a bus north to the port of Sokcho, the gateway to Seoraksan National Park, Korea's most spectacular **mountain park**. It's worth spending a day or two here exploring this picturesque region.

From Sokcho, take a bus down Korea's beautiful East Sea coast to Gyeongju, the ancient capital of the Silla Dynasty, when classical Korean civilization reached its height. You could spend weeks here exploring its **Buddhist temples, gardens** and **ruins**, but plan on at least two days.

After Gyeongju, take the short bus ride to Busan, Korea's second largest city and its busiest port. Busan's dramatic location, wedged between the mountains and the sea, results in spectacular scenery, especially at night. A couple of days here should be enough to absorb the city's distinctive sights, sounds and aromas.

The Korea Experience

3 Days
Day 1 Explore the city of Seoul.
Day 2 Continue exploring Seoul or visit Suwon Hwaseong Fortress.
Day 3 Visit Panmunjeom in the DMZ.

5 Days
Day 1–2 Explore the city of Seoul.
Day 3 Take the KTX head down to the ancient Korean capital of Gyeongju.
Day 4 From Gyeongju, take the short ride to Busan and experience that city.
Day 5 Take the KTX back to Seoul.

1 Week
Day 1–2 Explore the city of Seoul.
Day 3 Take a day trip to the DMZ.
Day 4 Head to the city of Sokcho to see beautiful Seoraksan National Park.
Day 5 From Sokcho, take a bus down to Gyeongju to check out its ancient monuments.
Day 6 Spend a morning in Gyeongju, and then take the bus to Busan.
Day 7 If your flight is in the evening, spend some time Busan, then take the KTX to Seoul.

From Busan, either fly or take a ferry to the charming volcanic island of Jejudo, a land of endless natural beauty and a fascinating culture distinct from that of the mainland. End your trip to Korea relaxing on Jejudo's beaches, climbing **Mt. Hallasan** or exploring one of the island's many scenic coastal hiking paths.

Urban Korea

While in Seoul, wander around the neighborhoods of **Myeong-dong**, **Dongdaemun**, **Hongdae** and **Gangnam**, all of which pulsate with non-stop energy.

From Seoul, take the commuter train to the historic port city of Incheon, where you can sample the exotic charm of the old waterfront and Korea's oldest **Chinatown**. To see the Korea of the future, also visit Incheon's gleaming **Songdo New City**, an ambitious experiment in 21st century urban planning.

Daejeon, a high-tech city that is Korea's answer to Silicon Valley. Be sure to visit **Expo Park** while you're there. From Daejeon, take the express train to Gwangju, southwest Korea's largest city, a growing cultural hub and home to some of Korea's finest cuisine. Explore the restaurants and galleries but it's also worth hiking **Mt. Mudeungsan**, Gwangju's guardian mountain.

From Gwangju, take an express bus to Daegu, a vibrant commercial and industrial city in southeast Korea. The city's **Traditional Medicine Market** and **old missionary sites** are fascinating, and thrill-seekers won't want to miss **83 Tower's SkyJump**.

From Daegu, it's just a short bus or train ride to the port of Busan, Korea's second largest city. Soak up its bustling, sometimes chaotic and oddly cosmopolitan charms.

Urban Korea

3 Days
Day 1 Spend a day (and night) exploring Seoul.
Day 2 Take the KTX to Busan.
Day 3 After exploring Busan, take the KTX back to Seoul.

5 Days
Day 1 Spend a day (and night) exploring Seoul.
Day 2 Spend another day in Seoul or head to Gwangju to experience its culinary and cultural landscape.
Day 3 From Gwangju, take a bus to the lively city of Daegu.
Day 4 From Daegu, take a bus or train to Busan.
Day 5 After exploring Busan, take the KTX back to Seoul.

1 Week
Day 1 Spend a day (and night) exploring Seoul.
Day 2 Take the subway to Incheon to take in its historic and modern sites. Return to Seoul.
Day 3 Take the KTX to Daejeon, Korea's Silicon Valley.
Day 4 From Daejeon, hop on the KTX to Gwangju to experience its cultural and culinary charms.
Day 5 From Gwangju, hop on a bus to the lively city of Daegu.
Day 6 After taking in Daeju, take the short bus or train ride to Busan, Korea's second city.
Day 7 After exploring Busan, take the KTX back to Seoul.

Depending on the season, you may want to check out **Haeundae Beach**, the "Korean Riviera," or rub shoulders with the stars during October's **Busan International Film Festival.**

Historic Korea

Any exploration of historic Korea should begin in Seoul, which has been Korea's capital for 600 years. Visit the **National Museum of Korea**, of course, but also tour Seoul's five **Joseon Dynasty palaces**, stroll about the quaint traditional alleyways of the **Bukchon neighborhoods**, hike the city's old city walls, and maybe check out the old churches, schools and legations in **Jeong-dong**, Seoul's old Western Quarter.

From Seoul, head down to Suwon and hike its magnificent **UNESCO-registered city walls**, built in the 18th century using technology and techniques from both East and West. After Suwon, head to the historic towns of Gongju and Buyeo, the former capitals of the ancient Baekje Kingdom, a culturally sophisticated kingdom that played a key role in transmitting Buddhism to Japan. Explore their ancient tombs, ruined palaces and other sites, but also be sure to take in the treasures housed in the Gongju and Buyeo **national museums.**

From there, keep heading south to Jeonju, the historic political and economic hub of the Jeolla provinces known for its great food and rich traditional arts culture. Enjoy a **Jeonju** *bibimbap*, maybe take in a *pansori* **performance**, but above all, spend a day walking around **Jeonju Hanok Village**, with its alleys lined by handsome *hanok* homes. From Jeonju, it might also be worth visiting the port of Gunsan to witness Korea's early modern history.

From Jeonju, head to Daegu and, from there, head north to Andong, the heart of Korea's Confucian culture. Everyone visits the preserved Joseon Dynasty **village of Hahoe**, a UNESCO World Heritage Site, but don't forget to visit the beautiful

Historic Korea

3 Days

Day 1 Explore Seoul's historic palaces.
Day 2 Spend a day walking around Bukchon Hanok Village and Insa-dong.
Day 3 Take the subway to Suwon and explore its impressive old city walls.

5 Days

Day 1 Explore Seoul's historic palaces.
Day 2 Take the subway to Suwon and explore its impressive old city walls.
Day 3 From Seoul, hop on the KTX to the ancient Korean capital of Gyeongju.
Day 4 Spend a full day exploring Gyeongju. In the evening, head back to Seoul.
Day 5 Spend the morning walking about Seoul's Bukchon Hanok Village.

1 Week

Day 1 Explore Seoul's historic palaces.
Day 2 Spend a day walking around Bukchon Hanok Village and Insa-dong.
Day 3 Take a bus to Gongju, the ancient capital of the Baekje Kingdom.
Day 4 Head to Daegu, and to Gyeongju.
Day 5 Spend a full day exploring Gyeongju.
Day 6 Take the bus or train to Andong. Be sure to visit Hahoe Village.
Day 7 From Andong, hop on a bus or train back to Seoul.

old Confucian academies of **Dosan Seowon** and **Byeongsan Seowon**, or the lovely Buddhist temple of **Bongjeongsa**. While at Hahoe, take in a performance of the town's famous **mask dance**.

From Andong, head to Gyeongju, a virtual outdoor museum to the brilliance of the ancient Silla civilization. The highlight here is the grand Buddhist temple of **Bulguksa** and its **Seokguram Grotto**, possibly the finest piece of Buddhist art in the country, but you'll also want to spend a day hiking around **Mt. Namsan**, with its countless Buddhist rock carvings, pagodas and ruins. While in Gyeongju, try to stop by **Yangdong Village**, another beautifully preserved Joseon Dynasty village and UNESCO World Heritage Site.

From Gyeongju, backtrack to Daegu again, and take the short trip from there to Haeinsa Temple, home of the Tripitaka Koreana, a vast collection of ingeniously preserved wooden printing blocks, carved in the 13th century, containing the entirety of the Buddhist canon.

Natural Korea

Oddly enough, you can find some of Korea's most spectacular nature along the DMZ, one of the world's most militarized frontiers. The lack of human activity in the DMZ has produced a unique ecosystem and an ironically tranquil landscape that is home to migratory birds and many species of rare plants and animals.

Mt. Seoraksan, on Korea's East Sea coast, is widely regarded as Korea's most beautiful nature park, with dramatic, jagged granite peaks, deep and thickly wooded valleys, and brilliant rock formations along the ocean coast. To properly appreciate it all, you need a

Natural Korea

3 Days

Day 1 Visit some of Seoul's natural sites like Seonyudo Park or Bukhansan National Park.
Day 2 Head to the DMZ and take in its natural splendor.
Day 3 Take a day trip to Taean National Park.

5 Days

Day 1 From Seoul, catch a bus to Sokcho, the town at the base of Seoraksan National Park.
Day 2 Spend a day hiking around Seoraksan National Park.
Day 3 From Sokcho, catch a bus to Wonju Airport and catch a flight to Jejudo.
Day 4 Spend a day exploring the natural wonder of Jejudo.
Day 5 Take a flight back to Incheon International Airport and transfer to your flight home.

1 Week

Day 1 From Seoul, catch a bus to Sokcho, the town at the base of Seoraksan National Park.
Day 2 Spend a day hiking around Seoraksan National Park.
Day 3 Take the long bus ride from Sokcho to Suncheon (you may have to transfer) to take in the sunset over Suncheonman Bay.
Day 4 Head to nearby Yeosu, and from there explore Dadohae Maritime National Park.
Day 5 From Yeosu Airport, take a flight to Jejudo.
Day 6 Spend a day exploring the natural wonder of Jejudo.
Day 7 Take a flight back to Incheon International Airport.

couple of days. While you're on the east coast, swing down to the small town of Samcheok and explore the beautiful underground landscapes of its massive limestone caves.

South of Seoul is Taean Haean National Park, where you can not only take in one of Korea's best sunsets, but also hike along beautiful seaside cliffs and experience the unique ecology of Korea's only sand dune.

The beachside resort of Boryeong is best known for **Boryeong Mud Festival**, Korea's greatest (and messiest) summer party, but nature lovers can better appreciate its extensive mud flats, produced by some of the world's most dramatic tides.

Southern Korea is dominated by the high massif of Mt. Jirisan. If you're a hiker, you could spend a full week here exploring its many trails and peaks. In its deep forests lives Korea's last remaining community of Asiatic black bears. Also near Mt. Jirisan is the protected wetland area of Upo, which provides a habitat to migratory birds and many endangered species of plants and animals.

Heading further south, there's the beautiful coastal wetland along Suncheonman Bay, known for its acres of mudflats, reeds and unspoiled ecology. The myriad islands off Korea's southern coastline, many of them contained within Hallyeo Maritime National Park and Dadohae Maritime National Park, are also highly recommended.

No tour of Korea's natural splendor would be complete without a visit to the volcanic island of Jejudo, recently voted one of the world's top sites of natural wonder. Between the scenic coastlines, the amazing lava tubes and the grand volcanic peak of **Mt. Hallasan**, you have enough here to keep you busy for weeks.

For the ultimate in Korean eco-tourism, set aside a couple of months to hike the Baekdu Daegan, a trail that runs the entire length of Korea's mountain spine.

Gourmet Korea

Despite its size, Korea is a nation of rich culinary diversity, and traveling around just to explore its food can be a rewarding, albeit waist-expanding, experience.

Seoul is home to many of Korea's finest restaurants, and certainly its best **international cuisine**. Seoul was the city of kings, so be sure to try at least one meal of royal palace cuisine, which should fill you up for at least a week.

You can experience Sino-Korean dishes like *jjajangmyeon* anywhere in Korea, but the best can be had in its home of Incheon's **Chinatown**. For something a bit spicier, take the train from Seoul to the pleasant lakeside town of Chuncheon and dine on the city's signature dish, *dak galbi*, pan-fried chicken ribs mixed with noodles, vegetables and rice cakes. In summer, also try *makguksu*, cold buckwheat noodles, for which the region is famous.

Just south of Seoul is the city of Icheon, which is famous for a) its centuries old ceramics culture, and b) *ssalbap*: steamed rice, soup and a table covered in side dishes. Further south, in the ancient city of Buyeo, be sure to order *yeonbap*—rice and nuts that have been wrapped in a lotus leaf and steamed. It looks as good as it tastes. If your culinary tastes tend more towards the liquid, historic **Sewang Brewery** in the small town of Jincheon is a great place to learn about the joys of *makgeolli*, milky Korean rice beer.

Southeast Korea is generally not known for its food, but if you know what you're looking for, you'll find some gems. Andong, in particular, has a well-regarded local cuisine that includes dried mackerel, *heotjesabap* ("fake memorial rites food"), Andong-style steamed chicken and, perhaps most famous of all, **Andong *soju***, Korea's best known traditional firewater. Busan, too, is a wonderful place to eat. **Jagalkchi Fish Market** is not only a great place to score raw fish, but a sight to behold in and of itself.

Korea's best cuisine, however, can be found in the country's southwest. The Jeolla provinces have long served as the nation's breadbasket, a fact reflected in their rich and highly developed local food. The best known regionally specialty is Jeonju *bibimbap*, rice mixed with vegetables and a tangy red pepper sauce, served with a dozen or so side dishes. Jeollanam-do, meanwhile, is famous for **Namdo cuisine**, which features a table packed with high-quality meats, seafood and vegetables from around the province. Once you've had this, you may find eating elsewhere unsatisfying. Adventurous eaters with a strong gag reflex will definitely want to try a local specialty, *hongeohoe*—sliced, fermented skate.

Gourmet Korea

3 Days

Day 1 Explore Seoul's culinary treasures, including royal palace cuisine.
Day 2 Take a day trip to Chuncheon and try out *dak galbi* (pan-fried chicken ribs) and *makguksu* (cold buckwheat noodles).
Day 3 Try out Chinese food, Korean-style, in Incheon.

5 Days

Day 1 Explore Seoul's culinary treasures, including royal palace cuisine.
Day 2 Take a day trip to Chuncheon and try out *dak galbi* (pan-fried chicken ribs) and *makguksu* (cold buckwheat noodles).
Day 3 From Seoul, hop on a bus or train to Jeonju and have a Jeonju *bibimbap*.
Day 4 Head to Gwangju, home to some of Korea's best food, and sample some Namdo cuisine.
Day 5 Head back to Seoul. Maybe stop by Incheon for some Korean-style Chinese food.

1 Week

Day 1 Explore Seoul's culinary treasures, including royal palace cuisine.
Day 2 Take a day trip to Chuncheon and try out *dak galbi* (pan-fried chicken ribs) and *makguksu* (cold buckwheat noodles).
Day 3 From Seoul, hop on a bus or train to Jeonju and have a Jeonju *bibimbap*.
Day 4 Head to Gwangju, home to some of Korea's best food, and sample some Namdo cuisine.
Day 5 From Gwangju, head to Busan to check out Jagalchi Fish Market.
Day 6 From Busan, head to Andong, home to a very unique local cuisine.
Day 7 From Andong, head back to Seoul.

ABOUT KOREA

Topography of South Korea

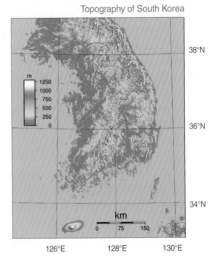

Topography

Korea is a peninsula that juts out from the southern reaches of Manchuria in Northeast Asia. The peninsula stretches 1,100 km from north to south, and has a total area—including islands—of 220,847 km². In terms of area, this makes the peninsula roughly the size of the United Kingdom. The peninsula is considerably wider at its northern frontier and narrows at the waist; Koreans often liken its shape to that of a roaring tiger.

For the purpose of this guide book, however, "Korea" will refer only to the southern half of the Korean Peninsula, that part of the peninsula that stretches from the inter-Korean Demilitarized Zone (DMZ) in the north to the southern coast and the offshore islands of Jejudo and Marado to the south. It is this part of the peninsula that is under the administration of the Republic of Korea, or "South Korea," and the part that is widely open to international visitors and tourists. The northern half of the peninsula, or "North Korea," is administered by a separate government, and beyond the purview of this book.

South Korea has a total land area of 100,033 km², making it roughly the size of the US state of Indiana. It takes just under three hours by high-speed train to travel from Seoul, in the north, to Busan, in the south and, generally speaking, few places are beyond a four or five-hour drive away.

Beautiful mountains of the Taebaeksan Range. Mountains account for most of Korea's area.

Over 70% of Korea's landmass is mountains, particularly along the east coast, where the high peaks of the Taebaeksan Mountain Range form the "backbone" of the country; and the south, which is dominated by the grand massif of Mt. Jirisan. The areas around the western coast tend to be flatter, with large plains on which you'll find some of Korea's most productive farmland.

Korea also has several sizable islands, most notably volcanic Jejudo, dominated by the massive shield of Mt. Hallasan (1,950 m), South Korea's highest peak. Other notable islands include Geojedo, a major scenic and industrial center near Busan; Jindo, a rural island off the southwest tip of Korea; Ganghwado, a historic island that has guarded the mouth of the Hangang River for centuries; and Ulleungdo, a small volcanic island in the East Sea and one of Korea's hidden gems.

Korea has several large rivers, including the Hangang River, which flows through Seoul; the Nakdonggang River, which flows through southeast Korea and empties out by Busan; the Geumgang River, which feeds the rich farmlands of west-central Korea; and the Yeongsangang River, which drains southwest Korea. The country doesn't have any large natural lakes, but it does have several large reservoirs as a result of 20th century hydro-electric projects, including Chungjuho Lake in central Korea and Paroho Lake in northeastern Korea.

Demographics

As of 2010, South Korea had a population of 48,580,000 people, with a population density of about 486 people per km². This is deceptive, though—as most of the country is mountainous, the bulk of the population lives along the river basins and west coast plains, or in valleys between the mountains. Moreover, Korea's population is highly urbanized. As of 2005, over 80% of Koreans lived in cities; fully one fifth of Koreans lived in Seoul alone. What this means is that while major cities and urban clusters like Seoul–Incheon–Gyeonggi-do can be incredibly crowded, much of the countryside is blissfully quiet and tranquil, and many mountain regions are hardly populated at all.

Ethnic Koreans make up the overwhelming majority of the population. Koreans are an ancient people, but there is no full agreement as to their historical root. It is widely believed Koreans are descended from peoples who migrated to the Korean Peninsula from Central Asia during the Paleolithic and Neolithic eras. Their unique language, Korean, is frequently classified as Altaic, making it a relative of Mongolian, Turkish, and the languages of Central Asia and Siberia, as well as possibly Japanese. Over the centuries, Koreans have adopted many cultural and political concepts from China, most notably Confucianism, while at the same time successfully maintaining a distinct cultural and national identity.

Traditionally, Korea has been pretty homogeneous ethnically, and proudly so. Until only recently, the only major ethnic minority was a small population of ethnic Chinese, or *hwagyo*, who began settling

Korean fans during World Cup 2002

in Korea at the very end of the 19th century. Things are changing, however. Korea's miraculous economic success has attracted more and and more foreigners to its shores, producing a society that is increasingly multicultural. In 2007, the number of foreigners residing in Korea topped 1 million for the first time ever. Many migrants come from China and developing nations in south, southeast and central Asia to work in Korea's labor-starved small and medium-sized factories. More recently, large numbers of younger foreign women have come to Korea as brides—Korea's demographics have produced a shortage of marriageable women, especially in the countryside. The cultural impact of these marriages, and the multi-ethnic children that result, is expected to be profound, especially in rural districts where so-called "international marriages" account for up to 40% of total marriages.

Another recent demographic trend being felt is aging. Not long ago, Koreans had large families; now, Korea has one of the lowest birth rates in the OECD. Again, this is especially noticeable in the countryside, where it sometimes seems there are no young people at all. As with multiculturalism, the aging phenomenon is expected to have a major impact on Korean society in the decades to come.

Economy

Korea is an advanced, industrialized economy, albeit one adjusting to its newly achieved status as a global trading powerhouse. Korea's nominal GDP was estimated at US$1.007 trillion in 2010. Adjusted for purchasing power parity, it stood at US$1.459 trillion, making Korea the 13th largest economy in the world. Nominal GDP per capita was US$20,265 but, adjusted for purchasing power parity, it was US$30,200. By means of comparison, this is roughly the EU average, and an amazing figure if you consider that in the late 1950s, Korea was poorer than many African states.

Since 1996, Korea has been a member of the Organisation for Economic Co-operation and Development (OECD).

Korea's economy is largely industrial and service-based; agriculture, which once accounted for the bulk of the economy, now accounts for less than 3% of its GDP. International trade is an important component of the economy—as of 2010, Korea was the world's 8th largest exporter, and the 11th largest importer. Major exports include semiconductors, IT equipment, automobiles, computers, steel, ships and petrochemicals. A net aid recipient for much of the post-Korean War period, Korea is now an international aid giver and a member of the OECD Development Assistance Committee.

Korea World Trade Center, Seoul

Government

Korea is a multi-party democracy and a presidential republic with power divided between the executive, legislative and judicial branches. The executive branch is led by an elected president who serves a five-year term. The president is assisted by an appointed prime minister and a cabinet, which is appointed by the president on the recommendation of the prime minister. Legislative responsibilities are handled by a unicameral, 300-seat parliament, the National Assembly; 246 of the lawmakers are elected, and 54 selected by proportional representation. Lawmakers serve four year terms.

The judicial branch is led by both a Supreme Court, the highest court of appeals in the land, and the

National Assembly Building, home of Korea's parliament

Constitutional Court, which deals primarily with issues of constitutionality. The Constitution of the Republic of Korea is the highest law in the land. The Korean constitution was promulgated in 1948, and last amended in 1988.

Security & Safety

Due to North Korea, South Korea is frequently depicted as a dangerous hot zone. At the risk of minimizing the tragedy of national division, however, Korea is a pretty safe place. Technically speaking, North and South Korea are still at war, and have been since 1950, but acts of violence between the two, while they do happen (such as North Korea's 2010 sinking of the South Korean warship ROKS Cheonan and the shelling of a South Korean island later that year), are rare and usually restricted to remote parts of the DMZ or the contested maritime boundary in the West Sea. Bill Clinton might have once called the DMZ the scariest place on Earth, but the fact that the DMZ is one of Korea's premier travel destinations, with scores of tourists visiting daily, should provide perspective.

Crime rates, too, are relatively low, especially compared to those of the United States. In Korea's big cities, some neighborhoods might be nicer than others, but what you won't find are crime-infested ghettos or slums. If you drop your phone or wallet, you even stand a chance of having it returned. Still, Korea is not completely crime free, and you should take the ordinary precautions you'd take anywhere when going out. Female travelers, in particular, will want to take care—sexual assaults against international travelers, while rare, do happen. Being aware of your surroundings and using common sense should get you through just fine.

It is also worth mentioning here Korea's time-honored tradition of street protests. Street protests are not an uncommon phenomenon, especially in Seoul. These protests are mostly harmless, but they can sometimes get rowdy, with violent clashes between protesters and riot police. To avoid getting caught up in something, try to avoid political demonstrations if you can.

South Korean MP at the DMZ

HISTORY OF KOREA

Prehistory & Gojoseon

Koreans state with pride that their nation has a 5,000 year history and, indeed, they are one of the few peoples on earth who can trace their national lineage back thousands of years.

Archaeological evidence such as stone tools and pottery shards indicate that the Korean Peninsula has been inhabited since at least the Stone Age; the Korean people of today, however, are believed to be descendants of Altaic tribes from Central Asia, Siberia and Manchuria who migrated to the Korean Peninsula in waves between the Stone and Bronze ages. Koreans traditionally date the founding of their nation to 2333 BC, when Dangun—the grandson of the King of Heaven— founded the kingdom of Gojoseon in what is now southern Manchuria. Dangun may have been a figure of legend, but the kingdom he was said to have founded was certainly real. The kings of Gojoseon ruled over a prosperous and sophisticated Bronze Age civilization that covered much of what is now North Korea and Manchuria from at least the 8th century BC until 108 BC, when the Chinese Han Dynasty invaded and liquidated the kingdom.

According to legend, the grandson of Heaven, the king Dangun Wanggeom, is said to have founded the first Korean nation, Gojoseon, in 2333 BC. It is theorized by some that the term Dangun Wanggeom refers not necessarily to an individual, but to a title, a king who combined temporal and religious authority. In 1919, Korea's government-in-exile designated 2333 BC as year one in a new calendar system still in use today.

The Three Kingdoms

In northern Korea, the victorious Chinese replaced Gojoseon with four Chinese commanderies, which were met with local hostility. Elsewhere on the Korean Peninsula and southern Manchuria, Korean tribes formed tribal confederations. The state of Buyeo arose in the north in the second century BC, while, in the south, three large tribal confederations, the Samhan ("Three Han"), took root. By the first century AD, these confederacies congregated into three great kingdoms: Goguryeo, a militarily powerful state that, at its height, ruled much of Manchuria and Korea as far south as the Hangang River valley; Baekje, a culturally sophisticated Buddhist kingdom that controlled most of southwest Korea and the Hangang River valley; and Silla, something of a late bloomer that ruled the mountainous but easily defensible lands of southeast Korea. An intense rivalry developed between these three kingdoms for domination of the Korean Peninsula, giving birth to the Three Kingdoms Period. The wars, alliances and betrayals of the Three Kingdoms Period defined Korean history for the first six centuries of the millennium.

Baekje was the first to blossom. Founded by a branch of the Buyeo royal family that had migrated south in 18 BC, Baekje consolidated its rule over central and southwest Korea, reaching its territorial height in the fourth century. Baekje maintained close ties with both Tang Dynasty China, from which it adopted many aspects of Chinese high culture and statecraft, and Japan, to which it played a leading role in transmitting the trappings of advanced continental civilization. In 384, the kingdom adopted Buddhism as the state religion; the faith would have a tremendous impact on Baekje's political, social and artistic cultures.

Three Kingdoms Period (5th Century)

The fifth century, however, was to be Goguryeo's. Like Baekje, Goguryeo was founded by a former Buyeo prince in 37 BC. Over the next three centuries, it strengthened its hold on the territories of southern Manchuria and northern Korea; constantly at odds with various Chinese dynasties and the rough-and-ready tribes of Manchuria, the kingdom developed a strong martial culture. Under the reigns of King Gwanggaeto the Great (r. 391–412) and his son, King Jangsu (r. 413–491), Goguryeo went on a conquering spree, acquring large swaths of Manchuria in the north and the Hangang River valley in the south through wars against Manchurian tribes and states and Baekje and Silla. By the first decades of the sixth century, Goguryeo ruled three-fourths of the Korean Peninsula, the Liaodong Peninsula, southern Manchuria and even parts of what is now the Russian Far East.

Goguryeo's Golden Age, too, was not to last. in 551, Baekje—in alliance with the third of the Three Kingdoms, Silla—invaded Goguryeo in a bid to retake the strategically and economically vital Hangang River valley. After a series of costly assaults on Goguryeo fortresses, Baekje succeeded in retaking the valley in 553, but was immediately betrayed by Silla, which quickly seized the region from exhausted Baekje forces. In 554, Baekje invaded Silla in

Murals from Goguryeo tomb, 5th century

retaliation, but the offensive ended in disaster at the Battle of Gwansanseong Fortress, when the Baekje army was decimated and the Baekje king killed.

According to historical texts, the kingdom of Silla was founded in 57 BC, but historians themselves believe the state was the last of the Three Kingdoms to centralize. With its capital in today's Gyeongju, Silla consolidated a hold on the tribes and city states of southeast Korea; in the mid-sixth century, it conquered the Gaya Confederacy, a group of city states that formed a buffer between Silla and Baekje. Internally, it grew a highly developed, stratified society ruled by a monarchy and several aristocratic families. In

528 AD, after some resistance, Silla adopted Buddhism as a state religion. The core of its military was formed by an elite of aristocratic young men trained in Buddhism and the martial arts, the *hwarang*.

The sixth and seventh centuries were a period of great tumult on the Korean Peninsula as Silla, Baekje and Goguryeo waged an all-out struggle for domination. Baekje, which never recovered from the Battle of Gwansanseong and was ruled by kings more interested in building Buddhist temples than a powerful army, was at a disadvantage. In 660, the forces of Silla, led by the great general Kim Yu-sin, invaded and conquered Baekje in alliance with Tang Dynasty China. In 668, the Silla–Tang alliance conquered Goguryeo, which had been fatally weakened by wars with the Chinese. After the fall of Goguryeo, the Chinese attempted to establish a colony of their own in Korea, but were forcibly kicked out of the peninsula by Silla after a decade of war. Silla had "united" the Korean Peninsula under one ruler.

Unified Silla and the North–South States Period

Koreans ofter refer to the period following Silla's conquest of Baekje and Goguryeo as the "Unified Silla Period." Silla's unification of the Korean Peninsula was not complete, however. In 698, a former Goguryeo general founded the kingdom of Balhae. This prosperous and cultured kingdom would rule much of northern Korea and southern Manchuria until 926, when it was conquered by a Manchurian people, the Khitan.

The Unified Silla Period was the zenith of Korean classical civilization. The royal capital of Gyeongju was one of the world's great cities, its palaces, gardens and temples famous even in China. Led by strong kings from the Kim clan, Silla developed a rich culture, with Buddhism playing a central role. Many of Korea's cultural treasures, including the beautiful Buddhist monastery of Bulguksa and its sublime Seokguram Grotto, date from this cultural Golden Age.

From the late eighth century, however, Silla was plagued by political instability as aristocratic families fought with one another for influence and control. The king became little more than a figurehead, and the capital's control of the provinces began to slip as leading families and individuals carved out virtual fiefdoms. Illustrative of this state of affairs was the story of Jang Bo-go, a low-born soldier who, from his base on the island of Wan-do off southwest Korea, carved out what amounted to his own transnational maritime empire before being assassinated in 841.

As the 10th century rolled around, Silla found itself in an almost constant state of civil war. Powerful figures in the north and southwest broke away from Silla, establishing the kingdoms of Later Goguryeo and Later Baekje, beginning the so-called Later Three Kingdoms Period. In 918, a Later Goguryeo general by the name of Wang Geon overthrew his king and took power for himself, renaming the kingdom Goryeo. Moving south, Wang Geon absorbed the rump state of Silla in 935, and defeated Later Baekje the following year. At last, Korea was, for the first time in its history, united under the rule of one king.

Dabotap Pagoda,
Bulguksa Temple, Gyeongju

Goryeo Dynasty

Like Silla before it, Goryeo—from which the English word
"Korea" is derived—was a devoutly Buddhist kingdom.
Wang Geon established his royal capital in his hometown
of Gaegyeong (today's Kaeseong, in North Korea); to
promote continuity, he married a Silla princess and
incorporated the Silla aristocracy into his new political
order. Under Goryeo, the arts and culture flourished—
Buddhist temples were constructed all across the
country, and Korean ceramics reached their pinnacle of
artistry with the development of so-called Goryeo
celadon, the blue-green ware for which Korea was
famous throughout the Far East. In 1234, a Goryeo official
crafted the world's first metal movable type, a full two
centuries before Johannes Gutenberg developed

Goryeo celadon was a highly valued
commodity in East Asia. © Yonhap

movable type in Europe. Economically, Goryeo was a vibrant trading state, conducting
trade with nations as far away as the Middle East. Goryeo ginseng was an especially
prized commodity. Goryeo was plagued by both foreign threats and domestic instability.
In the 11th and 12th centuries, the kingdom was forced to contend with invasions by
Manchurian tribes and peoples. In 1170, dissident generals launched a coup, turning the
Goryeo king into a figurehead and establishing a virtual shogunate that witnessed the
kingdom run by a series of military strongmen.

Early 13th world history is dominated by the rise of the Mongols and, in 1231, it was
Goryeo's turn to confront the horde. Overwhelmed, the Goryeo royal court fled to the
island of Ganghwa-do. In 1236, as an act of patriotic piety, the Goryeo king had carved
wood blocks of the entire Buddhist canon, the Tripitaka Koreana, which survives today at
the magnificent Buddhist monastery of Haeinsa. Unfortunately, it was ineffective as a
defense strategy: the Mongols were content to repeatedly trample and pillage the
defenseless mainland as the Korean royal family stewed on its island sanctuary. The
assassination in 1258 of the anti-Mongol dictator Choe Ui, the last of Korea's military
rulers, brought the Goryeo shogunate to an end, and the king finally surrendered to the
Mongols, keeping his throne in return for making Goryeo a Mongol vassal state.

The Mongols brought great changes to Goryeo. Goryeo crown princes were taken to the
Mongol capital, married to Mongol princesses and given Mongol names. Mongols,
Central Asians and pro-Mongol Koreans were put in positions of power and influence. As
part of the Great Mongol Empire, Goryeo was integrated into the Silk Road and other
global trade routes; Arab and Uighur merchants set up communities of their own in
Gaegyeong.

Goryeo experienced something of a revival under the reign of King Gongmin (r. 1351–
1374), who struggled to free his state from the yoke of the Mongols who would lose
power in China with the establishment of the Ming Dynasty in 1368. Gongmin was
assassinated in 1374, however, and was succeeded by a series of weak kings until 1392,
when a general by the name of Yi Seong-gye rebelled and seized the throne for himself,
bringing the Goryeo Dynasty to an end.

Joseon Dynasty

King Sejong the Great,
the most accomplished king
of the Joseon Dynasty

Coming to power with the assistance of powerful neo-Confucian scholars and officials, Yi removed from power and influence the Buddhist establishment, which was despised by the new leadership for its wealth and corruption under the previous dynasty. The founders of the new Joseon Dynasty wished to create the model neo-Confucian state, ruled by a king who in turn was assisted by a class of Confucian scholar-officials. In this aim, they largely succeeded, producing by the end of the dynasty's 500-year history what many call the world's most Confucian culture.

The early Joseon Dynasty was ruled by strong, capable kings. The most brilliant of these was King Sejong the Great (r. 1318–1450), the very model of the wise Confucian scholar-king. Sejong oversaw reforms that led to a flowering of Korean economy, culture and science. He is most famous for overseeing the creation of the *hangeul* alphabet, Korea's ingenious indigenous writing system.

Joseon society was highly stratified, led by an elite class of usually landed scholar elites known as *yangban*. Advancement in Joseon society was determined by the *gwageo*, the all-important state civil service exam. Passing the civil service exam required a mastery of the so-called Chinese classics (and, of course, written classical Chinese). Such mastery could only come after years of dedicated study, either through tutors or at a series of Confucian schools and academies. Underneath the *yangban* were lower classes, including merchants, artisans, clerks, artists and huge populations of peasant farmers and slaves.

In the 16th and 17th centuries, Joseon suffered two highly debilitating foreign invasions. The first, and by far the more destructive, was the Imjin War, a series of Japanese invasions between 1592 and 1598. Led by the warlord Hideyoshi Toyotomi, the Japanese—armed with arquebuses obtained from the Portuguese—nearly conquered the entire peninsula before they were stopped by an allied force of Koreans and Chinese troops sent by China's Ming Dynasty. At sea, the brilliant Korean admiral Yi Sun-sin inflicted defeat after devastating defeat on the Japanese fleet, eventually forcing a Japanese withdrawal from Korea. The invasions left Korea a smoldering ruin, however— many of its cities, shrine and temples were burnt to the ground, its farmland trampled, and countless civilians killed. Barely had Joseon recovered from the Imjin War when the Manchus, consolidating their hold in China, invaded Korea in 1627 and 1637 in a successful bid to force the Joseon court into a tributary relationship.

Under especially competent and visionary kings such as King Yeongjo and King Jeongjo, the 18th century witnessed a cultural and scientific renaissance as the kingdom achieved a full recovery from the invasions of the previous century. The 19th century, however, marked a period of decline as the royal court grew mired in endemic factional strife.

Daehan Empire

As the 19th century drew to a conclusion, Korea found itself subject to imperial pressures from the West and Japan. Raids by the French in 1866 (to avenge the death of French priests killed during a royal crackdown on Catholicism) and the Americans in 1871 (to avenge the burning of a US ship that had attempted to force open Korea for trade) failed to open up the country, which—having witnessed the Western powers' pillaging of China—pursued a strict policy of isolation that earned it the moniker "the Hermit Kingdom." In 1876, however, the Japanese—employing gunboat tactics similar to those used by Commodore Perry on them just 20 years earlier—succeeded in forcing Korea to open up three ports to foreign trade. In 1882, Korea and the United States signed a trade and friendship treaty, which was soon followed by similar treaties with other Western powers.

Emperor Gojong © Yonhap

King Gojong, the Korean monarch who ruled during much of this period, attempted to modernize his nation while fending off imperial threats, particularly from Japan and Russia. In 1895, Japan defeated China in the First Sino-Japanese War and, as a result, Korea's traditional relationship with China was severed. In 1897, Gojong renamed his kingdom the Daehan Empire to reflect the country's officially equal status with China. With the help of Western and Japanese advisors, Korea began to take on the trappings of a modern kingdom, with Western-style schools, hospitals, electrical lighting, railroad and tram services and running water.

Unfortunately, King Gojong's attempt to modernize Korea proved too little, too late. In 1905, Japan defeated Russia in the Russo-Japanese War, ending Russian influence in Korea and giving Tokyo a free hand on the peninsula. In 1907, Japan forced Korea to become a Japanese protectorate and, in 1910, officially annexed the country, beginning a 35 year period of colonial rule.

Japanese Colonial Rule

In typical colonial fashion, the Japanese exploited their Korean colony economically, socially and militarily in the name of "civilizing" it. Korea's rich farmlands were developed to feed Japan's burgeoning urban population, and the colonies' ports and railways were developed to facilitate the transport of troops and armaments to fuel Imperial Japan's growing wars in China. Nevertheless, a good deal of modernization did take place, too. The nation began to urbanize—in 1905, Seoul's population was just 250,000. By 1936, it had grown to 730,000, including a large number of Japanese settlers. Many symbols of modern civilization, such as automobiles, trains, hotels, and movie theaters began appearing at this time.

Culturally, colonial rule proved incredibly destructive. A period of relatively liberal rule in the 1920s allowed Korean culture to flourish but, in the 1930s, Japan reverted to a policy of intense Japanification. Koreans were encouraged to take Japanese names, and the Korean language was forbidden in schools. The Japanese had little respect for

Korea's cultural heritage. Symbolic of this was the almost complete destruction of Gyeongbokgung Palace, a symbol of the Joseon Dynasty and Korea's history as an independent nation, and its replacement by the imposing Japanese Government-General Building, designed in the shape of the Japanese character for Japan.

Resistance to Japanese rule, such as the massive independence protests of March 1, 1919, were put down with great brutality. As Korea entered the 1930s, Japan's wars in China, and eventually in the Pacific, took their toll in the colony as well in the form of military drafts, labor conscription and wartime deprivations.

Independence and the Korean War

War Memorial of Korea

With the defeat of Imperial Japan by the Allies in 1945, Korea at long last recovered its independence. This proved bittersweet, however—the victorious Allies placed Korea under their own administration, with Soviet troops occupying areas of the Korean Peninsula north of the 38th parallel and US troops occupying areas to the south. Initially intended as a temporary measure, this division—as in Germany—soon became permanent in the ideologically charged atmosphere of the Cold War. In 1948, the pro-Western Republic of Korea (i.e. South Korea) was declared in Seoul, soon to be followed by the declaration of the communist Democratic People's Republic of Korea (i.e. North Korea) in Pyongyang.

On June 25, 1950, tensions between the two hostile states came to a dramatic head when North Korea launched an armored blitzkrieg on the South. The Korean War did not start out well for the South—Seoul fell after just three days, and by August, South Korean forces, now joined by international (largely American) forces fighting under the UN flag, were pushed back to a small pocket around the southeastern port of Busan.

The defenders solidified, however, bringing the North Korean invasion to a halt and, on Sept 15, 1950, UN commander Gen. Douglas MacArthur pulled off a masterstoke, cutting the North Korean logistical lines with a daring amphibious landing at the West Sea port of Incheon. Unfortunately, this brilliant move was followed up by a poorly coordinated invasion of the North in a bid to reunify the Korean Peninsula, which in turn provoked a massive intervention by Chinese communist "volunteers." The Chinese pushed the South Koreans and their UN allies back past Seoul before the latter, regrouping and changing tactics, turned the tide again, pushing the front line back to the area around the 38th parallel by July of 1951. What followed was two years of brutal but, for the most part, territorially meaningless fighting while negotiators hammered out an armistice, which was finally reached on July 27, 1953.

Miracle on the Han

The 35 years of Japanese colonialism and the Korean War had left Korea in truly dire straits. Seoul was essentially a big refugee camp, its infrastructure largely destroyed during the war. The prospects for the Korean economy looked bleak. The country was dependent on foreign aid, and corruption and repression by the Rhee government, which had turned increasingly authoritarian, didn't help.

In April of 1960, massive anti-government demonstrations drove Rhee from power. His regime was replaced by a democratically elected parliamentary government led by President Yun Bo-seon and Prime Minister Chang Myon. This experiment in Korean democracy proved brief, however—Chang's government was plagued by constant instability and unrest, and could not solve the intractable economic and social problems facing the nation. On May 16, 1961, a group of military officers, led by Major General Park Chung-hee, seized control of the government in a bloodless coup.

For Park, the May 1961 coup marked the start of an 18 year reign as South Korea's leader. Retiring from the military to run as a civilian candidate, Park was narrowly elected president in 1963. At the top of his list of priorities was the development of the Korean economy. Prior to the election, in 1962, Park announced the first in a series of ambitious five year plans to industrialize and develop Korea through export-led growth. Partnering with Korea's large business conglomerate, or *jaebeol*, the government initially emphasized labor-intensive light industries like textiles and wig-making but, as the *jaebeol* accumulated their own capital and access to international capital, particularly from the United States and Japan, increased, the focused shifted to heavy industry such as steel, automobiles, ships and petrochemicals.

Considerable investments were made in infrastructure, too, including highways, railroads, ports and schools. The Park government also tried, with considerable success, to improve rural village life, too, through the New Village Movement, which emphasized self-help and cooperation to modernize farming and built rural infrastructure. Korea's unprecedented economic development during this period defied predictions by experts and international lending institutions, and earned the appellation, "Miracle on the Han," referring to the Hangang River, which flows through the heart of Seoul.

For all his contributions to Korean economic development, Park was essentially a military dictator, however, and ruled Korea with an iron fist. Opponents were harassed, arrested, tortured and sometimes killed. The electoral process was rigged in favor of Park and his Democratic Republic Party; despite this, Park barely won re-election in in 1967 and, after changing the Constitution to allow a third term, 1971. Even this was not enough for Park

View towards Yeouido, Seoul's financial district

and, in 1972, he declared martial law and adopted the so-called Yusin Constitution, which strengthened the power of the president—now to be indirectly elected to unlimited six-year terms—even more. As Park grew more dictatorial, the opposition grew stronger. In 1978, Park was indirectly elected to another term. The following year, massive protests rocked the country and, on Oct 26, 1979, Park was assassinated by his own head of intelligence, finally bringing his 18-year grip on Korea to an end.

Democracy, Olympics and the IMF

The end of Park did not lead to an end to dictatorship, however. On Dec 12, 1979, the caretaker government that took over from Park was overthrown in another military coup led by Major General Chun Doo-hwan. Solidifying his control, Chun declared martial law in May 1980, sparking widespread protests. In the southwestern city of Gwangju, long a hotbed of pro-democracy activism, bloody clashes between protesters and paratroopers turned into a full-scale insurrection as local militia, composed of students and ordinary citizens, drove government forces from the city. After a siege, the army retook the city with much loss of life. The Gwangju Democratic Movement or, as it was called at the time, the "Gwangju Massacre," severely compromised Chun's already challenged legitimacy, and remained a permanent stain on his government.

Under Chun, Korea continued its impressive economic development. The economy was liberalized considerably, and new growth engines like electronics and semiconductors took off. By 1989, Korea's GNP reached US$230 billion, compared to just US$2.7 billion in 1962. Per capita income, too, had grown from US$103.88 to US$5,438.24 during the same period.

In April 1987, Chun, facing increasing opposition, attempted to hand off power to his chosen successor without direct elections. The public fury was immediate, intense and widespread. Massive street protests brought the nation to a standstill. Faced with an unappetizing choice between what promised to be an incredibly bloody crackdown and concessions to the protesters, Chun gave in. The constitution was revised again and direct elections held to chose Chun's replacement. And so democracy, denied to Koreans since 1960, was reborn.

Despite Korea's phenomenal economic and social development, popular images in the West were still those of a poor, war-torn nation. This changed in 1988, when Seoul hosted the Summer Olympic Games. The games were a "coming-out" party for the nation, which used the opportunity to show off to the world Korea's new status as a global player.

The Korean economic miracle continued throughout the early 1990s. In 1996, its status as a developed nation was made "official" when it joined the OECD; by this time, its GDP per capita had surpassed the US$10,000 mark. The following year, however, Korea was hit hard by the Asian Financial Crisis of 1997 and forced to go to the IMF for help. The then-record-setting IMF bailout of Korea, attended by huge layoffs and headline-grabbing business failures, was a huge blow to the Korean psyche. Sacrifices and selfless acts of patriotism by ordinary Koreans to help repay the debt, such as housewives donating their gold jewelry for the cause, earned worldwide praise, however.

World Cup, Sunshine and Today

The so-called IMF crisis helped long-time dissident, democracy activist and lawmaker Kim Dae-jung win the 1997 presidential election. The first-ever opposition candidate to win the presidency, Kim handled the financial crisis deftly, promoting liberalization, economic reform and the development of the information technology (IT) sector. By 1999, the Korean economy was once again growing quickly and, in 2001, Korea repaid its debt to the IMF in full, three years ahead of schedule.

Kim is best remembered, however, for his efforts to improve South Korea's relationship with North Korea. Since the Korean War, inter-Korean relations had alternated between hatred and outright hostility, despite several dialogue efforts. North Korean acts of aggression and terrorism were not uncommon and, in 1994, the peninsula nearly went to war over suspicions that Pyongyang was building nuclear weapons. Changing tact, Kim sought to encourage North Korea to change through reconciliation. In June 2000, he surprised the world by going to Pyongyang and holding the first-ever inter-Korean summit with North Korean leader Kim Jong-il. For his efforts, the South Korean president was awarded the Nobel Peace Price that year.

In 2002, South Korea co-hosted with Japan another major international sports event, the FIFA World Cup. Like the Olympics, this proved an opportunity for Korea to show off its post-1997 recovery and its development into a high-tech IT powerhouse.

Kim Dae-jung's policies towards North Korea were largely continued by his successor, Roh Moo-hyun, a former activist who sought to further democratize Korea's political and social systems. In 2008, however, Korean voters returned conservatives to both the parliament and the presidential mansion with the election of former Seoul mayor and Hyundai Construction CEO Lee Myung-bak, who has emphasized economic growth and infrastructural development. In 2010, Korea successfully hosted yet another major international event, the G20 summit.

As Korea begins the second decade of the 21st century, it faces many challenges. Some, like climate change and sustainable development, are ones it shares with nations worldwide. While the Korean economy is still largely dependent on exports and manufacturing, efforts are being made to transition to a more knowledge-based economy to take advantage of Korea's highly educated workforce and its world-leading IT infrastructure. Korean democracy, relatively young by global standards, continues to entrench itself. The issue of national reunification—a much desired but extraordinarily expensive endeavor, given the enormous costs it would require to raise North Korea to anywhere near South Korea's standard of living—promises to be a major discussion topic in the years ahead, especially as continued economic troubles put the long-term survivability of the North Korean regime in doubt.

The 2010 G-20 Summit in Seoul

SEOUL

HIGHLIGHTS

• Wander around Seoul's historic royal palaces, especially the UNESCO-designated Changdeokgung Palace, the crown jewel of Joseon Dynasty architecture

• Explore the old alleyways of the Bukchon neighborhood, a charming piece of old Seoul

• Sit in a traditional Korean teahouse in Insa-dong, an alley known for its traditional atmosphere, culture and antique shops

• Dance the night away in one of the many clubs in Hongdae, the heart of Korea's youthful indie culture

• Shop till you drop in Myeong-dong, Dongdaemun, Namdaemun or one of Seoul's countless other shopping districts

• Rub shoulders with the (mostly) rich and famous in Gangnam, where the Korean economic miracle is on full display

Buam-dong
SAMCHEONG-DONG • BUKCHON • SEONGBUK-DONG
• Daehangno
Seodaemun Prison Museum • • SEOUL'S ROYAL PALACES
• INSA-DONG
Sinchon • Jeong-dong • City Hall Area • DONGDAEMUN MARKET
HONGIK UNIVERSITY AREA • Namdaemun Area • MYEONG-DONG
Yanghwajin •
• Seoul Forest
• ITAEWON
• Apgujeong-dong
• YEOUIDO • Cheongdam-dong
• COEX Mall • Lotte World
GANGNAM

KOREA'S DYNAMIC, EVER-CHANGING HEART

Seoul has been the capital of Korea for 600 years.
With a population of over 10 million, the city is home to almost one in five people in South Korea. Not only is it the undisputed political, economic, social, cultural and educational heart of the country, it is quickly becoming one of the world's truly great cities as a center of international trade, commerce and culture. Life here moves at a frantic, non-stop pace—New York City might bill itself as the city that never sleeps, but to see that slogan practically applied, come to Seoul.

If there is one constant in Seoul, it's change. The city is a microcosm of the Korean economic miracle: over the last 60 years, it has transformed itself from a poor, bombed-out Third World capital into an advanced, affluent and well-run global metropolis. In recent years, the city has made a major push to beautify its cityscape, which had previously favored function over form. How Seoul will look in a few years, nobody knows.

Like Korea in general, Seoul is a city of dynamic contrasts between the old and the new. Historic palaces, temples and gates blend seamlessly with skyscrapers and neon lights. The same goes for the residents—one moment you could be talking with a Buddhist monk, the next partying with hipsters in Hongdae. The city is also home to an increasingly large international community. The opportunities here are endless; all you need to do is explore.

Night view of the Hangang River and downtown Seoul.
N Seoul Tower looms in the background.

History

The area where the city of Seoul now stands—the fertile flood valley of the Hangang River—has been inhabited since the Stone Age. In the Amsa-dong region of what is now southern Seoul, archaeological evidence has been unearthed indicating that humans have lived here for some 3,000-7,000 years. During the Three Kingdoms Period (57 BC–AD 668), the strategic Seoul area was an object of inter-kingdom rivalry to control its fertile lands and important transportation routes. By the mid-6th century, the kingdom of Silla gained control of the region and kept it for the entirety of the dynasty.

Stone guardian stands sentry before Gyeongbokgung Palace

The subsequent dynasty, Goryeo (918–1392), established its capital in the present-day city of Gaeseong (in North Korea). Seoul (or the city that would one day become Seoul, anyway), meanwhile, grew bigger and more influential, too, largely owing to its location near the royal capital. In 1067, it was designated one of three sub-capitals and took on a new administrative importance. Palaces were built in the city, and as nearby subjects relocated to the growing town, the outline of Seoul's historic downtown area began taking shape.

In 1392, General Yi Seong-gye seized power following a successful coup against the last Goryeo king and founded a new dynasty, the kingdom of Joseon. This new kingdom, founded on the ideology of neo-Confucianism, would bring some 500 years of stability to Korea and establish the basis of much of what is now regarded as Korean traditional culture. Heeding the counsel of his friend and adviser, the Buddhist monk Muhak, Gen. Yi moved the capital of the new kingdom to Seoul, then called Hanyang (and later Hanseong). Royal palaces and shrines were built, and in 1394, the royal government officially took up residence in the new capital. Shortly thereafter, work began on an 18 km ring of walls to surround and protect the city—much of the walls still remain, as do several of their gates. By 1405, most of the city planning was complete. Much attention went into it, with palace, ministry, gate and road positions carefully determined by the demands of feng shui or Asian geomancy. In fact, Seoul's historic downtown area still holds true to this original plan. The Renaissance of Joseon-era Seoul was the mid-18th century, when Korea was ruled by the energetic and reform-minded King Yeongjo. Trade along the Hangang River flourished and commercial activity in the capital blossomed as trade linkages were established with provincial areas of the country.

With the opening of Korea to the West at the end of the 19th century, great changes came to Seoul. Missionaries set up modern schools and hospitals (as well as, of course, churches), while an American company established the city's first electric company, tram system and water treatment facilities. Western architecture was imported, and the city began to take on a decidedly modern appearance. When the Japanese colonized Korea in 1910, they established their government-general in Seoul, which they renamed Keijo. Under Japanese rule, Seoul both expanded greatly and modernized. In 1905, Seoul's population was just 250,000. By 1936, it had grown to 730,000, including a large number of Japanese settlers. Imperial rule proved harsh, with the colonial authorities showing little regard for

Seoul's cultural and historical heritage, tearing down the city's ancient walls and several of its gates to build roads and trams. Large parts of Seoul's royal palaces were demolished.

With the defeat of Imperial Japan by the Allies in 1945, Korea at long last recovered its independence. This proved bittersweet, however, as the peninsula was soon divided into the pro-Western Republic of Korea (i.e. South Korea) and the communist Democratic People's Republic of Korea (i.e. North Korea) in Pyongyang. On June 25, 1950, tensions between the two hostile states came to a dramatic head when North Korea launched an armored blitzkrieg on the South, igniting the Korean War. The three years of fighting left Seoul devastated. The city's infrastructure was ruined and much of its population—now swollen to 2.5 million due to an influx of refugees—was reduced to living in makeshift camps. With resources tight, rebuilding the city proved a difficult task, even with the aid of Korea's wartime allies. Gen. Park Chung-hee's bloodless coup on May 16, 1961 changed Seoul and Korea as a whole. Park ruled Korea with an iron fist for 18 years until his assassination in 1979. While dictatorial, Park nevertheless brought about unprecedented economic growth: during his rule, GNP per capita increased twentyfold through a program of export-oriented industrialization. The "Miracle on the Hangang River," as this rapid industrialization was called, continued on through the 80s and into the 90s, transforming Korea into one of the world's leading trade nations. Nowhere was this more apparent than in Gangnam, the area of Seoul south of the Hangang River, where this region was formerly nothing but farmland. Today, it is the city's most affluent area, home to upscale shopping districts, high-end residential neighborhoods and major international business districts. Seoul's "coming out party" was the 1988 Summer Olympic Games. Another sporting event, the 2002 FIFA World Cup Korea/Japan, again drew international attention to the city, which was widely praised for its successful hosting of the event and the enthusiastic outdoor celebrations that accompanied the matches. In recent years, the city has been focusing attention away from "hard" issues like construction and towards "soft" issues like quality of life and the environment. As Seoul rushes headlong into the future, environmental transformation and redevelopment are still at the forefront; expect the skyline to transform radically in the decades ahead.

Layout

Seoul is a big place, spread 605.21 km² over the floor of a basin surrounded by prominent mountains. The Hangang River bisects the city along an east-west axis, dividing into two sociological distinct regions, Gangbuk (the old city north of the river) and Gangnam (the affluent new city to the south). A series of bridges connect the two parts of the city. The city is big but, fortunately, most of its culturally and historically important sites are concentrated in the "old city" north of the river, centered on Gwanghwamun and Gyeongbokgung Palace. In theory, one can walk most of this but, in practice, some combination of bus/subway travel will be necessary.

One of the beautiful things about Seoul is that Mother Nature is always just a subway ride away. To the north of the city is Bukhansan National Park, home to dramatic granite peaks and beautifully forested hiking paths. To the south you'll find Mt. Gwanaksan and Mt. Namhansan, the latter home to the impressive Namhansanseong Fortress. Even in the heart of Seoul, you'll find some nice urban strolls on Mt. Namsan, Mt. Bugaksan, Mt. Inwangsan and Mt. Naksan.

SEOUL MAP

Gilsangsa Te
Suyeon Sanbang
Mt. Bugaksan
Gan
Mus

Cheong Wa Dae
(Blue House)
Seoul Selection
Bookshop
Gyeongbokgung Palace
Gwanghwamun
Cha
Pala

Anguk
Stn.

Gyeongbokgung Stn.
Jongno Tower
Insa-d

Digital Media Street
Digital Media City

World Cup Park

Independence Gate

City Hall

Myeong
Cathed

Yonsei Univ.

World Cup
Stadium Stn.

Euljiro 1-ga S

Seoul World Cup Stadium
Nanji Hangang Park

Ewha Womans Univ.

Sungnyemun

Myeong-dong
Hyundai
Dept. Store

Hongik Univ. Stn.

KT&G
Sangsang Madang

Namdaemun Market

Namsan Cable Car
N Seoul T

Ewha Womans
Univ. Stn.

Seoul Stn.

Mangwon
Hangang
Park

Sinchon Stn.

Hapjeong Stn.

Hongik Univ.

Playground
(Free Market)

Seonyudo Park

Yanghwajin

Millennium
Seoul Hilton

Seoul Marina

National Assembly

Yeouido
Hangang Park

Samgakji Stn.

Yongsan Electronics Market
Yongsan Stn.

War Memorial of Korea

Itaewon Marke

The National
Museum of Korea

Yeouido Stn.

63 Bldg.

Ichon Stn.

Ichon Hangang Park

Noryangjin Stn.

Hangang River

Sindorim Stn.

Noryangjin
Fish Market

Dongjak S

Guro Stn.

Guro Arts Valley

National Cemetery

Boramae Park

Sillim-dong Sundae Alley
(Korean Sausage)

Seoul Nat'l Univ.

Isu Stn.

Seoul Nat'l Univ. Stn.

Seongnagwon Garden

Dream Forest

Sangbong Bus Terminal

Choi Sunu's Old Home

Dongsoong Art Center

Daehangno

Marronnier Park

ng Palace

Heunginjimun

Gyeongdong Oriental Medicine Market

rine

ore

Dongdaemun Stn.

Cheonggyecheon Stream

Chungmu Art Hall

Sindang-dong Tteokbokki Alley

Jangchung Jokbal Restaurants

Dongguk Univ. Stn.

ok Village/

W Seoul Walkerhill

l Theater of Korea

Children's Grand Park Stn.

Ttukseom Stn.

Gwangnaru Stn.

Gwangnaru Hangang Park

Cheonhodaegyo

Seoul Forest

Children's Grand Park

Techno Mart

useum of Art

Seoul Waterworks Museum

Seongsudaegyo

Dong Seoul Bus Terminal

n Hotel

Dongbodaegyo

UN Village

Central Mosque

Hyundai Dept. Store

Galleria Dept. Store

Ttukseom Resort Stn.

Ttukseom Resort

Yeongdongdaegyo

Cheongdamdaegyo

Jamsildaegyo

Jamsicheolgyo (Railroad Bridge)

Olympicdaegyo

Hannamdaegyo

Jaseng Hospital of Oriental Medicine

Garosu-gil Street

Jamwon Hangang Park

Bongeunsa Temple

Cheongdam Stn.

Jamsil Sports Complex

Jamsil Hangang Park

Olympic Park

BK Dong Yang Plastic Surgery Clinic

Sinsa Stn.

ASEM Tower

COEX

Samseong Stn.

Lotte World (Lotte World Folk Museum)

Jamsil Stn.

Park

Gangnam Kyobo Tower

Central City

The Ritz-Carlton, Seoul

LG Arts Center

Express Bus Terminal Stn.

Seolleung Stn.

Yeoksam Stn.

Gangnam Stn.

Seoul Nat'l Univ. of Education Stn.

Nambu Bus Terminal Stn.

l Arts Center/ onal Gugak Center

Yangjae Citizen's Forest

SEOUL'S ROYAL PALACES

The royal capital of the Joseon Dynasty for 500 years, Seoul is blessed with no fewer than five royal palaces. Making masterful use of their surroundings, these palaces are the epitome of Korean traditional architecture with their fine craftsmanship, harmonious design and human scale. Changdeokgung Palace, with its splendid royal pleasure gardens, is especially breathtaking. During the Joseon Dynasty, these palaces were virtually cities onto themselves. Sadly, during the Japanese colonial era, they were much reduced in size as the colonial government tore down much of them to make way for roads, zoos and colonial offices. Since Korea regained its independence, work has been ongoing to restore Seoul's palaces to their former glory.

Gyeongbokgung Palace 경복궁 B2

Gyeongbokgung is the most prominent of Seoul's royal palaces, thanks to its commanding location in the downtown Gwanghwamun neighborhood. The palace has a tumultuous past. It was first built in 1394 by King Taejo, the founder of the Joseon Dynasty, as the nerve center of the new royal capital of Hanseong (now known as Seoul). It was, along with the Jongmyo Shrine and several other major altars, one of the first structures built in the new capital, and its location at the southern foot of Mt. Bugaksan 북악산 was carefully determined by the principles of *feng shui*.

Like the Forbidden City in Beijing, Gyeongbokgung Palace was a city unto itself, full of residences, offices and shrines attended to by an army of servants and officials. The complex was ringed by stone

Gyeongbokgung Palace from above

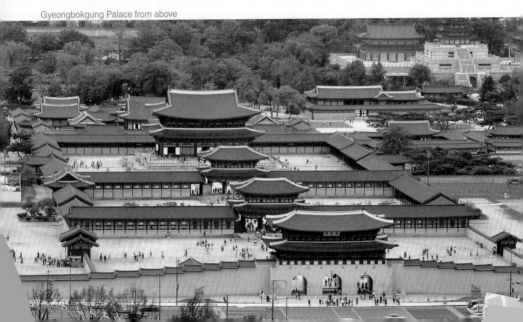

1 **Gwanghwamun Gate** 광화문 Restored to its original condition and form in 2010, this is the main gate to the palace and a Seoul landmark. **2** **Geunjeongjeon** 근정전 The massive main throne hall is surrounded by handsome cloisters. The stone markers in the courtyard mark where court officials stood during royal processions. **3** **Gyeonghoeru** 경회루 Used to host royal banquets, this impressive two-story banquet pavilion is surrounded by a large, picturesque pond. **4** **Hyangwonjeong Pavilion** 향원정 Sitting on a small island connected to land by a pretty wooden bridge, this pavilion blends in perfectly with the mountains that form its backdrop. **5** **Geoncheonggung** 건청궁 The newly restored Geoncheonggung is where Empress Myeongseong was assassinated in 1895. **6** **Jibokjae** 지복재 This old royal library (next to Geoncheonggung) is a mixture of Korean and Chinese architectural styles.

walls, passage through which was controlled by a series of imposing gates. In front of the palace, along what is now the broad boulevard of Sejong-ro 세종로, the royal government created "Yukjo Geori" ("Six Ministries Street"), where the ministries of the royal government were located.

During the Japanese invasions of 1592–1598, the palace was burnt to the ground, and Gyeongbokgung languished in ruin until 1867, when a major rebuilding project restored it to its former grandeur. This period of glory would not last long, however—in 1895, the strong-willed Empress Myeongseong was assassinated by Japanese agents (see p53), and King Gojong

fled the palace, never to return (see p37). After Japan's annexation of Korea, much of the palace was pulled down—only 10 buildings were left standing. Since Liberation, Gyeongbokgung has been the focus of much restoration effort—work continues to this day. In 2010, restoration work was completed on Gwanghwamun, the palace's iconic front gate.

Visiting a Korean palace can be a bittersweet experience. There is no doubting the ascetic beauty of the architecture, with its emphasis on harmony with the natural surroundings. Unfortunately, however, most of the buildings are empty, the palaces having been stripped of their artworks and furnishings during the Japanese colonial era.

⏰ 9 am to 6 pm (Mar–Oct), 9 am to 5 pm (Nov–Feb). Ticket sales stop one hour prior to closing. Closed Tuesdays 🎫 3,000 won 🚇 Gyeongbokgung Station, Line 3, Exit 5; Gwanghwamun Station, Line 5, Exit 1

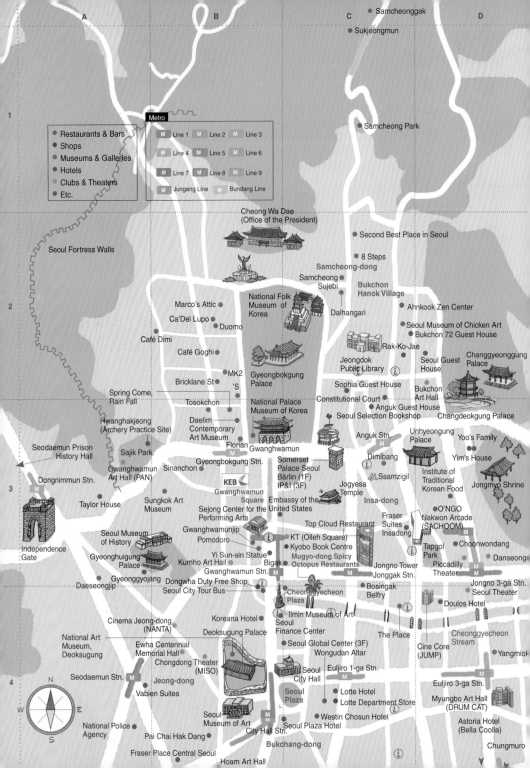

National Palace Museum of Korea 고궁박물관 B3
The National Palace Museum includes over 40,000 artifacts from the royal court of the Joseon Dynasty. ⊕ 9 am to 6 pm (weekdays), 9 am to 7 pm (weekends). Ticket sales stop one hour to closing. Closed Mondays 🎫 Free 🚇 Gyeongbokgung Station, Line 3, Exit 5; Gwanghwamun Station, Line 5, Exit 1 ✆ 02-3701-7500 🖰 www.gogung.go.kr

National Folk Museum of Korea 국립민속박물관 C2
Housing over 2,240 artifacts, the museum's exhibition educates visitors on how Koreans lived from traditional times to the present day. ⊕ 9 am to 6 pm (Mar–Oct), 9 am to 5 pm

TIPS

FREE GUIDED TOURS

Free guided tours for the palace in English are given at 11 am, 1:30 pm and 3:30 pm. Tours begin outside the information office inside Heungnyemun Gate 흥례문 and take about an hour. Tours are also given in Japanese and Chinese—inquire at the information office for times.

CHANGING OF THE GUARD

Changing of the Guard ceremonies take place every hour from 10 am to 3 pm in front of Heungnyemun Gate, which is located between Gwanghwamun Gate and the main courtyard.

EMPRESS MYEONGSEONG

History and Culture

The Empress Myeongseong (1851–1895), also known as Queen Min, is one of the most fascinating—and most tragic—figures of the late Joseon era. Born into the Min family, a once powerful clan that had grown impoverished over the ages, she was orphaned by age 9. Still, she drew the attention of the wife of the powerful prince regent, Heungseon Daewongun, who was tasked with finding a wife for his son, the young King Gojong (see p37). The future queen, born of a noble family but with no close relatives who might compete for influence, was the perfect choice. In 1866, she and King Gojong—two years her junior—were married.

Korean court politics had long been dominated by factionalism, and the young queen became a master of it. Before long, she headed a faction to rival that of the Heungseon Daewongun himself, with enmity between the two becoming quite public. When she finally succeeded in forcing the prince regent to retire from the palace in 1872, she gained complete control over the court, placing her relatives in high positions.

The queen oversaw a dramatic time in Korean history—internally, the country was beset by divisions between conservatives and reformers, while beyond Korea's shores, the Great Powers looked on with imperial ambitions. Her inclinations were generally with reformers and the West—much of Korea's modernization of the late 19th century took place under her patronage. This put her at odds with conservatives (led by the still influential Heungseon Daewongun) and, perhaps more importantly, Imperial Japan. On Oct 8, 1895, a gang of ruffians—widely believed to have been organized by Japanese resident minister Miura Goro—broke into Gyeongbokung Palace and assassinated the powerful queen. Although 65 men, including Miura, were charged in Japan for complicity in the killing, none were convicted.

Queen Min, posthumously made empress in 1902, has today become a symbol of the tragedy of Korea's history, a heroic figure who stood up to foreign aggressors and paid the ultimate price.

(Nov–Feb), 9 am to 7 pm (Sat, holidays). Ticket sales stop one hour prior to closing. Closed Tuesdays 🍴 Free 🚇 Gyeongbokgung Station, Line 3, Exit 5; Anguk Station, Line 3, Exit 1 ✆ 02-3704-3114 🖰 www.nfm.go.kr

Changdeokgung Palace 창덕궁 D3

Gyeongbokgung Palace may be Seoul's largest palace but for many, Changdeokgung Palace is the most beautiful. A UNESCO World Heritage Site, Changdeokgung is the epitome of Korean traditional architecture, its structures striking a fine balance with the natural landscape. The most beautiful part of the palace, however, is its rear garden, or Huwon, widely regarded as the finest example of Korean traditional gardening. If you are able to visit only one palace in Seoul, make it this one. You can tour the palace grounds freely (after paying admission, of course), but to enter the Huwon, you need to join a guided tour (see p56).

Construction of Changdeokgung began in 1405 and was completed in 1412. Like Gyeongbokgung, it was burnt to the ground during the Japanese invasions of 1592–1598, but, unlike Gyeongbokgung, it was rebuilt after the war for use as the royal residence. Fire proved a persistent problem—a blaze in 1623 destroyed almost everything except the main throne hall, and another in 1917 caused a great deal of damage. In order to "restore" the palace following the 1917 blaze, the Japanese took down and moved several buildings from Gyeongbokgung Palace to Changdeokgung Palace.

For 254 years from 1618 to 1872, Changdeokgung was the royal seat of government. In 1907, it briefly became the royal seat of government again, when Korea's last reigning monarch, Emperor Sunjong, ruled from the palace following the forced abdication of his father, Emperor Gojong. Furthermore, following its return from Japan in 1963, the Korean royal

The Huwon Garden's Aeryeonji Pond in autumn

1 **Donhwamun Gate** 돈화문 The original gate was built in 1412, while the current gate dates from 1609, making it the oldest of Seoul's palace gates. 2 **Geumcheongyo** 금천교 Constructed in 1411, this is the oldest stone bridge in Seoul. Be sure to check out its carvings. 3 **Injeongjeon** 인정전 The main throne hall was built in 1804. Note the beautiful folding screen behind the throne, the intricate carvings on the ceiling, and the somewhat out-of-place Western-style parquet floor, lights and curtains, installed in 1908. 4 **Nakseonjae** 낙선재 A small collection of buildings in the southeastern corner of the palace complex, the Nakseonjae was built in 1847 as a residence for a royal concubine and the royal mother and grandmother. From 1963 to 1989, Nakseonjae was the place of residence of the last descendants of the Korean royal family. Open for viewing on Friday, Saturday and Sunday.

family used a small portion of the palace as a residence until the death of the crown princess in 1989.

The palace complex—including its spectacular gardens—was registered with UNESCO in 1997. In registering the palace, the UNESCO committee called it "an outstanding example of Far Eastern palace architecture and garden design, exceptional for the way in which the buildings are integrated into and harmonized with the natural setting, adapting to the topography and retaining indigenous tree cover."

☺ See TIPS on p56. Closed Mondays
🎫 3,000 won (general tour), 5,000 won (Ongnyucheon and Nakseonjae tour), 15,000 won (open tour) 🚇 Exit 3 of Anguk Station, Line 3. Walk past the Hyundai Building 현대빌딩
📞 02-762-8261 🖥 www.cdg.go.kr

Huwon Garden 후원

The most beautiful spot in Changdeokgung Palace is Huwon Garden, the epitome of Korean traditional gardening. Like English gardens, Korean gardens seek to utilize the surroundings in as natural a way as possible—hillsides, streams, and rocks become integral parts of the garden. Nothing is forced: pavilions, ponds and other man-made elements are added to complement the landscape, not dominate it.

Huwon Garden is broken into three sections. The most visited is the area surrounding Buyongji Pond 부용지, a square-shaped artificial pond with a small, circular island in the middle—the shape of the pond and island is an expression of Korea's traditional view of the cosmos. The pond is surrounded by several beautiful pavilions, the most outstanding of which is Buyongjeong Pavilion, built in 1792.

Past Buyongji Pond area, just through the stone Bullomun Gate 불로문 ("No Aging Gate"), is Aeryeonji Pond 애련지, another pond that is particularly spectacular in autumn when the surrounding trees turn bright red. Also nearby is the spectacular Yeongyeongdang 연경당, a villa built in the style of a Joseon-era gentry residence by the crown prince in the early 19th century, and has a wonderful rustic beauty about it.

Past the Aeryeonji area are the inner parts of the garden. These sections were, until recently, closed to the general public. One of the highlights of the inner garden is Gwallamjeong Pavilion 관람정, a uniquely designed gazebo shaped like an open fan. Nearby is Jondeokjeong Pavilion 존덕정, a hexagonal gazebo dating from 1644. Further inward is the scenic Ongnyucheon Stream 옥류천, with an artificial waterway where the king and his court would play royal drinking games amidst the natural beauty.

TIPS

Admission, Guided Tours & All-Palace Tour

Admission to the Changdeokgung Palace itself is 3,000 won. This will allow you to walk freely around the palace and the Nakseonjae complex. It will NOT get you access to Huwon Garden, however.

To enter Huwon Garden, you need to join a separate guided tour. Tickets to this tour are 5,000 won, and can be purchased from the gate at the entrance of the garden. English tours are conducted twice daily—at 11:30 am and 2:30 pm. If you're a Korean speaker, or don't care about the guides' explanations, you could join a Korean tour, which are held almost hourly from 10 am to 4:30 pm. Tours in Japanese and Chinese are available, too.

In addition, you can also purchase a 10,000 won ticket that will get you one each entry into Changdeokgung Palace (including the Huwon Garden), Changgyeonggung Palace, Gyeongbokgung Palace, Deoksugung Palace and Jongmyo Shrine and is good for up to a month; these month-long passes be purchased at any of the palaces.

Changdeokgung Palace from above

Jongmyo Shrine 종묘 D3

Jongmyo Shrine houses the memorial tablets of the kings and queens of the Joseon Dynasty. One of the oldest Confucian shrines in Korea, its simple design is considered the epitome of Joseon-era Confucian architecture. Its long, unadorned halls, built to harmonize with the surrounding woods, display the modesty and love of nature so typical of Korean Confucianism, while its structure and layout encapsulate Confucianism's social hierarchy.

The shrine is also, along with Changdeokgung Palace, one of Seoul's two UNESCO World Heritage Sites. It is also the site of the annual Jongmyo Daeje rite 종묘대제, accompanied by the Jongmyo Jeryeak 종묘제례악, a piece of Korean traditional court music designated by UNESCO a "Masterpiece of the Oral and Intangible Heritage of Humanity."

As the memorial shrine of the dynasty, Jongmyo Shrine was one of the first structures built in Seoul when Yi Seong-gye—King Taejo—moved the capital of his new kingdom here in 1394. Like many other important structures, it was burned down in the Japanese invasions of 1592–1598, but rebuilt in 1601. Since then, the shrine complex has remained miraculously untouched in its original condition.

Today, the shrine—or at least its main hall—holds the memorial tablets of 19 kings and 30 queens. The rooms holding the memorial tablets are themselves simple and unadorned. The two-building complex itself, however, is appropriately stately—when it was first constructed, the shrine's main hall may very well have been the longest building in Asia. The complex is located to the east of Gyeongbokgung Palace; to the west of the palace was built another shrine, Sajikdan Altar 사직단.

The time to go to Jongmyo Shrine is the first Sunday in May, when it plays host to the Jongmyo Daeje rite, a spectacular annual performance of Korean traditional

court music and dance. In the Joseon era, the ceremony—a memorial rite to monarchs past—was held five times a year, led by the king and queen. Now it is held just once a year. During the highly ritual-conscious Joseon era, the ritual was considered absolutely vital to the nation's survival and prosperity.

⊕ **Mar–Oct**: 9 am to 6 pm (weekdays), 9 am to 7 pm (weekends, public holidays). **Nov–Feb**: 9 am to 5:30 pm (weekdays, weekends). Ticket sales stop one hour prior to closing. Closed Tuesdays ⊟ 1,000 won 🚇 Five minute walk from Jongno 3-ga Station (Exit 11 of Line 1, Exit 8 of Line 3, Exit 8 of Line 5) ✆ 02-765-0195 ⏱ http://jm.cha.go.kr

Changgyeonggung Palace 창경궁 D2
Changgyeonggung Palace has a rather odd history. It was originally built in 1484 as a residence for two former queens and the

History and Culture

CUTTING THE SPIRIT OF THE KINGDOM
Jongmyo Shrine used to be connected to Changgyeonggung Palace. In the Japanese colonial era, however, a road was built between the palace and shrine to symbolically sever the spiritual link between the royal family and its ancestors. Palace and shrine have now been reconnected via an overpass—if you are visiting Changgyeonggung Palace, it's worth visiting Jongmyo, too, although the closing time of the overpass entrance is a half hour earlier than the main entrance.

royal mother. The place was torched during the Japanese invasions, and rebuilt in 1616. In 1907, when Emperor Sunjong moved from Deoksugung Palace to Changdeokgung, Changgyeonggung was turned into a park, complete with a zoo and botanical garden. This "parkification" was completed by the Japanese in 1910, when they renamed the place from Changgyeonggung ("Changgyeong Palace")

Rear garden, Changgyeonggung Palace

1. Changgyeonggung Palace 2. Throne, Changgyeonggung Palace 3. Botanical Garden

to Changgyeongwon ("Changgyeong Garden") and opened it to the general public. In 1983, the zoo was removed and the compound restored to "palace" status. But it still feels like a park, and the botanical garden is still there.

Honghwamun Gate 홍화문 **and Okcheongyo Bridge** 옥천교 Eenter the palace through Honghwamun Gate, built in 1616. After the gate, there is a beautiful stone bridge, built in 1483, that crosses a small stream.

Myeongjeongjeon Hall 명정전 The main throne hall (built in 1616) is smaller than the throne halls of Gyeongbokgung or Changdeokgung, but it's beautifully designed with some particularly intricate cloisters behind it. To the left of the main hall is Munjeongjeon 문정전, the site of one of the most tragic stories of the Joseon Dynasty.

Chundangji Pond 춘당지 The site of Chundangji Pond was originally a royal farm plot but in 1909, a Japanese-style pond was dug, complete with a Japanese-style pavilion and boats. The pavilion and boats are now gone but the pond—lined by beautiful trees and a Chinese pagoda—still remains.

Botanical Garden The Victorian-style glasshouse of Changgyeonggung Botanical Garden 창경궁 대온실 was built in 1907 as Korea's first such glasshouse, and is home to rare Korean flora.

🕐 9 am to 6:30 pm (Apr to Oct), 9 am to 5:30 pm (Nov to Mar) 9 am to 5 pm (Dec to Feb). Closed Mondays 1,000 won 🚇 Exit 4, Hyehwa Station, Line 4. Walk 15 minute ☎ 762-4868~9 🖥 http://cgg.cha.go.kr

Deoksugung Palace 덕수궁 B4

Deoksugung Palace is the most "urban" of Seoul's palaces, located in the heart of the city just across from Seoul City Hall. In fact, it's two palaces in one—one a Korean traditional palace, complete with brightly colored tile-roofed structures, and the other a Western-style palace highlighted by the grand neoclassical Seokjojeon Hall.

Built as a villa in the 15th century, the palace was greatly expanded at the end of the 19th century as a residence for Emperor Gojong (see p37), who moved here in 1897 following a year's residency at the nearby Russian legation. In 1907, he was forced to abdicate under Japanese pressure, but he

TIPS

ENGLISH LANGUAGE TOURS

English language tours of the palace are given at 10:30 am on Tuesday to Friday, and 1:40 pm on Saturday and Sunday. Japanese, Chinese and Korean language tours are also available.

continued to live at the palace until his death in 1919.

⏰ 9 am to 9 pm (Ticketing closes 8 pm) Closed Mondays 💵 1,000 won 🚇 City Hall Station, Line 1, Exit 2; Line 2, Exit 12 ☎ 02-771-9951

Deoksugung Palace

Junghwajeon Hall (left), Seokjojeon Hall

Daehanmun Gate 대한문 The current main gate dates from a 1906 reconstruction. It is here that changing of the guard ceremonies (see p53) are held three times a day (11 am, 2 and 3:30 pm).

Junghwajeon Hall 중화전 The main throne hall of the palace, this splendid building burnt down in 1901 and was rebuilt in 1906.

Jeonggwanheon Pavilion 정관헌 One of Seoul's quirkier pieces of older architecture, this part-Korean, part-Romanesque pavilion was built by a Russian architect as a coffee house for Emperor Gojong.

Seokjojeon Hall 석조전 This massive neoclassical hall, designed by a Briton and completed in 1910, was built as Gojong's royal residence.

National Museum of Contemporary Art, Deoksugung Annex 국립현대미술관. 덕수궁 Another massive neoclassical building, this one was completed in 1939 as the so-called Yi Royal Family Museum. Today it is the Deoksugung Annex of the National Museum of Contemporary Art, one of the finest museums in the country.

⏱ 9 am to 6 pm (Tue–Thu); 9 am to 8:30 pm (Fri–Sun). Closed Mondays 🎟 Free to 5,000 won (depends on exhibition) ☎ 02- 368-1414

History and Culture

A Cup of Coffee for the Emperor

During his stay at the Russian legation, King Gojong developed a taste for coffee, prepared for him by Antoinette Sontag, the sister-in-law of the Russian minister and the founder of Seoul's first Western hotel. He took his newfound love of java with him when he left the Russian legation for his new home at Deoksugung Palace. The king commissioned Russian architect Aleksey Seredin-Sabatin to build a pavilion where he could sit and enjoy a cup of coffee.

The result was an amusingly eclectic building mixing Western Romanesque designs with Korean motifs—check out the deer and flower patterns in the railings and frieze. It is irregularly used for coffee and tea events even today, and is open to the public every Saturday.

Jeonggwanheon Pavilion

KING GOJONG AND THE RISE AND FALL OF THE DAEHAN EMPIRE

At the close of the 19th century, Korea was in trouble. Centuries of stability under the kings of the Joseon Dynasty had disintegrated in a perfect storm of internal conflict and external pressure from the imperial powers.

In 1895, a modernized Japan handily defeated the Qing Dynasty of China, making it the most powerful country in East Asia. Competing for influence in the region was Russia, with strong interests in northeast China. In the Korean court, already long plagued by factional strife, pro-Russian and pro-Japanese politicians struggled for dominance.

In 1884, pro-Japanese reformers staged a coup, taking control of the royal court. In 1895, the powerful pro-Russian queen of King Gojong, Queen Min, was assassinated at Gyeongbokgung Palace by ruffians (an event widely believed to have taken place at the behest of the Japanese legation), forcing the king and the crown prince to seek refuge at the Russian legation in Jeong-dong. During the king's yearlong stay at the legation, the Russians used their influence to replace the pro-Japanese court with pro-Russian figures.

This culminated with King Gojong leaving the Russian legation in 1897 and taking up residence at Deoksugung Palace. There, he declared the Daehan Empire, placing himself on equal footing to the Chinese emperor. The empire proved a dramatic time; needing to modernize or perish, Emperor Gojong worked to bring his country into the modern world. Diplomats, businessmen, missionaries and teachers flocked to the country. Modern schools and hospitals were built, railroads and streetcar systems opened, churches established, and electricity and water facilities developed. Treaties were signed with various countries, and foreign businessmen obtained concessions in mining, transportation and other industries throughout the country.

Unfortunately for the kingdom, the foreigners also brought imperial ambitions. In 1904, the competition between Japan and Russia for dominance in the region came to a head with the Russo-Japanese War, won by Japan in 1905. With the Russians out of the way and the Americans, British and French doing little to stop them, the Japanese strong-armed the Korean court into signing the Protectorate Treaty of 1905, giving control of Korea's foreign relations to Japan. When Emperor Gojong tried to fight this by sending a delegation to the Hague Convention of 1907, the Japanese forced him to abdicate in favor of the crown prince. Finally, on Aug 22, 1910, the Japanese made their rule over Korea complete with the Japan-Korea Annexation Treaty, thus starting 35 years of colonial rule.

With its harmonization of Korean traditional and "modern" Western elements, Deoksugung Palace is a symbol of the Daehan Empire.

TIPS

CHANGING OF THE ROYAL GUARD CEREMONY

Now the capital of a presidential republic, Seoul might no longer have a resident monarch, but it still has a changing of the royal guard ceremony.

In the days of the Joseon kings, the palace gates were guarded by an elite military unit called the Sumungun. The unit was tasked with opening and closing the gates and patrolling the area around the palace. This tradition fell out of practice with the end of the monarchy, but was revived in 1996 to give both residents and visitors a taste of the lost culture of the royal palaces.

Changing of the guard ceremonies 수문장교대식 take place in front of the Daehanmun Gate of Deoksugung Palace three times daily, at 11 am, 2 and 3:30 pm (no ceremonies Monday). In addition to period attire—various colors representing different ranks and positions—the affair is accompanied by the beating of drums, the barking out of orders and Korean traditional martial music. The pageantry of it all tends to be quite popular with visitors, as evidenced by the crowds of camera and camcorder-toting tourists that gather for the ceremonies.

Gyeonghuigung Palace 경희궁 B3

Built as a secondary palace in 1616, Gyeonghuigung became a royal residence in 1624, when Changdeokgung Palace was set alight as rebels occupied Seoul. Just prior to Japan's annexation of Korea in 1910, however, the palace was completely dismantled to make room for a school. In 1988, Seoul began to rebuild the old palace. Many of the major structures have been restored, including the old throne hall and surrounding cloisters. The front gate of the palace, Heunghwamun Gate 흥화문, is original.

🎫 Free ⏰ 9 am to 6 pm (weekdays), 10 am to 6 pm (weekends, holidays). Closed Mondays 🚇 Gyeonghuigung Palace is just behind Seoul History Museum 서울역사박물관, and is a 5 minute walk from Exits 1 or 8 of Gwanghwamun Station, Line 5. ☎ 02-724-0274~6

Gyeonghuigung Palace

SAMCHEONG-DONG 삼청동

To the east of Gyeongbukgung Palace is a trendy area of cafés, restaurants and boutiques known as Samcheong-dong. It's a great area to escape the urban jungle and relax amidst a pleasing harmony of the charmingly traditional with the fashionably modern. Located in the area of Seoul known as Bukchon 북촌, Samcheong-dong is known for its relatively high number of Korean traditional homes or *hanok*. Many of the *hanok* have been turned into cafés, restaurants and wine bars. Joining them are newer cafés and bars built in trendy modern styles. It's a popular place to walk around and, should the mood strike, enjoy a cup of coffee or a glass of wine in a charming setting. For shoppers, there are a good number of small boutiques carrying items such as clothes, shoes, handbags, and other accessories.

Samcheong-dong Road 삼청동길

Start your Samcheong-dong stroll from Samcheong-dong Road. The road follows along the eastern wall of Gyeongbokgung Palace. At the entrance to the road stands Dongsipjagak 동십자각, once the southeast guard tower of Gyeongbokgung. Later road development turned it into a traffic island.

To the left of the road is the beautiful stone wall of the palace—lined by an impressive row of ginkgo trees, this makes for one of the best walks in Seoul in autumn, when the trees turn bright yellow. To the right is a series of art galleries, including Gallery Hyundai, Kumho Museum of Art, Growrich Gallery, Gallery SUN Contemporary, Hakgojae Gallery,

Stone wall of Gyeongbokgung Palace, Samcheong-dong Road

Keumsan Gallery, Kukje Gallery and Gallery Ihn.

Follow Samcheong-dong Road up, and you'll eventually reach a fork—one fork heads to Cheongwadae 청와대 (the presidential mansion), while the other takes you to a road of cafés, restaurants and the Prime Minister's Residence 국무총리공관.

🚇 Samcheong-dong Road is approached via Exit 1, Anguk Station, Line 3 (walk towards Gwanghwamun Gate 광화문), or Exit 4, Gyeongbokgung Station, Line 3 (walk past Gyeongbokgung Palace). Once you see Dongsipjagak, head up that road.

TIPS

SEOUL SELECTION BOOKSHOP

Also on Samcheong-dong Road, near Dongsipjagak, is Seoul Selection Bookshop, one of Seoul's best places to score English-language books on Korea or DVDs of Korean films with English subtitles. It also has a café with helpful staff happy to provide tourist information. (Hours: 9:30 am to 6:30 pm. Closed Sundays, 02-734-9565, www.seoulselection.com)

Dongsipjagak, old guard tower of Gyeongbokgung Palace, entrance to Samcheong-dong

Restaurants & Cafés

Samcheong-dong is filled with restaurants, cafés and wine bars. Many of them make use of Korean *hanok* homes that have been renovated or newly built for the purpose, providing patrons with a refined and tranquil ambiance quite distinct from other neighborhoods of Seoul. A number of places have rooftop seating with nice views of the historic surroundings. In addition to restaurants and cafés, Samcheong-dong has tons of small boutiques and shops that are popular with young Seoulites.

- **8 Steps** C2 European cuisine in a charming old Korean *hanok* setting. (02-738-5838)
- **Cook'n Heim** C2 Brings together hamburgers, art and a Korean garden. (02-733-1109)
- **Cave de La Petite France** B2 Good French cuisine and French wine in a cozy, exotic atmosphere. (02-739-1788)
- **Samcheong-dong Sujebi** 삼청동수제비 C1 Great potato noodle soup shop. And always crowded. (02-735-2965)
- **Second Best Place in Seoul** 서울에서 두번째로 잘하는집 C1 An old-style teahouse legendary for its *patjuk* (red bean porridge). (02-734-5302)
- **Maple Tree House** 단풍나무집 C1 Delicious meats in a relaxed and nicely lit atmosphere. (02-730-7461)
- **Yongsusan** 용수산 C1 Does Gaeseong-style Goryeo royal cuisine in a luxurious setting. Highly recommended. (02-732-3019)
- **Sosonjae** 소선재 C1 Decently priced Korean traditional cuisine made from seasonal vegetables and local ingredients. (02-730-7002)
- **Yeon** 연 C2 This *hanok* café welcomes travelers, and is a great place for a cup of tea or after-work drink. (02-734-3009)
- **Dalhangari** 달항아리 B2 While the interior might seem rather café-esque, this Samcheong-dong restaurant does organic Korean course cuisine (*jeongsik*) that is both tasty and good for you. (02-733-7902)

TIPS

CHEONGWADAE TOUR

The impressive presidential mansion of Cheongwadae 청와대, also known as the Blue House (from the color of its roof tiles), is the center of power in Korea. Security around here is tight—take note of the plainclothes security personnel as you walk along the road leading to the complex. Tours are conducted four times a day (10, 11 am, 2, 3 pm) from Tuesday to Saturday, but you need to apply at least 10 days in advance to go through the proper security screening. Visit the Cheongwadae website (http://english.president.go.kr) for more information.

Museums & Galleries

The Samcheong-dong area has a number of interesting museums and galleries, including:

- **Gallery Hyundai** 현대갤러리 A3 This gallery of modern art includes both Gallery Hyundai proper and the nearby Gallery Dugahun. ⊙ 10 am to 6 pm. Closed Mondays 🎫 Free ✆ 02-734-6111~3 🖰 www.galleryhyundai.com
- **Kumho Museum of Art** 금호미술관 A3 This museum opened in 1989 with the goal of discovering and supporting local Korean artists. ⊙ 10 am to 6:30 pm. Closed Mondays 🎫 2,000 won ✆ 02-720-5114 🖰 www.kumhomuseum.com
- **Kukje Gallery** 국제갤러리 B2 Recognizable by Jonathan Borofsky's statue of a walking woman on its roof, Kukje Gallery holds regular exhibits of local and international modern artists. ⊙ 10 am to 6 pm (Mon–Sat), 10 am to 5 pm (Sun) 🎫 Free ✆ 02-735-8449 🖰 www.kukjegallery.com
- **Hakgojae Gallery** 학고재갤러리 A3 Housed in a lovely Korean traditional house, Hakgojae Gallery holds exhibits of Korean and overseas modern artists. ⊙ 10 am to 7 pm (Tue–Sat), 10 am to 6 pm (Sun). Closed Monday 🎫 Free ✆ 02-720-1524~6 🖰 www.hakgojae.com

BUKCHON 북촌

To get a feel for what Seoul was like prior to its late 20th century modernization, head to the Bukchon area between the palaces of Gyeongbokgung and Changdeokgung. This neighborhood, composed of winding alleys and Korean tile-roof homes, is the perfect place in which to get lost—few places in the city are as charming.

Owing to its politically strategic location between the palaces, Bukchon—or "North Village"—was long the preserve of Seoul's high-official elite. In the early 20th century, its large estates were broken up into smaller units to accommodate the city's growing population. It's at this time that the neighborhood took its current form of winding alleys with Korean *hanok* homes packed so closely together that, when seen from above, it appears to be a sea of black tiles.

In recent years, Bukchon has received a good deal of attention from city authorities who view the area as a tourism resource. This has been a mixed blessing: while the city has been pumping money into the neighborhood to protect and restore its *hanok*, the growing tourist trade has prompted some *hanok* owners to turn their properties into commercial establishments such as guest houses, cafés and wine bars. This has proven controversial, with some critics decrying its harm to the residential neighborhood's original traditional character.

Given the lay of the neighborhood, it would be difficult to give a precise A to B-style walking course. Broadly speaking, there are two main *hanok* clusters—31

31 Gahoe-dong, Bukchon Hanok Village

Gahoe-dong to the west and 11 Gahoe-dong (where many of the galleries are located) to the east. Use the map only as a general guideline because you're best off just wandering from spot to spot, discovering as you go.

🚇 Bukchon is best approached via Exit 1, 2 or 3 of Anguk Station, Line 3. From there, you're best off looking at the map on p64 for more detailed directions.

31 Gahoe-dong 가회동 31번지 C2 This is Bukchon's most famous cluster of *hanok* homes. Located on a gently sloping hill, the road provides outstanding views both at the bottom and at the top, where you can view modern downtown Seoul beyond the traditional tile roofs of Bukchon.

Simsimheon 심심헌 C2 On the left side of 31 Gahoe-dong, this stunning *hanok* is open to the public and well worth the 10,000 won entrance. Visitors get English explanations and homemade plum tea, too. Operated by the National Trust of Korea.
🕐 9 am to 6:30 pm. Closed Mondays 🎫 10,000 won 📞 02-763-3393 🖱 simsimheon.com

Bukchon Cultural Center 북촌문화센터 D3 This lovely *hanok* home was built in 1921 and is modeled on the Yeongyeongdang villa of Changdeokgung Palace. It is now owned by Seoul Metropolitan City and used as an information and cultural center, providing tours of the neighborhood and hosting classes and workshops.
🕐 9 am to 6 pm 🎫 Free 📞 02-3707-8388 🖱 http://bukchon.seoul.go.kr

Gahoe Museum 가회박물관 D2 This *hanok* gallery is home to one of Seoul's best collections of traditional folk paintings and amulets. Craft programs are available and visitors are also treated to green tea! 🕐 10 am to 6 pm Closed Mondays 🎫 3,000 won 📞 02-741-0466 🖱 www.gahoemuseum.org

Han Sang-su Embroidery Museum 한상수자수박물관 D2 Features the work of master embroiderer Han Sang-su. Hands-on programs also available. 🕐 10 am to 5 pm. Closed Mondays 🎫 3,000 won 📞 02-744-1545 🖱 www.hansangsoo.com

Dong-Lim Knot Museum 동림매듭박물관 D2 This museum is dedicated to *maedeup*, Korean traditional decorative knots. Like many other Bukchon museums, participatory programs are conducted. 🕐 10 am to 6 pm. Closed Mondays 🎫 2,000 won 📞 02-3673-2778 🖱 www.shimyoungmi.com

Dugahun 두가헌 A3 Formerly the residence of a relative of the royal family, this 100-year-old *hanok* has been renovated as a café/wine bar/French-Italian restaurant. A tad pricey, but it's a great place to spend the evening (and even has a Cuban cigar menu). 🕐 **Tea Time:** 2:30 to 4 pm. Closed Mondays; **Wine Time:** 10 pm to 12 am. Closed Sundays 📞 02-3210-2100 🖱 www.dugahun.com

Restaurants & Cafés

• **Hwangsaengga Kalguksu** 황생가칼국수 B3
Handmade Korean noodles and dumplings.
Extremely popular, especially at lunch time.
(02-739-6334)

• **Bukchon Gamasot Seolleongtang** 북촌가마솥
설렁탕 B3 Not far from Bukchon's Jeongdok
Public Library 정독도서관, this place specializes
in *seolleongtang* 설렁탕, a rich beef broth
soup made from ox bone. (02-725-7355)

• **Ramyeon Ttaengineun Nal** 라면땡기는날 B3
Wildly popular, this cheap ramyeon noodle
restaurant is near Jeongdok Public Library.
(02-733-3330)

• **Coffee Mill** 커피방앗간 B3 Terrific *hanok*
coffee house with a great atmosphere, very
good cakes and waffles, and excellent
coffee. (02-732-7656)

TIPS

BUKCHON GUEST HOUSES

A number of the *hanok* homes in Bukchon
have been renovated for use as guest
houses. These places give visitors a chance
to experience a Korean traditional home and
are popular with foreign visitors. Most
provide Korean meals, and some even host
cultural events and programs. For a list, see
the Accommodation section on p154.

CULTURAL SENSITIVITY

Bukchon is an area so beautiful that you
sometimes forget that people actually live
there. Bukchon is, first and foremost, a
residential area, and a quiet one at that.
When you visit—and especially if you're
staying there—please keep the neighbors
in mind.

History and Culture

Hanok

Literally meaning "Korean home," the term *hanok* came into being after Korea's
opening to the West in order to differentiate Korea's traditional architecture from the
newer Western-style buildings. The major characteristics of a *hanok* are a) the use of
flues to heat the floor (a system called *ondol*), and b) large unheated wooden floors,
or *maru*, to keep the home cool in summer. Wealthier homes, such as those found in
Bukchon, have black-tile roofs (commoner homes were traditionally roofed with
straw), are multi-structured, and have central courtyards called *madang*.

Hanok are built solely from wood, stone and earth—the yellow earth used in the
walls, called *hwangto* in Korean, is said to have physical benefits for the occupants.
Windows and sliding doors are usually made from Korean paper, or *hanji*, although

more modernized *hanok* use glass. Like
other Korean traditional structures,
hanok are deliberately modest—they
are rarely, if ever painted, and they
emphasize "human" scale. Bukchon
hanok often have elegant front gates.

You never wear shoes in a *hanok*. You
sleep on the floor on a brightly-colored
cushioned mat called a *yo*.

INSA-DONG 인사동

Insa-dong is one of Seoul's best-known destinations to foreign visitors. The neighborhood, which in the old days was called (for reasons unknown) "Mary's Alley," is lined with antique shops, small galleries, traditional craft shops, cafés and restaurants. So popular is it with tourists that in recent years it has become, well, touristy, but it's still a fascinating area with some history to it.

Insa-dong has a "main drag," so to speak, that runs from its entrance near Anguk Station to opposite Tapgol (Pagoda) Park. From this main street radiate many smaller alleyways that are well worth exploring. Also in the Insa-dong area are several areas of historical and cultural interest, including Unhyeongung Palace, Minga Daheon, Cheondogyo Central Temple, Jogyesa Temple and Seung Dong Presbyterian Church 승동교회.

A number of sites in and around Insa-dong, including Tapgol Park, Cheondogyo Central Temple and Seung Dong Presbyterian Church, are closely tied with the March 1 Independence Movement (see p74) of 1919.

🚇 The north end of Insa-dong is approached via Exit 6 of Anguk Station, Line 3. The south end is reached via Exit 1 of Jongno 3-ga Station, Line 1, 3 or 5.

One of the many craft shops of Insa-dong

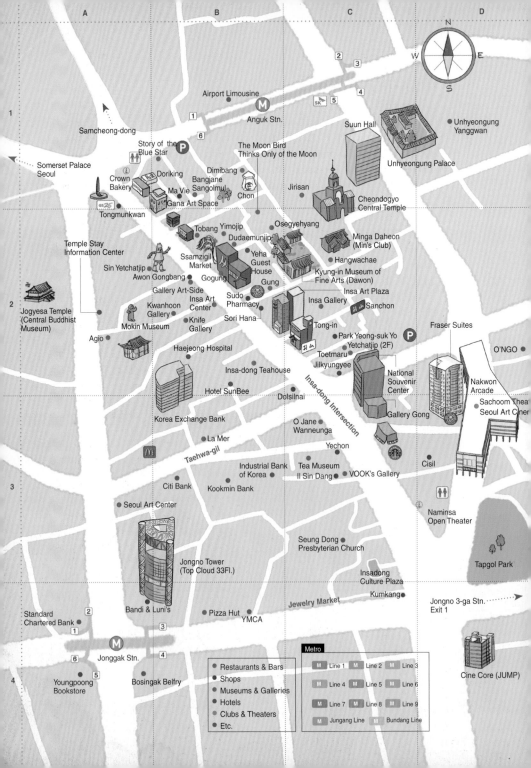

Map labels:

A B C D

N / W E / S

1

Samcheong-dong

Somerset Palace Seoul

Airport Limousine

Anguk Stn.

Story of the Blue Star

Crown Bakery
Doriking
Ma Vie
Gana Art Space

Dimibang
Bangjane
Sangolmul
Chon

The Moon Bird Thinks Only of the Moon

Jirisan

Suun Hall

Unhyeongung Yanggwan

Unhyeongung Palace

Cheondogyo Central Temple

Tongmunkwan

Temple Stay Information Center

Sin Yetchatjip
Awon Gongbang

Gallery Art-Side
Kwanhoon Gallery

Mokin Museum

Agio

Jogyesa Temple (Central Buddhist Museum)

Tobang Yimojip
Dudaemunjip
Ssamzigil Market
Gogung
Insa Art Center
Knife Gallery

Osegyehyang

Yeha Guest House
Gung

Sudo Pharmacy

Sori Hana

Minga Daheon (Min's Club)

Hangwachae

Kyung-in Museum of Fine Arts (Dawon)

Insa Art Plaza

Insa Gallery

Sanchon

Haejeong Hospital

Insa-dong Teahouse

Hotel SunBee

Korea Exchange Bank

La Mer

Taehwa-gil

Citi Bank
Kookmin Bank

Seoul Art Center

Jongno Tower (Top Cloud 33Fl.)

Bandi & Luni's

Dolsilnai

O Jane
Wanneunga

Yechon

Industrial Bank of Korea
Il Sin Dang
Tea Museum

VOOK's Gallery

Seung Dong Presbyterian Church

Insadong Culture Plaza
Kumkang

Tong-in

Park Yeong-suk Yo Yetchatjip (2F)
Toetmaru
Jilkyungyee

National Souvenir Center

Gallery Gong

Insa-dong Intersection

Fraser Suites

O'NGO

Nakwon Arcade

Sachoom Thea
Seoul Art Ciner

Cisil

Naminsa Open Theater

Tapgol Park

Jongno 3-ga Stn. Exit 1

Standard Chartered Bank

Jonggak Stn.

Youngpoong Bookstore

Bosingak Belfry

Pizza Hut
YMCA

Jewelry Market

Cine Core (JUMP)

Restaurants & Bars
Shops
Museums & Galleries
Hotels
Clubs & Theaters
Etc.

Metro

M Line 1   M Line 2   M Line 3
M Line 4   M Line 5   M Line 6
M Line 7   M Line 8   M Line 9
M Jungang Line   M Bundang Line

History & Culture

Jogyesa Temple 조계사 A2 Jogyesa Temple is the headquarters of the Jogye Order of Korean Buddhism, Korea's largest Buddhist sect. This is one of Seoul's most active Buddhist temples—be sure to visit during the Buddha's Birthday festivities, usually held in late April or early May. There's also a Buddhist history museum located on the complex. ✆ 02-732-2183 ⌂ www.jogyesa.kr

Templestay Information Center 템플스테이통합정보센터 A2 Just across from Jogyesa Temple is a massive new Temple Stay Information Center, which, as the name would suggest, provides information on stays at one of Korea's beautiful Buddhist monasteries. The center also has a restaurant (serving vegetarian Buddhist cuisine) and a café. ⊙ 9 am to 6 pm. Open all year round ✆ 02- 2031-2000 ⌂ eng.templestay.com

Unhyeongung Palace 운현궁 C1 This residence is notable as the home of Heungseon Daewongun, the conservative prince regent who was the effective ruler of Korea during Gojong's minority and for a good time afterwards. The palace, built between 1863

and 1873, is a typical upper-class Korean home, characterized by the rustic Confucian modesty so characteristic of the period. ⊙ 9 am to 6 pm (Nov–Mar), 9 am to 7 pm (Apr–Oct). Closed Mondays ▤ 700 won. Free for lunch hours (noon to 1 pm, Tue–Fri) ✆ 02-766-9090 ⌂ www.unhyeongung.or.kr

Cheondogyo Central Temple 천도교중앙대교당 C1 Built in 1921, this massive red brick Art Nouveau building, located just across from Unhyeongung Palace, is the central place of worship of Cheondogyo, a strongly nationalist religious group that mixes Korea's traditional faiths with elements of

1. Unhyeongung Palace 2. Jogyesa Temple 3. Cheondogyo Central Temple 4. Tapgol Park 5. Antique shop, Insa-dong

March 1 Independence Movement

History and Culture

Japan's annexation of Korea in 1910 marked the start of a dark period of brutal colonial rule. Opposition to Japanese rule reached a peak in 1919, when President Woodrow Wilson's proclamation of the right of self-determination at the Paris Peace Conference sparked a nationalist uprising in Korea. On March 1, 1919, 33 Korean nationalists met at a restaurant in Insa-dong to read a declaration of independence. In Tapgol Park, a Korean student recited a copy of the declaration before a massive crowd, while copies of the declaration were read throughout the country. The crowds evolved into processions and demonstrations that were put down with great brutality by the Japanese, who killed and arrested thousands of Koreans.

The March 1 Independence Movement is considered a catalyst of the Korean nationalist movement. To commemorate the movement, March 1 has been declared a national public holiday in Korea.

Christianity. During the colonial era, the Cheondogyo faith produced many independence activists, including a large number of the leaders of the March 1 Independence Movement of 1919.

Tapgol Park 탑골공원 D3 Tapgol Park has the distinction of being Seoul's first modern park, designed in 1897 by John McLeavy Brown, a British advisor to King Gojong. In 1919, independence protests here led to the March 1 Independence Movement. The highlight of the park is the 10-story Wongaksa pagoda 원각사지10층석탑, carved in marble during the Goryeo Dynasty.

Museums & Galleries

Kyung-in Museum of Fine Arts 경인미술관 C2 This fine gallery blends the modern and the traditional. It includes a Korean traditional home, Korean garden and traditional teahouse. ⏰ 10 am to 6 pm 🎫 Free ✆ 02-733-4448~9 🖱 www.kyunginart.co.kr

Gallery Art-Side 갤러리아트사이드 B2 Founded in 1999, this gallery focuses on Asian contemporary art. ⏰ 10 am to 6 pm. Closed Mondays & public holidays. ✆ 02-725-1020

Insa Art Center 인사아트센터 B2 This impressive six-floor art complex boasts four exhibition halls that presents a diverse range of styles and artworks for visitors to enjoy. ⏰ 10 am to 7 pm 🎫 Free ✆ 02-736-1020 🖱 www.insaartcenter.com

Kwanhoon Gallery 관훈갤러리 B2 Opened in 1979, this is one of the neighborhood's earliest display spaces for modern art—accordingly, it has helped to launch the career of many a young artist. ⏰ 10:30 am to 6:30 pm 🎫 Free ✆ 02-733-6469 🖱 www.Kwanhoongallery.com

Mokin Museum 목인박물관 A2 This intriguing museum contains some 8,000 wooden figures of people and animals. The Korean collection includes figures carved from the Joseon era to the present day. ⏰ 10 am to 7 pm. Closed Mondays. 🎫 5,000 won ✆ 02-722-5066 🖱 www.mokinmuseum.com

Insa Gallery 인사갤러리 C2 Opened in 1994, this modern art gallery has introduced to

the public many works by both veteran and up-and-coming artists. ⊙ 10 am to 6:30 pm (Mon–Sat); 10:30 am to 6 pm (Sun) 🎫 Free ✆ 02-735-2655

IBK Jump Theater 점프전용관 D4 A dazzling comic martial arts show, *Jump* combines traditional Korean taekwondo with *taekkyeon* and other modern Asian martial arts for a spectacular nonverbal performance. ⊙ Mon 8 pm/Tue to Sat 4, 8 pm/Sundays & public holidays 3 & 6 pm 🎫 40,000–50,000 won 🚇 Jonggak Station, Line 1, Exit 4 ✆ 02-722-3995 🖱 www.hijump.co.kr

Shops

Insa-dong is mostly known as a place to pick up art, antiques, craft supplies and traditional clothing—indeed, its history as a center of arts and antiques goes back over a century. If you're looking for distinctly Korean souvenirs, this would be a good place to look.

Ssamzigil Market 쌈지마켓 B2 This trendy, four-floor complex is a market within a market. Contains 70 shops including handicraft stores, souvenir shops, art galleries and restaurants. ⊙ 10 am to 8:30 pm ✆ 02-736-0088 🖱 www.ssamzigil.co.kr

Tong-in 통인 Founded in 1924, this is one of Insa-dong's best-known antique shops and carries many exquisite items including furniture. ⊙ 10 am to 7 pm (Apr–Sep); 10 am to 6 pm (Oct–Mar) ✆ 02-733-4867

Jilkyungyee 질경이 C2 This designer specializes in "modernized" *hanbok* or Korean traditional clothing. ⊙ 9 am to 9 pm ✆ 02-734-5934 🖱 www.jilkyungyee.co.kr

Tongmunkwan 통문관 A1 Opening in 1934 and run by the same family for three generations, this shop bills itself as the nation's oldest bookshop. ⊙ 10:30 am to 5:30 pm. Closed Sundays. ✆ 02-734-4092 🖱 www.tongmunkwan.co.kr

Park Yeong-suk Yo 박영숙요 C2 A ceramics shop famed for Queen Elizabeth II's 1999 visit, and well worth a look. ⊙ 10 am to 6 pm ✆ 02-730-7837

Sori Hana 소리하나 B2 One of the most popular traditional craft shops in Insa-dong, approximately a third made by famous designers (the other two thirds reproduction crafted by the shop itself). ⊙ 9:30 am to 8 pm ✆ 02-738-8335

Il Sin Dang 일신당 C3 If you'd like to take up the art of calligraphy or papercraft, Il Sin Dang has been selling, for 20 years, calligraphy brushes, traditional paper, and ink, among others. ⊙ 9 am to 8 pm ✆ 02-733-8100

WHAT TO EAT

• **Min's Club** 민가다헌 C2 Located in a beautiful *hanok* near Cheondogyo Central Temple, this place features fusion cuisine in an early 20th century setting. (02-733-2966)

• **Sanchon** 산촌 C2 Run by a former Buddhist monk, Sanchon is one of Seoul's best-known restaurants and specializes in vegetarian Buddhist temple cuisine. Music and dance performances take place in the evenings. Lunch: 22,000 won. Dinner: 39,600 won. Folk performances: 8 to 8:40 pm. Hours: 11:30 am to 10 pm. (02-735-0312)

• **Toetmaru** 툇마루 C2 Most famous for its barley rice *bibimbap* 보리비빔밥, a mixture of barley and rice covered with soybean paste stew, and crab marinated in soy sauce. Reasonably priced, too. (02-739-5683)

• **Bärlin** 베얼린 C3 The best German restaurant not just in Seoul, but in all of Korea. A very classy place with a distinctively German feel. (02-722-5622)

• **Top Cloud** 탑클라우드 C3 Located at the top of the distinctive Jongno Tower, this Western restaurant is better known for its outstanding views. (02-2230-3001)

JEONG-DONG 정동

A pleasant tree-lined neighborhood to the west of the Deoksugung Palace, Jeong-dong is where many of Seoul's first foreign legations, schools and churches were built in the late 19th and early 20th century. As such, the area was a major entry point for the introduction of foreign culture into Korea—Seoul's first Protestant churches, first modern schools and first modern hotel were all built there. Today, the area retains a somewhat exotic foreign charm, and a good number of historical buildings—many designed by Americans, Britons and Russians—still remain.

🚇 Exit 2 of City Hall Station, Line 1 or Exit 12 of Line 2.

Seoul Anglican Cathedral 서울성공회성당 This beautiful Romanesque-style granite church, built in 1926, is the mother church of Korea's Anglican faithful. English services are held 9:30 Sunday morning in the cathedral crypt chapel and 5:00 Sunday evening in the main cathedral. ✆ 02-739-0785

Seoul Museum of Art 서울시립미술관 Formerly the home of the Supreme Court, this museum is home to a collection of 1,432 works of art in such genres as Western painting, oriental painting, sculpture, crafts, photography and calligraphy.

🕐 10 am to 8 pm. Closed Mondays 🎫 Free
✆ 02-723-2491 🔖 http://seoulmoa.seoul.go.kr

Pai Chai Hak Dang 배재학당 Korea's first modern intermediate school, the school was founded in 1885 by American Methodist

Beautiful Romanesque exterior of Seoul Anglican Cathedral

1. Seoul Museum of Art 2. Former Russian Legation 3. Pai Chai Hak Dang
4. Chungdong First Methodist Church 5. Statue, Chungdong First Methodist Church

missionary Henry Gerhard Appenzeller, who also founded Chungdong First Methodist Church just down the street.

Chungdong First Methodist Church 정동제일감리교회
This stately American-style Gothic church of red brick was built in 1897 and is Korea's oldest existing Protestant church.

Salvation Army Headquarters 구세군본부
Completed in 1928, this massive neoclassical structure is hidden away on the road that passes in front of the US ambassador's residence.

Seoul Municipal Hall 서울시의회건물
This modernist structure was built in 1935 as a cultural hall. After Liberation, it was home to Korea's first parliament.

Jungmyeongjeon 중명전
Built in 1900, this Russian-designed building, now a museum, is important as the site for the signing of the Protectorate Treaty in 1905, under which Korea signed away its foreign policy decision-making to Japan.

Ewha Hak Dang 이화학당
Founded in 1886 by American Methodist missionary Mary F. Scranton, Ewha Hak Dang eventually grew into Ewha Middle and High Schools and Ewha Womans University, one of the world's largest women's universities. Check out the museum on the grounds.

Former Russian Legation 구러시아공관
Following the assassination of his queen, Empress Myeongseong, Emperor Gojong fled along with the crown prince to the Russian Legation, where they stayed for a full year. Most of the old embassy was burnt down during the Korean War; all that remains is its central tower.

Chongdong Theater 정동극장
Chongdong Theater has presented a 90 minute traditional performance every day of the year since 1997 in an effort to keep the spirit of Korean traditional performing arts alive in modern day. Shows are primarily geared towards foreign visitors; all performances are accompanied by English subtitles, and performers are available for pictures in their traditional garments after each performance. Tickets run between 20,000 won and 40,000 won.

ⓒ 02-751-1500 www.mct.or.kr

Former Russian Legation

Salvation Army Headquarters

Cheonggyecheon Stream

Seoul Municipal Hall

Junmyeongdang

Seoul Anglican Cathedral

Ewha Girls High School's Simpson Hall

Jungmyeongjeon Hall

Jeonggwanheon

Sontag Hotel

Seokjojeon

Hamnyeongjeon City Hall Plaza

Deoksugung Palace

Line 5 Seodaemun Stn.

Chungdong First Methodist Church

Deoksugung Palace Wall

Seoul Museum of Art

Pai Chai Hak Dang

Line 1,2 City Hall Stn.

Nanta Theater 난타전용관 A unique performance that draws around 300,000 visitors each year, "Nanta" is a nonverbal performance that combines traditional Korean *samulnori* rhythms with modern music, comedy, martial arts and dance, all in the setting of a kitchen. Tickets range from 50,000 won to 60,000 won, with three performances daily. There are two more Nanta theaters, in Hongdae and Myeong-dong, too ⓒ 02-739-8288 ⓑ http://nanta.i-pmc.co.kr

Deoksugung Palace Wall 덕수궁돌담길 The stone wall running along the south side of the palace is one of Seoul's most favored strolling spots, particularly in fall.

Deoksugung Palace Wall

DANGEROUS FOR YOUR RELATIONSHIP?

History and Culture

According to a popular saying, if you stroll along Deoksugung Palace Wall with a loved one, you'll split up by the time you reach the end. As for the origins of this saying, there are two popular theories. The first notes that the family court used to be located nearby, so couples seeking a divorce would, by necessity, pass by the stone wall. The second theory is that the spirits of female palace servants—who forwent marriage to serve the court, often doing the difficult work court ladies refused to do—still reside in the neighborhood.

CITY HALL AREA 서울시청 부근

The City Hall area, with its mixture of old Korean charm and modern-day energy, is a microcosm of the dynamic contrast between old and new that is Korea. Beautiful and intriguing at any time day or night, this wonderful district is a place where you could spend an entire day wandering around, soaking in history while getting a glimpse of the future.

City Hall Station, Line 1 or 2

Seoul City Hall 시청 **& Seoul Plaza** 서울플라자 C4, p52 Built in 1926 by the Japanese colonial government, original Seoul City Hall is an imposing, almost menacing gray faux-stone building. At the time of the writing of this book, City Hall is undergoing a major renovation, with the old building being included in a new, massive, state-of-the-art City Hall complex (to be completed in 2012). Seoul Plaza, the large oval-shaped lawn in front of City Hall, has been a favorite leisure spot for Seoul residents since it opened in 2004. In winter, a large outdoor ice rink is set up on the plaza.

Bukchang-dong 북창동 C4, p52 Behind Seoul Plaza Hotel and across from Seoul Plaza is the neighborhood of Bukchang-dong, known for its vibrant nightlife.

Seoul Finance Center 서울파이낸스센터 **& Mugyo-dong** 무교동 C4, p52 The Seoul Finance Center, a new 30-story building, is a good place to go for international dining. The first and second floor basements are full of eateries serving up food from all corners of the globe, including Thailand, Vietnam, India, Japan and China and there's also a deli. But for something truly Korean, try Mugyo-dong Octopus Alley 무교동낙지골목.

Gwanghwamun Square

Cheonggyecheon Stream

This is home to one of Seoul's most famous dishes, Mugyo-dong stir-fried octopus (*nakji bokkeum* 낙지볶음). If you like spicy food, this is a very good place to start. A two-person serving will run you about 18,000 won. For a bit more, you can enjoy live octopus (*san nakji* 산낙지)—consuming a still-squirming octopus is a dining experience you're unlikely to forget.

Cheonggyecheon Plaza 청계천광장 C4, p52 Cheonggyecheon Plaza marks the head of Cheonggyecheon Stream, one of Seoul's newest and most talked-about leisure spots. For decades an unsightly elevated highway, the urban waterway was restored and opened to the public in September 2005. The stream runs some 5.8 km and is a popular walking course with its distinctive bridges and diversity of neighborhoods. The plaza is dominated by "Spring," a 20-meter-high blue-and-red sculpture in the shape of a marsh snail by American pop artists Claes Oldenburg and Coosje van Bruggen; admittedly, it's not for everyone. There are several ways to get around

Cheonggyecheon. One, of course, is to walk it. Another is to take one of the special double-decker buses—there are five tours a day, departing from in front of Dongwha Duty Free Shop in Gwanghwamun.

Ilmin Museum of Art 일민미술관 C4, p52 Ilmin Museum of Art served as the headquarters of The Dong-A Ilbo newspaper from 1926 to 1992. It is now a 3-story contemporary art museum with a public documentary archive. ⏱ 11 am to 7 pm. Closed Mondays 🎟 Free ☎ 02-2020-2055·

Kyobo Book Centre 교보문고 C3, p52 Korea's largest book store, this monster shop in the basement of the Kyobo Insurance Building has Seoul's largest collection of foreign language books, making it very popular with resident foreigners. It also houses a large stationery store with a wide selection of goods. ⏱ 9:30 am to 10 pm ☎ 1544-1900

TIPS

WONGUDAN ALTAR 원구단 C4

Also near Seoul Plaza is Wongudan Altar, one of Seoul's truly hidden gems. Tucked away in the garden of Westin Chosun Hotel 웨스틴조선호텔, the three-story octagonal shrine, built in 1899, brings to mind the Temple of Heaven in Beijing. Following the proclamation of the Daehan Empire in 1897, Emperor Gwangmu (formerly King Gojong) would visit the altar to pray for a bountiful harvest. The Wongudan cuts a dramatic figure against a backdrop of skyscrapers and electronic signboards.

Sejong Center for the Performing Arts

Seoul Museum of History

Bigak 비각 C3, p52 This monument housed in a Korean-style pavilion located just in front of the landmark Kyobo Building, was built in 1902 to celebrate the 40th anniversary of King Gojong taking the throne.

Gwanghwamun Square 광화문광장 B3, p52 In August 2009, work was completed on a new square in the heart of the old downtown. Stretching from Gwanghwamun Gate to the Kyobo Building, Gwanghwamun Square is a pedestrian-friendly public space highlighted by two imposing statues of war hero Admiral Yi Sun-sin and King Sejong the Great. In summer, the square's water fountain—lit up at night—is a popular attraction, particularly for families.

Sejong Center for the Performing Arts 세종문화회관 B3, p52 Established in 1978, the Sejong Center features a wide range of performing arts, including drama, various musical genres and art. For up-to-date information on current performances in English, check out the Sejong Center homepage at www.sejongpac.or.kr/english ℂ 02-399-1111

Seoul Museum of History 서울역사박물관 B3, p52 Opened in 2002, this museum presents the history and culture of Seoul from prehistoric times to the modern age. A recently created highlight is a 1:1,500 scale model of the entire city. ⊕ Weekdays 9 am to 9 pm; weekends & holidays 9 am to 7 pm (Mar–Oct), 9 am to 6 pm (Nov–Feb) 🎫 Free ℂ 02-724-0274 🌐 http://museum.seoul.kr

TIPS

BOSINGAK 보신각
A short walk from Kyobo Book Store in the direction of Jonggak Station (Line 1) brings you to a large, Korean-style belfry. In Joseon times, its bell was rung to announce the daily opening and closing of Seoul's city gates. The evening and morning bells also marked the beginning and end to the nighttime curfew enforced in the royal capital. So central was this bell to city life that the street on which it is located—which was, as it is today, one of Seoul's most important roads—was named "Jongno" or "Bell Street."
The current pavilion dates from a post-Korean War reconstruction. In today's Korea, it is most famous for the bell-chiming ceremony held here at midnight of New Year's Eve, when crowds gather here to watch Seoul's mayor and other city notables ring in the new year.

MYEONG-DONG 명동

Myeong-dong is, above all else, a shopping district, and most of the people who visit do so either to drop money or watch other people drop money. As one of the city's chief fashion centers and a popular nightlife spot, Myeong-dong tends to attract a younger crowd (and a significant number of Japanese tourists). Stores are in the mid to high price range, with a large number of major international brand outlets as well. There are also the department stores, including the landmark Shinsegae and flagship branch of Lotte, as well as fashion emporium, Migliore.

Myeong-dong has a single "main drag," so to speak, where you'll find many of the high-end brand-name shops. The alleyways, meanwhile, are where you'll find mid-range and cheaper brands. Several of the department stores are located just outside the main area.

History

Myeong-dong began its life as a quiet residential village in the Joseon era. With the coming of the Japanese in the early 20th century, however, the neighborhood was transformed into the colonialists' primary commercial hub. It was at this time that much of the neighborhood's historic buildings were constructed, and Myeong-dong became one of Seoul's treasure troves of colonial-era architecture.

The Korean War left much of Myeong-dong in ruins. When it was rebuilt in the late

1. Bank of Korea Museum 2. Shinsegae Department Store
3. Myeong-dong Theater 4. Myeong-dong street scene

1950s, many bookshops and tea houses opened up in the area, in large part thanks to the presence of the National Theater, which attracted Seoul's artistic and cultural elite. The National Theater would eventually move, and Myeong-dong's reign as Seoul's cultural heart passed, but soon enough, upper-end shops began moving into the area, and with them Seoul's fashion mecca was born. Today, Myeong-dong is one of Seoul's main commercial and financial hubs, home to many large banks and brokerage companies, business headquarters and, of course, shops, eateries and drinking establishments.

▣ The Myeong-dong area can be reached via Myeong-dong Station, Line 4 or Euljiro 1(il)-ga Station, Line 2.

Bank of Korea Museum 한국은행박물관 C4
Located at Myeong-dong Intersection, this castle-like neo-Renaissance building, completed in 1912, first served as the headquarters of the Bank of Choson, the central bank of Japan's Korean colony, and is now a museum to Korean banking history. ⏱ 10 am to 5 pm. Closed Mondays ☎ 02-759-4881

Korea First Bank 제일은행 C4 Originally the Choson Savings Bank, this imposing neoclassical office across from the Bank of Korea Building was completed in 1933.

Shinsegae Department Store 신세계백화점 C4
Formerly the Mitsukoshi Department Store

and completed in 1930, the Shinsegae Department Store next to Korea First Bank is the last of Seoul's colonial era department stores. Seoul's oldest department store comprises a historic "old store" and a large, newly built "new store" next door. ⏱ 10:30 am to 8 pm ☎ 1588-1234

Former National Theater of Korea 옛국립극장 E2
The Baroque-style former National Theater of Korea was built in 1934 as a movie theater; after Liberation, it was used as the National Theater and is now Myeong-dong Theater, a state-of-the-art performing arts and culture center.

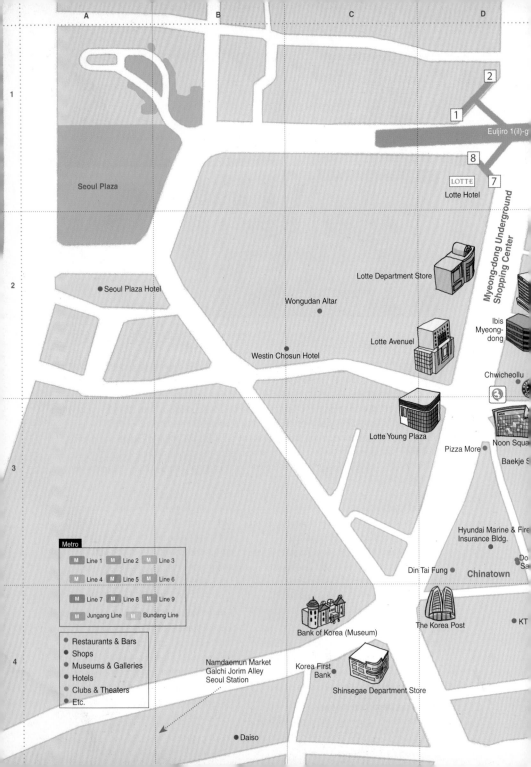

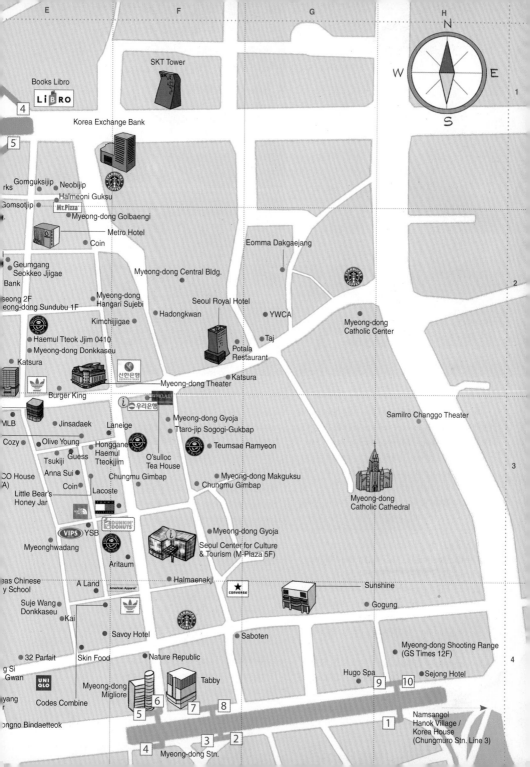

1. Myeong-dong Cathedral 2. Interior, Myeong-dong Cathedral 3. A Chinese restaurant in Myeong-dong

Myeong-dong Cathedral 명동성당 G3 Designed by French missionary priests and built by Chinese masons, Myeong-dong Cathedral was completed in 1898. It is a Gothic masterpiece, built of locally produced red and black brick and featuring a high vaulted ceiling. There's a crypt chapel, too, containing the relics of several martyrs. In addition to being a house of worship, the cathedral has played a major role in Korea's political and social history. In the 1980s, when Korea was ruled by a military dictatorship, pro-democracy demonstrators took refuge in the church, which the police were reluctant to storm. ⏰ English masses are held at 9 am on Sundays. ☎ 02-774-1784

Myeong-dong Chinatown 차이나타운 D3 The closest thing Seoul has to a true Chinatown is located just behind the massive Korea Post Tower, near the old Chinese Embassy and the century-old Hansung Chinese Elementary School. Basically, it consists of two alleys of Chinese restaurants and bookshops. If you're in the mood for Chinese mooncakes, there's a bakery here selling them.

Myeong-dong Migliore 명동밀레오레 F4 This department store at the entrance to Myeong-dong's main drag contains about 1,000 shops specializing in clothing and accessories. ⏰ 11 am to 11:30 pm. Closed Mondays ☎ 02-2124-0001

Lotte Department Store 롯데백화점 D2 The Myeong-dong branch of the Korean-Japanese shopping giant. If you're going really upscale, check out Lotte Avenuel next door. ⏰ 10:30 am to 8 pm ☎ 02-771-2500

Lotte Young Plaza 롯데영플라자 D3 This department store, which specializes in ladies' apparel, caters to younger women. ⏰ 11:30 am to 9:30 pm ☎ 02-771-2500

Lotte Young Plaza and Lotte Avenuel

WHAT TO EAT

• **Myeong-dong Donkkaseu** 명동돈까스 E2 A well-known specialist in the fine art of Japanese-style pork cutlets. (02-776-5300)

• **Ttaro-jip Sogogi-Gukbap** 따로소고기국밥 F3 *Gukbap*, literally "soup rice," is a bowl of rice served with a beef-broth soup, usually served with clots of beef blood (actually, quite yummy). In winter, this is a perfect tummy-warmer. (02-776-2455)

• **Potala Restaurant** 레스토랑 포탈라 F2 Run by a 10-year Tibetan resident of Korea, this restaurant near Myeong-dong Cathedral does wonderful Tibetan and Nepali food and drink, including a variety of Tibetan dumplings, Tibetan butter tea and Tibetan booze. (070-8112-8848)

• **Chungmu Gimbap** 충무김밥 F3 Cheap-but-filling Chungmu *gimbap* (small rice and seaweed rolls served with sliced spicy squid) and *tteokbokki* (spicy ricecakes). (02-755-8488)

• **Myeong-dong Gyoja** 명동교자 F3 A Myeong-dong institution that has been serving up great food since 1969. Specializes in *kalguksu* or handmade, knife-cut noodles and *mandu*, Korean-style dumplings. (02-776-5348)

• **Din Tai Fung** 딘타이펑 D3 The Myeong-dong branch of the famous Taiwanese dumpling chain. (02-771-2778)

• **Woo Rae Oak** 우래옥 A3, p106 This 50-year-old establishment near Euljiro 4-ga (not far from Myeong-dong) has a reputation for two things: being pricey and serving very, very good food. It's most famous for its Pyongyang-style *naengmyeon* (cold wheat noodles), which are said to rival those of Pyongyang itself, but its meat dishes are absolutely heavenly. If you're willing to part with a bit of cash, you won't be disappointed. (02-2265-0151)

• **Baekje Samgyetang** 백제삼계탕 E3 This Myeong-dong eatery has been around for about 40 years, and specializes in *samgyetang* (Korean ginseng chicken soup), a summertime favorite. (02-776-2851)

MT. NAMSAN 남산

At 265 m high, nobody will ever confuse Mt. Namsan with K2. That said, Seoul's "South Mountain," with the landmark N Seoul Tower crowning its peak, makes for a wonderful urban hike that provides some of the best views in Seoul. Mt. Namsan was regarded as Seoul's southern "protective spirit." It also marked the southern limit of the old royal capital of Seoul—sections of the old fortress wall can still be found along its slopes. There are a ton of ways up this mountain. Easy paths start from Dongdaemun, Myeong-dong, Itaewon and elsewhere. The National Theater of Korea (see p108) on the north side of the mountain and Hyatt Hotel on the southern side are good places to start. Getting there to N Seoul Tower and the summit takes about 30 minutes.

N Seoul Tower N서울타워

One of Seoul's most recognizable landmarks, N Seoul Tower—originally named Namsan Tower or Seoul Tower—was built in 1969 as a communication tower and opened to the public as a park in 1980. In 2005, the tower's new owners—the CJ Corporation—gave the tower a major face lift, renovating the facilities and making it a much nicer place to visit, especially with a date. There are several restaurants, including the upscale N Grill, a revolving restaurant with killer views, and the stationary Korean restaurant Hancook, which has just as nice views with a much more affordable menu. There's also an observation deck and one of the most jaw-dropping restrooms you're likely to ever use.

🕙 10 am to 11 pm 🎫 9,000 won
📞 02-3455-9277 🚇 The tower sits atop a 262 m-high mountain—how you climb it is up to you. There are regular buses to the tower that depart from near Exit 2 of Chungmuro Station, Line 3 or 4 between 8 am and midnight. There's also a cable car—the lower terminal is a 10-minute walk from Myeong-dong Station, Line 4, Exit 3. A round-trip ticket is 7,500 won, while a one-way ticket is 6,000 won. You could also hike it—it's not particularly strenuous, and will take you about 40 minutes to get to the top.

View of Seoul from plaza of N Seoul Tower

N Seoul Tower (left), Namsangol Hanok Village

Namsan Botanical Gardens 남산식물원 Located on the southern side of the mountain just beside the Hyatt Hotel, this area of walking paths, trees and flowers is a pleasant enough place to have an evening stroll.

Patriot Ahn Choong-gun Memorial Hall

안중근의사기념관 This memorial located near Namsan Public Library 남산도서관 is dedicated to Korean freedom fighter Ahn Choong-gun, who assassinated former Japanese prime minister and resident-general of Korea Ito Hirobumi in 1909.

Namsangol Hanok Village 남산골한옥마을

In a small valley on the northern slope of Mt. Namsan is Namsangol Hanok Village, a wonderful collection of historic Korean homes that were moved to the spot and lovingly restored. The homes, of various social classes, were restored and adorned with class-appropriate furnishings to give visitors a sense of Joseon-era lifestyles.

The village hosts various events and programs to give visitors a taste of Korean traditional culture, including art and craft classes. On the Chuseok and Seol (Thanksgiving and Lunar New Year) holidays, the place is overrun with visitors. Those with an interest in Korean traditional music will want to check out Namsan Gugakdang 남산국악당.

🕘 9 am to 9 pm (Apr–Oct), 9 am to 8 pm (Nov–March). Closed Tuesdays 🎫 Free
📞 02-2264-4412 🚇 Chungmuro Subway Station, Line 3 or 4, Exit 3 or 4

Korea House 한국의 집 Just in front of Namsangol Hanok Village is Korea House, one of Korea's most famous Korean restaurants. Modeled after one of the halls of Gyeongbokgung Palace, the beautiful *hanok* eatery is more than a restaurant—it's a cultural experience. Lunch and dinner is served, with the house specialty being *hanjeongsik* (Korean banquet cuisine, see p685). Folk performances are staged in the evenings as well. The venue is also frequently used to host Korean-style weddings.

🕘 Noon to 2 pm (lunch), 5:30 to 7 pm (dinner I), 7 to 8 pm (performance), 7:20 to 8:50 pm (dinner 2), 8:50 to 9:50 pm (performance)
📞 02-2266-9101~3 🚇 Chungmuro Subway Station, Line 3 or 4, Exit 3 or 4 🖥 www.koreahouse.or.kr

NAMDAEMUN AREA 남대문일대

The Namdaemun area, so named for Namdaemun Gate, is the home of Seoul's most famous outdoor market, Namdaemun Market. This colorful market, spread out over several blocks, attracts visitors from far and wide with its energy, great deals and exotic charm. Traders flock to it to buy goods wholesale for resale in their home cities and nations. Also in the Namdaemun area are several sites of historic interest, including Sungnyemun Gate (now under reconstruction after a 2008 fire), Seoul Station and Yakhyeon Catholic Church.

🚇 Namdaemun Market is best approached via Hoehyeon Station, Line 4. Seoul Station and Yakhyeon Catholic Church, meanwhile, are reached via City Hall Station, Line 1 & 2.

Namdaemun Market 남대문시장

Namdaemun Market has a history that goes back 500 years to the start of the Joseon era, when merchants set up shop just outside the city walls near the current location of the market. Today's incarnation dates from 1922 and is, along with Dongdaemun Market, one of Seoul's two largest markets.

The market has over 10,000 shops, both large and small. It's most known for clothing, agricultural goods, everyday goods, foodstuffs and medical supplies, although these are but a few of the things that can be found. Foreign tourists find the ginseng products, seaweed and curios to be of particular interest, but even if you're not buying anything, it's great just to stroll

Culture Station Seoul 284 (formerly Seoul Station), one of Seoul's most impressive colonial-era buildings

Namdaemun Market scenes

around and take in the market atmosphere, with vendors hawking their wares and customers engaging in serious haggling. You might also want to check out the so-called *dokkaebi* market 도깨비시장, filled with off-market goods.

Layout and Hours

Namdaemun Market is a pretty sprawling place ringed by eight entry gates. As in many Korean shopping districts, shops tend to congregate by kind, so clothing shops will be gathered in one spot, eyeglass shops in another, fabric shops in another, and so on. Be sure to consult the map on p92.

The market is open both day and night. Shop hours differ from place to place, but the thing to remember is that the wholesalers operate primarily at night. Sunday is probably not the best day to go, but many shops are open nonetheless.

Sungnyemun Imported Goods Arcade 숭례문수
입상가 Located near Gate 1, this underground shopping arcade is chock-full of imported

TIPS

HAGGLING
Unlike in the big department stores and brand-name shops of Myeong-dong, haggling and bargaining is a perfectly accepted means of doing business in Namdaemun. In fact, it's encouraged, but don't expect deep price cutting, either.

CHECK THE QUALITY!
Namdaemun sells a lot of low-cost stuff, which is nice, but you need to check the quality first, lest you spend your hard-earned won on near junk.

GALCHI JORIM
In the bowels of Namdaemun Market is an alley of restaurants specializing in *galchi jorim*, a cheap, spicy stew of boiled hairtail fish and radish. It's a local specialty, and particularly nice with a bowl of milky Korean rice wine or *makgeolli*. The most popular restaurant for this dish is Hee-rak (02-755-3449).

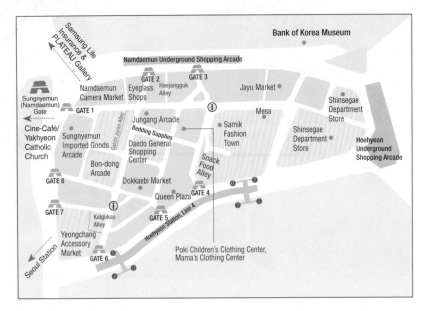

goods like clothing, food and electronics.

Jungang Arcade 중앙상가 Clothing, cosmetics, electronics, dry goods, folk crafts and handicrafts, mostly sold wholesale. This is also a great place to pick up kitchenware and Korean traditional clothing.

Daedo General Shopping Center 대도상가 Kitchenware, decorative goods, men's accessories like Zippo lighters, and more.

Samik Fashion Town 삼익패션타운 A combination market/department store for fashion.

Mesa 메사 A shopping mall for men's and women's fashions. ⓒ 02-2128-5000

Dokkaebi Market 도깨비시장 Underneath the Namdaemun market is another shopping area with a ton of goods, including imported foods and liquors. The entrance is near Namdaemun Gate.

Namdaemun Camera Market 남대문카메라시장 Along the edge of the market nearest Namdaemun Gate is a collection of camera shops. This is the best place in Seoul to pick up camera equipment, including used supplies.

Eyeglasses Namdaemun area is famous for its large number of eyeglass shops that produce high-quality and fashionable eyewear for much less than you'd probably pay at home. If you've been looking to buy new glasses or contacts, this is the place to do it and usually produce your prescription specs (eye exam included) within an hour or two. See the map for location.

Culture Station Seoul 284 (left), Sungnyemun Gate

Seoul Station 서울역

Seoul Station is one of the world's busiest train stations. This is where you catch trains—including the high-speed KTX—to Daejeon, Daegu, Busan and other destinations south and east of Seoul. The station also comes equipped with a gleaming shopping center. Prior to the completion of the new steel and glass station, the city was served by the old Seoul Station 구서울역사, the pretty, Renaissance-style brick building next to the new station. Built in 1925, the old station has now been renovated as an art gallery and culture space named Culture Station Seoul 284.

Sungnyemun Gate 숭례문

Prior to a fire in February 2008, Sungnyemun Gate—or Namdaemun (Great South Gate)—was the oldest building in Seoul and one of the city's most recognizable landmarks. The tragic fire—an incomprehensible act of arson—destroyed the gate's wooden superstructure and left a nation in tears. Now undergoing reconstruction, the gate will be restored to its previous glory by 2013.

DOKKAEBI? DOKKAEBI MARKET?

History and Culture

The *dokkaebi* is one of the most popular of Korean cultural motifs, found in countless myths, folk paintings and temple murals. A Korean goblin or troll, the *dokkaebi,* is the transformed spirit of inanimate objects—often, discarded home objects like brooms and fireplace pokers. Something of a lovable, if mischievous, rogue, the *dokkaebi* enjoys playing tricks on the wicked and rewarding the virtuous. They're also keen to challenge wayward travelers to roadside matches of Korean wrestling or *ssireum*, for right of passage. They tend to live in caves, abandoned homes, old trees and deep valleys, and come out at night. Interestingly enough, *dokkaebi* traditionally have only one leg.

In lore, the *dokkaebi* usually carries a large club—he can use this club to grant you any object you wish. Be warned, however: whatever you receive has been stolen from someone else, as the club can summon only objects that currently exist.

Dokkaebi Markets, on the other hand, are open air flea markets—they usually specialize in used goods, although smuggled goods (often from US military bases) can frequently be found, too. People will offer varying explanations of the market's name, but in fact, it's a mispronunciation of the correct name for such markets—*dottegi* market, which means "market where you can get anything."

SEONGBUK-DONG 성북동

Seongbuk-dong is a relaxing neighborhood of Korean gardens and historic homes. As an added bonus, if you're visiting in May or October, it's also home to one of Korea's best museums, the Gansong Museum of Art. Most of the primary sites are within easy walking distance of one another, although Samcheonggak and Gilsangsa Temple are a bit out of the way and may require a cab ride.

🚇 The nearest subway access to the Seongbuk-dong sites is Exit 6 of Hansung University Station, Line 4. From there, you can either start walking (about 15 minutes), catch a cab or take bus No. 1111 or 2112 to Hongik Middle and High School 홍익중고등학교, which is near the Choi Sunu House.

Seongnagwon Garden 성락원 C3

Seongnagwon Garden was originally a villa used by Sim Sang-eung, a high-ranking official under King Cheoljong (r. 1849–1863). Later, it was used as a detached palace by Yi Gang (Prince Imperial Ui), the fifth son of King Gojong. In fact, it was here that Yi Gang died in 1955. This hidden gem is one of the finest Korean gardens in the city. (**Note:** The garden is closed for renovation as of this writing.) ☺ Closed Sundays 🚇 Getting here is a bit tricky. The easiest way is to take a taxi from Exit 6 of Hansung University Station, Line 4. ☎ 02-920-3412

Suyeon Sanbang teahouse

1. Seongnagwon Garden 2. Samcheonggak 3. Gate, Gilsangsa Temple
4. Lotus lanterns, Gilsangsa Temple 5. Samcheonggak

Choi Sunu House 최순우옛집 C3 Not far from Seongnagwon is the former home of the late Choi Sunu, a renowned Korean art historian and director general of the National Museum of Korea. The home, which was built in the 1930s, is a perfect example of the adaptation of *hanok* architecture to 20th century living.
🕐 10 am to 4 pm (Open only Apr–Nov). Ticketing closes at 3:30 pm. Closed Mondays & Sundays 🎟 Free 🚇 Just a short walk from Seongnagwon Garden ☏ 02-3675-3401

Samcheonggak 삼청각 A1 Hidden in the hills overlooking Samcheong-dong is Samcheonggak, a beautiful Korean garden/cultural center built initially as a venue for the inter-Korean Red Cross talks of 1972. Throughout the 70s, it was one of Seoul's three most famous restaurants, and served as an exclusive entertainment venue for high-ranking officials and politicians, who came to wine, dine and be merry with comely female entertainers known as *gisaeng* (similar to Japanese geisha). Located at the site is a pricey Korean restaurant and tea house. For visitors, it offers beautiful views of the surrounding mountains. When you're at Samcheonggak, sit on the outdoor terrace and order a cup of coffee or tea—the views of the city and mountainsides are worth it.
🕐 Open 24 hrs 🎟 Free 🚇 Take a 10 minute taxi ride from Gwanghwamun Station, Line 5 or Gyeongbokgung Station, Line 3.
☏ 02-765-3700 🖰 www.samcheonggak.or.kr

Gilsangsa Temple 길상사 C2 Gilsangsa Temple is an oasis of Zen tranquility in the heart of the city. It regards itself as surrounded by, but not a part of, the secular world, and visitors are likely to agree. The site where the temple now sits was originally the Daewongak, an elite restaurant and *gisaeng* house remotely located in the hills overlooking Seoul, far from prying eyes. In 1987, however, the owner of the restaurant—a former *gisaeng* herself, then residing in Los Angeles—donated it and its considerable real estate to a famous Buddhist monk so that it might be converted into a Buddhist temple, which it duly was. Much of the temple is spread throughout a densely forested mountain

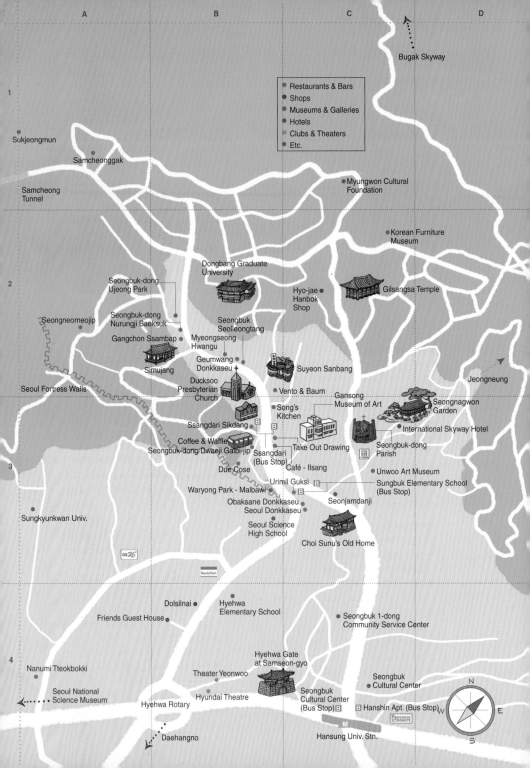

A B C D

1

Bugak Skyway

- Restaurants & Bars
- Shops
- Museums & Galleries
- Hotels
- Clubs & Theaters
- Etc.

Sukjeongmun

Samcheonggak

Myungwon Cultural
Foundation

Samcheong
Tunnel

Korean Furniture
Museum

2

Seongbuk-dong
Ujeong Park

Dongbang Graduate
University

Hyo-jae
Hanbok
Shop

Gilsangsa Temple

Seongneomeojip

Seongbuk-dong
Nurungji Baeksuk

Seongbuk
Seolleongtang

Gangchon Ssambap

Myeongseong
Hwangu

Jeongneung

Simujang

Geumwang
Donkkaseu

Suyeon Sanbang

Seoul Fortress Walls

Ducksoo
Presbyterian
Church

Vento & Baum

Gansong
Museum of Art

Seongnagwon
Garden

Song's
Kitchen

International Skyway Hotel

Ssangdari Sikdang

Coffee & Waffle

Seongbuk-dong
Parish

Seongbuk-dong Dwaeji Galbi-jip

Take Out Drawing

Ssangdari
(Bus Stop)

3

Due Cose

Café - Ilsang

Unwoo Art Museum

Urimil Guksi

Sungbuk Elementary School
(Bus Stop)

Waryong Park - Malbawi

Obaksane Donkkaseu

Seonjamdanji

Seoul Donkkaseu

Sungkyunkwan Univ.

Seoul Science
High School

Choi Sunu's Old Home

GS25

FamilyMart

Dolsilnai

Hyehwa
Elementary School

Seongbuk 1-dong
Community Service Center

Friends Guest House

4

Nanumi Tteokbokki

Hyehwa Gate
at Samseon-gyo

Seongbuk
Cultural Center

Seoul National
Science Museum

Theater Yeonwoo

Seongbuk
Cultural Center
(Bus Stop)

Hanshin Apt. (Bus Stop)

Hyehwa Rotary

Hyundai Theatre

N
W E
S

Daehangno

Hansung Univ. Stn.

valley that is beautiful every season of the year. Its remote location makes it an ideal place for the practice of Zen—the temple's meditation hall, the House of Silence, is open every day from 10 am to 5 pm. The temple also has a teahouse and benches where you can take a break from the weary world.

🗺 Free 🚌 Buses for Gilsangsa depart from Dongwon Mart 동원마트 some 30 m past the Bus No. 1111 stop near Exit 6 of Hansung Univ. Station, Line 4. Buses leave at 8:30, 9:20, 9:40, 10 am, noon, 1, 3 and 4:30 pm. ☏ 02-3672-5945~6 🌐 www.kilsangsa.or.kr

Simujang 심우장 B2 This simple *hanok* home was the residence of Buddhist monk, poet and independence activist "Manhae" of Han Yong-un. Built in 1933, it is quite unique in that, unlike most *hanok* which face south, this one faces north. The reason for this is simple, actually—Han did not want his house to face the Government-General building, the nerve center of the Japanese colonial administration.

Suyeon Sanbang 수연산방 C2 A wonderfully atmospheric teahouse, Suyeon Sanbang is truly a hidden gem. Built in the 1930s, this

GISAENG: SPEAKING FLOWERS

History and Culture

Perhaps no figure from Korea's past has been so romanticized as the *gisaeng*, the female courtesans of the Joseon era. Somewhat similar to the more famous *geisha* tradition of Japan, these remarkable women entertained wealthy and powerful men—in order to do this, they were trained in such arts as dance, music and poetry. Among the most educated and cultured women of their age, some even became noted poets and artists in their own right. They were also called *haeeohwa*, which means "flowers that can understand words."

Usually coming from humble families, aristocratic families fallen on hard times or born to *gisaeng* themselves, *gisaeng* often began their training at special schools—called *gyobang*—before the age of 10. Their careers tended to be short— few *gisaeng* managed to continue their careers past their early 20s, and all were required by law to retire by age 50. If a *gisaeng* was lucky, she could become the concubine of a wealthy man; if not, she often found herself at work or even owning a drinking establishment of her own. Not all *gisaeng* entertained, per se—some were dressmakers, while others specialized in traditional medicine.

The *gisaeng* system continued throughout the Joseon period and into the Japanese colonial era, with training centers in Seoul and Pyongyang growing particularly famous. During Korea's post-independence development and modernization drive, however, many aspects of Korean traditional culture disappeared as social customs and norms changed. Today, the *gisaeng* exists only in TV dramas and silver screen historical epics, a romantic symbol of Korea's past.

Suyeon Sanbang teahouse

hanok was the home of Korean novelist Lee Tae-jun. His granddaughter converted his home into a Korean traditional teahouse, and so it remains. The teahouse has a large garden where, season and weather permitting, you can sit and enjoy your tea amidst natural splendor. ⏰ 11:30 am to 10 pm ☎ 02-764-1736

Gansong Museum of Art 간송미술관 C3
Gansong Museum of Art is probably the best museum in Korea you've never heard of. The country's first private art museum, it was created in 1938 from the personal collection of Jeon Hyeong-pil, a wealthy Korean art collector who worked tirelessly to protect Korea's artistic heritage at a time when countless works of art were being virtually plundered by Japanese collectors. The collection, housed in a stately building from the late 30s, includes 12 national treasures and 10 other national cultural properties. The only drawback to the museum is that it holds month-long

TIPS

LOOKING FOR GIFT IDEAS?

Just across from Gilsangsa is Hyojae, a shop run by Lee Hyojae, *hanbok* (Korean clothing) and Korean fabric designer. In addition to clothing, you'll find *bojagi* 보자기 (Korean wrapping cloths), tea mats, cushions, table clothes and a wide variety of other goods designed by Lee herself. Give it a look. (02-720-5393)

exhibits just twice a year, in the months of May and also October.

⏰ 10 am to 6 pm (Open only May & October) 🎫 Free ☎ 02-762-0442

• **Ssangdari Sikdang** 쌍다리식당 B3 Rice, grilled pork, side dishes—what more do you need? They also do a good *budaejjigae* 부대찌개 ("Army Base Stew," a stew of *kimchi*, *ramyeon* noodles, sausages, baked beans and etc). Incredibly popular. (02-743-0325)

• **Song's Kitchen** 송스키친 B3 Run by a proprietor who is both a food stylist and an interior designer, this quaint restaurant is nothing if not picturesque. The "vintage" atmosphere is helped by all the antiques on display. Menu highlights include seafood and

cheese *tteokbokki* 치즈떡볶이 (spicy pan-fried rice cakes) and good pizza. (02-747-1713)

• **Seongbuk-dong Dwaeji Galbi-jip** 성북동돼지갈비집 B3 One of the oldest restaurants in the area, this place specializes in grilled pork, served with rice and consumed in leaves of cabbage. (02-764-2420)

• **Geumwang Donkkaseu** 금왕돈가쓰 B2 This place does a roaring trade in breaded pork cutlets served Korean-style, which is to say, big and fat. Hours: 9:30 am to 10 pm. (02-763-9366)

WHAT TO EAT

BUAM-DONG 부암동

If Seongbuk-dong is tranquil, nearby Buam-dong is even more so. Relatively untouched by developers, this lovely piece of urban undevelopment is regarded as a little slice of the countryside in the big city. This is no joke—if you didn't know better, you'd have no idea you were in Seoul. The peaceful, rural atmosphere of the neighborhood lends itself to cafés and galleries, and these you will find in abundance. Sections of Seoul's old city walls can be found intact—these offer fine views of the surrounding mountains. ▣ Take Bus No. 1020, 7022 or 7018 from Exit 3 of Gyeongbokgung Station, Line 3 and get off at Buam-dong Office.

Changuimun Gate 창의문 At the entrance to Buam-dong is Changuimun Gate, also known today as Jahamun Gate 자하문 (the "Violet Mist Gate"), one of several lesser gates that controlled access to the royal capital.

Fortress Walls Snaking up and down Seoul's surrounding mountains is a series of ancient fortress walls, which for centuries had protected the capital from enemies both foreign and domestic. Construction began in 1396 and the walls were built by some 200,000 laborers in just one year, an impressive piece of engineering considering the ruggedness of the terrain. See p103 for more information.

Whanki Museum 환기미술관 This museum contains over 1,000 works by the abstract artist Kim Whanki, housed in a stunning museum that incorporates the natural elements found in Kim's work. ☺ 10 am to 6 pm. Closed Mondays 🎟 7,000 won ▣ Take green Bus No. 7022, 1020 or 0212 from Exit 3 of Gyeongbokgung Station, Line 3. ✆ 02-391-7701~2

Gallery Curiosity, Buam-dong. "Life is Suddenly" was written by movie director Lee Joon Ik.

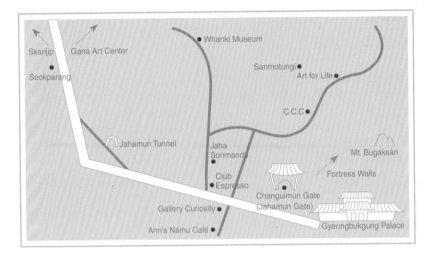

Seokparang 석파랑 In addition to being one of Seoul's most luxurious Korean restaurants, Seokparang is also a cultural property in and of itself. Parts of the 150-year-old Korean mansion originally belonged to a villa owned by Heungseon Daewongun, the prince regent of Korea who was a major figure in the late Joseon era. The restaurant specializes in Korean palace cuisine—meals come with rice, soup and a dizzying array of side dishes. Fine dining doesn't come cheap, however—set-menu prices vary from 45,000 to 100,000 won per person. ⏱ Noon to 3 pm (lunch); 6 to 10 pm (dinner) 🚃 Leave Exit 3 of Gyeongbokgung Station, Line 3 and take green Bus No. 0212, 1020, 1711, 7018, 7022 to Sangmyung University 상명대학교. ☏ 02-395-2500 🖱 www.seokparang.co.kr

Gana Art Center 가나아트센터 With the largest floor space in the country, this beautiful gallery—designed by noted architect Jean-Michel Wilmotte—is not only a great place to take in modern art but also a wonderful place to relax, with an especially pleasant outdoor sculpture garden. ⏱ 10 am to 7 pm 🎫 3,000 won 🚃 Take Bus No. 1020 or 1711 from Exit 3, Gyeongbokgung Station, Line 3 ☏ 02-720-1020 🖱 www.ganaart.com

Changuimun Gate (left), Courtyard of Seokparang

What to Eat

• **Jaha Sonmandu** 자하손만두 With great views of the surrounding mountains, this restaurant specializes in handmade *mandu* or dumplings. *Manduguk* 만두국 (dumpling soup) and *tteok manduguk* 떡만두국 (dumpling soup with rice cakes) are popular, but if you're looking for something even more filling, try the *kimchi mandu jeongol* 김치만두전골, a bubbling stew of *kimchi* dumplings. (02-379-2648)

• **Art for Life** 아트포라이프 Part gallery, part concert hall, part Italian restaurant, this place—run by a couple who were musicians with the Seoul Philharmonic Orchestra—is located in a beautifully renovated *hanok*. Hours: 11:30 am to 10 pm, (breaktime: 3 to 5 pm weekdays, 3 to 4 pm weekends). Closed Mondays. (02-3217-9364)

• **Ssarijip** 싸리집 Located not in Buam-dong itself but nearby Gugi-dong 구기동, this is one of Seoul's best places to try *bosintang* 보신탕 or dogmeat soup. Located in a Korean-style *hanok* with a wonderful courtyard, the restaurant is packed in the summer, but is still a relaxing place to have a meal. A bowl of *bosintang* will cost you 15,000 won; a heavier stew or *jeongol* 전골, is worth the 28,000 won. Hours: 11:30 am to 9:30 pm. (02-379-9911)

• **Club Espresso** 클럽에스프레소 Outstanding fresh-brewed coffee in a pleasant atmosphere. Hours: 9 am to 11 pm. (02-764-8719)

1. Jaha Sonmandu 2. Art for Life 3. Ssarijip 4. Coffee house, Buam-dong

BUKHANSAN NATIONAL PARK 북한산국립공원

Guarding Seoul to the north are several mountains that make up Bukhansan National Park, a ridge of several magnificent rocky peaks, including Baegundae Peak, which at 836 m is Seoul's highest point. This rugged area provides some of Seoul's best (and most challenging) hiking, as well as some of the best rock-climbing in Korea.

Guarding the northern passes into Seoul, Bukhansan has long been of strategic significance. During the Joseon era, the mountain was ringed by impressive fortifications that stand to this day. Due to its thick forests and scenic beauty, the mountain is home to several Buddhist temples, including Hwagyesa Temple, a major Zen center famous for its large contingent of foreign monks.

🚇 **Doseonsa Course:** Take subway line 4 to Suyu Station. From there, take Buses No. 2, 120 or 153 to its final destination. **Jeongneung Course:** Take Buses No. 171, 1114, 1213 or 7211 from Gireum Station, Line 4. Get off at Bongguksa Temple 봉국사. **Hwagyesa Temple:** Take small Bus No. 2 from Exit 5 of Suyu Station, Line 4. Get off at Hanshin University 한신대학교 and walk up the path to the temple.

Seoul seen from Bukhansan National Park

Hiking

The area of Bukhansan National Park spans several dozen square kilometers, so not surprisingly, there are a number of paths up the mountain. The direct path to the peak can take as little as two hours (be warned—it's a strenuous two hours), while more scenic routes can take up to four or five. The most popular—and the shortest—route takes you from Doseonsa Temple 도선사 to the Yongammun Gate 용암문 of Bukhansan Fortress. From there, it's a slog along the ridgeline until you reach the granite peak of Baegundae 백운대—there are ropes and steps to assist you in the task.

Bukhansan Fortress 북한산성

As a strategically vital area, Bukhansan has played host to fortifications of one sort or another for about 1,900 years. Following the Japanese invasions of the late 16th century and Manchurian invasion of the mid-17th century, Korea's rulers felt compelled to strengthen and expand the mountain's fortifications. In 1711, work got underway on a 9.7 km ring of fortifications along the ridges of the mountain. With 14 gates, the walls are some of the most extensive Joseon-era fortifications in Korea.

Hwagyesa Temple 화계사

Hwagyesa is a relaxing Buddhist temple on the lower slopes of the park. It is most famous as the home of the Hwagyesa International Zen Center (02-900-4326), opened in 1994 by Zen Master Seung Sahn (1927–2004). As the founder of the Kwan Um Zen School, Seung Sahn played an active role in promoting Buddhism in the West; accordingly, Hwagyesa is home to a prominent community of Western monks. For foreigners interested in Zen, the Zen Center holds Sunday mediation sessions and Dharma talks beginning at 1pm.

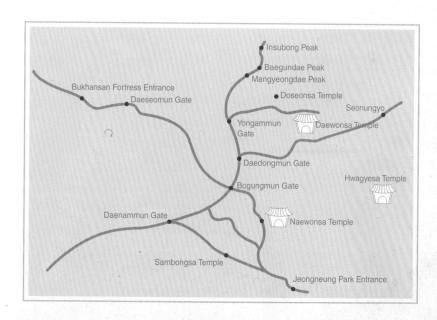

DONGDAEMUN MARKET 동대문시장

Twenty-six shopping malls, 30,000 specialty shops and 50,000 manufacturers. All within a 10-block radius. Welcome to Dongdaemun Market.

Dongdaemun Market is the place to go for fashion, period. Apgujeong-dong, south of the Hangang River, might have the luxury brands, and Myeong-dong the international brand outlets, but for fashion junkies looking for unique designs at decent prices, Dongdaemun is the place to go. Heck, even if you're not into clothing, it's a great place to visit, particularly at night when all its lights, action and crowds make for an impressive show of human energy.

Dongdaemun is open pretty much all day and all night, but retailers and wholesalers keep different hours. Retailers are usually open from 10 am to 5 am the next morning, while wholesalers are open from 8 pm to 8 am the next morning. Many shops close Mondays. Dongdaemun Market sprawls over several city blocks south of Cheonggyecheon Stream, split in two by a main north-south street. Major landmarks include the 34-floor Doosan Tower, Migliore fashion center and Dongdaemun Design Plaza & Park. Broadly speaking, the newer, glitzier Dongdaemun of bright lights and towering malls is to the west of the main road, while the older, grittier Dongdaemun of smaller shops is to the east around what was formerly Dongdaemun Stadium.

🚇 Two subway stations service the sprawling Dongdaemun Market, Dongdaemun Station (Lines 1 & 4) and Dongdaemun History & Culture Park Station (Lines 2 & 4).

Migliore and Doosan Tower

Doosan Tower 두산타워 B3 This 34-floor landmark, known colloquially as Doota, gets about 100,000 customers a day, which should probably tell you something. Clothing, accessories, beauty supplies—it's all there. ⊕ 7 pm to 5 am next day (Mon–Tue), 10:30 am to 5 am next day (Tue–Sat), 10:30 am to 11 pm (Sun) ⓒ 02-3398-3114

Migliore 밀레오레 B3 The Dongdaemun branch of the Korean department store, a total of nine floors of fashion. ⊕ 10:30 am to 5 am next day. Closed Mondays ⓒ 02-3393-0001

Pyeonghwa Market 평화시장 A3 This is one of the oldest wholesale markets in the country. The market played an important role in the Korean labor movement—see the momument to labor activist Chun Tae-il in front of the market next to Cheonggyecheon Stream.

Gwangjang Market 광장시장 A3 One of Seoul's oldest markets, Gwangjang Market is most famous for its silks and *hanbok* (Korean traditional clothing) market. Also noted for its alley of street food stalls, with *bindaetteok* (mung bean pancake) something of a specialty. In fact, the market is worth visiting just to eat! ⊕ 7 am to 7 pm ⊟ Exit 8, Jongno 5-ga Station, Line 1

History and Culture

DONGDAEMUN GATE 동대문

Since a disastrous 2008 fire destroyed the Sungnyemun (Namdaemun) Gate, the Dongdaemun Gate is—along with Sukjeongmun Gate on Mt. Bugaksan—one of only two of Seoul's old main city gates still standing. More properly called Heunginjimun 흥인지문, the gate has a history going back to 1396, when Seoul's old city walls were

first constructed, although the current structure dates from 1869.

The gate consists of a solid stone base with a two-story wooden superstructure. A unique feature is the half-moon wall built in front of the main gate, which was used for additional defense. Unfortunately, the gate is not usually open to the public.

A B C D

1

Hyehwa Rotary

Filipino Market
Caterina
Sungkyunkwan
Univ.
Platters
Chunnyun Jazz Bar
Hakrim
Dabang
Arko Arts
Theater
Hyehwa Stn.
Beer Cabin
Marronnier Theater
Platters
Seoul Nat'l
Univ. Hospital
Arko Art Center
Daehangno
Former
Daehan
Hospital
Marronnier
Park
Korea National Open Univ.
(Former National Industry Institute)
Daehangno Theater

Dongsoong Art Center
Drawing Show Theater

Hansung Univ.

Naksan
Park

Changsin Stn.

Naksan
Myogaksa

Gyeongdong
Oriental
Medicine Marke

2

Metro
M Line 1   M Line 2   M Line 3
M Line 4   M Line 5   M Line 6
M Line 7   M Line 8   M Line 9
M Jungang Line   M Bundang Line

● Restaurants & Bars
● Shops
● Museums & Galleries
● Hotels
● Clubs & Theaters
● Etc.

Doosan Art Center

Two Hotel

Pharmacy Area

Ewha Womans Univ.
Dongdaemun Hospital
Everest

Dongmy
Dongmyo
Stn.
Dongmy
Shrine

Heunginjimun
(Dongdaemun Gate)

Jongno 5-ga Stn.
Broiled Fish Alley

Somunnan Dak
Wonjo Hanmari

Dongdaemun
General Market

Dongdaemun Stn.

Gwangjang Market
Cheonggyecheon
Stream

Wedding Goods Market
Used Books Alley

Best Western Hotel

Jungang Mark

3

Bangsan Market
Woo Rae Oak

Pyeonghwa Market
Cerestar

Doota

New Pyeonghwa
Market
Dong Pyeonghwa
Market

Cheong Pyeonghwa Market

Hullyeonwon
Park

Migliore

Jungbu Market

National
Medical Center

Dongdaemun Design Plaza
and Park—under construction

Designer
Club

Chungmu Art Hall

Hwanghak-dong
Flea Marke

Western Co-op
Residence Hotel

Hello apM
U:US
Nuzzon

Darkhan
Samarkand Café

Good Morning City

Dongdaemun History
& Culture Park

Sindang Stn.

Ala-Too Café

Central
Asia Village

Dongdaemun Stadium Stn.

Hanyang Technical
High School

Ojang-dong
Naengmyeon Alley

Gwanghuimun Gate

I Love Tteobokki

Hyundai Residence

Kyungdong
Presbyterian Church

Sindang-dong
Tteokbokki Alley

Mabongnim Halmeoni
Tteokbokki

Chungmuro

Jongjeom

Pyeongyang Myeonok

Jangchung-dong
Jokbal Restaurant Street

4

Grand Ambassador Seoul
Fat Grandma's Place

Pyeongan-do Jokbaljip

Dongguk Univ. Stn.

Original Jangchungdong
Grandmother's Place

Cheonggu Stn.

Dongguk Univ.

5F
Noblian Branch Clinic of Jaseng
Hospital of Oriental Medicine

National Theater of Korea

Shilla Seoul

N
W   E
S

TIPS

DONGDAEMUN DESIGN PLAZA & PARK

A landmark redevelopment project by famed Iraqi-British architect Zaha Hadid, this eye-catching complex—which organically blends landscaping and architecture—is scheduled for completion in 2013, and will contain outdoor green space, exhibition halls, shops, restaurants and more. Part of it—Dongdaemun History & Culture Park—is already open to the public and is well worth the visit.

Gyeongdong Market 경동시장 B2 Not too far from Dongdaemun is Seoul's largest Oriental medicine market, Gyeongdong Market (also called Seoul Yangnyeongsi). It's a fascinating place to walk around, just to take in the incredible selection of exotic herbs and medications, including the ever-popular (with foreign tourists, anyway) bottles of snake liquor—snake cured in alcohol. Ginseng, of course, is the most popular product. ⏲ 9 am to 7 pm. Closed Sundays 🚇 Exit 2 of Jegi Station, Line 1

Medicinal herbs, Gyeongdong Market

Hwanghak-dong Flea Market 황학동벼룩시장 D3 At this streetside market, you can find just about anything if you look hard enough. Home to about 500 shops, this used to be the place to go for antiques but, nowadays, the goods on display have greatly diversified. ⏲ 9 am to 7 pm.

Central Asia Village 중앙아시아촌 B3 In recent years, Seoul has witnessed an influx of foreign residents as the Korean economy grows and globalizes. One of the best places to witness this is the so-called Central Asia Village near the former Dongdaemun Stadium. The village is a small collection of shops, businesses and restaurants near Dongdaemun Stadium run and frequented by Korea's increasingly large population of Central Asian immigrants. Although this is not a residential district like the ethnic communities that have formed in many North American and European cities, the Cyrillic signboards, exotic cuisine and distinctly Central Asian faces and dress that visitors find when they visit give the neighborhood its distinct character—Korea meets the Silk Road. For the Western visitor, the neighborhood's draw is its exotic Central Asian restaurants, especially Mongolian and Uzbek.

National Theater of Korea

Dongmyo Shrine 동묘 D2 Built in 1601, this shrine to the east of Dongdaemun Gate, in the middle of Hwanghak-dong Flea Market, is quite unique in that it was built to honor the Chinese General Guan Yu (AD 162–219), famed for his exploits during China's Three Kingdoms Period. In the 16th century, Ming Chinese generals dispatched to Korea to help defeat the Japanese in the Imjin War (the Japanese invasions of 1592–1598) demanded the shrine be built, and the Korean court—dependent on Chinese military aid—was not in a position to refuse. The shrine incorporates Chinese elements into its design, including the brilliant brick masonry and radiant decoration. 🖼 Free 🚇 Dongmyo Station, Line 1 and 6

Sindang-dong Tteokbokki Alley 신당동떡볶이골목 C3 Not far from Dongdaemun, around Sindang Station, is an alley way specializing in the Korean dish *tteokbokki*, rice cakes cooked in sweet and spicy red pepper sauce

with ramen noodles, fried dumplings and an assortment of other ingredients. Great in wintertime, and best enjoyed with a shot of *soju*.

National Theater of Korea 국립극장 A4 The National Theater of Korea is a unique performing space designed to accommodate a wide range of performance styles. It is home to the national drama, Korean opera, national orchestra and national dance companies of Korea. 🚇 Dongguk University Station, Line 3, Exit 6 ☎ 02-2280-4115~6 🖱 www.ntok.go.kr

Jokbal

• **Jangchung-dong Jokbal Street** 장충동족발골목 B4 Jangchung-dong *Jokbal* (pig's feet) Street specializes in, well, boiled pig's trotters, one of Korea's best loved cuisines. The meat is served in slices, which are consumed typically wrapped in lettuce. It is usually eaten with a bottle of *soju*.

• **Everest** 에베레스트레스토랑 C2 Located on the second floor of a nondescript building in an equally nondescript neighborhood not far

from Dongdaemun Station is one of the best (and most popular!) Nepali restaurants in Seoul—get here at the wrong time, and you'll need to wait in line. For your curry fix, this is a highly recommended place; the food is awesome and the prices surprisingly reasonable. (02-766-8850)

• **Samarkand Café** 사마리칸트 B3 Samarkand Café does fine Uzbek cuisine in a friendly atmosphere. Quite popular and pretty cheap, too. (02-2277-4261)

• **Darkhan** B3 A Mongolian restaurant popular with Korea's large Mongolian worker population. (02-2278-4633)

• **Ala-Too Café** B3 Another friendly Uzbek place, this one on the second floor above an Uzbek/Russian bakery, is also recommended. (02-2277-9212)

WHAT TO EAT

DAEHANGNO 대학로

Daehangno, or "University Street," gets its name as the former location of Korea's most prestigious university, Seoul National University, which moved south of the Hangang River in the 1970s (the College of Medicine still remains, however). Today, the neighborhood has become Seoul's "theater district," with over 300 small theaters that put on regular performances. Small theaters in the neighborhood include the noted Saemtoh Parangsae Theater 샘터파랑새극장, Jeongbo Small Theater 정보소극장 and Hakjeon Theater 학전소극장. Most of the area's theaters are tiny places with no more than a few dozen seats (some, however, are larger, with 100 seats or more), giving performances a truly intimate feel.

The area is virtually synonymous with "youth culture," as university students from all over gather in places such as Marronnier Park to take in outdoor performances and frequent the many cafés and restaurants. Daehangno also has a bit of history, with a number of impressive pieces of colonial architecture.

Performance at one of Daehangno's small theaters

Former Daehan Hospital (left), "Art Makes Life More Interesting than Art," Arko Art Center

Arko Art Center 아르코아트센터 A1 Part of Marronnier Park, the red brick Arko Art Center has played an important role in the development of Korean modern art by providing an accessible place for local artists to hold exhibits. ⊕ 11 am to 8 pm (Mar–Oct), 11 am to 7 pm (Nov–Feb). Closed Mondays 🎫 2,000 won ⓒ 02-760-4850~2

Dongsoong Art Center 동숭아트센터 A1 One of Daehangno's major performing arts venues, Dongsoong Art Center hosts a wide variety of shows. ⊕ Depends on programs ⓒ 02-766-3390

Marronnier Park 마로니에공원 A2 This small urban space often plays host to outdoor theatrical and musical performances, especially on weekends, and as such is packed with young people.

Former Daehan Hospital 구대한의원 본관 A2 Now a museum, the former Daehan Hospital, located just in front of Seoul National University Medical Center, was created in 1907 as Korea's top medical facility.

Sungkyunkwan University 성균관대학교 A3, p96 One of Seoul's best and oldest universities, Sungkyunkwan University traces its illustrious history back some 600 years to 1398, when it was founded as the country's

TIPS

LIVE JAZZ
If jazz is your thing, check out Chunnyun Jazz Bar—it's one of Seoul's best jazz clubs. Admissions are 8,000 won (Mon–Thur) & 10,000 won (Fri–Sun), although if you order a meal or cocktail, this is waived. (02-743-5555)

top Confucian academy. The university museum (Hours: 10 am to 4 pm, closed weekends) is well worth visiting, as is the campus's Joseon-era Confucian shrine.

Filipino Market 혜화동필리핀시장 Head to Hyehwa Catholic Church (near Hyehwa Rotary) on a Sunday to check out the Filipino Market, a makeshift bazaar of Filipino food, Filipino groceries, Filipino CDs and DVDs, phone cards and other goods from the sunny archipelago. ⊕ 9 am to 5 pm, Sunday

•**Caterina** 카테리나 A1 A popular area wine bar and Italian restaurant with a charming atmosphere. (02-764-3201)

•**Platters** 플래터스 A1 Near Marronnier Park, Platters is a 1950s-style American diner complete with good burgers, milkshakes and Philly cheesesteaks. (02-744-7651)

•**Nanumi Tteokbokki** 나눔이떡볶이 A4 A popular hole-in-the-wall that has attained legendary status with students at nearby Sungkyunkwan University. (02-747-0881)

WHAT TO EAT

SINCHON 신촌

When you mention Sinchon to average Seoulites, they immediately think of colleges. In the Sinchon area are some of Korea's most prestigious universities, including Yonsei University, Ewha Womans University, Hongik University and Sogang University. The streets in front of these institutes of higher learning are packed with young people shopping, eating and drinking, especially on a Friday or Saturday evening when the area becomes one big party.

🚇 Sinchon Station, Line 2

Yonsei University 연세대학교 C2 One of Korea's top three universities, Yonsei possesses a storied history dating back to 1885. Yonsei University Medical School and Severance Hospital trace their lineage back to Korea's first modern hospital, the Gwanghyewon, founded by American Presbyterian missionary, doctor and diplomat Horace Allen. The rest of the school traces its lineage to Chosun Christian College, founded in 1915 by Allen's fellow missionary, Horace Grant Underwood.

🚇 10–15 minute walk from Exits 2 or 3 of Sinchon Station, Line 2

Ewha Womans University 이화여자대학교 D2 Founded in 1886 by American Methodist Episcopal missionary Mary F. Scranton, Ewha Womans University began as Ewha Hak Dang, now the site of Ewha Girls High School in Jeong-dong. Ewha produced

Yonsei University

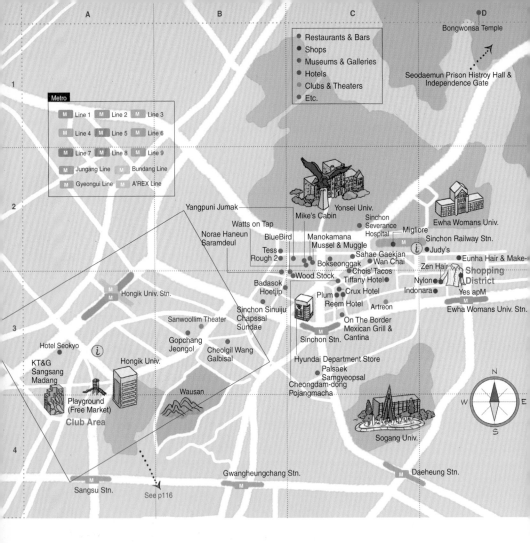

many of Korea's female "firsts," including Korea's first female PhD, female lawyer, female Constitutional Court justice and its first female prime minister. Of the historic buildings, the most impressive is the grand Pfeiffer Hall (1935), the administrative main hall of the university. The Ada Prayer Chamber, a small Gothic chapel on the third floor, is a hidden gem. On a much more modern note is the artificial steel and glass valley connecting the main entrance with the Pfeiffer Hall. Designed by world-famous French architect Dominique Perrault, it was completed in 2008.

🚇 Five minute walk from Exits 2 or 3 of Ewha Womans University Station, Line 2.

Ewha Shopping District D3 The area in front of Ewha Womans University is a noted shopping area for women's clothing, accessories, beauty supplies, and other things feminine. Many renowned—or at least well-appointed—hair and nail salons can be found in the area as well.

MISSIONARIES AND KOREAN CHRISTIANITY

History and Culture

Christianity first came to Korea in the 18th century, when Catholicism entered the country from China. At the end of the 19th century, Protestant missionaries from the United States, Great Britain, Canada and Australia began missions in Korea following its opening to the West. In addition to their religion, these missionaries brought social and political change—Christians were at the forefront of improving the lot of women in Korean society, for instance, and many Christians were active in the independence struggle against the Japanese.

Today, Christianity is Korea's second largest religion, and the country now produces the world's second largest number of Christian missionaries next to the United States. One of the most enduring contributions of Western missionaries was the creation of modern schools and universities. Many of the first missionaries were educators in addition to being preachers, setting up many of Korea's first high schools and universities. Yonsei and Ewha universities are just two examples.

WHAT TO EAT

Restaurants

• **Bokseonggak** 복성각 C2 A Chinese restaurant frequented by students. (02-392-1560)

• **Choi's Tacos** 초이스타코 C2 A taco place. Run by a man named Choi. Does a really good trade. (02-362-2113)

• **On The Border Mexican Grill & Cantina** 온더보더 C3 The largest Mexican restaurant chain in the United States has a shop near Sinchon Station. Good place to go for a margarita. (02-324-0682)

• **Manokamana** 마노카나마 C2 Indian and Nepali cuisine not far from the front gate of Yonsei University. (02-338-4343)

• **Mussel & Muggle** 머슬앤머글 C3 With a French-trained chef in the kitchen, this place near Sinchon's Hyundai Department Store does Belgian-style mussels, mussel pasta and even a mussel pizza. (02-324-5919)

Pubs & Bars

When we're talking about Sinchon, we're talking about drinking and having a good time. Many of the bars in the area are popular with foreigners, although unlike Itaewon with its large (but decreasing) US military contingent, most of the foreigners you find in Sinchon are local English teachers and exchange students.

• **Norae Haneun Saramdeul** 노래하는사람들 B3

Somewhat cramped, this bar gets a good mix of Westerners and Koreans, and lots of dancing on the weekend. (02-325-7808)

• **Woodstock** 우드스탁 C3 As the name would suggest, this local institution specializes in classic rock with décor to match. (02-334-1310)

• **Watts on Tap** 왓츠온탭 C2 This Canadian-owned pub, popular with the expat crowd, mixes a good beer selection with decent pub food. (010-5552-5568)

• **BlueBird** 블루버드 C3 One of Sinchon's better-known jazz bars. Wonderful atmosphere. (02-332-3831)

• **Mike's Cabin** 마이크스캐빈 C2 Run by a Korean American, this cozy bar is also popular with the expat crowd. Tends to be quieter than Norae Haneun Saramdeul.

• **Bar Tei** C2 Armed with an exotic Bohemian atmosphere, with a good selection of classic rock, alternative rock, Brit pop and modern rock, not to mention cheap beer, this bar is quite popular. (02-365-3824)

• **Gopchang Jeongol** 곱창전골 B2 Located not far from Sanwoolim Theater, this Hongdae bar is famous for its large collection of Korean classic rock LPs. There's a decent choice of Western and Korean beverages and, if you're hungry, the food is pretty good too. (02-3143-2284)

HONGIK UNIVERSITY AREA 홍대

Hongik University or "Hongdae," as it usually called, is one of Korea's top art and design schools; accordingly, the area around campus has a distinctively artsy feel with tons of privately-run art schools, art supply and framing shops, a few galleries and tons of tiny, unique shops and cafés in the surrounding neighborhood. On the weekends, you can purchase arts and crafts—all created by local artisans—at the Hope and Free markets held in front of the university.

The area around Hongik University is best known as an entertainment district, especially for its many music and dance clubs. Indeed, Hongdae is the beating heart of Korea's "indie" culture, where young people challenge the conservative cultural mores that dominate much of the rest of Korean social life.

🚇 Hongik University Station, Line 2

Hope and Free Markets 희망시장, 프리마켓 E3
The Hope and Free markets, held in a playground in front of Hongik University every Saturday and Sunday, respectively, offer crafts for sale, handmade by local students and professional artisans. Similar to an artist fair—the items are unique, original creations. It's a great place to pick up reasonably priced crafts and artworks by young, up-and-coming talent.

B-Boy dancing in Hongdae

Hongdae scenes

KT&G Sangsang Madang 상상마당 F3 This nine-level cultural complex, easily recognizable by its commanding, organically inspired building, gives local indie artists a venue to show off their stuff, and holds a cinema, gallery, performance hall and café, as well as a design shop on the first floor. ☺ 10 am to midnight (1 am on weekends), but each floor keeps its own hours ☎ 02-330-6200

B-Boy Theater C2 B-Boy Theater presents an open run of the wildly popular nonverbal performance, "Battle B-boy." This unique performance combines street B-boy dancing with hip-hop, Korean traditional dance and East Asian music for an engaging nonverbal performance that appeals to audiences of all ages. 🎫 50,000 won 🚇 Hongik University Station, Line 2, Exit 9 ☎ 02-323-5233 🖥 www.sjbboys.com

Hongdae Club Scene

The clubs in front of Hongik University have something of an interesting history. Unlike the clubs of Itaewon, Hongdae's music and dance clubs most started out as artists' studios that were later transformed into clubs. Beginning in the 1990s, these clubs

TIPS

CLUB DAY & LIVE DAY

"Club Day"—held every last Friday of each month—was the highlight of the Korean club scene, when a 20,000 won ticket got you into 21 different local clubs (see below). In February 2011, however, the event was suspended amidst talk that it had become over-commercialized. In May, a local association announced Club Day would restart. Live music clubs, meanwhile, would put together a "Sound Road" every last Sunday from July. Readers are advised to check individual clubs for details.

ELECTRONIC: M2 (02-3143-7573), Via (02-3141-2046), Tool (010-3112-0338), JokerRed (019-345-7122)
HIPHOP: Harlem (NB1) (02-326-1716), Q-Vo (02-3143-7574), DD Club (011-783-4024), Hooper (02-336-3445), Saab (02-324-6929),
MIXED: Ska 2 (010-8004-4635), Myoungwolgwan (02-3142-1357)
ROCK: Freebird (02-335-4576), DGBD (02-322-3792), Soundholic (02-3412-4203), FF (011-9025-3407), Spot (02-322-5956)
JAZZ: Evans (02-337-8361), Watercock (02-324-2422)

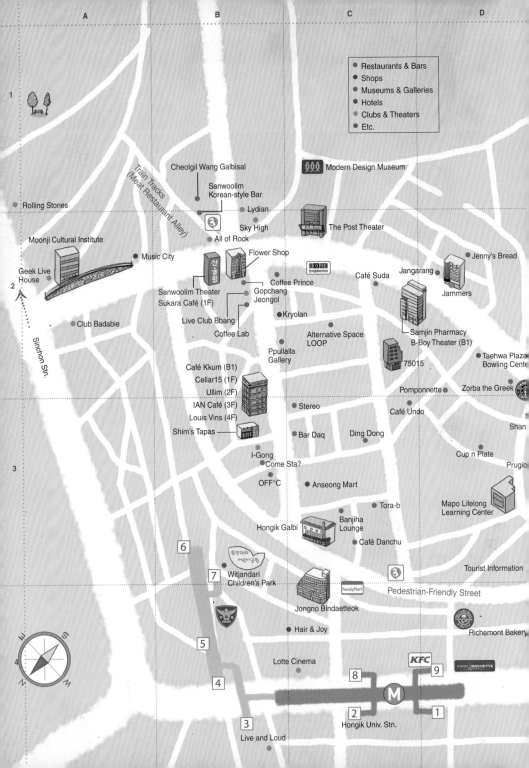

A **B** **C** **D**

1

- Restaurants & Bars
- Shops
- Museums & Galleries
- Hotels
- Clubs & Theaters
- Etc.

Cheolgil Wang Galbisal

Sanwoolim Korean-style Bar

Modern Design Museum

Rolling Stones

Lydian

Sky High

The Post Theater

All of Rock

Moonji Cultural Institute

Music City

Flower Shop

Geek Live House

2

KOTC

Café Suda

Jangarang

Jenny's Bread

Jammers

Sanwoolim Theater

Coffee Prince

Sukara Café (1F)

Gopchang Jeongol

Live Club Bbang

Kryolan

Club Badabie

Coffee Lab

Samjin Pharmacy

Alternative Space LOOP

B-Boy Theater (B1)

Ppullalla Gallery

75015

Taehwa Plaza Bowling Center

Sinchon Stn.

Café Kkum (B1)

Cellar15 (1F)

Pomponnette

Zorba the Greek

Ullim (2F)

Café Undo

Shan

IAN Café (3F)

Louis Vins (4F)

Stereo

Shim's Tapas

Cup n Plate

Prugio

3

Bar Daq

Ding Dong

I-Gong

Come Sta?

OFF°C

Anseong Mart

Mapo Lifelong Learning Center

Tora-b

Hongik Galbi

Banjiha Lounge

Café Danchu

Tourist Information

6

7 Witjandari Children's Park

Jongno Bindaetteok

FamilyMart

Pedestrian-Friendly Street

Richemont Bakery

5

Hair & Joy

Lotte Cinema

KFC

9 PARIS BAGUETTE

4

8

M

2 Hongik Univ. Stn.

1

3

Live and Loud

Train Tracks (Meat Restaurant Alley)

E F G H

Metro

M Line 1	M Line 2	M Line 3
M Line 4	M Line 5	M Line 6
M Line 7	M Line 8	M Line 9
M Jungang Line		M Bundang Line
M Gyeongui Line		M A'REX Line

3

2

Kkini

M

Sangsu Stn.

4

1

Hakata Bunko

Dongchunhong

Gyahaha

ik Univ.

Rainbow Cream

Bok A'

Parking Lot Alley

Far East Broadcasting Co.

Unit

Sk@

Vinyl

D'Avant

Noise Basement (NB2)

Kunstbe

Old Rock

Rolling Hall

Kokoro Bento

Samgeori Pocha

Evans
Tool

JokerRed

Café Alley

DD

Saab

FF

Design Museum aA

Hooper

Ska2

Mural Alley

Tinpan

Jenny's Café

Eunhasu Dabang

Inn Bar

405 Kitchen

Gamssarong

Mulgogi

Swing Guitar

Ice Waffle

Myeongwolgwan

B-hind

Spot

Harlem (NB1)

Agio

Del Mundo

Gaenari Mart

ogno

Playground

Little Terrace

Re

Zari

FamilyMart

Hope & Free Market

Freebird

Margaux

Soo Jewelry

ar

Greek Joy

Castle Praha

DGBD

Watercock

Rainbow Sea

KT&G
Sangsang
Madang

Seoul Resource Center
for Young Women

Tyche

Coffee Prince

M2
Q-vo

Multicultural Museum

The Café Roro

Ramyeon

Su Noraebang

Su Noraebang

Ziller Zone

Sapience 7

Publishing Alley

DUNKIN'
DONUTS

Gallery Hut!

Dada Bldg.

Club Mansion

oon Café

Hongik Bossam
2F Gamjatang

Nanta

Myth Hong

Mindeulle
Yeongto

GS25

Moonji Publishing Co., Ltd.

Live Space V-Hall
Club Vera

Kyusoodang Wedding Hall

Youngbin Wedding Hall

GS25

Le Tre
Campane

Mimine

Bobo Hotel

Omato Tomato

Hotel Seokyo

Hapjeong Stn.

Bulgogi Brothers

우리은행

1

2

3

4

provided a much-needed space for Korea's burgeoning punk and indie music scene.

This is a neighborhood that basks in its alternative chic, and the clubs here have not been without controversy. The performances, relatively tame compared to those in the West, have occasionally sparked outrage from more conservative elements of the Korean public. In 2005, for instance, a local punk group flashed viewers during a popular TV program, leading city authorities to threaten a crackdown on clubs. This never came to pass, as most appreciate a space for independent musicians to do their thing. All visitors are likely to find lots of opportunities to join the fun. ▣ The "Hongdae" club area is reached from Exit 9 of Hongik University Station, Line 2

• **106 Ramyeon** 일공육라면 D3 This Hongdae place does instant noodles—and only three kinds at that—but what they do is good. Try the spicy *budae jjigae ramyeon*, which comes with sausage. (02-3142-1241)

• **Yangpuni Jumak** 양푼이주막 C2 A Korean-style pub, the house specialty is its *gyeran mari* (egg roll) and *pajeon* (fried green onion pancake), which goes well with a bowl of *dongdongju* (Korean rice beer). (02-338-3285)

• **Little Terrace** 리틀테라스 F3 Or more precisely, "This Little Terrace Has Mesmerized Me," this fifth-floor wine bar serves affordable wines in a romantic atmosphere, including its eponymous terrace complete with nice views. (02-333-3310)

• **Castle Praha** 캐슬프라하 G3 A taste of the Czech Republic in Korea, this European-style beer hall houses a microbrewery (run by a Czech brew master) that produces dark and wheat beers in addition to your standard Pilsener. (02-334-2121)

• **Redemption Bar** 리뎀션 레게바 Possibly the only venue in Seoul where you can sit in a tent, pitched indoors, while drinking wine

and listening to reggae. The bar is also associated with efforts to help Tibet. (02-322-5743)

• **Le Tre Campane** F4 레 뜨레 깜빠네 A great place to go for genuine thin-crust, oven baked pizza and other Italian dishes. (02-336-3378)

• **Le Petit Four** 르쁘띠푸 Chef Kim Dae-hyun's French desserts are to die for. The macarons are especially delightful. (02-322-2669)

• **Gam Salon** 감싸롱 G2 So named because the place is made from the wood of the persimmon (*gam*) tree, Gam Salon is best known for its delicious hand-made burgers. (02-337-9373)

• **Cheolgil Wang Galbisal** 철길왕갈비살 B1 A particular favorite of this writer, this place does wonderful Korean *galbi* served with outstanding bean-paste soup, or *doenjang jjigae*. Reasonably priced, too. (02-332-9543)

• **Greek Joy** 릭조이 E3 Near Hongik University, this is one of the best (and one of the few!) Greek eateries in Korea. (02-338-2100)

WHAT TO EAT

SEODAEMUN INDEPENDENCE PARK 서대문독립공원

Seodaemun Independence Park, the focal point of which is Seodaemun Prison History Hall, pays tribute to the sacrifices of those who fought for Korea's independence throughout the 35 years of Japanese colonial rule (1910 to 1945).

Independence Gate 독립문 A3, p52 The entrance to Independence Park is Independence Gate, a massive stone gate modeled on the Arc de Triomphe in Paris. Designed by a Swiss engineer with funds collected by Korean independence activists, the monument was erected in 1896. Its history is a bit complex, with a twist of irony. The gate was placed in the location of an older gate, Yeongeunmun Gate, where, during the Joseon era (1392-1910), Korean kings would welcome Chinese envoys—at the time, China and Korea shared an "elder brother–younger brother" relationship in accordance with the traditional Confucian view of international relations. When Japan defeated China in the first Sino-Japanese War in 1895, this relationship between Korea and China was severed, and Korea became "independent." The old gate was razed and the new Independence Gate built in its place. By removing Chinese influence in Seoul, Korea's "independence" simply gave the Japanese a free hand to do as they liked in Korea. Ironically, Korea's "independence" turned out to be the first step on the road to colonization. 🚇 Exit 4 of Dongnimmun Station, Line 3.

Independence Gate

Seodaemun Prison History Hall

Seodaemun Prison History Hall 서대문형무소역사관 A3, p52 For a real sobering look at Korea's colonial past, the place to go is Seodaemun Prison, now a museum and the former "place of residence," so to speak, of many Korean independence activists during the dark ages of Japanese colonial rule. It's a monument preserved so that future generations of Koreans never forget their painful history of oppression and victimization at the hands of foreign aggressors. Some of the prison buildings are open to the public. The engineering wing, in fact, has been set up complete with graphic displays of the torture inflicted on prisoners and an educational video. One of the cell blocks has been opened to allow visitors to look around and enter some of the cells. This is probably the most impressive part of the prison—the cells have been left just as they were, and their cold walls say more than a thousand propaganda videos. Near the prison complex are a number of other statues and monuments to Korea's independence movement. ⊙ 9:30 am to 6 pm (Mar–Oct), 9:30 am to 5 pm (Nov–Feb). Closed Mondays 🎫 1,500 won 🚇 Exit 5 of Dongnimmun Station, Line 3 ⓒ 02-360-8590 ⊕ www.sscmc.or.kr

Sajik Park 사직공원 A3, p52 Sajik Park is home to Sajikdan Altar, where the kings of Joseon used to perform the Sajikdaeje, a religious service to two gods: Sasin (the god of earth) and Jiksin (the god of the harvest). The rite was a prayer for peace and a bountiful harvest, and featured processions, sacrificial offerings, special attire, and music and dance. While most of Sajikdan was destroyed by the Japanese, two stone altars still remain. Also remaining is its stately front gate, which dates from 1720. 🚇 Walk 10 minutes from Exit 1 of Gyeongbokgung Station, Line 1.

THE KOREAN FLAG

History and Culture

The flag of the Republic of Korea—the Taegeukgi—is arguably the world's most philosophical flag. In its center is a large red and blue Taoist *yin-yang*, which represents the harmony of opposites that is the origin of all things. The four trigrams that surround the *yin-yang* symbolize justice, wisdom, vitality and fertility. They are also references to the classical elements. The white background, meanwhile, symbolizes the purity of the Korean people.

King Gojong proclaimed the Taegeukgi Korea's national flag in 1883. After Korea's colonization by Japan, the flag continued to be used by the Provisional Government of the Republic of Korea in China, and was brought back once the Republic of Korea was established in 1948.

ITAEWON 이태원

Now the heart of Seoul's expatriate community, Itaewon got its start in the early 20th century, when it was a residential district for Japanese colonialists. The Japanese left in 1945 following their defeat in the Pacific War, but were replaced by the Americans, who set up shop in the massive Japanese military compound in Yongsan (now the US Army Garrison—Yongsan). Itaewon, located next to the base, became a GI playground, and over the ensuing decades would acquire a well-deserved reputation for its rowdy, somewhat unsavory character.

Times, however, have changed dramatically. Over the last decade, Itaewon's streets have grown increasingly diverse—today, you are just as likely to meet a Pakistani laborer or a Chinese tourist as you are a US soldier. High atop a hill in the heart of the neighborhood, Seoul's largest Islamic mosque looms majestically, while below, shoppers and fun-seekers of all nationalities flock to the area's famous shops and foreign eateries. Koreans—who used to avoid Itaewon like the plague—now flock here in droves; on a weekend, you can find countless Korean couples and families strolling about its streets, taking in its exotic sights, tastes, smells and sounds.

The heart of Itaewon is the "main drag," which runs east-west starting from Noksapyeong Station in the west. It's along here that you'll find many of the neighborhood's notable shops, eateries and bars. You'll find quite a bit in the alleyways off the main drag, too, particularly south of Itaewon Station—it's here that you'll encounter some of the seedier joints as well as Seoul's largest concentration of gay bars and clubs—and behind the Hamilton Hotel, where you'll find more upscale establishments.

🚇 Itaewon Station, Line 6 drops you off right in the heart of Itaewon. The Haebangchon area, however, is easiest reached via Noksapyeong Station, Line 6.

Seoul Central Mosque

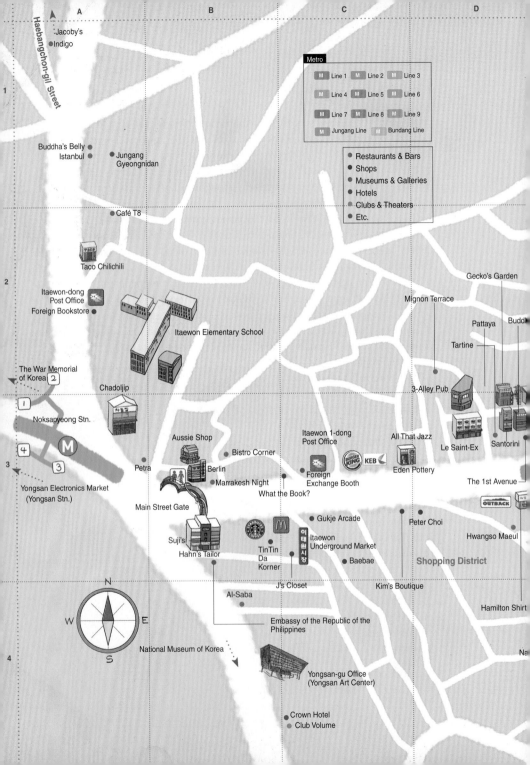

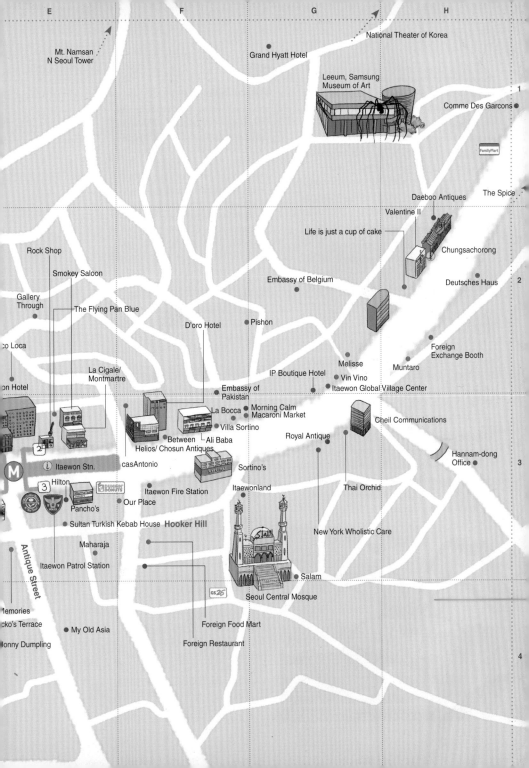

National Theater of Korea

Mt. Namsan
N Seoul Tower

Grand Hyatt Hotel

Leeum, Samsung
Museum of Art

Comme Des Garcons

FamilyMart

1

Daeboo Antiques

The Spice

Valentine II

Rock Shop

Life is just a cup of cake

Chungsachorong

Smokey Saloon

Deutsches Haus

Gallery
Through

The Flying Pan Blue

Embassy of Belgium

2

co Loca

D'oro Hotel

Pishon

Foreign
Exchange Booth

Melisse

Muntaro

La Cigale/
Montmartre

on Hotel

IP Boutique Hotel

Vin Vino

Itaewon Global Village Center

Embassy of
Pakistan

La Bocca

Morning Calm
Macaroni Market

Cheil Communications

Villa Sortino

Between

Ali Baba

Royal Antique

Helios/ Chosun Antiques

Hannam-dong
Office

3

casAntonio

Sortino's

M

Itaewon Stn.

Itaewonland

Thai Orchid

3

Hilton

DUNKIN
DONUTS

Itaewon Fire Station

Pancho's

Our Place

New York Wholistic Care

Sultan Turkish Kebab House   Hooker Hill

Maharaja

Itaewon Patrol Station

Salam

Antique Street

GS25

Seoul Central Mosque

Memories

cko's Terrace

My Old Asia

Foreign Food Mart

4

onny Dumpling

Foreign Restaurant

Seoul Central Mosque 이슬람중앙사원 G3 Sitting atop a hill, Seoul Central Mosque—a beautiful white beacon of human decency looking down upon the decadence of Itaewon—is Korea's largest Islamic house of worship, built in 1976. The area around the mosque has a number of good Middle Eastern restaurants and shops specializing in religious items and goods imported from the Middle East. ℂ 02-793-6908

Leeum, Samsung Museum of Art 리움삼성미술관 G1 One of Seoul's finest art museums can be found in Itaewon on the lower slopes of Mt. Namsan north of the "main drag." The architecturally stunning Leeum Samsung Museum of Art, which opened in 2004, was designed by renowned designers Mario Botta, Jean Nouvel and Rem Koolhaas. It is home to many masterpieces of Korean traditional and Western art, including several beautiful national treasures, as well as Louise Bourgeois' famed spider sculptures outside. ⊙ 10:30 am to 6 pm. Closed Mondays 🎫 10,000 won ℂ 02-2014-6900

'Hooker Hill' F3 While much of the rest of Itaewon is in the process of gentrification, you can still find some of the old-time sleaze on the appropriately named "Hooker Hill," an alley of seedy bars and clubs to the south of Itaewon's main drag.

TIPS

TAILOR-MADE SUITS

Itaewon's main drag is home to many tailors who specialize in tailor-made suits. In fact, as you're walking along, you'll likely be approached by at least one tailor. Suits can run anywhere from 300,000 won to over a million won, depending on materials. Hahn's Tailor (02-793-0830, B3) gets good reviews from customers. Also recommended for tailored shirts is Hamilton Shirts (02-798-5693, D3), which will deliver directly to your hotel room.

LANGUAGE BARRIER NO MORE

Most of the establishments in Itaewon have staff who speak English and Japanese, so don't worry about communication difficulties.

HOMO HILL F3

While times are changing, Korean society is still rather conservative, and it cannot be said Seoul has a thriving gay nightlife scene. Itaewon is a rare exception—on a hill not far from Hooker Hill is a collection of gay and lesbian bars and nightclubs, and some clubs catering to the transvestite/transgender population.

HAEBANGCHON

A short walk from Itaewon, past Noksapyeong Station and up towards Namsan Third Tunnel is Haebangchon, a residential neighborhood originally founded after the Korean War by refugees from North Korea (hence the name, which literally means, "Liberation Village"). Today it is inhabited by a large number of foreigners, particularly English teachers from the West, Nigerians and Filipinos. Accordingly, it is home to a number of decent foreign restaurants. Give it a look.

Leeum Samsung Museum of Art

Shopping

Tailor-Made Suits D3 Tailors—many of them around for decades—line Itaewon's main drag, and you're likely to be asked more than once if you'd like to have a suit or shirt made to measure.

Antiques E3 Itaewon, along with Insa-dong, is Seoul's best place to purchase antiques. Unlike Insa-dong, however, most of the shopkeepers here speak English and Japanese. In shops like Chosun Antique (02-793-3726, F3) and Kim's Antique Gallery (02-796-8841, F3), you can find handsome old Korean dressers and tables, Korean doors, brasswork and much, much more. Of course, expect to pay top antique prices.

Hamilton Shopping Center 해밀턴쇼핑센터 E3 Located next to the Hamilton Hotel, the Hamilton Shopping Center is four stories of shops specializing in clothing, souvenirs and traditional goods.

Leather Goods D3 You'll find leather goods in abundance—handbags, shoes, jackets and accessories—factory-made and often inspired by famous designer labels.

WHAT TO EAT

Yongsan—or at least Itaewon—is THE place to come in Seoul for international eats. You'll find eateries from all over the world—standard Western fare, Middle Eastern cuisine, Thai food, Indian curries, Korean barbecue and more. In recent years, the restaurants have grown increasingly upscale—or at least less grungy.

• **Sortino's** 소르티노스 F3 One of the best Italian restaurants in Seoul, owned by an expatriate Italian Canadian who also runs the more upscale and intimate Villa Sortino. (02-797-0488)

• **La Cigale Montmartre** 라 시갈 몽마르뜨 E3 Famous for its Belgian-style mussels, this classy place is particularly popular in summer, when its outdoor seating is a blessing. (02-796-1244)

• **Le Saint-Ex** 르생텍스 D3 The oldest French restaurant in Seoul, this cozy bistro is run by a long-time French expatriate. (02-795-2465)

• **Gecko's Terrace** 게코스테라스 E3 Overlooking Itaewon Station, this European-style pub has good pub food and a cozy atmosphere, although it does get crowded on weekends. (02-749-9425)

• **Buddha's Belly** 부다스벨리 A1 A Thai-themed wine bar that serves Thai cuisine in a classy setting. (02-796-9330)

• **casAntonio** 까사안토니오 F3 Along with Sortino's, one of the best Italian restaurants in Seoul. Perfect combo of fine cuisine and class atmosphere. (02-794-8803)

• **Taco Chilichili** 타코칠리칠리 A2 A short walk up from Noksapyeong Station, this very popular Mexican restaurant has burritos to die for. (02-797-7219)

• **Jacoby's** 자코비버거 A1 Some of the best burgers in Korea can be found here. Just be sure to go on an empty stomach: these monsters aren't light eating. (02-3785-0433)

• **Salam** 살람 G3 A good Turkish restaurant near Seoul Central Mosque. (02-793-4323)

• **The Spice** 더스파이스 H1 Fine European dining: the head chef studied under Gordon Ramsay. Pricey, but not terribly so. Trendy atmosphere. (02-749-2596)

• **Petra** 페트라 A3 Good Middle Eastern cuisine perched on a hill overlooking Noksapyeong Station. (02-790-4433)

• **La Bocca** 라보카 F3 This outstanding Italian café, deli and wine bar mixes good food with a relaxing atmosphere. Good for brunch, too. (02-790-5907)

• **Indigo** 인디고 A1 A pleasant little Haebangchon café with good food and a warm atmosphere. (02-749-0508)

MORE YONGSAN SITES

National Museum of Korea
국립중앙박물관

The National Museum of Korea—previously located in the Gwanghwamun area—opened in its new home in Yongsan in October 2005. And an impressive home it is—almost half a kilometer in length and six stories in height, it's the largest museum in Asia and the sixth largest museum in the world in terms of floor space, covering 28,542.3 m². Its massive design is said to resemble a Korean traditional fortress, and the museum grounds are decked out with ponds, Korean traditional gardens and other facilities that make it a pleasant enough place to visit even before you walk through the door. The museum makes use of the cutting edge in museum technology to ensure that its invaluable collection of artifacts could survive anything short of a direct nuclear hit.

All in all, the museum has a collection of 150,000 artifacts and works of art, although only a fraction of these are on display at any given time. The collection includes many of Korea's most treasured cultural objects, including Silla-era Buddhist art, Goryeo-era celadon ceramics and Joseon-era paintings. In the awe-inspiring main lobby is the giant Gyeongcheonsa Temple Pagoda, a beautifully carved 13 meter marble structure dating from the Goryeo era.

The museum regularly hosts special exhibits that are well worth the price of admission. Guided tours of the museum are also given—hour-long English language tours available, once daily at 2:30 pm.

National Museum of Korea

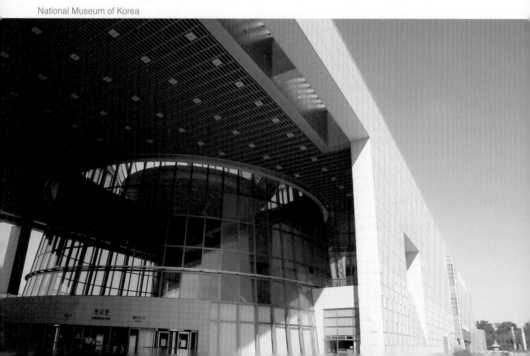

Artillery piece & Two Brothers Statue, The War Memorial of Korea

🕘 9 am to 6 pm (Tue, Thur, Fri), 9 am to 9 pm (Wed, Sat), 9 am to 7 pm (Sun, holidays) 🎫 Permanent exhibits are free but there's an entry fee for special exhibits (fee depends on exhibit). In addition to the exhibits, the museum has a good deal of other facilities as well, including performance halls and a theater. 🚇 Ichon Station, Line 4 or Jungang Line, Exit 2 ☎ 02-2077-9045~7 🖱 www.museum.go.kr

The War Memorial of Korea
전쟁기념관

The War Memorial of Korea is a massive space that includes both indoor and outdoor exhibition halls. The most moving aspect of the entire complex is the Memorial Hall: upon the walls running along the entire front perimeter of the building are inscribed the names of all the soldiers whose lives were lost during the Korean War. The list of names goes on forever—Korean casualties are listed by unit, while UN casualties are listed by nation, with the exception of the United States, whose war dead are listed by state. The outside exhibition showcases tanks, armored vehicle and other pieces of equipment used in the Korean War, as well as the Korean War Monument and Two Brothers Statue.

🕘 9 am to 6 pm. Ticketing stops one hour prior to closing. Closed Mondays 🎫 Free 🚇 Samgakji Station, Line 4 or 6, Exit 12 ☎ 02-709-3139 🖱 www.warmemo.or.kr

Yongsan Electronics Market
용산전자상가

To buy gadgets on the cheap, head to Yongsan Electronics Market, a collection of several markets and malls located behind Yongsan Station. You'll find stereo equipment, computers and computer

Cameras on sale at Yongsan Electronics Market

supplies, software, office equipment and other electronic goodies for prices approximately 20% less than elsewhere—and in the case of imported goods, up to 50% less. PC users have found the Promised Land—you'll find many small shops where you can have top-of-the-line desktops built for under US$1,000. Mac users, on the other hand, will find fewer shops catering to their needs, but the growing popularity of Apple products in Korea has been a boon for Mac users—there's an Apple authorized reseller on the first floor of the ETLAND mall. Most of the shops are open from 10 am to 8 pm, and are closed on the first and third Sundays of the month. 🚇 The market is located near Yongsan Station, Line 1 or Sinyongsan Station, Line 4

Yongsan Station 용산역 & I'Park Mall 아이파크몰

Attached by a skyway to the electronics market are Yongsan Station and I'Park

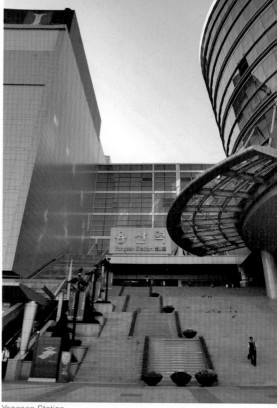
Yongsan Station

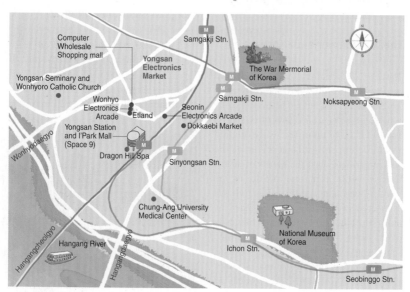

Mall, one of Seoul's newest, with everything you'd expect in a shopping complex, including restaurants, huge discount retailer E-mart, one of Seoul's best movie multiplexes and, next door, the foreigner-friendly Dragon Hill Spa. Yongsan Station is Seoul's second largest train station and the primary point of departure for destinations in Korea's southwest, such as Jeonju, Gwangju and Mokpo.

Yongsan Seminary 용산신학교 & Wonhyoro Catholic Church 원효로성당

Just a 10-minute walk from the Yongsan Electronics Market, on the campus of Sacred Heart Girls High School, is one of Seoul's hidden treasures, the Yongsan Seminary and Wonhyoro Catholic Church. Completed in 1902, the chapel is one of the oldest churches in the country.

Wonhyoro Catholic Church

US ARMY GARRISON — YONGSAN

History and Culture

Sprawling over 2.5 km² of prime Seoul real estate just south of Mt. Namsan, the US Army Garrison—Yongsan is both a symbol of the "alliance forged in blood" between Korea and the United States, and a historical reminder of Korea's painful past.

In the late 19th century, the Qing Dynasty occupied a strategic location on the Hangang River before it was kicked out by the Japanese, who established a massive military compound and headquarters. When the Japanese were defeated in World War II, out went the Japanese troops and in came the Americans. In fact, a number of historic buildings in the garrison, including the headquarters of the 8th US Army, were built by the Japanese.

Needless to say, hosting a massive foreign military complex in the heart of their capital has proven controversial among Koreans. In 2003, Korea and the US agreed to transfer Yongsan back to Korea; the US side would move its headquarters to the city of Pyeongtaek, some 90 km to the south, by 2012. Seoul Metropolitan City announced it would use the land to build a massive park, something akin to New York City's Central Park. In 2008, however, the new presidential administration of Lee Myung-bak, fearing a weakening of US resolve to defend Korea, pushed the transfer date back to 2016.

US Army Garrison—Yongsan is off-limits to all but US military personnel, US military civilians and Korean civilian workers on the base, although on-base friends can sign you in for a visit (depending on your nationality).

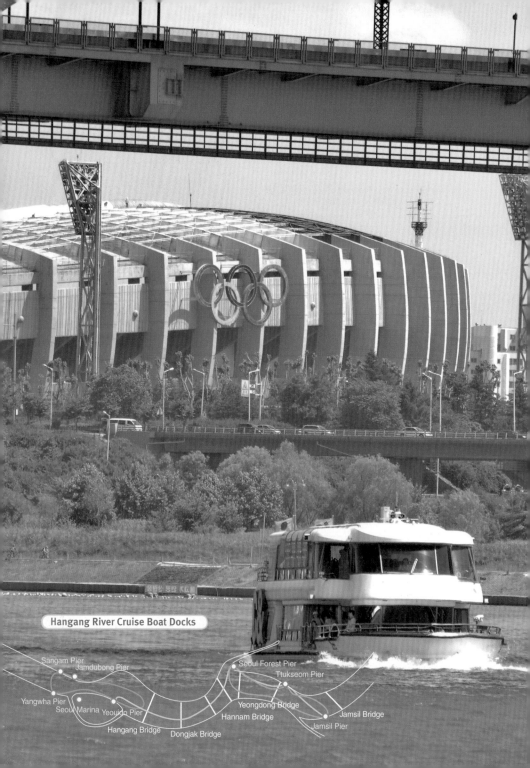

Hangang River Cruise Boat Docks

Sangam Pier
Jamdubong Pier
Yangwha Pier
Seoul Marina
Yeouido Pier
Hangang Bridge
Dongjak Bridge
Hannam Bridge
Yeongdong Bridge
Seoul Forest Pier
Ttukseom Pier
Jamsil Bridge
Jamsil Pier

RIVER CRUISES 한강유람선

The best way to see the river is via one of the city's popular river cruises. These cruises run from about midday to late at night, although the evening cruises—especially around sunset—tend to be most popular. This is an extremely pleasant way to spend an hour or so, and a great way to take in riverside landmarks such as the Hangang River bridges and the golden tower of 63 City.

You can board ferries at one of three piers—Yeouido 여의도, Jamsil 잠실 and Ttukseom 뚝섬. One-way and round-trip courses are available—see the time tables below.

TIPS

HANGANG RIVER BRIDGES

A total of 27 bridges cross the Hangang River in the Seoul area. Some of these are lit up at night to provide spectacular night views. The futuristic Olympic Bridge in the eastern part of the city is particulary stunning.

Some of the bridges are quite historically significant, as well. Hangang Railway Bridge A, for instance, was completed in 1900, and several others were built in the Japanese colonial era.

Courses

Type	Pier	Travel Time	Fee
Standard Cruise	Yeouido, Jamsil, Ttukseom	1 hour	11,000 won
Live Music Cruise	Yeouido, Jamsil, Ttukseom	70 min	15,000 won
BBQ Cruise	Yeouido	90 min	60,000 won
Buffet Cruise	Yeouido	90 min	60,000 won

*Reservations required for the BBQ and Buffet ferries.

• **Yeouido:**   Yeouido ⟶ Banpo Bridge ⟶ Yeouido
• **Jamsil:**   Jamsil ⟶ Banpo Bridge ⟶ Jamsil
• **Ttukseom:** Ttukseom ⟶ Banpo Bridge ⟶ Ttukseom

• **Yeouido Pier** Exit 3 of Yeouinaru Station, Line 5 • **Jamsil Pier** Exit 7 of Sincheon Station, Line 2. Walk about 20 minutes (or take taxi) • **Ttukseom Pier** Exit 8 of Ttukseom Station, Line 2. Walk about 10 minutes ⊕ www.hcruise.co.kr (C&Hangangland)

YEOUIDO 여의도

Koreans often refer to Yeouido as the "Manhattan of Seoul," and while this is no doubt an exaggeration, the comparison is not completely without basis. Like its New York counterpart, Yeouido is a river island, and it is Seoul's political, financial, commercial and media heart. The 63 Building (officially named "63 City"), is Seoul's landmark skyscraper, and is located here.

Yeouido is very much a product of Korea's post-war economic miracle. Prior to industrialization starting in the 1960s, Yeouido was a flood-plagued sandy island with a name meaning, literally, "Useless Island." During the Japanese colonial period, the imperial authorities built Korea's first international airport on the island. In the 70s, Korea's development-minded president Park Chung-hee pushed an ambitious program to turn the erstwhile "useless island" into a new commercial and political center. In 1975, the green dome of the National Assembly Building was completed, providing a new home to the Korean parliament. Korea's major political parties, media companies, banks and investment houses and other major companies soon followed.

TIPS

YEOUIDO SAETGANG ECOLOGICAL PARK

The wetlands on the south side of Yeouido island have been turned into an aquatic park, complete with wooden walking paths. If you're in the neighborhood, it might make for a nice stroll. See the map on p223.

If you're expecting towering, Art Deco-style skyscrapers à la New York, you'll likely be disappointed—Yeouido is, in fact, not an especially exciting place. Still, there are a number of things to see.

Saetgang Bridge over Yeouido Saetgang Ecological Park

63 City 63시티 249 meters high, this golden monolith was an architectural wonder when it was completed in 1985. The name refers to the number of floors, although this is somewhat misleading—only 60 floors are above ground. The building houses a shopping center, IMAX Theater and a popular aquarium, in addition to restaurants, conference centers and, of course, offices. The most popular destination, however, is the observation deck which offers some of the best views of the city. ⏰ 10 am to 10 pm 🎫 **Observation deck** 12,000 won **Aquarium** 17,000 won **IMAX Theater** 12,000 won **Total package** 33,000 won (10% discount if you bring passport/foreigner ID card) ☎ 02-789-5663

National Assembly Building 국회의사당 Home of the Korean parliament, the National Assembly Building offers tours—apply at the visitor center. ⏰ 9 am to 6 pm (weekdays), 9 am to 5 pm (weekends). Admission closes one hour prior to closing ☎ 02-788-2885

Yeouido Park 여의도공원 Formerly an asphalt plaza that doubled as a parade ground and emergency airstrip, Yeouido Park was transformed into a beautiful stretch of green in 1999. The park consists of three separate zones, including a lovely Korean traditional garden. There's also a bike path

63 City (top), National Assembly Building

TIPS

SEOUL MARINA

Newly opened in April 2011, Seoul Marina Club & Yacht rents its fleet of 45 yachts to the public at rates much lower than elsewhere in Korea, with one- to three-man sailboats available for 4,000 won an hour per person. Even six-man cruisers are available for just 15,000 won per person. The beautiful marina, complete with restaurants, cafés, and seminar rooms in a snazzy glass building scenically placed right behind the landmark National Assembly Building, has moorings for up to 90 boats. You need an hour of training before you can rent a yacht and, if you're more ambitious, sailing lessons are available, including Korea's first-ever sailing lessons for children. The marina even offers a "bike ferry" service to ferry Seoul's growing number of cyclists across the mighty Hangang River. ☎ 02-423-7888 🖥 www.seoul-marina.com

popular with both bikers and rollerbladers—bike rentals are available. Behind the National Assembly Building is Yunjung-ro Street, famous throughout Korea for its beautiful cherry blossoms in spring. ℘ 02-3780-0562 🚇 Yeouido Station or Yeouinaru Subway Station, Line 5

Noryangjin Fish Market 노량진수산시장 Seoul's largest fish market, Noryangjin Fish Market is a 24-hour affair, although the fish auctioning takes place in the wee hours of the morning before 6 am. Here you can find the bounty of the sea in its countless manifestations. Much of the produce is sold while alive, while nearby restaurants will be happy to cook up your fish (or slice it up raw) for you. ⊕ 24 hours 🚇 Noryangjin Station, Line 1

Springtime in Yeouido
The time to visit Yeouido is spring, when the island's countless cherry blossoms bloom. Yeouido Park hosts the Yeouido Cherry Blossom Festival at this time—it's Seoul's most popular cherry blossom event, and is accompanied by music and other cultural events.

TIPS

HALLELUJAH!

Yoido Full Gospel Church, located near the National Assembly, is the mother of all megachurches—830,000 members as of 2007, it is the largest Christian congregation in the world. Not bad considering that when it was founded by Rev. David Yonggi Cho in 1958, the Pentecostal church was little more than a tent church.

Services take place almost all day Sunday—these truly are impressive events of faith and devotion. Foreign language services in English, Chinese, Japanese, Spanish, Indonesian and Russian are also provided. See http://english.fgtv.com for more information.

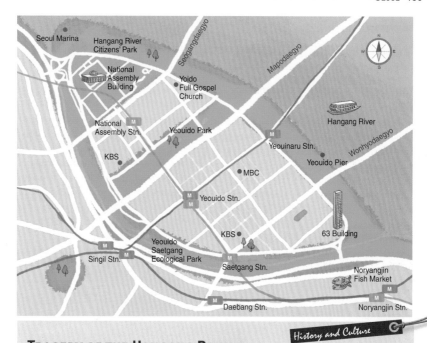

Seoul Marina
Hangang River
Citizens' Park
Seogangdaegyo
Mapodaegyo
National Assembly Building
Yoido Full Gospel Church
Hangang River
National Assembly Stn.
Yeouido Park
Yeouinaru Stn.
Wonhyodaegyo
KBS
Yeouido Pier
MBC
Yeouido Stn.
KBS
63 Building
Yeouido Saetgang Ecological Park
Singil Stn.
Saetgang Stn.
Noryangjin Fish Market
Daebang Stn.
Noryangjin Stn.

TRAGEDY OF THE HANGANG BRIDGE

History and Culture

When the Korean War started on June 25, 1950, South Korea was caught off-guard. Within three days, North Korean troops had entered Seoul. South Korea hastily moved its capital to Daejeon and, in a panic, prepared the bridges over the Hangang River for demolition to slow the enemy advance.

On the morning of June 28, the order came to blow the bridges. Unfortunately, in the case of the Hangang River Bridge, it was clogged with refugees and retreating soldiers, and no effort was made to clear them—not even a warning. In a great explosion, several bridge spans were dropped into the river, sending an estimated 300–800 people to their deaths.

If this wasn't calamitous enough, the bridge was destroyed with three divisions of the South Korean Army still on the northern side of the river, along with much of the army's heavy equipment. Many of these troops were captured and killed by the North Koreans, and it was a long time before the South Korean army could recover from the losses. In September of that year, the colonel who ordered the demolition—perhaps on orders from above—was court-martialed and shot, although a posthumous trial 16 years later cleared him of wrongdoing.

YANGHWAJIN 양화진

Yanghwajin Foreigners' Cemetery
양화진외국인선교사묘원

A short walk from Hapjeong Station (Line 2 and 6) on a little plot of land overlooking the Hangang River is Yanghwajin Foreigners' Cemetery, founded in 1890. Currently, 551 individuals are buried at Yanghwajin, including 279 Americans, 31 Britons, 19 Canadians and 18 Russians. Although the spot is technically named "Yanghwajin Foreign Missionaries' Cemetery," only 167 of the occupants were missionaries; also buried here are soldiers, diplomats, journalists and others. Because of the international character of the dead, the headstones come in an assortment of sizes and styles, from simple blocks of stone to Celtic crosses and elaborately decorated obelisks. Epitaphs can be found in English, French, German, Italian, Russian, Chinese and Japanese, and are quite interesting to see. Homer B. Hulbert's gravestone, for instance, reads, "I would rather be buried in Korea than in Westminster Abbey."

🕐 10 am to 5 pm. Closed Sundays 🚇 Exit 7 of Hapjeong Station, Line 2 ✆ 02-332-9174

Jeoldusan Catholic Martyrs' Shrine, built where thousands of Korean Catholics were executed in the late 19th century

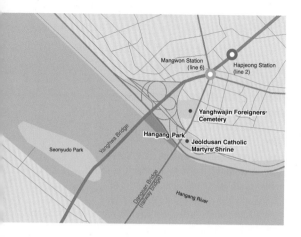

Jeoldusan Catholic Martyrs' Shrine 절두산순교성지

A short walk from Yanghwajin Foreigners' Cemetery brings you to Jeoldusan Catholic Martyrs' Shrine, one of the holiest places in the country for Korean Catholics. After its introduction in the 19th century, Catholicism in Korea experienced a period of great hardship. In 1866, the last and ultimately most severe of a series of persecutions of Catholics was launched. The royal government, then led by the xenophobic prince regent Heungseon Daewongun, executed nine French missionaries who had illegally smuggled themselves into Korea. In response, the French sent warships up the Hangang River, eventually landing at the cliffs of Yanghwajin. The ships were forced to withdraw, and in his fury Heungseon Daewongun declared that Yanghwajin, now soiled by the Westerners, had to be washed clean with the blood of those responsible for the foreign presence—the Catholic faithful. Over the next six years, thousands of Catholics were dragged to the top of the cliff and beheaded, their bodies cast off onto the rocks below. Afterwards, the cliff became known as Jeoldusan or "Decapitation Hill." Much later, in 1966, Catholics built a church and memorial hall atop the cliffs, with a fine perspective of the Hangang River. The area below the hill was turned into a park graced with many moving pieces of religious art. The memorial hall and church do a respectable job of teaching visitors about the early history of the Catholic Church in Korea and contain a number of relics from the martyrs, 103 of whom were canonized in 1925 and 1968 (granting Korea the status of having the fourth largest number of Catholic saints in the word).

KOREAN CHRISTIANITY

Spend any amount of time in Korea and you'll soon discover the country's vibrant Christian community. The Seoul skyline is dotted by neon crosses fixed atop the city's countless churches. Several of the world's largest churches, including the 830,000-man Yoido Full Gospel Church (see p134), are located here. It's estimated that about 28% of Korea's population is Christian (18% Protestant, 10% Catholic), the second highest percentage in Asia behind the Philippines. In terms of fervor and enthusiasm, however, Korean Christians are second to none. In fact, according to recent news reports, Korean

Stained glass, Myeong-dong Cathedral

churches dispatch the second largest number of Christian missionaries abroad (behind only the United States), a stunning accomplishment given Korea's significantly smaller population.

Korean Christianity wasn't always as flourishing, however. In the late 17th century, works by the Italian Jesuit missionary Matteo Ricci were first brought to Korea via royal tribute missions. By the latter half of the next century, reformist scholars had established a church led by a system of lay clergy. It was an experience almost unparalleled in Catholic history—a church establishing itself without the help of foreign missionaries.

The new faith was viewed with abject horror by Korea's Confucian establishment, however, and Catholicism underwent several bloody persecutions throughout the 19th century. Many Catholics were killed, and those who survived often fled to remote mountain villages where they established small communities of believers far from the persecution in the cities. Not even Western missionaries were immune—in the great persecution of 1866, for example, nine French priests were executed, sparking an armed conflict with France.

By comparison, Protestantism came later, and as a result had a much easier time of it. Unlike Catholics, who were forced for over a century to pray and proselytize illegally, often at great risk to life and limb, Protestant missionaries from the United States, Canada, UK and Australia entered Korea in the late 19th century as diplomats, doctors and educators, often with the support of royal authorities, who viewed them as agents of modernization. Indeed, Protestant missionaries played an important role in Korea's modernization, establishing many of the country's first modern hospitals, schools and universities, as well as churches.

Korean Christianity went through a rough patch under Japanese imperial rule. The

Japanese distrusted Western missionaries (most of whom were expelled at the start of the Pacific War) and viewed churches—many of which had become centers of anti-Japanese nationalist activities—with suspicion. Still, at least until the 1930s, the religion continued to flourish. Christian activity in northern Korea was so vibrant, in fact, that the city of Pyongyang (ironically enough, now the capital of atheist North Korea) was called the "Jerusalem of the East."

Liberation from colonial rule, post-war economic development and Korea's close relationship with the United States provided the environment for a second boom in Korean Christianity. The number of Korean Protestants jumped from just over 623,000 in 1960 to over 8 million in 2005. Their influence on society grew, too—of Korea's post-Liberation presidents, three (Syngman Rhee, Kim Young-sam and Lee Myung-bak) were Protestants and two (Kim Dae-jung and Roh Moo-hyun) were Catholics. In particular, Christians played a major role in Korea's democratization movement of the 1970s and 1980s.

While Korean Christianity is certainly more vibrant than many of its counterparts in the West, the country's newfound affluence has not been without its effects—in recent years, there's been a drop in the growth rate of Korean churches. This has been accompanied with a resurgent interest in Korea's more traditional faiths, particularly Buddhism. Not that you'd be able to tell this from the clamor of Korean churchgoers, however.

Relief of martyrs, Jeoldusan Catholic Martyrs' Shrine

RIVERSIDE PARKS

Hangang Citizens' Park 한강시민공원

Much of the Hangang River's banks has been transformed into park space in the form of Hangang River Citizens' Park. This is really 12 separate parks rather than one large one, with separate areas in (from west to east) the Gangseo, Nanji, Yanghwa, Seonyudo, Mangwon, Yeouido, Ichon, Banpo, Jamwon, Ttukseom, Jamsil and Gwangnaru districts. Each section is unique and equipped with sports and leisure facilities like tennis courts, swimming pools and picnic grounds.

Seonyudo Park 선유도공원 p137 Of the 12 districts, Seonyudo Park is one of the best known. The park, originally the site of an old water treatment plant, makes use of its industrial past to create a wonderful ecological zone. Linking the park, which is actually on an island in the middle of the river, is the beautiful arched Seonyugyo Bridge, a pedestrian walkway that is lit up in the evening to make one of Seoul's most beautiful night views.

🕐 6 am to midnight 🚇 Seonyudo Park is best reached via taxi from Exit 1 of Dangsan Station, Line 2. ✆ 02-3780-0590

World Cup Park 월드컵공원 There was a time not so long ago when the Nanji district of Seoul was something of a national shame. For over a decade Seoul's primary landfill, the area amounted to little more than a big, noxious-smelling mountain of garbage. Due

World Cup Park

to the strong odors emitted by the eyesore, the entire area was covered with a layer of topsoil after the landfill was closed in 1993.

Then something amazing happened—plants and animals began returning to the Nanji area, which had since been deserted by humanity. Encouraged, city authorities spent six years stabilizing the waste and another year building the 3,471,090 m² park known today as World Cup Park. The park opened in May of 2002, just in time to celebrate its namesake, the 17th FIFA World Cup co-hosted by Korea and Japan.

The park is huge—it actually consists of five smaller parks, including the area in front of the imposing World Cup Stadium and two massive ziggurats of green—formerly mountains of garbage—that have been transformed into Haneul (Sky) and Noeul (Sunset) parks.

1. Sebit Dungdungseom 2. Seonyudo Park 3. Haneul Park

Banpo Bridge Moonlight Rainbow Fountain

• **Pyeonghwa Park:** This area in front of World Cup Stadium includes a pond, picnic grounds and some beautiful marshland.

• **Nanjicheon Park:** A serene riverine environment following the Nanjicheon Stream.

• **Nanji Hangang Park:** A park area which runs alongside the Hangang River with a number of sporting facilities and a pier where you can catch boats for a small river cruise.

• **Haneul Park:** Once a mountain of garbage, this hill now provides some of the best views of Seoul in the city. Wind turbines at the top generate power for the park. The park is especially known for its scenic steps and beautiful reeds blooming in late autumn.

• **Noeul Park:** So named because this lesser of the two former trash heaps offers some of Seoul's best sunsets. Golf fans might also wish to make use of its nine-hole golf course. ⏱ 24 hours, but Haneul Park closes at sunset. 🚇 Exit 1 of World Cup Stadium Station, Line 6. There's a free shuttle to the park from the nearby Mapo Agriculture-Fisheries Market. ☎ 02-300-5500, 3780-0612 (Nanji Hangang Park)

Banpo Bridge Moonlight Rainbow Fountain
반포대교 무지개분수 **& Setbit Dungdungseom** 세빛
동동섬 If you'd like to see a real riverine spectacle, head to Banpo Bridge in the evening to see the Moonlight Rainbow Fountain. Five times a day (six on Friday, Saturday and Sunday) some 10,000 LED nozzles installed along the side of the bridge let loose with a 20-minute-long, multicolored barrage of water (sucked up from the river below with pumps) in time with musical selections from Beethoven, Vivaldi and others. Just next to the bridge, Sebit Dungdungseom—"Floating Island" in English—is Seoul's newest architectural gem. Floating on the Hangang River, the complex is designed to be a combined culture, convention and leisure facility. It is best seen at night when lit up. ⏱ Noon, 5 pm, 8 pm (weekdays); extra 9 pm show on weekends (Apr to Jun); noon, 6 pm, 8 pm, 9 pm (weekdays), extra 10 pm show on weekends (July to Aug) 🚇 The best place to witness the fountain is Banpo Hangang Park, which can be reached via Exits 8-1 or 8-2 of the underground arcade of Express Bus Terminal Station, Lines 3, 7 or 9.

SEOUL FOREST 서울숲

Seoul Forest, completed in 2005, likes to think of itself as Seoul's answer to New York's Central Park or London's Hyde Park. Central Park it is not, but it's a very pleasant place indeed, inter-crossed by walking paths and bridges, some of them quite architecturally pleasing.

Prior to the construction of the park, the Ttukseom area was a gritty industrial area in need of redevelopment. Now, it is a 1,156,498 m² oasis of green in a city trying to rediscover its ecological roots.

One of the star attractions of the park is its large population of Sika deer.

🕐 24 hours 🚇 Free 🚶 Walk 10 minutes from Exit 8 of Ttukseom Station, Line 2. By boat, cruises from Yeouido stop by Seoul Forest on the way to Jamsil. 📞 02-460-2901~2926

Bicycle built for two, Seoul Forest

APGUJEONG-DONG 압구정동
& CHEONGDAM-DONG 청담동

In a land of posh, the neighborhoods of Apgujeong-dong and Cheongdam-dong are the poshest of all. The very mention of the neighborhoods evokes visions of chic boutiques, designer labels, trendy bars and cafés, and imported luxury cars. This is pretty much what you'll find, so what you think of the place depends on what you think of the aforementioned. That said, many of the denizens here are not actually residents—attempts to appear so notwithstanding—so backpackers shouldn't feel completely out of place, and the cafés and sizzling nightlife should not be missed.

🚇 The main shopping area is actually a bit of a walk from Apgujeong Station, Line 3. You're probably best off taking a cab from the station. Garosu-gil, meanwhile, is best approached via Exit 8 of Sinsa Station, Line 3.

Apgujeong-dong 압구정동

This is Seoul's Beverly Hills, with its very own "Rodeo Street" where you can max out your credit card. Apgujeong-dong is filled with clothing shops, expensive cafés and young shoppers. One landmark is the eclectic Galleria Department Store.

Rodeo Street 로데오거리 C1, C2 This winding road linking Apgujeong-dong and Cheongdam-dong is everything its famous namesake in Los Angeles is, minus the palm trees. This is really Korea's fashion mecca—design trends begin here and move to Dongdaemun afterwards. If you're looking for big-name foreign brands like Prada, Gucci, Dolce & Gabbana, Cartier, Giorgio, Armani and Louis Vuitton, you've come to the right spot. In addition to these flagship shops, the street also has beauty salons, high-end restaurants and movie theaters.

Galleria Department Store 갤러리아백화점 E1 The most easily recognizable Apgujeong-dong landmark, the west wing of this luxury department store is covered with 4,330 LED glass disks that reflect light in the day and are lit up at night. The West

Wing carries all sorts of high-end items, while the East Wing (in an all together different building to the right) carries almost exclusively luxury brands and caters to well-heeled shoppers of real means. 🕐 10:30 am to 8 pm (Mon–Sat), 8:30 pm (Fri–Sun) ✆ 02-3449-4114

Galleria Department Store

1

A   B   C   D

Hanyang Apt.

S-OIL

신한은행 SHINHAN BANK

KB

하나은행

Apgujeong Stn. Line 3

Galleria

All Day Brunch

Bonjuk

H Cube Gallery

Little Saigon

Sotdae
Saju Café

UNIQLO

Yeongyang
Center

678

Gallery Hyundai
Gangnam

Ye-Hall

Andrew's Eggtart

Jeongdong Arcade

Hohwabanjeom

Tasty Boulevard

Princess Hotel

GS25

Rodeo Street

Adellia

Chadoljip

Mafia

Monkey Beach

Beans Bins

2

Jaseng Hospital of
Oriental Medicine

Ari

CONVERSE

Chicken Place

Schadheli

Mado

Hwajeonmin

Seoseogalbi

Boat Whistle

Badaro
Ganeun·Gisa

Wonjo Chogajip

Canon

Papa Bubble

De Chocolate
Coffee

Diesel

In the Box

Codes
Combine

General Idea

Saemaeul Sikdang

Toni & Guy

On

Zen Hideaway

Peppermint Dream

MINI
STOP

Sakkayana

Gangseomyeonok

Design Café

GS25

Kloo

Sanbong Hwaro Gui

Byugdoljib

Samgyeopsal &
Kimchijjigae

Milk Bar

Jaeminan Jogakka
Saju Café

SK

Macos Adamas

Dashing Diva
Han Style

3

Samwon Garden

Oriental Spoon

Mandarina Duck

MINI
STOP

Ed Hardy

Take Urban

Terry Gallery

De

Rock & Roll

Il Mare

Sketch

Dosan Park

Dosan Ahn Chang-Ho
Memorial Hall

MuiMui

BURGER
KING

Space*C, Coreana Art &
Culture Complex

Homestead Coffee

MINI
STOP

The Queen

Café Papergarden

Jeonjasinbal

Woolim Cheongda
Theater

Café Mou

Caffèra

Gorilla in the Kitchen

staSera

Paris Croissant Kitchen

Gulbi Maeul

RALPH LAUREN
Walking Slowly

KRAZE
burgers

Sony

Hak-dong Intersection

Kim Yeon Ju Boutique

IMART Gallery

Jahayun Clinic

Platinum
Microbrewery

JuJu

4

Atelier Hermès

Cine City

Cheongdam
Sundubu

FRIDAYS

BENNIGAN'S
GRILL • PASTA

Gangnam-gu
Office Stn. Line 7

Daily Pro

Triple O

Horim Art Center

Hwassi 167 Degrees

BMW

Dosan Intersection

Mercado

Seongsu Bridge

Cheongdam-dong 청담동

Named for a particularly nice pond that existed here some time in the distant past, Cheongdam-dong is now the wealthiest district in all of Seoul. Like Apgujeong-dong, it is known for its upscale boutiques, designers and clubs—only more so. Cheongdam-dong also attracts a more mature crowd than Apgujeong-dong, with local shoppers and patrons generally in their 30s and 40s.

Cheongdam-dong Gallery Street

Cheongdam-dong is more than just posh shops and cafés, mind you. In recent years, it has also become home to a number of hot new art galleries that cater to young and financially endowed collectors. About 50 privately owned galleries have gathered in the area, many specializing in cutting edge and experimental work by up-and-coming artists. Most of the galleries can be found on the stretch of road between Galleria

TIPS

GAROSU-GIL 가로수길

Garosu-gil—which basically translates as "Tree-lined Street"—is perhaps as close to Paris as you'll find in Seoul. This pleasant little road is indeed lined with trees (ginkgo trees, to be precise), and is chock-full of European-style streetside cafés and wine bars, with some cozy boutiques and shops thrown in for good measure. Sure, the prices are a bit pretentiously high, but it does make for a nice breather from some of Seoul's more, ahem, energetic neighborhoods. In part due to the influence of the popular US cable TV series "Sex and the City," American-style brunch has also become something of a neighborhood fad.

Interestingly enough, the area started as an artists' enclave, and many of the establishments still have a decidedly artsy feel to them, even if the artists themselves have since moved on to other neighborhoods.

Department Store and Cheongdam-dong Catholic Church.

Used Luxury Goods

While Cheongdam-dong plays host to the city's largest concentration of luxury brand names, Apgujeong-dong has a number of consignment shops that sell used luxury goods for up to 60% off what you'd spend for them new.

Eating and Drinking

When you're done shopping, Apgujeong-dong and Cheongdam-dong are overflowing with chic (and steep) cafés, bars and restaurants. As with shopping, places in Cheongdam-dong tend to be more expensive. The area around Dosan Park in Cheongdam-dong, in particular, is famous for its well-designed cafés.

While not Apgujeong-dong or Cheongdam-dong, the nearby tree-lined street of Garosu-gil also has a large number of trendy bars, cafés and restaurants.

WHAT TO EAT

The Apgujeong-dong, Sinsa-dong and Nonhyeon-dong areas are filled with places to eat, drink and be merry.

• **Samwon Garden** 삼원가든 A3 One of the best meat restaurants in all of Seoul, this place has been around since 1976 and is owned by the father of LPGA golfer Grace Park. In addition to the wonderful food, it has a beautiful Korean-style garden. (02-548-3030)

• **Take Urban** D3 Organic coffees and teas. (02-512-7978)

• **Homyeondang** 호명당 H2 Specializes in organically made noodles. (02-511-9517)

• **Mercado** 메르까도 C4 Wonderful Brazilian barbeque place that will fill you up with enough red meat to last you a lifetime. (02-515-3288)

• **Sanbong Hwaro Gui** 산봉화로구이 C2 Does really high-quality barbecued meats, included Wagyu beef. And as a bonus, it's reasonably priced. (02-546-2229)

• **Saemaeul Sikdang** 새마을식당 C2 More grilled Korean meats done right. (02-6404-9989)

• **Eric's New York Steak House** The Yeoksam-dong branch of the Korean New York-style steak house chain. (02-2155-1636)

• **Oriental Spoon** C3 A café-like eatery specializing in Southeast Asian cuisine, particularly noodle dishes, with some Japanese and Chinese dishes. (02-512-0916)

• **Ganga** 강가 B1 This Indian cuisine is a bit pricey, but the food is good and the atmosphere refined. (02-2055-3610)

• **Gorilla in the Kitchen** A3 This stylish restaurant specializes in healthy, beautifully prepared dishes. Emphasis on the "healthy": the restaurant menu breaks each dish down by nutrients and kcals. (02-3442-1688)

• **Lab XXIV** 랩24 C1 Started by Korean celebrity chef Edward Kwon, this trendy eatery in Cheongdam-dong serves high quality contemporary cuisine at reasonable cost. (02-511-4523)

COEX MALL 코엑스몰 (SAMSEONG-DONG) C2

Located in the landmark Korea World Trade Center (KWTC) complex of Samseong-dong, COEX Mall is the largest underground mall in Asia. With over 260 shops, it's a great place to go on a rainy day. A very popular destination for foreign visitors, it has everything you'd expect in a mammoth shopping mall—stores, restaurants, cafés, a very popular movie theater, Korea's best aquarium, even a museum dedicated to Korea's gift to global culinary cuisine—kimchi. Also part of the complex are two luxury hotels and one of Seoul's best casinos. Just across from the mall is Bongeunsa Temple, one of Seoul's biggest Buddhist temples.

Buddha of Bongeunsa Temple looks out upon COEX

Shopping

As one of the biggest malls in Asia, COEX Mall is a place where you can find just about anything under the sun. The best place to score luxury goods is Hyundai Department Store, adjacent to the mall. For clothes-hounds, global casual brands like Nike and Levi's are represented, as are many Korean designers.

The COEX branch of Korean bookseller Bandi & Luni's is one of the best places in Korea to find English-language books. Nearby is Evan Music, one of Korea's largest shops for music and movies.

Movie Theater The COEX MegaBox Cineplex 코엑스메가박스 has 16 screens and features popular Hollywood releases and commercial Korea hits.

COEX Aquarium 코엑스아쿠아리움

COEX Aquarium is fascinating place and a great place to walk around even if you don't particularly fancy marine creatures in general. Especially cool is the "undersea tunnel," where you can get a bottom's up view of a wide variety of sea life, including sharks. ⊕ 10 am to 8 pm 🏷 17,500 won 📞 02-6002-6200

Kimchi Field Museum 김치박물관

Yep, it's a museum that's all about kimchi. Kimchi relics, kimchi displays, kimchi tasting rooms, kimchi in art, a kimchi store—more kimchi than you can shake a stick at.
⊕ 10 am to 6 pm (Tue–Sun). Closed Mondays 🏷 3,000 won 📞 02-6002-6456

TIPS

SEVEN LUCK CASINO

Seven Luck Casino's Gangnam branch is located at the Convention Annex Building of COEX Center in Samseong-dong. Like most of Korea's other casinos, it's strictly for foreigners but if you like to gamble, it's a fun place with an interesting East-meets-West atmosphere. All the favorite games—blackjack, Baccarat, Tai-Sai, roulette, Caribbean poker and slot machines—are represented. Hours: 24 hours, 365 days a year. (02-3466-6100)

BONGEUNSA TEMPLE

Just across from the Korea World Trade Center complex is the Buddhist temple of Bongeunsa, one of Seoul's largest. It was founded in 794, and although the temple was heavily damaged during the Korean War, a few old buildings survived, along with some precious examples of Buddhist art. Temple stay programs are available. The 23 meter tall statue of the Maitreya Buddha cuts an impressive figure as it looks out upon Korea World Trade Center skyscraper. Getting There: Exits 5 and 6 of Samseong Station, Line 2. (02-545-1448, www.bongeun.org)

Coex Aquarium (top), Kimchi Field Museum (bottom)

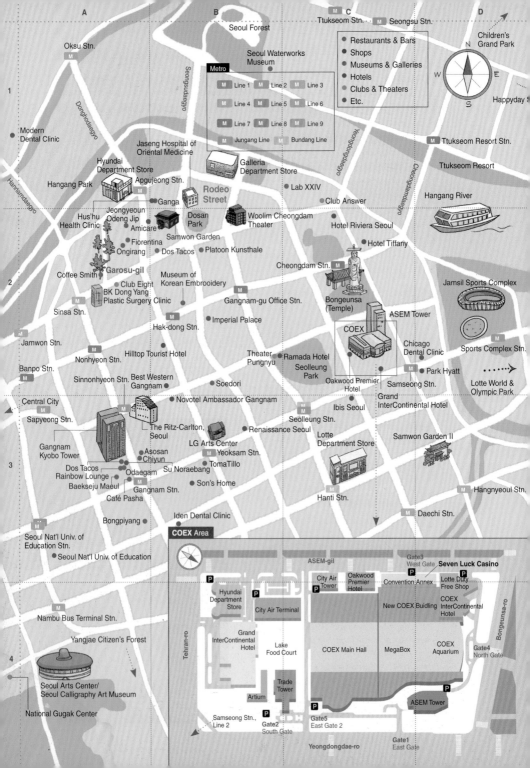

PERFORMING ARTS IN GANGNAM

The Gangnam area is home to several major performing arts venues, including the massive Seoul Arts Center complex and the National Gugak Center, Korea's leading center for Korean traditional music and dance.

Seoul Arts Center 예술의전당 A4 Seoul Arts Center showcases the diversity of Korea's cultural traditions,d including five arts buildings, each devoted to a different genre in a single compound. The Opera House, designed with a roof resembling a traditional Korean aristocrat's hat, is a seven-story building that includes the 2,300-seat Opera Center for marquee operas, the 700-seat Towol Theater for plays, and the Jayu Theater for experimental productions. Korea's national ballet and opera companies are based at the Arts Center. The Music Hall is Korea's first exclusively music-focused performance hall, with a 2,523-seat Concert Hall and a more intimate Recital Hall. It's also home base to Korea's national choir, the Korea and Seoul symphony orchestras, and the Seoul Performing Arts company.

Also included in the Seoul Arts Center complex are the Hangaram Art Museum, Seoul Calligraphy Art Museum and Hangaram Design Museum.

🚌 Take Bus No. 4429 from Exit 5 of Nambu Bus Terminal Station, Line 3 ☎ 02-580-1300 🖳 www.sac.or.kr

National Gugak Center 국립국악원 A4 Located adjacent to Seoul Arts Center, the center is comprised of two theaters, an outdoor performance area and a traditional performing arts museum. Every Saturday at 5 pm from May through December, the Yeakdang Theater presents a 90 minute show of traditional Korean folk songs, drumming, *pansori* and court dances for only 10,000 won per seat. From early May to early December, the Umyeondang Theater presents a show with similar content at the same price, but performed by younger artists. 🚌 Take Bus No. 4429 (green) after getting off at Nambu Bus Terminal Station, Line 3, Exit 5 ☎ 02-580-3300 🖳 www.gugak.go.kr

Seoul Arts Center (left), National Gugak Center

LOTTE WORLD 롯데월드 (JAMSIL)

Lotte World is not just an amusement park—it's its practically own city. According to one 2002 survey, it is the seventh most popular amusement park in the world. This sprawling complex in Seoul's Jamsil neighborhood includes the world's largest indoor amusement park, an outdoor amusement park, a folk museum, a department store, a major luxury hotel and Korea's best ice skating rink. If you have kids, they'll love it. Big kids will find plenty of things to do, too. Also nearby is the beautiful Seokchon Lake, which makes for fine walks.

⏰ 9:30 am to 10 pm (Mon to Thu) 9:30 am to 11 pm (Fri to Sun) 💳 38,000 won (day pass), 26,000 won (day admission); 31,000 won (night pass, after 4 pm), 22,000 won (night admission, after 4 pm) 15,500 won (night admission, after 7 pm). Reduced admission for youth and children. 🚇 Exit 4 of Jamsil Station, Line 2 and 8 ☎ 02-411-2000 ✆ www.lotteworld.com

Indoor Park "Adventure," Lotte World's indoor amusement park, is truly a sight to behold: four floors of fun, covered by a Victorian-style glass dome—the scale is almost surreal. In the center is a fine indoor ice skating rink that's popular with young couples. You've got your full assortment of games and rides, with festivals, parades, light shows and other spectacles thrown in for good measure. You can get a good view of the complex from the monorail that takes you around both the indoor and outdoor parks.

Outdoor park, Lotte World

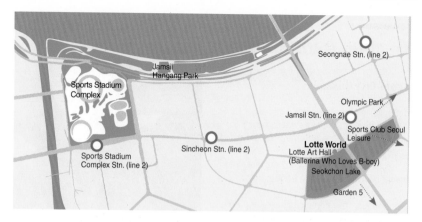

Outdoor Park The outdoor park is known as "Magic Island," because it's built on an island in Seokchon Lake. Like Disneyland, it's got a big magic castle. Here you have another wide range of rides and games, including the ever-popular Gyro Drop which drops you 70 meters in 2 seconds. There are also boat excursions on the lake.

Folk Museum The popular Folk Museum is Lotte's contribution to Korea's cultural heritage. Here you'll find an exhibit hall with Korean cultural relics, miniature palaces and villages, a performance hall and more.

Seokchon Lake 석촌호수 Originally a tributary of the Hangang River, this body of water was turned into an artificial lake in 1971; later road construction split the lake in two. The 2.5 km-wide lake makes for one of Seoul's best walking and jogging areas and is particularly nice at night when Lotte World's Magic Island is lit up.

Olympic Park 올림픽공원 Dedicated to one of Seoul's watershed moments, its hosting of the 1988 Summer Olympic Games, Olympic Park is one of the city's nicest pieces of greenery. This massive park is home to several large stadiums and arenas built for the Olympic Games, a plethora of monuments and sculptures (including the

impressive World Peace Gate), grass fields, sports facilities and even a velodrome. Ponds and pleasure pavilions add to the experience. Of more historical interest is Mongchon Toseong Fortress, an ancient earthen fortress constructed by the kingdom of Baekje (18BC-660AD), which established its first capital hereabouts. The area was excavated during the construction of the Olympic stadiums, providing a valuable glimpse of life in that era. The fortress is contained within the confines of the park. Olympic Park's stadiums are now frequently used as concert venues, particularly when popular international acts come to town.

🚇 Jamsil Station and Jamsillaru Station, Line 2; Olympic Park Station, Line 5; Mongchontoseong Station, Line 8

Olympic Park

GETTING AROUND SEOUL

SEOUL CITY BUSES

Seoul has a comprehensive bus system that provides easy access to/from all parts of the city and beyond. The bus system, which is highly efficient but labyrinthine, is comprised of three different types of buses: *ilban* ("regular"), *jwaseok* ("seated" express) and *maeul* ("town" or neighborhood). Bus service begins around 4:30 am and ends around 1 am. Over 8,500 city buses and 400 express buses are used to transport Seoulites every day. There are literally hundreds of available bus routes in Seoul and a comprehensive, searchable map is available online at http://bus.seoul.go.kr

• **Ilban buses:** Operating throughout the city, *ilban* buses are identified by three different colors: blue, green and yellow. Blue buses connect suburban areas to downtown Seoul. Green buses circulate within a particular district, connecting residential areas with subway lines and bus terminals. Yellow buses (with reduced fare of 900 won) can be found in downtown Seoul, concentrating on major tourist, shopping and business district.

• **Jwaseok buses:** These city express coaches are red and provide comfortable, speedy transport for inter-city commuters from neighboring cities such as Ilsan, Bundang, Suwon and Incheon. Every passenger is seated and base fare is higher (1,700-1,800 won).

• **Maeul buses:** Bright green in color and significantly smaller in size, these "village" buses serve local micro-routes usually connecting a few adjacent neighbourhoods with the nearby subway station (reduced fare of 700 won)

Bus fare is 1,050 won and is payable upon boarding with cash or transit card (see TIPS for more info). Like the subway, it operates on a multi-zone system and using a T-Money card offers a 100 won discount per fare. Transfers to/from subway and other buses, up to 30 minutes, are included with the fare—be sure to swipe the card on the sensor when disembarking to register your transfer or end the fare calculation of your journey. (Also note that lower *maeul* bus or yellow bus fares are upgraded to base fare rates when transferring to subway or other normal fare buses.)

SUBWAY

Seoul metro is extremely easy to navigate (each subway line is color-coded and numbered) and all signage, maps and announcements are in English—without

doubt the best method of public transportation for visitors. Subway service begins around 5am and ends around midnight. Travel time between stations is approximately 2 minutes; additional 5 minutes for transfers. Pick up a map at any station or tourist info kiosk. Refer to www.smrt.co.kr; cybermap available at www.seoulmetro.co.kr/eng

A subway map is also included in the book.

The subway, like the bus, operates on a multizone system: base fare covers the first 10 km and each additional 5 km is charged 100 won. Transfers are free. Using a T-money or transit card, base fare is 1,050 won. Using a single-journey card, available at ticket dispensing machines located at every station, the basic fare is 1,150 plus 500 won deposit which is returned with the card at deposit return devices similarly situated at each station.

For tourists wanting to do a lot of running around on both the bus and subway, the prepaid Seoul Citypass (15,000 won for 1-day pass; 25,000 won for 2-day; 35,000 won for 3-day) is good for up to 20 bus or subway rides daily (including free transfers), unlimited rides on Seoul City Tour Bus and coupons for admissions and attractions. It is non-transferrable and non-refundable.

CYCLING

Seoul is not the most bicycle-friendly city in the world. Between the hills and—more importantly—the aggressive drivers, you're best off leaving the bike at home. The city is trying to improve the situation, opening up bike paths in some neighborhoods and operating free bike rentals similar to the Velib System in Paris—for

TIPS

T-MONEY/ TRANSPORTATION CARDS

The most cost-efficient means of using the public transportation system is to use a T-Money or transportation card. A T-Money card is more convenient and offers discounted fares on all public transportation. Fares are 100 won less when you use the T-Money card rather than cash, and discounts are offered on transfers. When you transfer within 30 minutes of exiting the bus, the base fare remains the same for rides up to 10 km, and 100 won is added for each additional 5 km traveled. To register a transfer, the T-Money card must be swiped when you exit the bus, too.

A T-Money card costs approximately 2,500 won and can be purchased at automated machines in every subway station or in local convenience stores (Family Mart, GS25, Buy the Way and 7-Eleven). These cards can be recharged easily at an automated machine in the subway station. Another option is a credit-based transportation card, including debit cards, credit cards and e-cards. These cards tabulate the amount spent each month and deduct the total fare in one charge.

TIPS

Many taxis offer a free interpretation service via phone, but it is a good idea to have your destination written down in Korean to show your driver (For basic Korean expressions, see p708). Tipping is not expected.

example, in the scenic Bukchon area. But things are still at a rudimentary stage. One area that is rather pleasant to bike around is the Hangang River area. Hangang River Citizen's Park (see p140) and Ttukseom Seoul Forest (see p143) have bike paths (in the case of Hangang River Park, 36.9 km of bike paths), with a number of bike rentals along the way. The rental fee is 3,000 won per hour, or 6,000 won for a bike for two.

HANGANG RIVER WATER TAXI

In an attempt to lessen daily commuter traffic and frustration, Seoul Metropolitan City now offers the "Express Shuttle," an express water taxi service from Ttukseom to Yeouido and from Jamsil to Yeouido. Travel time from Ttukseom to Yeouido on the water taxi is 14 minutes. Morning commute water taxis run every 20 minutes between the hours of 7:10 am and 8:30 am, and evening commute water taxis run every 20 minutes from 6:30 pm to 8 pm. The last evening taxi departs from the station at 7:30 pm. Water taxi fare is 5,000 won each way, and each taxi holds seven passengers. Reservations can be made by calling the reservation hotline between the hours of 9 am to 10 pm at 1588-3960. Reservations can also be made online, although the site is only available in Korean. See www.pleasantseoul.com for more information.

SEOUL CITY TOUR BUS

The Seoul City Tour Bus offers tourists a comfortable and convenient means of transport between Seoul's most notable tourist attractions. You can choose from four tours: a daytime downtown tour, Cheonggyecheon and palace tour (double decker bus), and two night tours, one in a single decker bus and the other in a double decker. The downtown tour costs 10,000 won, while the night tour costs 5,000 won. The double-decker Cheonggyecheon and palace tour costs 12,000 won, while the double-decker night tour costs 10,000 won. The best part of the single-decker tours is that you can get on and off as much as you like for the price of one ticket (the Cheonggyecheon/Palace tour allows you to get off only at the palaces, while the double-decker night tour is non-stop). Tourists with a Seoul City Tour Bus ticket receive considerable discounts on admissions to the sites along the route. Also, each bus offers information about the sites visited in Korean, English, French, Japanese and Chinese. No tours on Monday. Buses depart from in front of Donghwa Duty Free Shop near Exit 6 of Gwanghwamun Station, Line 5. For more information, call 02-777-6090 or visit www.seoulcitybus.com.
• **Downtown Tour**: 9 am to 9 pm (last departure, 7 pm). Buses depart every 30 minutes • **Night Tour**: Bus departs at 8 pm
• **Cheonggyecheon/Palace Tour**: Every hour from 10 am to 5 pm • **Night Tour** (double decker): 8 pm

GETTING TO/FROM SEOUL

AIR

Incheon International Airport is Korea's primary gateway for destinations to and from overseas, but Gimpo Airport, about 40 minutes west of downtown Seoul, handles most of the city's domestic air travel needs. All of Korea's domestic airports are connected to Gimpo, but, truth be told, most travelers to Korea won't find much need for it—Korea's just not that big, and most destinations are more easily reached via bus or train. In fact, the only time you're likely to take a domestic flight is when you visit Korea's scenic island of Jeju-do.

Getting to Gimpo Airport: The easiest way to get to Gimpo is via Seoul Subway Line 5. If you prefer the bus, many limousine buses to Incheon International Airport stop at Gimpo Airport along the way—see www.airport.co.kr for details on stops and times.

TRAIN

Seoul has three primary train stations. By far the largest is Seoul Station, the northern terminus of Korea's Gyeongbu (Seoul—Busan) railway line. This line services Seoul, Daejeon, Daegu, Busan and a slew of smaller cities in central and southeast Korea. From Seoul, the KTX express train to Busan takes just under three hours.

Seoul's second most important train station is Yongsan Station, the northern terminus of the Honam Line, which services destinations in southwest Korea, including Daejeon's Seodaejeon Station, Iksan, Jeonju, Gwangju and Mokpo. From Seoul, the KTX express train to Mokpo takes three hours, 10 minutes. The other major train station in Seoul is Cheongnyangni Station, in the northeastern part of town. This station handles rail traffic to destinations in eastern Korea, especially in the province of Gangwon-do, but also cities and towns in central Korea like Wonju, Danyang and Andong.

BUS

• **Express Buses:** Buses depart Seoul from four major terminals: Seoul Express Bus Terminal (Gangnam Gosok Terminal), Dong Seoul Bus Terminal, Sangbong Bus Terminal and Nambu Bus Terminal.

• **Seoul Express Bus Terminal:** This two-building terminal is the main departure point for travel between Seoul and other major cities. For tickets and logistical information, call 02-536-6460~2 or visit www.kobus.co.kr. To reach the terminal, take subway Line 3 or 7 or 9 to Express Bus Terminal Station, Exit 1 or 7.

• **Dong Seoul Bus Terminal:** Serves similar destinations to Seoul Express Bus Terminal, but with fewer options and less frequent service. For ticket information, call 1688-5979. The terminal is adjacent to Gangbyeon Station, Line 2, Exit 3.

• **Sangbong Bus Terminal:** Operates routes to Cheongju, Daejeon, Jeonju and Gwangju. For ticket information call 02-323-5885. Take Line 7 to Sangbong Station, Exit 2.

• **Nambu Bus Terminal:** Operates to southern destinations like Pyeongtaek, Yongin, Anseong and Osan. For ticket information, call 02-521-8550. Take Line 3 to Nambu Terminal Station, Exit 5.

ACCOMMODATION LIST

H1 Luxury Hotel   **K** Hanok Guesthouse

H2 Mid-Range Hotel   **G** Guesthouse or Hostels

S Service Residence

GWANGHWAMUN AREA

H1 Seoul Plaza Hotel 서울플라자호텔
Central location near City Hall makes this an ideal location for businessmen. 📖 280,000–5,000,000 won ✆ 23 Taepyeongno 2-ga, Jung-gu ☎ 02-771-2200 🖱 www.hoteltheplaza.com/eng

H1 Westin Chosun 웨스틴조선 Korea's oldest international hotel, established in 1914, but recently refurbished with state-of-the-art facilities and Western-style services. 📖 220,000–1,500,000 won ✆ 87 Sogong-dong, Jung-gu ☎ 02-771-0500 🖱 http://twc.echosunhotel.com

H1 Koreana Hotel 코리아나호텔 A prime central location just across the road from City Hall, Seoul Plaza and Korea Press Center and within easy walking distance of many more key institutions. 📖 72,000–900,000 won ✆ 61-1 Taepyeong-ro 1-ga, Jung-gu ☎ 02-2171-7000 🖱 www.koreanahotel.com

H2 Best Western-New Seoul Hotel 베스트웨스턴 뉴서울호텔 Another centrally-located hotel, boasting excellent business facilities such as a dedicated business center and high-speed Internet service in each room. 📖 126,000–261,000 won ✆ 29-1 Taepyeongno 1(il)-ga, Jung-gu ☎ 02-735-8800 🖱 www.bestwesternnewseoul.co.kr

H2 Holiday Inn Seongbuk Seoul 홀리데이 인성북 Recently expanded and re-opened as a five-star business hotel, with diverse facilities for all-round comfort. 📖 US$ 160–330 ✆ 3-1343 Jongam-dong, Seongbuk-gu ☎ 02-929-2000 🖱 www.holiday.co.kr/eng/index.htm

H2 Biwon Hotel 비원호텔 Located just 10 minutes away from Changdeokgung Palace, Changgyeonggung Palace and Jongmyo shrine, this is a good hotel for sightseeing. 📖 100,000–160,000 won ✆ 36 Wonnam-dong, Jongno-gu ☎ 02-763-5555 🖱 www.biwonhotel.com

H2 Hotel SunBee 선비호텔 Ideal for both tourists and business travelers thanks to its location in Insa-dong, this hotel also prides itself on the best service. 📖 77,000–110,000 won ✆ 198-11 Gwanhun-dong, Jongno-gu ☎ 02-730-3451 🖱 www.hotelsunbee.com

K Anguk Guesthouse 안국게스트하우스 Provides traditional Korean-style rooms and hotel-standard comfort. Nearby parks and forest offer exercise and relaxation in a natural environment. Located in a beautiful neighborhood between the Gyeongbokgung and Changdeokgung palaces. Built under the supervision of the Korean Tradition Preservation Center of Seoul. 📖 50,000–80,000 won ✆ 72-3 Anguk-Dong, Jongno-gu ☎ 02-736-8304 🖱 www.anguk-house.com/lodging.htm

K Bukchon 72 Guest House 북촌게스트하우스 Experience the unique feel of a totally remodeled Korean traditional-style house at reasonable rates. Featuring Korean environmentally-friendly yellow earth walls and *ondol* (under-floor) heating, this guest house is located in a key cultural neighborhood and prides itself on its friendly staff. A great place to stay for a Korean sojourn with some character. 📖 40,000 (single)–90,000 won (triple) ✆ 72 Gye-dong, Jongno-gu ☎ 010-6711-6717 🖱 www.bukchon72.com

K Rak-Ko-Jae 락고재 Meticulously renovated by a Korean master carpenter according to traditional principles, Rak-Ko-Jae is not simply a traditional guesthouse. It's a cultural space where guests can experience the elegance of Korean traditional food, music, dance, art, poetry and the dignity of past scholars—as well as

Somerset Palace, Seoul   The Shilla Seoul   Park Hyatt Hotel

lodging. The ultimate cultural guesthouse experience within Seoul. 🍵 180,000–450,000 won ♠ 98 Gye-dong, Jongno-gu ✆ 02-742-3410 / 010-8555-1407 (En) 🖱 www.rkj.co.kr

🄺 Seoul Guesthouse 서울게스트하우스
Traditional Korean guesthouse located in a historic, protected neighborhood between two palaces. Within 15 minutes walk of Insa-dong. A chance to stay in an atmospheric area at reasonable prices. 🍵 40,000–220,000 won ♠ 135-1 Gye-dong, Jongno-gu ✆ 02-745-0057 🖱 www.seoul110.com

🄺 Sophia Guest House 소피아게스트하우스
A rare surviving example of a detached royal palace, Sophia Guest House makes use of buildings dating back more than 150 years. Staying here is a wonderful opportunity to experience the sense of time and Korean aesthetics offered by such traditional *hanok* architecture. Lying in the beautiful and tranquil cultural quarter of Bukchon, the guest house offers both a relaxing atmosphere and easy access to some of Seoul's most attractive tourist spots. Suitable for both tourists and business travelers. 🍵 35,000–70,000 won ♠ 157-1 Sogyeok-dong, Jongno-gu ✆ 02-720-5467 🖱 www.sophiagh.com

🄺 Tea Guest House 티 게스트하우스 Built carefully over a long period by skilled carpenters, Tea Guest House is another traditional-style establishment, opened in 2006. All rooms are in buildings made from old pine, bamboo and loess, which, together with the *ondol* heating system in winter, make for a healthy and relaxing night's

sleep. The guest house also boasts an attractive Korean-style courtyard and garden, and guests can sample the delights of Korean tea. This guest house is also situated in the attractive Bukchon cultural quarter. 🍵 60,000 (single)–160,000 won (special room) ♠ 15-6 Gye-dong, Jongno-gu ✆ 02-3675-9877 🖱 www.teaguesthouse.com

🄶 Yim's House 임스하우스
Another reasonably-priced hotel very close to Changdeokgung Palace, Jongmyo Shrine and Insa-dong. 🍵 35,000–45,000 won ♠ 33 Waryong-dong, Jongno-gu ✆ 02-747-3332 🖱 www.seoulbusinesshotel.com

🄶 Holiday in Korea Hostel 홀리데이인코리아호스텔 Located just a teapot's throw from Insa-dong, it offers easy walking access to the best of Seoul's old palaces and traditional neighborhoods. 🍵 17,000–44,000 won ♠ 53 Ikseon-dong, Jongno-gu ✆ 02-3672-3113 🖱 www.holidayinkorea.com

🄶 Banana Backpackers 바나나백패커스
Formerly named Seoul Backpackers, this Insa-dong establishment has now been colorfully rebranded and named after a popular yellow fruit. A good range of facilities includes free laundry, free luggage storage, free (wireless) Internet access and more (see website). 🍵 20,000 (dorm bed, off-peak)–65,000 won (family room, off-peak) ♠ 30-1 Ikseon-dong, Jongno-gu ✆ 02-3672-1973 🖱 www.bananabackpackers.com

🄶 Beewon Guest House 비원게스트하우스
Located next to Changdeokgung Palace. Facilities include dormitory rooms, private rooms, a family room, an *ondol* room with a heated floor, a kitchen, computers with

Internet and a washing machine. 🛏 19,000 (dorm)–65,000 won (room for three) 🏠 28-2 Unni-dong Jongno-gu 📞 02-765-0670 🖳 www.beewonguesthouse.com/en/

G Guesthouse Korea 게스트하우스코리아 Boasts a typical full portfolio of guest house facilities, as well as employing young Korean volunteers who enjoy sharing Korean culture and society with guests. 🛏 18,000 (dorm)–40,000 won (double) 🏠 155-1, Gwonnong-dong, Jongno-gu 📞 02-3675-2205 🖳 www.guesthouseinkorea.com

G Hostel Korea 호스텔코리아 This guest house's proximity to the huge shopping area in Dongdaemun means it is ideal for those whose number one priority in Seoul is picking up bargain clothes and shoes.

🛏 25,000 (dorm)–65,000 won (triple ensuite) 🏠 178-65 Sungin-dong, Jongno-gu 📞 02-762-7406 🖳 www.hostelkorea.com

S Fraser Suites Serviced Residences 프레이저플레이스 The first choice for expats with large budgets, these fully-serviced luxury apartments are ideally located in Insa-dong. Suitable for both temporary and long-term stays. 🛏 300,000–800,000 won 🏠 272 Nagwon-dong, Jongno-gu 📞 02-6262-8282 🖳 http://seoul.frasershospitality.com/

S Somerset Palace, Seoul 서머셋팰리스 The other luxury-serviced residence suite near Insa-dong, offering a similarly rounded portfolio of services and facilities at similar prices. Mid- to long-term stays are also the norm here. 🛏 140,000–260,000 won 🏠 85 Susong-dong, Jongno-gu 📞 02-6730-8888 🖳 www.somersetpalaceseoul.com

MYEONG-DONG AREA

H1 Lotte Hotel Seoul 롯데호텔 One of the five branches of Lotte Hotel throughout Korea, this super-deluxe hotel hosts major international events. Renowned for its top-notch duty free shop. 🛏 350,000–12,000,000 won 🏠 1 Sogong-dong, Jung-gu 📞 02-771-1000 🖳 www.lottehotel.com

H1 Millennium Seoul Hilton Hotel 밀레니엄서울힐튼 Located at the foot of Mt. Namsan, offering splendid views of this island of green in central Seoul. 🛏 230,000–360,000 won 🏠 395 Namdaemunno 5(o)-ga 📞 02-753-7788 🖳 www.hilton.co.kr

H2 Astoria Hotel 아스토리아호텔 Chungmuro's Astoria Hotel opened in 1959, making it one of Seoul's oldest hotels. Its distinctive New York-style Italian restaurant, Bella Coolla 63, is a great place to enjoy genuine Western food, while the Astoria's location makes it a good base for shopping and enjoying the bustling heart of Seoul. Staff at the front desk speak English and Japanese. 🛏 90,000–144,000 won 🏠 13-2 Namhak-dong, Jung-gu 📞 02-2268-7111

G Myeong-dong Guest House 명동게스트하우스 A guest house boasting the usual convenient points associated with a Myeong-dong location, this establishment claims to offer clean and modern facilities and cheaper prices than anywhere else in the area. 🛏 35,000–45,000 won 🏠 17 Namsan-dong 3-ga Jung-gu 📞 02-755-5437 🖳 www.mdguesthouse.com

G Namsan Guest House 남산게스트하우스 Located on Mt. Namsan, where you can breathe the fresh air and take in the hill's famous sites. 🛏 110,000 won (room for six) 🏠 50-1 Namsan-dong 2-ga, Jung-gu 📞 02-752-6363 🖳 www.namsanguesthouse.com

G Seoul Backpackers 서울백패커스 A newly-opened hostel located conveniently close to Seoul Station and Namdaemun Market—an area with few hostels. 🛏 45,000–60,000 won 🏠 205-125 Namchang-Dong, Jung-gu 📞 02-3672-1972 🖳 www.seoulbackpackers.com

DONGDAEMUN AREA

H1 The Shilla Seoul 신라호텔서울 Listed among the top hotels in the world, the Shilla is a good place to head if you want no-expenses-spared comfort and refined cultural performances. 🛏 230,000–7,200,000 won 🏠 202 Jangchung-dong 2

ga, Jung-gu ✆ 02-2233-3131 🖳 www.shilla.
net/en/seoul

H1 Grand Ambassador Seoul 그랜드앰배
서더서울 Boasts a full hand of services and
facilities following a recent 50-year
anniversary renovation. 🛏 167,000–413,000
won 🏠 186-54 Jangchung-dong 2(i)-ga,
Jung-gu ✆ 02-2275-1101~9 🖳 https://grand.
ambatel.com

H2 Dongdaemun Hotel 동대문호텔 A cozy
yet practical and elegant second-class hotel.
🛏 70,000 won (single), 80,000 won (double)
🏠 444-14 Changshin-dong, Jongno-gu
✆ 02-741-7811

G Windroad Guesthouse 윈드로드게스트
하우스 The guesthouse for theater-loving
backpackers, Windroad is just one block from
the gates of Sungkyunkwan University and
close to culturally vibrant quarter of
Daehangno. 🛏 11,000 (dorm)–60,000 won
(room for four) 🏠 85-5 Myeongnyun-dong
3-ga, Jongno-gu ✆ 02-6407-2013 🖳 www.
backpackerkorea.net

G Travelers A Hostel 트레블러스에이호스텔
This hostel is within easy reach of all
locations in the Dongdaemun area and offers
pleasant walks along the stream in either
direction. 🛏 40,000–100,000 won 🏠 106-2
Jugyo-dong, Jung-gu ✆ 02-2285-5511,
2265-2156 🖳 www.travelersa.com

**G Young Home Guest House &
Home Stay** 영홈게스트하우스 This hostel is
very close to Korea University, one of Korea's
leading higher education institutions.
🛏 900,000 won (one month) 🏠 122-513
Jegi-dong, Dongdaemun-gu ✆ 02-927-5546

SEODAEMUN AREA

H1 Grand Hilton Seoul 그랜드힐튼서울
Seoul's closest Super Deluxe Hotel to
Incheon International Airport. Located
outside the city center by a mountain
offering fresher air, and connected to
downtown areas by a shuttle bus service.
🛏 300,000–3,000,000 won 🏠 201-1
Hongeun-dong, Seodaemun-gu ✆ 02-3216-
5656 🖳 www.grandhiltonseoul.com

G Carpe Diem 카르페디엠 게스트하우스 This
is a guest house for women only. Its location
is ideal for those who want to enjoy the
fashionable Hongdae (Hongik University)
area. 🛏 20,000 won (all dorm beds) 🏠 26
Hansolgil, Mapo-gu ✆ 02-6497-6648 🖳 www.
carpediemkorea.com

G Kims' Guest House 킴스게스트하우스
This hostel is located near the Hangang
River, as well as being just one subway stop
away from the nightlife of Hongdae.
🛏 18,000–80,000 won 🏠 443-16 Hapjeong-
dong, Mapo-gu ✆ 02-337-9894 🖳 www.
kimsguesthouse.com

G Stay Korea Hostel 스테이코리아호스텔
Conveniently situated near the university
areas of Hongdae and Sinchon, this hostel is
run by a young couple that speaks French,
English and Japanese. Free facilities include
bicycles. 🛏 19,000 (dorm bed)–80,000 won
(four-person room) 🏠 566-4 Yeonnam-dong,
Mapo-gu ✆ 02-336-9026 🖳 www.staykorea.
co.kr

Hamilton Hotel

Grand Hilton Seoul

Ulji-ro CO-OP Residence

YONGSAN AREA

H1 **Hotel Capital** 캐피탈호텔 Located in the Itaewon area, this hotel is in a practical location for those needing access to both the north and south of the Hangang River. 🛏 180,000–500,000 won ✦ 22-76 Itaewon-dong, Yongsan-gu ✆ 02-6399-2000 🖳 www.hotelcapital.co.kr

H2 **Hamilton Hotel** 해밀턴호텔 Plant yourself in the middle of pulsing Itaewon for the most cosmopolitan atmosphere available in Korea. 🛏 90,000–213,000 won ✦ 119-25 Itaewon-dong, Yongsan-gu ✆ 02-794-0171 🖳 www.hamilton.co.kr

GANGNAM AREA

H1 **COEX InterContinental Hotel** 코엑스 인터컨티넨탈호텔 Situated within the Korea World Trade Center complex, it offers great access to the various conference centers and exhibition halls nearby. 🛏 310,000–2,800,000 won ✦ 524 Bongeunsaro, Gangnam-gu ✆ 02-3452-2500 🖳 www.seoul.intercontinental.com

H1 **Grand InterContinental Seoul** 그랜드인터컨티넨탈서울 Conveniently located near COEX and the Korea City Air Terminal, where luggage can be checked in before taking a limousine bus out to Incheon International Airport. 🛏 260,000–3,340,000 won ✦ 521 Teheran-ro, Gangnam-gu ✆ 02-555-5656 🖳 www.seoul.intercontinental.com/

H1 **Imperial Palace Hotel** 임페리얼팰리스호텔 Aims to provide a unique European ambiance and artistic interior at the heart of Gangnam. It is also home to Imperial Palace Medical Square, with a skincare clinic and dentistry that lets guests go home rested and healthier. 🛏 300,000–4,000,000 won ✦ 313 Eunju-ro, Nonhyeon-dong, Gangnam-gu ✆ 02-3440-8000 🖳 www.imperialpalace.co.kr

H1 **JW Marriot Seoul** JW매리어트호텔서울 Famed for being home to Asia's biggest spa and fitness club, the hotel is well furnished with Japanese, Chinese, buffet, and grill restaurants

The Ritz-Carlton, Seoul Hotel

to restore the calories you burn off there. 🛏 328,000–3,600,000 won ✦ 19-3 Banpo-dong, Seocho-gu ✆ 02-6282-6262 🖳 www.jw-marriott.co.kr

H1 **Park Hyatt Seoul** 파크하얏트서울 Regular deluxe rooms are spacious, boasting natural rock bathroom walls. The 24th-floor lobby offers breathtaking views of Seoul. 🛏 280,000–545,000 won ✦ 995-14 Daechi 3(sam)-dong, Gangnam-gu ✆ 02-2016-1234 🖳 http://seoul.park.hyatt.com

H1 **Lotte Hotel World** 롯데호텔 월드 Located slightly outside the center of Seoul, Lotte Hotel World is adjacent to the huge indoor theme park of Lotte World. 🛏 310,000–2,000,000 won ✦ 40-1 Jamsil-dong, Songpa-gu ✆ 02-419-7000 🖳 www.lottehotelworld.com

H1 **The Ritz-Carlton, Seoul** 리츠칼튼서울 A chance to enjoy marble baths and Frette cotton linens from Italy. 🛏 210,000–4,000,000 won ✦ 602 Yeoksam-dong, Gangnam-gu ✆ 02-3451-8000 🖳 www.ritzcarltonseoul.com

H1 **Novotel Ambassador Doksan, Seoul** 노보텔앰배서더 독산 Describing itself as a business hotel, this place has the usual business facilities plus banquet halls, a wedding hall and three meeting rooms. 🛏 Available on request; varies according to date and nationality ✦ 1030-1 Doksan 4(sa)-dong, Geumcheon-gu ✆ 02-838-1101 🖳 www.ambatel.com/doksan

H1 **Renaissance Seoul Hotel** 르네상스서
울호텔 Selected by English language daily The
Korean Times as Korea's best city hotel in
2000 and best food service in 2001. It is
located in Gangnam and includes no less
than 10 eating and drinking establishments.
🛏 312,000–4,700,000 won ☎ 676 Yeoksam-
dong, Gangnam-gu ✆ 02-555-0501, 556-0601
🖰 www.renaissanceseoul.com

H2 **Seoul Palace Hotel** 서울팰래스호텔 A
hotel that prides itself on offering
"personalized" service to suit every guest.
Its arcade includes an art gallery, a skin
management and a foot health center.
🛏 140,000–330,000 won ☎ 63-1 Banpo-
dong, Seocho-gu ✆ 02-532-5000 🖰 www.
seoulpalace.co.kr

S **Oakwood Premier COEX Center**
오크우드프리미어 코엑스센터 Another set of
serviced residences offering accommodation
for periods from one night to several years.
Provides a shuttle bus service to key
shopping and business locations. Situated
near the COEX and World Trade Center
complex. 🛏 255,300 won– ☎ 159
Samseong-dong, Gangnam-gu ✆ 02-3466-
7000 🖷 02-3466-7700 🖰 www.
oakwoodpremier.co.kr

S **Seoul Residence** 서울레지던스 This
hotel in the Gangnam area is ideally located
for access to the COEX complex, the City Air
Terminal, Bongeun-sa Temple, LG Arts Center
and much more. Stays of just one or two
nights are possible, but several weeks or
months is the norm. Accordingly, each room
is equipped with laundry and cooking
facilities. 🛏 110,000–150,000 won (per day),
3,600,000–4,200,000 (per month) ☎ 708-16
Yeoksam-dong, Gangnam-gu ✆ 02-6202-
3100 🖰 www.seoulresidence.co.kr

HANGANG RIVERSIDE & NEAR INCHEON INTERNATIONAL AIRPORT

H1 **Hyatt Regency Incheon** 하얏트리젠시
인천 This the only super-deluxe hotel in the
immediate vicinity of Incheon Airport and is
a nice place to eat Sunday brunch.

🖰 Available upon request; depends on date
of stay ☎ 2850-1 Unseo-dong, Jung-gu,
Incheon Hyatt ✆ 032-745-1234 🖰 http://
hyattregencyincheon.com

H1 **Sheraton Grande Walkerhill** 쉐라톤
그랜드워커힐 Offering outstanding views of Mt.
Achasan and the Hangang River. First
established in 1963, after which continuous
renovation has created a truly classy hotel.
🛏 from 200,000 won ☎ 21 Gwangjang-
dong, Gwangjin-gu ✆ 02-455-5000 🖰 www.
sheratonwalkerhill.co.kr

H1 **W Seoul - Walkerhill** W서울워커힐호텔
Only 15 minutes from the financial heart of
Seoul, the W is nonetheless situated in 180
acres of parkland on a mountain overlooking
the Hangang River. Its super-elegant design
puts it head and shoulders above many
other Seoul hotels and makes it
unquestionably the place to stay for
aesthetes. 🛏 375,000–5,850,000 won ☎ 21
Gwangjang-dong, Gwangjin-gu ✆ 02-465-
2222 🖰 www.wseoul.com

H2 **Best Western Premier Incheon
Airport** 베스트웨스턴프리미어 인천에어포트호텔
Located close to Incheon International
Airport, making it ideal for business
travellers. 🛏 120,000–300,000 won
☎ 2850-4 Unseo-dong, Jung-gu, Incheon
✆ 032-743-1000 🖰 www.airporthotel.co.kr

H2 **Hotel Dongseoul** 동서울호텔 This is a
hotel where the customer becomes a VIP as
soon as he or she steps into the lobby.
🛏 100,000–180,000 won ☎ 595 Guui-dong,
Gwangjin-gu ✆ 02-455-1100 (#0) 🖰 www.
idshotel.co.kr

H2 **Yoido Hotel** 여의도호텔 Located in
Yeongdeungpo, an industrial area just on the
south side of the Hangang River, this city-run
hostel provides clean rooms. 🛏 115,000–
200,000 won ☎ 10-3 Yeouido-dong,
Yeongdeungpo-gu ✆ 02-782-0121~9
🖰 www.yoidohotel.co.kr

INCHEON & GYEONGGI-DO

HIGHLIGHTS

• Explore the historic port of Incheon, a charming mix of colonial architecture, exotic tastes and home to Korea's largest Chinatown. Songdo New City, meanwhile, offers a glimpse at Korea's ambitious, high-tech future

• Escape to the West Coast island of Ganghwado with its beautiful Buddhist temples, historic fortresses and great seafood

• Experience Cold War history at Panmunjeom and explore less touristed regions of the Demilitarized Zone (DMZ), the ironically named border between North and South Korea

• Walk along the 18th century city walls of Suwon, a masterpiece of engineering and design, and the epitome of the Korean renaissance

• Take the kiddies to Everland, Korea's answer to Disneyworld and one of the most popular theme parks in the world

• Stroll amidst the royal tombs of the Joseon Dynasty, beautiful examples of Korean traditional landscaping recently registered with UNESCO

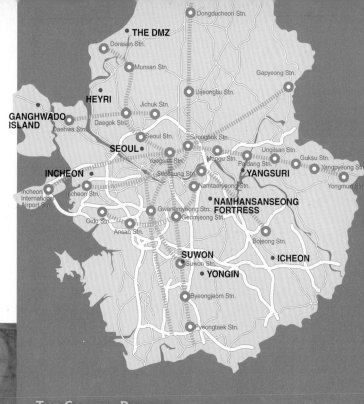

The following labels appear on the map:

Dongducheon Stn.
• THE DMZ
Dorasan Stn.
Munsan Stn.
Gapyeong Stn.
Uijeongbu Stn.
HEYRI
Jichuk Stn.
GANGHWADO
ISLAND
Daegok Stn.
Daehwa Stn.
Seoul Stn.
Seongbuk Stn.
Ungilsan Stn.
SEOUL •
Guksu Stn.
Yongsan Stn.
Mangu Stn.
Yangpyeong Stn.
Paldang Stn.
INCHEON •
Seolleung Stn.
• YANGSURI
Yongmun Stn.
Incheon
International
Airport Stn.
Incheon Stn.
Namtaeryeong Stn.
• NAMHANSANSEONG
FORTRESS
Gwangmyeong Stn.
Oido Stn.
Geumjeong Stn.
Ansan Stn.
Bojeong Stn.
SUWON •
• ICHEON
Suwon Stn.
• YONGIN
Byeongjeom Stn.
Pyeongtaek Stn.

THE CAPITAL REGION

Encircling the city of Seoul, the province of Gyeonggi-do is
essentially Seoul's backyard. For the last six centuries, its
history has been intimately tied with that of Seoul; in fact, its
name literally translates as "Province Near the Capital."
Gyeonggi-do forms with Seoul the economic, political, social
and cultural heart of Korea. Combined, the Seoul–Gyeonggi-do–
Incheon area accounts for nearly 50% of Korea's population.

There's plenty to see in the province, almost all of it within an
easy day trip's distance from Seoul. This includes the beautiful
scenery of the West Sea coast, the historic fortress town of
Suwon, and the exotic sites, sounds and tastes of Incheon.
Along the northern frontier of the province, which forms the
border with North Korea, the DMZ and the truce village of
Panmunjeom are tangible evidence of Korea's painful recent past.

Tri-Bowl, Songdo New City, Incheon

The landmark Incheon Bridge

INCHEON 인천

Perhaps best known for the dramatic Korean War battle that bears its name, Incheon has served as the world's gateway to Korea for more than a century. Even today, it is Korea's primary port of entry, with more than 20,000 travelers passing in and out of Incheon International Airport every day. In the era of steam and sail, the city's old town—then known as Jemulpo (or Chemulpo)—played host to a heady mix of races, cultures, religions and languages as the adventurous, ambitious, desperate and devout arrived on Korean shores in search of fortunes and souls. This heritage of cultural exchange has left an indelible imprint on the city. Stroll about Incheon's old town and you'll come across Chinese townhouses, Japanese banks, colonial-style saloons and Christian churches, all embraced in a Korean setting.

Incheon isn't just old colonial buildings, however. Just across the landmark Incheon Bridge from Incheon International Airport rises the impressive skyline of Songdo New City, a glittering monument—albeit one still very much under construction—to Korea's high-tech future.

History   For much of the 19th century, Korea did its best to earn its nickname, as the "Hermit Kingdom." Contact with the outside world was limited, and not without reason—the Koreans had witnessed the humiliation of China by the imperial West during the Opium Wars. Punitive raids on Korea by the French (1866) and Americans (1871) didn't endear Koreans to outsiders, either. In 1876, however, Japan, having learned the lessons of the Perry Expedition, used some gunboat diplomacy of its own to finally open Korea to foreign trade. The Treaty of Ganghwa opened three ports to Japanese trade—Incheon, Busan and Wonsan. Similar treaties with Western powers, including the United States (1882), soon followed.

The closest port to the royal capital of Seoul, Incheon—then known as Chemulpo—became Korea's premier "open port." Into what was little more than a fishing village poured sailors, adventurers, diplomats, missionaries, traders and rogues from faraway lands. Thatched roof huts were replaced by exotic European-style architecture. Life in Incheon differed little from life in China's treaty ports—the Japanese, Chinese and a collection of Western nations set up their own concession areas, complete with foreign consulates, where expatriates spoke their own languages, built homes in their own national styles, and followed their own laws. To accommodate the newly arrived foreigners, a Japanese businessman opened Korea's first Western-style hotel in 1888. On the hill overlooking the port, the foreigners built Korea's first Western-style park (a full nine years before Seoul) and even established a colonial-style club house. Anglican missionaries also opened Korea's first Western-style hospital. Incheon's foreign settlements were abolished in 1914, after Japan had colonized Korea. The imprint the settlements left on the face of Incheon, however, remains to this day.

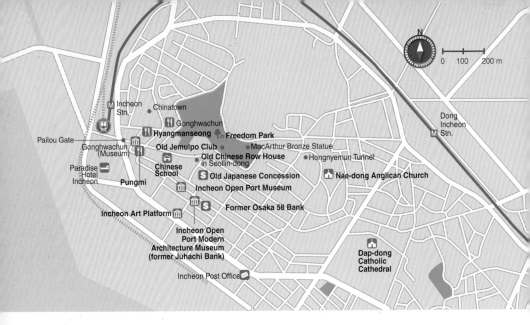

Map labels:
- Incheon Stn.
- Chinatown
- Pailou Gate
- Gonghwachun
- Hyangmanseong
- Freedom Park
- Gonghwachun (Museum)
- Old Jemulpo Club
- MacArthur Bronze Statue
- Paradise Hotel Incheon
- Chinese School
- Pungmi
- Old Chinese Row House in Seollin-dong
- Hongnyemun Tunnel
- Old Japanese Concession
- Nae-dong Anglican Church
- Incheon Open Port Museum
- Incheon Art Platform
- Former Osaka 58 Bank
- Incheon Open Port Modern Architecture Museum (former Juhachi Bank)
- Dap-dong Catholic Cathedral
- Incheon Post Office
- Dong Incheon Stn.
- N
- 0   100   200 m

Layout

With a population of more than 2.5 million people, Incheon is a pretty big place, with urban sprawl stretching almost as far east as Seoul. Also included in Incheon's municipal borders are Ganghwado Island and a number of other smaller island groups.

Fortunately, most of what you'll want to see (with the exception of Songdo) is within walking distance of Incheon Station. Chinatown is located just across from Incheon Station, in fact, and most of the historic downtown can be explored as a walking tour from the station. The resort area of Wolmido, too, can be reached on foot from Incheon Station, but you may find it easier to take the short bus ride there. Songdo, meanwhile, is virtually its own city, built on reclaimed land southwest of downtown Incheon. To get here, you'll need to take a bus, taxi or the subway.

Speaking of subway, Incheon is both attached to Seoul's subway system (specifically, Line 1) and has its own subway line. Seoul Subway Line 1 which ends at Incheon Station runs largely east–west, while Incheon Subway's single line runs largely north–south, with its southern terminus in Songdo.

Historic Downtown

Chinatown 차이나타운

Korea's oldest and largest Chinatown was born in 1884, when immigrants from China's Shandong Province settled down in Incheon as traders, importing sundries, salts and cereals and exporting alluvial gold. At one time the abode of some 100,000 Chinese, Chinatown was abraded by history—only 500 Chinese reside here today. Still, it is a colorful place that has undergone a renewal in recent years and is home to Korea's best Chinese food, Chinese shops, Chinese townhouses and a wonderfully exotic atmosphere found nowhere else in Korea.

Incheon is the last stop of Seoul Subway Line 1. The entrance to Chinatown is just across the street from Incheon Station. This is where you should begin your walk. www.ichinatown.or.kr

1 Pailou Gate 차이나타운 패루 Chinatown's entrance is marked by a Chinese traditional pailou gate. **2** Gonghwachun 공화춘 Opened in 1905, this former Chinese restaurant-turned-museum was where the popular Sino-Korean dish *jjajangmyeon* was born. **3** Chinese School 화교중산중학교 The Chinese School is the site of the old Qing consulate, part of which still remains on campus. **4** Chinese Row Houses in Seollin-dong 선린동 화교연립주택 You still find many traditional Chinese row houses, including this one from the 1930s. **5** Uiseondang Temple 의선당 Founded by Chinese immigrants in 1893, this temple mixes Buddhist and Taoist styles. It also served as a martial arts training center.

TIPS

TRY KOREAN CHINESE FOOD!

Sampling Chinatown's outstanding Chinese cuisine is a highlight to any trip to Incheon. Incheon's Chinatown is, in fact, the birthplace of one of Korea's favorite dishes, *jjajangmyeon*. Popular Korean Chinese dishes include:

• *Jjajangmyeon* 짜장면: Based on the northern Chinese dish zhajiangmian, this sweet dish of noodles in black bean sauce was a favorite dish during Korea's development years in the '60s, '70s and '80s. Even today, it is probably the single most popular takeout food in the country. Variations include *ganjjajang* 간짜장(served with sauce minus the starch) and *samseon jjajang* 삼선짜장 (served with seafood).

• *Jjamppong* 짬뽕: Originally a specialty of Nagasaki's Chinatown, the Korean version consists of noodles in a spicy seafood soup.

• *Tangsuyuk* 탕수육: Sweet and sour pork. Often consumed with a side of *jjajangmyeon*.

• *Mandu* 만두: Pork dumplings, served either fried (*gunmandu* 군만두) or boiled (*mulmandu* 물만두).

Another thing to try in Incheon is *onggibyeong* 옹기병, a dish of Chinese dumplings baked along the walls of large clay jars. There are a couple of places selling Chinese-style mooncakes as well.

There are tons of outstanding and venerable eateries for you to try, including:

• **Hyangmanseong** 향만성 (032-766-2916): This 80-year-old restaurant serves all your Chinese favorites. Highly recommended.

• **Pungmi** 풍미 (032-772-2680): Another venerable restaurant that has been doing Chinese food right for 50 years.

CHINESE-KOREANS: HWAGYO

Overseas Chinese, or *hwagyo* as they are called in Korea, are Korea's largest ethnic minority. Chinese immigration to Korea began in earnest from 1882, when Chinese traders, merchants and laborers were first allowed to settle in Korea. The Chinese population increased quickly—by 1890, there were about 1,000 Chinese in Incheon alone, where they had carved out their own settlement. In the Joseon Dynasty, Korea's highly Confucian society held merchants in contempt; the Chinese, on the other hand, held no such qualms about commerce, and flourished as a result. Almost every Korean city had a *hwagyo* community, which typically ran silk and clothing shops, general stores, barber shops and restaurants. By 1946, *hwagyo* accounted for 82% of Korea's total trade earnings.

The Chinese Revolution and the Korean War hit the *hwagyo* community hard, however. Official discrimination, especially under the Park Chung-hee administration, made life intolerable for many *hwagyo*, who fled in droves to the United States and other destinations abroad. By the 1990s, just 22,842 remained in Korea. Almost all operated Chinese restaurants, virtually the only job available to them.

The establishment of diplomatic ties between Korea and the People's Republic of China, economic globalization, the lifting of discriminatory laws and a new wave of Chinese immigration has breathed new life into the *hwagyo* community. It's difficult to determine how large the community is now—according to official statistics, there were 696,861 Chinese nationals in Korea as of 2011, but most (488,100) are actually ethnic Koreans from northern China. Ethnic Chinese residents of Korea totaled 21,978.

Hwagyo, Korea's largest ethnic minority

Hwagyo often come from families who have lived in Korea for generations, but many still retain Chinese citizenship, typically that of the Republic of China (a.k.a. Taiwan). To preserve Chinese culture and language, they frequently send their children to special schools for *hwagyo*, which teach the same curriculum as Taiwanese public schools.

Old Japanese Concession

The Treaty of Ganghwa of 1876 opened up the port of Incheon to international trade. Possessing imperial ambitions regarding Korea, the Japanese were quick to move in. The old Japanese concession, spread over several blocks in front of today's Jung-gu Office and separated from Chinatown by a landmark flight of stone steps, has a distinctively colonial feel with planned grid-like streets, stately Renaissance-style offices, Japanese-style residences and old brick warehouses. The Incheon Open Port Modern Architecture Museum (formerly the Japanese Juhachi Bank) is a good place to learn about the beauty and history of old Incheon.

6 **Jung-gu District Office** 중구청사 Built in 1933, this was originally the Japanese consulate, and later Incheon City Hall. 7 **Incheon Open Port Modern Architecture Museum** 인천개항장 근대건축전시관 Formerly a branch of Nagasaki's 18th Bank, this building, completed in 1890, is now a museum dedicated to Incheon's historic architecture. 8 **Incheon Open Port Museum** 인천개항박물관 The Renaissance-style former Incheon branch of Japan's Dai-ichi Bank, built in 1898, is now a museum to the Open Port era. 9 **Former 58th Bank** 전 일본제58은행지점 Built in 1939, this colonial bank is easily recognized by its French mansard roof. 10 **Hongnyemun Tunnel** 홍례문터널 Dug by the Japanese in 1905, this stately stone tunnel connected the old port with the interior. 11 **Former Incheon Post Office** 구 인천우체국 Constructed in 1924, the old post office displays a mix of Western styles, typical of Japanese colonial architecture.

Western Concessions

Unlike Korea's other so-called "open ports" which were inhabited almost exclusively by Japanese, Incheon was home to a significant Western community of missionaries and traders. Today, their legacy can be seen in Freedom Park (originally named All Nations' Park), a Russian-designed park that, in addition to being Korea's first modern park, is also home to the city's landmark statue of Korean War hero General Douglas MacArthur. It can also be seen in the old Chemulpo Club, a recently restored colonial-style watering hole that now serves as a museum, and the beautiful Nae-dong Anglican Church and Dap-dong Catholic Cathedral.

12 **Chemulpo Club** 제물포 구락부 Open in 1901, this Russian-designed landmark was a colonial-style watering hole for Incheon's foreign community. 13 **Freedom Park** 자유공원 Overlooking the waterfront, Korea's first Western-style park opened in 1888. 14 **Nae-dong Anglican Church** 내동 성공회성당 Founded by a British navy chaplain in 1891, this church was also the site of Korea's first Western-style hospital. 15 **Dap-dong Catholic Cathedral** 답동성당 This grand cathedral was built by French missionaries in 1897. 16 **Incheon Art Platform** 인천아트플랫폼 A collection of old colonial-era brick warehouses and offices has been brilliantly re-utilized as an arts and culture space.

Wolmido Island 월미도
& Harbor Cruises

Wolmido is translated as "Moon Tail Island," and at one time—until recently, in fact—it was an island that resembled the tail of a crescent moon. In the first half of the 20th century, Japanese colonists built a causeway and turned the island into a popular resort area, complete with hotels and seawater baths. Overlooking Incheon Harbor, the hilly island was also militarily strategic. During the Korean War, the North Koreans fortified the island, and the Americans made it their first objective during the brilliant Incheon Landing. Unfortunately, the naval bombardment that preceded the landing leveled most of the island, including the historic resort.

Post-war industrial development and land reclamation have integrated Wolmido into the mainland, so it is no longer an island, but still a popular weekend destination with a boardwalk lined with restaurants (mostly raw fish) and a small amusement park. The hill is now a park, with walking paths, gardens and an observation tower with great views of Incheon Harbor.

You can also catch ferry cruises of Incheon Harbor from Wolmido, too. The cruises, which take you from Wolmido past Yeongjongdo 영종도 (home of Incheon International Airport) and Incheon Bridge before returning to Wolmido, leave at noon, 2 pm, 4 pm and 6 pm. Cruises take an hour, 30 minutes, and cost 15,000 won per person.

🚍 From Incheon Station, take Bus No. 2, 23 or 45 and get off at the last stop, Wolmido. Likewise, you could just take a cab from the station—it's just a 5 minute ride.

Amusement park, Wolmido

Songdo District

Songdo New City 송도 신도시

Scheduled for completion in 2015, Songdo International Business District (IBD) 송도국제 업무단지—formerly Songdo New City—is very much a work in progress. But that doesn't mean it's not worth exploring.

To walk around Songdo is to experience Korea's high-tech, design-centric future. Even in its incomplete state, it already has one of Korea's most impressive skylines, punctuated by the nearly finished 68-story Northeast Asia Trade Tower (NEATT) 동북아 트레이드타워—one of Korea's tallest buildings—and views of the landmark Incheon Bridge 인천대교. Unlike the hyper-chaos of Korea's other major cities, cobbled together over centuries of growth, Songdo is an ambitious exercise in 21st century urban planning, a completely new city built upon land reclaimed from the sea, blessed with wide boulevards, pleasant parks and inspired architecture.

Within easy subway reach from Seoul, Songdo makes for a convenient weekend day trip even if, admittedly, the place can sometimes look like a ghost town due to the ongoing construction.

🚇 Central Park Station, Incheon Subway Line 1. Tri-Bowl is located at one of the exits.

Songdo Future Road

Rural towns have trekking paths that bring you closer to nature. Songdo has the Songdo Mirae-gil 송도미래길 or "Songdo Future Road," a trekking course that takes you into the future of 21st century urbanism.

Pop out of University of Incheon Station, Incheon Subway Line 1, and you'll find yourself at the appropriately named Tomorrow City 투모로우시티, the start of the course. Tomorrow City is a high-tech culture and exhibit space full of gadgets, galleries and displays presenting Songdo's vision of a "ubiquitous" future where IT technology is

Songdo New City and its landmark Northeast Asia Trade Tower

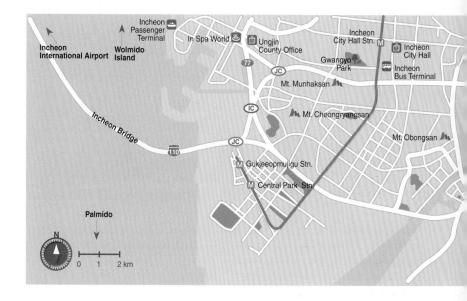

omnipresent. Even if you're not a complete tech geek, you'll find it fascinating.

From Tomorrow City, head to Central Park and walk along the beautiful salt-water canal that flows through the park. Like the more famous park of the same name in New York, Central Park is surrounded by high rise buildings, although none as magnificent as the Northeast Asia Trade Tower (304 m). Nearly complete, its 65th floor observation deck promises to provide stunning views when it opens.

As you approach the end of the canal, you'll come to Compact Smart City 컴팩트스마트시티, another impressively designed exhibit space showing off the city's high-tech future. Just beyond it is the Tri-Bowl 트라이볼, a landmark sculpture/exhibition space designed by US-based architect Yoo Kerl. As its name would suggest, it is composed of three connected bowls and is truly a sight to behold, especially at night when it is lit up and resembles a landing spaceship.

At the west boathouse (near the end of the

canal), cross the bridge and follow the path to Incheon Bridge viewpoint. Composed of shipping containers, a symbol of Incheon's role as a logistical hub, the viewpoint

 TIPS

CENTRAL PARK CRUISE

If you've got time to spare, take a cruise on the canal in Central Park. Boats depart from the East Boathouse on the hour from 10 am to 6 pm (except noon), with additional trips at night from July to August. Fare: 4,000 won.

Tri-Bowl, typical Songdo New City's futuristic architecture

provides wonderful views of the surrounding mudflats (depending on the tide) and the Incheon Bridge, a 12.5 km colossus spanning the approach to Incheon Harbor. The sunsets here can be inspiring and the bridge, lit up at night, is particulary stunning.

Once you've seen the bridge, head back up the canal (only on the other side) and follow the path to the so-called Canal Walk 캐널워크, a European-esque shopping complex named for the artificial waterway that flows through it. You'll find a variety of good restaurants in here, too. As elsewhere in Songdo, the Canal Walk beautifully harmonizes function and design.

It's time to revisit Central Park again, this time enjoying the other side of the seawater canal. Once you've reached the end, keep going until you've reached Songdo Convensia, a landmark convention center that brings to mind the Sydney Opera House.

 TIPS

What to Eat

For a romantic evening, try the seafood buffet, Fiesta 피에스타 (www.sd-fiesta.com) on the 21st floor of Michuhol Tower 미추홀타워 in Technopark 테크노파크 (Exit 4, Technopark Station, Incheon Subway Line 1). At 33,000 won a person on weekdays (38,500 won on a weekend), it's a bit pricey, but the food's good, the interior is classy, and the views of downtown Songdo and Incheon Bridge, weather permitting, cannot be beat. Even if you don't see a soul in the city itself, this place is often full so it's best to call ahead to reserve a table—give them a ring at 032-260-0088. Hours are 11:30 am to 10 pm, with a 3:30 pm to 5:30 pm break on weekdays.

A bit cozier but also with stellar views is the buffet restaurant, La Stella 라스텔라, on the 19th floor of the Songdo Park Hotel 송도파크호텔, with views of both Central Park and the ocean. On a weekend, lunch or dinner costs 37,000 won per person. This place tends to fill up, too, so make a reservation at 032-210-7360~1. The hotel is on the southwest side of Central Park.

While it doesn't have the bird's-eye views, the restaurant/tapas bar What's David's? is popular for its good pasta, pizza and steak and authentic European atmosphere. Open till midnight, the place is near the Korea Coast Guard headquarters, not far from Central Park. Call for more info at 032-833-1225.

Incheon Landing Operation
Memorial Hall 인천상륙작전기념관

A little bit outside of town, not far from Songdo New City, is Songdo Resort 송도유원지, an older amusement park and resort area popular with Incheon residents. One of the historical highlights of the area is the imposing Incheon Landing Operation Memorial Hall, an architectural tribute to the Korean War battle that made Incheon famous worldwide. Located on a hill overlooking what was "Blue Beach," one of the three landing zones during the operation, the memorial/museum—built almost entirely of concrete—features heroic reliefs, plenty of flags, an 18 m tall memorial tower and interesting displays of weapons, maps, uniforms and other Korean War-related items, including a whole section dedicated to UN Supreme Commander Douglas MacArthur. History buffs and fans of military history won't want to miss it.

🕘 9 am to 6 pm. Closed Mondays. 🎫 Free
📞 032-832-0915 🚇 The easiest way to get here is to take a taxi from Dongmak Station, Incheon Subway Line 1 (10 min). You could take Bus No. 6-1, 8 or 908 from Dongmak Station and get off at Songdo Resort, from where it is another 5–10 minute walk.

Incheon Landing Operation Memorial Hall

Incheon Bridge 인천대교

The world's seventh longest bridge at 12.3 km, Incheon Bridge is a truly awe-inspiring sight—it's said its imposing towers are, top-to-bottom, as tall as Seoul's landmark 63 Building. Its central span hangs some 74 meters above the waves, high enough to allow the passage of the mammoth supertankers and container ships that go to and from the bustling port of Incheon. A mega-project in every meaning of the term, the behemoth cable-stayed bridge took 52 months to build at a cost of US$1.4 billion. It was opened to traffic in October of 2009.

Assuming you don't have a private aircraft, there are two ways to see the bridge properly—by driving over it or from a boat below. Driving over the bridge can be an exhilarating experience that provides some jaw-dropping views, although the lack of observation platforms or rest stops does foreshorten the experience somewhat. It's also expensive: one-way toll for the bridge is 5,500 won (11,000 round-trip). Moreover, if you're taking a taxi from Incheon's Yeonan Pier 연안부두 (and if you are going to/coming from Palmido, you probably are), it's a long ride and the fare could come to about 25,000 to 30,000 won to Incheon International Airport, from where you could take a bus back to Seoul. On a positive note, even with the lack of

Top to bottom, Incheon Bridge's towers are as high as Seoul's skyscrapers.

true observation platforms, there's a small area where tourists—including taxis—like to stop to take in the bridge in all its majesty, especially around sunset.

Seeing the bridge from below might be an even more thrilling experience. All the boats to Palmido pass under the bridge and this is in fact one of the highlights of the trip. From the deck of a boat, you gain a true appreciation for the bridge's mammoth, almost dizzying, scale. Even tankers seem dwarfed by it. In the background looms the gleaming skyline of Songdo New City, punctuated by the nearly completed 68-story Northeast Asia Trade Tower.

Palmido 팔미도

The waters off Incheon are home to many islands but few are as charming as Palmido. Located 15.7 km south of Incheon Harbor 인천항, the small island was, for 106 years, a sensitive military zone off-limits to civilians. It's still sensitive, in fact—the island's only residents are ROK Navy personnel stationed there—but on Jan 1, 2009, the government re-opened the scenic and historic spot to tourism.

Atop the 60 m hill that is the island's chief topographic feature stands Palmido Lighthouse. Actually two lighthouses: the original from 1903 and a new, much larger one built in 2003. A short but sturdy

Palmido Island

structure with the elegant beauty so characteristic of architecture of its period, Old Palmido Lighthouse was designed by a Japanese engineer in the employ of the Korean imperial government with money loaned from France and completed in 1903. Korea's first modern lighthouse, it guided ships to and from Incheon Harbor for a century until, in 2003, a new state-of-the-art lighthouse was completed right next to it. During the Korean War, a joint CIA-military intelligence commando team landed on Palmido and relaunched the lighthouse, helping guide UN forces to the shore in the dramatic Incheon Landing on Sept 15, 1950.

The new lighthouse, while not nearly as historic, houses a museum dedicated to the lighthouse's history (replete with mock-ups of the CIA raid and Incheon Landing!) and a splendid observation deck from which to take in the surroundings.

INCHEON LANDING
History and Culture

If the Korean War is known for one battle, and one battle alone, it is the Incheon Landing. The Incheon Landing was the kind of masterstroke most generals can only dream about. In one bold, dramatic move, the bulk of the North Korean invasion force—grappling with the UN defenders on the Nakdonggang River—was outflanked, cut off and forced into a disorderly retreat. The battle turned the war on its head: it was now the North Koreans who were on the run as the UN rushed up the peninsula towards the Yalu River to reunite Korea under South Korean rule.

It is a miracle the battle was even launched. Lacking landing beaches, approached by narrow, shallow, and easily mined waterways guarded by prominent hills, cursed with dangerously quick tides, having a small anchorage surrounded by high seawalls and, worst of all, home to the world's most dramatic tides that could turn much of the landing area into huge mudflats, Incheon was regarded as a terrible place to attempt a landing. UN Commander Gen. MacArthur, however, was convinced a landing at Incheon would work. To a delegation of skeptical high-ranking military leaders, he declared, "We shall land at Incheon, and I shall crush them."

Preceded by naval and aerial bombardment and guerrilla operations, the Incheon Landing got underway in the early morning hours of Sept 15, 1950, the invasion armada guided by the lighthouse on Palmido. The North Koreans—possibly expecting a landing elsewhere—were caught completely unprepared. US Marines landed on Wolmido at 6:30 am. By 8 am, they had captured the strategic island. A little after 5:30 pm, the rest of the invasion force began landing elsewhere in the city, using ladders to scale the difficult seawalls. After the first day, some 13,000 Marines were on the ground. By morning the next day, UN troops had established a line around Incheon, cutting off the routes of escape for any North Koreans left in the city.

From its beachhead at Incheon, the UN invasion force moved to capture the vital Gimpo Airfield and, ultimately, the South Korean capital of Seoul. As supplies and reinforcements poured in through Incheon, the Marines advanced eastward. By the morning of Sept 18, Gimpo Airfield was in the hands of the Marines. The liberation of Seoul, however, would require another week of bitter, house-to-house fighting through the fortified city.

1. Old and new lighthouses of Palmido 2. People disembarking from a ferry
3. Mock-up of capture of Palmido in the Korean War

WHAT TO EAT

Palmido has no restaurants or even coffee machines. So be sure to bring a roll of *gimbap* or hot thermos in the winter—it can be quite cold and windy here. Snacks and drinks can be purchased on the boat. The boat also serves up plates of sliced, raw flounder for 15,000 won. By Yeonan Pier—well, all over Incheon, really—you'll find many seafood restaurants (the nearby Incheon Seafood Market is worth a look, too), and if sea creatures aren't your thing, Incheon's famous Chinatown boasts some of the best Chinese food in Korea.

TRANSPORT INFO

Boats to Palmido depart from Incheon's Yeonan Pier—from Dongincheon Station (Line 1), take a taxi or Bus No. 12 or 24 and get off at the pier. Hyundai Marine (http://palmido.co.kr) and Hyundai Excursions (www.partyboat.co.kr) operate boats that depart from behind the Hyundai Excursions Building, a short walk from Incheon Passenger Terminal. Hyundai Marine runs two cruises a day (10 am, 1:30 pm) on weekdays and hourly boats (10:30 am to 3:30 pm) on weekends. Hyundai Excursions runs three boats daily (11 am, 1:30 pm and 3:30 pm) on weekdays and three (11:30 am, 1:30 pm and 3:30 pm) on weekends. Do check the timetable, though, because schedules change frequently.
IMPORTANT: Weekday cruises are subject to demand. The trip to the island takes about 50 minutes, during which time you'll be entertained with live music and/or dance performances. Once you reach the island, you'll have about an hour to look around before the boat returns to Incheon.

WHERE TO STAY

Most travelers don't stay in Incheon, which is just an hour's subway ride from Seoul. If you're taking a flight out of Korea, though, you'll find a number of options near Incheon International Airport, including Incheon Airport Oceanside Hotel (032-746-0072, www.oceanside.co.kr), which is good value at 127,000 won a night on weekends. If you're a bit more flush, Premier Songdo Bridge Hotel (032-210-3000, www.songdobridgehotel.com, 200,000 won a night) and Sheraton Incheon Hotel (032-835-1000, www.sheraton.com/incheon, 330,000 won a night) in Songdo are lovely hotels, even if the local nightlife is, like Songdo itself, a work in progress.

GANGHWADO ISLAND 강화도

For centuries, Ganghwado Island has served as both a getaway—in the very literal sense—and a gatekeeper to Korea. In the 13th century, the Korean royal court fled to the island fortress, strategically located at the mouth of the Hangang River, as the Mongols swept down upon Korea. In the 19th century, French, American and Japanese invaders attacked the island, waging fierce battles below its bastion walls. Later, more foreigners, this time Christian missionaries from Britain and elsewhere, would set foot on the island and establish Korean-style churches that dotted the countryside, some of which still stand to this day.

Located just an hour's drive west of Seoul, Ganghwado Island still gets a large number of visitors, although mostly in the form of tourism. History buffs love its old walls and citadels, while its beautiful Buddhist monasteries provide weekend solace to world-weary refugees from Seoul. Hikers head for Mt. Manisan, with its ancient altar and spectacular views of the sea, while the more culinarily-inclined are content simply to consume the island's famous fresh blue crab, shrimp and other bounty from the surrounding waters and mudflats.

Gate of old Gwaseongbo Fortress, site of an American raid in 1871

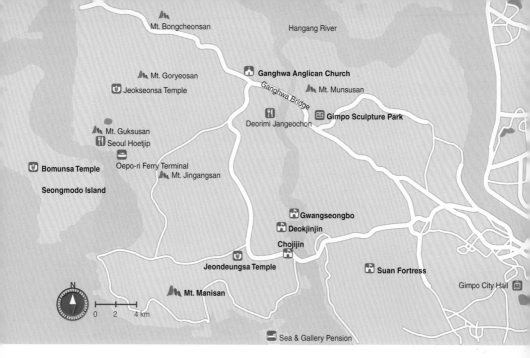

Mt. Bongcheonsan

Hangang River

Ganghwa Anglican Church

Mt. Goryeosan
Jeokseonsa Temple

Ganghwa Bridge

Mt. Munsusan

Deorimi Jangeochon

Gimpo Sculpture Park

Mt. Guksusan
Seoul Hoetjip

Bomunsa Temple

Oepo-ri Ferry Terminal

Mt. Jingangsan

Seongmodo Island

Gwangseongbo
Deokjinjin
Chojijin

Jeondeungsa Temple

Suan Fortress

Gimpo City Hall

Mt. Manisan

N

0   2   4 km

Sea & Gallery Pension

Old Goryeo Palace Site 고려궁지

Historically, Ganghwado is most famous for providing shelter to the Korean court during the dark days of the Mongol invasions of the 13th century. The first Mongol invasion, launched in 1231, led to a Korean surrender and a heavy tribute burden. Determined to resist, in the following year the royal court, led by King Gojong (r. 1213–1259) of the Goryeo Dynasty, evacuated the capital of Gaeseong (located just across the DMZ in today's North Korea) in favor of Ganghwado and safety from attack by the land-loving Mongols (whose fear of the water was so severe they would not cross even the narrow strait separating the island from the mainland). It was an impressive logistical undertaking for a medieval kingdom. The court stayed at Ganghwado until 1270, when it finally sued for peace with the Mongols, who had spent the better part of forty years laying waste to the Korean mainland.

Unfortunately, most of the old palace and fortifications were destroyed when the royal court returned to the mainland. In the Joseon era (1392–1910), a new palace complex was constructed after the Qing invasion of Korea in 1636 but this, too, was torched by French marines in 1866; only three buildings remain. Still, the old palace ground, located in the administrative hub of Ganghwa-eup, is worth seeing along with an old gate from the Joseon era town wall.

900 won ▮ The palace site is near Ganghwa Elementary School 강화초등학교 in Ganghwa-eup.

Old Fortresses

Standing sentinel at the mouth of the Hangang River, which was old Korea's highway to the royal capital, Ganghwado also hosted some of Korea's first interactions with the West in the late 19th century. These interactions were not entirely peaceable, however. In 1866, the French, enacting vengeance for a brutal crackdown on Catholics by the Korean royal court that

Old cannon, Gwangseongbo Fortress

left nine French missionaries dead, attacked the island. The raiders were repulsed, but not before they'd burned and looted much of the island in typical imperialist fashion. In 1871, American marines attacked Ganghwado's fortresses in retaliation for the burning of a US ship and to persuade (unsuccessfully, as history would have it) the Koreans to sign a trade treaty. Finally, in 1875, the Japanese attacked the island and forced the Korean king to sign the Ganghwa Treaty, which marked Korea's "opening" to imperial powers of the West and Japan.

The old fortifications are still very much in place along the island's western coast (i.e., guarding the strait with the mainland). The most impressive of these is the Gwangseongbo Citadel 광성보, a series of defense walls, gun emplacements and command posts where Korean defenders fought to the death against US Navy bluejackets in 1871. Other historic coastal batteries can also be found at Chojijin 초지진 and Deokjinjin 덕진진.

🚌 Buses to Gwangseongbo, Deokjinjin and Chojijin run from Ganghwa Bus Terminal.

Mt. Manisan 마니산

Ganghwado's most notable topographical feature (besides being surrounded by water) is Mt. Manisan, a 472 meter peak that rises gently out of the southern interior of the island. Crossed by well-kept hiking paths, including a full flight of stone steps to the top, it sees a good many weekend hikers

National Foundation Day rite, Mt. Manisan

Beautiful rooflines of Jeondeungsa Temple

from Seoul, even in winter. The peak offers fine views of the West Sea and the Korean mainland provided the weather is good.

The mountain is best known, however, for the Chamseongdan 참성단, a stone altar on its peak. According to legend, Dangun, who founded the Korean nation in 2333 BC, held sacrificial rites to heaven here. Annual rites are still performed at the altar on National Foundation Day (Oct 3). The upper ridge line is quite rocky: hiking boots are advisable. 🚌 Buses to Mt. Manisan run from Ganghwa Bus Terminal.

Jeondeungsa Temple 전등사

One of Korea's most beautiful Buddhist temples, Jeondeungsa has a history that goes back to AD 381. It is home to a plethora of cultural treasures, including its 17th century main hall and an 11th century Chinese temple bell that came into the temple's possession after World War II. When you visit, be sure to check out the corners of the main hall where you'll notice

carved figures of naked women holding up the roof. According to legend, the artisan building the temple fell in love with a barmaid in town. Unfortunately for him, she absconded with all his money. In revenge, the engineer worked her image into the temple, where, at least figuratively, she would have to hold up the temple roof for all eternity. 🚌 Buses to Jeondeungsa run from Ganghwa Bus Terminal.

Bomunsa Temple 보문사

Another wonderful temple to visit is Bomunsa, located on the small isle of Seongmodo 석도 (a 5 minute ferry ride from the Oepo-ri Ferry Terminal 외포리선착장, located on the west coast of Ganghwado). There's an ancient Buddhist grotto 마애석불좌상

Bomunsa Temple and its famous Buddhist relief

on the grounds of the temple, and in the granite cliffs above the complex is a 10 m high Buddhist relief, reached by a kilometer long flight of steps.

🔲 To get to Bomunsa, take a bus from Ganghwa Bus Terminal to Oepo-ri and take the ferry from there.

Hanok Churches

Ganghwado is also home to several *hanok* churches built in the traditional Korean *hanok* style during the early part of the 20th century. The most famous of these is Ganghwa Anglican Church 강화도 성공회성당, located on a hill in Ganghwa-eup. Consecrated in 1900 and built by a royal architect who participated in the reconstruction of Seoul's Gyeongbokgung Palace, the church harmonizes Korean palace architecture and Buddhist spatial principles with a Roman basilica interior. If you visit on a Sunday morning, you're more likely to gain admittance. There's another *hanok*-style Anglican church (built in a much simpler style) in Onsu-ri, near Jeondeungsa Temple.

More intrepid travelers can visit Seodo Central Methodist Church 서도중앙교회, located on the island of Jumundo, an hour and 40 minutes by ferry from Oepo-ri (two ferries a day, at 9:30 am and 3 pm, but the latter requires you to sleep on the island). Also in *hanok* style, it has a rather unusual second story above its entrance, originally used as a bell tower in imitation of Western church architecture.

🔲 Ganghwa Anglican Church is in downtown Ganghwa-eup. Onsu-ri Anglican Church is a short walk from Jeondeungsa Temple.

Ganghwa Anglican Church harmonizes east and west.

WHAT TO EAT

Being an island, Ganghwado is famous for its seafood. In particular, it is known for its delicious blue crab (*kkotge* 꽃게). Seoul Hoetjip 서울횟집 (032-933-5433), located in the port of Oepo-ri, is famous for its local crab stew (*kkotgetang* 꽃게탕), which you can order for 50,000 won a serving (feeds two). It's also a good place to take in the sunset over the winter sea.

Another specialty of Ganghwado is eel harvested from the island's famous mudflats. There are tons of restaurants specializing in eel—particularly roasted eel (*jangeo gui* 장어구이)—in the so-called "Deorimi Jangeochon" 더리미장어촌 near the Ganghwa Bridge 강화대교.

Jangeo gui (broiled eel)

TRANSPORT INFO

Buses to Ganghwado Island leave from Seoul's Sinchon Bus Terminal, a 100 m walk from Exit 7 of Sinchon Station, Line 2 (walk in the direction of the police station). The trip to Ganghwa-eup takes about an hour and 10 minutes. From Ganghwa Terminal 강화버스터미널, you can take local buses to destinations throughout the island.

WHERE TO STAY

A lot of folk do Ganghwado as a day trip from Seoul. Should you choose to spend the night, though, there are plenty of accommodations—homestay facilities (*minbak*) and rental houses (pensions) in particular—in the villages along the southern coast. Sea & Gallery Pension 펜션 씨앤갤러리 (032-937-0416, www.sngpension.com, Korean) as the name suggests, blends artwork and European interior rooms (70,000–150,000 won a night) with beautiful views of the sea. Advance booking is advisable.

Sunrise at Oepo-ri Ferry Terminal

THE DMZ

It's often said that the Korean Demilitarized Zone, or DMZ, is one of the most dangerous places on Earth. This distinction is probably technically true—the mountains and hillsides on both sides of the 4 km strip of land separating the two Koreas bristle with troops, guard posts, tanks, missile, bunkers, gun emplacements, land mines and other tools of death and destruction. A one-hole golf course at a military base in Panmunjeom, the truce village that has come to symbolize the world's last Cold War frontier, warns not to retrieve balls at the "world's most dangerous golf course."

Yet the DMZ is perhaps Korea's supreme irony. As you gaze out upon the DMZ from Checkpoint 3 of Panmunjeom's Joint Security Area, your attention is drawn not to the rare opportunity to peek into mysterious North Korea, the North Korean soldiers perched on the watchtower nearby or your chances of survival in a sudden re-opening of hostilities. Instead, you're captivated by the supreme tranquility—the quiet, the lush green hillsides, the rare birds swooping into untouched marshlands. Here, at the most militarized border on the planet, you feel completely at peace.

The DMZ stretches some 248 kilometers across the Korean Peninsula from the mouth of the Imjingang River in the west to the town of Goseong in the east. The demilitarized zone itself, where human activity has been greatly limited for the last half-century, has become one of Asia's greatest nature preserves. In the sparsely populated hinterlands just outside the zone, where it seems soldiers outnumber civilians, you can find both towering monuments to battles won and derelict ruins that stand witness to the tragedy of war.

Viewing a guard post in the DMZ

Panmunjeom 판문점

With the fall of the Berlin Wall, Panmunjeom became the world's last remaining outpost where democracy and communism literally stare each other down in a tense standoff, pregnant with political and historic meaning. This is not your ordinary tourist destination. Civilians cannot enter the DMZ without prior permission and tourists are allowed to visit Panmunjeom only as part of organized group tours. Even then, visitors must follow strict dress codes and, above all, follow closely the instructions of official guides, who are usually US soldiers.

Tours from Seoul first take you along Freedom Road 자유로, the flat and straight highway connecting the capital with the DMZ. The buses eventually reach the Imjingang River 임진강, crossed by the Unification Bridge 통일대교. This is the end of the line for most civilians. If you're with a tour group, however, you'll pass through an army checkpoint at the southern end of the bridge and cross into the Civilian Limit Zone and, a bit beyond that, the Joint Security Area 공동경비구역, or JSA.

The first stop on the tour is Camp Bonifas (named after a US soldier who was axed to death in the JSA in 1974), a large South Korean military installation that serves as the base camp of the United Nations Command Security Force—Joint Security Area. For most of post-Korean War history, the southern side of the JSA was jointly patrolled, but since 2004 it has been entrusted exclusively to the South Koreans (although a small contingent of Western, mostly American, troops remain). At the camp, you'll be briefed, usually by a US officer, on the history and regulations of

[Map]

Kaesong Industrial Complex
Northern Limit Line
GAESEONG
Panmunjeom
Southern Limit Line
Propaganda Village ● Freedom Village
Chopyeongdo Island
● 3rd Tunnel
Dora Station ● Imjingak
Imjingang Station
Sacheon Stream
● Munsan Station
Gyeongui Line
↓ Paju City
SEOUL
Imjingang River

Panmunjeom's Joint Security Area (JSA)

the JSA. There, you can also check out the short one hole par-3 on the base premises—just don't expect to retrieve your golf balls, as the fairway is surrounded by mine fields.

It's another short bus ride to the JSA. About 400 meters past Camp Bonifas, you come to a double-barbed wire fence manned by South Korean soldiers. This fence, which continues almost unbroken for the entire breadth of the Korean Peninsula, marks the start of the DMZ. Pass the fence and it's like entering a completely different planet: vegetation grows lush and, outside the bus, the scenery is eerily peaceful and, frankly, spooky. Some of the land is cultivated by the villagers of Daeseong-dong 대성동, the only civilian habitation in the southern half of the DMZ. But by and large, the only things that move are the birds; protected from human activity for a half century, the DMZ has become a habitat for many species of wild birds.

The Joint Security Area itself is iconic, especially if you've seen Park Chan-wook's 2000 film, *JSA*. This small cluster of buildings (some impressive, some humble) was built in 1953 following the Armistice

Agreement which brought the fighting to a halt. The signing of the document was done in the original village of Panmunjeom which was actually located about 800 meters to the north but has since disappeared. The JSA—widely referred to as "Truce Village"—was used for regular meetings between North Korean and UN military officials (the Military Armistice Committee or MAC) to supervise the implementation of the armistice and is still occasionally used for inter-Korean meetings.

The JSA is split down the middle by the Military Demarcation Line (MDL), the actual "border" between North and South Korea. On the southern side are the impressive Freedom House 자유의 집 and Peace House 평화의 집, which, aside from being splendid pieces of modern Korean architecture, are also used for North–South meetings. On the northern side of the MDL is the Panmungak 판문각, a gray Stalinist structure which, our guides will point out, is probably smaller than it actually appears. Soldiers from both sides stare down visitors and each other. Between the two borders is the sky-blue MAC building built in the 60s where, with a guide, you may briefly cross over into North Korean territory (permissible ONLY within the building).

Near the buildings is a highpoint called Checkpoint 3 from where you can get a sweeping vista of the DMZ. The tranquility of it all is unnerving. Who'd imagine that surrounding this beautiful stretch of untouched nature is one of the largest concentrations of military force in the history of man? In the near distance, the North Korean Potemkin village of Kijong-dong is home to the world's tallest flag post (160 meters), flying the world's largest flag.

WHAT TO
EAT

Your tour guide will bring you somewhere to eat, although you may have to pay for food separately depending upon the tour.

TIPS

PANMUNJEOM TOURS
You can't just drive up to Panmunjeom—you need to join a tour. The USO (02-795-3028), which provides morale and entertainment services to the US military, conducts very popular tours to Panmunjeom. Scheduled two times a week, the USO tour is reasonable (US$70 for civilians), but spots fill up fast. Call the USO for the exact schedule. TOURDMZ (02-755-0073) also conducts well-priced tours of the JSA at 77,000 won (weekdays) and 78,000 won (weekends). See www.tourdmz.com for more information. See also Panmunjeom Travel Center (02-771-5593, www.koreadmztour.com), which conducts tours for 77,000 won.
One note about the tours, however: most have dress codes. Be sure to inquire when you reserve a tour spot. You need to bring your passport and children under 11 may not join.

Imjingak Area 임진각국민관광지

A short train trip north of Seoul brings you to Imjingak, a small park on the Imjingang River. A solitary railroad bridge crosses the river and, next to it, lonely concrete pylons of a bridge long since destroyed. Across the river is the DMZ and, beyond that, North Korea.

For the general visitor, Imjingak is as close to North Korea as you can get without obtaining special permission. This, and its easy reachability from Seoul, has turned it into a literal shrine of national division. On the Korean autumn harvest celebration of Chuseok and the Lunar New Year holiday, North Korean-born South Koreans (and their descendants) gather at Imjingak to perform traditional ancestral rites ceremonies. Other visitors leave colorful ribbons with prayers of peace and reunification.

Imjingak Pavilion 임진각

The Imjingak Pavilion is a three-story building with restaurants, an exhibit of photos of North Korea, a convenience store, café and other facilities. What it is best known for is the views of the Imjingang River, DMZ and North Korea that can be seen from the rooftop observatory.

Mangbaedan Altar 망배단

Between 1945, when Korea was divided, and the start of the Korean War, an estimated 3.5 million North Koreans fled to the South to escape communist oppression. They were joined by countless more during the Korean War and, more recently, a growing number of defectors fleeing the famine and repression of today's North Korea. In Korean, these people are called *silhyangmin*, or "people who have lost their hometowns." The first generation of *silhyangmin* have spent the last 60 years without ever setting eyes on the land of their birth, and their plight, one of lost homes and separated families, is one of the enduring tragedies of the Korean War and national division.

In the old days, *silhyangmin* used to come to Imjingak on holidays and construct temporary altars at which they would perform the ancestral rites most Koreans perform in their hometowns. In 1986, however, the South Korean government constructed the Mangbaedan, a permanent altar for their use. The altar consists of an incense burner and seven stone slabs, each one representing a North Korean province. On each slab is carved an image from the province it represents.

Korean War Memorials

The park at Imjingak is a short walk from Imjingang Station, the last stop on the truncated Seoul–Shinuiju Line. Some of the park is quite kitsch, for instance, a 70's-like amusement park—a tad malapropos just 7 km south of a border former US President Bill Clinton in 1993 called "the scariest

Taking in the view, Imjingak

place on Earth" along with shops selling North Korean money, souvenirs and booze.

Other parts are more rewarding including the walkway to the pavilion where there are several Korean War and Cold War-related memorials. One of the largest is a memorial to the Korean cabinet ministers killed in 1983 when the North Koreans bombed the Martyr's Mausoleum in Rangoon, Burma in a failed attempt to assassinate then-South Korean president Chun Doo-hwan. A monument that is afforded particular pride of place is the one dedicated to the United States forces that fought in the war. Some 16 nations sent

Mangbaedan Altar, Freedom Bridge and old railway bridge

War monuments (left), Steam Locomotive of Jangdan Station

troops to Korea under the UN flag and each one has its own monument somewhere in the country—this is the American one. The marble cube is surrounded by flags and battle reliefs for the Army, Navy, Air Force and Marine Corps. The park also has some old tanks, fighter planes and other weapons on display.

Gyeonguiseon Railway Bridge 경의선철교

The trussed railway bridge crossing the Imjingang River is the Gyeonguiseon Railway Bridge. If you look carefully, you can see that at one time there were two bridges: the eastern one has been restored while only the pylons remain of the western one.

The bridges were built in 1905 as part of the Seoul-Shinuiju railway that linked Seoul with Pyongyang and, beyond that, the great railroad networks of Manchuria and Russia. After Korea's division in 1945, however, service along the line was cut and, during the Korean War, both bridges were destroyed, although one was later rebuilt. The bridges are located past the Civilian Control Line and are hence off-limits to civilians without special permission.

Freedom Bridge 자유의 다리

Just behind the Mangbaedan Altar is the so-called "Freedom Bridge," a simple wooden bridge that was a temporary span built over the Imjingang River in 1953 to carry home the 12,773 South Korean POWs following the Armistice Agreement. It was later moved to its current spot to be preserved as a memorial. At the northern end of the bridge is a barbed wire fence overlooked by a guard tower where the Civilian Control Line begins. Visitors often leave ribbons, banners, flags and handwritten notes on the fence.

Steam Locomotive of Jangdan Station 장단역 증기기관차

Near the Freedom Bridge is an old, rusted and very much battle-worn steam locomotive. For the better part of 60 years, the old train was left rusting in the DMZ but was moved to its current location in 2009 to allow visitors to see an important piece of history and symbol of national division.

According to the train's final operator, it was carrying a load of military supplies to UN forces in the North on December 31, 1950, but Chinese operations made it impossible to reach the destination. The train stopped to await further instructions before machine gun fire started ripping in—possibly from UN troops who worried it might be used by the communists—

resulting in the 1,020 bullet holes riddling the train body.

Along the side of the train is a barbed wire fence decorated with countless ribbons on which visitors write their prayers for peace, reconciliation and Korean reunification. Even if you can't read Korean, it is worth taking a look: many have been left by foreign visitors, some from other conflict zones around the world who leave behind prayers for peace in their own troubled lands.

Imjingak Pyeonghoa Nuri
임진각평화누리

Also part of the Imjingak is a field that has been transformed into a peace park, complete with an outdoor stage used for concerts and other cultural performances. It's a beautiful, tranquil place designed by respected Korean landscape architect Min Hyung-sik. The highlights here are the "Hill of Wind," a grassy hill covered in colorful pinwheels conceived by artist Kim Un-kyung; and installation artist Choi Pyung-gon's "Calling Unification," four grand bamboo figures advancing up the hill, facing northwards. The former reminds us that the wind freely crosses the DMZ, free of the restraints of ideology, while the latter is a quiet but powerful prayer for Korean reunification.

Ribbons of peace (top)
Imjingak Pyeonghoa Nuri

There are a number of restaurants around, including one in the Imjingak Pavilion itself. One thing the area is famous for are beans grown in the Jangdan area, or Jangdan *kong*. The restaurant in the Imjingak Pavilion cooks up a Jangdan bean stew (Jangdan *kong jeongol*, 장단콩 전골) that's worth trying.

WHAT TO EAT

Getting to Imjingak is a fairly simple matter. Just take the train from Seoul Station to Munsan (every 30 minutes during rush hour, every hour otherwise), and from Munsan change to the train for Imjingang Station (about once hourly between 6 am and 6 pm). The trip itself takes about an hour.

TRANSPORT INFO

HEYRI ART VALLEY 헤이리아트벨리

Bauhaus on the Imjingang River. Or so one could conceivably call Paju's Heyri Art Valley, a collection of art galleries, workshops, film studios, bookshops and cafés hidden away in an idyllic valley just an hour's drive north of Seoul. Along with nearby Paju Book City 파주출판도시, Heyri is a grand experiment in ecologically friendly architecture, design and urban planning, made all the more amazing—or surreal, depending on your point of view—by its location just a river's width from North Korea. An outdoor museum (with plenty of indoor ones, too) that even philistines without the slightest interest in the arts can enjoy, it's a place you could spend all day strolling about, dipping in and out of galleries and bookshops as the mood strikes.

Heyri Art Valley was born in 1997 as part of a larger effort to cultivate the cultural industries in a frontier region long underdeveloped and overmilitarized due to national division. The community is spread out in a quiet hillside valley beside the lower end of the Imjingang River, right where the waterway empties out into the larger Hangang River. Across the river is North Korea—on your way to the village you'll pass miles of barbed wire fence and watchtowers along the southern bank of the river, manned by South Korean troops. This in itself makes

Winter reeds and pond, Heyri Art Village

Keumsan Gallery, where architecture literally blends with nature

the village a symbol of peace and sustainability in a land scarred by war and destruction.

About 380 artists—including painters, sculptors, graphic artists, filmmakers and potters—live and/or work in Heyri. Korea's top architects were let loose to design the studio and art spaces, and the result—an outdoor display of the very best of eco-friendly Korean design—is absolutely breathtaking. Each and every building is an expression of the individuality of both its architect and owner. Yet all the structures strictly conform to the village's overriding principle of harmony with nature, designed to harmonize and complement the hills and streams. By regulation, none is more than three stories high. Tying the village together is a series of walking paths, winding roads and picturesque bridges.

GETTING AROUND AT HEYRI

Walking is easy but, if you'd like, take the electric car tour of the village at 8,000 won a person (15,000 won for couples, 18,000 won for three, 23,000 won for four). You can also rent a bike at 7,000 won for the first two hours (3,000 won for every extra hour). Bikes for two, however, cost 12,000 won for the first two hours (8,000 won for every extra hour). The bike rental/electric car station is near the Keumsan Gallery by Gate 3. Reserve by calling 070-7798-0875.

TAKE A MAP!

Even if you can't read Korean, be sure to pick up a map at information booths located in the village—they really help. There's also a general information center that can be reached at 1588-7385 or www.heyri.net

⊕ Heyri is a village, which means it is open 24 hours a day. The galleries, on the other hand, keep their own hours: many operate from 10 am to 7 pm, although cafés and restaurants close later.
⊟ Entry is free but many galleries charge admission. ▣ Take Bus No. 2200 from Exit 2, Hapjeong Station, Line 2 and get off at Heyri Art Valley. The trip, which runs along Freedom Road (Jayu-ro) through Goyang, takes about 50 minutes.

Total Art Space Book House, designed by Kim Jun-sung and New York's SHoP Architects PC (top), Han Hyang Lim Ceramic Museum

TIPS

NEARBY SITES

Paju Book City 파주출판도시: Like Heyri, Paju Book City—a collection of Korean publishing houses—is an outdoor exhibit of cutting-edge architecture and design, conceived to harmonize with its wetland environment. Bus No. 2200 passes through it on the way to Heyri.

Odusan Unification Observatory 오두산통일전망대: Almost within walking distance of Hyeri is the Odusan Unification Observatory which overlooks the confluence of the Imjingang and Hangang rivers. More notably, it overlooks North Korea, which is just 460 m away.

WHAT TO EAT

It feels as if Heyri has more cafés and teahouses per square foot than anywhere on the planet. Many of the bookshops and exhibit halls also serve as cafés and any attempt to list them would fall dreadfully short. One particularly popular café is the one in Gallery Touch Art 갤러리터치아트. With its usual assortment of coffees and teas (and waffles, to boot!)—but its real charm is its location overlooking Heyri's centrally located pond and Reed Square. If you want something more substantial than tea or coffee, a number of the cafés also have kitchens. Book House 북하우스 has a restaurant/ grill that does good food in lovely surroundings.

WHERE TO STAY

Most visitors to Heyri come as a daytrip from Seoul, but if you've got a bit of coin, architecturally spectacular Yonaluky (031-959-1122, www.yonaluky.com KR) is itself a work of art. Each room has an individual outdoor spa (walled for privacy). Rooms double as private art galleries, too, with works switched out every several months. Rooms range from 350,000 to 750,000 won (includes breakfast and dinner). Also architecturally eye-catching Motif 1 (031-949-0901, www.motif1.co.kr), a guesthouse owned and operated by photographer Lee An-soo and designed by hot Korean architect Cho Min-suk. Rooms harmoniously combine Western and Korean design elements with the natural surroundings. Many of its guests have been local and international artists. Rooms begin at 140,000 won a night. Another work of art is Forest Garden (010-2788-2660, www.forestgarden.kr), an architectural award-winning guest house that both surrounds and is surrounded by trees. Perfect harmonization of man-made and nature. Rooms begin at 170,000 won a night.

SUWON HWASEONG 수원화성

Built at the end of the 18th century by the brilliant King Jeongjo to house the remains of his father, the mad Prince Sado, Suwon's Hwaseong Fortress is the crown jewel of Joseon Korea's *silhak* intellectual school, a social reform movement within Korean Confucianism to focus on practical applications of learning with an emphasis on science and technology. Adopting in its design and construction the latest advances in engineering technologies and military science, including concepts imported from overseas, the bastion—designated a UNESCO World Heritage Site in 1997—emanates a feel that is distinctly Korean yet vaguely Western. Its six kilometers of walls are studded with imposing gates, watchtowers, sentry points, secret portals and command pavilions, providing visitors with an endless list of things to explore.

🚇 The fortress (Paldalmun Gate) is a 20 minute walk from Suwon Station, Line 1.

Hwaseong Fortress's northern entrance, Janganmun Gate is even larger than Seoul's Sungnyemun Gate.

KING JEONGJO, JEONG YAK-YONG & SILHAK

History and Culture

King Jeongjo

Despite the massive scale of the project, Hwaseong Fortress was completed in just two years, between 1794 and 1796, impressive even by today's standards. It was the brainchild of King Jeongjo (r. 1776–1800), an energetic reformer whose reign marked Joseon's cultural, intellectual and scientific renaissance.

There were several reasons behind the building of the fortress. Firstly, it would serve as a memorial to Jeongjo's father, Prince Sado, an allegedly sadistic man who would have become king had his father, King Yeongjo, not ordered him into a rice chest that was then locked and left in the hot sun for eight days until he died. Believing his father to be the victim of the Joseon Dynasty's endemic factional strife, Jeongjo ordered the fortress built to house the late prince's tomb.

Behind this act of filial piety, however, lay some more practical concerns. Korea had been invaded by the Japanese in the 16th century and the Manchus in the 17th century; both times, Korea's system of mountain fortresses failed. Clearly, more advanced defensive facilities were needed. Perhaps more importantly, however, Jeongjo hoped to relocate the royal capital to the new fortress, away from the bitter factional strife of Hanyang (today's Seoul). He failed in this latter objective, the capital remaining in Seoul.

Construction of the new fortress was entrusted to Jeong Yak-yong, better known by his pen name, "Dasan." Something of a polymath, Jeong was a brilliant scholar, philosopher and architect closely associated with the *silhak* ("practical learning") movement within Korean Confucianism. *Silhak* emphasized the practical over the metaphysical, focusing on temporal matters such as social science, industry and technology—Hwaseong Fortress was its crowning achievement. Jeong's blueprints incorporated the strengths of Korean, Chinese and Japanese design to produce a fortress that could serve in both defensive and offensive

Dasan Jeong Yak-yong

operations. It even drew upon elements of Western castle architecture and construction, such as its use of brick. The building process made use of an ingenious series of pulleys and cranes, operated by paid workers rather than corvée labor. The result was a fortress that was both functional and a work of art in its own right.

Hiking Hwaseong

Hwaseong Fortress forms a nearly full ring around Suwon's old downtown. At one time, the entire city was contained within its walls but urban development in the modern era has led to much of the city spilling out beyond the gates. Unusually for Korean fortresses that typically surround either a town or mountain top, Hwaseong does both, running along both flat lowlands and steep hillsides. You can walk the whole thing in about three hours, although you'll probably want to spend an entire day exploring. Hwaseong Fortress: 1,000 won.

❶ Janganmun Gate 장안문: The old north gate of the fortress, this massive portal with a two-story pavilion is Korea's largest gate, even larger than Seoul's Sungnyemun. Note the crescent-shaped demilune that offers the gate even further protection from enemies. The gate is beautiful both day and night.

❷ Hwaseomun Gate 화서문: Not only is Hwaseong's western gate striking in its own right; it's also protected by an imposing brick watchtower that cannot be found elsewhere in Korea.

❸ Hwahongmun Gate 화홍문: More of a bridge than a gate, this section of the wall was built with seven arches through which flows Suwoncheon Stream. Nearby is a pond and, on the hill overlooking it, a command pavilion. This is one of the most picturesque stretches of the wall.

❹ Paldalmun Gate 팔달문 **and Seojangdae Pavilion** 서장대: Now a traffic island surrounded by modern Suwon, the grand old south gate offers a dramatic contrast between the old and new. From the gate, follow the wall as it ascends Mt. Paldalsan

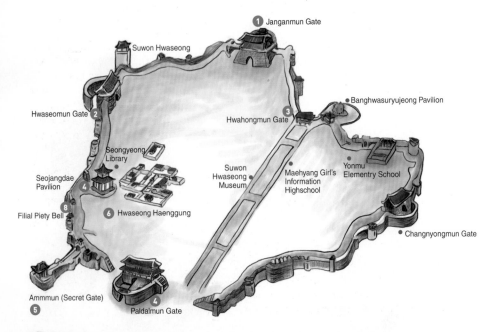

❶ Janganmun Gate

Suwon Hwaseong

Banghwasuryujeong Pavilion

Hwaseomun Gate ❷

Hwahongmun Gate ❸

Seongyeong Library

Seojangdae Pavilion ❹

Suwon Hwaseong Museum

Maehyang Girl's Information Highschool

Yonmu Elementry School

Filial Piety Bell

❽ ❻ Hwaseong Haenggung

Changnyongmun Gate

Ammmun (Secret Gate)
❺

❹ Paldalmun Gate

until you reach Seojangdae Pavilion. Located on the highest point of the wall, this command post offers breathtaking views of the fortress, city and hills beyond.

⑤ Secret Gates 암문: Called *ammun* in Korean, these hidden entrances were used to sneak supplies into the fortress and, if need be, let troops sally outside the fortress to attack a besieging enemy. The one in the southwest on the slope of Mt. Paldalsan is particularly interesting.

⑥ Hwaseong Haenggung 화성행궁: Built by Jeongjo as a royal residence for the king when he visited his father's tomb, this gorgeous temporary palace was restored in

2003, the original having been destroyed during the Japanese colonial era.
💷 1,500 won

⑦ Traditional Archery 전통궁도: There's a range in the fortress where you can try your hand at the Korean martial tradition of archery. Fee: 2,000 won for 10 arrows.

⑧ Filial Piety Bell 효원의종: Hwaseong was built as an act of filial piety; to celebrate this, the city hung a big Korean-style bell for visitors to ring. You ring it three times: once for your parents' health, once for your family's health, and once for your own personal development. Fee: 1,000 won for singles and doubles, 2,000 won for groups of three or four.

WHAT TO EAT

Suwon is quite famous for its *galbi* (barbecued ribs). Yeonpo Galbi 연포갈비 (02-255-1337), near Hwahongmun Gate 화홍문 is especially well known but there are literally a hundred restaurants specializing in this dish throughout Suwon.

WHERE TO STAY

Suwon is usually a day-trip from Seoul, but if you feel like spending the night, Hwaseong Guest House (031-245-6226, www.hsguesthouse.com) is very conveniently located just behind Paldalmun Gate, with dormitory rooms beginning at 15,000 won (private rooms with bath for 30,000 won). If you're exploring not only Suwon, but nearby Yongin, the colorfully named Hotel Amour & Symphony (031-206-0942, www.amourhotel.com) on the east side of town is a good value at 90,000 won a night.

YONGIN 용인

For many Seoulites, Yongin represents a nice day trip out of the big city. Within the lushly forested hillsides of this conveniently located Seoul suburb are some of Korea's most popular tourist destinations, including the massive Korean Folk Village and, of course, Everland theme park—one of the most visited theme parks in the known universe. If you're looking for somewhere to escape the masses, Yongin might not necessarily fit the bill; on any given weekend, the masses may very well follow you down there. But, owing to its proximity and entertainment facilities, Yongin's a fantastic place to bring the kids. And if a little adult tranquility is what you're looking for, the Ho-Am Art Museum and Hee Won Garden, the latter one of the finest examples of Korean traditional garden design anywhere in the country, are well worth the short bus ride out of Seoul.

Korean Folk Village 한국민속촌

Korean Folk Village is, natch, a Korean folk village—and a large one, at that. You could literally spend an entire day wandering around the place; or two days if you happen to get lost.

It's been said by some that Korean Folk Village is "artificial." This is true—unlike Andong's Hahoe Village or Suncheon's Nagan Eupseong, Korean Folk Village is

Everland, one of the world busiest theme parks

not a pre-existing historic village that has been preserved. It was purpose-built in 1974 as an open-air folk museum.

That being said, as folk villages go, Korean Folk Village has been done quite tastefully. The Joseon Dynasty-style homes and buildings—some 270 structures sitting on a grand total of 245 acres—have been painstakingly reconstructed as authentically as possible. So good are the reconstructions and atmosphere that the village is frequently used as a film set. The place is very picturesque—a camera is mandatory.

Korean Folk Village is surrounded by forest and split roughly in half by a long, narrow lake. The actual folk village is a short walk from the admission gate, just past the obligatory restaurants, tea houses and gift shops. Once inside, however, it's like being transported back in time to the Joseon era. As you meander throughout the village, you'll come across traditional dwellings from all regions and social classes of Korea, from the homes of Jejudo Island peasants with their distinctive thatched roofs tied with rope, and walls made from volcanic rock, to the dignified tile-roof homes of *yangban* scholar aristocrats. You can even find a massive county magistrate's complex and *seowon*, the Confucian schools that served the role of universities and higher learning in the Joseon era.

At some of these dwellings you can find staff in traditional garb engaging in traditional crafts such as spinning and straw crafts. Some events are more seasonal; during the Dano holiday, this writer watched as locals washed their hair with water boiled with calamus plants, a tradition once believed to make the hair shiny. The village also stages regular cultural performances and provides several hands-on activities for children.

During the hot summer months, be sure

to try a cup of *misutgaru* 미숫가루 (1,000 won), a cool drink made from toasted grain powder and honey—the traditional market is a good place to score one.

⊙ Winter: 9 am to 6 pm, summer: 10 am to 7:30 pm. Hours change slightly throughout the year and between weekdays and weekends.
🎫 15,000 won for adults, 12,000 won for teens, and 10,000 won for children. 🚌 From Exit 5 of Gangnam Station, Line 2, take the 5001-1 bus to the Korean Folk Village. The trip takes about one hour. ☎ 031-288-0000 🌐 www.koreanfolk. co.kr

Everland 에버랜드

When Seoulites think of Yongin, they think of **Everland**. The Everland Resort, owned by Samsung Corporation, is one of the largest amusement parks on earth. Sitting on 3,700 acres of prime real estate, the park ranked sixth worldwide in park attendance in 2002, and eventually worked its way to number five, beating out luminaries such as Epcot, Disney MGM and Disney's Animal Kingdom, and earning a place on Forbes' list of best amusement parks.

If you've been to Disneyland you know what to expect. If you're prepubescent, or just really into amusement parks, Everland is a dream come true. Even if you aren't, it's still worth visiting for the sheer scale and surrealness of it all. On a weekend, families from all over the country descend on the place in droves.

Everland is broken up into six zones— American Adventure, Magic Land, Aesop's Village, European Adventure, Zoo-Topia and Global Fair. Leave any hope you have of seeing it all in a single day at the ticket booth—you could spend a week wandering around and not see everything. And that's not even including Caribbean Bay 캐리비안베이, Everland Resort's summer water park, or its large zoo. Each section has its own unique rides and attractions. The architecture and atmosphere is very Disney-like— while the Disney Castle is missing, you'll be greeted at the entrance with mock-ups of St. Basil's Cathedral, the Hagia Sophia and what appears to be a giant wall-mural of a Tuscan village.

Also like Disneyland, there's stuff for big people to do, too. Fancy a round of golf? Try the Glen Ross Golf Club 글렌로스골프클럽; but be forewarned—at 220,000 won on a weekend, green fees tend to be steeper than elsewhere, outside of perhaps Japan or the most exclusive clubs. If you're a race fan, Everland Speedway 에버랜드 스피드웨이 (currently under reconstruction) is Korea's best raceway. It even provides classes for aspiring Mario Andrettis of the world to earn their racing licenses. Car nuts will also appreciate the nearby Samsung Transportation Museum 삼성교통박물관. A shuttle bus service takes you throughout the entire complex.

⊕ 9:30 am to 10 pm (subject to change, depending on season) 🎫 For adults, it's 31,000 won for a single-entry pass (23,000 won for children). A day pass will run you 38,000 won (29,000 won for children). Day tickets to Caribbean Bay are 35,000 won (adults) and 27,000 won (children). There is discounted admission for post-5 pm admission. 🚌 The fastest way to get to Everland is by Bus No. 5002 from Exit 6 of Gangnam Station, Line 2 (1

Everland, Korea's largest amusement park

hr). There are also buses from Seoul National University of Education and Sadang Stations, as well as Suwon Station. If going there from Korean Folk Village, take Bus No. 10-5 from the parking lot front. ☎ 031-320-5000 🖳 www.everland.com

Ho-Am Art Museum 호암미술관
& Hee Won Garden 희원

Also part of Samsung's Yongin fiefdom, the Ho-Am Art Museum really deserves separate mention. The largest private museum in Korea, it is undoubtedly one of the world's finest collections of Korean art. The museum houses the private collection of the late Samsung founder, Lee Byung-chul, and includes several pieces that were designated as national treasures by the Korean government.

The art collection aside, the museum is worth visiting for the setting alone. Spread in front of the museum is the splendor of Hee Won Garden, one of the most spectacular examples of Korean traditional garden design anywhere. Korean gardens are designed to appear as natural as possible—the human touches are unassuming yet brilliant in the way they blend harmoniously with the natural environment. A Silla-era stone pagoda here, a Goryeo-era Buddhist relief there—even the garden ornaments are precious cultural properties. The mountains and nearby lake are as much a part of the garden as the picturesque lotus pond. You can spend

Beautiful Hee Won Garden

hours here contently doing absolutely nothing but relaxing, listening to the sound of the wind and running water. Overlooking the garden atop stone terraces that blend in with the surroundings are the museum hall and a pleasant teahouse where you can enjoy a cool beverage.

If you manage to momentarily free yourself from the garden's mesmerizing tranquility, the museum itself is home to a vast collection of metalwork, Buddhist art, paintings and ceramics dating from the pre-historic period to the Joseon era.

🕙 10 am to 6 pm 🎟 4,000 won 🚌 Free shuttle bus service will take you to the museum from the ticket booth area of Everland (10 am to 4 pm, departs hourly except at noon) ☎ 031-320-1801~2 🖳 http://hoam.samsung.foundation.org

WHAT TO EAT

Everland has its obligatory restaurants and eateries, including international eats. The atmosphere is a bit on the young side, though. Out of the way, but very popular, is Sansarang 산사랑 (031-263-6080, www.sansalang.co.kr), a tranquil spot at the foot of a mountain serving Sannamul *jeongsik* 산마을 정식 (mountain vegetables, soup and rice served in a stone pot) for 14,000 won a person.

WHERE TO STAY

Almost always done as a daytrip from Seoul. If you'd like to combine your trip with a bit of skiing/snowboarding, though, the nearby Yangji Pine Resort 양지파인리조트 (031-338-2001, www.pineresort.com) has rooms for about 300,000 won a night, but more importantly, it also has six ski slopes, rated beginner to advanced.

NAMHANSANSEONG FORTRESS 남한산성

Namhansanseong Fortress is a picturesque mountain fortress that rings the hilltops overlooking the Seoul suburb of Bundang. The nearly 12 km of walls and gates, surrounded by richly forested hillsides, were built in the 17th century (and greatly rebuilt and restored in the 20th century), and contain temples, shrines and even a temporary palace for use by the king. The walls provide breathtaking views of the city of Seoul, especially from the West Gate 서문, from where sunsets and night views are particularly inspiring.

In addition to its scenic beauty, Namhansanseong is also famous for being the site of one the most humiliating defeats in Korean history (see next page).

The fortress is now a provincial park with well-maintained hiking paths to all points of interest. If you'd like to circumnavigate the walls, expect to set aside about three to four hours. There are tons of restaurants in front of the South Gate 남문, so don't worry about sustenance.

View of Seoul from Namhansanseong Fortress

SURRENDER AT NAMHANSANSEONG FORTRESS   *History and Culture*

Historically, the fortress is most famous for a dramatic siege that took place here in 1636. The Manchus, then in the midst of a war against China's Ming Dynasty, had invaded Korea after the court of King Injo rebuffed Manchu demands for recognition. The invaders, a motley crew of Manchu and Mongolian warriors, quickly dashed down the peninsula while Injo and his court retreated to safety of Namhansanseong Fortress. A massive Manchu force—personally led by Manchu leader Hong Taiji, the founder of China's Qing Dynasty—laid siege to the fortress which was defended by just a handful of Koreans. Despite the enemy's overwhelming numbers, the defenders held out bravely for 45 days before news came that the island of Ganghwado, where the royal family had taken refuge, had fallen, and Injo's queen, consorts and children were now captive. Injo decided to surrender but Hong Taiji, looking to make a point, demanded Injo surrender in person. Injo, the Crown Prince and a party of retainers left the fortress and headed to an altar on the south bank of the frozen Hangang River where Injo kowtowed to Hong, signaling Korea's submission to the Qing.

West Gate (left), Sueojangdae, the fortress's old command post

TRANSPORT
INFO

Most people take the subway to Sanseong Station (Line 8), then Bus No. 9 from Exit 2 of the station to the fortress's South Gate. The bus ride takes about 20 minutes. Another option is to take Line 5 to Macheon Station, from which a hiking path to the West Gate of the fortress starts. The hike to the gate takes about an hour.

ICHEON 이천

For half a millennium, Korea's finest ceramics have come from the kilns of Icheon, a small town about an hour southeast of Seoul in the province of Gyeonggi-do. Indeed, they still do —Icheon is home to about 300 active ceramics producers and 40 traditional firewood kilns that keep the region's time-honored artistic traditions alive. Here, amidst the plentiful wood and clay, artisans churn out beautiful works of art that are as functional as they are eye-pleasing.

In addition to producing wonderful ceramics, Icheon is also one of Korea's most fertile regions; its local cuisine is accordingly first-rate. Finish up a day of ceramic shopping with a meal at one of the town's many restaurants specializing in *ssalbap jeongsik* 쌀밥정식, an exquisite table d'hôte of rice, soup, meat and 20 or so side dishes—it's literally fit for a king.

Icheon Ceramics Village 이천도자기마을

Today, most of Icheon's ceramic producers are located in the rural hamlet of Sindun-myeon 신둔면, a short taxi ride from Icheon's express bus terminal. The producers have largely gathered in two "potters' villages," or *doyechon* 도예촌—one in Sindun-myeon proper and the other in a valley called Sagimakgol. Both are similar—dozens of studios and shops where you can spend days going through the beautiful wares, which include priceless vases and daily items like cups, plates and spoons—all works of art. The artisans are often manning the shops, so if you'd like to talk to the artist, there's plenty of opportunity to do so (assuming you speak some Korean). Both areas have traditional wood-burning

Icheon Ceramics Festival celebrates the town's proud pottery heritage.

kilns for good measure.

Classes are also offered for those who'd like to try their hand at pottery. One such place in Sagimakgol is Duseong Doye Gyosil 두성도예교실 (031-632-0130), with hands-on programs that begin at 20,000 won.

Haegang Ceramics Museum
해강도자기미술관

Haegang Ceramics Museum, located not far from the ceramics villages in Sindun-myeon, was founded in 1990 by the late "Haegang" Yoo Kun-hyung, a ceramics master who dedicated his life to rediscovering Korea's proud Goryeo celadon tradition. The museum is a good place to learn about Korea's ceramic history as well as to appreciate the beautiful collection of work.

ⓒ 031-634-2266~7 www.haegang.org

t

ICHEON CERAMICS FESTIVAL
TIPS

The best time of year to come to Icheon is from late April to late May when the town is in the midst of the month-long Icheon Ceramics Festival. This celebration of the town's proudest artistic tradition, going strong since 1987, brings people from all over to see and purchase the wares, enjoy hands-on experiences and take in the many cultural performances on hand.
www.ceramic.or.kr

THE BEAUTY OF JOSEON CERAMICS
History and Culture

While Korean ceramics date back to prehistory, their golden age was the Joseon era when ceramics became Korea's most beloved art form. The artisans of the previous dynasty, the Buddhist Goryeo Kingdom (918–1392), produced intricate porcelains renowned for their beautiful celadon glaze. With the overthrow of Goryeo by the neo-Confucian founders of the Joseon Dynasty (1392–1910), the ornate celadon styles fell out of favor. Taking their place was *baekja*, or Joseon white porcelain. These wares, pure white in color and almost completely unadorned, better reflected the simpler, austere tastes of the times.

The Icheon region, along with the neighboring towns of Yeoju 여주 and Gwangju 광주, became the center of the Joseon ceramics industry. This was partly thanks to the area's rich supply of kaolinite, or china clay. It also helped that the region was blessed with a good supply of water and wood as well as, perhaps most importantly, easy transport access to the royal capital of Seoul.

Toward the end of the Joseon era, a flood of cheaper foreign-produced ceramics and, later, imperial pressure led to a decline in Icheon's ceramics industry. Since Liberation in 1945, however, the kilns have been burning bright again as artisans gather in the region's valleys not only to keep alive the traditions of the past, but also to put their own spin on the ancient craft and share their knowledge with the public.

Off the Beaten Track

Silleuksa Temple 신륵사 & Mok-A Museum 목아박물관

Just to the east of Icheon is the small town of Yeoju which, like Icheon, is known for its age-old ceramics tradition. A short bus ride from "downtown" Yeoju brings you to the stunning Buddhist temple of Silleuksa. While most Korean temples are located on remote mountainsides, Silleuksa was instead built riverside with beautiful views of the Namhangang River.

The temple is believed to have been founded in the Silla era, and underwent its last major renovation at the beginning of the 18th century. In 1473, it received the honor of being named the supervisory temple for the tomb of King Sejong the Great, who was buried nearby. The precinct boasts of numerous treasures, the most impressive of which may be its Goryeo-era seven-story brick pagoda, a rarity in a country where most pagoda are built of stone. Be sure to check out some of the other beautiful pieces of masonry, too, including some memorial steles, an impressive stone lantern, a granite pagoda and an early Joseon Dynasty wooden hall dedicated to three great historic monks. Silleuksa's most picturesque site, however, is the simple pavilion and stone pagoda built on a granite slab overlooking directly the Namhangang River. The sunsets here are worth the visit.

It's good to combine a visit to Silleuksa with a visit to Mok-A Museum, founded by Korean traditional woodcraft artist Park Chan-su in 1993 as a repository for Buddhist art. There are some impressive indoor and outdoor displays; the woodcraft is especially inspiring.

⊕ **Mok-A Museum** 9 am to 5 pm (Nov to Feb), 9 am to 6 pm (Mar to Oct) ℂ **Silleuksa** 031-885-2505 **Mok-A Museum** 031-885-9952 🚌 **Silleuksa** 2,200 won, **Mok-A Museum** 5,000 won 🚍 From Icheon, take a bus for Yeoju (30 min). From Yeoju, take one of the frequent buses to Silleuksa from in front of Yeoju Bus Terminal (10 min). To get to Mok-A Museum, take a bus or taxi from in front of Silleuka (5 min). You could also take a taxi from Yeoju Bus Terminal to Silleuksa for about 5,000 won. From Seoul, buses to Yeoju depart from Dong Seoul Terminal and Express Bus Terminal (1 hrs 20 min).

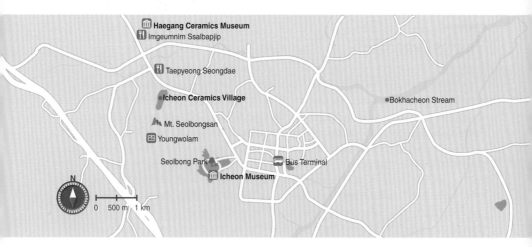

Haegang Ceramics Museum
Imgeumnim Ssalbapjip

Taepyeong Seongdae

Icheon Ceramics Village

●Bokhacheon Stream

Mt. Seolbongsan

Youngwolam

Seolbong Park
Bus Terminal

Icheon Museum

N

0 500 m 1 km

WHAT TO
EAT

In the popular consciousness, Icheon is associated with two things—ceramics and *ssalbap* 쌀밥, or rice. Icheon rice, in fact, was of such high quality that it was found atop the king's dinner table during the Joseon era. Simply put, this is a fertile area with good food.

Icheon's gift to Korea's culinary landscape is *ssalbapjip* 쌀밥집, restaurants that specialize in Icheon-style *jeongsik*. *Jeongsik* 정식, or table d'hôte, will differ slightly from place to place and in Icheon it generally consists of rice in a stone pot, meat, crab seasoned with soy sauce, a soup and an array of countless side dishes. It's as appealing visually as it is to the taste buds.

The area around Sindun-myeon—indeed, everywhere in Icheon—is full of places to have *ssalbap jeongsik*, and regularly attracts Seoulites in search of a good meal. The most famous of these restaurants is Imgeumnim Ssalbapjip 임금님쌀밥집 (031-6320-3626) in Sindun-myeon. Locals, however, recommend Taepyeong Seongdae 태평성대 (031-638-8088), a massive place just across from the Sagimakgol Village that seems to be doing a roaring trade.

Highly recommended for a very pleasant culinary experience is Deokjegung 덕제궁 (031-634-4811), an exquisitely appointed *hanok*-style restaurant located on a quiet hillside just off the road in Sindun-myeon. Dining areas are private, entered through Korean-style wood and paper doors—the peaceful, dignified atmosphere perfectly complements the outstanding cuisine.

TRANSPORT
INFO

Buses to Icheon depart from Seoul's Gangnam Express Bus Terminal—the trip takes about an hour. Once you're in Icheon, most of the ceramics-related sites are a short taxi ride away from the bus terminal. You may wish to take the taxi driver's business card when you reach your destination—to get to your next destination (or back to the bus terminal, for that matter), you may have to call him again. This is all quite easy to do and makes getting around much easier, especially if you're carrying around a bag of newly purchased ceramics.

YANGSU-RI 양수리

About 50 km west of Seoul, Yangsu-ri—literally, "Town of Two Waters"—is but a small village at the western extremity of the Gyeonggi-do county of Yangpyeong. It owes its name to the fact that the Bukhangang and Namhangang Rivers converge here to form the mighty Hangang River. Thanks to this strategic location, it used to be a thriving commercial port in the days when wooden boats plied Korea's rivers laden with grain and wood. The construction of the nearby Paldang Dam 팔당댐 in the 1970s and the subsequent designation of the river area as a "green belt" ended Yangsu-ri's days as an inland port, but its scenic beauty and convenient placement on National Road No. 6 6번국도 turned it into a popular driving and date destination for Seoulites. The recent extension of the Seoul subway's Jungang Line has made it even more accessible.

The most scenic spot in the town is a place called Dumulmeori 두물머리, a pure Korean translation of the Sino-Korean "Yangsu-ri" and, in fact, the name locals use for the town. Located at the southern end of an island in the Bukhangang River, the site overlooks the point where the two rivers merge. Marking the spot is a grand 400-year-old zelkova tree that has shaded visitors here for centuries;

Early morning at Yangsu-ri

1. Old zelkova tree, Yangsu-ri 2. Jangdokdae Fountain, Semiwon 3. Lotus blossoms, Semiwon

you might recognize it as it has featured in countless ads and TV dramas. Floating peacefully on the water are two yellow-sailed wooden boats—a common sight on the river not so long ago—these are reconstructions crafted by Kim Gwi-seong, Korea's only remaining builder of Korean traditional sailboats.

The best time to visit is about an hour before sunrise, especially in spring and autumn when the big gap between nighttime and daytime temperatures gives rise to a cover of mist and fog over the river.

Just across from Dumulmeori on the "mainland" is a pleasant garden called Semiwon 세미원, which takes its name from the old saying, "When you see water, wash your mind, and when you see flowers, beautify your heart." In addition to being a place of relaxation, it is also an exercise in natural water purification thanks to the garden's many aquatic plants. The garden is most famous for its paddies of lotus flowers which are best seen from early June to early August. Admission is 3,000 won but you receive a voucher redeemable for 3,000 won's worth of local agricultural goods.

Sujongsa Temple 수종사

Dumulmeori is where you can appreciate the scenery from up close. To get a bird's-eye view of the surroundings, head to Sujongsa, a Buddhist temple located high on Mt. Ungilsan 운길산, a peak overlooking Yangsu-ri. It takes about an hour to hike from the bottom of the mountain to the temple (if you're lucky, a passing car might offer you a ride), but it's more than rewarding.

Sujongsa dates from 1459. It is said that King Sejo (r. 1455–1468) was returning from the Geumgangsan Mountains when he stopped in Yangsu-ri to spend the night. As he was enjoying the evening scenery, he thought he heard the sound of a bell on Mt. Ungilsan. He sent men to investigate; they found a cave, the site of an old temple where water dripping from a crack produced the bell-like sound. The king ordered to be built on the spot a new temple which he named Sujongsa or "Water Bell Temple."

The temple is not particularly large, although it does have a couple of old pagodas and a stone stupa from the Joseon era. What people come here for, however, is the view and the tea. From the courtyard, visitors are treated to a panoramic view of Yangsu-ri, the rivers, Lake Paldangho 팔당호 and the surrounding mountains. The best view, however, can be had through the window of the Samjeongheon 삼정헌, a small teahouse located in the temple itself where visitors are served complimentary cups of green tea. Tea lovers have long praised the green tea boiled from the waters of Yangsu-ri; the great Joseon scholar Jeong Yak-yong

TIPS

NIGHT TRAIN

The first train to Yangsu-ri departs from Yongsan Station, Jungang Line 1, at 5:13 am; depending on the time of year, this may not get you there in time to see the sunrise. You might consider taking the last train to Yangsu-ri from Yongsan Station at 11:15 pm the night before and either staying at an inn or waiting in a PC room until dawn breaks.

(see p203) who was born and died at the foot of Mt. Ungilsan, was mad for the drink. It becomes much tastier, however, as you gaze from the Samjeongheon at the vista unfolding below you.

Because of Mt. Ungilsan's popularity as a hiking destination, Sujongsa gets more than its fair share of visitors, and because of this it can get a bit too noisy for the monks' liking. When you visit, be courteous and keep your voice down and, when you have your tea, take it with the meditative spirit of the milieu.

View of Yangsu-ri from Sujongsa Temple

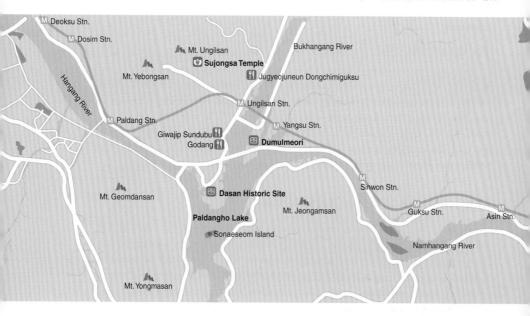

WHAT TO EAT

Being a popular getaway spot for Seoulites, there are a good many restaurants in and around Yangsu-ri. Giwajip Sundubu 기와집순두부 (031-576-9009), located in a *hanok* on the Namyangju 남양주 side of the river, is famous for its variety of soybean dishes, especially tofu. Also well-regarded is Jugyeojuneun Dongchimiguksu 죽여주는 동치미국수 ("Dongchimi Noodles That Will Knock You Dead") which serves noodles in a cold kimchi broth (031-576-4070). There are a ton of cafés in Yangsu-ri, too. A good one is Godang 고당 (031-576-8090), a *hanok* establishment serving great coffee brewed from beans they roast daily.

WHERE TO STAY

Yangsuri is most often visited as a daytrip from Seoul, but there are a couple of really nice nearby hotels worth mention. House of the Mind 생각속의 집 (031-773-2210, http://mindhome. co.kr [KR]) is a masterfully designed complex of six concrete homes that blend in harmoniously with the sublime natural surroundings of Yangpyeong. If you like spectacular architecture in beautiful locations, this is your place. Rooms begin at 200,000 won winter and mid-summer peak seasons (including breakfast). Rooms come with outdoor barbecue facilities, too. Equally spectacular is Over the Mountain 오버더마운틴 (031-585-7575, http://overthemountain. co.kr), located in the mountains a bit further up the river in Gapyeong. Its concrete units take advantage of the beautiful mountain landscape, with open glass walls providing unobstructed views. Rooms have private outdoor spas, and there's a swimming pool, too. Pick-up service provided from Cheongpyeong Station. Both hotels are even more lovely in rainy and foggy weather.

TRANSPORT INFO

Yangsu-ri is easily reached from Seoul via the Jungang Line—just get off at Yangsu Station. The trip takes between 45 minutes and an hour from Seoul, depending on where you embark. From Yangsu Station, it's a 20 minute walk across a bridge and along a pleasant riverside walking path to reach Dumulmeori. If you're planning to visit Sujongsa first, however, you want to get off at Ungilsan Station rather than Yangsu Station.

JOSEON ROYAL TOMBS 조선왕릉

In 2009, UNESCO designated Korea's Joseon Dynasty royal tombs World Heritage sites. And for good reason—the tombs account for the entire lineage of the Joseon Kingdom, from King Taejo (r. 1392–1398) to Emperor Sunjong (r. 1907–1910). Easily accessible from Seoul, the tombs are exquisite examples of Korean landscaping and provide visitors with insight into the history and worldview of the Confucian-inspired dynasty of Joseon.

Characteristics of Joseon Royal Tombs

The majority of the 40 Joseon royal tombs are located between 10 to 100 *ri* (4 to 40 km) from Gyeongbokgung Palace, some in Seoul itself but mostly in Gyeonggi-do. The location and arrangement of the tombs are highly informed by Confucianism and feng shui. In accordance with Confucian etiquette, each tomb is divided into three spaces: an entrance, usually marked by a simple red gate and a stone bridge; a place to conduct rites, usually a T-shaped Korean-style hall; and the burial spot itself, with the grave and stone monuments. The burial grounds are typically located on hillsides with mountains to their rear for protection and streams nearby to let energy flow. Much care went into the surrounding landscapes: tombs are usually surrounded by splendid forests of pine and oaks.

Intricate stonework at Seonjeongneung Tomb, Samseong-dong, Seoul

Donggureung Tomb Complex 동구릉

(Guri 구리, Gyeonggi-do)

The largest of the Joseon tomb clusters, Donggureung is the final resting place of seven kings and 10 queens, including the founder of the Joseon Dynasty, King Taejo (r. 1392–1398). The tomb of King Seonjo (r. 1567–1608) is particularly grand while King Taejo's tomb is unique as it is covered in rushes from the northern Korean town of Hamheung, Taejo's hometown.

⏰ 6 am to 6:30 pm (Mar–Oct), 6 am to 5:30 pm (Nov–Feb). Ticket sales stop 1 hour prior to closing. Closed Mondays. 💰 1,000 won 🚍 Take Bus No. 1-1 or 9-2 from Gangbyeon Station, Line 2 and get off at Donggureung (40 min).

Seonjeongneung 선정릉

(Samseong-dong 삼성동, Seoul)

The burial place of King Seongjong (r. 1469–1494) and King Jungjong (r. 1506–1544), Seonjeongneung is today located in the heart of one of Seoul's busiest commercial districts. The visual contrast between the tombs and the surrounding urban landscape is striking. Despite the location, the site is surrounded by rich forests and is quite tranquil, making it an excellent urban park.

⏰ 6 am to 9 pm (Mar–Oct), 6:30 am to 9 pm (Nov–Feb). Ticket sales stop 1 hour prior to closing. Closed Mondays. 💰 1,000 won 🚍 Exit 8 to Seolleung Station, Line 2.

Taereung 태릉

(Gongneung-dong 공릉동, Seoul)

Also located in Seoul, this tomb belongs to one of Korean history's most powerful queens, Queen Munjeong, who served as the virtual ruler of Korea throughout much of the mid-16th century as regent to her son, the young King Myeongjong (r. 1545–1567), who is also buried at the site.

⏰ 9 am to 6:30 pm (Mar–Oct), 9 am to 5:30 pm (Nov–Feb). Ticket sales stop 1 hour prior to closing. Closed Mondays 💰 1,000 won 🚍 Exit 7 of Taereung Station, Line 6 and 7, and take Bus No. 1155 or 1156 to Taereung Gongneung (10 min).

Gwangneung 광릉

(Namyangju 남양주, Gyeonggi-do)

Located in one of Korea's most beautiful forests (which is also home to Gwangneung National Arboretum 광릉국립수목원), Gwangneung is the tomb of King Sejo, one of the dynasty's most energetic kings. This is a particularly beautiful place to visit in autumn when it can be combined with a visit to the arboretum for which you'd better make advance reservation.

⏰ 9 am to 6:30 pm (Mar–Oct), 9 am to 5:30 pm (Nov–Feb). Ticket sales stop 1 hour prior to closing. Closed Mondays. 💰 1,000 won 🚍 Take Bus No. 7-5, 7-8 or 707 from Cheongnyangni Station to Gwangneungnae (40 min). From there, switch to Bus No. 21 and get off at Gwangneung.

Hongneung 홍릉 & Yureung 유릉

(Namyangju 남양주, Gyeonggi-do)

These two tombs are unique in that they are the burial places of emperors: Emperor Gojong (r. 1863–1907) and Emperor Sunjong (r. 1907–1910) of the Daehan Empire, along with their queen consorts. As befitting an emperor's resting place, the tombs are modeled on the Xiaoling Tomb, the burial place of Emperor Hongwu, the founder of China's Ming Dynasty. Unlike Korea's other royal tombs where the stone guardians and animals are located just in front of the burial mound, here they are located along the path to the rites pavilions. The pavilions themselves have been turned into grand, palatial structures with the masonry exhibiting a distinctively foreign influence as the tombs were built when Korea was a Japanese colony.

⏰ 9 am to 6:40 pm (Mar–Oct), 9 am to 5:30 pm (Nov–Feb). Ticket sales stop 1 hour prior to closing. Closed Mondays. 💰 1,000 won 🚍 Take Bus No. 9202, 30, 330-1, 765 or 9205 from Cheongnyangni Station and get off at the tombs (40 min).

GANGWON-DO

HIGHLIGHTS

- Relax and enjoy the local cuisine in the charming lakeside town of Chuncheon

- Hike the breathtaking mountainous expanses of Seoraksan National Park and experience some of Korea's most fantastic peaks

- Get in touch with your spiritual side at the beautiful Buddhist temples of Odaesan National Park

- Take the overnight train from Seoul to the East Coast village of Jeongdongjin, home to Korea's most romantic sunrise

- Get subterranean in the surreal limestone caves of Samcheok

- Visit the sobering Korean War ruins at the DMZ town of Cheorwon

- CHEORWON
- HWACHEON
- SOKCHO
- SEORAKSAN NATIONAL PARK
- NAKSAN PROVINCIAL PARK
- CHUNCHEON
  - Chuncheon Stn.
- ODAESAN NATIONAL PARK
- GANGNEUNG
  - Gangneung Stn.
  - Jeongdongjin Stn.
- JEONGDONGJIN
  - Mangsang Stn.
  - Donghae Stn.
- DONGHAE
- WONJU
  - Auraji Stn.
- PYEONGCHANG
- JEONGSEON
- SAMCHEOK
  - Samcheok Stn.
  - Wonju Stn.
- CHIAKSAN NATIONAL PARK
  - Mindungsan Stn.
  - Bongyang Stn.
  - Yeongwol Stn.
- DONGGANG RIVER
- TAEBAEK
  - Taebaek Stn.

LAND OF MOUNTAINS & SEA

Korea's most mountainous province, Gangwon-do, is also the country's most beautiful. This is a land of high, craggy peaks, deep valleys, rushing rivers, and small towns and villages wedged into what little space is left. The Taebaeksan Mountain Range which forms the backbone of the Korean Peninsula comprises much of the province and is its defining geographical feature. Much of the population lives along the narrow strip that runs along the East Sea coast.

The spectacular peaks of Mt. Seoraksan National Park are the biggest draw but hidden in the mountains are countless temples, gorges, caves and other scenic spots. The coastal city of Gangneung is home to a rich cultural heritage and one of Korea's most popular summertime destinations. The northern frontier, which runs along the DMZ, is also worth exploring for its Korean War ruins.

Chuam Beach, Donghae

Famed redwood rows of Namiseom Island

CHUNCHEON 춘천

Nestled in the rugged snow-capped peaks of the province of Gangwon-do, the warm and inviting provincial capital of Chuncheon is a land of mountains, lakes and rivers. Thanks to recently upgraded rail and road links, it gives world-weary Seoulites a place to escape the urban jungle for a day or two to rejuvenate amidst beautiful scenery and enjoy some good food before returning once again to the daily grind.

Layout

Chuncheon sits on a large lake, as you'll no doubt notice as your train pulls into Chuncheon Station. Not so long ago, Chuncheon was known as a city of mountains. In addition to mountains, however, the town was blessed with fast flowing rivers, a blessing not unnoticed by civil engineers who, starting in the 60s, proceeded to build some of Asia's largest dams and hydroelectric plants here. This turned Chuncheon from a mountain railway junction to a city of man-made lakes. Today, the city is surrounded by Uiamho Lake to the west, Chuncheonho Lake to the north and, further east, the massive Soyangho Lake, which is so large as to almost qualify as an inland sea. Home to numerous resort islands including Namiseom Island, Jungdo Island 중도 (of which there are actually two) and Wido Island 위도, the lakes provide visitors with plenty of water sport activities in the summer months and beautiful vistas in winter. Downtown Chuncheon, which sits on Lake Uiamho, is a relatively large provincial capital and a major educational center with several universities. It's a pleasant enough place to walk around and, although by Korean standards it's relatively new, it does have a few historical sites of interest including a number of Korean War memorials and two Catholic churches founded by Irish missionaries in the mid-20th century.

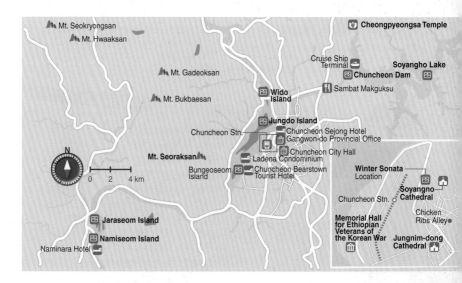

Namiseom Island (left), Namiseom Zip Wire

Namiseom Island 남이섬

The most famous of Chuncheon's islands is Namiseom, located about 30 minutes southwest of downtown Chuncheon. Namiseom is a scenic island of tree-lined walking paths that are especially beautiful when the snow falls in winter. One redwood-lined path is particularly famous as a film set in the popular Korean mini-series *Winter Sonata* (see below).

The natural surroundings here are absolutely beautiful, and much effort has been put into preserving the island's environment—you'll find no telephone polls, for instance. Namiseom is also home to one of the region's nicer places to stay, the beautiful Naminara Hotel (see p232).

 To reach Namiseom, it's best to get off the train at Gapyeong Station and taxi it to the ferry pier—there are frequent ferries from 7:30 am to 9:40 pm.

 TIPS

NAMISEOM ZIP WIRE

If ferries aren't your thing, there's another way to get to Namiseom—by air! Near the ferry dock you'll notice a high metal tower. This is the tower for the Namiseom Zip Wire which uses pulleys suspended on an inclined cable to transport you across the river to the island using gravity. It's an exhilarating experience—the ride begins at 80 m high, and brings you 940 m across the river at speeds of 60–80 km per hour (1–1.5 min).

You can also take the Zip Wire to nearby Jaraseom Island, the venue for autumn's Jaraseom International Jazz Festival. Admission is 38,000 won (includes Namiseom entrance and boat fare back).

History and Culture

WINTER SONATA

Chuncheon has become something of a pilgrimage site for fans of the Korean TV mini-series *Winter Sonata*, which set Asia—Japan in particular—ablaze after it debuted in 2002. Throughout Chuncheon, you'll find signs and banners—usually in Japanese—marking the various locations that appeared in the drama. These include the lakeside area, Myeong-dong alley and, most prominently, Namiseom Island, where there's an actual statue of the show's two stars, Bae Yong-joon and Choi Ji-woo.

Jungdo Island 중도

Most people come to Chuncheon for the lakeside scenery. Jungdo Island---actually, three islands---is a pleasant resort area within easy reach of downtown. The islands are home to grass fields, walking and biking paths, camp grounds (1,500 won a night), picnic areas, a pool and other leisure facilities. Bike and electric bike rentals available. There are some wood cabins available for rent, too, at 55,000 won a night (peak season).

5,300 won (1,300 entry, plus 4,000 ferry charge). Take a cab from Chuncheon Station to the ferry dock near Hotel Bears.

War Memorials

Because of its strategic location, Chuncheon is known as something of a military town. Several large Korean bases ring the area, and, until recently, there was also a sizable US military base in the city across from Chuncheon Station.

Along Uiamho Lake 의암호 you'll find Peace Park 평화공원, a memorial to the Battle of Chuncheon, fought at the very opening of the Korean War on June 25, 1950. In the battle, South Korean defenders badly mauled a superior North Korean force,

Memorial Hall for Ethiopian Veterans

holding the invaders at bay and buying the South Korean army valuable time.

One of the more intriguing war memorials in Korea can be found along Gongjicheon Stream 공지천. A large hall built in the shape of three African huts marks the Memorial Hall for Ethiopian Veterans of the Korean War 에티오피아한국전참전기념관, built to honor the Ethiopian troops who were sent to Korea in 1951 as part of the Kagnew Battalion.

Jungnim-dong Cathedral 죽림동 성당

A simple but beautiful stone church completed in 1952, Jungnim-dong Cathedral is the work of Irish Catholic missionaries who served in this region of Korea. In back of the church is a small

Jungnim-dong Cathedral, built by Irish missionaries around the time of the Korean War.

cemetery that includes the graves of Irish missionaries martyred by invading North Korean troops in the early days of the Korean War.

Nearby is architecturally interesting Soyangno Catholic Church 소양로성당, also designed by Irish missionaries as a memorial church for one of the martyred Irish priests. Both churches have been registered as national cultural properties.

Soyangho Lake 소양호
& Cheongpyeongsa Temple 청평사

A short bus ride (or 10,000 won taxi drive) to the northeast will take you to Soyangho Lake, a massive reservoir that actually serves as a transport conduit in the mountainous Korean interior. Because of its size, the lake is often referred to as an "inland sea."

The lake is the creation of the Soyang Dam 소양댐, the largest rock-filled dam in Asia. Built in 1973, the dam is an impressive sight and the ride to the top—along a winding road that runs up the side of a scenic gorge—is breathtaking. The dam's massive sluice gates look like they'd put on quite a show if opened, but don't count on

Cheongpyeongsa Temple

it happening during your visit—the gates have been opened only seven times since the dam was built. The dam is surrounded by numerous restaurants and a café with views of the lake. A wintertime specialty is icefish tempura—grab a bag for 10,000 won.

If you're so inclined, you can take a boat from the dam to the town of Yanggu 양구 in the heart of Gangwon-do. When water levels permit, you can even travel by lake all the way to Inje 인제 and the spectacular Seoraksan National Park 설악산국립공원 (see p239)—the trip takes about three hours.

If you don't have the time or you're looking for something more relaxing, take

Uiamho Lake

the 10 minute boat ride to Cheongpyeongsa Temple—a roundtrip ticket is only 5,000 won. Cheongpyeongsa Temple is one of Chuncheon's most famous tourist attractions. While it's not one of Korea's biggest temples nor is it particularly architecturally significant, it *is* quite remote, requiring a boat ride and a 4 km walk to reach. In winter, be sure to bundle up because it can get quite cold. The path to the temple follows a mountain stream with a beautiful waterfall.

The front gate of the temple is registered as Treasure No. 164. Isolated high in the mountains of this remote part of Korea, you really do feel as if you've entered a new world. Have 1,000 won handy to pay the entrance fee. If you're feeling hungry, there are several restaurants along the path to the temple.

THE TRAIN TO CHUNCHEON

History and Culture

Until December 2010, most people got to Chuncheon from Seoul by train. This used to be one of Korea's most romantic train treks—the train would chug along the Bukhangang River amidst splendid mountain scenery. In the early morning hours, the river and reservoirs (resulting from large dams) are shrouded in fog—a beautiful sight it was.

In December 2010, the existing train line was replaced by a rapid transit line that essentially integrated Chuncheon into Seoul's subway line. This has greatly facilitated travel to Chuncheon by cutting down time and expense, but for those who remember the old train, the trip has lost a touch of romance. The scenery out the window is still beautiful, though, even if it passes by at a faster pace.

On the way to Chuncheon you'll stop in a couple of small Korean resort towns including Gapyeong 가평, Cheongpyeong 청평 and Gangchon 강촌. In the summer months, these towns bristle with tourists and students who flock here to enjoy water sports. In winter, people come to take in the scenery and enjoy a cup of coffee at one of the many picturesque cafés.

If you're not on a schedule—and here, you shouldn't be—it is worth getting off the train at one of these stops to have a drink, perhaps eat lunch and walk around a bit before continuing your journey to Chuncheon (either by train or bus). Britons, Canadians, Australians and New Zealanders with a taste for history will probably want to stop at Gapyeong, the site of the Battle of Gapyeong in April, 1951 between Commonwealth forces and the Chinese. Monuments to these brave troops can be found here.

CHICKEN RIBS ALLEY

In the center of downtown Chuncheon not far from Chuncheon City Hall 춘천시청 is Myeong-dong 명동, a shopping street that resembles its more famous Seoul cousin, albeit smaller and less crowded. On a weekend, you'll find tons of young people—both tourists and locals—strolling around, doing a bit of window shopping and people watching.

The food highlight of Myeong-dong is Dak Galbi Alley 닭갈비골목. For many, in fact, this is the highlight of coming to Chuncheon. Located in the alley are some 20 restaurants specializing in one of Chuncheon's most famous contributions to Korean cuisine—Chuncheon *dak galbi* 춘천 닭갈비 or Chuncheon-style chicken ribs. You'll find restaurants serving this dish all over Korea but nowhere will you find it as authentic—or as tasty—as you'll find it here.

To make Chuncheon *dak galbi*, seasoned boneless chicken, vegetables, noodles, sweet potato, rice cakes and other ingredients are pan-fried in a large steel pan at your table. While you watch the food cook, you can talk with your friends over a shot of Korean liquor, *soju*. If you like spicy dishes, this is one dish you'll adore. After you've finished the chicken, mix the remaining sauce and vegetables and fry them up with rice. A meal of Chuncheon *dak galbi* is a great way to spend an evening and is bound to leave you feeling warm—and quite full. A note, though—be sure to bring along at least one friend because the dish isn't served in solo portions.

Chuncheon's other specialty is *makguksu*, a buckwheat noodle dish served cold. For this dish, try Saembat Makguksu 샘밭막국수 (033-242-1702), one of Chuncheon's best-known eateries.

As a popular tourist destination, Chuncheon has a wide range of accommodations, including the relatively upscale Chuncheon Sejong Hotel 세종호텔춘천 (033-252-1191), Chuncheon Hotel Bears 춘천베어스관광호텔 (033-256-2525) and Ladena Condominium 라데나콘도미니엄 (033-240-8000). There are also plenty of cheaper motels and *yeogwan* as well. The key is to book early, especially on a weekend, since rooms fill up fast.

WHERE TO STAY

One of the best places to stay in Chuncheon is the Naminara Hotel 나미나라호텔 on Namiseom. Not only is the hotel surrounded by terrific scenery; the building itself is a work of art—quite literally. The hotel's rooms—done up in a variety of themes—have been decorated with the works of noted artists, turning a night here into a cultural experience. A stay here is highly recommended but do book early! On a weekend, a night in one of the "gallery" rooms will cost 99,000 won. Give them a call at 031-580-8000 or, if you read Korean or Japanese, visit their homepage (www.namihotel.com).

Chuncheon is the eastern terminus of the Gyeongchun (Seoul–Chuncheon) commuter train line. Trains depart from Seoul's Cheongnyangni Station (1 hr). Chuncheon Station is located in the heart of Chuncheon, right on Uiamho Lake. Frequent buses to Chuncheon depart from Seoul's Dong Seoul Bus Terminal (1 hr 30 min). Chuncheon's Express and Inter-city Bus terminals are located in the southwest part of town, near Namchuncheon Station 남춘천역. This is where you'll want to go to get to other parts of Gangwon-do and beyond. As the provincial capital, Chuncheon is well connected to the rest of Gangwon-do, and makes a convenient and pleasant base for exploration.

TRANSPORT INFO

SOKCHO 속초

Not far from the border with North Korea, the East Sea fishing port of Sokcho is best known as the gateway to Seoraksan National Park, considered by many to be Korea's most spectacular mountain park. The town itself is not large (around 90,000 people), but it is an important fishing port and the constant influx of tourists gives it a surprisingly lively feel. Its dramatic location, wedged between the East Sea and Mt. Seoraksan, make this a very pleasant place to spend a day or two.

Sokcho Town

Sokcho's charms are more natural than man-made. With the East Sea in the foreground and Mt. Seoraksan 설악산 forming the backdrop, the city boasts some fine scenery. Of particular scenic interest are the town's two large lagoons, Yeongnangho Lake 영랑호 and Cheongchoho Lake 청초호, which are popular local leisure spots for jogging and walking. The later was also the primary venue for the 1999 Gangwon International Tourism Expo, and is where you'll find the landmark Expo Tower 엑스포타워 and a visually striking commemorative hall. From the top of the tower, visitors are provided panoramic views of Cheongchoho, Sokcho and Mt. Seoraksan. Don't miss it.

Along the coast, you'll find a couple of harbors used by the local fishing fleet, including Dongmyeonghang Port 동명항 and Daepohang Port 대포항. Dongmyeonghang is

Mt. Seoraksan looms over Sokcho

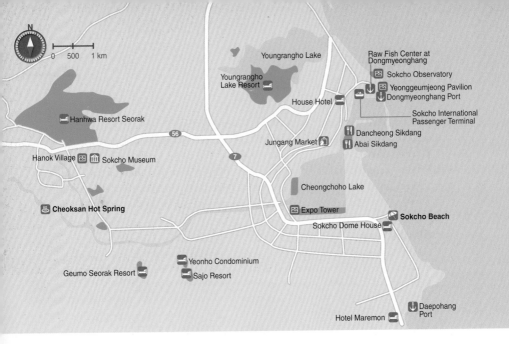

N
0   500   1 km

Youngrangho Lake

Raw Fish Center at
Dongmyeonghang

Youngrangho
Lake Resort

Sokcho Observatory

House Hotel

Yeonggeumjeong Pavilion

Dongmyeonghang Port

Sokcho International
Passenger Terminal

Hanhwa Resort Seorak

Dancheong Sikdang

Jungang Market

Abai Sikdang

Hanok Village   Sokcho Museum

Cheongchoho Lake

Cheoksan Hot Spring

Expo Tower

Sokcho Beach

Sokcho Dome House

Yeonho Condominium

Geumo Seorak Resort

Sajo Resort

Hotel Maremon

Daepohang
Port

also where to go for the best sunrises in town—look for the Yeonggeumjeong Pavilion 영금정, two Korean-style pavilions atop a hillock overlooking the sea and on a wave-beaten rock in the sea itself (the latter attached to land via a pedestrian suspension

Expo Tower

TIPS

EXPO CRUISE TOUR

From the Expo venue on Cheongchoho Lake, you can take round-trip sightseeing cruises to some nearby coastal scenic spots. Round-trip trips between Sokcho and Naksan take 90 minutes and cost 16,800 won. These cruises are a pleasant way to take in the spectacular local scenery.

bridge). There's also a walking path connecting the pavilions to a nearby disused lighthouse that now serves as an observatory. Again, the views back over the city and the mountains are breathtaking.

Abai Village 아바이마을

One particular neighborhood of note is Abai Village, located on a strip of land between Cheongchoho Lake and the East Sea. The fishing village was founded after the Korean War by villagers who had fled their homes in North Korea's Hamgyeong-do region; most residents are either the

Yeonggeumjeong Pavilions

original founders or their descendants. The village's name, Abai, means "father" in the dialect of Korean spoken in Hamgyeong-do, and is a reference to both the origins of the community and the large number of elderly who call it home. The neighborhood looks like it stepped straight out of a 70s Korean TV drama (in fact, it was actually used as the set of a popular 2000 drama, *Autumn in My Heart*), which lends it much of its charm. A symbol of the village is the hand-pulled ferry that connects the village with downtown Sokcho: once the main means of transport in and out of the village prior to days before roads were built, you'll now find it often loaded with tourists. To many Koreans, Abai Village is most famous for its tasty sausages, Abai *sundae*.

Sokcho Beach 속초 해수욕장

Sokcho Beach is a 2 km long strip of white sand (of which only 450 m are open to the public) backed by craggy pine trees. It's not quite as popular as Gyeongpodae (see p261), Haeundae (see p592) or Daecheon (see p379), but it still gets quite crowded during the summer months. A popular nighttime activity is to come here and light

fireworks—many of the convenience shops around the beach sell them.

Cheoksan Hot Spring 척산온천

In the western part of town is the Cheoksan Hot Spring District, a collection of spas and resort hotels with natural mineral rich spring water drawn from 500 m underground. The waters are said to be good for stress, neuralgia, arthritis and geriatric diseases. See "Where to Stay" on p237 more information.

TIPS

SOKCHO'S LOCAL CUISINE

Being a fishing port, you'll be tripping over fresh seafood restaurants. Indeed, next to Mt. Seoraksan, raw fish is probably Sokcho's biggest tourist draw. The bustling Jungang Market 중앙시장, the waterfront restaurants of Daepohang 대포항 and the Raw Fish Center at Dongmyeonghang 동명항활어직판장 are good places to score raw fish—a plate of *modeum-hoe* 모듬회 (a plate of mixed raw fish) will run you about 80,000–100,000 won. After your meal you can ask for the fish bones and any leftovers to be boiled up in a spicy soup called *maeuntang* 매운탕 for 20,000–25,000 won. Accompany your meal with a bottle of *soju* 소주 or *cheongju* 청주 (a clear rice wine not unlike *sake*, the most popular commercial brand of which being Cheong Ha 청하). Although not always a perfect indicator of quality, it's a good idea to look for the busiest places—there's got to be a reason everyone's flocking there, right?

Another local specialty—and one blissfully not fish-related—is *dak gangjeong* 닭강정, fried chicken coated in a sweet and spicy sauce. Manseok Dakgangjeong 만석닭강정 (033-632-4084) inside Jungang Market is the place to go for these, as evidenced by the long line-ups in front of the joint. A box will cost you 15,000 won.

Finally, no discussion of Sokcho's food scene would be complete without mention of *sundae* 순대, steamed Korean blood sausage typically stuffed with noodles, vegetables and bean curd. Abai Village is known for its own particular variety of *sundae*, Abai *sundae*, which uses as the sausage wrapper the thicker large intestine of the pig rather than the thinner, more commonly used small intestine, a recipe residents brought with them from North Korea. Dipped in a sauce of salted shrimp before eating and served with a side of kimchi, it makes for a good, hearty meal. Give

Abai Sikdang 아바이식당 (033-635-5310) or Dancheong Sikdang 단청식당 (033-632-7828) a try—a plate will cost 10,000–30,000 won, depending on size. These places also do a variation on the *sundae* theme called *ojingeo sundae* 오징어순대—gutted squid stuffed with noodles and vegetables, steamed, sliced up and served.

Another local specialty is Hamheung-style *naengmyeon* 함흥냉면, a North Korean dish of cold buckwheat noodles topped with hot sauce and sliced fish. You can find places serving this dish in Abai Village.

At the high end, Youngrangho Resort 영랑호리조트 (033-633-0001) has a tower condo, villa-style condos and a spectacular location on the side of Lake Yeongnangho. During the peak season (Jul 16–Aug 21), rooms begin at 220,000 won a night but rates come down significantly during off-peak months. Hotel Maremons 호텔마레몬스 (033-630-7000) is a luxury hotel overlooking the sea near Daepohang; the upper floors offer panoramic views of the city and mountains. Rooms begin at 230,000 won.

In the Cheoksan Hot Spring District, the Hyundai Soo Condominium 현대수콘도미니엄 (033-635-9090) has comfortable rooms in pleasant surroundings beginning at 200,000 won a night—check out its in-house bowling alley. Nearby, Seorak Pine Resort 설악파인리조트 (033-635-5800) is another major resort hotel with an indoor/outdoor spa and rooms beginning at 120,000 won a night. The mother of all Sokcho spa resorts, however, is the Tuscan-style Hanwha Resort

Seorak Sorano 한화리조트 설악쏘라노 (033-635-7711), where rooms begin at 274,000 won a night.

Hanwha Resort Seorak Sorano

Seorak Sorano's main draw is Seorak Waterpia 설악워터피아, a spa/theme park with a variety of pools (including an artificial wave pool), baths and slides using water drawn from the Cheoksan Hot Spring—fun for whole family. Seorak Sorano also operates one of Korea's most scenic golf courses, the Seorak Plaza Country Club 설악플라자컨트리클럽, where rental fees are 160,000 won for non-members on weekends.

For budget accommodation, The House Hostel 하우스호스텔 (033-633-3477) by Sokcho Intercity Bus Terminal is very popular with backpackers for its clean, basic rooms, eclectically decorated communal lounge and friendly, English-speaking owner more than happy to give you the low-down on Sokcho's scenic spots. Rooms are 50,000 won in the peak season (Jul 2–Aug 15) and fall to 30,000 won non-peak.

One of the more unusual places to stay is Sokcho Dome House 속초돔하우스, just on the other side of the pine trees lining Sokcho Beach 속초해수욕장. This pension consists of 21 single-room domes, each with its own outside picnic table. Rooms go for 120,000 won a night (during weekends and peak season of Jul 1–Aug 31).

There are many accommodation options in front of Seoraksan National Park, at Osaek Hot Springs 오색온천 and on Mt. Seoraksan itself. See the "Seoraksan National Park" section for more information.

From Seoul, buses to Sokcho depart from Dong Seoul Terminal and Seoul Express Bus Terminal (3 hrs 10 min). From Busan, it's a six hour trip. From Gangneung, it's just an hour trip. Be advised that Sokcho has two bus terminals, an Express Bus Terminal (with buses to Seoul and Incheon) just south of Cheongchoho Lake and an Inter-city Bus Terminal (with buses everywhere else) downtown, not far from Dongmyeonghang.

The magnificent granite spine of Mt. Seoraksan's Ulsanbawi ridge

SEORAKSAN NATIONAL PARK 설악산국립공원

Spread some 398 km² over three counties, Seoraksan National Park is Korea's most spectacular mountain park. Not terribly far from North Korea's famous Geumgangsan Mountains, which Koreans have lauded for their beauty for centuries, Mt. Seoraksan 설악산 ("Snow Crag Mountain") is a land of high granite peaks sculpted by the elements into spectacular shapes, overlooking the white capped expanses of the East Sea. Imagine the mythical landscapes of ancient Korean and Chinese watercolor paintings and you'll have a good idea of what awaits you. It's enchanting any time of year but especially so in autumn when the hillsides are ablaze in hues of red and gold, and winter when the park becomes a glistening, snow-covered wonderland. Home to 2,000 animal species, including the endangered Amur goral, and 1,400 rare plant species, the park was designated a UNESCO Biosphere Reserve in 1982.

Seoraksan National Park can be divided into three sectors. Outer Seorak 외설악 (or Oeseorak) is the region of the park closest to the sea and is the most frequently visited part. The western part of the park is called Inner Seorak 내 설악 (or Naeseorak), and is further subdivided into North Inner Seorak and South Inner Seorak. Inner Seorak is more remote, less touristed, and more natural. The park contains several peaks over 1,200 m, including Daecheongbong Peak 대청봉 (1,708 m), Korea's third highest.

In addition to its natural splendor, the park is also home to two major Buddhist temples, Sinheungsa 신흥사 and Baekdamsa 백담사.

 There is a 2,500 won entrance fee to the national park.

TIPS

SINGLE VS MULTI-DAY HIKES

Seoraksan National Park lends itself to both single and multi-day hikes. Its trails are extensive and well-maintained, and there are mountain huts strategically placed throughout the park. If planning a multi-day hike, however, it's strongly recommended that you pick up a map of the park from one of the information centers (usually located at the start of the trails).

Be warned that the mountain huts operate on a first-come, first-served basis and during the peak autumn season they can fill up quick. If you're planning to stay at Jungcheong Shelter 중청대피소, right below Daecheongbong Peak, make a reservation at 033-672-1708.

SEORAKSAN SUNRISE

The sunrise from Daecheongbong Peak is truly awe-inspiring—the sun rising over the East Sea, the clouds caught in the valleys and craggy peaks below. To do this, you'll probably need to spend the night at one of the mountain huts near the peak, preferably Jungcheong Shelter.

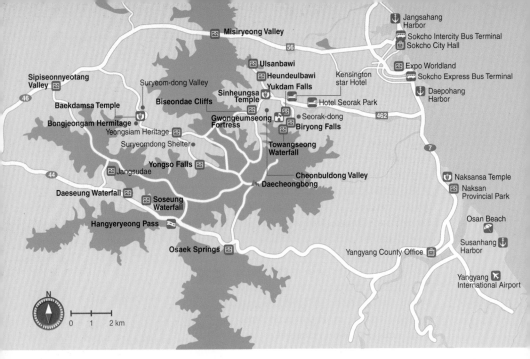

Outer Seorak 외설악

With easy access from Sokcho, Outer Seorak is the most visited part of Seoraksan National Park. It's also where most of the really spectacular peaks are located. If you're not athletically inclined, the easiest way to enjoy the park is to take the cable car (fare: 9,000 won, round trip) that connects Seorak-dong 설악동 (the tourist village in front of the park entrance) and Gwongeumseong Fortress 권금성, a Goryeo-

era fortification atop a 1,200 m high peak. The 1.5 km cable car ride takes 30 minutes, and from the top it's another 20 minute hike to the fortress. The views from the fortress over the rest of the range, as well as Sokcho and the East Sea, are pretty dramatic.

Another popular and relatively easy course is to follow the path from Seorak-dong to the Biryong ("Flying Dragon") Falls 비룡폭포. This takes you past some of the park's most picturesque waterfalls, including the six-tiered Yukdam ("Six Pools") Falls 육담폭포 and, finally, Biryong Falls which is especially pretty in autumn. The 2.4 km hike takes about two hours. There is also a very difficult, somewhat hazardous path from there that leads to the towering Towangseong Falls 토왕성폭포, a three-tiered waterfall cascading some 320 m from the cliffs above, but due to its dangerous nature it is closed to the public, save for one day a year in winter when the park hosts its annual ice climbing event.

Towangseong Falls (left), Cheonbuldong Valley

A slightly harder but more rewarding hike takes you from Seorak-dong to Biseondae Cliffs 비선대 via the Cheonbuldong Valley 천불동계곡, the main valley of the park, aptly named for the many craggy peaks and cliffs that flank it and are said to resemble 1,000 statues of the Buddha. In autumn, the dramatic white cliffs, red and gold forests and cobalt sky do make for some impressive visuals. The cliffs of Biseondae ("Flying Fairy Cliff") are so named because they bring to mind Taoist fairies flying to the heavens; Western visitors may liken it to face of a great cathedral. The 3.6 km hike to Biseondae takes about two hours. From there, it may be possible to continue hiking the long path to the park's highest peak, Daecheongbong 대청봉, but park authorities sometimes shut this route down to prevent forest fires. At any rate, for beginning hikers the easiest route to Daecheongbong begins at the Hangyeryeong Pass 한계령 (reached by bus from Sokcho via a spectacularly windy mountain road)—the hike from the pass to Daecheongbong and down again via the Cheonbuldong Valley will take you about 12 hours.

Finally, there's the path to Ulsanbawi 울산 바위, a magnificent, 4 km long granite spine. The views from the top are jaw-dropping

Sunrise from Daecheongbong Peak

Buddha, Sinheungsa Temple (left), Stone cairns in the Baekdam Valley

but the final section of the 3.8 km hike is not for the faint of heart—you must ascend a steel staircase screwed into the sheer granite cliffs. If you suffer from vertigo, you may wish to consider a different hike. Along the way, you'll pass Gyejoam Hermitage 계조암 and, just in front of it, Heundeulbawi 흔들바위 ("Shaking Rock"), a 5 m high bolder balanced seemingly precariously on another large rock. With a bit of effort you can rock it a bit, but if you're thinking of rolling it off the mountain, good luck—millions have tried before you and failed. Makes a nice photo, though.

Sinheungsa Temple 신흥사

Sinheungsa Temple is the primary temple of Outer Seorak, and is a short walk from the Seorak-dong entrance of the park. Founded in AD 652, the temple occupies a lovely location at the head of the main valley up Seoraksan. It's home to a number of historically important properties including a three-story stone pagoda (Treasure No. 443) from the Unified Silla Era (668–935) and a main hall dating from the 17th century. Be sure to check out the temple's stupa garden where the stone monuments of the temple's greatest monks are gathered.

The most eye-catching part of the temple is the 14.6 m tall bronze statue of a sitting Buddha completed in 1997 after a decade

of fundraising. Erected as a prayer for national reunification, the statue houses three pieces of the remains of the cremated Buddha that were donated by the government of Myanmar.

🚌 Bus No. 7 or 7-1 from downtown Sokcho goes to Seorak-dong, the tourist village in front of the park entrance (30 min).

Inner Seorak 내설악

If Outer Seorak is defined by its jagged, wind-carved peaks and granite cliffs, then Inner Seorak is defined by its beautiful natural valleys, relatively untouched by man. Inner Seorak is itself divided into two zones, a northern one centered on Baekdamsa Temple and some of the other northern valleys, and a southern one, focused on the Osaek Springs 오색약수터.

The most popular hike in this part of the park is the 7 km walk from the Baekdam Information Center 백담탐방지원센터 to Baekdamsa Temple through the Baekdam ("100 Pools") Valley 백담계곡. The walk is a bit long (one and a half to two hours), but pretty easy, and the surrounding mountain scenery is gorgeous. If you're not inspired to walk or pressed for time, there's a shuttle bus to the temple, too. From Baekdamsa Temple, it's another 4.7 km hike through the scenic Suryeom-dong Valley 수렴동계곡 to Suryeom-dong Shelter 수렴동대피소, passing Yeongsiam Hermitage 영시암 along the way. At Suryeong-dong Shelter, you have a

Formerly a small hermitage, Baekdamsa is now a large temple and the gateway to Inner Seorak.

decision to make—return the way you came, or press ahead and hike the 6 km trail (about three hours) to Bongjeongam Hermitage 봉정암 through the Gugokdam Valley 구곡담계곡, one of most magnificent stretches of trail in the entire park. In autumn, the colors here are mind-blowing and the path passes along a series of beautiful waterfalls and pools. From Bongjeongam Hermitage, it's another roughly two hour hike to Daecheongbong Peak, the highest peak in the park, but unless you set out really early, this would probably make it a two-day hike. Fortunately, there are two well-appointed mountain huts near the peak, Daecheong Shelter 대청대피소 (sleeps 120, 5,000 won a night, 1,000 won for blanket rentals), which is about 50 minutes away from the peak on the path from Bongjeongam, and Jungcheong Shelter 중청대피소 (sleeps 120, 8,000 won a night), which is right under the peak itself. From Daecheongbong, you could head back down to Baekdamsa or descend through Outer Seorak via the Cheonbuldong Valley.

Baekdamsa Temple 백담사

Founded in AD 647, Baekdamsa Temple was once a small temple hidden deep in this valley of Inner Seorak. Today, however, it is a fairly large one, largely thanks to former Korean president Chun Doo-hwan, who lived here for nearly three years after stepping down from power in 1988. Chun, a general who came to power in a military coup in 1979, came here to pay penance for his misdeeds, not the least of which being his brutal crackdown on pro-democracy demonstrators in the city of Gwangju in May of 1980 (see p443).

The temple's other famous guest—of whom it is most proud—was the early 20th century Buddhist poet, social reformer and independence activist Han Yong-un, who was ordained here in 1905. While you're here, be sure to see the temple's beautiful 18th century wooden Buddha statue.

From Sokcho Intercity Bus Terminal, take a bus headed for Wontong 원통 and get off at Yongdae-ri 용대리 (30 min). From there, it's a 1 km walk to the park entrance.

Daeseung Waterfall

Daeseung Falls 대승폭포
& Jangsudae 장수대

Another scenic point worth checking out in Inner Seorak is Daeseung Falls, one of Korea's three most famous waterfalls (the other two being in North Korea). The stream here cascades 88 m down a granite cliff; an observation platform has been built for better viewing. The waterfall is said to have been a favorite resting spot of King Gyeongsun (r. 927–935), the last king of the Silla Kingdom.

The path to the waterfall begins at Jangsudae 장수대, a Korean *hanok*-style mountain villa built by a Korean Army general in 1959 to commemorate the soldiers who perished in the brutal fighting that took place in these mountains during the Korean War. In the past, hikers could spend the night here, but no longer. There's a rest stop for on supplies nearby, too.

If you so choose, continue hiking from Daeseung Falls to Daeseungnyeong Pass 대승령 (1,210 m), and from there down the colorfully named Sibiseonnyeotang ("12 Nymph Bathing Pools") Valley 십이선녀탕계곡, with its picturesque waterfalls and pools.

From Sokcho Intercity Bus Terminal, take the bus to Wontong (via Hangyeryeong 한계령) and get off at Jangsudae (1 hr 10 min). If you descend via the Sibiseonnyeotang Valley, take the bus back to Sokcho from the village of Namgyo-ri 남교리.

South Seorak 남설악
& Osaek Springs 오색약수터

The southern part of Inner Seorak is usually regarded as a separate entity. The center of this part of the park is Osaek ("Five Colors") Springs. "Springs" is meant in the plural—there's a hot spring and a cold spring—with the cold spring a short walk from the Osaek Ranger Station 오색분소. The refreshing mineral water that springs up from here is rich in iron, and the well itself does have an iron red color. When drunk, the water is said to help a number of conditions including stomach problems and—unsurprisingly, given the iron content—anemia. The information board also boasts that it can kill intestinal parasites and that you can drink as much as you like without getting a stomachache. The name comes from the fact that the water supposedly has "five tastes," although you might only detect the iron taste. It is a slightly fizzy taste though, like a carbonated beverage, thanks to its high level of carbonic acid.

In the nearby village of Osaek-ri 오색리, you'll find the hot springs. Here, the water pipes up at a nice 42 degrees Celsius. As you'll find at most of Korea's hot springs, the waters here are generally enjoyed in hotel bathhouses. You can use the bathhouse of the pleasantly simple Sorak Springs Motel 설악온천장 (033-672-2645) for

4,000 won or for free if you're a guest (70,000 won peak season, 30,000 won non-peak). A bit more upscale is Osaek Green Yard Hotel 오색그린야드호텔 (033-670-1000), which tries—not entirely unsuccessfully—to emulate a Swiss chalet. Rooms begin at 120,000 won during the peak season. You can use the hotel bathhouse for 9,000 won (5,000 won for hotel guests). Oddly enough, the hotel also has a collection of Aztec and Mayan art on permanent exhibition.

From Sokcho Intercity Bus Terminal, take a bus for Osaek Oncheon 오색온천 (40 min).

WHAT TO EAT

You'll find plenty of restaurants, especially in Seorak-dong but also at Osaek-ri. If you're visiting the Osaek Hot Springs, consider Namseorak Sikdang 남설악식당 (033-672-3159), which serves a *dolsotbap jeongsik* 돌솥밥정식 (rice steamed in a stone pot with soup and plenty of side dishes) and rice boiled with water from the Osaek Spring.

WHERE TO STAY

If you're not staying in Sokcho, the Osaek Hot Springs or on the mountain itself, there are plenty of places to stay in Seorak-dong, the gateway to Outer Seorak.

The most upscale place here is the Kensington Stars Hotel 켄싱턴스타호텔 (033 635-4001), an English-themed hotel with surreally English décor. It's a bit kitsch but still rather pleasant. Rooms begin at 169,000 won but if you're independently wealthy, for 2,200,000 won a night, you can stay in the Presidential Suite which was built for the exclusive use of late Korean president Park Chung-hee—the views of Seoraksan through its 12-layer bulletproof glass are astounding.

Seoraksan Tourist Hotel 설악산관광호텔 (033-636-7101, rooms begin at 65,000 won) and Hotel Sorak Park 설악파크호텔 (033-636-7711, rooms begin at 99,000 won a night) offer decent tourist hotel-style accommodations. There are some good budget options such as Arirang Resortel 아리랑리조텔 (033-636-6628), where rooms begin at 60,000 won on peak weekends, and Seorak Morning 설악의 아침 (033-632-6677), with clean, Western-style rooms for 50,000 won peak season.

TRANSPORT INFO

From Sokcho Intercity Bus Terminal, take a bus for Osaek Oncheon 오색온천 (40 min).

Kesington Stars Hotel

NAKSAN PROVINCIAL PARK 낙산도립공원

Located just up the coast from Gangneung, Naksan Provincial Park is a 24 km strip of coastline highlighted by several popular beaches. The largest of these beaches is Naksan Beach 낙산해수욕장, a 1.8 km stretch of white sand that is extremely popular with families in summer thanks to its shallow water, which lends itself to wading and swimming. But the smaller Hajodae Beach 하조대해수욕장 might be the most scenic—also white and sandy, yet backed by a granite cliff from which a gnarled old pine emerges. Some of the best sunrises in Korea can also be viewed from the top of this cliff.

Beautiful rocky coastline of Naksan Provincial Park

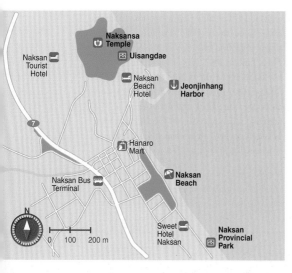

Naksansa Temple

Naksan Tourist Hotel

Uisangdae

Naksan Beach Hotel

Jeonjinhang Harbor

7

Hanaro Mart

Naksan Bus Terminal

Naksan Beach

N

0 100 200 m

Sweet Hotel Naksan

Naksan Provincial Park

Naksansa Temple 낙산사

One of the most famed sites of Naksan Provincial Park is the seaside Buddhist temple of Naksansa. Only a handful of Korean Buddhist temples overlook the sea, and this is one of the best known.

Naksansa was founded in 671 by the renowned Silla monk Uisang, one of brightest minds ever produced by Korean Buddhism and a prolific founder of temples. Having just returned from Tang Dynasty China, where like many scholar monks he'd gone for advanced study, Uisang had come to the area upon hearing that Avalokitesvara, the Bodhisattva of Mercy, lived in a cave near the beach. The master spent 14 days praying in the cave before Avalokitesvara finally appeared. She told the monk to build a temple above the cave, which he did, dedicating it to the bodhisattva.

Despite the beauty of the location, the temple has had something of a traumatic history; it has been destroyed several times due to both natural and manmade causes. The temple was completely destroyed in the Korean War and rebuilt in 1953. Sadly, a massive forest fire in April 2005 destroyed it again. Almost all of what is seen today is a post-fire reconstruction.

A couple of things did survive the blaze, however. The Hongyemun 홍예문, the old stone gate at the entrance of the temple, was erected in 1467 to mark a visit that

1. Hongnyeonam Hermitage 2. Uisangdae 3. Statue of Avalokitesvara, Naksansa Temple

year by King Sejo. The old stone pagoda in the courtyard dates from the early Joseon Era—itself significant in that it shows that even under the Confucian kings of Joseon, Buddhism lived on—and is capped by a bronze finale unusual for Korea that brings to mind the Tibetan-style pagodas of Yuan Dynasty China.

In front of the temple, on a hill overlooking the sea, is a 16 m tall statue of Avalokitesvara built in 1977. If this fails to impress, a short walk from there is Uisangdae, a simple Korean pavilion atop a cliff overlooking the water. Built in 1925, the pavilion is one of the few buildings at the temple that survived the 2005 fire. Uisang used to sit here and meditate: one look from the spot at the dramatic scenery, and you'll understand why. The sunrises here are profoundly inspiring; so much so that in tribute, Uisang penned:

"After the pear-tree flowers have fallen and when the cuckoo cries sadly, beyond the hill east of Naksan at Uisangdae, I get up in the middle of night to see the sun rise. The auspicious clouds look like they are blooming, and the sun looks as if it is being held up by six dragons. As the sun rises majestically from the sea to the sky, the whole world shakes and the sun rises swiftly, shining more brightly than a thousand candles."

- Uisang

A short walk along the bluff overlooking the water will bring you to Hongnyeonam 홍련암 or "Red Lotus Hermitage," a small hermitage built atop a cave overlooking the waves. The hermitage is so named as legend has it that as Uisang was meditating near here, a red lotus flower blossomed in the sea. It's not especially ornate, but its location overlooking the sea is exhilarating.

WHAT TO EAT

A little north of Naksansa, you'll find the uniquely designed Seorakyeok 설악역 (033-671-7896), a wooden café/French restaurant famous for its lobster dishes. A large, butter-grilled lobster will run you 59,000 won. Several kilometers up the coast from Naksansa is the fishing port of Daepohang 대포항. This is a favorite destination for fans of raw fish, and the place is awash with *hoetjip* (raw fish restaurants). Just look for the ones with lots of people—you can't go wrong.

WHERE TO STAY

The swankiest place on the beach is the Daemyung Sol Beach Hotel and Resort 대명쏠비치리조트 (033-670-3502, www.solbeachlahotel.com), where rooms have their own private spas and terraces with whirlpool baths. This kind of luxury goes for 500,000 won a night.

The appropriately named Naksan Beach Hotel 낙산비치호텔 (033-672-4000) is a pleasant place on a hillside overlooking the sea right next to Naksansa Temple. Rooms start at 130,000 won a night; rooms seaside offer great views of the sunrise. There's a seawater sauna, too. A couple of kilometers up the beach north of Naksansa is the Condotel Hillhouse 힐하우스 (033-671-2883). The views of the sea, especially from the upper floors, are fantastic, and rooms have cooking facilities. Breakfast is provided, too. Rooms with a sea view begin at 44,000 won a night but during the peak season the price climbs to 120,000 won. Along Naksan Beach you'll also find a number of pensions. During the high season, these places can go for more than 150,000 won a night.

TRANSPORT INFO

Express buses to the town of Yangyang depart from Seoul's Dong Seoul Terminal and Express Bus Terminals (2 hrs 55 min). From Yangyang Bus Terminal 양양버스터미널, take bus No. 9 or No. 9-1 to Naksansa Temple (10–15 min). Taxi is also an option—the trip takes just 10 minutes.

ODAESAN NATIONAL PARK 오대산국립공원

Located in the heart of Korea's mountainous spine just west of Gangneung, Odaesan National Park is one of Gangwon-do's several glorious mountain parks. At 1,563 m, Mt. Odaesan ("Five Peak Mountain") is a big mountain by Korean standards, with several peaks over 1,000 m in height. The park doesn't see quite as many visitors as Mt. Seoraksan to the north but is a remarkably beautiful place all the same, especially in autumn when the mountain's pristine forests—Korea's largest—turn color. In addition to the peak itself, Sogeumgang Valley in the eastern part of the park is a place of remarkable scenic beauty, eulogized by no less a figure than the great 16th century Joseon scholar Yi I (better known by his pen name of Yulgok), who likened the landscape to a smaller version of the famously beautiful Geumgangsan Mountains, now part of North Korea.

In addition to its natural splendor, the park is home to two major Buddhist temples, Woljeongsa and Sangwonsa, both lovely places in their own right, and to rich collections of Korean heritage items. Sangwonsa Temple, in fact, is only one of five temples in Korea to keep remains of the Sakyamuni Buddha, making it, and Mt. Odaesan itself, a holy site.

Sogeumgang Valley, one of the most lovely stretches of nature in Korea

Hiking Mt. Odaesan

Mt. Odaesan is a largely rounded peak—its hiking trails, while long, are not especially steep or treacherous. The most popular route takes hikers along a gentle 7 km course (hiking time: 3 hours, 10 minutes) from Sangwonsa Temple to the highest peak, Birobong 비로봉 (1,563 m), in the western part of the park. When the weather is good, the views from the top are outstanding—it seems the ridge lines of the surrounding mountains go on forever and to the east lie striking views of the East Sea.

Another very popular hike takes you up the Sogeumgang Valley 소금강계곡 to Noinbong Peak 노인봉 (1,338 m). This is a pretty long slog at 13.3 km (hiking time: 7 or 8 hours), but the scenery, especially along the valley, makes it worth the effort. The valley, actually a gorge, follows a crisp, cool mountain stream that cascades from somewhere near Noinbong. The hiker is surrounded by lush forests, and along the way passes enchanting natural pools, fantastic rock formations and a series of nine waterfalls called the Guryong ("Nine Dragon") Falls 구룡폭포. So eye-catching is it

Sogeum Falls

that, in 1970, the Korean government designated it National Scenic Spot No. 1. Once you've reached the top, come down the same way you came or take the 4 km hike along a relatively gentle path to the Jingogae Pass 진고개, where there's a road and rest stop (from which you can take a taxi to nearby Jinbu-myeon 진부면 and, from

there, buses to Seoul and other local towns).

There is a large mountain hut near Noinbong Peak. If you're game and there's room (the hut sleeps 30 on a first-come, first-served basis), you can sleep here; it is a good place to watch the sunset or good rest spot if you're hiking the Baekdu Daegan Trail.

The Birobong Trail begins at Sangwonsa Temple. The Sogeumgang Valley trail, on the other hand, begins at Sogeumgang Information Center, which is reached via Bus No. 303 from Gangneung Station (1 hr).

Woljeongsa Temple 월정사

Hidden away in the forests south of the main peaks of Mt. Odaesan, the Buddhist temple of Woljeongsa was founded in 642 by the great Silla monk Jajang, who founded a number of important temples around the country (most notably Tongdosa Temple 통도사 near Busan, one of Korea's largest monasteries). History has been rough to the temple, which has suffered numerous calamities, most notably

during the Korean War when it was burned down by the South Korean army to prevent the communists from claiming it, a tragedy inflicted on many historic temples during the war.

Fortunately, not everything old was destroyed. The temple's pride and joy is its splendid nine-story stone pagoda from the 10th century, which stands in the main courtyard. Standing 15.2 m high, the beautifully preserved monument is considered a masterpiece of Goryeo religious art. Also quite intriguing is the very unusual stone statue of a bodhisattva, kneeling on one knee and seemingly making an offering to an unknown recipient. The one in the courtyard is a replica; the original, carved in the 11th century, can be found in the temple museum, which houses a number of other pieces of valuable Buddhist art, both from Woljeongsa and other temples.

Woljeongsa Temple and its stunning 10th century pagoda, a masterpiece of Goryeo Dynasty art

Stone bodhisattva, Woljeongsa Temple

⏰ **Museum**: 9:30 am to 6 pm (Apr–Oct), 9:30 am to 4:30 pm (Nov–Mar) 💳 2,500 won ✆ 033-339-6800 🚌 Take a bus from Gangneung to the town of Jinbu (50 min), and from Jinbu take a bus to Woljeongsa (15 min).

Sangwonsa Temple 상원사

Some believe Sangwonsa Temple, like Woljeongsa, was founded by the Buddhist monk Jajang in 643, although others point to a slightly later founding by the sons of the Silla king. What we do know for certain is that it was rebuilt several times, first in 705, then again in 1947 following a fire in 1946. Sangwonsa managed to avoid the fate of Woljeongsa and survived the Korean War intact, mostly on account of its head monk who refused to abandon the temple, challenging South Korean soldiers to burn it with him inside (which, thankfully, they refused to do). Its most important treasure is the splendid bronze temple bell 상원사동종 (Treasure No. 36), crafted in 725 during the Silla Kingdom. It was once quite famous for its beautiful sound, which could be heard throughout the valley; due to preservation concerns, it is no longer rung. Originally the town bell of the southeastern city of Andong

Sangwonsa Temple miraculously survived the Korean War.

Bronze bell of Sangwonsa Temple (left), Buddhist statues, Sangwonsa Temple

(see p551), it was moved to the temple in the 15th century. In the past, temple bells were prized targets of invaders and pirates; sadly, this is one of only three surviving Silla bells that remain in Korea.

In the main hall of Sangwonsa is a wooden statue of a young Manjusri, the Bodhisattva of Wisdom 목조문수보살좌상. It was carved in 1466 at the commission of the daughter of King Sejo as a prayer for a male child. It is also said to be an artistic reincarnation of the young Manjusri whom, according to legend, King Sejo of the Joseon Dynasty met during a visit to Sangwonsa.

The hike to Mt. Odaesan's Birobong Peak begins from Sangwonsa Temple. Along the way, you'll pass the architecturally unusual Saja-am Hermitage 사자암 with its bizarre roofed terraces, and Jeongmyeolbogung 적멸보궁, the "treasure palace" that holds relics of the Sakyamuni Buddha brought from China by the Ven. Jajang when he founded the temple. The building dates from the Joseon Dynasty (1392–1910) and, as it holds actual relics from the Buddha, it contains no statues. As one of only five sites in Korea where relics of the Sakyamuni Buddha reside, it is a very popular pilgrimage destination for Korean Buddhists.

🍱 2,500 won ✆ 033-332-6666 🚌 Take a bus from Gangneung to Jinbu (50 min), and from Jinbu take a bus to Sangwonsa (40 min).

WHAT TO EAT

There are plenty of restaurants in front of Woljeongsa Temple. Give Birobong Sikdang 비로봉식당 (033-332-6597) a try—it does a *bibimbap* made from mountain greens picked from Mt. Odaesan.

WHERE TO STAY

There is one upscale place to stay near Mt. Odaesan, Kensington Flora Hotel 켄싱턴플로라호텔 (033-330-5000), a luxury hotel with great views from the upper floors. As the name would suggest, there's a floral theme here with the hotel providing all sorts of floral and herbal care and treatments, including aromatherapy. Western rooms begin at 180,000 won a night. If you'd prefer somewhere simpler, there are some *minbak* (homestay) and pension facilities on the road to Woljeongsa Temple, including the charming Healthy House Happy 700 헬시해피하우스700 (033-336-8770), with walls built of yellow clay, which is said to have therapeutic effects. During the peak season, rooms that sleep four go for 120,000 won a night, but this comes down to 70,000 won in the off-season. About halfway between Woljeongsa and Sangwonsa, you'll find the Dongpigol Camp Site 동파골야영장, where you can pitch your tent for 2,000 won a person during the peak season.

Beautiful lotus pond of Seonggyojang, an impressive 18th century mansion

fffffffffff

GANGNEUNG 강릉

With a population of nearly 230,000, Gangneung is the largest city on Gangwon-do's East Sea coast, and something of a commercial center for the isolated coastal region of a province cut off from the rest of the country by the high Taebaeksan Mountain Range 태백산맥. It's got quite a bit of history, too. For centuries, its mountains and seaside charms attracted Korea's political and intellectual elite. It was also the place of birth of the 16th century scholar "Yulgok" or Yi I, one of the greatest Confucian minds of the Joseon Dynasty.

Gangneung gets quite a few visitors, especially in summer when droves of merrymakers flock here to take in the fun and sun at Gyeongpo Beach, one of Korea's most popular beaches. Also popular with visitors is Gyeongpoho Lake (actually an enclosed bay) and Gyeongpodae Pavilion, scenic spots lauded for their beautiful views of the moon. Culture and history buffs will want to stop by the Ojukheon where Yulgok was born and check out some of the town's beautiful old Korean homes and gardens, like the spectacular Seongyojang, one of the largest Korean manor houses remaining from the Joseon Dynasty. There's plenty to see around Gangneung, too, including the seaside scenic spot of Jeongdongjin 정동진 and the high grasslands of Daegwallyeong Pass 대관령.

A good time to visit is springtime when the city hosts its annual Dano Festival, an ancient shamanist rite registered on UNESCO's list of "Masterpieces of the Oral and Intangible Heritage of Humanity."

Gyeongpo Beach is a popular summer destination.

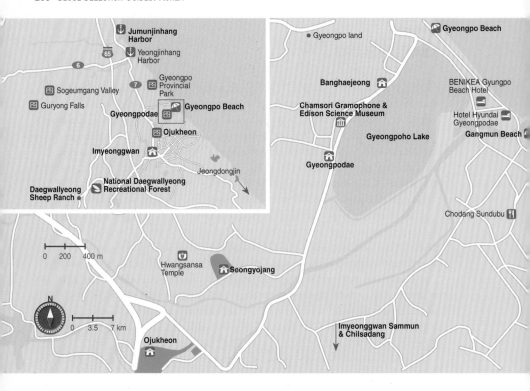

Layout

While most visitors come for the beach, most of Gangneung is located about a kilometer or so from the coast, built along the Namdaecheon Stream 남대천. There's not a whole lot to see downtown but it does have plenty of shops, motels and restaurants. There's also got the train station (pretty much smack downtown) and the main bus terminal (out on the western part of town).

In addition to Gyeongpo Beach, the entire coastline of the municipality of Gangneung is dotted with ports and harbors. Many of these are tiny but others, like Jumunjin 주문진, are quite large and home to substantial fishing fleets which, in turn, supply a thriving seafood eatery industry. There are several smaller beaches as well, the most famous being Jeongdongjin.

Imyeonggwan Sammun 임영관삼문 & Chilsadang 칠사당

One downtown site certainly worth seeing is Imyeonggwan Sammun (formerly the Gaeksamun), the front gate of what was, in Goryeo and Joseon times, a large government guest house which, in turn, was part of a much larger government complex. The simple, unpainted gate was built in 936, making it the single oldest surviving wooden structure in Korea and only one of a handful of wood buildings remaining from the Goryeo Dynasty. Unlike the gates of the later Joseon Dynasty, the brackets that support this gate are exposed, allowing the viewer to appreciate the beautiful craftsmanship.

The guest house, the Imyeonggwan 임영관,

Signboard, Imyeonggwan

was built at the same time as its gate, and
managed to survive all the way until 1929
when the Japanese colonial authorities tore it
down to make way for a school sports field
(an indication of the little regard that the
Japanese colonial regime held for Korea's
cultural heritage). In 2006, the guest house
was rebuilt in its original style. One of the
guest house buildings, Jeondaecheong 전대청,
has an old signboard penned by none other
than Goryeo's King Gongmin (r. 1351–
1374) during a royal visit to Gangneung.

Also nearby is another handsome Korean
hall, Chilsadang, the current incarnation of
which dates from a late 19th century
reconstruction. Along with Imyeonggwan
Sammun, it is pretty much all that's left of
Gangneung's old government complex.
Imyeonggwan Sammun is right in front of
the back gate of Gangneung City Hall.

Seongyojang 선교장

Out towards Gyeongpoho Lake is a large,
well-preserved manor house from the
Joseon Dynasty, called Seongyojang. Yi
Nae-beon (1703–1781), a local nobleman,
began work on the home in 1756;
subsequent generations of Yi's clan have
continued to add to it. In fact, a descendant
of Yi continues to live here, albeit in a
newly built annex off to the side from the
historic buildings.

As is typical of Korean aristocratic
residences, the complex is composed of
separate halls tied together into several
clusters by open courtyards, with separate
halls for the men and women of the house.
In the Joseon Dynasty, Gangneung was a
popular place for scholars and officials to
come to relax, and the manor—quite unlike
other private homes—has many small
rooms where visitors could stay. The most
unusual of its buildings is the Yeolhwadang
열화당, a wooden hall built in 1815 as the
men's quarters. What makes it particularly
unique is its terrace, built sometime around
the turn of the 20th century. Topped by a
Russian copper-plated roof, the terrace is
said to have been a gift from the Russian
consul, who may have stayed here on a visit.

Just in front of the main manor complex

Seongyojang was built in 1756 as the home of a local nobleman whose descendants live here to this day.

and a bit off to the side is a square lotus pond overlooked by a Korean pavilion. Built in 1916, it's an especially beautiful place in summer when the lotus blossoms bloom in a pond that also hosts a couple of pine trees right in its middle. The view of the pond and pines from inside the pavilion is sublime—the epitome of Korean traditional aesthetics. For a private residence, the pond is quite large and brings to mind the Buyongji Pond of Changdeokgung Palace.

In the old days, the Seongyojang was literally lakeside, as Gyeongpoho Lake came all the way up to the house which could thus be reached by boat. Since then, however, the lake has shrunk in size considerably, and the shore is now some distance away.

🕐 9 am to 6 pm (summer), 9 am to 5 pm (winter) 💳 3,000 won 🚌 Take Bus No. 202 from Gangneung Station (30 min) or Gangneung Express Bus Terminal (15 min). 📞 033-646-3270

Ojukheon 오죽헌

Also on the road to Gyeongpoho Lake, Ojukheon ("Black Bamboo House") is a lovingly preserved Joseon Dynasty house most famous for being the birthplace of Yi I (1536–1584), the celebrated 16th century Confucian intellectual and government official whose visage graces the front of the 5,000 won bill (along with an image of the house itself). It is just as famous as the home of Yi's mother, Lady Sin Saimdang (1504–1551), who to this day is held up as a model of Confucian motherhood.

Ojukheon, so named for the grove of black bamboo behind the home, was originally built by the Joseon official Choe Chi-un (1390–1440) some time in the early 15th century. This makes it one of the oldest surviving private residences in the country. Through marriage, the home eventually passed into the possession of the Yongin Yi clan. The home's golden age was the early 16th century when Sin and, later, her son Yi I were born here. Yi's descendants maintained

Ojukheon, home of the famed Confucian scolar Yi I

'YULGOK' YI I & SIN SAIMDANG

Yulgok Yi I

Gangneung's favorite son is Yi I (1536–1584), widely considered one of the two greatest Confucian scholars of the Joseon Dynasty (the other being his contemporary elder, Yi Hwang of Andong). He's better known by his pen name, Yulgok, or "Chestnut Valley," a name he took from the village in Paju, Gyeonggi-do where he spent his childhood.

Yi was born at the Ojukheon House in Gangneung, the son of a royal official and Sin Saimdang, an accomplished cultural figure in her own right. When he was eight, his family moved from Gangneung to his father's home in Paju, Gyeonggi-do. Under the devoted guidance of his mother, he soon proved a prodigy, mastering the Confucian classics at a young age and passing the national literary examination at the age of 13. When he was 16, however, his mother died. For three years, he tended to her grave, living just next door, and then left for a temple in the far-off Geumgangsan Mountains of northern Korea to study Buddhism. The following year, he left the temple and returned to Gangneung, where he refocused his attention on Neo-Confucianism. In this he excelled, receiving the top score in the *gwageo*—the Confucian civil service exam of the Joseon Dynasty—no fewer than nine consecutive times.

Unlike many Neo-Confucian scholars who focused on more esoteric, metaphysical topics, Yi was more concerned with practical matters. Accordingly, he was an active figure in politics, serving about 20 years in several administrative and ministerial positions, including a stint as minister of defense. He was also a reformer, arguing that the state and its systems should change with the times, lest it risk collapse. Most memorably, he called for the maintenance of a 100,000-man army to defend Korea from attack. Typically, this suggestion was ignored due to factional politics, and Korea found itself ill-prepared when Japan invaded soon after Yi's death.

Yi's mother, Sin Saimdang (1504–1551), was one of Joseon Dynasty's most accomplished women. Raised in a household without sons, Sin received an education ordinarily granted only to sons of the family. Even after her marriage, she continued her scholarly and artistic pursuits, becoming a much respected poet, painter, calligrapher and embroiderer. She focused the greatest portion of her attention, however, on educating her children, no easy task given that she had four sons and three daughters.

Even in modern times, Sin has been held up as a model of Korean womanhood, the *hyeonmo yangcheo* or "wise mother and good wife." In 2009, her visage was even put on the new 50,000 won bill. This is increasingly coming under fire from Korean feminists, however, who feel the idealization of the woman who sacrifices herself for her husband and children perpetuates patriarchal social values.

Sin Saimdang

the property until 1975, when the government took over responsibility for its upkeep. The home has three rooms, one of which is Mongnyongsil 몽룡실 ("Dragon Dream Room"), where Yi was born, so named because Sin is said to have dreamed of a dragon the day she conceived him.

Also in the complex you'll find several other structures, the most interesting of which is Eojegak 어제각, a small pavilion built in 1788 on the order of King Jeongjo, an admirer of Yi. The pavilion houses the ink well used by Yi when he was a child, as well as the preface of "Gyeokmong Yogyeol," a text Yi wrote in 1577 for students just beginning their studies.

Also on site is the Gangneung Municipal Museum 오죽헌시립박물관, which houses a good collection of local cultural properties and folklore, including drawings and other art works by Sin Saimdang.

⊕ 8 am to 6 pm (Mar–Oct), 8 am to 5:30 pm (Nov–Feb) 💵 3,000 won 🚌 Take Bus No. 202 or 303 from Gangneung Station (25 min) or Gangneung Express Bus Terminal (15 min). ☏ 033-640-4771

TIPS

GANGNEUNG DANOJE FESTIVAL 강릉단오제

Taking place on the fifth day of the fifth lunar month, Dano was one of traditional Korea's biggest holidays. Believing that celestial bodies of the universe converged on that date, Koreans regarded Dano as an especially auspicious day, when the world was most filled with *yang* (positive) energy. When Korea was an agricultural society, it was also a time— coming as it did right upon the completion of the spring planting—when farmers could, if just for a day, relax and have some fun. Women would don beautiful dresses and ride on swings, hoping to attract the gaze of eligible men, while young men would show off their strength in bouts of Korean traditional wrestling or *ssireum*. Women would wash their hair in water boiled with calamus to give it extra shine. Shaman rituals were also held, and special foods—especially rice cakes cooked with mugwort and other medicinal roots— were prepared. Fans were also gifted to one another; after all, the hot summer was approaching.

In modern times, the holiday is not as celebrated as it used to be. In Gangneung, however, the old traditions are maintained, and in grand fashion. The Gangneung Danoje Festival is a month-long celebration featuring shaman rites, parades, Korean wrestling, swing rides, Korean traditional mask dramas and, of course, food and drink. The festival begins on the fifth day of the fourth lunar month with the brewing of the so-called *sinju* or liquor of the gods, at the Chilsadang in downtown Gangneung. On the 15th day of the fourth lunar month, a shaman rite is held for the mountain god at a shrine at Daegwallyeong Pass. The festival really gets off the ground on the third day of the fifth lunar month, when a grand procession is held through downtown Gangneung to a shaman altar on Namdaecheon Stream 남대천.

A highlight of the festival is the Gwanno Mask Drama 관노가면극, a non-verbal regional folk play set to musical accompaniment rarely seen outside of Gangneung on Dano. There's a ton of other stuff going on as well, including markets, wrestling and music performances. In recognition of the importance of the Gangneung Danoje Festival, it was designated a "Masterpiece of the Oral and Intangible Heritage of Humanity" by UNESCO in 2005.

Gyeongpo Beach

Gyeongpo Beach 경포해수욕장
& Gyeongpoho Lake 경포호

The most famous of Korea's east coast beaches, Gyeongpo Beach is also one of the most crowded, at least in summer, when the place can be wall-to-wall people (or wall-to-wall beach umbrellas, as it were). Fine white sand, backed up by verdant pine forests, extends up and down the coast for about 6 km. There's plenty of motor-boating opportunities at the beach, too—just look for the boats (30,000 won for a short trip).

Also along the beach is a strip of motels and restaurants—sort of like Miami Beach, just with less Art Deco and more love motels and raw fish joints.

Right behind the beach, Gyeongpoho Lake was originally a narrow-necked bay but sand and rock carried in by the tides eventually blocked it up, creating a shallow, placid lake. Its name means "clear like a mirror," a reference to the stillness of its waters in contrast to the choppy water of the sea. Originally, the lake was a full 12 km in circumference but, thanks to silting over the years, it is now just 4 km. In the center of the lake is a small rock island with a single Korean pagoda—it seems to be a popular resting place for the birds. The lake is especially pretty in spring when the cherry trees that ring it are in full bloom.

On a hill overlooking the lake is Gyeongpodae 경포대, a handsome Korean

Gyeongpoho Lake

pavilion with a fine view of the surroundings. It is famously said that from this pavilion, you can see "five moons" simultaneously: one in the sky, one reflected in the sea, one reflected in the lake, one reflected in your wine glass and the one reflected in your lover's eyes.

🚌 Take Bus No. 202 from Gangneung Express Terminal and get off at Gyeongpo Beach. The trip takes about 20 minutes.

Chamsori Gramophone & Edison Science Museum 참소리축음기 에디슨과학박물관

Certainly one of the most unusual—and unexpected—museums in Korea, the Chamsori Gramophone & Edison Science Museum was founded in 1992 by Son Seong-mok, a collector who has spent the last half century traveling the world in search of gramophones. So far, he's managed to obtain nearly 5,000 gramophones and 150,000 phonographic albums. Along the way, he also picked up about 1,000 inventions by famed American inventor Thomas Alva Edison. Amongst the many rare and fascinating items in the collection are five of the world's six remaining first-generation tinfoil phonographs produced by Edison himself in 1877, as well as a Model T Ford and an Edison-produced electric car. Perfect for both children and adults, this place really is a must-visit.

🕐 9 am to 6 pm (summer), 9 am to 5:30 pm (winter) 🎫 7,000 won 🚌 Take Bus No. 202 from Gangneung Express Bus Terminal and get off at Gyeongpodae. The museum is right there (20 min). ☎ 033-655-1130, 🖰 www.edison.kr (KR)

No trip to Gangneung is complete without trying Chodang *sundubu* 초당순두부 (6,000 won), a culinary simplicity at its most sublime—pure white tofu in clear broth. Gangneung is famous for making its tofu with sea water, which imparts to the dish a light but delightfully salty taste. The soup is usually accompanied by *biji jjigae* 비지찌개, a rich, creamy stew made from soy pulp. If you've been looking for a break from spicy fare, you're at the right place. There's a so-called "Chodang Sundubu Village 초당순

Chodang sundubu

두부마을" located in the forested area south of the beach—here you'll find several restaurants specializing in the dish, including Wonjo Chodang Sundubu 원조초당순두부 (033-652-2660), which boasts of having been founded by the woman who invented the dish in the 30s. Bus No. 230 from Gangneung Express Bus Terminal comes to the village. If seafood is what you're after, a few kilometers up the coast from Gangneung proper is the fishing port of Jumunjin 주문진. This place is full of raw fish restaurants, including four major multi-restaurant seafood emporiums around the waterfront.

As one might expect, most of the higher-end accommodations are along Gyeongpo Beach. The best views can be had at Hotel Hyundai Gyeongpodae 호텔현대경포대 (033-651-2233), with rooms that overlook either Gyeongpo Beach or Gyeongpoho Lake. Western-style rooms begin at 140,000 won a night. Also between the lake and the beach is BENIKEA Gyungpo Beach Hotel 베니키아경포비치호텔 (033-644-6699), with rooms starting at 120,000 won. There are also plenty of other hotels and motels along the beach strip. If you don't want to pay to stay by the beach, there are reasonably priced love motel-style *yeogwan* (inns) around Gangneung Bus Terminal. If the

Sun Cruise Resort

best sunrises are what you're after, those can be found at the appropriately named Sun Cruise Resort 썬크루즈리조트 (033-610-7000, http://english.esuncruise.com) at Jeongdongjin. This is also one of the single-most unusual accommodations we'll recommend in this book—it's built in the shape of a huge cruise ship sitting atop a bluff overlooking the beach, as if sailing into the sunrise. Seen from the beach, it might be a great, gaudy blight upon the natural scenery, but from the resort itself, the views are fantastic. Rooms begin at 70,000 won per night. Also near Jeongdongjin is the beautiful Haslla Museum Hotel 하슬라뮤지엄호텔 (033-644-9414~5), which as the name suggests is part museum, part hotel. Maintained by a husband-wife team of sculptors, the hotel itself is a work of art, with terrific views to boot. If they've got a room (there are only 24) and you can part with 280,000 won a night, this is a great place to stay.

Express buses to Gangneung depart from Seoul's Dong Seoul Terminal and Gangnam Express Bus Terminal (3 hrs). Express buses to Gangneung can also be taken from Chuncheon 춘천, Wonju 원주, Donghae 동해, Sokcho 속초 and other regional cities and towns. If you'd prefer to go by rail, there are six trains daily to Gangneung from Seoul's Cheongnyangni Station 청량리역, but be warned: it's a long trip through Korea's mountainous backbone—6 hours. On the plus side, it can be a very picturesque trip, especially in winter when the train treks through the heart of Korea's snow country.

JEONGDONGJIN 정동진

Listed in the Guinness Book of World Records as the closest train station to the sea, Jeongdongjin Station 정동진역 opens up literally onto the beach. The station was established in 1962 and was an important transport hub for the local mining industry, but with the decline of mining in the early 90s it fell into almost complete disuse. In 1995, however, it appeared in the popular Korean TV series *Hourglass*. Almost overnight, it was reborn as a major tourist destination, where throngs flock to take in the spectacular sunrises. As is often the case with such places, fame has changed Jeongdongjin. There has been much development, some of it of questionable taste. Block out that and the crowds (especially if you go on Jan 1), though, and you'll find the sunrises inspirational. Couples will love it. The most charming spot consists of a couple of wind-swept pines and a simple bench not far from the station itself, a reminder of the peaceful, forlorn Jeongdongjin of old. If you don't want to watch the sunrise from the beach, there's a pavilion atop Goseongsan 고성산, a small hill overlooking the water.

🚃 The classic way to get to Jeongdongjin is to take the night train from Seoul's Cheongnyangni Station, which departs at 11 pm and arrives at 4:40 am. If you're in Gangneung, just take Bus No. 109 from in front of Gangneung Intercity Bus Terminal and get off at Jeongdong (30 min).

Sunrise over Jeongdongjin

NEW YEAR'S SUNRISE

On New Year's Day, Jeongdongjin is packed with revelers. If you're lucky enough to get a train ticket (unlikely if you didn't book in advance), be prepared for some crowds. Of course, if you like people, this isn't so bad, and there will be plenty to do, see, eat and drink while you wait for the sun to come up.

Unification Park 통일공원

Off the Beaten Track

A few kilometers north of Jeongdongjin is Unification Park, home to two retired warships. The larger of the two is the destroyer ROKS Jeonbuk (formerly the USS Everett F. Larson), launched by the Americans in 1945 and transferred to the Korean Navy in 1972. In 1999, the destroyer was decommissioned and turned into a museum ship.

The smaller one is, surprisingly, a North Korean submarine. On Sept 15, 1996, a North Korean submarine dropped off a team of commandos on the South Korean coast near Gangneung to conduct surveillance on military facilities in the area. On Sept 18, however, the submarine ran aground while trying to retrieve the commandos. Unable to free the submarine, the North Koreans resolved to make it back home overland. A local taxi driver spotted the submarine, however, and informed the authorities. What followed was a massive, 49 day manhunt by South Korean troops and police that ended with 24 North Koreans killed, one captured and one presumed to have escaped to North Korea. Of the 24 North Korean dead, 11—mostly the submarine's crew—are presumed to have committed suicide on the first day rather than risk capture. The South Koreans also took casualties, both military and civilian, including several killed in incidents of friendly fire.

On Dec 28 of that year, North Korea issued a rare "apology," expressing deep regret for the incident. The South Koreans kept the submarine, later moving it to its current location as the centerpiece of Unification Park, which opened in 2001.

🎟 3,000 won ⏰ 9 am to 5:30 pm (Mar–Oct), 9 am to 4:30 pm (Nov–Feb) ☎ 033-640-4469
🚌 Take Bus No. 11-1 from Jeongdongjin Station (about 15 min)

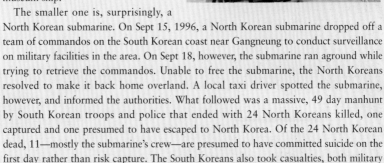

DONGHAE 동해

Named for the body of water on which it sits, the city of Donghae ("East Sea") is an important East Sea port, with a population of just over 100,000. It is also home to Ssangyong Cement's Donghae production line, one of the biggest cement factories in the world. Unless you've got a keen interest in cement, however, the city itself is rather non-descript, and you're unlikely to visit for its urban charms. It does have weekly ferry connections to Vladivostok in Russia and Sakaiminato in Japan, though, which makes the town a place of interest for travelers going further afield. It is also one of the best places to catch ferries to the volcanic island of Ulleungdo 울릉도. It used to be that you could take ferries from here to North Korea's scenic Geumgangsan Mountains, too, but the recent cooling in relations between the two Koreas has led to a suspension of service, and as of the writing of this book, the future of the Geumgangsan Mountains Tourism project is very much in doubt.

While the city has little to capture one's interest, some mountains and valleys that surround it are lovely, especially the scenic Mureung Valley 무릉계곡, with its magnificent rock formations, thick forests and beautiful waterfalls. Another scenic spot, this one on the coast, is Chuam Beach 추암해수욕장's Chotdaebawi 촛대바위, a candlestick-shaped rock (some might liken its shape to something else) famous for its captivating sunsets, which have inspired legions of photographers.

Chuam Beach. Chotdae Bawi ("Candlestick Rock") is in the far left.

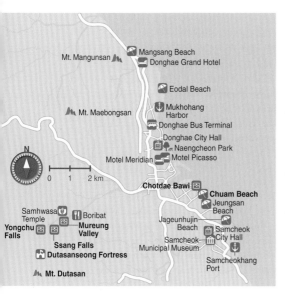

Mangsang Beach
Mt. Mangunsan
Donghae Grand Hotel

Eodal Beach

Mt. Maebongsan

Mukhohang
Harbor

Donghae Bus Terminal

Donghae City Hall

Naengcheon Park

Motel Meridian
Motel Picasso

Chotdae Bawi

Chuam Beach

Jeungsan
Beach

Jageunhujin
Beach

Samwhasa
Temple
Boribat

Samcheok
City Hall

Yongchu
Falls
Mureung
Valley

Samcheok
Municipal Museum

Ssang Falls

Dutasanseong Fortress

Samcheokhang
Port

Mt. Dutasan

N

0 1 2 km

Layout

The city stretches north–south along the narrow strip of land between the sea and mountains. Donghae Station is located in the far south of town, not far from Donghae Passenger Ferry Terminal 묵호항여객선터미널, from whence boats to Russia and Japan depart. The fishing port of Mukhohang 묵호항, where you catch fast boats to Ulleungdo, is in the north of town. The bus terminal is almost equidistant from Donghae Station and Mukho. Trains to Donghae also stop at Mukho Station, near Mukhohang Port, so if the ferry to Ulleungdo is your objective, this is where you should get off. Chuam Beach is just south of town, along the rail line to Samcheok 삼척.

Chuam Beach 추암해수욕장 & Chotdae Bawi 촛대바위

Chuam Beach is a 150 m stretch of white sand with shallow water perfect for wading in the summer months. Most people, however, come here for the fantastic rocks and coastal cliffs. The most famous of these is Chotdaebawi or "Candlestick Rock," a 5–6 m tall rock that stands at the edge of the sea. The sunrises here are mesmerizing—so much so, in fact, that the image of the sunrise at Chotdaebawi is often seen at the beginning of the video that accompanies the Korean national anthem. Bring a camera, by all means, but be prepared to fend off the rest of the tripod-toting crowd.

Take Bus No. 61 from Donghae Station (20 min) or Donghae Bus Terminal (45 min) and get off at Chuam. You could also take a taxi—it's just 5 minutes by cab from Donghae Station.

Chotdae Bawi, or "Candlestick Rock"

Mureung Valley 무릉계곡

Mureung Valley is yet another stunning gorge, the likes of which Gangwon-do is blessed. In the old days, they said Taoist fairies would come down from the mountains to play in its waterfalls and pools. It's easy to see why—the place can seem like an earthly paradise.

Mureung Valley was formed by a stream that tumbles down from the heights of Mt. Dutasan 두타산 (1,353 m). At the entrance of the valley is a huge slab of granite on which the names of countless scholars who visited this scenic spot over the centuries have carved their names. Follow the valley upwards and you'll come to Samhwasa 삼화사, a small Buddhist temple blessed with an iron-seated Vairocana Buddha from the Unified Silla era (668–935) and a well-preserved stone pagoda from the late 9th century. Go past the temple and you'll pass a series of ravines, pools and waterfalls, the most impressive of which are Ssang ("Twin") 쌍폭포 and Yongchu 용추폭포 waterfalls, the former eponymously named because it is, in fact, a twin waterfall with two stunning cascades emptying into a crystal clear pool. Once you're at the Yongchu Waterfall—4 km from the start of the park—you can return from whence you came.

There's a path up Mt. Dutasan, too, along with a longer trail that links Mt. Dutasan with neighboring Mt. Cheongoksan 청옥산 (1,403 m). The views can by beautiful, even in wet weather when the mist heightens the area's mysterious, otherworldly vibe. It's a long slog, though (about 30 km if you do both peaks, or roughly 13–14 hours), so plan on a full day excursion if you decide to go up.

⊕ 2,000 won ☎ 033-534-7306~7
🚌 Take a bus to Mureung Valley from Donghae Bus Terminal (1 hr).

Ssang Falls, Mureung Valley

WHAT TO EAT

While Donghae, like every other Korean city, has tons of places to dine, the best place is in front of Mureung Valley. One good place to try is Boribat 보리밭 (033-534-7051), where you can get *bibimbap* 비빔밥 made from mountain vegetables and *deodeok gui* 더덕구이, grilled marinated bellflower root.

WHERE TO STAY

Donghae Grand Hotel 동해그랜드호텔 (033-534-6682), on Mangsang Beach 망상해수욕장 north of town, is a three-star place with great views, especially at sunrise. Its indoor and outdoor pools are worth checking out, too. Rooms with an ocean view start at 130,000 won a night in July–August, although this comes down to 80,000 won/96,000 won on weeknights/weekends during off-peak months. Located downtown near Naengcheon Park 냉천공원, Meridian Motel메르디앙모텔 (033-533-7800) is clean and pleasant, with rooms going for 50,000–60,000 won a night. Nearby, the flashy-looking Motel Picasso 피카소모텔 (033-533-2500) has a variety of rooms between 80,000 and 150,000 won a night; rates come down considerably during off-peak months. You'll find several other good motels in this neighborhood, too.

TRANSPORT INFO

Trains are available to Donghae from Seoul but it's a long haul—there are six daily trains that depart from Cheongnyangni Station for Donghae, and the trip takes six hours. Much easier on your derriere are buses. There are frequent buses to Donghae from Seoul's Dong Seoul Terminal, and the trip takes just three hours. Donghae is also well connected via bus to other cities in Gangwon-do, including Gangneung, Sokcho and Samcheok. Regarding the ferry, DBS Cruise Ferry (033-531-5611-2, www.dbsferry.com) carries passengers to Vladivostok and Sakaiminato on the triple-deck Eastern Dream. The schedule as follows:

To Vladivostok Depart 3 pm Sunday, arrive 3 pm, Monday. Economy class tickets cost 220,000 won. Private room with beds, though, go with the Junior Suite: 462,000 won.

To Sakaiminato Depart 6 pm Thursday, arrive 9 am Friday. Economy class tickets: 141,000 won. Private room with beds in the Junior Suite: 330,000 won.

Squid dries at Chuam Beach.

SAMCHEOK 삼척

Just south of Donghae, Samcheok is a small coastal city that, to its credit, is home to a branch of Kangwon National University 강원대학교. What is worth seeing here is Hwanseongul Cave, one of Asia's largest limestone caves, situated in the mountains west of town. Samcheok is also home to one of Korea's quirkier tourist sites, Haesindang Park, a coastal park dedicated to, well, the penis.

Hwanseongul Cave 환선동굴

The karst hills west of Samcheok are home to many limestone caves, but Hwanseongul Cave is by far the greatest. At 6.5 km long, it is one of Asia's largest limestone caves. Only 1.6 km of it is open to visitors, but this will still take about an hour to explore. Inside the mammoth cave where the ceiling reaches heights of 20–30 m, you'll find a variety of fantastic rock formations, stalagmites and stalactites; there are also numerous pools, waterfalls and streams. The complex is linked together by stairs and bridges, and is well lit, although the red, green and purple neon might turn some visitors off. At one point, you pass under a heart-shaped hole in the ceiling—if you're with your significant other and pledge your love to him/her underneath it, the love will last forever, it is said. At another point, you

At 6.5 km, Hwanseongul Cave is one of Asia's largest limestone caves.

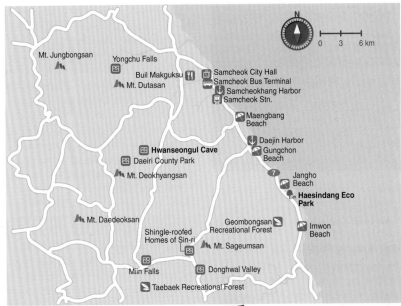

Mt. Jungbongsan

Yongchu Falls

Buil Makguksu
Mt. Dutasan

Samcheok City Hall
Samcheok Bus Terminal
Samcheokhang Harbor
Samcheok Stn.

Maengbang
Beach

Daejin Harbor
Gungchon
Beach

Hwanseongul Cave
Daeiri County Park
Mt. Deokhyangsan

Jangho
Beach

**Haesindang Eco
Park**

Mt. Daedeoksan

Shingle-roofed
Homes of Sin-ri

Geombongsan
Recreational Forest

Imwon
Beach

Mt. Sageumsan

Miin Falls

Donghwal Valley

Taebaek Recreational Forest

cross the Jiokgyo 지옥교 ("Bridge of Hell")
into the Jiokgyegok 지옥계곡 ("Valley of
Hell")—abandon hope all ye who enter
here. Cross the "Bridge of Confession," 참회
의다리 though, and all your sins disappear—a
blessing celebrated with a neon rainbow on
the cave wall. The temperature inside stays
at 10–14°C, making it a nice summer
reprieve.

The cave is located at an elevation of 500
m. The walk from the parking lot to the
cave entrance is long and steep, taking
about 30 minutes to climb by foot.
Fortunately, there's also a monorail that'll
do most of the work for you, taking you
directly to the mouth of the cave for the
cost of a 3,000 won ticket (5,000 won
round-trip).

Near the parking lot along the path to
the monorail terminal, you can also check
out a couple of traditional homes unique to
this region of Korea. Roofed with wooden

DAEGEUMGUL CAVE

While you're in the neighborhood, it's
also worth checking out Daegeumgul
Cave 대금굴, discovered in 2003 and
opened up to the public in 2007. The
cave is 1,610 m long, of which you can
explore 793 m. Unfortunately, you need
to a) join a guided tour (groups of 40),
and b) pre-order a ticket (12,000 won)
online at http://samcheok.mainticket.
co.kr (Korean only). The ticket price also
includes fare for the cable car to the
cave, and also allows you to see
Hwanseongul Cave at no added charge.
The entry gate for Daegeumgul Cave is
just past the ticket booth for
Hwanseongul Cave.

shingles of pine or oak rather than tile or
rice straw, these homes were once common
throughout the mountain interior of
Gangwon-do where slash-and-burn farmers
eked out their livings for centuries.

⊕ 8 am to 7 pm (Mar–Oct), 8:30 to 5 pm (Nov–Feb) 📧 4,000 won ⓒ 033-541-9266
📱 Take a bus from Samcheok Bus Terminal to Hwanseongul Cave (40 min).

Haesindang Park 해신당공원

You won't find many places in Korea like Haesindang Park, located in the small fishing village of Sinnam 신남마을. Imagine seaside walking paths, a pleasant pine forest...and hundreds of penises. Dedicated to Korea's folk tradition of phallicism, the park is home to countless sculptures of the penis, some fanciful, others more anatomically correct. Between the penis cannon, the penis zodiac carvings, an exhibit with life-like sculptures reenacting scenes from Joseon Dynasty pornography, and groups of middle-aged women having their photos taken straddling a huge stone phallus, it can be quite surreal.

Once you've had your fill of penises, there's also a museum with displays on the lifestyles of local fishermen.

Now, there's a reason for all this: according to legend, five centuries ago, a young virgin from the village perished in the stormy seas as she was collecting seaweed. Bitter and lonely, her spirit drove away the fish and the village suffered. Then, one day, one of the local fishermen dropped his drawers to urinate in the sea and the fish returned. Putting two and two together, villagers began carving wooden phalli, which they tied together with rope and hung as offerings from a shrine overlooking the sea in hopes of soothing the spirit's loneliness.

In fact, many of the fishing villages along the East Sea coast have similar legends, and for centuries performed annual rites in which they hung wooden phalli as offerings in hopes that the Sea Spirit would grant safety and abundance. Over time, however, most of these villages ceased to perform the rite, or replaced it with modified rites sans phallus. Sinnam Village is virtually the only village that still performs the rite, which it does every Daeboreum holiday (15th day of the first lunar month) and on the first five days of the 10th lunar month.

⊕ 9 am to 6 pm 📧 3,000 won 📱 Take Bus No. 20, 90 or 90-1 from Samcheok Bus Terminal to Haesindang Park (50 min)

The many phalli of Haesindang Park

WHAT TO EAT

Downtown Samcheok has plenty of eateries. The best known place in town is Buil Makguksu 부일막구수 (033-572-1277), which does *makguksu* 막국수 (buckwheat noodles) and *suyuk* 수육 (boiled meat). Samcheok's signature dish, however, is *gomchiguk* 곰치국, a spicy soup made from moray eel. Until very recently, Korean fishermen considered the aesthetically challenged moray inedible. Then somebody discovered that boiling it up in a spicy broth did wonders for a hangover. The place to go for this is Donga Sikdang 동아식당 (033-547-5870) near Samcheokhang Harbor 삼척항. A bowl of *gomchiguk* will set you back 12,000 won. Their other specialty is *seonggye baekban* 성게백반 (10,000 won)—soup, side dishes and rice, mixed *bibimbap*-style with cooked sea urchin.

WHERE TO STAY

You'll find some moderately priced inns and hotels near Samcheok Bus Terminal 삼척버스터미널, including the clean Moon Motel 문모텔 (033-572-4436), where rooms begin at 60,000 won a night (40,000 won off-peak). Off the beaten track, but a really picturesque trip back into a more rustic Korea, are the *minbak* (homestay) opportunities (033-552-1659) at the old *neowajip* village 너와집마을 at Sin-ri (see below). Rooms that sleep up to eight begin at 80,000 won.

TRANSPORT INFO

From Seoul, buses to Samcheok depart from Seoul Express Bus Terminal (3 hrs 30 min). There are frequent buses to and from Donghae (30 min), Gangneung (50 min) and other cities in Gangwon-do.

Shingle-roofed Homes of Sin-ri 신리민속마을 *Off the Beaten Track*

On the road to Taebaek, deep in the Taebaek Mountain Range, is the village of Sin-ri 신리. Formerly a community of slash-and-burn farmers, this rustic village is home to several well-preserved examples of the shingle-roof homes that used to be common in the hardscrabble communities of the Taebaek Range. Throughout most of the country, Koreans traditionally used tile (aristocrats) or straw thatch (commoners) to roof their homes. In the rough Taebaeksan Range, however, where the winters are cold and there's little land to grow rice (and produce straw), locals turned to the most plentiful material they could find—wood.

In Sin-ri, most of the homes are *neowajip* 너와집—houses roofed with shingles cut from red pine. In other villages, locals roofed their homes with tree bark. The homes are an exercise in harmonizing man and nature. In dry weather, the shingles contract, letting light into the homes. In wet weather, they expand, preventing rain from leaking into the home. In winter, snow completely covers the roof, providing much-needed insulation. Sadly, however, these homes began disappearing from the 1970s; today, very few remain. The most impressive of the homes is Kim Jin-ho House 김진호가옥, a larger home surrounded by a stone wall. In addition to the homes, you can also find an old mill and a rare surviving example of a Korean waterwheel. There are *minbak* (homestay) facilities, too. ✆ 033-552-1659 🖳 http://neowa.invil.org (KR) 🚌 The best way to get there is to take a bus from Samcheok Bus Terminal to Dogye 도계, then take a taxi from there. It's actually easier to get here from Taebaek—buses from Taebaek headed for Hosan 호산 pass by the village and take about 30–40 minutes.

Snow-encrusted trees and white peaks, Mt. Taebaeksan

TAEBAEK 태백

This small mountain town high in the Taebaek Mountain Range 태백산맥 used to be a major center of the Korean coal mining industry. In the 1980s, however, Korea's coal industry went into terminal decline as the country turned to more refined, cleaner fuel sources. All that remains of Taebaek's mining days is a museum and an old mine that is now a historical site. The death of the mining industry hit Taebaek hard and, truth be told, it has yet to fully recover. In an effort to aid and ameliorate, the government did allow the town to open Kangwon Land Casino 강원랜드 카지노, which is not only the nation's largest casino but also the only one allowed to admit Koreans (the rest are foreigner-only).

In addition to the Korean punters and those with a keen interest in the history of coal mining, the town draws its fair share of visitors who come for its splendid mountain scenery. Particularly visit-worthy is the magnificent peak of Mt. Taebaeksan, one of Korea's most sacred mountains due to its connection with the national foundation myth.

Taebaeksan Provincial Park
태백산도립공원

The best reason to come to the town is to hike up Mt. Taebaeksan 태백산 ("Great White Mountain"), one of Korea's tallest peaks at 1,567 m. It's a big mountain but not a particularly difficult one to climb—there are no cliffs to negotiate and the path is blissfully smooth. From the upper reaches, the views of the surrounding Taebaeksan Range are breathtaking. If you bring a flashlight and get to the peak early (a 2 hour climb, if you go up the shortest route), the sunrises are spectacular.

In winter, the mountain receives heavy snow, which makes the climb even more beautiful. The snow encrusts the windswept trees and bushes: these "snow flowers"

Sacred yew trees, Mt. Taebaeksan

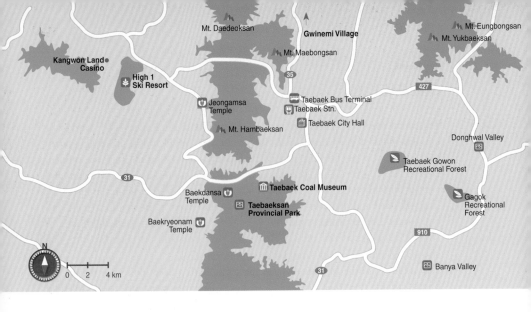

Mt. Daedeoksan

Gwinemi Village

Mt. Eungbongsan

Mt. Yukbaeksan

Mt. Maebongsan

Kangwon Land
Casino

High 1
Ski Resort

35

427

Jeongamsa
Temple

Taebaek Bus Terminal

Taebaek Stn.

Taebaek City Hall

Mt. Hambaeksan

Donghwal Valley

Taebaek Gowon
Recreational Forest

31

Baekdansa
Temple

Taebaek Coal Museum

Gagok
Recreational
Forest

Taebaeksan
Provincial Park

Baekryeonam
Temple

910

N

0   2   4 km

31

Banya Valley

produce a fantastic, almost otherworldly landscape. Spring is another good time to visit when the peak's many royal azaleas bloom.

In addition to the scenic splendor, Mt. Taebaeksan is worth climbing for its spiritual and cultural importance. Thanks to its shamanist and Buddhist heritage, Korea has many spiritually important mountains and peaks, but Mt. Taebaeksan is one of the most sacred. According to legend, it was here that Hwanung, the son of the King of Heaven, came down from Heaven to found his own sacred city and teach men how to live. Accordingly, the entire mountain is dotted with shrines, altars and Buddhist temples, the most impressive of these being the stone altar complex of Cheonjedan 천제단, atop the highest peak itself. Every day, the shrines and altars bustle with activity, with shamans from throughout the country making regular pilgrimages here. The biggest rites are held at Cheonjedan every Oct 3, Korea's National Foundation Day holiday.

Climbing Mt. Taebaeksan

The most popular course takes you from Danggol Ticket Booth 당골매표소 (near the Coal Museum, see p278) through the Danggol Valley 당골계곡 to the Banjae Ridge 반재, and from there to the Cheonjedan Altar Complex (1,560.6 m) and Janggunbong Peak 장군봉 (1,566.7 m). Along the way, you'll pass Manggyeongsa Temple 망경사, which at 1,470 m is one of Korea's highest Buddhist temples. Be sure to taste the well water—they say it is the best in Korea. You'll also pass a monument to

National Foundation Day rites at Cheonjedan Altar

Manggyeongsa Temple (left), Cheonjedan Altar

King Danjong, a 15th century monarch who died at age 16 after he was deposed and exiled by his own uncle. The path, which is pretty gentle, is 4.4 km long, and should take about two and half hours to climb. Another option is a more direct hike from Yuilsa Temple 유일사 to Cheonjedan, a 4 km hike that takes two hours.

The Cheonjedan complex is composed of three altars aligned in a north–south line. The largest of these is the circular Cheonwangdan 천왕단, or "Altar to the King of Heaven," where on Oct 3 offerings are made to Heaven to pray for national peace and prosperity. When many people refer to Cheonjedan, they are referring to this altar. To the north is a smaller, square-shaped altar called the Janggundan, and to the south is an even smaller, practically disused altar called the Hadan 하단. When these altars were first built is unknown, but it's believed ceremonies have been held atop the mountain since at least the Three Kingdoms period (57–668).

From Cheonjedan Altar, you can go down the way you came up, or hike the 3 km ridge to Munsubong Peak 문수봉 (1,517 m), a peak holy to Buddhists (you'll find a

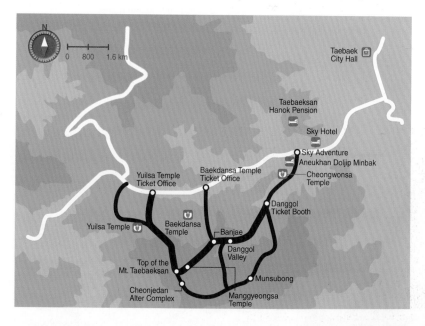

number of stone towers up here), and from there follow the path down to Danggol Ticket Booth.

The peaks and main ridge afford dramatic views of the surrounding mountains. The vegetation at the higher altitudes is alpine; particularly impressive are the ancient, weatherbeaten yew trees, regarded as sacred by Korean shamanists.

🏷 2,000 won ✆ 033-550-2741 (Danggol Ticket Booth), 033-550-2746 (Yuilsa Temple Ticket Booth) 🚌 Danggol Course: Take a bus from Taebaek Bus Terminal for Danggol and get off at the park's parking lot (25 min). Yuilsa Temple: Take a bus from Taebaek Bus Terminal for Yeopyeong/Sangdong and get off at Yuilsa Temple (35 min).

Taebaek Coal Museum 석탄박물관

Taekbaek was the heart of Korea's coal industry, the dominant industry in southern Gangwon-do from the 1930s, when the Japanese colonialists first began exploiting the region's rich coal deposits, to the 1980s, when Korea's shift to nuclear power and other fossil fuels all but killed domestic coal mining. Taebaek Coal Museum, which opened in 1997, educates visitors about the

important role coal mining in Taebaek played in Korea's national development and the sacrifices made by the legions of miners who braved difficult and dangerous conditions in the mine shafts below. You'll find all sorts of mining equipment on display here, as well as mock-ups of mining life above and below ground.

🕘 9 am to 6 pm 🏷 2,000 won ✆ 033-552-7730 🚌 The museum is near the head of the Danggol trail of Mt. Taebaeksan.

Kangwon Land Casino 강원랜드카지노 & High 1 Resort 하이원리조트

Actually in the nearby town Jeongseon 정선, Kangwon Land Casino—now part of the High 1 Resort—has the distinction of being the only casino in Korea where the locals can gamble. There are other casinos throughout Korea, especially in Seoul, but all cater exclusively to foreign tourists and residents. In 1995, the Korean government permitted Jeongseon to open up a casino as a way to help the region recover from closure of the coal mines.

Las Vegas it's not, but if you're itching to

High 1 Resort

drop some money on blackjack, roulette or craps, you're in the right place. Kangwon Land is the largest casino in Korea, with 132 tables and 960 slot machines and video games. Table games include blackjack (45 tables for non-members), Baccarat, roulette, the Big Wheel, tai sai, Caribbean stud poker and casino war.

High 1 Resort, meanwhile, is one of Korea's newer ski resorts, complete with luxury hotels and condos, a golf course, and even a revolving restaurant on the peak of a 1,340 m mountain. The resort has 18 slopes, the longest of which is 4.2 km. The basic lift and gondola rate (morning, afternoon or night) is 46,000 won; all-day access is 72,000 won. If you just want to ride the gondola sans skiing, it'll cost you 12,000 won. Rental skis/snowboards available.

🕐 **Casino:** 10 am to 6 am the next morning (Weekdays, Saturday), all day Sunday
🎫 **Casino:** 5,000 won. Chips begin at 1,000 won. 🚌 Take a bus (or train) from Taebaek to the small town of Gohan-ri 고한리, and from there take a shuttle bus from Gohan Train Station or take a taxi (10 min). ✆ 033-590-7700 🖱 www.high1.com

WHAT TO EAT

You'll find plenty of restaurants at the Danggol entrance of Taebaeksan Provincial Park. In downtown Taebaek, a good restaurant to try is Neowajip 너와집 (033-553-4669) near Taebaek Fire Station 태백소방서, which serves fantastic *sanchae bibimbap* 산채비빔밥 (rice mixed with mountain vegetables, 7,000 won) and *jeongsik* 정식 (Korean banquet cuisine—rice, soup and a table full of side dishes, starting at 20,000 won). Also try the *memil jeonbyeong* 메밀전병 (buckwheat crepes wrapped around a filling of seasoned vegetables and tofu. Not only is the food spectacular, but the restaurant itself is in a 120-year-old wooden shingle home, the likes of which were once common in these parts of Korea.

WHERE TO STAY

Downtown Taebaek has some moderately priced lodging, although some of it is a bit run-down. The biggest, and one of the nicest, hotels is Sky Hotel 태백스카이호텔 (033-552-9912~3), on the road from Taebaek to Taekbaeksan Provincial Park. Rooms begin at 80,000 won on weekends during the peak season (Jun 1–Aug 31, Dec 1–Feb 28). If you're looking for something more remote, there's Taebaeksan Hanok Pension 태백산한옥펜션 (033-554-4732, 011-820-4732), a *hanok* bed-and-breakfast in a valley off the road to Taebaeksan Provincial Park. During the peak season (July 19–Aug 16), rooms for two begin at 90,000 won.

The Danggol entrance of Taebaeksan Provincial Park has a *minbak* village (033-553-7440), so if you've come to hike Mt. Taebaeksan, this is probably a more convenient, and more pleasant, option. Rooms for two go for 45,000 won. Take a look at Aneukhan Doljip Minbak 아늑한 돌집민박 (033-553-3432), too, where rooms for two (with walls made from Korean red clay) run 40,000 won during the peak season (Jul–Aug, mid-Dec–mid-Feb, and regional festivals). If you've come for Kangwon Land Casino and you still have money left when they're through with you, High 1 Resort has a number of lodging options for the better-heeled, including High 1 Hotel (033-590-7700), where rooms begin at 157,300 won.

TRANSPORT INFO

Thanks to Taebaek's history as Coal Town Korea, it's linked by rail and road to the rest of the country, but its mountain location means it takes a bit of time to get there. There are regular buses to Taebaek from Seoul's Dongseoul Bus Terminal (3 hrs 30 min). There are also regular buses to other cities throughout Gangwon-do.

There are six trains a day to Taebaek from Seoul's Cheongnyangni Station. It's a long trip (4 hours, 30 minutes), but as the train cuts through some spectacular mountain scenery, it can be quite picturesque.

Off the Beaten Track

Jeongseon Rail Bike 정선 레일바이크

Like Taebaek, the town of Jeongseon 정선 is a former mining town hidden in the mountainous highlands of southern Gangwon-do. While the mines have long since closed, the town's beautiful mountain scenery still remains.

A fun way to take in the rural charm is by rail bike. Making use of a disused, 7.2 km track of the old coal railroad running from Gujeol-ri Station 구절리역 to Auraji 아우라지, the rail bike passes through some beautiful mountain scenery, especially in autumn when the hillsides turn a bright crimson. The path runs mostly downhill, past mountains, rivers and farms; bikes run smoothly enough that even solo travelers can easily peddle their way along. Combined with stops at other destinations in the area, it's a very pleasant way to spend an autumn afternoon. Once you've reached Auraji, there's a free train service that will bring you back to Gujeol-ri Station.

At old Gujeol-ri Station, you'll also find "The Katydid's Dream," 여치의 꿈 a landmark spaghetti house/café made of two railway cars stacked together, painted green and, with some creative steelwork, made to look like a katydid. There's also a small accommodation facility with cute, colorfully painted two-person "houses" made from steel cylindrical capsules (70,000 won a night).

On a cultural note, the final destination of Auraji sits aside a pool in the Namhangang River, and is the birthplace of the Jeongseon version of the famous Korean folk song "Arirang." The confluence of two rivers, Auraji was, during the Joseon Dynasty, where boatmen carrying timber used to begin their riverine trip to the royal capital of Seoul. Like boatmen everywhere, they were fond of singing and their voices used to fill the air. The

slow, sad "Jeongseon Arirang," one of the best-loved versions of the song, tells of a woman waiting for the return of her husband, a boatman who left for some far-off destination.

⊕ 8:40 am, 10:30 am, 1 pm, 2:50 pm, 4:40 pm 🚲 22,000 won (two-person bike), 32,000 won (4-person bike) 🚌 First, from Taebaek, take a bus (or train) to Jeongseon. From Jeongseon Bus Terminal, take a local bus to the village of Yeoryang. From Yeoryang, there are mini-buses to Gujeol-ri Station. ⓒ 033-563-8787 🖱 www.railbike.co.kr (KR)

Gwinemi Village 귀네미마을

If you're in Taebaek in summer, do try to visit Gwinemi Village, a small community high in the mountains north of Taebaek off the road to Samcheok. And by "high in the mountains," we mean "high in the mountains"—the village is at an elevation of over 1,000 m, positively Himalayan by Korean standards. What makes this place so unique, though, is its spectacular scenery. Taking advantage of the clean mountain air and cool temperatures, the locals have taken to vegetable farming, particularly Korean cabbage, so visitors are treated to a beautifully exotic tapestry of rolling hills covered in green farms, not unlike the tea plantations of Boseong. Also thanks to the altitude, the village gets some spectacular sunrises.

While the village is quite beautiful, its inhabitants, ruefully, are not there entirely by their own volition—the village was formed in the 1980s by residents of another small village in Samcheok that was flooded due to dam construction.

🚌 Take a bus from Taebaek Bus Terminal in the direction of Hajang and tell the driver you're getting off at Gwinemi Village (40 min).

DONGGANG RIVER 동강

A tributary of the Hangang River, the Donggang River cuts a rugged, winding 60 km path through the mountains of Jeongseon 정선 and Yeongwol 영월 counties. This is beautiful, wild country with whitewater rapids, weather-beaten limestone cliffs, fields of wild flowers, rare animals such as otters and Mandarin ducks, and rustic villages hidden on sharp bends of the river. So beautiful is it that it's sometimes likened to China's famously scenic Li River. In the late 90s, plans by the government to erect a dam on the river—in part sparked by a disastrous 1993 flood that submerged much of Yeongwol—nearly spelled the end for this environment, but the public outcry was so great that in 2000, the authorities announced that they had abandoned the plan.

The Donggang offers a variety of opportunities for outdoor sports, including rafting, trekking and biking. A particularly striking route takes hikers from the village of Jeomjae 점재마을 to the peak of Mt. Baegunsan 백운산 (882.5 m) and down again to the villages of Jejang 제장마을 and Munhui 문희마을. The river here snakes through the mountains in a convoluted series of oxbows, the banks dotted with small villages bathed in the shade of limestone cliffs. As a hiker, you have many different options here—you could go along the ridge lines or stay low and follow

The meandering Dongang River

1. Rafting on the Donggang River 2. Donggang's beautiful natural scenery 3. Baengnyong Cave.

the river. Atop the hill across the river from Jejang, there are the remains of an old mountain fortress, and just down the river from Jejang in the direction of Munhui, you'll find Baengnyong Cave 백룡동굴, a 12 km long limestone cave first opened to the public only in 2010. Aside from the views of the dramatically meandering river from the top of Mt. Baegunsan, the villages along the river each have their own special charm, and it's worth spending a day leisurely exploring.

For rafting, the best section of the river is the Eorayeon Valley 어라연계곡, where you'll find stretches of whitewater (especially around the Doen Kkokkari Rapids 된꼬까리 여울), as well as dramatic mountain scenery. It's a good place to hike, too—it'll take you about three hours to hike from the Geoungyo Bridge 거운교 to the peak of Jatbong 잣봉 (537 m), down to the Eorayeon and back along the river to Geoungyo Bridge. Eorayeon is a well-known scenic spot, a sharp bend in the river that, when seen from above, looks like the Korean Peninsula in miniature.

In the village of Geoun-ri 거운리, you'll find plenty of tour companies offering rafting trips along the Donggang River. Those inexperienced in rafting needn't worry—experienced guides will accompany you. Most companies offer 10 km (3 hours), 13 km (4 hours) and 30 km (8 hours) courses (or distances similar), with most ending at Geoungyo Bridge. Look to spend about 30,000–90,000 won per person, depending on the distance. The two-hour Munsannaru 문산나루 → Geoungyo Bridge (Seopsae) course is the most popular at 30,000 won.

WHERE TO STAY

If you're staying overnight, one recommended place is Hanbando River Pension 한반도리버펜션 (033-375-0099), a bed and breakfast across the river from Eorayeon (a.k.a. the bend in the Donggang River that resembles the Korean Peninsula). Rooms for two begin at 80,000 won on peak weekends (July 15–Aug 25). The pension also has a small museum with local artifacts and old log rafts of the type that used to ply these waters—the pension owner can take you out on one of these and show you the sights while belting out old boatmen songs, including the "Jeongseon Arirang" (see p282).

TRANSPORT INFO

First, you need to get to the small town of Yeongwol 영월. From Seoul, buses to Yeongwol depart from Dong Seoul Terminal (2 hrs). You could also take a train from Seoul's Cheongnyangni Station (2 hrs 30 min). From Taebaek, take a bus to Yeongwol (1 hr 30 min), and from Yeongwol Bus Terminal, take a bus to Geoungyo (6:20 am, 8:40 am, 12:30 pm, 3:20 pm, 6 pm).

Peak of Mt. Balwangsan, Yongpyong Ski Resort

PYEONGCHANG 평창

The mountain town of Pyeongchang is smack in the middle of Korea's snow country. In winter, the surrounding mountains, passes and highland plateaus are inundated by Korea's heaviest snowfalls, making it perfect for winter sports. Not surprisingly, the town is home to some of Korea's top ski resorts, including the very popular Yongpyong Ski Resort.

Pyeongchang was little known outside of Korea until 2011, when it was named the host city of the 2018 Winter Olympic Games. For now, the town is, as ski resorts go, a small, sleepy place—visitors are unlikely to confuse it for Innsbruck or Vail. In preparation for the games, however, it will undergo a major facelift in the coming months, so what you read here won't be the case for much longer. While Pyeongchang is known mostly as a winter destination, it's lovely throughout the year. In particular, it is home to Korea's largest highland meadows, where you can hike around picturesque sheep ranches and wind farms, breathing in the clean mountain air as you take in the beautiful landscape.

Pyeongchang and the southwestern town of Muju 무주 (host of the 1997 Winter Universiade) form the two poles of Korean winter sports. The nation's growing horde of skiers and snowboarders descends upon the town each winter to take advantage of the deep snow. Yongpyeong is also becoming an increasingly popular destination for international travelers, especially those from warmer climes like Southeast Asia.

Yongpyong Ski Resort 용평스키리조트

It may not be Whistler but Yongpyong ("Dragon Valley") is still Korea's top ski resort and, indeed, one of the best in East Asia. It has an astounding 31 slopes (covering the whole range, from beginner to expert), 15 ski lifts and Dragon Plaza, the largest ski house in Asia. The longest run is the intermediate-level 5.6 km Rainbow Paradise, approached via cable car from Dragon Plaza—the views of the surrounding Taebaek Mountain Range are incredible.

The most scenic part of the park is Dragon Peak 드래곤피크휴게소 (1,459 m), the summit of Mt. Balwangsan 발왕산. On the summit—reached by gondola—is a picturesque Swiss-style chalet with drop-dead views of the mountains and, on a clear day, even the East Sea. Located in the chalet are a

2018 WINTER OLYMPICS

On July 6, 2011, Pyeongchang was named the host city of the 2018 Winter Olympic games. For the visitor, what this means is that Pyeongchang is likely to be in a state of flux between now and the Olympics. The massive Alpensia Resort (partially open: www.alpensiaresort.co.kr) is being developed as the primary venue of the games. New hotels, including the Apensia's Intercontinental and Holiday Inn, are being constructed, and the town's food and nightlife scene is expected to change dramatically. There are even plans to link Pyeongchang by KTX high-speed train with Seoul and Incheon International Airport.

café and (Korean-style) Western restaurant known for its spaghetti. If you're a morning person, the sunrises here are gorgeous.

Daytime lift and gondola passes are 71,000 won. Daytime+evening passes go for 97,000 won. Ski rentals are 26,000 won (daytime), while snowboards can be rented for 34,000 won. In addition to the skiing, the resort also has public and private golf courses. The green fee for non-members on the public course is 150,000 won on weekdays, and 190,000 won on weekends.

Yongpyong Resort is also popular—especially with Japanese tourists—as a filming locale of the 2002 Korean TV mini-series *Winter Sonata*, which was exceptionally popular in Japan.

Like any proper ski resort, Yongpyong

DAEGWALLYEONG SNOW FLOWER FESTIVAL

In January, Hoenggye-ri 횡계리 hosts the Daegwallyeong Snow Flower Festival, a celebration of Daegwallyeong's best known meteorological phenomenon. The festival features a good many fun events, including sledding, sleigh rides, skating, snowman making and mountain hiking. For more information, call 033-336-6112 or visit http://www.snowfestival.net.

has plenty of accommodation, including hotels, condos and a youth hostel. As a welcome change from elsewhere in Korea, some of these are actually tastefully designed, especially the Birch Hill Condominium 버치힐콘도 (members only, sadly), which is modeled on the Beaver Creek Resort in Colorado. The most popular place to stay is Dragon Valley Hotel 드래곤밸리호텔, where rooms begin at 250,000 won a night. It books out fast in the winter, though, so be sure to make a reservation first. The youth hostel is a good option, especially if you're in a group—rooms of five go for 70,000 won a night.

🚌 Free shuttle buses for Yongpyong Resort leave from Hoenggye Post Office. There are also direct buses to the resort from Seoul. Buses depart from near Exit 4, Jamsil Station, Line 2 and Exit 2, Sports Complex Station, Line 2 (2 hrs 30 min. Fare: 15,000 won one way, 28,000 won round-trip). Visit www.yongpyong.co.kr or call 02-2201-7710 for more details, including bus schedule. ☎ 033-335-5757 🖳 www.yongpyong.co.kr

Daegwallyeong Sheep Ranch
대관령 양떼목장

Granted, sheep are probably not the first thing to pop into mind when considering Korea's top tourist destinations. Perhaps this is what gives Daegwallyeong Sheep Ranch, deep in the highlands of Taebaek Mountain Range, its charm. It's just so exotic—rolling treeless hills of grazing land, so very unlike anywhere else in Korea. Some liken it to Switzerland with its peaks, grassy fields and, well, sheep. It's both relaxing and inspiring—unless you've just gotten off the plane from Scotland or New Zealand.

The ranch is open all year round—in fact, you're more likely to spot the sheep grazing in the hills in summer than in chill winter months when they are kept warm inside. Yet the ranch is an incredibly popular winter tourist destination, largely thanks to its beautiful winter scenery. The

The distinctly non-Korean landscape of Daegwallyeong Sheep Ranch

Daegwallyeong area—a key gateway through the Taebaek Mountain Range—gets the heaviest snowfall in Korea. Even without the snow, the area has a stark highland beauty, of barren rolling hills beneath a cloudless cerulean sky.

Pyeongchang's Daegwallyeong region is South Korea's largest plateau area, with the landscape dominated by grassy meadows punctuated by craggy mountain peaks. Due to its high altitude—the plateau is over 800 meters high with a number of peaks surpassing 1,000 meters—Daegwallyeong is known as the "first village under the sky." The region has served as an important pass through Korea's rough mountainous interior.

The sheep ranch is approached via the small mountain town of Hoenggye 횡계, on the eastern edge of the plateau. The town itself doesn't have much beyond the all-important bus station, although it does

have some decent places to stay and eat.

Most visitors come to the ranch for the scenery and a walking path of about 1.2 km takes you around the grassland which reaches a peak altitude of 980 meters. It gets cold and windy up here, so be sure to dress warmly.

The higher parts of the ranch offer some beautiful views of the surrounding highlands. After it snows—and when it snows up here, it snows a lot—it's like a glistening white tapestry thrown over the hills, meadows and peaks. It doesn't quite have the same intimidating vastness of the Scottish Highlands, but it's not dissimilar, either. And in the Korean context, it's quite unique.

🕘 9 am to 5 pm Ⓒ 033-335-1966 👆 www.yangtte.co.kr. 🚌 Buses to Hoenggye-ri run from Seoul's Dong Seoul Bus Terminal. The trip takes about two and a half hours. From Hoenggye-ri Bus Station, take a taxi to the ranch—the fare will be about 10,000 won.

WHAT TO EAT

As for food, the area is famous for its beef, dried pollack and *osam bulgogi* 오삼불고기 (spicy pan-fried squid and pork). You'll find many such restaurants in Hoenggye—the Napjak Sikdang 납작식당 (033-335-5477) does a mean *osam bulgogi*.

WHERE TO STAY

Conceivably, this could be done as a day trip—the first bus leaves Seoul at 6:35 am, and the last bus back leaves at 8 pm. There are several small hotels and motels in Hoenggye, but another option is to make use of one of the several rental houses or "pensions" 펜션. A two-person room could run you 100,000–140,000 won a day during ski season. Some ones to check out are Wildfloaroma 대관령들꽃향기펜션 (033-335-6873), Jajaknamu Pension 자작나무펜션 (033-335-3691) and Woorimaul Pension 우리마을펜션 (033-336-4580).

WONJU 원주

With a population of just over 320,000 people, the city of Wonju is the largest city in the province of Gangwon-do and a major transportation hub, with rail and highway connections to Seoul. It's also an important educational center, home to several notable universities including a campus of prestigious Yonsei University. The city's important transportation links have given it a strategic significance, too—no less than three major battles were fought for control of the city in the Korean War. Accordingly, the city and its surroundings are home to a number of large Korean military bases, including the headquarters of the Republic of Korea 1st Army, and, until very recently, two American bases.

Wonju's convenient rail and road access to Seoul, and its location in the far southwestern corner of the province, almost make it seem like a satellite city of the capital. Like most cities of this size, there are a lot of shops, restaurants and motels but, truth be told, it's not an especially riveting place—the city was almost completely rebuilt after the Korean War. The downtown has little of historical interest, save perhaps the old water tower next to Wonju Station, which once serviced the steam locomotives of the Japanese colonial era. Most travelers who come to Wonju do so to visit nearby Chiaksan National Park, a scenic mountain park popular with hikers from Seoul.

Chiaksan National Park

Chiaksan National Park 치악산국립공원

Mt. Chiaksan ("Pheasant Crag Mountain") is a steep, rugged mountain with several peaks over 1,000 m high, including its highest peak, Birobong 비로봉 (1,288 m). Its slopes are covered in thick, verdant forests that hide deep valleys and picturesque waterfalls. Thanks to its relative proximity to Seoul, its trails can get quite busy on weekends, especially in autumn when its maples turn bright crimson.

Most hikers approach the mountain from the north via Guryongsa Temple 구룡사, the mountain's largest Buddhist monastery. The path takes you through thick forest (with some centuries-old pines) and past a couple of pretty waterfalls before commencing what seems like an endless series of stairs up the mountain to Birobong Peak. The first part of the trail is pretty tame but the stairs are fairly steep—bring a bottle of water. The hike to the peak is 5.7 km and takes about three and half hours. From Birobong, head back down the way you came or descend via

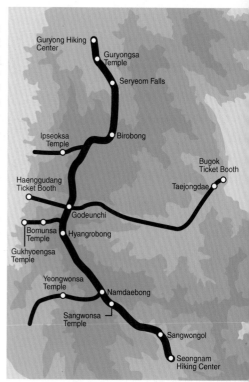

THE GRATEFUL PHEASANT

History and Culture

Mt. Chiaksan takes its name from a legend associated with the peak. Many years ago, a traveler was walking along one of the mountain's paths when he came across a pheasant, around which a snake was wrapped. Feeling bad for the pheasant, he took his bow and fired an arrow at the snake, killing it and rescuing the pheasant. Later that night, he was looking for a place to spend the night, and met a woman who kindly invited him to spend the night at her place. During the night, however, the woman turned into a snake and, vowing revenge for the death of her husband, wrapped herself around the sleeping traveler, promising to kill him if the bell of nearby Sangwonsa Temple 상원사 did not ring thrice before dawn. Learning of the man's plight, the grateful pheasant ran to Sangwonsa Temple and bashed its head into the bell three times, killing itself but saving the man. This tale is recounted in visual form in a wooden engraving that hangs in the belfry of Sangwonsa Temple, near Namdaebong Peak 남대봉.

Hwanggol Valley 황골계곡 (4.1 km). There's also a campsite near Guryongsa Temple; during the peak season, pitch a tent for 2,000 won a night.

Explore the southern end of the park (including Sangwonsa Temple) around Namdaebong Peak 남대봉 (1,181 m), but to do this, begin at Seongnam-ri 성남리.

🚩 3,200 won ⓒ 033-762-5695 🚌 Take Bus No. 41 from Wonju Station to Guryongsa Temple (40 min). If you're going to Seongnam-ri, take bus No. 21 (30 min). Bus No. 82 will take you back to Wonju from the Hwanggol Valley.

TIPS

PANDAE ICE PARK

If you're into extreme sports, Wonju is home to one of Korea's finest artificial ice-climbing parks. Wonju Pandae Artificial Ice Park is, essentially, a natural cliff covered by a 100 m wall of ice, overlooking a frozen river. It's 90 degree climbing here and not for beginners or the faint of heart. Bring your own screws and other gear, too. You need to reserve a spot before you go (033-761-4177). You're going to need your own wheels or take a cab from Wonju.)

Wonju Pandae Artificial Ice Park

There are plenty of places at the Guryongsa entrance to get nourishment. Many of the eateries here do *deodeok gui* 더덕구이 or roasted, seasoned bellflower root.

WHAT TO EAT

Assuming you're in Wonju to hike Mt. Chiaksan, Wonju makes an easy day trip from Seoul. If you'd like to spend the night here, though, it's probably more pleasant to stay at the entrance to Chiaksan National Park than in Wonju itself. You'll find your usual collection of *minbak* (homestays) and pensions near the Guryongsa entrance. Also near the entrance, more creature comforts are offered at Chiaksan Hotel 치악산호텔 (033-731-7931), where rooms go for 80,000 won a night on peak weekends.

WHERE TO STAY

From Seoul, buses to Wonju depart from Dong Seoul Terminal and Express Bus Terminal (1 hr 40 min). Trains to Wonju depart from Seoul's Cheongnyangni Station (1 hr 20–30 min). As Gangwon-do's largest city, the town is also well-connected by bus to other cities inside and outside the region, including Chuncheon, Gangneung, Daejeon, Daegu and Busan.

TRANSPORT INFO

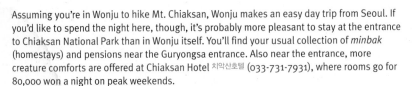

CHEORWON 철원

Just across the provincial border from Gyeonggi-do, in the mountainous region of Gangwon-do is the town of Cheorwon, home to some of the country's most impressive Korean War ruins. Once a large, prosperous railroad and road junction controlling the Geumhwa Valley 금화계곡, a vital north-south passageway to Seoul, the town was virtually wiped off the map in the bitter fighting during the Korean War. After the war, the town was rebuilt several kilometers away. Where the old town once stood, all that remains are shattered ruins in the rice fields.

While the Workers' Party of Korea office is the most famous of Cheorwon's Korean War ruins, there are some others to see as well. A short walk down the road from the historic office brings you to the remnants of the Cheorwon Methodist Church 철원감리교회, an old American mission church from the 1930s that was later used as a North Korean barracks. If you venture past the Civilian Control Line 민통선, there is more, including an old ice cellar, bank and agricultural inspection office. Most of what you will see, however, are rice fields.

Ruins of Workers' Party of Korea office are a reminder of the tragedy of the Korean War.

Ruins of Workers' Party of Korea Building 철원노동당사

The ruins of the old Cheorwon office of the Workers' Party of Korea, the ruling party of North Korea, is perhaps Korea's most haunting symbol of division and war. One of only a few buildings in Cheorwon whose walls remained standing once the guns fell silent, the bombed-out skeleton, with its bullet and shell-scarred facade, recalls images of postwar Germany. Around it are nothing but fields and hills where a once prosperous downtown had been—a jarring reminder of the complete devastation the war visited upon the city.

The original building was constructed in 1946 by the North Koreans using Soviet engineering techniques. The result was a sturdy, three-story concrete building of the Soviet style frequently encountered in North Korea and the former Eastern Bloc. The office was erected, it is said, using forced labor and contributions of rice squeezed from the locals.

As the headquarters of the local branch of the communist Workers Party of Korea, within its walls party leaders kept an eye on the local population, planned espionage and guerrilla activities against the South, and questioned and tortured those accused of anti-communist activities. Bones, bullets and barbed wire were discovered in a tunnel behind the office.

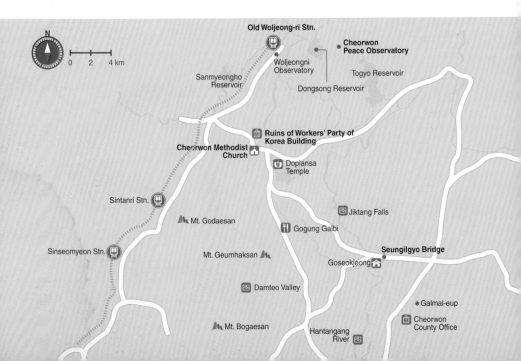

Like the rest of Cheorwon, the old building suffered greatly in the battles for the Iron Triangle in mid-1951. Repeated shelling left it a burnt-out shell. The steps leading to its entrance bear the marks of tank treads. It is all very tragic and surreal.

Today, the ruins are seen as a symbol of Korea's division and the horror of fratricidal war. On occasion, the site is used for concerts and performances.

Old Woljeong-ri Station 월정리역 & Cheorwon Peace Observatory
철원평화전망대

Located just in front of the southern side of the DMZ is a small train station. Old Woljeong-ri Station—actually a 1988 restoration—is the closest train station to the DMZ in South Korea, although trains stopped running this far north long ago. It is kept around for symbolic reasons. Behind the station is an old train platform, a rusting sign and the twisted skeletal remains of a North Korean transport train bombed by the Americans during the war.

In the old days, Woljeong-ri Station was a whistle stop on the Gyeongwon Line.

Linking the capital city of Seoul with the East Sea port of Wonsan (now in North Korea), the line was completed by the Japanese in 1914 using local Korean labor and White Russian émigrés. The railroad opened Seoul's market to Cheorwon's rice and Wonsan's seafood, bringing prosperity to both towns. The division of Korea and subsequent Korean War severed the line, however. Now, the last stop on the line is Sintan-ri in the neighboring county of Yeoncheon 연천.

Nearby is an observatory for crane watching—cranes flourish in the tranquil, generally uninhabited DMZ—and the Cheorwon Peace Observatory. Recently built and equipped with a state-of-the-art monorail, it offers a rare chance to look out into the DMZ and beyond into North Korea (tickets: 3,000 won).

Seungilgyo Bridge 승일교
Several kilometers from the old Workers' Party of Korea building is the Seungilgyo Bridge, a handsome, if somewhat aged, concrete arch bridge that spans a gorge of the Hantangang River 한탄강. It is a

Seungilgyo Bridge, which according to legend was started by North Korea and finished by South Korea

Korean War ruins, Cheorwon

particularly beautiful spot any time of year, especially if you like old bridges.

According to popular belief, construction of Seungilgyo Bridge was started by the North Koreans in 1948 and completed by the South Koreans after the war. If you look closely, you will see that the north and south halves of the bridge—notably the decorative arches—are clearly different. There has been some debate about the name: some claim it is taken from the names of the South and North Korean leaders at the time (Rhee Syngman—pronounced Lee Seung-man in Korean—and Kim Il-sung), while others claim it is named for Col. Park Seung-il, who was killed in action after leading his troops across the Hantangang River.

Because of the tragic history of national division and war that the bridge architecturally represents, it is sometimes referred to as Korea's "Bridge on the River Kwai."

While no one doubts the tragic romance of the bridge's history, it may not, in fact, be true. Recent research has turned up journal entries and photos that suggest that the bridge was begun by the colonial Japanese and completed by the US 79th Engineer Construction Battalion. This is the explanation given on the bridge's tourist information board. In summer, the waters underneath the bridge are a popular rafting area.

A local specialty is pork ribs, or *pokeu wang galbi* 포크 왕갈비. This flavorful meat dish consists of specially selected pork marinated in medicinal herbs and fruit, and is served at room temperature. Gogung Galbi 고궁갈비(033-455-1535) in Dongsong-eup 동송읍 is a good place to savor this. Otherwise, there are plenty of eateries all over Cheorwon including its new downtown, Galmal-eup 갈말읍. Cheorwon's Korean beef, *hanu*, 한우 is particularly well regarded.

WHAT TO EAT

There is no real need to stay in Cheorwon, as it can be visited as a day trip from Seoul. If you do want or need to stay, though, there are a good many small motels and inns in Dongsong-eup and Galmal-eup. Highly recommended is the Hantan River Spa Hotel 한탄리버스파호텔 (033-455-1234, www.hantanhotel.co.kr), a lovely spa with indoor and outdoor facilities overlooking a scenic ravine in the Hantangang River.

WHERE TO STAY

To get to the ruins of the Workers' Party of Korea, just take Seoul Subway Line 1 to Dongducheon 동두천, transfer to the Gyeongwon Line commuter train and get off at the last stop (and we do mean last—any further and you're in North Korea) of Sintan-ri 신탄리. From Sintan-ri, there are buses that pass by the ruins. All told, it takes about two hours. To get to some of the sites across the Civilian Line of Control, you need a car. Access to the area is open four times a day on weekdays (9:30, 10:30 am, 1 pm, 2:30 pm, closed Tuesdays)—you need to inform the Iron Triangle Tourism Office (033-450-5558) in the hamlet of Goseokjeong 고석정 at least 20 minutes beforehand. On weekends, you must take a shuttle bus (8,000 won) from the aforementioned office. If you don't have a car, you can hire a taxi (about 60,000 won). To get to the Seungilgyo Bridge, just take a taxi from Goseokjeong.

TRANSPORT INFO

HWACHEON 화천

Rugged mountains, deep blue lakes and rushing rivers—that's what Hwacheon's all about. Just getting to Hwacheon is itself an adventure, with buses from Chuncheon (the nearest transportation hub) following a winding route along the craggy banks of Chuncheonho Lake and the Bukhangang River 북한강. Traveling about the district involves bus and car rides through steep valleys and high mountain passes that offer stunning views over the wilds of central Korea.

For most of the year, Hwacheon is little more than a sleepy mountain town (albeit a beautiful one) frequented mainly by a) sportsmen hoping to do a little fishing, and b) Korean military personnel, who actually outnumber residents in this sparsely populated county near the DMZ. In January, however, its frozen rivers play host to one of Korea's most popular winter festivals, the Hwacheon Sancheoneo Ice Festival. The festival aside, however, Hwacheon's scenic beauty alone justifies the two and a half hour bus ride from Seoul, and history buffs will appreciate the Korean War history hidden amidst the county's mountains and waterways.

Created in 1944, scenic Paroho Lake ("lake where the barbarians were smashed") was the site of some of the worst fighting of the Korean War.

Peace Dam Park

N
0 3 6 km

Mt. Ilsan

Bimok Park

Hwacheon Dam

Myeongga

Cheonil Makguksu

Hwacheon County Office
Hwacheon Bus Terminal

Paroho Lake

Hwacheon
Eojuktang

Eobu Hoetjip

Paroho Lake 파로호

Hwacheon, like neighboring Chuncheon, is in the heart of Korea's lake country. Granted, most of the "lakes" are actually reservoirs, the product of massive dam projects during the middle part of the 20th century, but the resulting scenery is beautiful nonetheless. They also provide a venue for leisure activities like sport fishing and boating.

Created in 1944 with the construction of the Hwacheon Dam, Paroho Lake 파로호 is the largest of Hwacheon's reservoirs. Known prior to 1951 as the Hwacheon Reservoir 화천저수지, it was given its current name—which translates as "lake where the barbarians were smashed"—by Korea's first president, Syngman Rhee, to commemorate the seizing of the strategically important body of water (and, just as important, its valuable hydroelectric plant) from Chinese forces in the Korean War.

Rimmed by snowy peaks in winter, the deep blue lake is quite picturesque, especially in the morning, when it is covered in fog. There is a small lakeside village that has a number of restaurants where you can enjoy the bounty of the reservoir's plentiful fish stock. Also lakeside are a couple of Korean War battle monuments and a small museum dedicated to the bloody battles fought to control the lake.

On weekends and holidays, there are tour ferries that depart from a dock at the west end of the lake for a 24 km, 80 minute trip to Peace Dam Park. There is one boat a day from Nov to Apr (1 pm), and two from May to Oct (9:30 am, 2 pm). The fare is 8,000 won one way, 15,000 round-trip.

Korean War memorial

Hwacheon Dam, built by the Japanese between 1939 and 1944

Hwacheon Dam 화천댐

Built by the Japanese between 1939 and 1944, the massive Hwacheon Dam is still one of Korea's largest dams and an important source of electrical power. In fact, at the time of the Korean War, it was one of South Korea's only sources of power, and for this reason—and the fear that the communists could use it as a weapon to flood the Hangang River valley—some of the Korean War's fiercest battles took place around the dam and Hwacheon Reservoir. Sturdily built, the dam survived intense bombings from US B-29 heavy bombers, although its sluice gates were eventually taken out by aerial torpedoes dropped by US Navy aircraft in a daring raid reminiscent of the Death Star scene in "Star Wars." There are a couple of Korean War monuments by the dam, which itself cuts a rather spectacular image against the backdrop of the lake and forested hills beyond.

Buses to Paroho Lake depart from Hwacheon's city bus terminal. To get to Hwacheon Dam, however, you should take a cab from downtown Hwacheon (the fare is about 15,000 won).

TIPS

HWACHEON SANCHEONEO ICE FESTIVAL

Hwacheon's population skyrockets every winter when it plays host to the Hwacheon Sancheoneo Ice Festival, recently named one of the world's best winter festivals by the Lonely Planet and CNN. Dedicated to the *sancheoneo*, an indigenous freshwater mountain trout that thrives in the county's ice cold rivers, the festival's signature event is ice fishing. There will be equipment on hand, although if you like (and some do), you could try it barehanded, too! It's really quite good fun, and even if fishing activities don't appeal to you, there's plenty else going on like sledding and skating.

Peace Dam 평화의댐
& Bimok Park 비목 공원

Hwacheon is perhaps best known as home to the Peace Dam, a rather curious piece of Cold War history. In 1986, the North Koreans began work on a mammoth dam just across the DMZ. South Korea—then preparing for the 1988 Summer Olympics—feared the North Koreans might use the dam to flood the Hangang River and wreak havoc in Seoul. So work began on a dam of their own, dubbed the "Peace Dam" to block potential flood waters from the North. A nationwide campaign to gather money for the dam was undertaken—school children would donate their lunch money for the cause—but construction was suspended when public opinion turned against the project, which came to be regarded as an embarrassing white elephant.

The dam got another lease on life in 2002, when cracks began appearing in the North Korean dam across the DMZ. The North Koreans added to worries in 2005 when—without bothering to warn anyone—they released water from the dam, causing considerable damage to border

Bimok Park

areas in South Korea. Work thus began again on the Peace Dam, which was finally completed in October 2005.

At 601 meters long and 125 meters high, the Peace Dam is truly gargantuan in scale. True to purpose, it lacks a reservoir; it was built to keep water out, not hold it back. Located in a remote mountain valley near the DMZ, the surroundings couldn't be any more gorgeous. The dam is now part of a "peace park," and surrounding the dam wall are a number of belfries in which hang massive Buddhist bells crafted from casings and shells collected from 30 conflict zones around the world. It is said that when rung, the bells can be heard for a hundred kilometers.

Also near the dam is a humble stone

The Peace Dam was erected to stop North Korea from flooding Seoul.

tomb with a rusty steel helmet and a cross made of gnarled wood. This is a replica of an actual tomb found not far from here in 1964 by a young lieutenant named Hahn Myung-hee. Hahn later penned the song "Bimok" ("Wooden Cross"), which became one of the most famous Korean tunes of the 1970s. The tomb symbolizes the tragedy of a nation torn apart by fratricidal war.

📖 Buses to the Peace Dam run from Hwacheon's Intercity bus terminal (50 min). The road to the dam passes through rugged mountain country, including the Haesan Scenic Spot, a high mountain pass that offers wonderful vistas. You can make better use of the scenic spot if you have your own car or take a taxi.

Old North Korean Barracks

Located above the 38th parallel, Hwacheon was controlled by North Korea prior to the Korean War. An interesting reminder of this history is an old North Korean barracks

Old North Korean barracks

building located about a 20 minute drive from downtown Hwacheon. A sturdy stone building with little in the way of decoration, it was recently restored. You'll need a taxi here—ask the driver for Inmingun Saryeongbu Maksa 인민군사령부막사.

WHAT TO EAT

With its many rivers and lakes, Hwacheon is famous for its fish, often served raw. Myeongga 명가 (033-442-2957), not far from Hwacheon Bus Terminal, is famous for its freshwater trout (*sancheoneo* 산천어), roasted freshwater eel (*jangeo-gui,* 장어구이) and freshwater mandarin fish sashimi (*ssogari-hoe,* 쏘가리회). Raw fish can be expensive, though, so be forewarned. Hwacheon Eojuktang 화천어죽탕 (033-442-5544), located in front of Hwacheon Hydroelectric Power Station 화천수력발전소, does a

Makguksu

mean *eojuktang* 어죽탕 (spicy fish stew) on the cheap. Eobu Hoetjip 어부횟집 (033-442-3131), located near the pier of Paroho Lake, has been serving its raw fish for over 30 years. If you'd prefer something less fishy, behind the bus terminal you'll find Cheonil Makguksu 천일막국수 (033-442-2127), which specializes in *makguksu* 막국수—spicy buckwheat noodles served cold and a regional specialty.

WHERE TO STAY

There are about 20 or so motels and Korean-style inns (*yeogwan,* 여관) in Hwacheon Town. Most are pleasant enough and offer rooms at around 35,000–50,000 won a night, depending on size and time of year. If you're looking for something a bit more luxurious, you might want to look in Chuncheon, where there is a much wider range of accommodations.

TRANSPORT INFO

Buses to Hwacheon depart from the Dong Seoul (14 buses daily) and Sangbong (13 buses daily) terminals. The trip takes about three hours, with all buses passing through the provincial capital of Chuncheon first. From Chuncheon, frequent buses to Hwacheon take just one hour.

CHUNGCHEONGBUK-DO

HIGHLIGHTS

- Take a cruise boat on Chungjuho Lake, a virtual inland sea surrounded by beautiful mountains and dramatic rock formations

- Soak your aches and pains away at Suanbo Hot Springs

- Spend a day or two at the Korean lakeside resort town of Danyang

- Hike the lovely peaks of Songnisan National Park and check out the fascinating Buddhist temple of Beopjusa

- Check out the museums and historic sites of the provincial capital of Cheongju

- Trek across Sobaeksan National Park, home to the massive Buddhist complex of Guinsa

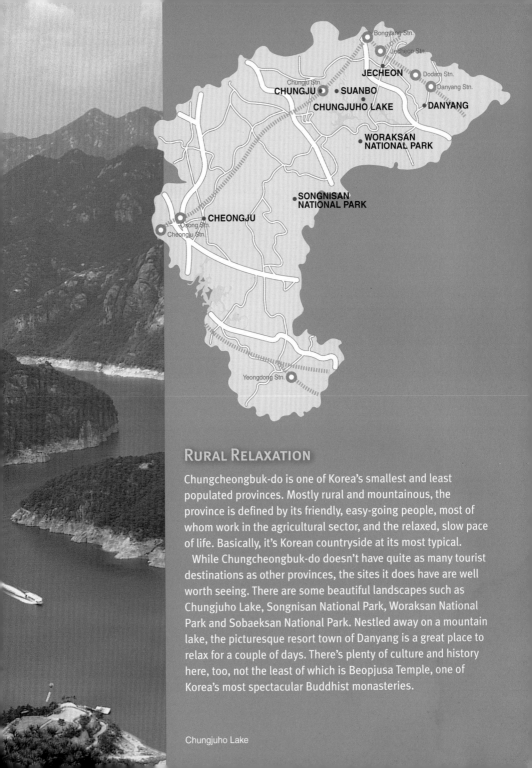

Bongyang Stn.
Jecheon Stn.
JECHEON
Chungju Stn.
Dodam Stn.
Danyang Stn.
CHUNGJU ● **SUANBO**
CHUNGJUHO LAKE
● **DANYANG**
WORAKSAN NATIONAL PARK
● **SONGNISAN NATIONAL PARK**
Osong Stn.
● **CHEONGJU**
Cheongju Stn.
Yeongdong Stn.

RURAL RELAXATION

Chungcheongbuk-do is one of Korea's smallest and least populated provinces. Mostly rural and mountainous, the province is defined by its friendly, easy-going people, most of whom work in the agricultural sector, and the relaxed, slow pace of life. Basically, it's Korean countryside at its most typical.

While Chungcheongbuk-do doesn't have quite as many tourist destinations as other provinces, the sites it does have are well worth seeing. There are some beautiful landscapes such as Chungjuho Lake, Songnisan National Park, Woraksan National Park and Sobaeksan National Park. Nestled away on a mountain lake, the picturesque resort town of Danyang is a great place to relax for a couple of days. There's plenty of culture and history here, too, not the least of which is Beopjusa Temple, one of Korea's most spectacular Buddhist monasteries.

Chungjuho Lake

The 18th century walls of Sangdangsanseong Fortress

CHEONGJU 청주

The provincial capital of Chungcheongbuk-do, Cheongju—not to be confused with the nearby town of Chungju or the Jeollabuk-do provincial capital of Jeonju—has been an important economic and administrative center for the region for centuries. Today, it is a commercial, economic and transportation hub of more than 660,000 people, home to several universities and even its own airport. Over the last century, however, the city has come to be overshadowed by the nearby metropolis of Daejeon.

Cheongju is a nice enough town, its road and rail connections are convenient, and it has a few points of interest. The Cheongju Early Printing Museum marks the site where, in 1377, Korean monks produced the first book printed using metal movable type. Cheongju National Museum is also worth a visit to learn about the culture and history of the province. Overlooking the city atop a hill just east of town, the old stone fortress of Sangdangsanseong Fortress offers great views and makes for a nice hike.

Layout Cheongju's old downtown, including the Chungcheongbuk-do Provincial Office 충청북도청 and Cheongju City Hall 청주시청, is in the eastern part of the city. Cheongju's intercity and express bus terminals, meanwhile, are next to one another on the western edges of town. Cheongju Station 청주역 is actually a couple of kilometers west of town, so to get back and forth from there, you'll need to take a bus or cab. The same goes for Cheongju International Airport 청주공항, which is several kilometers north of the city. Cheongju National Museum and Sangdangsanseong Fortress are just east of town, while Cheongju Early Printing Museum is smack dab in the center of the city.

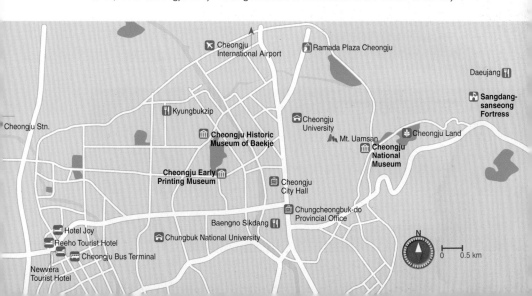

Cheongju Early Printing Museum
청주고인쇄박물관

Opened in 1992, Cheongju Early Printing Museum was built on the site of the old Buddhist temple of Heungdeoksa 흥덕사. In 1377, monks printed a copy of the *Jikji*, an anthology of Zen teachings compiled by the Korean Buddhist monk Gyeonghan (better known by his pen name, Baegun), using metal movable type. This was the first time in world history that metal movable type was used, a full 78 years before Johannes Gutenberg introduced movable type to Europe. In recognition of this breakthrough in mankind's cultural development, the *Jikji* was registered by UNESCO as a "Memory of the World" in 2001; in 2004, UNESCO created the Jikji Prize to recognize institutions that have contributed to the preservation of mankind's documentary heritage.

The Cheongju Early Printing Museum has in its possession some 650 artifacts, including a number of historic printed documents from the Goryeo and Joseon dynasties. There are also displays explaining the development of metal type print and detailing the printing process itself. Sadly, what you won't find here is a copy of the *Jikji* itself most of which was lost. The final volume survives, mind you, but it was purchased by French diplomat and antiquities collector Victor Emile Marie Joseph Collin de Plancy at the turn of the 20th century and shipped to France. You can find it today in the Oriental Manuscripts division of the National Library of France. Korea has lobbied the French to return the volume to the land of its creation, but so far the French have refused.

⏰ 9 am to 6 pm. Closed Mondays 🎟 Free
📞 043-200-4515 🖥 http://jikjiworld.cjcity.net
🚌 Take Bus No. 831 or 831-1 from Cheongju Bus Terminal and get off at Cheongju Arts Center 청주 예술의전당. The museum is just across the street.

Cheongju National Museum
국립청주박물관

Dedicated to preserving and promoting the historical and cultural heritage of Chungcheongbuk-do, Cheongju National Museum has a permanent collection of 2,300 artifacts, including Paleolithic stone tools and Goryeo-era celadon ceramics. There's a children's museum, too, if you need something for the kids to do. The museum is in a lovely location in a forested valley on the way to Sangdangsanseong Fortress. Built in 1987 by one of Korea's greatest architects, the late Kim Swoo-geun, it is a modern interpretation of Korean traditional architecture.

⏰ 9 am to 6 pm (Tue–Fri), extended hours on weekends. Admission ends one hour prior to

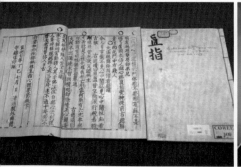

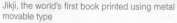
Jikji, the world's first book printed using metal movable type

Artifacts, Cheongju National Museum

Sangdangsanseong Fortress provides wonderful views of Cheongju.

closing. Closed Mondays. 🛗 Free ✆ 043-229-6300 🖳 http://cheongju.museum.go.kr 🚌 Take Bus No. 821, 822-1 or 826 from Cheongju Intercity Bus Terminal to City Hall. At City Hall, transfer to Bus No. 861-2 to the museum. The trip takes about 40 minutes.

Sangdangsanseong Fortress 상당산성

Snaking its way along around the peak of Mt. Uamsan 우암산, Sangdangsanseong is a typical mountain fortress of the Joseon Dynasty (1392–1910). Its impressive stone walls, standing 4.7 m high, form a 4.4 km loop around the hilltop. Once the military headquarters of the Chungcheong region, the fortress was a city unto itself, home to a garrison of 3,500 troops and Buddhist warrior monks. Its walls were filled with administrative buildings, ponds, barracks, armories, warehouses and other military facilities. Most of those are long gone but its main east, south and west gates still remain, as do two smaller "secret" gates that allowed reinforcements to enter the fortress unnoticed when it was under seige. The current walls mostly date from a 1716–1719 reconstruction (with restoration work done in the 1970s), but it is believed the ancient Baekje Kingdom first built a fortress here during the Three Kingdoms era (57 BC–AD 668).

It takes about two hours to walk the entire length of the wall. The western sections provide beautiful views of the city of Cheongju. Just inside the fortress is a collection of Korean traditional *hanok* homes that now function as restaurants—this is a good place to eat.

🕐 24 hours 🛗 Free ✆ 043-200-2227 🚌 Take Bus No. 513-1, 515, 314, 717, 311-1 from Cheongju Bus Terminal and get off at Chungcheongbuk-do Provincial Office. Transfer to Bus No. 862 to Sangdangsanseong.

Baeksuk

What to Eat

The *hanok* village inside Sangdangsanseong is a good place to score good food. One particularly well-known place up here is Daeujang 대우장 (043-252-3306), which does *hanbang baeksuk* 한방백숙 (30,000 won), chicken boiled in a broth of medicinal herbs—the meat just falls off the bone. Korean presidents, who until recently spent their summers at the nearby presidential retreat of Cheongnamdae 청남대, often frequented this restaurant while on vacation. Be sure to also order a bottle of *daechusul* 대추술, a smooth, locally produced wine made from jujube fruit.

Another *baeksuk* option is Kyungbukzip 경북집 (043-211-9200~1, www.kbzip.kr), where instead of chicken they use a variety of fresh water fish. This is serious eats for the ardent epicurean: a small serving of mandarin fish boiled with ginseng, dates, chestnuts and other ingredients will run you 80,000 won (for two). The catfish is cheaper at 60,000 won for two. *Maeuntang* 매운탕, a spicy fish soup, is also on the menu.

Cheongju's signature dish, however, is *yangnyeom samgyeopsal* 양념삼겹살—slices of fatty pork belly bathed in a sauce of Korean chili paste and grilled on a sheet of tin foil. Baengno Sikdang 백로식당 (043-259-9611), a Cheongju institution across from the provincial office, is a good place to score this delight, although they call it *gochujang bulgogi* 고추장불고기 (9,000 won a person). When the meat is finished, a bowl of rice is poured into the remaining sauce and cooked in tin foil.

In addition to the usual places where one would find restaurants (i.e., the bus terminal), the area in front of Cheongju University 청주대학교 has a ton of restaurants. You'll also find a good many cheap eats around Chungbuk National University 충북대학교.

Where to Stay

The Ramada Plaza Cheongju 라마다플라자청주 (043-290-1000, www.ramadakorea.co.kr) is probably the nicest hotel in central Korea. Located in the northern part of town near Cheongju University, it's got everything you'd expect in a 4 star hotel including Western, Japanese and Chinese restaurants, a sky bar, fitness center and pool. Rooms offer views of Mt. Uamsan or downtown Cheongju. It's not the most convenient location but with rooms beginning at 230,000 won a night, if you're staying here, you can afford the taxi ride. If you'd like to stay near the bus terminal but in comfort, you can try Newvera Tourist Hotel 뉴베라관광호텔 (043-235-8181~4) or Reeho Tourist Hotel 리호관광호텔 (043-233-8800). Both are clean and comfortable with rooms that start around 96,000 won. There are plenty of motels/inns of the gaudy "love motel" variety by the bus terminals, too. Hotel Joy 호텔조이 (043-234-1845) sports rooms with modern decor and home theaters that begin at 60,000 won a night.

Transport Info

Cheongju does have a train station but it's a bit out of town, and sits on the relatively minor Chungbuk Line which links the Gyeongbu (Seoul–Busan) Line and the Jungang Line that connects Seoul and Gyeongju. Cheongju's bus connections are much more convenient. Frequent express buses for Cheongju depart from Seoul's Dong Seoul Terminal and Express Bus Terminal (1 hr, 40 min). From Daejeon's Dongbu Terminal, inter-city buses for Cheongju depart every 10 minutes (1 hr). There are also express buses to Cheongju from Daegu (both Dongdaegu and Seodaegu), Busan and Gwangju.

Lest it be forgotten, Cheongju has an international airport, too. There are about 10 flights a day to Jejudo, as well as several flights a week to Beijing and Osaka. Direct buses to the airport depart from Bukcheongju Terminal and Daejeon's Dongbu Terminal.

Nogeun-ri Incident Site 노근리 사건 유적지

Off the Beaten Track

A few kilometers outside the small town of Yeongdong 영동 is a double railway bridge in the quiet village of Nogeun-ri (or, as it is often spelled in the foreign press, No Gun Ri). It was here that one of the most tragic—and controversial—incidents of the Korean War took place. Between July 26 and 29, 1950, an undetermined number of civilian refugees were killed here by elements of the US 7th Cavalry Regiment, some as they hid under the bridge. Pockmarked with bullet holes, the bridge still bears the scars of what transpired, a grim reminder of the brutality of war.

The Korean War turned much of Korea's population into refugees in their own country. In the face of the North Korean invasion, some four to six million refugees fled to cities in the south like Busan. Refugees even became factors on the battlefield; refugee-clogged roads hindered movement and logistics, and North Korean infiltration of refugee columns created havoc in UN rear areas and led to some of the most tragic episodes of the war.

What exactly happened at Nogeun-ri is still debated. What is known is that US troops, panicky and on the retreat, killed South Korean refugees at the railway bridge. How many were killed depends on who you ask—one US military historian put the figure as low as eight to 35, while Korean witnesses quoted by Associated Press (AP), which won a Pulitzer for a series of articles on the Nogeun-ri killings in 1999, put the death toll near 400. The town of Yeongdong claims 248.

In 2001, then-US President Bill Clinton offered a statement of regret for the killing of Korean civilians at Nogeun-ri. Work is currently underway to turn the area around the old bridge into a history park. Activist groups frequently visit the site, leaving behind signs, letters and other items which give the site a memorial feel.

📵 Buses to Yeongdong depart from Cheongju's Intercity Bus Terminal. In Yeongdong, take a bus to Hwanggan from Yeongdong Bus Terminal and get off at Nogeun-ri.

Off the Beaten Track

Sewang Brewery 세왕양조

Sewang Brewery is one of only a handful of historic breweries still in operation in Korea. Run by the same family for three generations, it's a piece of living history. The old brewery building, designed by a Japanese architect and built of pine cut from the thick forests of sacred Mt. Baekdusan, was completed in 1930, and has changed very little since then. Indeed, so perfectly was it designed for its intended task that it hasn't had to; the building's natural ventilation is so good that when repair work was done in 2006, it was found that its framework hadn't rotted at all. Even the clay jars in which the booze ferments date from the 1930s.

Sewang Brewery specializes in fermented beverages like *makgeolli* 막걸리 and *yakju* 약주. *Makgeolli*, which seems to be all the rage nowadays, is a milky rice beer that has long provided hard-working Korean farmers with some welcome midday relief. *Yakju* ("medicinal wine"), on the other hand, is a more refined rice wine and is usually clear.

Depending on how busy they are, you might be able to look around the brewery itself, and if you're really lucky, you might be able to check out the fermentation room where you can see the booze bubbling away in old clay jars. Next door, there's a tasting center and gallery—designed in the shape of an oak barrel, clay jar and *yakju* bottle—where you can learn more about Korean alcohol and the history of Sewang Brewery and have something to eat (make a reservation ahead of time, though, at 043-536-3567). Some of the old scrapbooks on hand are fascinating, with old photos, advertisements and documents related to the brewery. As hard as it may be to believe, the brewery was almost demolished in 2001 to make way for road construction. Fortunately, in 2003, it was listed as a registered cultural property.

There are frequent buses to Jincheon 진천 from Cheongju. From Seoul, buses to Jincheon depart from Nambu Bus Terminal. The trip takes about two hours. Once you're in Jincheon, you can take a local bus to Deoksan-myeon 덕산면. Get off at Deoksan Bus Stop (Yongmong Intersection 용몽사거리), and walk about 500 m in the direction of Deoksan Middle School 덕산중학교. The brewery is on your left.
www.icnj.co.kr

SONGNISAN NATIONAL PARK 속리산국립공원

One of the most popular hiking destinations in Korea, Songnisan National Park straddles the boundary between the provinces of Chungcheongbuk-do and Gyeongsangbuk-do. Mt. Songnisan's many sharp peaks, deep valleys and thick forests form so beautiful a landscape that the area has been praised as a "Little Geumgangsan," a reference to the spectacular Geumgangsan Mountains of northern Korea.

The park encompasses almost 275 km², stretched out largely north to south along the ridge of Mt. Songnisan 속리산. The mountain has more than a dozen peaks, including several over 1,000 m, most notably the tallest peak, Cheonwangbong 천왕봉 (1,058 m) and Munjangdae (1,054 m), a scenic pinnacle that is the objective for most hikers.

At the foot of the mountain is the spectacular Buddhist temple of Beopjusa, which attracts just as many visitors as the mountain itself. The precinct is a cornucopia of cultural treasures, including the magnificent Palsangjeon Hall, one of only a handful of surviving wooden pagodas in Korea. It's also home to Korea's largest statue of the Buddha, a 33 m tall copper Maitreya Buddha covered in gold leaf.

A refreshment shack atop Munjangdae Peak (1,054 m)

Beopjusa Temple 법주사

Beopjusa Temple was founded in 553 but substantially rebuilt in 776. In the early Joseon era, it was one of the largest Buddhist temples in Korea with about 60 buildings and 70 hermitages under its control. Like most of Korea's Buddhist temples, it was completely destroyed during the Japanese invasions of 1592–1598, but rebuilt in 1624. Repairs and additional construction continued in the ensuing centuries.

While not as big as it was during its heyday, it's still a big temple by contemporary Korean standards, with about 30 halls and control over numerous hermitages that dot Mt. Songnisan. It is also blessed with a wealth of Korean cultural treasures, including a stone lantern with a twin lion base 쌍사자석등 from the 8th century; another 8th century stone lantern with

Big rice cauldron, Beopjusa

carvings of the Four Heavenly Guardians 사천왕석등; and an impressive Silla-era stone lotus basin and a gigantic iron cauldron 철확 that was used to cook rice for the 3,000 monks who lived here at the temple's zenith. The real gem, though, is the five-story pagoda-esque Palsangjeon, a showpiece of Korean Buddhist architecture. One does pay for the privilege of seeing it—entry to Mt. Songnisan National Park through the

Beopjusa Temple and its beautiful Palsangjeon Hall, built in the 17th century and one of Korea's best remaining wooden pagodas.

Beopjusa Temple entrance costs 4,000 won, and the issue of entry fees has a source of friction between the temple and other concerned parties. Some things to look for during your visit to Beopjusa are:

Palsangjeon Hall 팔상전 One of the true masterpieces of Korean traditional architecture, the five-story Palsangjeon ("Eight Picture Hall") is a surviving example of wooden pagoda architecture, a rarity in Korea. Designated National Treasure No. 55, the hall was completed in 1626, and took 21 years to build. It houses eight murals depicting the life of the Sakyamuni Buddha. Be sure to check out the system of pillars and beams that keep this hall standing, as well as the beautifully faded murals on the woodwork that give this hall a historic feel. Also note the wooden dwarfs at the corners of the second-floor eaves, posed as if they are holding up the roof.

Daeungbojeon 대웅보전 Beopjusa's impressive Daeungbojeon, or main hall, is one of only a few two-story Buddhist main halls in Korea, and was completed in 1624. It houses a large gilt bronze Buddhist triad— one of Korea's biggest—which dates from the construction of the hall itself.

Bronze Maitreya Buddha 청동미륵대불 Probably the first thing you see at Beopjusa, the colossal gilded bronze statue of the Maitreya Buddha was erected in 1990 as a prayer for national reunification. It stands 33 m tall, weights 160 tons and is covered in 80 kg of gold leaf. This act of piety and patriotism cost US$4 million. Historically, the temple did have a large, gilded bronze statue of the Maitreya Buddha which was erected in the 8th century. In the 1860s, however, it was confiscated by the conservative Confucian government of Heungseon Daewongun, the powerful prince regent, to be melted down and used for the reconstruction of Gyeongbokgung Palace in Seoul.

Hiking Mt. Songnisan

The path most favored by hikers is the one that leads from Beopjusa Temple to Munjangdae 문장대 (1,054 m), a flat-topped rock that offers panoramic views of the surrounding ridges and valleys. For most people, the nearly 7 km hike takes about two and a half hours to the peak, and

Bronze Maitreya Buddha

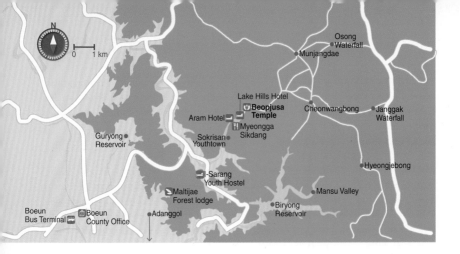

about the same to come down. It's a pretty easy hike—the paths are well-worn and the inclines fairly gentle. The view from the top, though, is worth the time and effort, especially in autumn when the hills turn color. Besides, by visiting Munjangdae, you'd be in good company—King Sejo stood atop the peak in 1464, and even composed a poem up here (though of course he was carried up by palanquin).

From Munjangdae, you could come down the way you came or take a scenic detour via Sinseondae, a large, flat rock with great views over the valley below.

🏛 3,000 won ℗ 043-542-3006 ⓐ http://english.knps.or.kr

History and Culture

JEONGIPUM PINE TREE 정이품송

Near the entrance of Songnisan National Park stands a graceful 600-year-old pine tree. In its old age, the tree needs the help of metal braces to support some of its limbs, but still projects a sense of quiet dignity.

The tree is most famous for the legend that is associated with it. In 1464, King Sejo, the seventh king of the Joseon Dynasty, visited Onyang Hot Springs and Mt.

Songnisan to cure an illness from which he was suffering. The royal traveling party was on the way to the mountain when it found the path obstructed by the tree, its limbs preventing Sejo's palanquin from passing. Sejo ordered the limbs be cut, but the tree—completely on its own—lifted its limbs so that the king could pass. Impressed by the courteous actions of the tree, Sejo bestowed upon the tree the rank of *jeongipum*, or minister of the second rank.

You'll find a ton of restaurants in the obligatory tourist village in front of Beopjusa Temple. If you like mushrooms, try the wild *neungi* mushroom stew 능이버섯전골 (*neungi beoseot jeongol*, 32,000 won for two) at Myeongga Sikdang 명가식당 (043-542-5188).

The nicest place to spend the night is Lake Hills Hotel Songnisan 레이크힐스호텔 (043-542-5281~8), located at the entrance of the park. It's got a coffee shop, Korean restaurant and bar. Rooms with a bed begin at 160,000 won a night.

There are two youth hostels near the park, too, Study & Training Youth Hotel 수련연수유스호텔 (043-542-5799) and Sokrisan Youthtown 속리산유스타운 (043-540-7777), both charging approximately 45,000 won. You'll also find a number of cheap inns and motels near the Beopjusa entrance to the park, including the venerable Aram Hotel 아람호텔 (043-543-3791). If you have a tent, there's a camp ground near the entrance to the park, too — rent a space for 1,600 won during the off-peak season, and 2,000 won during the peak season.

Highly recommended — if you can get a space — is Adanggol 아당골선씨가옥(선병국가옥) (043-543-7177), a 350-year-old aristocrat's mansion near Mt. Songnisan that is the ancestral home of the Boseong Seon clan. Its current mistress, Kim Jeong-ok, is a noted expert and producer of Korean soybean paste and sauce — the hundreds of earthen sauce pots in the courtyard make for an impressive sight. There are five guest rooms available, the cheapest one at 50,000 won a night. To get here, you'll have to take a local bus from Boeun 보은 for Jangan 장안. Adanggol is a short walk from Jangan bus stop.

Adanggol

The small town of Boeun is the usual gateway to Songnisan National Park. Frequent buses to Songnisan National Park depart from Boeun Bus Terminal (20 min). There are frequent buses to Boeun from Seoul's Dong Seoul Bus Terminal, Daejeon's Dongbu Terminal and Cheongju. From Seoul, there are 13 buses to Songnisan National Park that depart from Dong Seoul Terminal, and three buses from Central City Bus Terminal (3 hrs 30 min). There are direct buses to Songnisan National Park from Daejeon's Dongbu Terminal (1 hr 40 min).

CHUNGJU 충주

Chungju is a rather typical small town in the agricultural plains along the Namhangang River 남한강. Historically, the Chungju region was the hotly contested borderland between the ancient Korean kingdoms of Silla, Baekje and Goguryeo, fought over for its rich farmlands and vital transportation routes. Today, however, it's a rather slow, relaxed sort of place, with two universities in town that give it a bit of life. The town's present claim to fame is that it's the birthplace of current UN Secretary-General Ban Ki-moon.

What Chungju does have going for it is beautiful Chungjuho Lake, a scenic reservoir set amidst the mountains and cliffs of central Korea. Chungju is also a good base from which to explore the rugged peaks of Woraksan National Park. Also nearby is the popular hot spring resort of Suanbo where you can soak your travel aches and pains away.

Chungjuho Lake and its surrounding mountains showcase much scenic beauty.

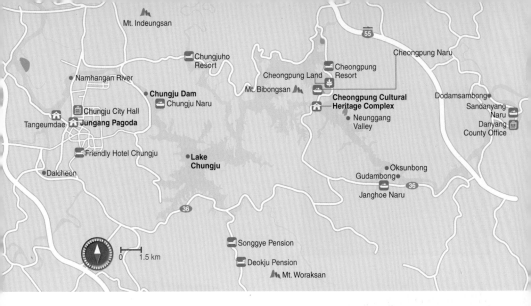

Chungju Town 충주시내
& Jungangtap Pagoda 중앙탑

The town of Chungju has shops, restaurants, motels and, of course, a bus terminal and train station. For the tourist, it's a transit hub to get where you want to go.

A little past Tangeumdae 탄금대 (see p318), on a terrace overlooking Namhangang River, is the imposing 7-Story Stone Pagoda of Tappyeong-ri 중원탑평리칠층석탑 or, as the locals call it, the Jungangtap ("Central Pagoda"). The largest stone pagoda from the Unified Silla era (668–935), the monument is believed to have been erected during the 8th century. It is said the pagoda was raised to mark the center of the Silla kingdom, hence its common name.

The pagoda certainly cuts an impressive figure against the surrounding landscape. A riverside sculpture park now surrounds it and makes for a pleasant evening walk. Also near the pagoda is Chungju Museum, where you can learn about the region's "Jungwon" culture, the product of the area's unique interaction with the Silla, Goguryeo and Baekje kingdoms.

🚌 Take Bus No. 400 from Chungju Intercity Bus Terminal.

Jungangtap Pagoda

Jungwon Goguryeo Stele 중원고구려비

This 1.44 m tall stone marker was erected by Goguryeo's King Jangsu (r. 413–491). It is covered in Chinese writing on all four sides—the text boasts of the accomplishments of King Gwanggaeto the Great (Jangsu's father) and Jangsu himself in expanding the borders of the kingdom. It also marked the border between Goguryeo and its southern neighbor, the kingdom of Silla.

Jungwon Goguryeo Stele

Like the Jungangtap Pagoda, the stele—the only Goguryeo stele in South Korea—has been designated a National Treasure. Overall, it resembles the massive, 7 m tall King Gwanggaeto the Great Stele in Manchuria, also erected by Jangsu as a memorial to his father, a great Korean conquerer who greatly expanded Goguryeo power in Manchuria and the Hangang River valley.

📱 Take Bus No. 400 from Chungju Intercity Bus Terminal.

UREUK, THE GAYAGEUM AND GENERAL SIN RIP   *History and Culture*

About three kilometers outside of town there's a small hillock overlooking the confluence of the Namhanghang River and one of its tributaries, the Dalcheon Stream 달천. In the old days called Daemunsan Hill 대문산, it is now called Tangeumdae 탄금대. It's a lovely little place associated with two pieces of history, one musical and one military.

In the 6th century, there lived a master musician named Ureuk. Ureuk was the court musician of King Gasil of the Gaya Confederation, a collection of small kingdoms along the lower Nakdonggang River valley that served as a buffer of sorts between the powerful kingdoms of Silla and Baekje. One day, Gasil observed a Chinese zither, or *guzheng*, and asked Ureuk why no such instrument existed in Korea. Ureuk responded by developing the *gayageum* 가야금, a 12-string zither similar to other traditional zithers in Asia, including the *guzheng* and the Japanese *koto*. He also wrote 12 songs for the new instrument.

In the mid-6th century, political instability came to Gaya, and Ureuk fled to the Silla Kingdom. He took up residence in Chungju, where he passed his days at Tangeumdae, playing the *gayageum* while admiring the scenery. In his honor, the hill on which he played was rechristened Tangeumdae or "Zither Plucking Rock."

Over 1,400 years later, Ureuk's invention is still Korea's most popular traditional musical instrument. Good places to hear the *gayageum* at work are Seoul's National Gugak Center and Namsan Gugakdang; you could also pick up a CD by Hwang Byung-

Gayageum

ki, Korea's most renowned *gayageum* master. If the traditional repertoire is not to your liking, buy a CD by the Sookmyung Gayageum Orchestra, a 24-string *gayageum* ensemble famous for their arrangement of Western classical and pop music like Pachelbel's "Canon" and "Let It Be" by The Beatles.

In the 16th century, Tangeumdae

Chungjuho Lake 충주호

Not so long ago, the area that is now Chungjuho Lake was a deep valley in the Sobaeksan Mountains 소백산맥, filled with farms and villages. In 1978, however, the government began construction of the massive Chungju Dam 충주댐 on the Namhangang River. When construction was finally completed in 1985, the valley had been completely flooded, producing Korea's second largest lake.

So big that some call it an "inland sea," Chungjuho Lake winds its way along the mountains of central Korea for 67.5 km². Surrounded by high peaks and dramatic cliffs, it is blessed with mesmerizing scenery, best seen from one of the cruise boats that ply its waters. It's also a water sports destination, popular with boaters and water skiers, as well as one of Korea's top fishing destinations.

became famous for a very different reason. In late May of 1592, the forces of Japanese warlord Toyotomi Hideyoshi invaded Korea with the intention of conquering the nation and marching on China. Armed with great numbers and arquebus guns introduced to Japan by the Portuguese, the Japanese quickly overran the Korean defenders in Busan and began racing north towards Seoul. The royal court dispatched Gen. Sin Rip, a well-respected general with experience fighting nomadic raiders in the wild Korean north, to stop them.

To break into the plains leading to Seoul, a large part of the Japanese force would have to pass through the strategic Saejae Pass in Mungyeong 문경새재 (see p557), where even a greatly outnumbered army could successfully bottle-up a larger attacking force in the narrow passage through the steep mountains. Bewilderingly, Sin left the pass unguarded and instead set up a position at Tangeumdae, where he felt the force—mostly cavalry—could perform better. He may have also believed that with a river to their back and nowhere to run, his troops would fight harder against the Japanese.

On June 8, Sin's army met the Japanese at Tangeumdae. What followed was more a slaughter than a battle. The Korean calvary proved no match for the Japanese arquebuses, who cut the Korean horses down as they charged. The Koreans began the battle with 8,000 men; when the dust settled, almost all were dead or captured. Sin himself escaped to the river where, rather than surrender, he jumped in and drowned. The Japanese suffered only a handful of casualties.

Sin's defeat at Tangeumdae left the path to Seoul wide open. The Korean king fled northwards and the Japanese took the royal capital soon after. The war would rage on for seven more years before the Japanese invaders were finally driven from Korea.

Memorial for the Battle of Tangeumdae

Chungjuho Lake Cruises

The best way to see Chungjuho Lake is by cruise boat. This is a wonderful way to pass an hour or three, depending on how far you go and which boat you take. Passengers are treated to spectacular scenery as the boat passes the lake's many picturesque cliffs and rock formations, each one backed with a local legend or two.

There are four piers, or, in Korean, *naru*, along the lake: Chungju Naru 충주나루, near Chungju Dam; Cheongpung Naru 청풍나루, on the south shore of the lake about halfway to Danyang; Janghoe Naru 장회나루, at a scenic spot also on the south shore of the lake, close to Woraksan National Park; and Sindanyang Naru 신단양나루, near the resort town of Danyang.

You have a choice of two kinds of boat—high-speed ferries or larger, three-story boats that take longer but have open upper decks to take in the scenery while the wind musses your hair. Cruises are as follows:

- **Chungju Naru Cruise (18 km, 1 hr):** This round trip takes you around the western part of the lake. Decent views of Mt. Woraksan. Good if your time is limited. 🎫 12,000 won

- **Chungju Naru ⟶ Janghoe Naru (38 km, 2 hrs):** Probably the most popular cruise, this takes you past most of the lake's scenic sites. Janghoe Naru is a good place to begin exploring Woraksan National Park (see p324). You can also take a bus from there to Danyang. Large boat only; boat leaves when it fills up (80 passengers). 🎫 17,000 won

- **Chungju Naru ⟶ Janghoe Naru Round Trip (76 km):** Time: 2 hrs 40 min (high-speed ferry); 4 hrs 20 min (large boat). 🎫 34,000 won

- **Chungju Naru ⟶ Cheongpung Naru (25 km):** Cheongpung Naru is near the Cheongpung Cultural Heritage Complex (see p322) and Woraksan National Park. Time: 50 min (high-speed ferry); 1 hr 10 min (large boat). 🎫 12,000 won.

- **Chungju Naru ⟶ Sindanyang Naru (53 km):** This is the longest haul, and the one you want to take if you're going to the resort town of Danyang. Time: 1 hr 50 min (high-speed ferry); 2 hrs 50 min (large boat). 🎫 20,000 won.

*Cruises are canceled in winter due to low water levels on the lake. Boats operate hourly 9 am to 4:30 pm in summer, and every other hour 10 am to 3 pm in winter. Note that cruises can get a bit crowded in summer.

"Alligator Island," Chungjuho Lake

Oksunbong ("Jade Bamboo Peak") 옥순봉: One of the "Eight Scenic Spots of Danyang," Oksunbong brings to mind a piece of jade held high by a bamboo shoot. Or so they say. It's a dramatic cliff that plunges straight into the lake. Old paintings of the peak show it was even more dramatic before the lake submerged the lower half of the mountain. According to local legend, Oksunbong used to be part of the town of Cheongpung, but famed Joseon-era scholar and official Yi Hwang (1501–1570) tried to have the scenic peak incorporated into Danyang when he was the local magistrate, supposedly at the behest of the courtesan Duhyang. The magistrate of Cheongpung refused this request but Yi went ahead and carved in the cliff the Chinese characters "Dan Gu Dong Mun," meaning that the peak was the gate to Danyang. After Yi died, Duhyang, overcome with grief, is said to have leaped to her death from another nearby cliff.

Gudambong ("Turtle Peak") 구담봉: Also one of the "Eight Scenic Spots of Danyang," this 343 m peak just before Janghoe Naru is so-named because its rock faces are said to resemble a turtle, and its reflection in the water supposedly a tortoise shell pattern; it has also been likened by some to a folding screen. No matter, one can still appreciate the dramatic beauty of its craggy cliffs broken up by lovely clumps of trees.

Oksunbong

Gudambong

Chungju Dam 충주댐

Completed in 1985, Chungju Dam is Korea's second largest dam, and the largest concrete gravity dam. Standing 97.5 m high and 464 m wide, the mighty dam provides electrical power and water to the region and plays an important role in flood control. As an example of a massive work of civil engineering, it's a staggering sight. Particularly impressive is when they open the sluice gates. There's an observation deck, too, and the dam is lit up at night.

While the dam has contributed mightily to Korea's economic development by producing power, providing water and solving the issue of flooding along the Namhangang River, for the tourist, its primary contribution has been the creation of Chungjuho Lake. The pier for cruise boats is right behind the dam.

🚌 From Chungju Bus Terminal, take a bus to Chungju Dam Pier. Buses are infrequent, however, so you might want to take the 20 minute taxi ride.

Cheongpung Cultural Heritage Complex 청풍문화재단지

As noted above, when the Chungju Dam was completed, the mountain valleys that are now Chungjuho Lake were flooded, submerging age-old towns and villages beneath the waves. One of the towns submerged was the historic riverside port of Cheongpung, an important regional trading and administrative center during the Joseon Dynasty. Not all was lost, however. Dozens of historically and culturally important buildings and artifacts from the flood zone were disassembled and relocated to a scenic hilltop overlooking the new lake.

The result was the Cheongpung Cultural Heritage Complex. The complex has 43 government-listed cultural properties, four old private residences and about 1,600 artifacts from the old days. Its pride and joy is the charming Hanbyeongnu 한벽루 (Treasure No. 528), an old party pavilion with a wonderful view over the lake.

Chungju Dam

Cheongpung Cultural Heritage Complex (left), Hanbyeongnu Pavilion

Another designated treasure here is a Goryeo-era stone Buddha that once stood in Cheongpung. You'll also find an old fortress gate that once served as the entrance to the Cheongpung magistrate's office (now the entrance of the complex), an old Confucian school, the old Cheongpung magistrate's office, tile-roofed and thatched-roof homes, Joseon-era stone monuments, Korean pavilions and sections of old fortress wall. Keep an eye out for the intertwined pine trees, too—they're a symbol of love. All in all, it's a thoroughly relaxing place to wander about for an hour or two, and the views can't be beat.

🕐 9 am to 6 pm (5 pm from Nov–Feb)
💰 3,000 won ✆ 043-641-4301
🚌 From Chungju, the best way to get here is to take the cruise boat from Chungju Dam to Cheongpung Naru, and then walk (uphill) from the dock to the complex. You could also take a bus from the nearby town of Jecheon. Bus No. 90 from Jecheon Bus Terminal goes to Cheongpung; the trip takes about 40 minutes.

WHAT TO EAT

You'll find restaurants in Chungju, of course, but the better eats can be found in the resort towns of Suanbo and Danyang. There are a ton of Korean restaurants at the entrances to Woraksan National Park, too. You'll also find a cluster of restaurants specializing in freshwater fish in front of Cheongpung Cultural Heritage Complex.

WHERE TO STAY

If you're not staying at the nearby resort towns of Suanbo or Danyang, you'll find some options in Chungju. In downtown Chungju, Friendly Hotel Chungju 충주후렌드리호텔 (043-848-9900) lives up to its name. The rooms are clean, and they provide a free English or Korean newspaper to guests. Guests also get a discount when they use the men-only sauna. There's a coffee shop, too. Standard Western-style rooms go for 80,000 won a night.

If you've got a bit more cash, Chungjuho Resort 충주호리조트 (043-851-2580) sits at the base of a mountain overlooking Chungjuho Lake and Oksunbong Peak. Rooms go for 150,000 won a night but can accommodate up to five. The views are gorgeous. Similar is Cheongpung Resort 청풍리조트 (043-640-7000) opposite Cheongpung Naru 청풍나루. It has two hotels, the pricier Lake Hotel and the more reasonably priced Hill Hotel. Views here are enhanced by a fountain in the lake that shoots water 162 m in the air, making it one of the largest fountains in Asia. Rooms begin at 152,000 won a night. Packages available: see http://cheongpungresort.co.kr for more info.

There are also a couple of pensions in the area including Songgye Pension 송계펜션 (043-651-8519) and Duckju Pension 덕주펜션 (043-653-1531, 011-482-9611) near Woraksan National Park. Expect to pay at least 100,000 won a night during the summer high season.

TRANSPORT INFO

From Seoul, buses to Chungju depart from Central City Bus Terminal (2 hrs 10 min). From Daejeon, buses to Chungju depart from Daejeon Dongbu Intercity Bus Terminal (2 hrs 30 min).

WORAKSAN NATIONAL PARK 월악산국립공원

Mt. Woraksan, or "Moon Crag Mountain," is an especially jagged mass of peaks in the heart of central Korea where the east-west Sobaeksan Mountains 소백산 meet the north-south Songnisan Mountains 속리산. Its highest peak, Yeongbong, stands at 1,097 m, but there are over 20 peaks along the ridges and valleys that make up the park. The mountain is covered in lush forests of pine and Mongolian oak, and throughout the park you'll find rushing streams and enchanting waterfalls. The upper heights offer inspiring views of Chungjuho Lake and surrounding mountains.

Compared to other national parks, Woraksan gets fewer visitors, although you'll still find lots of people here on a summer weekend, especially in or along the cool, refreshing streams of the lower valleys. The hikes here are not extremely difficult but some sections get quite steep—be sure to wear appropriate hiking gear, especially in winter.

Hiking Mt. Woraksan

Woraksan National Park is a big place. Broadly speaking, it can be divided into three sections: an eastern section composed of peaks and valleys near Danyang and Chungjuho Lake (Oksunbong and Gudunbong are part of the park); a middle section of wonderful mountain streams along the Yongha Gugok Valley 용하구곡, and a western section around the Songgye Valley 송계계곡, including the main body of Mt. Woraksan. The western part of the park, approached via Chungju, is the most popular with hikers, and is discribed below.

Deokjusanseong Fortress, site of a divinely assisted victory over Mongol invaders in 1256

36

Chungjuho Lake

Songgye Valley

Mt. Daemisan

Yeongbong Peak

Mt. Eoraesan

Sinreuksa Temple

Mt. Haseolsan

Mt. Malmoesan

Deokjusanseong Fortress

Deokjugol Valley

Jikmarijae

Mangdaebong

Haneuljae Pass

Woraksan National Park

Sajo Village Ski Resort

Songgye Valley

Mt. Bukbawisan

Mansu Valley

N

0   1   2 km

Bakjwibong

Jungwon Mireuk-ri Temple Site

Sinseonbong

Mt. Poamsan

There are a number of ways to reach Yeongbong Peak 영봉 (1,097 m). The quickest path up begins at the Dongchanggyo Rest Stop 동창교 휴게소. At 4.3 km, you could, in theory, reach the peak in about two hours, 40 minutes, but the path gets quite steep in places. The path is also thickly forested, obscuring views. A more popular path up the mountain is via the Deokjugol Valley 덕주골. The path is a bit longer (6 km), but considerably gentler. Plan on taking about 3 hours 40 minutes to reach the peak, and six hours round trip. The Deokjugol Path has the further advantage of passing along the way a number of natural and historical points of interest.

Sajabinsinsajiseoktap Pagoda
사자빈신사지석탑

This wonderful piece of 11th century stonework (Treasure No. 94) isn't on the actual path—it's a short walk up the Songgye Valley past the entrance to the trail. Originally nine-storied, the now four-story pagoda is held up by a base of four lion statues. In between the lions is a Buddha statue. The pagoda was erected as

Sajabinsinsajiseoktap Pagoda

a plea for Buddha's protection against invading Khitan nomads from Manchuria.

Sugyeongdae 수경대
The water in this natural stone pool on the way to Deokjusa is crystal clear and an entrancing shade of blue. Don't think about jumping in, though—entering is forbidden.

Deokjusanseong Fortress 덕주산성

Deokjusanseong Fortress is a weathered series of stone fortifications that snakes for around 10 km along the hills and valleys of the southern district of the park. Three gates still remain—the north, south and east gates, the last of which you pass at the entrance to Deokjugol Valley. Sections of the wall have been recently restored.

Deokjusanseong Fortress is one of many stone fortresses that guarded the strategic mountain passes of central Korea. Its most famous moment was in 1256, during the Mongol invasions of Korea. When the Mongols took Chungju, the residents fled to the safety of Deokjusanseong Fortress. A Mongol army laid siege, but the battlefield was suddenly enveloped in clouds, fog, rain, wind, thunder and lightening. Believing God to be in the defenders' corner, the Mongols broke off the attack.

Deokjusa Temple 덕주사

Founded in 587 AD, Deokjusa Temple is Woraksan's largest Buddhist temple. Unfortunately, the temple was destroyed during the Korean War so most of the buildings you see are new. What certainly is not new, however, is the gorgeous relief of the Buddha 마애여래입상 carved into the cliff behind the temple. Designated Treasure No. 406, the 13 m tall relief is believed to have been carved in the 11th century, and shows the characteristically stocky face common in Buddhist sculptures of the Goryeo Dynasty (918–1392). According to legend, the image was carved by Princess Deokju, the sister of the last crown prince of the Silla kingdom. She and the prince fled to the mountain after the fall of their kingdom; while she was carving this image, her brother was erecting the giant Maitreya Buddha statue at the nearby ruins of Mireuksa 미륵사.

Yeongbong Peak (1,097 m) is basically a big, craggy, cliff-faced rock.Reaching it involves climbing a lot of stairs but the views of Chungjuho Lake and the verdant hills that continue endlessly into the horizon are worth the effort.

Jungwon Mireuksa Temple Site 중원미륵사지

On the south end of the park at the Chungju end of the Haneuljae Pass are the ruins of the once important Buddhist temple of Mireuksa 미륵사. The temple was founded in the 11th century during the Goryeo Dynasty and, judging from the sheer amount of stoneworks that remain, it must have been quite large. Unlike most other Korean Buddhist temples which face south, this one faces north, an archaeological expression of the Goryeo Kingdom's determination to reconquer the Manchurian territories of the ancient kingdom of Goguryeo. Sadly, this didn't seem to work out as intended and, in the 13th century, the temple was burnt to the ground by the invading Mongols. The site languished in obscurity until 1977 when Korean archaeologists began uncovering and restoring the masonry.

The star of the temple site is the 10.6 m tall statue of the Maitreya Buddha 미륵리석불입상(Treasure No. 96). Carved of six stones and assembled like a stone pagoda, the Buddha has a massive head atop a simple, cylindrical body, not unlike other large Buddha statues in the Chungcheong-do region. It posseses a rustic, almost child-like charm. Before the temple was destroyed, the Buddha stood in the center of a covered grotto, like Seokguram Grotto in Gyeongju (see p533). Also on site are two stone pagodas, including a five-story pagoda designated Treasure No. 9, some stone lanterns, a massive stone turtle and other pieces of masonry.

Beautiful 11th century Maitreya Buddha, Jungwon Mireuksa Temple Site

Haneuljae Pass 하늘재

The Haneuljae Pass or "Sky Pass" is one of the oldest roads in Korea, dating back to 156 AD when King Adalla of Silla had it built through the mountains to allow his troops to invade northwards. Linking the Silla-dominated lands of the Nakdonggang River valley in the southeast with the Goguryeo and Baekje-dominated lands of the Hangang River valley in the north, the road brought together not just regions, but cultures.

The road continued to be a vital transportation route through the Goryeo Dynasty, but fell out of use in the Joseon Dynasty in favor of the nearby Mungyeong Saejae Pass 문경새재. Thanks to this period of disuse, thick forests of fir, oak and pine have since grown along the sides of the old pathway. If you like nature walks, you're in luck.

The path is quite short (3.2 km), linking the Mireuksa ruins in the west with the village of Gwaneum-ri 관음리 in Mungyeong in the east. It crests at 525 m—a stone marker indicates the high point. From the crest to Gwaneum-ri, there's also a paved road, which is not nearly as fun. From the Mireuksa ruins to the crest and back should take about three hours.

⊙ No hiking between sunset and two hours prior to sunrise. 🚆 Free ⓒ 043-422-5062~3 🖱 http://english.knps.or.kr

TRANSPORT INFO

From Seoul, there are eight direct buses to the park from Dong Seoul Bus Terminal. The trip takes about three hours. From Chungju Bus Terminal, you can take Bus No. 222 for Songgye 송계 and get off at the entrance to the park. If you want to go directly to the ruins of Mireuksa and Haneuljae, however, you should take Bus No. 246 from Chungju Bus Terminal. To explore the peaks around Chungjuho Lake such as Oksunbong, there's a park entrance at Janghoe Naru ferry terminal. To go to Yongha Gugok Valley, take a bus to Cheongpung from the town of Jecheon and get off at Dojeon-ri in Deoksan-myeon.

SUANBO 수안보

Nestled in the mountains just southeast of Chungju (of which, administratively, it is a part), the hot spring resort of Suanbo has been a favorite destination of Korean kings and presidents for centuries (not to mention the common folk). Records of the area's natural sulfur spring go back to the 11th century. During the Joseon Dynasty (1392–1910), Suanbo became something of a royal resort/sanitarium. King Taejo, the founder of the dynasty, visited the springs to relieve skin inflammation. Countless other royal personages flocked here throughout the dynasty to bathe in the restorative waters. In 1885, a modern-style outdoor bath was opened, and in the 1920s and 30s, the Japanese—never ones to pass up a good hot spring—turned the area into a Japanese-style hot spring resort. The development continued after Korea regained its independence in 1945, with Korean presidents Rhee Syngman and Park Chung-hee among the dignitaries who went for a dip here.

Today, the resort town is a popular weekend and holiday retreat for Seoulites, thanks to easy road access from Seoul. The spring water, piped up from 250 m underground, is a nice, warm 53°C; the acidity level of 8.3 keeps things sterile. The water is rich in minerals like lithium, calcium, natrium, fluorine and magnesium, and credited with a wide variety of therapeutic benefits—a spa manager in the 1940s even testified that one girl was cured of leprosy after spending 15 days at the spa. While it can't be promised that a visit to Suanbo will cure debilitating any illnesses, there are certainly worse ways to spend a day, especially after a couple of days on the road.

Hot tub at Suanbo Park Hotel (source: Suanbo Hot Spring Tourism Association)

TIPS

WHERE TO BATHE

Like most Korean hot spring resorts, most visitors enjoy the baths at one of the many hotels that have set up shop in the area. The big three tourist hotels are Suanbo Sangnok Hotel 수안보상록호텔 (043-845-3500), Suanbo Park Hotel 수안보파크호텔 (043-846-2331-6) and Chosun Tourist Hotel 수안보조선관광호텔 (043-848-8833). Rooms at the Sangnok and Chosun Tourist hotels begin at 120,000 won and 165,000 won, respectively. If you'd just like to use the baths at the Sangnok, it'll cost 7,000 won (guests: 5,000 won)

Suanbo Park hotel is a bit more expensive, with rooms beginning at 204,000 won a night, but by way of compensation, the hotel is blessed with a) a peaceful location surrounded by forests, and b) one of the finest outdoor baths in Korea (women only), with stunning views of Mt. Woraksan, especially on a snowy winter's day. If you're on a budget, though, you can use the hotel's sauna for 10,000 won. There are two major spas in town unattached to hotels: Suanbo Hi Spa 수안보하이스파 (043-846-8898) and Nakcheontang 낙천탕 (043-846-2905). The former has a large pool that accommodates up to 500 people. These are good options if you're just passing through.

Sajo Resort 사조리조트

Opened in 1989, Sajo Resort (043-846-0750) has six slopes for skiers and snowboarders. It won't compete with Korea's other ski destinations like Pyeongchang and Muju, but it is cheap—morning lift tickets are 42,000 won while half-day ski rentals are just 20,000 won. There's a sledding hill, too, for the kids (10,000 won) or your inner child (12,000 won). The resort is a bit out of town, but in winter, there's a regular shuttle bus service from Suanbo Bus Terminal.

WHAT TO EAT

No resort town would be complete without good eats. Suanbo is particularly noted for two items: pheasant (*kkwong*, 꿩) and marsh snails (*olgaengi*, 올갱이). Pheasant meat can be prepared in a variety of ways, be it raw, marinated and grilled, or even in dumplings. Daejanggun 대장군 (043-846-1757) has been around for 25 years, and does a seven-course pheasant dinner (50,000 won for two) once served only to Korean kings. The meal includes raw fish, pheasant *bulgogi* 꿩불고기 and pheasant dumplings 꿩만두. Marsh snails, on the other hand, are most frequently eaten in *olgaengi haejangguk* 올갱이해장국, a rich, spicy soup usually eaten after a hard night's drinking for its purported ability to stop a hangover.

The Tugari Sikdang 투가리식당 (043-846-0575) is the place to try this. You'll also find restaurants specializing in mountain vegetable (*sanchae*, 산채) and mushroom (*beoseot*, 버섯) cuisine.

WHERE TO STAY

If you're not staying at one of the big hotels mentioned above, you'll also find a ton of medium-range and budget hotels/motels/inns in town. Just walk around until you find something appealing. A real budget option is Il Yang Youth Hostel 일양유스호스텔 (043-846-9200), where a bed in a room of 16 goes for 9,000 won a night (closed to spring 2012). The hostel is also in a lovely mountainside location.

TRANSPORT INFO

There are regular buses to Suanbo from Chungju Bus Terminal. The trip takes 35 minutes.

DANYANG 단양

Sitting on a bend on the Namhangang River, Danyang is a charming little lakeside resort community nestled at the foothills of the Sobaeksan Mountains 소백산. Technically speaking, what you see today is actually Sindanyang or "New Danyang"—most of "old" Danyang was flooded with the completion of the Chungju Dam in 1985, so the town was relocated to a new site upstream.

Set amidst a backdrop of mountains, lakes and rivers, Danyang retains a rustic, small-town charm that accentuates its wondrous scenery. There's plenty to do here for a couple of days, be it exploring the town's magnificent limestone caves, taking in the sunset over the Dodam Sambong rocks, or just lazily relaxing lakeside. It's worth coming here any season of the year, but it's especially lovely in autumn, when the hillsides transform into a tapestry of gold and crimson.

Layout Danyang is essentially a one-road town on the bow of the river. The main intercity bus terminal sits riverside, although a newer station is currently under construction a bit further upstream. Danyang Station, however, is located on the opposite side of the river, a taxi or bus ride from the downtown area.

Sunset at Dodam Sambong, the most famous of Danyang's "Eight Scenic Wonders"

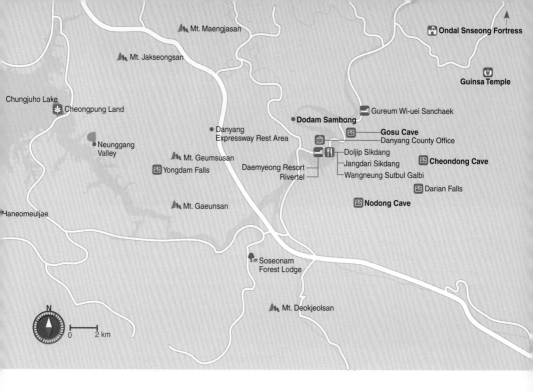

Eight Scenic Wonders of Danyang

The "Eight Scenic Wonders of Danyang," or Danyang Palgyeong 단양팔경, are, as the name would suggest, eight particularly scenic locations—mostly funky cliffs and rock formations—located around Danyang. The list was compiled by legendary Joseon-era scholar Yi Hwang (1501–1570) while he was serving as Danyang's magistrate in what can only be called an early example of tourism promotion.

1. Dodam Sambong 도담삼봉: These three jagged, pointy rocks in the middle of Namhangang River, just upstream from downtown Danyang, are Danyang's most famous tourist destination. According to legend, the rocks were once a husband, his wife and his concubine. The husband and wife, while very much in love, were unable to conceive so the husband took a concubine. The concubine did give birth to a son but, as soon as she did, she began to mistreat the wife. This made God spiteful, so he turned the quarrelsome threesome into stone. Today, the big rock in the middle—the one with a Korean pavilion perched upon it—is called the "husband rock," the one upstream the "wife rock," and the one downstream the "concubine rock." The best views can be had at sunrise or sunset. It's especially lovely in misty weather when the three rocks exude a mysterious beauty. Tour boats are available to show you around the rocks and nearby Seongmun—5,000 won will get you from here to Seongmun and back. To get to Dodam Sambong, just take a short taxi ride from Danyang Bus Terminal.

2. Seongmun 석문: Basically, this is a big stone arch overlooking the Namhangang

Dodam Sambong (left), Sainam

River, not far from Dodam Sambong, from where it can be seen. The gate is visible from the tour boats that depart from Dodam Sambong but you'll need to do a bit of hiking if you want to see the thing up close and personal.

3. Gudambong 구담봉: This fantastic cliff is best seen from a tour boat on Chungjuho Lake. For more information about the cliff and the tour boats, see the Chungju section (p 320).

4. Oksunbong 옥순봉: Also best seen from a tour boat on Chungjuho Lake. See the Chungju section for more information.

5. Sainam 사인암: Overlooking a clear mountain stream, this craggy red cliff crowned by pine trees looks like something straight out of an old Korean painting, and has been a favorite relaxation spot for centuries. To get here, walk from the bus terminal to the main drag, get on a bus for Banggok 방곡 and get off at Jikti 직티 (1 hr). The cliff is a short walk from there.

6. Haseonam 하선암, **7. Jungseonam** 중선암, **8. Sangseonam** 상선암: These three rocks can be found in Woraksan National Park's Seonam Valley 선암계곡, also known, thanks to the rocks, as the Samseon Gugok 삼선구곡, or "Three Fairy Valley." Admittedly, the rocks themselves are not especially exciting in and of themselves but they do punctuate a very beautiful stretch of valley deep in the

Oksunbong Peak

Sangseonam (left), Haseonam

mountains where clear brooks, thick forests and surreal rock formations can be found in abundance; it's especially refreshing in summer. Be prepared to pay a 1,600 won park entry. To get here, take the bus for Seonam Valley from Danyang Bus Terminal. You can find buses to these sites from Danyang Bus Terminal.

Gosu Cave 고수동굴

In addition to its Eight Scenic Wonders, Danyang is also famous for its limestone caves, of which Gosu Cave is the most spectacular. This extensive cave system stretches for a length of 1,300 m, and is full of pools, waterfalls and 120 fantastically formed stalactites and stalagmites. Stairs

and lighting have been installed to give the non-spelunking masses access to this intriguing subterranean landscape, or at least 600 m of it (to preserve the environment, the rest has been placed off-limits to visitors). It's like strolling through a Dali painting, except colder—the temperature here stays at 15°C all year round. This makes it a very popular destination in summer, even if crowds make it even more claustrophobic. Still, if you're in the area, you'd be a fool to pass this place up.

🕓 9 am to 5:30 pm (Apr–Oct); 9 am to 5 pm (Nov–Mar) 🎫 5,000 won 📞 043-422-3072
🚌 Take a bus to Gosu Donggul (Gosu Cave) from Danyang Bus Terminal, or simply take a taxi—it's just a 5 minute ride out of town.

Stalagmites of Gosu Cave

Cheondong Cave 천동동굴

If Gosu Cave isn't enough to satisfy your spelunking needs, check out Cheondong Cave, another limestone cave a little further out of town. At 450 m, it's not nearly as extensive as Gosu Cave but its landscape has been likened to depictions of Nirvana in Buddhist art. Be forewarned—it can get pretty narrow in here so if you're tall or a little husky, be prepared to do some bending and squeezing.

🕐 9 am to 5:30 pm (Mar–Nov), 9 am to 5 pm Dec–Feb) 💵 5,000 won 📞 043-422-2972 🚌 Buses to Cheondong Cave leave from Danyang Bus Terminal (20 min).

Guinsa Temple 구인사

The head temple of the Cheontae Order of Korean Buddhism, Korea's second largest Buddhist order, Guinsa is a virtual Buddhist city hidden in a steeply walled valley in the Sobaeksan Mountains. Unlike most of Korea's other Buddhist temples, which boast of histories dating back millennia, Guinsa was founded only in 1945, and work on the current complex began in the 60s.

What the temple lacks in lineal pedigree, however, it makes up in sheer scale and ambitious civil engineering. About 50 buildings have been wedged into a steep, narrow valley; to accommodate, the complex was built "up" rather than "out," with buildings nearly on top of one another.

The head temple of the Cheontae Order of Korean Buddhism, Guinsa is virtually a city unto itself.

Halls have been built in a Korean style, but of concrete rather than wood, and many are multi-story, giving the temple vertical lines found at no other Buddhist temple in the country. The Main Dharma Hall, one of the largest Buddhist temple buildings in Korea, is five stories high, with each floor serving a separate function. The temple has enough space to house up to 10,000 monks. At the top of the valley, with a fine view of the rest of the complex, is a three-story wooden hall which serves as a shrine

to the late Master Sangwol, who refounded the Cheontae Order in 1967.

All the buildings are ornately painted and decorated, and in contrast to the black roof tiles you'll find at most Korean Buddhist temples, some of the structures here are topped with golden orange roof tiles. You'll find shops and restaurants at the entrance of the temple.

ⓒ 043-423-7100 🚌 Buses for Guinsa depart from Danyang Bus Terminal (40 min). There are also direct buses from Seoul's Dong Seoul Terminal (3 hrs).

Ondalsanseong Fortress 온달산성

A bit out of town, on a strategic hilltop overlooking a bend in the Namhangang River, is an old stone bastion called Ondalsanseong Fortress. It's not particularly large—the walls are just 682 m in length—but the views over the river and hills are pretty dramatic. The walls are said to have been erected in the 6th century by the Goguryeo general Ondal (see next page) to protect the Hangang River valley from attacks by Silla.

🚌 Take a bus from Danyang Bus Terminal to Yeongchun 영춘 where the fortress is located.

Ondalsanseong Fortress, built by a Goguryeo general in the 6th century.

ONDAL THE FOOL & PRINCESS PYEONGGANG

According to legend, the heroic Goguryeo General Ondal came from humble beginnings—born poor, ugly and stupid. He spent his youth roaming town in rags, begging and selling scrap wood to support his mother. Unlearned and slow, he was given the nickname "Ondal the Fool."

So pitiful was his situation that he became something of a bogeyman by whom fathers could frighten daughters with threats of marriage. One such father was King Pyeongwon of Goguryeo (r. 559–590), who had a daughter, Princess Pyeonggang, who frequently cried. Whenever she cried, the King would threaten, "If you don't stop crying, I will marry you off to Ondal the Fool." A severe threat indeed, but not even this could get her to stop crying.

When Pyeonggang turned 16, the king arranged to marry off his daughter—who, thankfully, had by this time outgrown her crying—to a young man of noble birth. Pyeonggang, however, had taken her father's threats to heart, and protested that she was supposed to marry Ondal the Fool. Needless to say, the King was not amused, but Pyeonggang persisted until her father finally threw her out of the palace, telling her to go find Ondal and marry him.

Which she did. Clearly, though, for Princess Pyeonggang, Ondal was a bit of a project. She taught him the scholastic and martial arts, trading her jewels for a home, books, a sword and a horse. Ondal worked hard, and managed to transform himself into a skilled warrior.

To show himself off, he participated in the King's annual hunt, attended by the kingdom's top warriors. With his skill and bravery, he impressed the king, who to this point still had no idea who he was. The King called Ondal over and asked his name. When Ondal answered, the King was shocked, but pleased that after all these years, his daughter had proven herself correct. The King asked Pyeonggang to return to the palace with her husband, whom the King made a general in his army.

General Ondal proved a good general, leading Goguryeo forces to victory over invading Manchurian nomads attacking the kingdom from the north. In 590, Goguryeo made a bid to retake the Hangang River valley from Silla. Ondal led an assault on Achasan Fortress, an old Goguryeo bastion near Seoul that Silla had taken some years ago. Ondal was hit by an arrow, however, and died.

Ondal's body was placed in a coffin to be taken back to Goguryeo but, mysteriously, the coffin would not move, no matter how hard his men tried. When Princess Pyeonggang arrived, she embraced the coffin and cried. Only then would the coffin move, and Ondal could finally be brought home.

WHAT TO
EAT

Danyang's known for its garlic, and garlic cuisine is indeed the local specialty. Doljip Sikdang 돌집식당 (043-422-2842) is a good place to try *maneul ssam jeongsik* 마늘쌈정식, a meal consisting of lettuce leaves, garlic rice cooked in a stone pot accompanied by a plethora of garlic side dishes (10,000 won a person). Another good place to try is Jangdari Sikdang 장다리식당 (043-423-3960), which has a variety of garlic-centric meals in the 12,000–25,000 won price range. Meat eaters will want to stop by Wangneung Sutbul Galbi 왕릉숯불갈비 (043-423-9292), which does garlic *galbi* (ribs) for 10,000–25,000 won, depending on the cut.

WHERE TO
STAY

Being a resort town, Danyang's got plenty of places to stay. The snazziest establishment is Daemyung Resort Danyang 대명리조트단양 (043-420-8311), a condo that also operates Aquaworld, a large pool/bath complex using Danyang's very own natural mineral water spring. The views are terrific but they'll cost you—a room that sleeps four goes for 264,000 won a night.

Also offering nice views of the river is Danyang Tourist Hotel Edelweis 단양관광호텔에델바이스 (043-423-7070), where rooms start at 69,000 won (98,000 won on a weekend) but inflate to 140,000 won during the summer peak season. There are more reasonably priced motels and inns along the lake, too, including Rivertel 모텔리버텔 (043-421-5600), where rooms go for 35,000 won a night.

One particularly charming pension worth checking out—if you don't mind staying a bit out of town—is Gureum Wi-ui Sanchaek 구름위의 산책 (011-260-9708), or "Walk Above the Clouds," so named because it sits on a potato farm about 500 m up a 700 m mountain overlooking the Namhangang River. Rooms start at 200,000 won a night, which you won't mind paying if the morning weather is right and the clouds and fog get caught in the river valley below for a truly magical view. To get here, take a taxi from Danyang Bus Terminal—the fare should come to around 5,000 won.

TRANSPORT
INFO

Buses to Danyang run every hour, on the hour, from Seoul's Dong Seoul Bus Terminal (2 hrs 30 min). There are also frequent buses to Danyang from Chungju and Cheongju. You can also take one of the frequent trains that pass through Danyang from Seoul's Cheongnyangni Station (3 hrs). Lastly, a cruise boat is available to Danyang from Chungju and, in fact, this is the recommended way if you're coming from Chungju. Boats don't run to Danyang in winter, however, so you'll need to get off at Janghoe Naru and transfer to a bus. See the Chungjuho Lake section for more details.

DAEJEON &
CHUNGCHEONGNAM-DO

HIGHLIGHTS

- Discover the beauty of Baekje civilization in the historic cities of Gongju and Buyeo

- Have filthy beachside fun at the Boryeong Mud Festival

- Relax at the Taean Haean National Park, one of Korea's most beautiful stretches of coastline

- Learn about Korea's tumultuous past at Cheonan's Independence Hall

- Meditate for a while at lovely Sudeoksa Temple

- Enjoy the creature comforts of Daejeon, one of Korea's better planned cities

Gyeonggi-do

TAEAN HAEAN
NATIONAL PARK

SEOSAN

CHEONAN

Sinchang Stn.   Asan Stn.   Cheonan Stn.

HONGSEONG

Chungcheong
buk-do

Hongseong Stn.

Cheonsuman
Bay

Magok-sa

Osong Stn.

Jochiwon Stn.

GONGJU

Daejeon
Jochajang Stn.

DAECHEON
BEACH

Daecheon Stn.

GYERYONGSAN
NATIONAL PARK

Daejeon Stn.

Yellow Sea

BORYEONG

DAEJEON

Seo-Daejeon Stn.

BUYEO

Gyeryong Stn.

Nonsan Stn.

GEUMSAN

Janghang
Stn.

Jeollabuk-do

THE HEART OF ANCIENT MAGNIFICENCE

The region of Chungcheongnam-do, including the separately administered metropolitan city of Daejeon, is a land of rich farmland, beautiful coastlines and abundant cultural heritage.

During the dramatic days of the Three Kingdoms Era, this was the heartland of the mighty kingdom of Baekje, famed throughout Asia for its cultural sophistication. While Baekje fell in the 7th century to its longstanding rival, the kingdom of Silla, the ancient temples and splendid tombs in the old royal capitals of Gongju and Buyeo testify to the magnificence of its civilization.

When you're done exploring Baekje's historical heritage, spend a day or two taking in the natural splendor of the Taean Haean National Park, or enjoy a wild weekend at the Boryeong Mud Festival, the biggest—and dirtiest—summer party in the country. If you're in need of creature comforts, you can always pop into Daejeon, one of Korea's more pleasant urban environments.

Baekje Cultural Land, Buyeo

Tower of Great Light of Expo Park, venue of Daejeon Expo '93.

DAEJEON 대전

A major transportation hub and educational center, Daejeon—Korea's fifth largest city with about 1.5 million residents—is a relatively new city, born as a railway town in the early 20th century. It is also a fairly well-planned city, its broad avenues and grid-like neighborhoods a far cry from the chaos of other major Korean urban centers. Home to some of Korea's leading research universities, R&D centers and high-tech industries, especially around the so-called "Daedeok Innopolis" (formerly Daedeok Science Town), the city has earned a reputation as Korea's answer to California's Silicon Valley.

While a pleasant city to live in, especially if you're a lab geek or techie, for travelers, the city is often seen as a place to pass through rather than linger. It has few of the historical and cultural draws of some of Korea's other cities, but its excellent rail and road links make it an outstanding base for exploring the mountains, temples and communities of central Korea, including the nearby towns of Gongju and Buyeo, the capitals of the ancient Korean kingdom of Baekje.

History

Daejeon's early history is best summed up by the city's name, which translates as "Big Field." Prior to the start of the 20th century, there was little here but the city's namesake. In 1898, Korea's royal government awarded the Japanese—who for economic and military reasons were keen to develop Korea's transportation infrastructure—a concession to build the Seoul–Busan railroad. The line opened in 1905, with a station in Daejeon. Japanese settlers began moving in, a process that accelerated with the opening of the southwestern Honam line railroad in 1914, with its junction in Daejeon. By 1940, the once-tiny village was home to 70,000 people. In 1932, the Japanese colonial government transferred the provincial capital of Chungcheongnam-do from Gongju to Daejeon, making the city the economic, political and social center of the region.

After Korea's liberation in 1945, Daejeon continued to be a thriving railway town. When the North Koreans captured Seoul at the start of the Korean War in June of 1950, the national capital was briefly moved to Daejeon before being moved again to Busan. In July of that year, Daejeon, too, was captured by the North Koreans in the brutal Battle of Daejeon, a three-day engagement that witnessed bitter street-to-street fighting between the North Koreans and the US 24th Infantry Division. The battle left the city in ruins.

After the war, Daejeon was rebuilt. In the 1960s, the city's transportation infrastructure and central location—far from the inter-Korean DMZ—attracted the attention of Korean President Park Chung-hee, who undertook efforts to transform Daejeon into a hub of science and technology. The Korea Advanced Institute of Science and Technology (KAIST), Korea's top research university, was founded in the city in 1971, and Daedeok Science Town—a research cluster akin to Japan's Tsukuba Science City—was established in 1973. Daejeon's reputation as a city of science and technology was further enhanced when it hosted the 1993 Expo.

Daejeon today is one of Korea's fastest growing cities. In 1997, the national government, looking to relieve population pressures in Seoul, moved a number of government offices to the newly constructed Daejeon Government Complex. The opening of the KTX high-speed rail service in 2004 cut travel time between Daejeon and Seoul to under an hour, turning the city, for all practical purposes, into a giant suburb of Seoul.

Layout

Sitting in a broad plain, Daejeon is a sprawling town that, thanks to its history, has two downtown areas: an old one in the southeast of town near Daejeon Station and the old Chungcheongnam-do Provincial Office, and a newer one in the northwest of town around Daejeon Government Complex. The district of Yuseong, home to KAIST, Chungnam National University, Daedeok Innopolis and Yuseong Hot Spring, is even further to the northwest, just beyond the Gapcheon Stream 갑천.

A largely planned city, Daejeon's urban grid is relatively easy to navigate. It is serviced by two major train stations, both across town from each other. Daejeon Station, in the east of town, sits on the Seoul–Busan line. Seodaejeon Station, in the west of town, sits on the Seoul–Mokpo line. Both enjoy KTX services. The city also has three bus terminals: the Daejeon Express Bus Terminal and Dongbu Bus Terminal in the east of town, and Seobu Bus Terminal in the west. The city's lone subway line connects Daejeon Station and the old downtown with the Yuseong area.

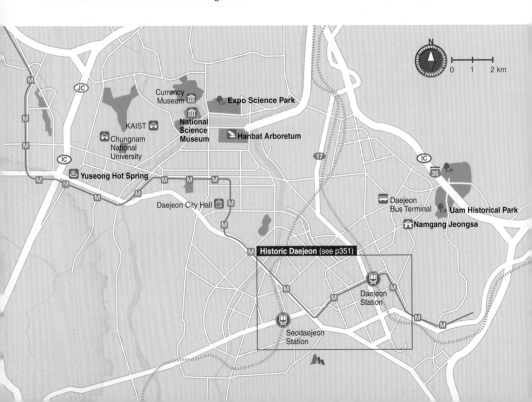

The city is also surrounded by a number of peaks, the most notable being Mt. Gyeryongsan 계룡산, a national park to the west of town. To the east is Daecheongho Lake 대청호, a large reservoir and popular city getaway.

TIPS

DAEJEON CITY TOURS

If you've got a day to kill in Daejeon but are not particularly keen on planning your own tour or discovering the joys of Daejeon's public transportation system, the City of Daejeon operates city tour buses that will bring you in comfort to many of its tourist spots for a mere 2,000 won. Tour buses depart from Daejeon Station. There are three tours available:

Science Tour: Twice daily on Tuesday and Thursday. Highlights: Expo Park, National Science Museum, KAIST (3 hrs 30 min)

History & Culture Tour: Twice daily on Wednesday, Friday and Sunday. Highlights: Hanbat Museum of Education, Dongchundang Park, Uam Historical Park (3 hrs 40 min)

Ecology & Environment Tour: Twice daily on Tuesday, Thursday, Saturday. Highlights: Daecheongho Lake area (3 hrs 30 min)

More Info: 042-253-0005

Expo Park 엑스포공원

Like many former expo sites, the venue of Daejeon Expo '93 was turned into a commemorative park. The park mostly serves as an educational space for science and technology, with a ton of conventional and hands-on exhibits, theaters, games and rides. It's not quite Epcot but it tries, and your kids will love it. Adults with an interest in science and technology will enjoy it, too. Many of the halls and exhibits are free but some, including the Simulation Theater and the Imax Dome Theater, charge admission.

At night, the park's landmark Tower of Great Light 한빛탑, erected in 1993 and a symbol of Daejeon, is lit up. Also illuminated at night is the nearby Expo Bridge, which also features a bridge fountain that shoots multicolored streams of water from nozzles attached to the bridge's side. Taken together with the tower and the Gapcheon Stream over which it passes, the bridge makes for one of Daejeon's most beautiful nighttime scenes.

Expo Bridge, one of Daejeon's best nighttime scenes

⊙ 10 am to 6 pm (Mar to Oct), 10 am to 5:30 pm (Nov to Feb). Admission ends 30 minutes prior to closing. Closed Mondays. ⊟ Free. Individual exhibits cost extra (1,500 won to 10,000 won). ⊟ Take Bus No. 606 from Daejeon Station. ℂ 042-869-5114 (press 5 for help)

National Science Museum 국립중앙과학관

Another lifesaver if you've got kids, the National Science Museum houses about 4,000 items documenting Korea's natural and technological history. The highlight here is the planetarium, housed under Korea's largest dome. Another highlight, especially for youngsters, is the Science Alive Discovery Center 창의나래관, a massive interactive space dedicated to science.

⊙ 9:30 am to 5:50 pm. Closed Mondays. ⊟ Free, with an additional 1,000 won for the planetarium. Admission for the Science Alive Discovery Center is 2,000 won. ⊟ Take Buses No. 180, 513, or 814 from Daejeon Station. ℂ 042- 601-7894~6

Planetarium of the National Science Museum

TIPS

MAGLEV TRAIN 자기부상열차

Connecting Expo Park and the National Science Museum is a 44-seat Maglev train, the only one in operation in Korea. Maglevs use magnetic levitation to suspend, guide and propel the train along its track, offering a smoother and quieter ride. The Maglev runs 10 times daily: five times from Expo Park to the National Science Museum, and five times in the opposite direction. The 1 km ride takes under 5 minutes.

Hanbat Arboretum 한밭수목원

Just across the Gapcheon Stream from Expo Park, this patch of greenery bills itself as Korea's largest artificial arboretum in an urban area. If you find yourself spending a summer night in Daejeon, it makes for a

Daejeon Culture & Arts Center, Hanbat Arboretum

Uam Historical Park 우암사적공원 & Namgan Jeongsa 남간정사

A relatively modern city, Daejeon is not generally known for its plethora of Korean traditional architecture but one site worth checking out is Uam Historical Park. Located at the foot of a forested hillock, this collection of wooden Korean halls, pavilions, shrines and gardens was where noted Joseon-era scholar and official Song Si-yeol (1607–1689) lived and taught his students. Song, known by his pen name of Uam, served as an official for over 50 years, and is mentioned no fewer than 3,000 times in the *Annals of the Joseon Dynasty*, the official history of the dynasty.

The highlight of the complex is the exquisite Namgan Jeongsa, a one-story structure built in 1638 over a running

rather pleasant evening stroll, when the gardens and ponds are lit up. The arboretum is also home to a number of cultural facilities, the most notable of which are Daejeon Museum of Art 대전시립미술관 (admission: 500 won) and Daejeon Culture & Arts Center 대전문화예술전당.

🕐 9 am to 6 pm. Admission ends one hour prior to closing. Closed Mondays. 🎟 Free 🚇 15 minute walk from Government Complex, Daejeon Station, Line 1. Leave Exit 3 and swing a right at Dunsan Police Station. ✆ 042-472-4972

Uam Historical Park, the former home of 17th century scholar Song Si-yeol

Nangam Jeongsa masterfully blends man-made with nature.

stream that empties out into a pond dug in front of the building. It's a lovely example of Korean traditional architecture and landscaping that one Korean pundit referred to as "the world's first Fallingwater," referencing the Frank Lloyd Wright masterpiece that also sits over a running stream. Song used it as a classroom, and the sound of the water running underneath must have made for a wonderful study environment, indeed.

🕐 Park: 5 am to 9 pm (Mar to Oct), 6 am to 8 pm (Nov to Feb). Namgan Jeongsa: 10 am to 5 pm 🎫 Free 🚌 Take bus No. 311 from Exit 7 of Daedong Station. ✆ 042-673-9286

Yuseong Hot Spring 유성온천

Yuseong Hot Spring, located in Daejeon's northwestern Yuseong district, is the city's most popular attraction with domestic tourists. The hot (27–56°C), mineral-rich waters that bubble up from the natural spring of Yuseong area are famous for their healing properties: according to one legend, a Baekje warrior wounded grievously in battle against the rival Silla kingdom was almost instantly healed upon dipping into the waters. Historically, however, Koreans favored cold water baths over hot, and it was the hot spring-mad Japanese who first began developing the Yuseong area as a resort early in the 20th century. After the opening of the railway, tourists began flocking to the area. Koreans, too, began taking to the hot springs and by the 1930s entrepreneurial Koreans began building baths and hotels. After Liberation, the area continued to develop and thrive as a resort. Today, Yuseong's hot springs see more than 20 million tourists a year. Accommodating them are 13 major tourist hotels, approximately 100 motels and inns, and countless restaurants, bars and other entertainment facilities.

To enjoy the hot spring waters, you need to go to either a hotel spa or a public bath. The veritable Yousung Hotel 유성호텔 (042-820-0100, 5 am to 10 pm), with a history that goes back to 1915, has a popular public spa with indoor and outdoor pools. Admission is 5,000 won. Another good choice is the Hotel Riviera 리비에라호텔 (042-823-2111, 6 am to 10 pm), where 12,000 won will gain you access to the bath and saunas—if you don't like the wet sauna and its Korean medicinal herbs, give the Finnish sauna a try.

If you're short of time or can't swing a full spa experience, there is a public foot bath near the Kyeryong Spatel 계룡스파텔— reward your tired feet with a dip in the soothing 41°C waters.

BATTLE OF DAEJEON

History and Culture

The Korean War did not start off well for South Korea and its American allies. On June 25, 1950, the war began with a North Korean blitzkrieg across the 38th parallel, the inter-Korean border. Just three days later, Seoul had fallen and, by mid-July, the North Korean juggernaut was pressing on the central Korean city of Daejeon, an important road and rail junction. The US 24th Infantry Division, led by Maj. Gen. William F. Dean, was tasked with blunting the North Korean assault, an unenviable task as his troops were outnumbered and outgunned by the North Koreans. His troops were largely ill-prepared to fight, too, as they had been pulled from cushy occupation duty in Japan. Previous encounters between the 24th Division and the North Koreans had gone badly for the Americans.

Maj. Gen. William F. Dean

On July 12, the Americans began setting up a defensive line along the Geumgang River to the north of Daejeon. North Korean pressure proved too great, however and, unable to hold the line, US forces dropped back to Daejeon itself. On July 18, Dean was ordered to hold the city until July 20, when American reinforcements would arrive in Korea and set up a defensive line further south.

Surrounding the city, the North Koreans began their assault on Daejeon on July 19. What followed were two days of brutal house-to-house warfare; as communications broke down in the firestorm that was Daejeon, the battle descended into a disorganized mess. Even Gen. Dean jumped into the fray, taking a small team and a bazooka onto the battle-torn streets in search of North Korean tanks.

Battle of Daejeon Memorial

As the day came to a close on July 20, Dean ordered a withdrawal from the city. During the withdrawal, his jeep took a wrong turn and got lost. For over a month, the general wandered Korea's hillsides in search of the American lines. He was captured by the North Koreans and spent the rest of the war—nearly three years—in a North Korean prison camp. He was the highest ranking American officer captured since the US Civil War. While imprisoned, he was awarded the Congressional Medal of Honor.

The 24th Infantry Division was nearly destroyed in the battle, forfeiting more than 900 lives. The time it bought allowed fresh American units to set up stronger defensive positions along the Nakdonggang River, where the North Korean offensive would finally be brought to a halt.

Historic Daejeon

Thanks to the Korean War and urban development, not a whole lot remains of Daejeon's history as a colonial railway town, but if you're interested and willing to put in some footwork, you can find some significant reminders of the past. Notable examples include:

① Old Railway Warehouses 구 철도청대전지역사 무소재무과보급창고(3호) (1958): The old railway station was leveled during the Korean War but these old warehouses, located behind Daejeon Station, were built soon after the war using colonial-era techniques.

② Old Chungcheongnam-do Provincial Office 구 충남도청사 (1932): The most impressive of Daejeon's colonial edifices, this grand office covered in scratch tile is remarkably well preserved—be sure to check out the beautiful period lobby.

③ Chungcheongnam-do Governor's Residence (1932) 충남도지사공관: Built in mixed Japanese-Art Deco style, the governor's residence is still in use, but may soon be turned into a museum. The street on which it is located—formerly a neighborhood for colonial officials—is lined with Japanese-style homes.

④ Old Korea Development Bank Building 구 산업은행 대전지점 (1937): Built in Renaissance style, this sturdy old bank is now an eyeglass shop.

⑤ Old Daejeon Branch of the Oriental Development Company 구 동양척식회사 대전지점 (1921): This colonial-style office was the local branch of Japan's answer to the British East India Company. Now a bathroom tile shop.

⑥ Former Chungcheong Regional Office of National Agricultural Products Quality Management Service 구 국립농산물품질관리원 충청지원(1958): Now used as an art gallery, this quirky functionalistic structure with window louvers and a Korean tile roof was designed by Korean architect Bae Han-gu.

1. Former Chungcheong Regional Office of National Agricultural Products Quality, Management Service
2. Old Auditorium, Daejeon Girls Middle School 3. Mok-dong Catholic Church 4.Ojeong-dong Missionary Village

7 **Mok-dong Catholic Church** 거룩한 말씀의 수녀회 성당 (1921): Built by French missionaries, this beautiful white Gothic church is now the chapel for a Congregation of the Sacred Word convent, formerly a Franciscan monastery.

8 **Old Auditorium, Daejeon Girls Middle School** 구 대전여중 강당 (1937): The roof lines of this small but graceful Art Nouveau building are said to resemble those of a Korean thatched roof house.

9 **Old Teacher's College School Headmaster's Residence** (1930s) 구 사범부속학교 교장 사택: A striking combination of Japanese and Western styles, this home is now used as a residence by the pastor of nearby Seongsan Church.

10 **Ojeong-dong Missionary Village** 오정동 선교사촌 (1956): Located on the campus of Hannam University 한남대학교, these picturesque homes—constructed in American fashion but with Korean roofs— were built by the American missionaries who founded the university.

11 **Battle of Daejeon Memorial** 대전지구전투기념비: Located in a park on Mt. Bomunsan 보문산, this memorial tower and statue commemorates the bitter Battle of Daejeon (see p 349), one of the most important engagements of the early part of the Korean War. The man with the bazooka is Maj. Gen. William F. Dean, the commander of the US 24th Infantry Division, who famously went tank hunting in the midst of the battle.

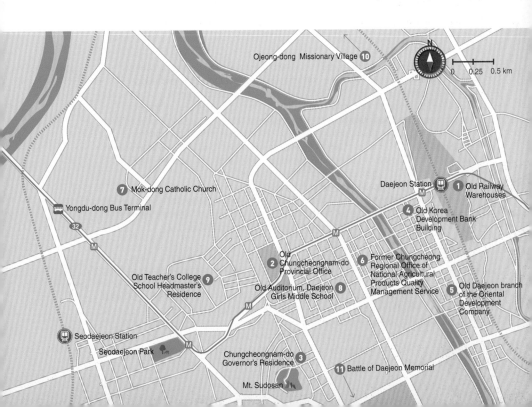

GETTING AROUND DAEJEON

TRANSPORT INFO

🚌 Daejeon has a well-developed bus system. Most major stops have digital schedules posted; even if you can't read Korean, you might be able to make out much of the info. Ⓜ Daejeon has its own single-line subway (1,100–1,200 won) running east–west, linking the old city with the new. It's especially useful for reaching the Yuseong Hot Spring area (Yuseong Spa Station). Unlike the Seoul subway, Daejeon's subway uses round, plastic tokens, which are cute if nothing else.

GETTING TO / FROM DAEJEON

✈ The nearest airport is Cheongju International Airport, about 40 minutes north by bus from Dongbu Bus Terminal. The only domestic flights from Cheongju go to Jejudo, however. There are a few flights a week to China and Japan. 🚆 Daejeon is serviced by two train stations. Daejeon Station is on the Seoul–Busan line. The KTX (every 10–20 minutes from Seoul, 22,900 won) brings you to and from Seoul in under an hour. Saemaeul trains (13 trains a day from Seoul, 15,500 won) will bring you to and from Seoul in about an hour and 50 minutes. KTX trips to and from Busan (every 20 minutes, 32,700 won) take under two hours. Seodaejeon Station is on the Seoul–Mokpo line, so this is where you get on or off to and from Seoul's Yongsan Station, Gwangju or Mokpo. The KTX (every 25 minutes from Yongsan, 22,700 won) brings you to and from Seoul's Yongsan Station in one hour. To Mokpo (24,300 won) takes 2 hours, 20 minutes. 🚌 Daejeon has three major bus terminals: Express Bus Terminal, Dongbu (East) Bus Terminal and Seobu (West) Bus Terminal. If you're traveling to major cities like Seoul, Busan or Gwangju, use the Express Bus Terminal. Express buses to and from Seoul's Express Bus Terminal (every 15 minutes) take about 2 hours. Dongbu Bus Terminal services cities to the east, north and south, while Seobu Bus Terminal services cities to the west like Gongju, Buyeo, Boryeong and Taean.

WHAT TO EAT

The areas around the train stations and bus terminals are always good places to find inexpensive places to eat. In fact, the entire area around Jungangno Subway Station 중앙로역 is full of Korean eateries where you can fill up on the cheap. One local Daejeon specialty is *dubu duruchigi* 두부 두루치기, or tofu stir-fry. Jillojip 진로집 (042-226-0914), hidden in an alley near Chungcheongnam-do Provincial Office 충청남도청, has been doing this dish (10,000 won) for 40 years. Another local specialty is *kalguksu* 칼국수, or hand-made noodle soup. From the outside, Hanbat Kalguksu 한밭 칼국수 (042-254-8350) looks run-down, but its *dubutang* (8,000 won for two), a spicy tofu soup into which noodles are added, is to die for. You can find it near the Mokcheon Market 목천시장, near Jungangno Subway Station.

The most happening bar scene can be found around Dunsan-dong 둔산동, Daejeon's "new" downtown around Daejeon City Hall (City Hall Station). Start in the streets across from Galleria Department Store. You'll find a great many bars in front of Chungnam National University 충남대 (near Yuseong Oncheon Station) and around Yuseong hot springs district, too.

WHERE TO STAY

There are major clusters of reasonably priced motels and *yeogwan* (Korean inns) near Daejeon's Dongbu/Express bus terminals, Seobu Bus Terminal and along the stream in front of Daejeon Station. On weekends, expect to pay 40,000 won a night. Motel California 모텔 캘리포니아 (042-252-7999) near Daejeon Station and the Limousine Motel 리무진모텔 (042-621-1004) near Dongbu Bus Terminal are clean and have typical motel amenities. An even cheaper option is sleeping in a *jjimjilbang* (Korean sauna), many of which have communal sleeping rooms. Rodeo Land 로데오랜드 (042-485-9270), near Daejeon City Hall, is big, clean, and will cost you just 8,000 won a night for the *jjimjilbang*. If you're flush, the nicer places are clustered in the hot spring resort area of Yuseong.

GYERYONGSAN NATIONAL PARK 계룡산국립공원

Literally "Chicken Dragon Mountain," this mountain park between Daejeon and Gongju is so named because, it is said, the mountain's ridgeline resembles a dragon with a chicken's crest atop its head. Visitors may or may not see the resemblance but there's no denying the natural beauty of the craggy mountain, home to no fewer than 15 peaks, the tallest of which is Cheonhwangbong 천황봉 at 845.1 m. Scattered about the mountain are dramatic rock formations, verdant valleys, beautiful waterfalls and plenty of other eye-candy.

In addition to the mountain itself, the park is also home to two major Buddhist temples, the monastery of Gapsa 갑사 in the west and the nunnery of Donghaksa 동학사 in the east. In the southwest of the park is another Buddhist temple, Sinwonsa 신원사, which is better known for a unique nearby shrine to the mountain spirit.

Mt. Gyeryongsan is beautiful all year round but the valley around Gapsa Temple is especially beautiful in autumn when the surrounding forests turn color. Donghaksa Valley 동학사계곡, meanwhile, is best visited in spring when its locally famous cherry blossoms bloom. The park is best approached from either Daejeon or Gongju. 💰 Free, but temples charge 2,000 won entrance ☎ 042-825-3004

Beautiful mountain scenery of Gyeryongsan National Park

Hiking Mt. Gyeryongsan

The most commonly used hiking trail runs from Gapsa Temple in the west to Donghaksa Temple in the east (or visa versa). It's a bit steep in spots, particular around the highpoint of Gwaneumbong Peak 관음봉 (816 m), but the route provides terrific views over the ridgeline and takes you past most of the park's cultural treasures. You'll pass some pleasant waterfalls along the way, too, most notably, Eunseon Falls 은선폭포. The 10 km course takes about four hours to hike.

Gapsa Temple 갑사

On the western slopes of Mt. Gyeryongsan resides Gapsa Temple. Founded in the first year of the reign King Guisin (420 AD) of Baekje by the Goguryeo monk Ado, Gapsa is one of Korea's most historic temples and a magical place to spend one's time. Amidst the lush forests and cool running streams, this is the perfect place to immerse oneself in a perfect blend of spiritual energy and nature's majesty.

During the Unified Silla era (668–935),

Gapsa was one of the 10 greatest temples of the Avatamsaka school of Buddhism, which emphasized the teachings of the Avatamsaka Sutra. Today, the temple is home to many handsome, wizened old structures and stone monuments. One of the more impressive sites is a stone stupa 갑사부도 located a short walk from the main compound. Fashioned in the Goryeo (935–1392) era, the stupa's intricate carvings of dragons and spirits are still vivid—Korean Buddhist art at its most sublime. Unique to the temple is an iron pole 갑사철당간 from which Buddhist banners were once unfurled—dating from the Unified Silla Era, it is one of only two of its kind still in existence in Korea. The temple also has in its possession a beautiful Buddhist tapestry from the 17th century, a national treasure that is still occasionally hung in the temple's main courtyard on special days.

Just next to the temple is a charming traditional teahouse next to a running brook that is all the more lovely in autumn, when the woods around it transform into a riot of color. If you continue from Gapsa Temple from the teahouse, you'll enter the lush Gapsa Valley from which the hiking path up Mt. Gyeryongsan begins.

💷 2,000 won ✆ 041-857-8981

Gapsa Valley

Stone stupa, Gapsa Temple

Donghaksa Temple 동학사

Located in a lovely valley on the east side of the park, Donghaksa Temple is one of Korea's largest Buddhist nunneries, home to approximately 150 Buddhist nuns both in training and ordained.

According to legend, Donghaksa was founded as a temple for male monks by the Silla monk Ven. Hoeui in 724, and expanded in the 9th and 15th centuries. Much of the temple was destroyed during the Korean War, so most of what you see is post-war reconstructions. A few of the older buildings, however, date from the 19th century. Like other Buddhist nunneries, the grounds are exceptionally

well kept; there's certainly a feminine touch here. One building worth noting is the Samseonggak 삼성각 ("Three Spirit Hall") behind the Main Hall where images of Chilseong (the Big Dipper), Sansin (the Mountain Spirit) and Dokseong (the Solitary Saint) are kept, representing a merging of Korea's Taoist, Shamanist and Buddhist traditions, respectively.

Also near the temple is another shrine, the Songmojeon Hall 속모전. This shrine is not Buddhist but Confucian, and holds the memorial tablets of King Danjong, who at the age of 13 was deposed by his uncle in a violent coup where six court officials were executed for their loyalty to the deposed monarch. ☎ 042-825-3004

Donghaksa Temple

WHAT TO EAT

As is the case with most Buddhist temples in Korea, there are a ton of restaurants in front of both Gapsa and Donghaksa temples, many specializing in *sanchae bibimbap* 산채비빔밥 (rice bowl mixed with mountain vegetables).

WHERE TO STAY

Most people stay in either Daejeon or Gongju, but if you'd prefer something closer, there are a number of small inns and *minbak* (homestay) facilities near Gapsa and Donghaksa. Also in front of Gapsa is Kapsa Youth Hostel 갑사 유스호스텔 (041-856-4666), where clean—albeit spartan—family rooms go for 55,000 won a night. If you've got a tent, there's also a camp ground (042-824-6005) near Donghaksa where you can set up for the night for 4,000 won (2,000 won electricity cost).

TRANSPORT INFO

Donghaksa Valley is best approached via Daejeon. Just take bus No. 107 from Daejeon Station—the trip takes about an hour. Gapsa, meanwhile, is best approached via Gongju. Just hop on one of the many local buses to Gapsa from Gongju Bus Terminal. The trip takes about 30 minutes.

'BROTHER AND SISTER PAGODAS'

About 20 minutes up the path to Gapsa from Donghaksa, you'll come across a pair of old stone pagodas. The pagodas—one seven stories, the other five—are believed to have been erected in the 12th century and were once part of a temple that was burned down in the Japanese invasions of the late 16th century. They are called the "Nammaetap," 남매탑 or "Brother and Sister Pagodas," a name attributed to a legend— of which there are several versions—associated with the pagodas.

In 660 AD, as the kingdom of Baekje fell before an invasion by Silla and Tang China, a young nobleman from the Baekje royal family fled into the forests of Gyeryongsan to take up life as a Buddhist monk. Bereft of his kingdom, he chose to live a simple life, building a small hermitage where he passed his days in prayer.

One snowy winter's day, the monk was doing his devotions when he heard an animal roar. He went outside and saw a great tiger, its mouth open and in obvious pain. The monk—clearly with little regard for his own well-being—took a look inside the tiger's mouth and found an animal bone lodged in its throat. He pulled the bone out, but not without admonishing the tiger for taking the life belonging to the bone. The grateful tiger registered its appreciation and disappeared into the woods.

The tiger did not reappear for some time after that, but one day, it suddenly showed up at the hermitage with a wild boar in its mouth. It dropped the boar before the monk as an act of gratitude. The monk, however, would have none of it, and instead admonished the tiger again for taking another life.

A few days later, the monk was praying when he heard a sound outside. When he looked to see what it was, he found a beautiful young woman—done up for a wedding—lying on the ground, unconscious. He brought her inside to tend to her. When she came to, he asked how she came to be at a remote mountainside hermitage in the middle of the night. She said that she was from the town of Sangju, and that on

her wedding day, a big tiger appeared. She passed out from fright and, when she awoke, she was at the hermitage. Since it was winter and the snow was deep, and Sangju quite a distance away, the monk and the young lady had little choice but to live together until things warmed up.

While they lived together, the two fell in love, and the woman asked the monk to marry her. The monk, remaining true to his vow of celibacy, refused, so instead they took a vow to live as brother and sister. And so they did, living the rest of their lives at the hermitage as Buddhist monks, even entering Nirvana (a.k.a. dying) on the same day.

To commemorate their memory, monks erected the two pagodas that you see today.

GEUMSAN 금산

Geumsan is a small market town south of Daejeon best known as the ginseng capital of Korea. A provincial backwater it might seem, but the town handles 70 to 80% of Korea's ginseng trade.

Geumsan has been famous for its ginseng since the Goryeo Dynasty (918–1392). Much of the trading gets done at the sprawling Geumsan Ginseng & Herbal Medicine Market 금산인삼약령시장 (041-753-3219), Korea's largest herbal medicine market. This is a fascinating—and aromatic—place to stroll and take in the vast array of Korean medicinal herbs on sale. At the International Ginseng Market 금산국제인삼시장, you'll find about 190 shops selling white ginseng (fresh ginseng that has been dried); on market days, they'll sell up to six tons of the stuff. If you'd prefer undried ginseng, there's another market for that, and if that's not enough, there's another nine-story general ginseng shopping complex 금산인삼종 합쇼핑센터 which, in addition to selling ginseng products, hosts even a ginseng sauna.

Prices for ginseng are 20 to 50% cheaper in Geumsan than elsewhere in Korea. The best days to go are days ending in 2 or 7, when sellers and buyers from all over the country descend on the market. The fun begins from 2 am (the market is closed on the 10th, 20th and 30th of every month). Geumsan Ginseng & Herbal Medicine Market is within walking distance of Geumsan Bus Terminal.

Geumsan Ginseng Festival

TIPS

GINSENG, THE MAGIC ROOT

Korean ginseng—Panax ginseng C.A. Meyer—has been a prized commodity for centuries. In East Asia, ginseng root is used as a tonic: its rejuvenating properties are widely lauded (even if scientific studies of its effects have proven inconclusive).

Korean ginseng (or *insam* 인삼) is usually called Goryeo ginseng, named for the medieval Korean kingdom that oversaw great developments in Korea's ginseng cultivation. The ginseng root is sold in three forms:

- **Undried Ginseng (*susam* 수삼):** This is fresh ginseng, straight from the ground. It spoils easily, however, making it difficult to transport.

- **White Ginseng (*baeksam* 백삼):** Grown for four to six years and then peeled and sun-dried, white ginseng tends to be cheaper, but supposedly has less of a therapeutic effect.

- **Red Ginseng (*hongsam* 홍삼):** Grown for six years and then steamed unpeeled, red ginseng is considered of the highest medical value among commonly available ginseng.

If you're lucky, you might happen upon some mountain ginseng, or *sansam* 산삼. Its restorative properties are the stuff of legend—it's said wild ginseng roots can be several hundreds of years old, and one such root recently sold for US$54,400. Ten year-old wild ginseng roots will usually run you about 100,000 won.

Ginseng also finds itself in a variety of foods and teas. Chicken ginseng soup, or *samgyetang*, is a popular dish in summer time. The soup is composed of a whole young chicken, stuffed with sticky rice, ginseng, dried jujube and other ingredients. Ginseng tea is also easy enough to find—served with honey, it's a great pick-me-up.

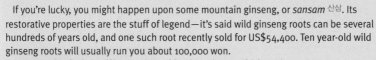

When in the Capital of Ginseng, eat ginseng. As you walk through the market, you'll even find stalls selling ginseng tempura, a treat you won't find anywhere else in the country.

Korea's best known ginseng dish is *samgyetang* 삼계탕 (chicken ginseng soup), a summertime specialty that is tasty and fortifying year-round. A good place to try this is the locally famous Wonjo Samgyetang 원조삼계탕 (041-752-2678) in the Ginseng & Herbal Medicine Market—the "special" *samgyetang* will set you back 14,000 won.

WHAT TO EAT

Frequent buses to Geumsan depart from Daejeon's Dongbu Bus Terminal. The trip takes about 50 minutes. If you wanted to get there from Seoul, buses to Geumsan depart every hour and a half from Seoul's Express Bus Terminal in Gangnam. The trip takes about 2 hours, 40 minutes.

TRANSPORT INFO

Gongju 공주

Today, Gongju is a small but very pleasant provincial town on the bank of the Geumgang River, about an hour's drive from Daejeon. To first-time visitors, it might not seem like much but, in fact, this town was, along with nearby Buyeo, a capital of the ancient kingdom of Baekje (18 BC–AD 660). The once mighty Korean dynasty's highly sophisticated Buddhist culture left a lasting impact on both Korea and Japan; in the latter, Baekje traders, monks, scholars and artisans played a major role in transmitting Buddhism, Chinese characters, pottery and other aspects of continental culture to the Japanese.

The Baekje kingdom may be long dead but the kingdom's heritage is still alive and well in Gongju, where you'll find fortresses, royal tombs and other relics of the town's royal past. Also worth visiting is the Gongju National Museum 공주국립 박물관, home to countless pieces of art and other artifacts from the Baekje era.

While you're in town, you'll also want to visit the beautiful Buddhist monastery of Magoksa 마곡사, an architectural gem hidden away in the forested mountains north of town. Gongju is also a good base from which to explore Gyeryongsan National Park (see p353).

Mesmerizing Goryeo Dynasty artwork on stone pagoda, Magoksa Temple

History

In Korea, the first centuries of the Common Era were defined by the epic struggles between the rival kingdoms of Goguryeo, Baekje and Silla for dominance over the Korean Peninsula. The kingdom of Baekje, which dominated southwestern Korea, developed a sophisticated culture thanks to its ties with China and adoption of Buddhism as the state religion. Baekje's profound regional influence played the leading role in transmitting Buddhism and Chinese culture to Japan.

In AD 475, the Baekje capital located near Seoul fell to Goguryeo. The kingdom established its new capital on the banks of the Geumgang River, naming it Ungjin, or "Bear Port" (see next page). For 63 years, Ungjin (current day Gongju) was the center of the thriving kingdom, complete with grand palaces and spectacular temples. It was at this time that Buddhism was declared Baekje's state religion.

For internal political reasons, the kingdom moved its capital to nearby Buyeo in 538. Nevertheless, the city thrived until the destruction of Baekje by a Chinese-Silla invasion in 660. The town continued to serve as one of the cultural, economic and political centers of the Chungcheong-do region well into modern times. It was the capital of the province of Chungcheong-do from 1602 to 1895, and with the division of the province into north (*buk*) and south (*nam*), the capital of Chungcheongnam-do from 1896 to 1932, when the provincial capital was moved to the new but booming railway town of Daejeon.

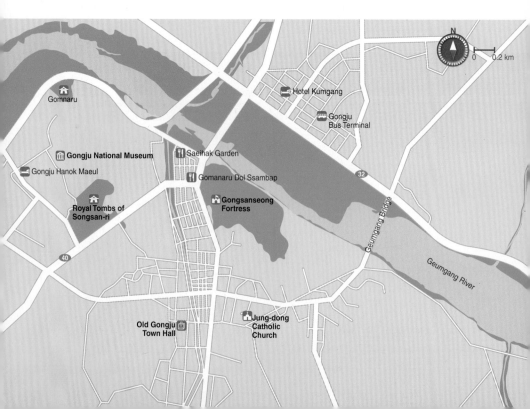

Gongsanseong Fortress, a Baekje Dynasty fortress with views over Geumgang River

Today, Gongju is a small provincial city and something of a local educational center with several universities and high schools. Its place in the urban pecking order may or may not be set for a dramatic change, however, depending on the fate of an ambitious regional development scheme to build a new national administrative city in parts of Gongju and a neighboring county (see p 363).

TALE OF THE SHE-BEAR

History and Culture

One day, a female bear, lonely after years of watching humans go about their business, kidnapped a local fisherman to make him her husband. At first, the fisherman was afraid and refused, so the bear trapped him in her cave by blocking its entrance with a large boulder. She took good care of him and after a couple of years some degree of affection developed between the two. The couple even had two cubs. Figuring she could trust her husband not to leave, the bear left the cave unblocked as she went to gather food. The husband bolted from the cave after sensing freedom for the first time in years. When she discovered that her husband had fled, the bear, overcome with sadness, jumped into the river with her two cubs and drowned.

The waters of the Geumgang River grew rough after the bear's death. To ease the resentment of the dead bear's spirit and calm the waves, local fishermen built a shrine for the bear. It is from this shrine that Gongju took its classic name, Ungjin ("Bear Port"). To this day, on a bend in the Geumgang River in the west of town, there is an old ferry crossing (no longer in use) called Gomnaru 곰나루 (a purely Korean term for "Bear Port"), where you'll find a small shrine (of recent manufacture) housing a stone bear carving from the 6th century.

Gongsanseong Fortress

Gongsanseong Fortress 공산성

With a commanding view of the Geumgang River, Gongsanseong Fortress was originally built during the Baekje era, although the current stone walls and pavilions date from the Joseon era and later. The fortress makes for a pleasant walk with nice views of the river, and it's not too far from the royal tombs of Songsan-ri (see right).

The walls—which are about 6 m high and 3 m wide—run for about 3 km, so you can probably walk the fortress in its entirety in two and a half hours. Along the way you'll pass a number of gates and pavilions, including the Manharu Pavilion 만하루 overlooking the Geumgang River 금강 and, just behind it, a well-preserved stone-walled water well excavated in the 1980s. Near the Manharu Pavilion is also the Buddhist temple of Yeongeunsa 영은사 which is famous for producing the soldier-monks who fought to defend Korea during the Japanese invasions of the late 16th century.

Geumgang Bridge 금강대교

Right next to Gongsanseong Fortress is Geumgang Bridge, built over the Geumgang River in 1933 as a way of compensating Gongju for moving the provincial capital to Daejeon. Parts of the bridge were blown up by American troops during the Korean War to stop the North Koreans from crossing the river. The bridge is lit up at night.

Royal Tombs of Songsan-ri 송산리고분

On a hillside near the Geumgang River is one of Gongju's most visited attractions—seven royal tombs from when Gongju was the capital of the Baekje kingdom. Some of the tombs were discovered in the early 20th century, although the most famous, the Tomb of King Muryeong (also known as Tomb No. 7), was accidentally discovered in 1971 during maintenance of the others. The discovery proved to be one of the biggest finds in the history of Korean archeology. The long-lost tomb, undisturbed by grave robbers, contained some 2,906 artifacts—12 of which were designated National Treasures—including

Geumgang Bridge

royal crowns, gold jewelry and other valuables. Interestingly, it is the only Korean tomb dating back to the Three Kingdoms Period in which the entombed individual and the year of construction have been identified.

Another one of the tombs, Tomb No. 6, is noted for its beautiful, albeit greatly faded, wall murals of the four mythical guardians of the cardinal directions: Blue Dragon to the east, White Tiger to the west, Red Phoenix to the south and Black Turtle to the north.

The tombs of Songsan-ri are built of brick with arched ceilings, covered over with a mound of earth. They resemble similarly

Tomb No. 7, Songsan-ri

A NEW CAPITAL?

Due to overcrowding in Seoul and the over-concentration of economic, social and political clout in the capital, Korean leaders have been talking about moving the capital from Seoul for quite some time. The Chungcheong provinces, due to their central location (far from the DMZ and North Korea) and politically critical role as "swing" provinces have been the favored location for the transfer. In the 1980s, Daejeon was the city most often discussed as a potential new capital; indeed, several government agencies were moved to Daejeon in 1997, when a new government complex opened in the city.

In August 2004, however, the Korean government decided on a multi-billion dollar project to build a new capital city by 2030. For the site of the new city, the government chose a nearly 73 square km plot that includes parts of rural Gongju and the neighboring town of Yeongi. In October 2004, however, the Constitutional Court of Korea ruled that the relocation of the national capital was unconstitutional, explaining that something of that magnitude required either a national referendum or amendment of the Korean constitution. To get around this, the government submitted a revised plan that would move almost the entire government to the new city but leave the presidential mansion of Cheong Wa Dae in Seoul, allowing the latter to remain, at least technically, Korea's capital. In 2007, the government released a detailed plan to build a so-called Multi-functional Administrative City, named Sejong Special Autonomous City, after the brilliant 15th century monarch, which would house nine ministries, several other government bodies and about 500,000 people. This plan was passed by the National Assembly with support of both the ruling and opposition parties.

As of the writing of this book, construction was ongoing at the site of the new city, the first stages of which are expected to be completed by 2015.

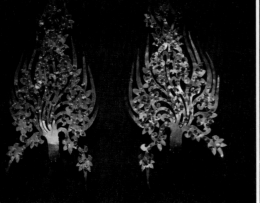

Baekje crown ornaments, Gongju National Museum (left) Mythical stone beast, Gongju National Museum

arched brick tombs built in southern China, indicating the close relations and vibrant cultural exchange between Baekje and China.

It used to be that you could enter the tombs but they are now permanently closed to protect them. On a positive note, there is an exhibit at the foot of the hill with re-creations of the tombs that visitors are encouraged to enter and experience. Many of the artifacts discovered inside the tombs are now kept at the Gongju National Museum. ⏰ 9 am to 6 pm 🎫 1,500 won ☎ 041-840-2548

Gongju National Museum 국립공주박물관

The Gongju National Museum moved to its current home, an impressive cutting-edge facility, in 2004. Thanks to its fine collection of Baekje-era artifacts, many of them from the Tomb of King Muryeong, the museum is one of Korea's finest and well worth a visit.

The museum has three exhibition halls—a special exhibit hall, a hall dedicated to the artifacts removed from the Tomb of King Muryeong, and another for artifacts from Gongju's stint as the royal capital. Among the most impressive artifacts are gold ornaments from the crowns of King Muryeong and his queen (National Treasure No. 154), a stone statue of a legendary animal that guarded the tomb (National Treasure No. 162), and a Buddhist stele with breathtaking carvings and inscriptions (National Treasure No. 108). The only incovenience is that the museum is situated somewhat out of the way from Gongju's other historic sites.

⏰ 9 am to 6 pm (weekdays), 9 am to 7 pm (weekends). Special night hours to 9 pm every Saturday (Apr to Oct). Closed Mondays. Admission ends one hour prior to closing. 🎫 Free 🚌 Take Bus No. 8 from Gongju Bus Terminal or walk about 20 minutes from the Royal Tombs of Songsan-ri. ☎ 041-850-6336 🌐 http://gongju.museum.go.kr

Old Gongju Town Hall 구 공주읍사무소

Built in 1920, this small but impressive European-style structure was used as Gongju Town Hall from 1930 to 1986. It

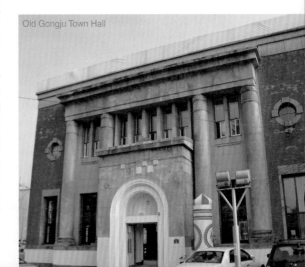

Old Gongju Town Hall

Jung-dong Catholic Church, built by French missionaries in 1937

was later used as an art academy before being transformed into an art and design space. In addition to hosting art exhibits, it is also home to a rather pleasant café. The area around it has been turned into a small art park.

Jung-dong Catholic Church 중동성당

Sitting high atop a hill overlooking downtown Gongju, this beautiful Gothic red-brick church was built in 1937, although the church itself was founded by French missionaries in 1897.

WHAT TO EAT

There's some good eating to be had at Gomanaru Dol Ssambap 고마나루 돌쌈밥 (041-857-9999), just across from the Gongsanseong Fortress parking lot. Order the *dolssam jeongsik* 돌쌈정식 (20,000 won), and you'll get *bulgogi*, a table full of side dishes and rice mixed with beans and vegetables steamed in a stone pot. You put a spoonful of rice in a lettuce leaf, top it with a slice of meat and some veggies, wrap it up and eat. Minimum order is two persons, though. Also across from Gonsanseong Fortress is Saeihak Garden 새이학가든 (041-854-2030), a local institution that has been doing Gongju specialties *gukbap* 국밥 (rice in meaty broth, 8,000 won) and *seokgalbi* 석갈비 (marinated pork ribs, 11,000 won) for over 60 years.

WHERE TO STAY

The selection of places to stay isn't great compared to Daejeon. The swankiest place in town is the Hotel Kumgang 금강관광호텔 (041-852-1071) a nice enough, mid-range place near Gongju Bus Terminal that'll run you 40,000 won a night (50,000 won on weekends).

If you're in a group, another option is Gongju Hanok Maeul 공주한옥마을 (041-840-2763), a cluster of some recently built Korean traditional *hanok* homes used as guesthouses. Rooms cost 120,000 won a night, with each room holding up to eight. The complex is out by Gongju National Museum, so use bus No. 8 to get there.

TRANSPORT INFO

Getting Around Gongju: Gongju Bus Terminal is just on the north side of the Geumgang River. Most of the historic sites are within walking distance of each other on or near the south bank of the river. Gongju National Museum, however, is probably best reached via bus or taxi.
Getting to/from Gongju: From Gongju Bus Terminal (041-855-8114) there are frequent buses to Daejeon (4,000 won, 1 hr), Seoul (7,700–8,600 won, 1 hr 50 min) and Buyeo (4,000 won, 1 hr).

Magoksa Temple 마곡사

Magoksa Temple is one of the most beautiful Buddhist monasteries in the country. The complex is a cornucopia of protected cultural properties, including five nationally registered treasures. As if this weren't enough, the temple is surrounded by verdant hillsides as far as the eye can see. Hidden away among these hillsides, the temple gets far fewer visitors than you'd expect for one of its size.

Depending on which legend you believe, the temple was founded in either AD 642 or 847. Located in the middle of nowhere, the monastery has served as a place of refuge throughout Korea's turbulent past. It survived the Japanese invasion of 1592 (when most of Korea was burnt to the ground), and sheltered even the legendary Korean independence fighter Kim Gu, who hid there after escaping from prison in 1898. Kim is said to have planted the lovely Chinese juniper tree that grows in the temple's main courtyard.

Once you cross the stone bridge over the wide stream in front of the temple, you're in a different world. After a fire, the temple was rebuilt in 1651; much of the current complex dates back to this reconstruction.

The most magnificent hall is the Daeungbojeon 대웅보전, a massive two-story wooden hall housing images of the Sakyamuni Buddha, flanked by the Amitabha Buddha and Medicine Buddha. According to legend, if you hug one of its huge wooden pillars, you're assured entry into Nirvana. The hall sits on a terrace overlooking the rest of the monastery.

Just below the Daeungbojeon is the Daegwangbojeon 대광보전, another large wooden hall housing an image of the Vairocana Buddha. Unusually, the Buddha faces east rather than south, as is most common in Korean Buddhist temples.

The simple Yeongsanjeon Hall 영산전, located at the front of the complex, contains 1,000 Buddha statues, all of which—if you look closely—are slightly different from one another.

Also unusual is the five-story pagoda in front of the Daeungbojeon. Erected in the Goryeo (935–1392) era, it is topped by a bronze crown similar to those found in Lamanist countries such as Tibet, indicating the influence of the Mongol-ruled Yuan Dynasty that occupied Korea in the latter Goryeo era.

WHAT TO EAT

The obligatory tourist village at the entrance to the temple has plenty of places to eat. One particular place of note is the Taehwa Sikdang 태화식당 (041-841-8020) which does traditional mountain vegetable cuisine. If you're in a group, give the *deodeok jeongsik* 더덕정식 (grilled bellflower root with rice, soup and side dishes) for 14,000 won; or have the *sanchae bibimbap* 산채비빔밥 (rice mixed with mountain veggies, 7,000 won).

TRANSPORT INFO

Bus No. 7 from Gongju Bus Terminal goes to Magoksa. The trip takes about 40 minutes.

Opened in 2006, Baekje Cultural Land gives us a rare glimpse at Baekje's cultural sophistication.

BUYEO 부여

Few places in Korea exude as strong a rustic charm as Buyeo. A small provincial town today, Buyeo was once the proud capital of a mighty kingdom whose cultural influence could be felt as far afield as Japan. Its mighty temples and palaces now lie in ruins, but reminders of the kingdom's golden age are scattered throughout the town. Because both cities were capitals of their respective realms during the Three Kingdoms Period, Buyeo is often compared to Gyeongju. The comparisons, however, only go so far. While both towns have more than their fair share of historical remains, Gyeongju is far larger and historically was the recipient of far greater government largesse. Although it enjoys a great deal more tourism than most towns of its size, Buyeo is still pretty sleepy.

That being said, Buyeo's mellow nature is part of its attraction. If Gyeongju is characterized by triumphalism, Buyeo is touched by the sweet sadness of a defeated capital. Its ruins remain, for the most part, just that—ruins. Its most renowned tourist site is where several thousand court ladies committed mass suicide (at least according to legend). The former royal garden Gungnamji Pond 궁 남지 is a microcosm of the town's esprit de corps—you could happily spend the day with a bottle of *makgeolli* rice wine, watching the willow trees and contemplating the city's former greatness.

History Buyeo's glory days marked the cultural height of the Baekje kingdom, one of three ancient Korean kingdoms that vied with one another for domination of the Korean Peninsula during the Three Kingdoms Period (57 BC–668 AD). In 538, King Seong of Baekje moved his capital from Ungjin, modern Gongju, to a well-protected bend in the navigable Baengmagang River 백마강. This capital would be called Sabi, modern Buyeo. It was during Baekje's so-called "Sabi Period" that Baekje culture— often regarded as the most sophisticated among those of the Three Kingdoms—truly blossomed. In particular, with royal patronage, Buddhism flowered. Baekje's kings worked hard to spread the faith not only within their own borders but overseas—in 538, a Baekje royal mission introduced Buddhism to Japan.

Baekje's rich culture was not enough to protect it from its enemies, however. In 660, Baekje's sometime ally (and sometime enemy) Silla concluded an alliance with Tang China, the superpower of its day. The two allies then launched a joint invasion of Baekje, overrunning its defenses and laying siege to Sabi. The capital quickly capitulated and the last Baekje king, King Uija, surrendered his kingdom. A later attempt by one of his sons to restore the kingdom ended in failure.

Even in defeat, however, Sabi played an instrumental role in the development of East Asian culture. When Constantinople fell to the Turks in 1453, learned Greek refugees flooded the West, lending impetus to the Renaissance. Likewise, the flood of Baekje refugees to Japan in the wake of the fall of Sabi contributed mightily to the development of Asuka culture in Japan.

Layout Buyeo's urban area is small enough that you could, theoretically, make your way everywhere by foot, although if you're traveling from one end to the other (say, from Busosanseong Fortress in the north to Gungnamji Pond in the south), you'll probably want to cab it. Most of Buyeo's major sites are located in the town itself. The major exception to this is the Baekje Culture Land complex, located north of the Geumgang River. Getting there requires a bus ride.

Jeongnimsa Temple Site 정림사지

In the middle of town is the former site of Jeongnimsa, one of the Baekje capital's most important temples. The temple, which flourished during the Baekje and Goryeo eras, has since disappeared, yet the massive stone pagoda and a seated stone Buddha remain. The pagoda is a particularly valuable cultural property (designated National Treasure No. 9) since it's one of only two remaining Baekje pagodas. Its narrow base and thin roof stones indicate

that it was built to resemble the graceful wooden pagodas that used to be commonplace at temples throughout the kingdom (and are still commonplace at temples in Baekje's cultural protégé, Japan).

After the fall of Buyeo in 660, Chinese General Su Dingfang defaced the pagoda by etching praise of his conquering of the Baekje kingdom—look carefully, and you can still see it on all four sides of the base. The sitting stone Buddha, meanwhile, dates from the Goryeo era. There's a small

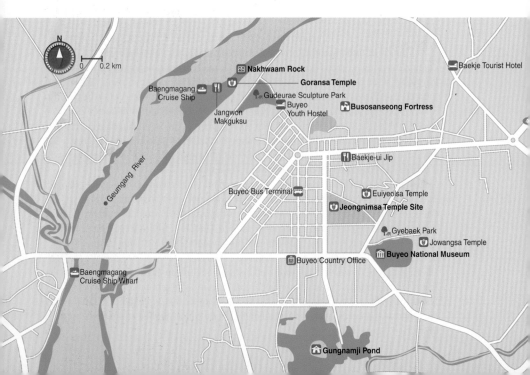

Jeongnimsa Pagoda (left), Model of old Jeongnimsa Temple

museum dedicated to the temple and Baekje culture, too.

⏰ 10 am to 5 pm (Oct–Mar), 9 am to 7 pm (Apr–Sep) 💴 1,500 won 📞 041-830-2721
🌐 www.jeongnimsaji.or.kr

Buyeo National Museum 국립부여박물관

The Buyeo National Museum, located on the southern outskirts of town, is one of Korea's largest repositories of Baekje history and culture, home to some 13,000 items. The museum is very visitor-friendly and a genuinely pleasant place to stroll around.

The museum's pride and joy is the gilt-bronze Incense Burner of Baekje 백제금동대향로, a national treasure. Excavated from a temple site in 1993, the incense burner is one of the country's finest works of Baekje art. The lid—a bronze representation of a Taoist paradise—is covered with some 75 mountain peaks populated by all sorts of figures, human, animal and mythical. The lid is capped by a phoenix. The body of the burner is decorated with lotus blossom patterns, while the stand is a dragon. You could stare at it for hours and not feel the time pass.

⏰ 9 am to 6 pm (7 pm on weekends). Open till 9 pm on Saturday, Apr to Oct. Closed Mondays
💴 Free 🌐 buyeo.museum.go.kr

Gungnamji Pond 궁남지

This pleasure pond, built by Baekje King Mu in 634 as Korea's first artificial pond, is arguably Buyeo's most relaxing spot. In the middle of the willow tree-lined pond is an island connected to the shore by a narrow wooden bridge. You could lie all day in the cool shade of the island's handsome Korean

Beautiful Baekje incense burner

Famed lotus blossoms of Gungnamji Pond, one of Korea's most idyllic spots

pavilion, sipping a beverage and watching the long willow branches sway with the summer breeze. The pond exerts a romantic charm that doesn't easily let go.

Beginning from May, the pond is covered with beautiful lotus blossoms, so make sure you've got your camera handy. The pond and pavilion are also lit up at night, which makes them the perfect place to spend a summer evening.

Busosanseong Fortress 부소산성

At the north end of town, located on a bend in the Baengmagang River, is a small hillock with some old earthworks. This hillock, called Busosanseong Fortress, used to serve as the rear garden of the Baekje royal palace (long since destroyed), a northward defense position and, in times of war, an emergency palace where the king could remain protected behind its stone and earthen walls that ringed the hillock and cliffs that plunged into the Baengmagang River.

Today, there's not much left of the fortress or the palace facilities that adorned it, other than some earthworks and the foundations of old temples and pavilions. In more recent decades, some Korean traditional pavilions and other structures

have been built on or moved to the hillock.

All in all, Busosanseong is a pleasant place to stretch your legs—the hillock is criss-crossed with walking paths that are pleasantly shaded by trees of the forest that surrounds the park. 💰 2,000 won

Nakhwaam Rock 낙화암

At the north end of Busosanseong Fortress is a cliff that plunges into the Baengmagang River. Atop this cliff is a rocky outcrop that has come to be known as Nakhwaam ("Falling Flower Rock"). This beautiful name masks the heart-rending tale associated with the site.

In 660, the southeastern kingdom of Silla made up its mind to bring the warfare of the Three Kingdoms Period to an end once and for all. Silla and its ally, Tang China, launched a two-pronged invasion of Baekje. The allied force, led by legendary Silla commander Kim Yu-sin and Chinese general Su Dingfang (who would later earn glory expanding Chinese influence in Central Asia), defeated Baekje's army which was led by the tragically heroic General Gyebaek at the Battle of Hwangsanbeol and laid siege to the royal capital of Sabi, modern Buyeo.

King Uija and the crown prince managed

Murals at Goransa Temple

to escape to Ungjin, modern Gongju, but the rest of the court took protection behind the walls of Busosanseong Fortress. There was nothing the defenders could do, however, and the fortress fell. *Samguk Yusa*, a 13th century history of Korea, records that, rather than surrender themselves to the Silla and Chinese troops, some 3,000 court ladies leapt to their deaths from Nakhwaam, their fluttering robes resembling falling flower petals as they crashed into the waves of the Baengmagang River below.

The rock, capped by a pavilion built in 1929, provides an outstanding view of the broad, meandering Baengmagang River and the surrounding countryside. Definitely worth the time and effort to reach it.

Goransa Temple 고란사

Just below Nakhwaam Rock and overlooking the river is Goransa Temple. A small Buddhist temple it may be, but what it lacks in size it makes up in other enchantments. In back of the main hall is a very famous mineral spring where the water, according to legend, would make

you younger. The kings of Baekje drank water from this well everyday, it is said. Nowadays, the water's ability to turn back the clock is looked upon with skepticism in some quarters but it's nevertheless quite refreshing on a hot summer's day.

Be sure to look at the wall murals in the back of the main hall—especially the one telling the tale of the 3,000 court ladies who plunged to their deaths nearby.

 TIPS

RIVER CRUISES

When in Buyeo, take the short cruise on the Baengmagang River past Nakhwaam. You're afforded some outstanding views, and the experience proves quite relaxing. There's a pier right next to Goransa Temple; this is where you get on the regular cruise boats. Most boats will drop you off at Gudeurae Park 구드래공원, a pleasant picnic ground on the banks of the Baengmagang River. If you like, you can also take the boat all the way down to Subukjeong Pavilion 수북정, which overlooks the bend in the river south of town, near Gungnamji Pond.
[FARES] Goransa–Gudeurae Park: 3,500 won one way, 5,500 won round-trip. Goransa–Subukjeong Pavilion: 6,000 won one way, 9,000 won round trip. More info: 041-830-2523

Nakhwaam Rock, where 3,000 Baekje court ladies leaped to their deaths

THE BALLAD OF SEODONG

History and Culture

The 13th century history book *Samguk Yusa* ("Memorabilia of the Three Kingdoms") relates the tale of King Mu (600–641), the 30th king of Baekje. As a young man, when he went by the name of Seodong, he fell in love with a beautiful princess of the rival Silla kingdom, Princess Seonhwa. The clever Seodong devised a brilliant (if perhaps a tad outside-the-box) plan to win her hand. He intentionally spread a scandalous song—the Seodongyo ("Ballad of Seodong")—about himself and the princess amongst Silla's people. Hearing the song, the outraged King Jinpyeong of Silla had the princess banished from his kingdom. Taking refuge in Baekje, the princess in her misfortune was comforted by Seodong, and the two went on to marry.

According to legend, Seonhwa would sail about Gungnamji Pond in a rowboat with King Mu to soothe the former Silla princess's homesickness.

Baekje Cultural Land 백제문화단지 & Baekje History & Culture Museum 백제역사문화관

On the northern side of the Baengmagang River you'll find the massive Baekje Cultural Land complex, which, its theme park-esque name aside, is really an impressive collection of reconstructions of Baekje architecture, including a recreated Baekje palace, a royal Buddhist temple, an entire Baekje village and some Baekje tombs moved to the site from other places

in Buyeo. The complex opened in 2006; it is mostly finished, although work is scheduled for final completion in 2013.

A visit to the park gives visitors a chance to appreciate the grandeur and sophistication of Baekje culture, at least in terms of architecture. Prior to the construction of the park, we could appreciate the craftsmanship of Baekje only through Japanese temples like Nara's Horyuji (whose architecture reflects Baekje techniques and influence), Baekje-

Baekje Cultural Land

influenced Silla architecture, and the few remaining Baekje stone monuments in Korea. The most eye-catching piece is the five-story wooden pagoda at the recreated Buddhist temple. If you've visited Japan's Kyoto or Nara, you will no doubt recognize the similarities, further evidence of the cultural impact Baekje had on Korea's neighbor across the East Sea.

Also part of the complex is Baekje History & Culture Museum, a good place to introduce yourself to the glories of Baekje culture. The museum is heavy on recreations rather than real artifacts (for those, go to the Buyeo National Museum), but if you're at Baekje Cultural Land, it's worth a visit.

🕐 9 am to 6 pm (Mar to Oct), 9 am to 5 pm (Nov to Feb). Admission ends one hour prior to closing 🎟 9,000 won. Includes admission to the Baekje History & Culture Museum 🚌 Take a bus to Baekje History & Culture Museum from Buyeo Bus Terminal. 📞 041-830-3400 🖥 www.bhm.or.kr

TRANSPORT INFO

There are frequent buses to Buyeo from Seoul, Daejeon and Gongju. Buses to Buyeo depart from Seoul's Dong Seoul Terminal. The trip costs 14,400 won and takes about two and a half hours. Buses from Daejeon's Seobu Bus Terminal to Buyeo cost 6,600 won, and the trip takes about an hour. Buses from Gongju to Buyeo cost 4,000 won, and the trip takes about 40 minutes.

WHAT TO EAT

Like in Gongju, *dolssambap* 돌쌈밥 (stone pot-cooked rice and meat eaten wrapped in lettuce leaves) is a local specialty. Gudeurae Dolssambap 구드래 돌쌈밥 (041-836-9259), near Gudeurae Park, is the place to try this—the *bulgogi dolssambap* 불고기 돌쌈밥 will cost you 14,000 won.

Another local specialty to try is *yeonipbap* 연잎밥—rice wrapped and steamed in lotus leaves—at Baekje-ui Jip 백제의집 (041-834-1212) in front of Busosanseong Fortress. The *soburi yeonbap* 소부리 연밥 (12,000 won) comes with the *yeonipbap* and *bulgogi*. *Yeonipbap* is said to have originated at the Buddhist temples of the Buyeo area—one local newspaper called it "a mandala on the table." For something a bit simpler, try the rustically charming Jangwon Makguksu 장원막국수 (041-835-6561), where you can score some delicious *memil makguksu* 메밀 막국수 (cold buckwheat noodles) for 5,500 won.

WHERE TO STAY

Blending traditional Baekje form and artistry with stylish modern design, the architecturally stunning Lotte Buyeo Resort 롯데부여리조트 (041-939-1000, www.lottebuyeoresort.com) is the place to stay if money is no concern. Hotel and condo rooms are available—the big difference being that you can cook in the latter. Rooms begin at 120,000 won. The spa costs extra (21,000 won) but those staying at the resort receive 30% discounts. The resort, which opened in September 2010, is located right next to Baekje Cultural Land. Construction of other facilities, including a golf course, is ongoing. Another good option is Samjeong Buyeo Youth Hostel 삼정부 여유스호스텔 (041-835-3101, www.buyeoyh.com), a pleasant establishment near Gudeurae Park where clean, hostel-style rooms go for 16,000 won a night. It also has a nice "pension" or villa section where you can rent a small cottage for 44,000 won (for 3 to 4 people) to 70,000 won (for 7 people) a night on weekends. Overlooking the Baengmagang River in the north of town, the Baekje Tourist Hotel 백제관광호텔 (041-835-0870) is Buyeo's other swanky place with rooms going for 78,000 to 350,000 won a night. There are numerous small motels and inns around town, too, with most going for 30,000 won a night. Finally, south of Gungnamji Pond is the Baekjegwan 백제관 (041-832-2721), an 18th century Korean aristocrat's home now used as a guesthouse. There are only four rooms, ranging in rates from 50,000 won to 100,000 won a night, so you need to book early. The home is gorgeous, though, and a marvelous opportunity to experience the beauty of old Korea.

THE KINGDOM OF BAEKJE

FOUNDING

According to the *Samguk Sagi*, a 12th century Korean history text, the kingdom of Baekje was founded in 57 BC by King Onjo. The son of King Dongmyeong, the founder of the northern Korean kingdom of Goguryeo, Onjo, his brother Biryu and their followers left Goguryeo to settle the fertile Hangang River basin. Onjo established a city, Wiryeseong, on the Hangang River in today's Seoul. He called his new country Sipje, or "Ten Vassals." Biryu, meanwhile, chose to settle in today's Incheon. Onjo's settlement prospered while Biryu's did not. Biryu demanded his brother's throne and when this demand was rejected, he declared war. After losing the war, Biryu committed suicide, and his followers left the Incheon area for Wiryeseong. His kingdom thus enlarged, Onjo renamed his country Baekje ("One Hundred Vassals").

MOVE TO UNGJIN AND SABI

In the fifth century, the kingdom of Goguryeo, under the energetic leadership of King Gwanggaeto the Great (r. 391–412) and his son King Jangsu (r. 413–491), launched a series of wars of territorial expansion, pushing the borders of their kingdom deep into Manchuria in the north and to the Hangang River valley in the south. In 475, the Hangang River valley, including Baekje's capital of Wiryeseong, fell to Goguryeo. After this loss, Baekje moved its capital to Ungjin (today's Gongju), a more defensible position thanks to the surrounding mountains and Geumgang River. Ungjin would serve as Baekje's capital until 538. Under capable kings such as King Muryeong (r. 501–523) and King Seong (r. 523–554), the kingdom attempted to regain its lost territory in the north in alliance with its neighbor to the east, the kingdom of Silla.

In 538, King Seong moved his capital from Ungjin to Sabi (today's Buyeo), a site blessed with more room for urban growth and better access to trade routes with China and Japan and the kingdom's vital southern provinces (today's Jeolla-do provinces). In the early 550s, Seong was able to recapture from Goguryeo the prized Hangang River valley after a costly campaign. This success was quickly followed by betrayal when Silla, breaking its alliance with Baekje, seized the strategic region for itself. Seong ordered a retaliatory invasion of Silla but this met with disaster at the Battle of Gwansanseong (554), in which Seong and nearly 30,000 Baekje troops fell on the field of battle.

DECLINE AND FALL

The Battle of Gwansanseong marked the beginning of a long, interminable decline for Baekje. The kingdom would last for another century—indeed, this period witnessed a flowering of Baekje culture—but militarily, it could no longer compete with the rising power of Silla, with which the kingdom was now locked in a relationship of bitter and permanent enmity. In addition, since the death of King Seong, the authority of the royal court had begun to diminish as power shifted to the kingdom's aristocracy.

Under King Mu (r. 600–641), Baekje undertook an ambitious program of temple and palace construction, but at the cost of ignoring national defense, a mistake for which his kingdom would soon pay dearly. His son, King Uija, struck an alliance with Goguryeo and in 642 attacked Silla. The invasion was quite successful—Baekje took some 40 fortresses from Silla—but led Silla to enter into an alliance with China's ruling Tang Dynasty, the superpower of its day. With the support of Tang, Silla set its sights on conquering Baekje and unifying the Korean Peninsula. In 659, Uija attacked Silla again but this prompted the Chinese to intervene. The combined forces of Silla and Tang invaded Baekje and, in 660, Tang and Silla laid siege to the Baekje capital of Sabi, which quickly surrendered. The kingdom of Baekje was no more. King Uija was exiled to Tang China, while many of Baekje's elite fled to Japan.

BAEKJE'S CULTURAL ACCOMPLISHMENTS

Even as the kingdom's geopolitical fortunes declined, Baekje culture blossomed. While fundamentally Korean, Baekje culture adopted many aspects of Chinese culture, as is readily apparent in Baekje brick tombs, temple architecture and Buddhist art. Baekje art was especially renowned for its refinement, subtlety and decorative sophistication, especially when compared to the simpler designs of Silla art. To better understand this contrast, check out the famous pair of pagodas in the main courtyard of Gyeongju's Bulguksa Temple: the intricate construction and decoration of the Dabotap Pagoda is representative of the Baekje aesthetic, while the simpler lines of the Seokgatap are characteristic of Silla tastes. Perhaps the most sublime piece of Baekje art is the jaw-droppingly beautiful bronze statue of a half-sitting Maitreya Bodhisattva (housed at the National Museum of Korea in Seoul); its beguiling, subtle "Baekje smile" entrances the viewer and puts one at ease. Just as mesmerizing is the gilt-bronze incense burner at the Buyeo National Museum, with its intricate depictions of a Taoist paradise.

Even after Baekje's fall, its culture continued to have a lasting impact on Korea. Countless Baekje artists and artisans offered their services to Silla, which valued Baekje's cultural sophistication. It was a Baekje architect, for instance, that erected the legendary nine-story wooden pagoda of Gyeongju's Hwangnyongsa Temple, a renowned piece of engineering that was famous even in China.

Baekje's cultural impact on Japan was also profound. According to the *Nihon Shoki*, an 8th century Japanese history text, Buddhism was introduced to Japan in 552 by a Baekje delegation sent by King Seong. Scholars, monks, artists and artisans from Baekje played a leading role in transmitting continental culture to Japan, where such culture was in high demand. The exquisite Buddhist monastery of Horyuji in Japan's Nara prefecture that was built, it is believed, with the participation of a large number of Baekje artists and craftsmen, may in fact be the finest example of Baekje architecture anywhere in the world. Baekje artisans influenced Japanese metal-working, ceramics and even tomb construction. The cultural impact of Baekje on Japan continued even after the kingdom's fall as Baekje aristocrats fled across the East Sea, taking their learning and cultural sophistication with them.

Off the Beaten Track

Gwanchoksa Temple 관촉사

In Nonsan, the next town over from Buyeo, is the Buddhist temple of Gwanchoksa, known for its giant stone statue of the Maitreya Bodhisattva, the "future Buddha." Standing just over 18 m tall, the bodhisattva is the largest stone Buddhist statue in Korea. It was completed in 1006, and took over 30 years to erect. The granite giant is typical of the early Goryeo Era (936–1392)—it's not a particularly skillful work but what it lacks in artistry and refinement it makes up in passion and enthusiasm. The Bodhisattva's head, crowned by a canonical crown, is disproportionately large, and on its face is an expression that would never be mistaken for enlightenment.

🪙 1,500 won 🚌 There are frequent buses to Nonsan from Daejeon Seobu Bus Terminal, Buyeo and Gongju. Trains from Seodaejeon Station pass through Nonsan, too. From Nonsan Intercity Bus Terminal, it's a 3,000 won taxi ride to Gwanchoksa. You can also take the bus to Konyang University and get off at Gwanchoksa (10 minute ride). ☎ 041-736-5700~2

Nabawi Catholic Church 나바위성당

Also in Nonsan, but almost on the provincial border of Jeollabuk-do, is historic Nabawi Catholic Church, a beautiful old church conceived in a synthesis of Korean and Gothic styles. Designed by French missionary Father Joseph Vermorel, the church was built in 1906 with laborers brought in from China. The church features a Gothic steeple with a Korean *hanok* roof—the mixture of East and West makes it one of the most beautiful churches in Korea. Particularly nice are the wood interior and the cloisters lining the body of the church.

Father Kim Dae-geon, Korea's first Catholic priest, gave his first sermon on the very site of this church in 1845. In back of the church is a walking path lined by the Stations of the Cross. At the top of the hill is a memorial pagoda for Father Kim.

🚌 From Nonsan (see Gwanchoksa Temple above), first take a bus (or train) to the hamlet of Ganggyeong, and from there take city Bus No. 50 or express city bus No. 333 for Iksan from Gangyeong Station and get off at Nabawi.

BORYEONG 보령 & DAECHEON BEACH 대천해수욕장

The small coastal town of Boryeong is best known as the home of Daecheon Beach, a 3.5 km stretch of white sand and seashells (and, depending on the time of day, extensive mud flats) on the West Sea coast that is one of Korea's most popular summertime destinations. Daecheon Beach's history as a summer resort goes back to the 1930s, when Western missionaries established a seaside compound of cabins and lodges, some of which remain to this day in a wooded area at the south end of the beach. Today, Daecheon is largely filled with hotels, motels, restaurants, bars and other entertainment facilities aimed at summer revelers from Seoul and elsewhere. In the high season, this place is wall-to-wall with people, so don't come here expecting a quiet stretch of seashore where you can get away from it all. Like at some of Korea's other summer resorts, however, what you will find is energy and fun in spades.

If you visit Daecheon in the winter, however, you'll find it much quieter. Unless you're up for a polar bear swim, this obviously isn't the best time to venture into the water, but the quiet, wind and waves do lend themselves very nicely to a pensive walk or romantic stroll along the beach.

Daecheon Beach, a popular summer seaside getaway

TIPS

BORYEONG MUD FESTIVAL

The highlight of Daecheon Beach's year—indeed, quite possibly *the* event of the Korean summer, especially for international tourists and resident expats—is the annual Boryeong Mud Festival held every July. This festival is nine days of very dirty and frequently very intoxicated fun featuring mud dancing, mud baths, mud mobs, mud prisons (don't ask), mudpool slides and more. Basically, it's a beach full of young, mud-caked bodies rollicking like there's no tomorrow. Foreigners make up a good percentage of the revelers.

The West Sea coast of Korea is home to extensive mud flats, produced by some of the most dramatic tides this side of Canada's Bay of Fundy. The mud found along the Boryeong coast contains unusually high levels of minerals, germanium and bentonite, which are good for the skin. The mud also emits large amounts of far-infrared rays (FIR), a form of light that, while invisible to the naked eye, ionizes and activates water molecules in our cells and blood, which in turn improve oxygen levels in our bodies, remove toxins and fats from our

bloodstream, eliminates waste and improve nervous functions. Boryeong city officials claim Daecheon's mud is better for you than even the famed mud of the Dead Sea, which has been used in high-end cosmetics since the days of Cleopatra. You'll find plenty of locally produced cosmetics using Boryeong mud on sale at reasonable prices.

The Boryeong Mud Festival may be Korea's most popular festival, especially with international visitors.

WHAT TO EAT

The Daecheon Beach area is chock-full of restaurants, especially raw fish eateries. Daecheon's signature dish, however, is oysters. Several kilometers up the coast from Daecheon Beach is the small fishing port of Cheonbuk 천북, home to Cheonbuk Oyster Town 천북굴단지, a stretch of about 100 restaurants and stalls serving oyster dishes, especially *gul gui* 굴구이 (roasted

oyster), *gul bap* 굴밥 (oyster rice) and *gul kalguksu* 굴칼국수 (oyster noodles). *Gul gui* goes for 25,000 won but the portion should be enough to feed several people. Winter is the oyster season so if it's mollusks, not mud, you're craving, visit between November and March. To get to the port of Cheonbuk, take a local bus from Daecheon Bus Terminal to Jangeun-ri and get off at Jangeun-ri. The trip takes about an hour.

WHERE TO STAY

As befitting a summer resort, there's a wide selection of tourist hotels, motels and *minbak* (home stay) accommodations along Daecheon Beach. The nicest place in town is the Hanwha Resort 한화리조트 (041-931-5500), a condo with great views of the beach. Rooms start at 293,000 won a night on the weekend. Another nice option is the LeGrand Fun Beach Hotel 레그렌드펀비치호텔 (041-938-9000) with rooms that start at 198,000 won a night during the mid-July to mid-August high season.

Most of the motels in Daecheon will cost you 130,000 or more a night on the weekend during the high season, more than double their off-season rates.

TRANSPORT INFO

There are frequent buses to Boryeong from Seoul, Daejeon and other places in Chungcheongnam-do. From Boryeong Bus Terminal, take one of the frequent buses to Daecheon Beach. Boryeong is also on the coastal Janghan rail line linking Cheonan (on the Seoul—Busan line) and Iksan (on the Honam line). There are frequent buses to the beach from Daecheon Station, too.

Taean Haean National Park
태안해안국립공원

Consisting of the Taean Peninsula 태안반도, the big island of Anmyeondo 안면도 and more than one hundred small islands (an area of about 330 square km), Taean Haean National Park is one of the most scenic of Korea's seashores. The area is blessed with a diversity of environments, including beaches, mountains, sea cliffs and sand dunes. Also in the park is the lovely Cheollipo Arboretum, founded by an expatriate American and home to 7,000 plant species.

Taean's name translates to "Big Comfort" as, historically, the region has been blissfully free of natural disasters. Man-made disasters, however, are a different matter. In 2007, an offshore collision involving an oil tanker produced one of the worst oil spills in Korean history. Much of the Taean coast—and its wildlife—was tarred in black oil. Thanks to a prodigious clean-up effort that included help from an astounding one million volunteers, the coast has been almost completely restored to its original pristine state.

Taean Rock, one of many scenic spots along Taean's seashore

Taean Town 태안시

Downtown Taean is not much to look at, but it's where most buses to Taean drop you off, and it is where you'll want to transfer to local buses that take you to Taean's most scenic spots.

🚌 Buses depart from Seoul's Dong Seoul, Nambu and Central City Bus Terminal to Taean (2 hrs 20 min). Buses depart from Daejeon's Dongbu Intercity Bus Terminal (3 hrs).

Mallipo Beach 만리포해수욕장

This lovely, crescent-shaped stretch of white sand beach backed up by pine forests is very popular in summer thanks to its shallow, warm water. If you like wading out into the sea, this is your beach. It can get very crowded, though. You'll find a good many motels and restaurants here, too, especially seafood joints.

🚌 Take the bus to Mallipo Beach from Taean Express Bus Terminal.

Sinduri Coastal Sand Dune 신두리해안사구

At 2,640,000 m², the sand dune system at Sinduri is Korea's largest coastal sand dune, formed over the millenniums by strong northwesterly winds in winter depositing coastal sand in its current location. No, it's not the Western Sahara or the Gobi but it's a beautiful landscape all the same, and home to a rich variety of wild life. The dune system encompasses several different ecosystems, including the Duung Marsh, Korea's first marsh conservation area.

🚌 Just take a bus from Taean Express Bus Terminal to Sinduri.

Cheollipo Arboretum 천리포 수목원

Cheollipo Arboretum is the creation of Carl Ferris Miller (1921–2002), an American expatriate banker and arborist who passed away in 2002 after living for 57 years in Korea. Blessed with a green thumb, Miller—who became a naturalized Korean citizen in 1979—transformed a barren piece of seaside real estate he'd purchased in 1962 into Korea's first private arboretum. Today, the arboretum is home to about 7,000 plant species spread out over seven different areas. It's a wonderful place to visit any time of year, although spring and

Cheollipo Arboretum

Taean Lily Festival

⏱ 9 am to 5 pm (Apr–Sep), 9 am to 4 pm (Oct–Mar) 💶 7,000 won (Apr to Oct), 5,000 won (Nov to Mar) 🚌 Take a local bus to Cheollipo Arboretum from Taean Express Bus Terminal. ☎ 041-672-9982 🌐 www.chollipo.org

Anmyeondo Island 안면도

Anmyeondo is Korea's sixth largest island today, but at the start of the Joseon Dynasty, it was an extended cape that projected south from the Taean Peninsula. Geographically, however, this proved a bit of a pain for transporting the government-imposed grain tax, so a channel was dug separating Anmyeondo from the mainland. A bridge now crosses that channel, allowing tourists to visit the island without taking a ferry.

Anmyeondo is famous for its lovely beaches, thick pine forests and beautiful sunsets. It has 14 beaches in all, but none quite as beautiful as Kkotji Beach꽃지해수욕장, which boasts one of the most stunning sunsets in Korea. Hordes of photographers come here, especially in October and November, to capture the setting sun as it descends into the ocean between two forested rock outcrops in the sea, the

autumn are particularly nice. Every single tree or bush you see here was planted from somewhere else (of the 7,000 species, about 6,000 are not indigenous to Korea), but thanks to Miller's horticultural skills, the landscapes unfold naturally. There are a number of *hanok* homes hidden throughout the arboretum, too, moved here by Miller so that they might be preserved.

Kkotji Beach is even lovelier at sunset.

so-called Grandfather and Grandmother rocks. The two rocks stand like guardians of the beach and, come sundown, the light reflecting off their craggy, weather-beaten faces produces a cornucopia of color. Also worth stopping by when you're on the island is Anmyeondo Recreational Forest 안면도 자연휴양림 (041-674-5019, Admission: 1,000 won), some 430 hectors of natural pine forest, criss-crossed by walking paths. In summer, the shade of the forest provides a welcome respite from the heat, and the scent of the old pine can be quite entrancing. The forest also has a collection of cabins and even Korean traditional *hanok* homes where you can stay the night—see "Where to Stay" below.

WHAT TO EAT

Seafood is the name of the game here. A town specialty is *baksok milguk nakjitang* 박속밀국낙지탕, in which an entire small octopus is boiled in a soup with fresh squash. The octopus is removed and eaten, and wheat noodles are then boiled in the soup. The Wonpung Sikdang 원풍식당 (041-672-5057), located in downtown Wonbuk-myeon, not far from Sinduri, has attained local acclaim for this dish. Taean is also renowned for its blue crabs (*kkotge* 꽃게). You can find

places selling steamed blue crab aplenty in the fishing port of Anheung, at the far eastern tip of the Taean Peninsula, and the port of Baeksajang at the northern tip of Anmyeondo.

WHERE TO STAY

There are a number of accommodation options available, although in the summer you'll want to book a room ahead of time. In particular, you'll find a great many "pensions" (similar to B&B's) in the Taean area, especially around the beach areas. One particularly interesting one is Ppalganpungseon Pension 빨간풍선펜션 (010-8932-8049, http://redballoons.co.kr), on the coast south of Taean—its 10 rooms are eclectically decorated with lace drapes, stuffed animals and colorful wall murals, and if you ask (and pay), they do meat and seafood barbecues. The beach is just a five-minute walk away; also nearby is the Orchid Town arboretum 오키드 식물원 (admission: 5,000 won), home to about 1,000 species of orchids and 100 kinds of Eastern and Western herbs. Rooms go for 170,000 won in the high season (Jul 23–Aug 15), but rates come down significantly during the semi-high season (Jul 17–22, Aug 16–21) and low season. Somewhat similar, although with a direct view of the sea and slightly more expensive, is Party Party Pension 파티파티펜션 (010-3588-9557, www.partypartypension.com) where rooms can run for 290,000 won a night during the high season. Another good option if you're on Anmyeondo is Anmyeondo Recreational Forest 안면도 자연 휴양림(041-674-5019, www.anmyonhuyang.go.kr). Log cabins, Korean-style *hanok* homes and even clay-walled, thatched roof huts are available. Book ahead in summer. Prices depend on lodging type and number of people; the Korean-style *hanok*, for instance, goes for 78,000 won a night for up to eight persons. If none of this appeals to you, try the Anmyon Plaza Resort Hotel 안면도 프라자 리조트 (041-674-9674, www.anmyonplaza.com), where rooms start at 90,000 won in the high season.

TRANSPORT INFO

Buses to Anmyeondo depart from Taean Express Bus Terminal—the trip takes about 30 minutes. When you get to Anmyeon, the biggest town on the island, you can transfer to local buses to Kkotji Beach and Anmyeondo Recreational Forest (or take a 5 minute taxi ride to either destination). There are also direct buses to Anmyeondo from Seoul's Central City Terminal.

SEOSAN 서산

The town of Seosan is a pleasant little rural community just to the west of Taean. The town itself is pretty quiet, but nearby are a number of historic sites that are worth popping by, time permitting.

Haemieupseong Fortress 해미읍성

Haemieupseong Fortress is one of Korea's best preserved examples of Joseon-era fortress architecture. Most Korean fortresses were built atop hills or mountains; this one, however, was built on a flat plain. During the old days, major towns were ringed by fortress walls but precious few examples of these walls exist today. During the modern era, much of the fortress was destroyed to make room for development but, in 1973, major restoration work was undertaken. The fortress's South Gate is original while the others are restorations. A walk along the entire length of the fortress wall takes about an hour.

Completed in 1491, the fortress was a major defense point protecting Korea's West Coast from marauding Japanese pirates. It was also a military command post with responsibility over the Chungcheong-do region. Architecture aside, the fortress's historical importance is closely tied with the history of the Catholic Church in Korea. It was here that many Catholics were executed during the Byeongin Persecution of 1866 (see History & Culture: Korean Catholicism), and the fortress and its surroundings are considered holy ground

The spring flowers might be lovely, but Haemieupseong Fortress has a grim past.

Yeosutgol Holy Ground

by Korean Catholics. Some 1,000 Catholics living in Chungcheong-do were brought to Haemieupseong Fortress, where they were imprisoned and sentenced to death. Prior to being led into the fortress through the West Gate, the Catholics were forced to desecrate Catholic objects like rosaries and crucifixes. Those who refused were executed on the spot. A memorial now stands just outside the West Gate.

🚌 Take a local bus from Seosan Bus Terminal to the village of Haemi. The trip takes about 15 to 20 minutes.

Yeosutgol Holy Ground 해미순교성지

Near the fortress is Yeosutgol Holy Ground, where Catholics were buried alive, drowned and otherwise killed en masse. The name "Yeosutgol" has a rather interesting derivation—it's said that when the victims were brought here, they kept murmuring to themselves, "Yesu, Maria. Yesu, Maria," i.e., "Jesus and Mary. Jesus and Mary." The non-Catholic locals hadn't the faintest idea what they were saying, and called the spot "Yeosu mori," i.e., "Yeosu Head," which became "Yeosutgol."

The site is now a major Catholic pilgrimage site. Sadly, most of the remains were washed away in floods, although some were discovered in 1935. The site is now home to a gigantic memorial hall paying tribute to those martyred here.

🚌 Walking distance from Haemieupseong.

WHERE TO STAY

Seosan is usually seen as a day trip from somewhere else but if you do spent a night here, moderately priced, clean motels can be found near Seosan Bus Terminal.

TRANSPORT INFO

From Seoul, buses to Seosan depart from Central City Bus Terminal. The trip takes one hour, 40 minutes. There are also buses to Seosan from Daejeon's Dongbu Bus Terminal (takes two hours, 20 minutes) and Cheonan (takes two hours, 30 minutes). Frequent buses run between Seosan and Taean, too.

Off the Beaten Track

Rock-carved Buddhist Triad of Yonghyeon-ri 용현리 마애여래삼존상

On a little-visited cliff west of town is one of the most spectacular works of Baekje art still in existence. Here, you'll find an ornately carved Buddhist triad, believed to have been crafted in the late 6th century or early 7th century. The carving consists of a Buddha standing upon a lotus leaf, flanked by two Bodhisattva; unusually, the Bodhisattva on the Buddha's left sits half-seated. The faces all bear that gentle, enigmatic "Baekje smile" so characteristic of Baekje art. The triad is presumed to express the historic, future and past Buddhas that appear in the Lotus Sutra. The region where the carving is located used to be Baekje's gateway of cultural exchange with China, and is a symbol of that vibrant cultural exchange. The carving has been designated a National Treasure but, despite its beauty, gets relatively few visitors due to its isolation.

🚌 Take a local bus from Seosan Bus Terminal for Unsan 운산 where you need to change to another local bus for Yonghyeon-ri.

Gaesimsa Temple 개심사

While not the biggest temple or particularly easy to get to, Gaesimsa Temple rewards the diligent traveler with some tranquility amidst charming surroundings, especially in spring when its cherry blossoms bloom. Much of the temple's charm is in its woodwork. Korean traditional architecture aims to harmonize with nature. At Gaesimsa, you're treated to Korean Buddhist architecture at its most natural, its most intimate and its most unpretentious. Take notice of the crooked pillars in some of the buildings. They might make the buildings look crooked, but that's the whole point—nature, by and large, is not straight.

The temple's Main Hall was built in 1484, making it one of only a handful of wood buildings that date past the 17th century. It houses a wooden seated Amitabha Buddha believed to have been carved in the 14th century. Also in the temple's possession is a hanging mural painted in the 15th century. In front of the temple is a pond crossed by a single, narrow wooden beam.

🚌 Take a bus to Haemi from Seosan Bus Terminal; from Haemi take a bus to Gaesimsa.

Buddhist triad of Yonghyeon-ri (left), Gaesimsa Temple

Ganworam Hermitage sits on a tidal island.

Ganworam Hermitage 간월암

Just off the coast is a small tidal island—during low tides, it is attached to the mainland via mudflats—on which is built Ganworam, a tiny Buddhist hermitage founded at the start of the Joseon Dynasty (1392–1910) by Muhak Daesa, monk adviser to Joseon founder Yi Seong-gye. Muhak is most famous for selecting Seoul as the capital of the new dynasty, a decision still in effect six centuries later.

Most of the buildings are new but it's a pretty place that features beautiful sunsets. Migratory birds flock to the surrounding waters in winter, making the area a favorite destination of birdwatchers. During low tides, you'll find locals harvesting oysters from the mud flats. There are quite a few restaurants nearby specializing in *yeongyang gulbap* 영양굴밥—steamed rice with oysters served in a stone pot. Keun Maeul Yeongyang Gulbap 큰마을 영양 굴밥 (041-662-2706) is a good place to try it.

🚌 Take a bus to Ganworam from Seosan Bus Terminal.

HONGSEONG 홍성

Hongseong is an old walled town on the West Sea coast. Like many small Korean towns, it's not an especially exciting place but sections of the old city walls still survive, and the town is a convenient point of entry to explore the fantastic Buddhist temple of Sudeoksa 수덕사 and Deoksan Provincial Park 덕산도립공원.

Hongjuseong Fortress 홍주성 & Joyangmun Gate 조양문

In pre-modern Korea, most cities and towns were surrounded by stone walls for protection. In the 20th century, most cities tore down their walls to make way for development. In Hongseong, however, about 800 m of the original 1,772 m of walls still remain or were restored in 1975. The walls, referred to as Hongjuseong Fortress, are not especially high but nonetheless make for a pleasant evening walk—they begin from Hongseong County Office, in back of which you'll also find an old Joseon-era administrative building, a charming 19th century pavilion on an island in the middle of an artificial pond. In days bygone, officials must have gathered here to relax and make merry.

The most impressive remnant of the old fortress is Joyangmun Gate, the old eastern entrance into the town. The imposing gate, topped with a wooden superstructure, now sits in the middle of a downtown traffic rotary. Much of the gate was dismantled by

The main hall of Sudeoksa Temple dates from 1308, making it the oldest wooden building in Korea.

Guardians of Sudeoksa Temple

the Japanese, who fought a particularly vicious battle here against Korean patriotic fighters in 1905, but it was restored to its original condition in 1975. Scars from the battle can still be seen in the gate's stones.

Sudeoksa Temple 수덕사 & Deoksan Provincial Park 덕산도립공원

Located on the lower slopes of beautiful Mt. Deoksungsan 덕숭산—whose peaks are lauded as the "Mt. Geumgangsan of west-central Korea" after the famed Mt. Geumgangsan ("Diamond Mountain") of North Korea—Sudeoksa Temple has a history that dates back to 597, when the first incarnation of the temple was founded by the eminent Baekje monk Jimyeong. Sudeoksa was one of 12 Buddhist temples in Baekje mentioned in the *Samgukyusa*, a 13th century Korean history book, and the only one that has continued on to the present day.

The crown jewel of the temple—indeed, one of the crown jewels of Korean traditional architecture—is its stunning Main Hall, one of only a handful of surviving wood buildings from the Goryeo Dynasty (918–1392). Typical of buildings built in this era, it possesses an elegantly unadorned beauty. Unlike the colorfully painted temple buildings of later eras, the Main Hall is a rustic yellow-brown. Its wood pillars and eaves have been left unpainted. Holding up the sloping gabled roof is a simple system of brackets atop the tapered wood pillars. Its profile is especially spectacular, giving full view of its effortless beam and pillar structure.

According to an inscription on one of its wood beams, the hall was erected in 1308, making it the oldest surviving wooden building in Korea. It houses a wooden Buddhist triad brought to Sudeoksa from another temple in the early 20th century; interestingly, they, too, were carved in 1308. There is a small museum near the front of the temple complex that houses a number of other temple treasures, too.

Historically, Sudeoksa played a major role in the development and preservation of Korea's *Seon* (Zen) tradition, and even now is a major Zen practice and training center. The late 20th century was an especially rich time for the temple, when it was led by three of Korea's greatest Zen masters, the monks Gyeongheo (1846–1912), Mangong (1872–1946) and Hyeam (1886–1985).

Mangong's contributions to Korean Zen were particularly great. He protected the tradition of clerical celibacy when Korea's Japanese colonial rulers were pressuring monks to marry as Japanese monks do and, extraordinarily for his time, included women amongst his students. Today, around the temple are a number of hermitages where *bhikkhuni* (Buddhist nuns) reside.

Behind Sudeoksa are the lovely valleys and peaks of Deoksan Provincial Park. At 495 m, Mt. Deoksungsan—the park's central mountain—is not the tallest peak in the world but for what it lacks in height it makes up in beautiful waterfalls, rock formations and forests. There are a number of important Buddhist hermitages scattered amongst the valleys and forests, too, most notably Sorim Chodang 소림초당, a tiny thatched roof hut built atop a cliff by Zen Master Mangong in the 1920s; just up the hill behind it is a 7.5 m tall stone statue of the Bodhisattva of Mercy, erected by Mangong in 1924. The path up the mountain begins from Sudeoksa, and takes you past Sorim Chodang and Jeonghaesa Temple 정해사 before reaching the peak. To hike from Sudeoksa to the peak should take about an hour, with another hour to return to the temple.

💰 2,000 won 🚌 Take a bus to Sudeoksa Temple from Hongseong Bus Terminal. The ride takes about 1 hour. ☎ 041-339-8932~3

At Sudeoksa, you'll find many good restaurants near the temple entrance specializing in *sanchae* 산채 (mountain vegetable) cuisine like *sanchae bibimbap* 산채비빔밥 (a bowl of rice mixed with mountain vegetables and seasoned with Korean chili sauce). If you're looking for a good place to eat in downtown Hongseong, try Daedong Sikdang 대동식당 (041-632-0277), where you can score a very good *ureong ssambap* 우렁쌈밥, a rice dish served with soybean paste mixed with snail meat accompanied by lettuce wraps and a ton of side dishes, all for just 6,000 won.

WHAT TO EAT

The nicest place in downtown Hongseong is Hongseong Oncheon Tourist Hotel 홍성온천관광호텔 (041-633-7777), which also doubles as a spa of sorts. Western-style rooms are 40,000 won and suites go for 60,000 won. Two people per room can use the hotel's hot spring baths for free. In Deoksan Provincial Park, you'll find Gaya Tourist Hotel 가야호텔 (041-337-0101~7, www.gayahotel.co.kr) which like the Hongseong Tourist Hotel doubles as a spa. With better facilities and a more pleasant location it costs more, too, with rooms beginning at 78,650 won a night. If you want the real rural experience, though, try Geobugi Maeul 거북이마을, a charming farming village just west of town. Some of the village homes–including several Korean-style *hanok* homes–rent rooms to visitors (but a Korean speaker will need to make the arrangements). More info (in Korean) can be found at http://geobuki.go2vil.org. If none of this appeals to you, you'll find plenty of reasonably priced motels in downtown Hongseong.

WHERE TO STAY

From Seoul, you can get to Hongseong by express bus from Seoul's Central City Bus Terminal (2 hrs). Buses also connect Hongseong with Daejeon, Boryeong, Taean, Gongju and other regional towns. You can get to Hongseong by train, too. Hongseong is connected by rail to Seoul's Yongsan Station, Cheonan, Seodaejeon and Iksan. From Seoul's Yongsan Station, the trip takes two hours.

TRANSPORT INFO

CHEONAN 천안

For centuries, Cheonan was an important road junction where the old roads from the southeast and southwest merged before leading into the royal capital of Seoul. It's still an important transportation hub—Korea's main highways and rail links with Seoul all pass through here—but now it is also a bustling commercial, industrial and educational center in itself with a population of more than half a million. The recent opening of a KTX service to the city, bringing people from Cheonan to downtown Seoul and vice versa in just 35 minutes—and the extension of Seoul's commuter train line to the city have virtually transformed it into a Seoul suburb, leading to further growth.

Like similar medium-sized cities in Korea, Cheonan is full of shops, motels, restaurants, bars and other creature comforts for the traveler. The presence of several universities in and around Cheonan also adds a youthful element.

Cheonan's two major draws are the Cheonan Independence Hall, a truly impressive museum/monument to Korean nationalism; and Gagwonsa Temple, home to one of the biggest Buddha statues in all of Asia. The opening of the Arario Gallery Cheonan in 2002 has also put the city on the map of Korea's contemporary art scene. The gallery is well worth a look.

Korean flags, Cheonan Independence Hall

Cheonan Independence Hall
천안독립기념관

For visitors, the regional center of Cheonan is best known as the home of Independence Hall, a truly awesome memorial to Korean independence and one of Korea's best museums.

Independence Hall opened to the public in 1987 as a museum and research center to preserve the history of Korean opposition to Japanese colonial rule. The complex, built at a time when Korea was ruled by a military dictatorship, is in some respects almost Stalinist in scale—note the intimidating concrete Grand Hall of the Nation, which the museum boasts is the largest tile-roofed structure in Northeast Asia. The hall was built in Korean traditional style to house a social realist tribute to the triumph of Korean nationalism over the forces of Japanese imperialism. The sprawling courtyard has more gargantuan monuments to the Korean nation. It's all very impressive, and on a positive note, at least Korea had the wisdom to wait until after its post-war economic boom was well underway before splurging on this massive project.

After you've taken in the massive outdoor exhibits, step in the Main Exhibition Hall and make your way through the museum's seven exhibitions, most of which are dedicated to various aspects of the anti-Japanese struggle. The countless exhibits and photos on display are fascinating, especially if you have an interest in Korean history. As you can imagine, the nationalism here comes at you fast and furious. Some of the displays can be quite shocking, and nobody will accuse the museum of presenting the Japanese in a favorable light—one of the more popular exhibits is a series of recreations of Japanese torture of Korean independence activists, with smirking Japanese soldiers inflicting cruel treatment on beaten, bleeding Koreans. The history of the colonial era is probably more complicated than the museum would like to admit, but the bitterness is not without reason—the period of Japanese colonial rule was one of Korea's harshest, as the imperial masters systematically attempted to denigrate Korea's unique history and culture and involve the colony in Tokyo's imperial aggression in the region.

⏲ Hours 9:30 am to 6 pm (Mar to Oct), 9:30 am to 5 pm (Nov to Feb) Ticket sales stop one hour prior to closing. Closed Mondays 🎫 Free 🚌 From Cheonan Express Bus Terminal, take Bus No. 400 to Independence Hall (about 30 min); From Cheonan Train Station, take Bus No. 400 to Independence Hall (about 20 min). ☎ 041-560-0114 🖰 www.i815.or.kr

Gagwonsa Temple 각원사

Located on the lower slopes of Mt. Taejosan 태조산, about 20 minutes outside town by bus, is the Buddhist temple of Gagwonsa. It's not exactly ancient—it was erected only in 1977—but for what it lacks in history it attempts to make up in pure mass. The main attraction is its massive bronze statue of a sitting Amitabha Buddha. Some 15 m tall and weighing 60 tons, it is one of the largest Buddha statues in Asia—its ears alone stretch 1.75 m! The Buddha was erected by an ethnic Korean from Japan in 1976 as a prayer for the reunification of Korea.

Not to be outdone, the temple's wooden buildings subscribe to the same philosophy—size does matter. Particularly impressive is the Main Hall, said to be one of the largest wooden buildings in Korea.

🚌 Take bus No. 24 from either Cheonan Station or across from the Express Bus Terminal. The trip takes about 20 minutes.

Opened in 1987, Cheonan Independence Hall is both a fascinating museum and stirring monument to Korean nationalism.

Giant Buddha statue of Gagwonsa Temple

Arario Gallery Cheonan
아라리오 갤러리 천안

Prior to 1989, few people visited Cheonan only for the city itself. In that year, however, the Seoul-based Arario Gallery— one of Korea's top modern art galleries, founded by millionaire businessman and art collector Kim Chang-il, a native of Cheonan—opened up an exhibit space in one of Cheonan's department stores. In 2002, the gallery opened up its own wonderfully designed, spacious premises near Cheonan Express Bus Terminal, transforming the neighborhood into one of Korea's hottest art destinations.

The Arario Gallery Cheonan is surrounded by a modern art park known as Arario Small City. Here you'll find outdoor installations by some of the world's best known modern artists displayed in public for all to see. The pride and joy of this collection is BritArt bête noire Damien Hirst's "Hymn," a 6.1 m high anatomy dummy placed in its own glass pavilion. Another Hirst work, "Charity," also stands in the park.

The gallery itself holds regular exhibits by top modern artists from both Korea and abroad.

⊙ 11 am to 7 pm, closed Monday 🚊 3,000 won
🏢 Just next to Cheonan Express Bus Terminal
🖐 http://arariogallery.co.kr

WHAT TO EAT

You'll find plenty of restaurants around Cheonan Station and Cheonan Bus Terminal. The Galleria Department Store, attached to the bus terminal, also has a food court that is a good place to eat.

If a local specialty is what you're after, take a local bus from Cheonan Station or Cheonan Bus Terminal to the small village of Byeongcheon-ri 병천리. There, in the historic Aunae Market, you'll find a street full of restaurants specializing in *sundae* 순대, a Korean blood sausage made of noodles and vegetables. These are served either steamed or in a soup (*sundaeguk* 순대국). They're cheap, filling and delicious. It used to be that these were sold only on market days (dates that end in 1 or 6), but you can now enjoy them every day.

Another specialty—indeed, what Cheonan is probably most famous for—is walnut cakes (*hodo gwaja* 호도과자). Walnut trees have been cultivated in Cheonan since a local Buddhist monk brought back a walnut tree from China in 1290. The walnut cakes, however, are a more recent invention, dating back to the 1930s. Walnut cakes are also something of a Korean train travel tradition—all trains sell them onboard. Cheonandang 천안당 (041-555-5112), near Cheonan Station, is a good place to buy them. Also good is Hakhwa Hodo Gwaja 학화 호도과자, (041-551-3370) next to the station, which is run by the granddaughter of the baker who invented the treat.

WHERE TO STAY

You'll find plenty of options, although not as many as in Seoul or Daejeon. At the upper end is Cheonan Metro Tourist Hotel 천안 메트로 관광 호텔 (041-622-8211), a three-star place right across from Cheonan Station. Rooms begin at 130,000 won a night. Also serviceable is Cheonan Central Tourist Hotel 센트럴 관광 호텔 (041-564-9100), where rooms begin at 77,000 won a night.

Cheaper, but with fantastically decorated rooms, is Hotel Elli 호텔 엘리 (041-575-4201), west of Cheonan Station. On a weekend, rooms start at 60,000 won a night.

Reasonably priced motels and inns can be found clustered near Cheonan Station and Cheonan Bus Terminal. Expect to pay about 40,000–50,000 won a night at most of them.

TRANSPORT INFO

Cheonan is very well connected to the rest of Korea. It shares a KTX express train station with the nearby city of Asan—the trip from Seoul Station to Cheonan—Asan Station takes about 35 minutes. The station is a bit west of Cheonan's main downtown area.

Cheonan Station, meanwhile, is serviced by both non-express trains and Seoul subway line 1. By subway/commuter train, the trip from Seoul takes about two hours. Cheonan Station is also the junction of KORAIL's Seoul–Busan line and the Jangang Line to destinations like Boryeong.

Buses to Cheonan depart from Seoul's Central City Bus Terminal (1 hr). Buses also connect Cheonan with plenty of other destinations, including Daejeon, Gongju, Buyeo and Taean.

JEOLLABUK-DO

HIGHLIGHTS

- Eat till you're sated in Jeonju, home of the famous Jeonju *bibimbap*, then take a stroll through Jeonju Hanok Village, with its alleys of traditional Korean homes

- See the beautiful Baekje pagoda at the ruins of Mireuksa Temple

- Soak in the exotic charm of Gunsan's old waterfront

- Experience the mystery and awe of Mt. Maisan, the "Horse Ear" mountain

- Hike around Byeonsanbando National Park, where mountains, seaside and culture meet

- Take in the romance of Namwon, Korea's "City of Love"

GUNSAN

DEOGYUSAN
• NATIONAL
PARK

Iksan Stn.

JEONJU

Jeonju Stn.

MAISAN
PROVINCIAL
PARK

Gimje Stn.

BYEONSANBANDO
NATIONAL PARK

Jeongeup Stn.

GOCHANG

NAEJANGSAN
NATIONAL PARK

NAMWON

Namwon Stn.

KOREA'S BREADBASKET

For centuries, the rich, fertile plains of Jeollabuk-do have been
Korea's breadbasket. Even today, the region is known for
having the country's best local cuisine, symbolized by Jeonju
bibimbap, one of Korea's signature dishes. Countless tourists
come here simply to eat.

Once you've set down your spoons, there's plenty to see in
this relatively bite-sized province. One of Korea's most
important centers of traditional cultural and art, Jeonju
beckons with its charming old alleyways. The surreal twin
peaks of Mt. Maisan, and its mysterious temple, Tapsa, make
for a memorable trek off the beaten path. With its colonial
homes and offices, the port of Gunsan offers a trip back into
Korea's more recent past. The old fortress town of Gochang is
a pleasant place to pass the time, and nature lovers shouldn't
miss the vistas of Byeonsanbando National Park or Mt.
Deogyusan, one of Korea's premier winter sports destinations.

Pampas grass at Byeonsanbando National Park

Korean door and courtyard of Jeonju Hanok Village, where charms of old Korea are found in abundance

JEONJU 전주

Walking though the alleyways of Jeonju is like stepping into a more genteel era of culture and sophistication. Stroll amidst the handsome curved tile roofs of the city's historic Jeonju Hanok Village, for example, and you'll discover something new at each turn. A teahouse here. A gallery there. The sounds of *pansori* coming from beyond a clay and tile fence.

The southwestern town of Jeonju is one of Korea's most important centers for traditional arts and culture. If you're looking for a taste of the elegance of Korea's yesteryear, you've come to the right place. Whether it's strolling through Jeonju Hanok Village, taking in a performance of *pansori* 판소리 (lyrical storytelling), eating a dish of the famed Jeonju *bibimbap* 비빔밥 (rice mixed with vegetables and Korean hot pepper sauce) or meditating in the mystical Buddhist monastery of Geumsansa, Jeonju's got plenty for everyone.

History

Jeonju has, for ages, been the political, economic and cultural center of the Jeolla provinces. Although in modern times it's been eclipsed in size by the city of Gwangju, Jeonju remains a compelling destination in the region. It sits in the heart of Honam Plain, a wide stretch of lowland that possesses Korea's most fertile farmland and, hence, is known as the breadbasket (or rice bowl, as it were) of Korea. Jeonju is rightfully famous for having the best food in the country, with the city's *bibimbap* acquiring particular acclaim.

Jeonju's prime location naturally endowed the town with much economic and political importance as a market and administrative capital for the region. The ruling family of the Joseon Dynasty, the Jeonju Yi family, hailed from the town, a fact evidenced by the presence of Gyeonggijeon Shrine, which holds a portrait of Yi Seong-gye, the founder of the dynasty. Even today, the city is the administrative capital of Jeollabuk-do and the region's center for business, culture and education.

Like other ancient cities in Korea, the winds of development have blown strong, dramatically changing Jeonju's urban landscape. Gone are the imposing fortress walls that used to ring the city, and the downtown is dominated by the concrete and glass office towers that you'd see in any other major Korean city. Nevertheless, large pockets of Jeonju's past still exist, and the town retains its well-earned reputation for the traditional arts, most notably in paper crafts and music.

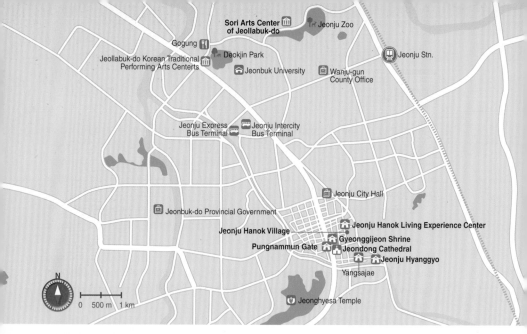

Sori Arts Center
of Jeollabuk-do
Jeonju Zoo
Gogung
Jeollabuk-do Korean Traditional
Performing Arts Centerts
Deokjin Park
Jeonju Stn.
Jeonbuk University
Wanju-gun
County Office
Jeonju Express
Bus Terminal
Jeonju Intercity
Bus Terminal
Jeonju City Hall
Jeonbuk-do Provincial Government
Jeonju Hanok Living Experience Center
Jeonju Hanok Village
Gyeonggijeon Shrine
Pungnammun Gate
Jeondong Cathedral
Jeonju Hyanggyo
Yangsajae
Jeonghyesa Temple

N

0   500 m   1 km

Jeonju Hanok Village 전주한옥마을

No place epitomizes old Jeonju better than
Jeonju Hanok Village. Located in
Pungnam-dong 풍남동, the village is home to
one of Korea's largest collections of *hanok*
homes. Here, you can leisurely stroll
through block upon block of hundreds of
elegant wooden Korean homes, many of
which have now been converted into
guesthouses, museums, galleries and
teahouses. You could literally spend the day
wandering through the neighborhood's
romantic clay wall-lined alleyways,
discovering the neighborhood's treasures.

Like Bukchon Hanok Village in Seoul,
most of Jeonju's *hanok* homes were built in
the 1920s and 30s, as Jeonju's population
increased in the wake of the city's
modernization. Likewise, the *hanok* here
have been modified to suit the urban
environment—they are so closely grouped
together, for example, that when seen from

Curved Korean roofs, Jeonju Hanok Village

Hanok, Jeonju Hanok Living Experience Center (left), Gyeonggijeon Shrine

higher vantage points like Omokdae Pavilion 오목대, their roof eaves almost seem to touch, forming a sea of curved black tile roofs. ⓒ 063-281-5044 ⬥ http://tour.jeonju.go.kr

Jeonju Hanok Living Experience Center 전주한옥생활체험관

Jeonju Hanok Village isn't a place to simply look at, it's a place to experience. Several of the *hanok* have been converted into places where tourists can experience Korean traditional culture and living. The Jeonju Hanok Living Experience Center (063-287-6300, www.jjhanok.com), for instance, gives visitors the chance to spend a night in a Korean traditional *hanok*, and offers classes on Korean traditional etiquette, arts and crafts, and a tea ceremony.

Yangsajae 양사재 (063-282-4959, www.

jeonjutour.co.kr) is another guesthouse offering traditional Korean accommodation for the evening. For weary travelers, there's nothing quite as relaxing as reclining on the floor of a Korean traditional home, looking out upon a courtyard garden or simply gazing at the handsome wood and clay ceiling above.

Gyeonggijeon Shrine 경기전

At the entrance of Jeonju Hanok Village is Gyeonggijeon Shrine, a wonderful example of Joseon-era Confucian architecture. The shrine holds a portrait of Yi Seong-gye, the local son who founded the Joseon Dynasty in 1392, as well as portraits of several other later kings. The current complex was built in 1616.

THE LAND OF *Bibimbap*

Many Koreans associate Jeonju with good food. And there's a reason for this—the local cuisine is simply outstanding. It's so good, in fact, that once you've eaten here, eating anywhere else is likely to be disappointing by comparison.

The star of Jeonju's cuisine is Jeonju *bibimbap*. A representative dish of the Joseon era and one of the most popular Korean foods today, Jeonju *bibimbap*—rice mixed with vegetables, meat, egg and other ingredients—is packed with flavor and nutrients, and served with a table full of side dishes. There are numerous places where you can taste Jeonju *bibimbap*—any taxi driver could probably recommend you one—but the most famous of the city's *bibimbap* houses is Gogung 고궁 (063-251-3211) in Deokjin-dong 덕진동, not far from Sori Arts Center of Jeollabuk-do and Jeollabuk-do Korean Traditional Performing Arts Center. Here, a *bibimbap* will run you 11,000 won, but oh, is it worth it.

Jeondong Cathedral (left), Jeonju Hyanggo

Jeondong Cathedral 전동성당

Across from Gyeonggijeon Shrine is Jeondong Cathedral, a local landmark and major Catholic pilgrimage site. The imposing church, built by French missionaries in 1914, beautifully mixes Romanesque and Byzantine elements—it's well worth taking a peek inside. Just next to the church is a handsome old red brick building that used to be the residence of the local bishop.

Pungnammun Gate 풍남문

Also nearby is Pungnammun Gate, which used to serve as the south gate of the city. It's Jeonju's only surviving city gate, the other three having been demolished in 1905. The gate has much in common with Seoul's landmark Namdaemun Gate.

Jeonju Hyanggyo 전주향교

Jeonju Hyanggyo served as a school for learning the Confucian classics during the Joseon era. Like the Gyeonggijeon Shrine, it's a wonderful example of Confucian architecture from the period.

Sori Arts Center 소리문화의 전당

The massive Sori Arts Center of Jeollabuk-do, located in Deokjin-dong 덕진동, is dedicated to Jeonju's musical heritage. The state-of-the-art facility, with both indoor and outdoor stages, is home to the Jeonju International Sori Festival, an autumn celebration of music that is Korea's preeminent "world music" festival. Located nearby is Jeollabuk-do Korean Traditional Performing Arts Center 전라북도립 국악원, home to one of Korea's best traditional music orchestras, as well as some of the nation's best traditional dancers and *pansori* vocalists.

Pungnammun Gate, the only surviving gate of Jeonju's old city walls.

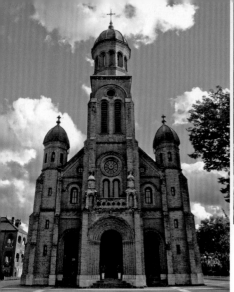

TIPS

JEONJU INTERNATIONAL SORI FESTIVAL

Held every September, the Jeonju International Sori
Festival is not only Korea's best Korean traditional
music festival but also a celebration of world music.
The festival usually features all sorts of Korean musical
genres, including instrumental work, fusion music and
dance, but at its heart is *pansori*, the lyrical storytelling
for which Jeonju (and indeed, all of southwest Korea) is famous. *Pansori* is often compared
to "folk opera," or the bluegrass tradition of American Appalachia. It's a form of musical
storytelling featuring a single vocalist accompanied by a drummer, and is particularly
representative of Korea's musical culture. This is an unmatched opportunity to see some of
Korea's top *pansori* artists performing their craft. To give the festival a bit of an international
flavor, overseas world music groups are invited, too. Most of the events are held at the Sori
Arts Center of Jeollabuk-do, but some are also held in Jeonju Hanok Village and elsewhere
(www.sorifestival.com).

WHAT TO EAT

In addition to the bibimbap (see Travel Tip), another Jeonju specialty is *kongnamul gukbap*, a
spicy, clear soup with soybean sprouts and rice. It's cheap and great for taking the edge off a
hangover. Waengi Kongnamul Gukbap (063-287-6980) near Gyeonggijeon does a fine bowl for
5,000 won. Another good place to try for kongnamul gukbap is Hyeondaeok (063-228-0020),
across the stream from Jeollabuk-do Provincial Office.

For some hearty eating, try Jo Jeom-nye Nammun Pisundae (063-232-5006) in the Nambu
Market just south of Pungnammun Gate. A plate of *pisundae*, a Korean blood sausage with a
lovely rich taste, goes for 8,000 won. A bowl of sundae *gukbap* (rice soup with blood sausage)
goes for 5,000 won.

WHERE TO STAY

If you'd like to stay in Jeonju Hanok Village, try Jeonju Hanok Living Experience Center (063-
287-6300, www.jjhanok.com), where rooms with a communal bathroom go for 70,000 won
(including breakfast). Larger rooms with private bathrooms available, too. The spectacular
Hagindang House (063-284-9929), a Korean-style mansion built in 1908, has rooms beginning
at 60,000 won (not including breakfast). Cultural programs are available, too.

Another wonderful hanok guest house is Dongnagwon, a restored hanok that also serves as
a museum to American missionary W.M. Junkin, who lived here after coming to Jeonju in 1895.
Even more hanok guesthouses can be found at http://tour-eng.jeonju.go.kr.

There are plenty of reasonably priced motels and inns around Jeonju Station, and there's a
"motel village" in Junghwasan-dong, in the south of town, where you can find rooms usually
for 40,000 won a night. BENIKEA Jeonju Hansung Tourist Hotel (063-288-0014~5), near Jeonju
City Hall, has rooms going for 50,000 won a night (weekdays). Each room is decorated with
hanji (Korean paper). Roughly similar is Jeonju Tourist Hotel (063-280-7700), with rooms
beginning at 60,000 won a night.

TRANSPORT INFO

There are four KTX express trains a day from Seoul's Yongsan Station to Jeonju (2 hrs). There
are several slower trains, too, that take about three hours, 20 minutes. Buses to Jeonju depart
from Seoul's Dong Seoul and Central City Bus terminals (2 hrs 50 min). From Daejeon, buses to
Jeonju depart from Jeonju Express Bus Terminal (1 hr 20 min), and from Gwangju, they depart
from U Square (1 hr 20 min).

Geumsansa Temple 금산사
& Moaksan Provincial Park 모악산도립공원

Once you've had enough of downtown Jeonju's charms, you might wish—time permitting—to take a half-hour bus ride (take the No. 89 bus from Pungnammun Gate) out of town to nearby Gimje 김제, home to the massive Buddhist monastery of Geumsansa, one of Korea's most important Buddhist temples.

It's believed that the temple was founded in the first year of the devoutly Buddhist King Beop of Baekje, or 599 AD. From 762 to 766, Precept Master Jinpyo, one of early Korea's greatest Buddhist monks, expanded the temple into a major monastery. During the Japanese invasion of 1592, most of the temple was burnt to the ground, so many of its current structures date from the reconstruction of 1635.

Geumsansa Temple is a trove of Korean cultural treasures, both of stone and wood. The centerpiece of Geumsansa is the awe-inspiring Mireukjeon Hall 미륵전. Designated National Treasure No. 62, this massive structure is the only remaining three-story traditional structure in Korea. The building was constructed to house an equally massive gilded statue of the Maitreya Buddha; its roof is so heavy that each floor requires separate support pillars. The current hall dates from the 1635 reconstruction, although it's been repaired

Mireukjeon Hall

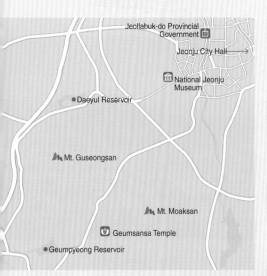

several times since.

Mireukjeon Hall is only one of several important cultural properties in the monastery's possession. Several stone pagodas, stone lanterns and wooden halls have also been designated national treasures by the government. The mountain on whose slopes the temple rests, Mt. Moaksan 모악산, is considered spiritually important by Korea's shamanist community. You should set aside at least half a day if you're to appreciate Geumsansa fully.

Geumsansa: 🎫 3,000 ⓒ 063-548-4441 ⓥ www. geumsansa.org (KR) 🚌 Bus No. 79 from Jeonju Bus Terminal (40 min.)
Moaksan Provincial Park: 🎫 3,000 ⓒ 063-222-7816 🚌 Bus No. 970 on Paldallo 팔달로 (40 min.)

1. Daejangjeon Hall 2. Geumsansa 5-story Pagoda 3. Buddhas in Main Hall

Mireuksa Temple Site 미륵사지

Off the Beaten Track

In a field about an hour's drive north from Jeonju are the ruins of Mireuksa 미륵사, the greatest temple of the Baekje Kingdom. The temple itself has long since disappeared but its massive stone pagoda still remains, standing sentinel over its patch of the fertile Honam Plain.

According to the *Samgukyusa*, a 13th century Korean history book, Mireuksa ("Maitreya Temple") was founded during the reign of King Mu of Baekje (r. 600–641). The king and his wife, the Silla princess Seonhwa, were traveling to Sajasa Temple to see the Ven. Jimyeong, a respected Baekje monk. Along the way, they passed a pond at the foot of Mt. Yonghwasan, and in the pond appeared the Maitreya ("Future Buddha"), flanked by two Bodhisattva. Impressed by what she saw, Princess Seonhwa had the pond filled up and a grand temple built on the location. Naturally, the temple was named for the Maitreya Buddha.

Judging from what survives today—admittedly, it's not much—including the foundation stones and what has been excavated, we can easily see that the temple was one of the largest in Korea, if not all Northeast Asia. Most temples have a single main dharma hall. Mireuksa had three, each with its own courtyard with its own massive pagoda. In front of the central main hall, which was the largest, stood a truly gargantuan wooden nine-story pagoda that must have been an architectural marvel in its day. In the east and west courtyards, stone pagodas modeled on the wooden one were erected.

We know that the temple survived through the Buddhist Goryeo Dynasty, but was closed and fell into ruin sometime in the Joseon Dynasty, when the dynasty's Confucian elite worked to discourage Buddhism. By the 18th century, the ruins of one of the stone pagodas were abandoned in the middle of a rice paddy; local farmers would climb atop the eaves to take midday naps.

What remains today is the western stone pagoda, a stone base for a Buddhist flag pole, and a good many foundation stones. This is enough, however, for us to picture the grandeur of the old monastery. The western pagoda (National Treasure No. 11) is only partially intact—three of the original nine stories have fallen to the ground, and the entire back half of the pagoda has collapsed. Still, at 14.24 m high, it's Korea's tallest pagoda, and also its oldest. Excavation and restoration work—in part to repair shoddy preservation work by the colonial Japanese—has been ongoing.

The eastern pagoda disappeared without a trace, but in 1992 it was completely reconstructed, using the remains of the western pagoda as a model. There's a museum, too, with displays of the many objects archaeologists have excavated from the site, as well as drawings and models of how the temple appeared in its golden age.

⊕ 9 am to 6 pm. Museum closed Mondays. 🚪 Free 🚌 From Jeonju Bus Terminal, take a bus to Geumma-myeon 금마면. At Geumma-myeon, transfer to Iksan 익산 Bus No. 41 or 60 and get off at Mireuksa Temple Site. 🖥 www.godoiksan.go.kr

Daedunsan Provincial Park 대둔산도립공원

Straddling the towns of Nonsan and Geumsan in Chungcheongnam-do and Wanju in Jeollabuk-do, Mt. Daedunsan 대둔산 (878 m) is a scenic mountain known for its craggy granite peaks, which are said to resemble the silk folding screens traditionally found in Korean homes. Take a cable car up most of the mountain but from the drop-off point, the trail to the peak is a steep and sometimes spooky one. Be warned—if you've got a fear of heights, this is not a hike for you. The highlight of the climb is Geumgang Gureum Bridge 금강구름다리, a 1 m wide suspension bridge linking two rock peaks over an 80 m ravine, followed by a vertigo-challenging ascent up a steep, narrow 127-step steel staircase up the face of a sheer granite cliff. From the top of the stairs, it's another 20 minute hike to Macheondae Peak 마천대, the highest peak. If you do make it to Macheondae, however, you're rewarded with fine views over the surrounding landscape. If you take the cable car, the hike will take you about two hours, round trip.

⊙ 7 am to 6:30 pm 🚌 There are direct buses to Daedunsan Provincial Park from Jeonju Bus Terminal (1 hr). It's actually easier to get there, however, from Daejeon's Seobu Intercity Bus Terminal (40 min). ✆ 063-263-9949

Clouds and valleys, Daedunsan Provincial Park (top)
Just 127 steps to the peak! (bottom)

Geumgang Gureum Bridge

GUNSAN 군산

A thriving center of trade and commerce during the Japanese colonial period, Gunsan is home to Korea's largest collection of imperial-era buildings and relics. The city charms visitors with its exotic atmosphere, but beneath the genteel colonial exterior of this former treaty port is a painful history of expropriation and exploitation, the aftereffects of which are still felt today.

History Prior to 1899, Gunsan was little more than a small West Sea fishing village. In 1899, however, the harbor was opened to international trade, and the waterfront area became a foreign-run concession territory. Imperial Japan, desperate for additional rice supplies to feed its growing population of urban workers, turned a covetous eye to the surrounding Honam Plain, Korea's most agriculturally productive region. Ambitious Japanese landlords established massive plantations in the countryside while Japanese traders and businessmen set about turning Gunsan into a modern port capable of handling the large amount of rice being exported back to the home islands. By 1919, the port was home to some 6,581 Koreans and 6,809 Japanese.

When Liberation came in 1945, the Japanese went home, but their homes, offices, farms and businesses remained to be taken over by local Koreans (with the exception of the large Japanese airbase just outside of town, which was taken over by the Americans who remain there to this day).

Japanese-style Dongguksa Temple, built in 1909

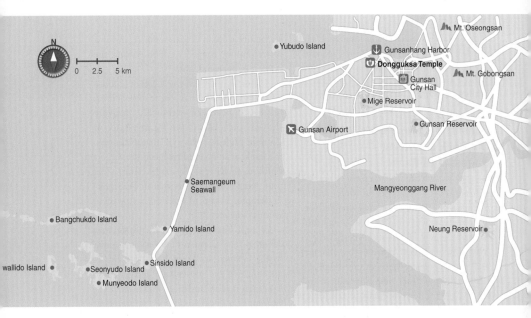

Gunsan is now a bustling port town taking advantage of burgeoning trade with China. For much of the post-Liberation period, the town suffered from relative neglect due to the development of other port cities and discriminatory development policies. But thanks in part to this neglect, much of its colonial-era architectural legacy has thus far avoided the developer's wrecking ball.

Dongguksa Temple 동국사

Perhaps the most intriguing—and certainly one of the most beautiful—of Gunsan's colonial-era buildings is Dongguksa Temple, located in Geumgwang-dong 금광동. Founded by a Japanese monk in 1909, Dongguksa is Korea's only remaining Japanese Buddhist temple still functioning as a temple. As you pass through the gate, you are awestruck by the distinctly Japanese lines of the temple's woodwork. With its severe right angles, almost complete lack of exterior embellishment, and steeply inclined roof, the temple is a picture of Edo-period Japanese temple design.

Inside, the Main Hall is solemnly painted in white and brown, quite a contrast to the

Interior, Dongguksa Temple

colorfully painted interiors of Korean temples. The Main Hall, monks' quarters and bathrooms are connected by internal corridors in traditional Japanese fashion. As if to put to rest any doubt as to the temple's origins, the bell that hangs in the temple's bell pavilion is distinctly Japanese, having been crafted in Kyoto in 1919.

🏯 Free 🚌 Bus No. 11 through 18 from Gunsan Station (30 min) ✆ 063-462-5366 🖥 www.dongguksa.or.kr (KR)

Gunsan Customs House 옛군산세관, Old Bank of Choson 구조선은행 & Nagasaki 18 Bank 나가사키 18은행

By the waterfront of Naehang Port 내항 ("Inner Port") are several spectacular examples of early Western-style architecture. The best preserved of these is the Old Gunsan Customs House, which dates back to 1908. Designed most probably by a French architect (some say German, although the first customs officer being French would suggest the former) and built of red bricks imported from Belgium, the Customs House is an eclectic mix of European architectural styles—a Gothic roof, Romanesque windows and an English-style door. This eclecticism characterized early modern architecture in Japan and throughout its empire.

The money to build the Customs House was provided by Korea's royal government, although the Japanese oversaw the use of the funds and construction of the building. In theory, the levying of customs on incoming ships should have helped the struggling Korean economy; instead, most of the money earned went to paying the interest on foreign loans.

A short walk from the Customs House will take you to a massive, nearly derelict red-brick structure with a distinctively shaped roof. This is the former Bank of Choson. Built in 1923 by Chinese laborers, the bank once boasted of being the largest building in Korea outside of Seoul. The roof, steeply inclined like that of Dongguk-sa Temple, is said to resemble a Japanese samurai's helmet.

Legend has it that the building was designed by a German POW taken captive by the Japanese in World War I, but this is unconfirmed and most likely untrue. After Liberation, the building was used as a Gunsan Branch of Hanil Bank before being turned into a nightclub. Since a fire several years ago, it has been an empty shell, although the city hopes to one day restore it as a museum.

Nearby are several other old colonial offices and structures, including the handsome former home of Nagasaki 18 Bank. With cream-colored walls and a green roof, the bank was built in 1907 and was instrumental in providing funds for local Japanese to purchase Korean land. Also nearby is Haemanggul Tunnel 해망굴,

Former Gunsan Customs House (left), Former 18th Bank

built in 1926 to link the port with the old downtown area. The tunnel is built through a hillside that itself is a park offering superb views of the port, and a nice spot to stretch your legs.

Old Japanese Homes of Yeonghwa-dong 영화동

The neighborhood of Yeonghwa-dong is a literal treasure trove of Japanese colonial architecture. Unlike the buildings near the waterfront, which are mostly official structures, those in Yeonghwa-dong were—and still are—private residences. One could spend hours wandering around its streets, taking in the plethora of old Japanese-style wooden homes—it's like walking onto a film set, which, in fact, is how the neighborhood is often used.

The most impressive of the homes is the former Hirotsu House 히로츠 가옥. Located near Gunsan Girls High School 군산여자고등학교, it's the best preserved traditional Japanese home in Korea, bar none. The large wooden *yashiki* (Japanese mansion) was built by a wealthy drygoods merchant by the name of Hirotsu to show off his wealth in a town where the elite were mostly plantation owners. Inside, you'll find tatami rooms and interior passageways typical of Japanese homes. Outside is a beautiful Japanese garden complete with a (now empty) koi pond. Until very recently, the home was empty and in need of repair, but it is now undergoing a proper restoration.

Yi Yeong-chun House 이영춘가옥 & Old Shimatani Plantation 구 시마타니농장

A short bus ride outside of town brings you to the vast rice fields of the Honam Plain. Peaceful as they may appear today, they have a bitter history—with yields some four times higher than in Japan but at only one tenth the price, they attracted the keen attention of Japanese landlords who established vast plantations worked by thousands upon thousands of Korean sharecroppers who led nearly slave-like existences.

One bittersweet reminder of this age is the former home of Dr. Yi Yeong-chun 이영춘가옥, one of Korea's earliest Western doctors and often called "Korea's Albert

Hirotsu House, an old Japanese colonial mansion

Schweitzer" for his work among the peasants of the Gunsan area.

Prior to coming into Lee's possession, however, it was a villa belonging to his employer, Japanese landowner Kumamoto Rihei, one of the biggest landowners in colonial Korea. Kumamoto's vast holdings amounted to fields more than 10 times the size of Yeouido in area, and were worked by some 20,000 Korean tenant farmers.

The former Kumamoto Villa, located next to Gunsan Nursing College 군산간호대학, was rarely used by Kumamoto himself, who preferred to live in Seoul. Nevertheless, it was luxuriously constructed and furnished, built with only the finest imported materials. The cost of construction was similar to that of the Japanese governor-general's residence.

Another short bus ride away, in back of the Balsan Elementary School 발산초등학교, is more evidence of the region's colonial past. There, you'll find a collection of Korean stone pagodas and stone lanterns, some designated national treasures. You'll also find an imposing concrete storehouse with heavy metal doors (marked "Made in the USA").

This used to be the plantation of Shimatani Yasoya, who came to Korea in 1903 and founded a rice plantation to produce cheap grain for his sake brewery in Japan. Shimatani was a tremendous lover of Korean traditional art. So great was his love for Korean art, in fact, that he plundered a great deal of it. The stone pagodas and lanterns behind Balsan Elementary School, for example, were moved to their current location for use as garden ornaments. The storehouse, meanwhile, was used to keep safe Shimatani's vast collection of Korean pottery and art.

🚌 To get to the old Kumamoto Villa, take Bus No. 86 from Gunsan Intercity Bus Terminal and get off at Gunsan Nursing College. To get to the old

Shimatani Plantation, take Bus No. 21 from the terminal and get off at Balsan Overpass and walk to Balsan Elementary School. Either trip should take you about 30 minutes.

Eocheongdo Island 어청도

Located some 70 km west of Gunsan, Eocheongdo is a pleasant little island blessed with a natural harbor favored by local fishermen. Its main scenic spots are the lovely old lighthouse on the west end of the island, erected in 1912, and the migratory birds who stop over on their way to and from China. There's (usually) only one boat to the island, so plan on staying overnight. There are a couple of small inns in town—most cost around 40,000 won a night.

🚌 Take Bus No. 7 from Gunsan Station to Gunsan Coastal Ferry Terminal (90 min), and from there take a ferry to Eocheongdo (2 hrs 30 min, fare: 22,900 won). There is one boat a day on weekdays (9 am), and two on weekends (7:30 am, 1:30 pm).

Lighthouse, Eocheongdo Island

Seonyudo Island (left), Saemangeum

Seonyudo Island 선유도

A popular destination in summer is Seonyudo Island, a small island in the heart of the Gogunsan archipelago 고군산군도. A little piece of old rural Korea, the island is inhabited by mostly fishermen, except in summer when the population gets a boost from large numbers of tourists from the mainland. Most come for its lovely beaches but another fun activity is to rent a bicycle (10,000 won) and spend the day biking around the island. There are some inns and restaurants on the island, and it's a pleasant place to spend the night.

🚌 Take Bus No. 7 from Gunsan Station to Gunsan Coastal Ferry Terminal (fare: 16,650 won, 45 min), and from there take a ferry to Seonyudo Island. There are six to seven ferries a day, except during the summer, when the number is increased to 13 to 14.

Saemangeum 새만금

Not so much a tourist spot as much as a marvel of modern engineering, Saemangeum is one of the greatest land-reclamation projects in the history of man. Its massive 33 km seawall is the longest seawall in the world, edging out the Netherland's Zuiderzee Works. By 2020, the project will have produced over 40,000 hectares of new farmland.

🚌 Take Bus No. 08, 09, 82, 91 or 92 from Gunsan Bus Terminal.

WHAT TO EAT

Gunsan is a port, which means there's plenty of seafood to be scored. Kunsan Seafood 군산횟집 (063-442-1114) is an eight-story raw-fish center right on the waterfront. Look to spend 80,000–100,000 won here. Also near the old waterfront is Binhaewon 빈해원 (063-445-2429), a historic Chinese restaurant that has been serving tasty Chinese cuisine for over 60 years. The rooms on the second floor—usually kept for customers with reservations—still maintain their exotic, historic charm. Gunsan's most famous eatery is Lee Sung Dang 이성당 (063-445-2772), Korea's longest continuously operating bakery. Opened first in the 1920s, it was taken over by Koreans in 1945. It is particularly famous for its *danpatppang*, or red bean buns.

WHERE TO STAY

You'll find plenty of cheap motels around Gunsan City Hall and Gunsan Intercity Bus Terminal. There's also a "motel village" in Naun-dong 나운동 in the west of town.

TRANSPORT INFO

The best way to get to Gunsan is to take the KTX from Yongsan Station in Seoul to Iksan, and then transfer to a train to Gunsan (2 hrs 30 min). Gunsan Station is a bit outside of town, so you'll need to take a bus or cab to get downtown. Gunsan's express and inter-city bus terminals are within walking distance of the historic waterfront. Buses to Gunsan depart from Seoul's Central Central City Terminal (2 hrs 30 min).

Gunsan is also well-connected by bus to Jeonju, Iksan and other cities in Jeollabuk-do. Gunsan also has an airport, although the runway is mostly used by the adjoining US Air Force base. There are two flights a day from Gunsan to Jeju-do—call 063-471-5001 or visit http://gunsan.airport.co.kr for more information.

BYEONSANBANDO NATIONAL PARK 변산반도국립공원

"Have a cup of tea before you go," reads the sign on the tea house of Naesosa Temple. This weary traveler, not one to turn down such a welcoming offer, steps inside the teahouse of Naesosa Temple and boils himself a nice kettle of green tea, a welcome treat. Outside the open sliding doors sits a weathered old stone pagoda and, beyond it, the tile roofs of the temple; further still are the forested hillsides of the beautiful mountains.

In a land filled with beauty, few places match the natural splendor of Byeonsan Peninsula. Jutting out from the small town of Buan 부안 in southwestern Jeollabuk-do Province, Byeonsan Peninsula—long protected as part of Korea's National Park system—has something for everyone. Its gorgeous mountains, dotted with dramatic cliffs, waterfalls, lakes and ancient Buddhist temples, beckon the hiker and cultural tourist, while lovers flock to its beaches to take in spectacular sunsets.

Naesosa Temple blends fine craftsmanship with splendid natural surroundings.

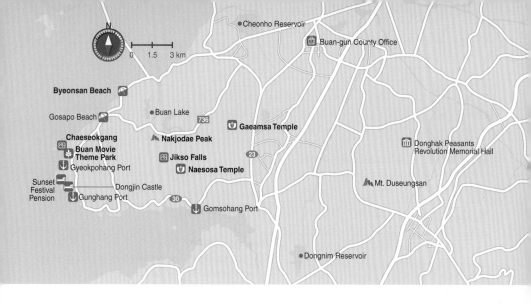

Map labels:
- Cheonho Reservoir
- Buan-gun County Office
- Byeonsan Beach
- Gosapo Beach
- Buan Lake
- 736
- Gaeamsa Temple
- Chaeseokgang
- Nakjodae Peak
- Donghak Peasants Revolution Memorial Hall
- Buan Movie Theme Park
- Jikso Falls
- Gyeokpohang Port
- 23
- Naesosa Temple
- Mt. Duseungsan
- Sunset Festival Pension
- Dongjin Castle
- Gunghang Port
- 30
- Gomsohang Port
- Dongnim Reservoir

0   1.5   3 km

Layout

Inner Byeonsan or 내변산 "Naebyeonsan" is the lovely mountainous interior of the Byeonsan Peninsula. It's here you'll find most of the quality hiking opportunities, with Jikso Falls and Nakjodae Peak (roughly 450 m) as two popular options. The interior is also home to Naesosa and Gaeamsa, two of Korea's most underrated Buddhist temples. Once you've had enough of the mountains, head to Outer Byeonsan or Oebyeonsan 외변산, and enjoy some of the peninsula's maritime scenery.

Naesosa Temple 내소사

Naesosa Temple is Byeonsan Peninsula's most visited temple. It's not hard to see why—the stroll to the temple set amidst towering pine trees is simply magical. The temple itself is blessed with a dramatic mountain backdrop and is home to two treasures: a temple bell from the Goryeo era (National Treasure No. 277) and an absolutely spectacular Main Hall (National Treasure No. 291). Be sure to check out the designs on the finely crafted doors. Also, look around the many other buildings on the compound—it's a treasure trove of Korean traditional architecture.

🎫 2,000 won ⓒ 063-583-7281 🖥 www.naesosa.org (KR) 🚍 Take Bus No. 350 or 301 to the temple (50 min) from Buan Bus Terminal.

Teahouse, Naesosa Temple

Jikso Falls 직소폭포

Jikso Falls is one of the peninsula's best known scenic spots, and one of the easiest to reach in Inner Byeonsan—it's a 4 km hike from Naesosa Temple. The scenery along the hike—past beautiful mountains, rivers and stone faces—makes for a pleasant stroll.

Nakjodae Peak 낙조대

Nakjodae Peak is reputed to have the finest sunsets in Korea. You have to work hard to see that sunset, though. The hike to the peak from Namyeochi Ticket Office 남여치매 표소 isn't easy—it's one hard hour-long slog. Bring your hiking boots—you'll need them.

Not far from Nakjodae is Wolmyeongam 월명암, a small Buddhist hermitage. If you're really ambitious, try to visit the hermitage before dawn—you'll be greeted with unforgettable views of the mist hanging in the hills.

🚌 From Buan, take a bus for Gyeokpo 격포 and get off at Byeonsan 변산 (20 min). From there, take a taxi to Namyeochi Ticket Office (15 min). Otherwise, you can hike there from Naesosa, but it's a three hour journey.

Gaeamsa Temple 개암사

While not quite as visited as Naesosa, Gaeamsa Temple allows you to enjoy your temple experience in peace and tranquility—amidst some fine mountain scenery, one should add. The Main Hall,

Jikso Falls (left), Gaeamsa Temple (right)

which dates from 1636, is a masterpiece of Korean wooden architecture. If you're the meditating sort, be sure to spend some time inside.

☎ 063-583-3871 🚌 From Buan Bus Terminal, take a bus for Julpo 줄포/ Gomso 곰소 or Gyeokpo 격포 /Naesosa and get off at the entrance of Gaeamsa (15 min).

Seaside Drive

If you've got a car, take a leisurely drive along the seaside road—start on Route 30 and keep going. Once you get to Gosapo Beach, the road will split off into a "seaside drive road" that will eventually meet up again with Route 30.

Chaeseokgang 채석강
& Jeokbyeokgang 적벽강

Chaeseokgang is a rocky, stratified cliff overlooking the sea. At the bottom of the cliff are a series of caves that you can enter at low tide. While the cliffs themselves are quite impressive, the spot is more famous as a place from which to take in the sunrise. About 1 km away is a similar set of cliffs known as Jeokbyeokgang, which is also a great place to witness the dawning sun.

🚌 From Buan Bus Terminal, take a bus for Gyeokpo (40 min)

Chaeseokgang (top), Jeokseokgang

WHERE TO STAY

While there are accommodations in downtown Buan-gun, where you really want to stay are the seaside hotels in Byeonsanbando National Park itself. Ones to try include Chaeseok Resotel Oakvill 채석리조텔오크빌 (063-583-8046), Sunset Festival Pension 해넘이축제 (063-582-0405) and Dongjin Castle 동진캐슬펜션 (063-583-0179), to name a few. Prices usually start at 40,000 to 50,000 won for a two-person room.

TRANSPORT INFO

Express buses to Buan-gun leave hourly from Seoul's Central City Bus Terminal. The trip takes about 3 hours, 10 minutes. From Buan, there are local buses that take you to the major tourist sites such as Naesosa Temple and Chaeseokgang.

GOCHANG 고창

Located in the southwestern corner of the province, Gochang is a friendly but very rural town known nationally for its excellent raspberry wine or *bokbunjaju* 복분자주. There's not a whole lot happening in the town itself—life moves pretty slowly in these parts—but it does have a very well-preserved Joseon Dynasty fortress that's worth a visit. Just outside of town, too, are the beautiful Buddhist monastery of Seonunsa and ancient dolmen sites that are designated a UNESCO World Heritage Site.

Gochangeupseong Fortress 고창읍성

Ringing a forested hillock in the south of town is Gochangeupseong Fortress (also known as Moyangseong 모양성), a well-preserved ring of stone walls from the early Joseon Dynasty. Its exact date of construction is uncertain, but evidence suggests it was built either in the 15th or 16th century. While most surviving fortresses in Korea are mountain fortresses ringing high mountaintops (*sanseong*), this is one of only a handful of remaining lowland fortresses (*eupseong*) that were built to defend coastal towns from the endemic raids by Japanese pirates during the Goryeo and Joseon dynasties. And unlike other lowland fortresses, such as Naganeupseong Fortress, these walls never encircled an actual town.

Gochangeupseong Fortress, one of Korea's few remaining lowland fortresses and site of the annual Dapseong Nori procession

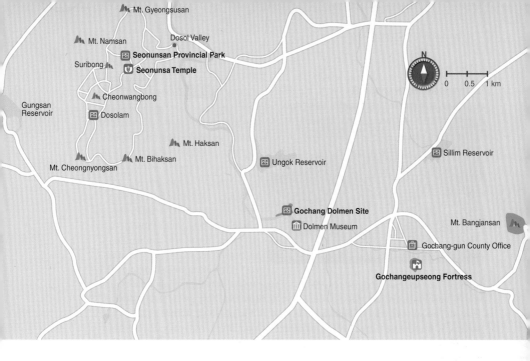

Instead, it housed a large government complex where the local magistrate and other officials lived and worked.

The fortress roughly forms a ring with a 1,684 m circumference, with walls four to six meters high—to walk completely around it takes about 30 minutes. It has three gates (themselves protected by additional crescent-shaped walls), two floodgates and six defensive bastions. In the old days, the fortress was also surrounded by a moat for added protection. Inside, the government complex disappeared ages ago, but 14 of the original 22 building have been reconstructed. Of these, the most important was the *gaeksa*, an official guesthouse where royal emissaries stayed and where local officials regularly performed ceremonies to honor the king. The fortress is especially beautiful in spring time when it is surrounded by a sea of bright pink royal azaleas.

🛋 1,000 won 🚏 10-minute walk from Gochang Bus Terminal ☎ 063-560-2313

Gochang Dolmen Site 고창고인돌공원

Dolmen (*goindol* in Korean) are single-chamber stone tombs, usually several upright stones supporting a large, flat capstone. They can be found throughout much of the ancient world but are especially plentiful in Korea, where dolmen-building cultures held sway throughout the Neolithic and Bronze ages.

Gochang has a particularly large number of dolmen, with no fewer than 447 of them

Gochang Dolmen Site, a UNESCO World Heritage Site

DAPSEONG NORI 답성놀이 &
GOCHANG MOYANG FORTRESS FESTIVAL 고창모양성제

History and Culture

The fortress' relatively good state of preservation is partially thanks to a tradition practiced by Gochang's womenfolk. In spring, women would gather to walk the entire length of the walls carrying a stone on their head. At the end of the walk, they would drop the stone at the fortress gate. This aim was to harden the fortress walls, which would loosen in spring, and provide a supply of stone for use as artillery or fortress repairs. For women involved, a single walk around the fortress was said to prevent disease, two times would bring good health and a long life, and three times around grant them entry into paradise. According to tradition, this was particularly effective in lunar leap months, and especially on the 6th, 16th and 26th of the lunar leap month, when the gates to heaven were said to be open.

Nowadays, this tradition has been moved to mid-October, when Gochang hosts the annual Gochang Moyang Fortress Festival. If you're in the region in October, don't miss this event—the parade of *hanbok*-clad women carrying stones upon their head as they stroll along the fortress walls truly is a sight to behold. 🚶 www.gochang.go.kr/festival

found at the Gochang Dolmen Site south of town near the village of Jungnim-ri 죽림리. Here you'll find a large, roadside grass field covered with dolmen, some as large as 300 tons. This spot, along with several others across the country, is registered as a UNESCO World Heritage Site.

A 700 m walk to the south of the site, at another group of dolmen in the village of Dosan-ri 도산리, is Gochang Dolmen Museum 고창고인돌박물관 (063-560-2576~8), where there are displays of prehistoric and Bronze Age life in Korea. And if you've ever wondered how the ancients moved the massive stones from the quarry to the dolmen sites, there's a hands-on exhibit where you can try to pull a dolmen stone on wooden runners.

🕐 9 am to 6 pm. Closed Mondays, 9 am to 5 pm (Nov–Feb) 🎫 Free. Outdoor sites are free but museum admission is 3,000 won 🚌 From Gochang Bus Terminal, take a bus for Gochang-Jungnim and get off at Gochang Dolmen Museum (20 min). From there, it's a 700 m walk north across the river to the dolmen site. ✆ 063-560-8666 🖳 www.gcdolmen.go.kr

Seonunsa Temple 선운사 & Seonunsan Provincial Park 선운산도립공원

Seonunsa Temple is a lovely Buddhist temple and popular weekend destination for residents of southwestern Korea. Not so long ago, this was a pretty big monastery, with 189 buildings and 89 hermitages in the late Joseon Dynasty. It's nowhere near as big now, but is still one of the more important temples in this part of the country. Unlike some of the other big temples in the region, this one was saved from being burning down during the Korean War when the police officer in charge of local security refused orders to destroy it.

Seonunsa was founded in 577 by the Baekje monk Geomdan. Back then, this was bandit country, so in addition to the usual sutra reading and meditation, the good monk also taught the locals more legitimate professions, including papermaking and drying salt from the nearby sea. To repay their debt to Geomdan, villagers would offer their salt to the temple twice a year. The sea salt production of the village of Sadeung has continued the tradition to this day every autumn, when the villagers dress in Baekje-era clothing, load up an ox with sacks of salt and march to Seonunsa Temple to deliver the cargo.

Seonunsa has a long Seon (Zen) tradition, as its name—which translates as "Meditation Cloud Temple"—would suggest. The precinct is blessed with a number of handsome old buildings, including Daeungbojeon 대웅보전 (Main

Daffodils, Seonunsa Temple

Hall), built in 1618. Don't miss the 17th century murals on the wall behind the altar. The temple feels its age—in a good way—with its faded colors lending an antique charm not found nearly enough at Korea's older temples. Be sure to check out the wildly crooked beams holding up the

It's not big, but Seonunsan Provincial Park is a pleasant mix of nature and culture.

Maitreya Buddha, Seonunsan Provincial Park

Hugging the temple is Mt. Seonunsan 선운산 (335 m), or as it was originally called, Mt. Dosolsan 도솔산. It's not tall but its pretty valleys and thick forests have led to comparisons, albeit greatly exaggerated, to North Korea's scenic Geumgangsan Mountains. The forests are quite colorful in spring and autumn. The most popular hiking trail takes you from Seonunsa Temple up Dosol Valley 도솔계곡, through a cave and to Dosoram 도솔암, a small Buddhist hermitage near which you'll find a giant 15.6 m tall cliff carving of the Maitreya Buddha from the Goryeo Dynasty. Also nearby, up a flight of stone steps, is Naewongung 내원궁, a small wooden hall built atop a big rock. The views of the mountain here are beautiful, and be sure to check out the Goryeo Dynasty gilt bronze seated Bodhisattva in the hall itself.

From Dosoram, you can either return to Seonunsa Temple or press on a bit more to Nakjodae 낙조대 ("Sunset Rock") and Cheonmabong Peak 천마봉. The entire hike should take you three hours, round trip.

🍽 3,000 won 🚌 Take a local bus from Gochang Bus Terminal to Seonunsa (30 min). ⓒ Seonunsa Temple 063-561-1422, Seonunsan Provincial Park 063-563-3450 🖱 www.seonunsa.org

ceiling of the Manseru Hall 만세루, a dramatic demonstration of Koreans' preference for natural lines over artifice. Seonunsa Temple is most picturesque in spring when its famous camellia grove behind the main hall blooms in full color.

A tasty local specialty is the Pungcheon eel 풍천장어, caught where Gochang's freshwater streams meet the salt waters of the Pacific. Marinated and broiled, the eel has a wonderfully rich, savory flavor. It's best consumed with Gochang's greatest contribution to Korean cuisine, *bokbunjaju*, a sweet fruit wine made from black raspberries. You can find restaurants doing this dish in front of Seonunsan Provincial Park 선운선도립공원. Expect to pay about 20,000 won.

WHAT TO EAT

If you'd like to stay downtown, there are some cheap inns near Gochang Bus Terminal. Just west of town is Hotel Hidden 히든모텔 (063-562-1006), a pleasant motel with its own beauty spa with rooms beginning at 35,000 won a night. There are some hotels and inns at the entrance of Seonunsan Provincial Park, too, including the Seonunsan Tourist Hotel 선운산관광호텔 (063-561-3377, 70,000 won a night) and Seonunsan Youth Hostel 선운산유스호스텔 (063-561-3333, 40,000 won a night).

WHERE TO STAY

Gochang is connected by bus from Gwangju (1 hr 10 min), Jeonju (1 hr 20 min), Jeongeup (30 min) and other towns in Jeollabuk-do.

TRANSPORT INFO

NAEJANGSAN NATIONAL PARK 내장산국립공원

Straddling the boundaries of Jeongeup 정읍 and Jangseong 장성 like a great amphitheater, Mt. Naejangsan (763 m) is best known for its spectacular autumn foliage, some of most colorful in Korea. Two lovely Buddhist temples, Naejangsa and Baegyangsa, complement the breathtaking scenery.

Hiking Naejangsan National Park

Mt. Naejangsan is not especially high but the trails are steep, and following the ridgeline can be an exasperating experience as you go up and down the series of peaks. Most hikers begin at Naejangsa Temple 내장사, where there are two half-ridge hikes (about 4 hours each) or, if you're feeling up to it, a full ridge hike (11 km, 7 hours). There's also another trail linking Naejangsa and Baegyangsa via the main ridgeline and the rocky peak of Baekhakbong 백학봉 (10.9 km, 7 hours) and the Sunchang Saejae Pass 순창새재. Whichever way you go, be prepared for a slog.

Enjoying the Foliage

Fortunately, you don't need to hike the mountain to enjoy its autumnal splendor; in fact, most visitors don't. The delightfully long stroll from the parking lot to Naejangsa Temple, underneath an increasingly thick canopy of crimson maple leaves, is rewarding enough. A popular

Naejangsan National Park's brilliant autumn foliage is some of the finest in the country.

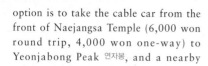

observation pavilion with wonderful views of the ridgeline, and then walk leisurely back down from there to Naejangsa. Another option is to take the relatively less taxing trail up the Geumseon Valley 금선계곡, with its beautiful waterfalls and, of course, foilage galore. The best time to take in the autumn colors at Naejangsa is early November, but this can change depending on weather conditions.

Naejangsa Temple 내장사

Naejansa Temple was founded in the 7th century, when this part of the country was part of the Baekje Kingdom. Tragically, aside from the collection of old stupa in

option is to take the cable car from the front of Naejangsa Temple (6,000 won round trip, 4,000 won one-way) to Yeonjabong Peak 연자봉, and a nearby

Naejangsa Temple

Baegyangsa Temple is just magical in autumn.

front of the precinct, the temple has very little to show for its history—it was burned to the ground during the Korean War. What you see today is a post-war reconstruction.

The newness of its buildings aside, in terms of location, Naejangsa can't be beat, hidden away in a beautiful valley that erupts into a riot of color come fall. One spot particularly popular with local photographers is a pond and a small pavilion along the path to the temple, right in front of the cable car terminal.

🚌 3,000 won 📞 063-538-7878
🖥 www.naejangsa.org (KR)

Baegyangsa Temple 백양사

While included within Naejangsan National Park, Baegyangsa Temple is at the foot of a separate mountain, and is most easily reached on a separate trip.

Like Naejangsa Temple, Baegyangsa is an ancient monastery (founded in 632) that was sadly burnt down during the Korean War, save for its Daeungjeon 대웅전 (Main Hall) and Geungnakjeon 극락전 (Nirvana Hall), which managed to survive. Also, like Naejangsa, the temple's location beneath the dramatic rocky peaks of Mt. Baegamsan 백암산 is simply breathtaking. The most scenic spot is a pond just in front of the temple where the reflection of the mountain and one of the temple's wooden pavilions is simply magical.

It can't be emphasized more that the autumn foliage here is truly gorgeous. Baegyangsa is also famous for its spring colors, too, so much so that a proverbial saying goes "Baegyangsa in spring, Naejangsa in autumn." 🚌 3,000 won 📞 061-392-7502 🖥 www.baekyangsa.org

TRANSPORT INFO

To get to Naejangsa, you must first go to the town of Jeongeup 정읍—you can do this by bus or train from Jeonju 전주 (1 hr), or by bus from one of the surrounding towns. From Jeongeup Bus Terminal, take bus 171 to Naejangsan National Park (30 min). To get to Baegyangsa, you first need to go to the town of Jangseong 장성 (35 minutes by bus from Jeongeup), and from there take a bus to Baegyangsa. There are also direct buses to Baegyangsa from Gwangju's U-Square (1 hr 20 min).

The main gateway to Maisan Provincial Park is the small town of Jinan. From Seoul, buses to Jinan depart from Seoul Central City Bus Terminal (3 hrs 30 min). Buses from Jeonju, meanwhile, take just 30 minutes.

MAISAN PROVINCIAL PARK 마이산도립공원

Maisan Provincial Park is a bizarre, almost a surreal place. Mt. Maisan ("Horse Ear Mountain") is not so much a mountain as it is two huge pointed outcrops of sedimentary rocks, each one over 600 m high. Between the two peaks sits one of the most unusual Buddhist temples in Korea, featuring easily one of the country's most mysterious landscapes.

Mt. Maisan 마이산

Some 100 million years ago, the area that is now Mt. Maisan was a freshwater lake where the weight of the water had compressed the sand and pebbles into aqueous rock. Then, 60 to 70 million years ago, crustal movements thrust the sedimentary rock upwards, forming Mt. Maisan. Aquatic fossils can be found on the mountain even today.

The legend behind the mountain's creation is a bit more colorful, though. Once, two fairies—one male and one female—came down from the heavens to live as humans. While on Earth, they had two children. One day, however, they decided it was time to return to the heavens. There was a catch, though—if anybody saw them trying to leave, they would be stuck on earth forever. The male wished to leave at night but the female, afraid of the dark, insisted on leaving in the morning. When they were preparing to take off, however, a local villager saw them and screamed. Now unable to leave, the rock family returned to earth. The husband, angry at his wife, snatched his two children and pushed his wife away. He turned himself into the eastern peak; its two attached sub-peaks are his children. The western peak is his wife,

The surreal "horse ear" peaks of Maisan National Park

Tapsa Temple's roughly 80 stone pagodas were erected by a single hermit.

her head hung in shame.

The eastern peak (680 m) is called Sutmaibong 숫마이봉 ("Male Horse Ear Peak"), and the western peak (686 m) Ammaibong 암마이봉 ("Female Horse Ear Peak"). Most visitors don't actually climb the peaks, though. Rather, they transverse the park from the northern parking lot to the southern one via the pass between the two peaks, passing the Buddhist temple of Tapsa along the way. The trail takes about two hours to complete.

Tapsa Temple 탑사

On the south side of the pass, in the shadow of the peaks, is Tapsa Temple. It's a small temple but in its courtyard are no fewer than 80 pagodas made from hand-piled stones. These pagodas were erected over the course of thirty years by a hermit, Yi Gap-nyong (1860–1957), who retreated to Tapsa at the age of 25 after the death of his parents. Wishing to realize a better world based on a combination of Confucianism, Buddhism and Seon (Zen), he began erecting stone pagodas—one level

a day—as a prayer to cleanse the sins of the world. During the day he gathered rocks, and at night he would pray and erect his towers. Most of the rocks came from Mt. Maisan itself, but he also made pilgrimages to other sacred mountains throughout Korea, bringing back with him stones to use in his pagodas. Yi built his towers stoutly, erecting canonical pyramids topped off with flat stone finials. He originally built 108 pagodas, a reference to Buddhism's 108 Defilements. Some of these are truly impressive feats of construction, including the 13.5 m tall twin pagodas behind the main hall, which took three years to build. While some of the pagodas have collapsed due to tourists touching them, none have fallen due to the elements.

As if the vibe of the place wasn't mysterious enough, when monks leave bowls of water outside in the winter, the water freezes into towers (a phenomenon called ice spikes).

🚌 2,000 won ⓒ Tapsa Temple: 063-433-0012, Maisan Provincial Park: 063-433-3313 🖱 www.maisantapsa.co.kr (KR)

TRANSPORT INFO

The main gateway to Maisan Provincial Park is the small town of Jinan. From Jinan, it's a short bus or taxi ride to the park (5 min). From Seoul, buses to Jinan depart from Seoul Central City Bus Terminal (3 hrs 30 min). Buses from Jeonju, meanwhile, takes just 30 minutes.

DEOGYUSAN NATIONAL PARK 덕유산국립공원

Located near the town of Muju 무주, Mt. Deogyusan is known largely as a skiing and winter sports destination—the mountain hosted the 1997 Winter Universiade. The mountains here get some of the heaviest snowfalls outside of Gangwon-do Province, and the winter scenery can be quite spectacular. Even if you're not a skier, the peaks and valleys of Deogyusan National Park offer plenty of quality hiking opportunities.

Deogyusan National Park
덕유산국립공원

Mt. Deogyusan has a number of peaks, including its highest Hyangjeokbong 향적봉, which tops out at 1,614 m. If you'd like to hike the whole ridgeline, you could do it in about 12 hours—the mountain is high but broad, so it's not steep, and the lack of tree cover in the higher altitudes allows for wide views over the surrounding landscape. One particular area that gets a good deal of attention is Gucheon-dong Valley 구천동계곡, with its so-called "33 Scenic Spots." Most are odd or slightly dramatic rock formations or waterfalls but, taken together, it's all quite nice and worth the stroll.

🪙 Free 🚍 Take a bus from Muju Bus Terminal to Gucheondong Bus Stop. ✆ 063-322-3473 🖰 http://english.knps.or.kr

Mt. Deogyusan's winter scenery is truly breathtaking.

Deogyusan Ski Resort is one of Korea's top winter sports destinations.

Deogyusan Ski Resort 덕유산리조트

Deogyusan Ski Resort (formerly Muju Resort) competes with Pyeongchang's Yongpyong Resort as Korea's finest ski destination. There are six slopes in all, including both Korea's longest and steepest—the 6 km Silk Road slope and the appropriately named Raiders slope, with its 60 degree incline. At the top of the peak is a Korean-style wooden and concrete pavilion that cuts a pretty dramatic form, especially with the snow and wind; the views from the top can be spectacular.

The resort tries to model itself on Austrian ski resorts, and with some degree of success. You'll find about 1,000 Austrian-style condos for rest, in addition to the imposing, five-star Hotel Tyrol. Day passes are 81,000 won, half-day passes are 66,000 won.

🚌 There's free shuttle bus service to the resort from the back gate of Muju Terminal. ✆ 063-322-9000 🌐 www.deogyusanresort.com

WHERE TO STAY

Deogyusan Resort has several accommodation options. The nicest by far is Hotel Tirol 호텔티롤 (063-320-7200), an Austrian-style luxury hotel with Austrian Larch interiors. During the winter peak season (Dec 24, 31, Jan 7, 14, 21 and 28) rooms begin at 430,000 won, although these rates come down considerably during off-peak and weekdays. For family travelers, the condo-style Family  Hotel 가족호텔 (063-320-7000) has two-bedroom rooms beginning at 400,000 won a night. Finally, the Kookmin Hotel 국민호텔 (063-322-9000) has clean, comfortable rooms beginning at 80,000 won a night. Deogyusan Resort's accommodations fill up quickly in winter, however, so you may have to find lodging elsewhere. At the entrance of the Gucheon-dong Valley of Mt. Deogyusan are several motels and pensions, including the pleasant Dasup Pension 다숲펜션 (063-322-3379), with rooms beginning at 60,000 won during peak-season weekends.

WHAT TO EAT

Deogyusan Resort has plenty of places to eat, but if you'd like something a bit more rustic, Geumgang Sikdang 금강식당 (063-322-0979) near Muju County Office does a mean *eojuk* 어죽 (a heart rice and fish porridge) for 6,000 won.

TRANSPORT INFO

From Seoul, buses to Muju depart from Nambu Bus Terminal (2 hrs 30 min). There are also direct buses to the Gucheondong Valley 구천동계곡 (3 hrs). From Daejeon, buses to Muju depart from Dongbu Intercity Bus Terminal (50 min). From Jeonju, buses take one hour, 50 minutes.

NAMWON 남원

Nestled at the foot of Mt. Jirisan, Namwon is a delightful little town known to Koreans as the "City of Love." It is most closely associated with the "Tale of Chunhyang," Korea's best-known love story, and the town's sites are largely connected with the tale. Once you've gotten your fill of Chunhyang, pay a visit to Silsangsa Temple to take in its truly memorable collection of Buddhist art.

Gwanghallu Pavilion 광한루

Most famous as the spot where Yi Mong-nyong first spotted his beloved Chunhyang, and where the two tearfully said goodbye when Yi was called to Seoul with his father, the Gwanghallu Pavilion and its garden have been a lauded scenic spot since the 15th century. A beautiful elevated pavilion of the type where local officials and aristocrats would host parties and banquets, Gwanghallu was given its current name—which means "Moon Palace Pavilion"—by the 15th century scholar and regional governor Jeong In-ji, who likened the scenery to a mythical palace on the moon.

The present pavilion was built in 1626, making it one of the oldest in Korea. The bridge that spans the pond in front of it, the Ojakgyo 오작교 ("Crow and Magpie Bridge"), is even older (1582). It gets its name from another old folktale of love. It is said the daughter of the King of Heaven fell in love with a handsome herder. The king was persuaded to allow the marriage, but the young couple soon grew lazy. Angered, the king decreed that they should live apart, except on one day, the seventh day of the seventh lunar month. When that day arrived, however, they could not meet as they lived on opposite sides of the Milky

Built in 1626, Gwanghallu Pavilion was the setting of Korea's best known love story.

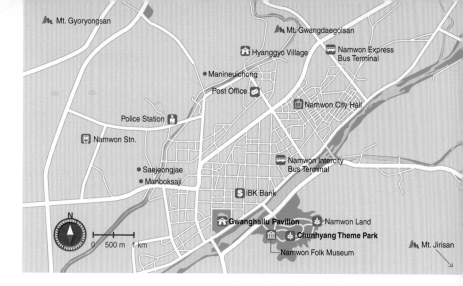

Way. The crows and magpies took it upon themselves to build a bridge across the Milk Way, allowing the lovers to meet. It is said that couples who walk on the bridge at least once a year are guaranteed happiness for that year.

Gwanghalluwon Garden 광한루원, itself, is one of the most beautiful Korean gardens in the region. Typical of Korean gardens, it strives to look natural with subtle elements pregnant with meaning. The three islands in the pond, for instance, symbolize Korea's three most important mountains. The garden also has a number of other pavilions added at later dates, a reconstruction of Chunghyang's home, as well as a small exhibit hall.

🕐 8 am to 8 pm 💷 2,000 won (evenings are free between 7 and 8 pm) 📞 063-620-8901~3 🚕 Five-minute taxi ride from Namwon Express Bus Terminal 🌐 www.gwanghallu.or.kr (KR)

Chunhyang Theme Park 춘향테마파크

If Gwanghallu didn't satisfy your need to things Chunhyang-related, or you prefer something a bit more kitsch, try Chunhyang Theme Park on the other side of the Yocheon River 요천. The park is divided into different sections that recount the tale of Korea's most famous lovers. To get to the park from downtown, cross Chunhyanggyo Bridge over the stream, passing through a big heart-shaped gate, and that's pretty much it—but it's not a bad place to spend an hour or two. Worth checking out is the Namwon Folk Museum 남원향토박물관, with exhibits that shed light on the history and heritage of the Namwon area.

🚕 Short taxi ride from Namwon Express Bus Terminal. 💷 3,000 won 📞 063-620-6836 🌐 www.namwontheme.or.kr (KR)

Silsangsa Temple 실상사

If you're traveling solo, and all the couples in Namwon are getting you down, take heart—in a field on your way to the mountains outside of town is Silsangsa Temple, a much welcome piece of tranquility. Silsangsa was founded in 828 in the chaotic final days of the Silla Dynasty, when political collapse and social turmoil led some Buddhist monks to truly retreat from the world in search of inner truth. Across Korea, they founded nine Seon (Zen) temples, of which Silsangsa was the first.

The temple was founded at its current location based on the very particular geomantic calculation that if a temple were not built on the site, Korea would be taken over by Japan. In fact, there is a saying that if Japan thrives, Silsangsa goes to ruin; and if

SONG OF CHUNHYANG 춘향가

The Chunghyangga ("Song of Chunyang") is one of five surviving *pansori* (see p717) tales, and probably the most beloved. It is a classic tale of love, loyalty, sacrifice and justice, set against a backdrop of Joseon Korea's deeply striated Confucian society.

Yi Mong-nyong, a young *yangban* and son of Namwon's magistrate, is standing on the Gwanghallu, a garden-side pleasure pavilion, taking in the flowers one summer morning when, in the distance, he spots a beautiful young woman sitting on a swing beneath a tree. Asking his servant who she is, he is told she is Chunhyang, the daughter of a retired *gisaeng*, the female entertainers who entertained powerful men.

Intrigued, Mong-nyong sends his servant to Chunhyang to tell her his master wishes to meet her. Chunhyang, however, plays hard to get, so Mong-nyong goes to her mother and asks permission to marry her. Permission is granted, and the two are married that day. The marriage, however, was informal, and conducted in secret—in the hierarchical society of the Confucian Joseon Dynasty, the aristocratic son of a *yangban* and the daughter of a *gisaeng*—technically slaves of the state—could never marry.

Soon after the two were married, however, Yi's father was appointed a royal minister, so father and son were recalled to Seoul. Unable to go to Seoul together, the young couple said their tearful goodbyes at the Ojakgyo, an old stone bridge near the Gwanghallu.

Chunyang promised to remain faithful to her husband until he could come to bring her to Seoul.

A new magistrate soon took over in Namwon, but he proved to be a corrupt lech who almost immediately set his eyes on the beautiful Chunhyang. He ordered her to sleep with him. When she refused, he had her put into prison. Mong-nyong, meanwhile, excelled at his studies in Seoul, and was appointed a royal inspector. Disguised as a beggar, he returned to Namwon. Upon arriving, however, he found the peasants squeezed by the local officials of their harvests, Chunhyang soon to be put to death for disobeying the magistrate, and almost everyone disgusted with Mong-nyong, who they accused of abandoning his wife to a terrible fate.

Still dressed as a beggar, he met Chunhyang at prison. Ever loyal, his wife still loved him, despite what seemed to her his apparent failure in Seoul. The next day, Mong-nyong gathered his retinue—also disguised as beggars—and crashed an official banquet hosted by the magistrate. Mong-nyong begged one of the guests for food, which the guest, the magistrate of a nearby town, provided. Feigning gratitude, Mong-nyong offered a poem as thanks for the food. When the magistrate read the poem, he was shocked—it was a pointed criticism of the officials, who were gathered for a banquet while the peasants starved under rapacious taxes. It was only then that they realized Mong-nyong was no beggar, but a royal inspector. He had Chunhyang released from prison, and for his licentiousness and corruption, he had the magistrate of Namwon stripped of his position and banished to a distant island.

In the 18th century, the Song of Chunhyang was turned into a novel. It's a tale that resonates even today—the story has been retold countless times in adapted forms for television, screen and stage.

Silsangsa thrives, Japan goes to ruin. To keep Japan in check, in its main hall, Bogwangjeon Hall 보광전, there's a map of the island chain right on the bell itself—struck so many times that much of Japan is no longer visible.

Since its founding, the temple has witnessed more than its fair share of ups and downs. Most recently, during the Korean War, it was occupied by the South Korean Army during the day and by communist guerrillas at night; yet, miraculously, it was never burned. The temple and some of its nearby hermitages are a cornucopia of late Silla craftsmanship. The twin pagodas in the main courtyard are especially handsome, as is the 9th century iron seated Medicine Buddha inside one of the halls. The most spectacular work of art here, however, is the intricately carved three-story stone pagoda in front of Baekjangam Hermitage 백장암, a short walk from the main temple. And don't forget to check out the very funky stone guardians in front of the bridge to the temple.

From Namwon Intercity Bus Terminal, take a bus to Baengmu-dong or Baemsagol and get off at Inweol Terminal. From there, take a bus to Silsangsa (1 hr 30 min). 063-636-3031 www.silsangsa.or.kr (KR)

WHAT TO EAT

There are plenty of restaurants at the entrance to Jirisan National Park and around the Gwanghallu. One place in the park just south of the stream is Cheonnyeon Dolsotbap 천년돌솥밥 (063-626-3453), which serves a very tasty *yeongyang dolsotbap* (7,000 won)—rice in a stone pot, mixed with chestnuts, ginseng, jujubes, green peas, corn, mushrooms and other ingredients. Also comes with soup and side dishes. Namwon is especially well-known for its *chueotang* 추어탕, a rich soup made from boiled mudfish caught in the local streams. One of the better patronized places for this dish is Saejip Chueotang 새집추어탕 (063-625-2443), just on the stream not far from Gwanghallu. A bowl goes for 7,000 won, but if you want to try the mudfish in all its incarnations, go for the *jeongsik* 정식 (40,000 won and up). Another local specialty is the meat of the black pigs raised on the slopes of Mt. Jirisan. If you're in the Baemsagol Valley 뱀사골, give Jirisan Sikdang 지리산식당 (063-626-8800) a try. The *doejigogi sanchae jeongsik* 돼지고기 산채정식 (pork, mountain vegetables, rice and soup) goes for 15,000 won a person.

WHERE TO STAY

There are plenty of places to stay in both downtown Namwon (near Namwon Bus Terminal) and at the entrance to Jirisan National Park. If you don't mind staying a bit out of town, Greenpia Motel 그린피아모텔, south of the Yocheon Stream 요천 (063-636-7200) is comfortable and clean with rooms starting at 70,000 won a night in the peak season. At the entrance to Mt. Jirisan's Baemsagol Valley is Jirisan Baemsagol Jayeon Land 지리산 뱀사골자연랜드, with cabins for rent for 120,000 won a night during the peak season, but just 50,000 won non-peak.

TRANSPORT INFO

From Seoul, trains to Namwon depart from Yongsan Station. Most take about 4 hours, but there are two KTX high speed trains a day (2 hrs 30 min). Namwon sits on the Jeolla Line, giving it rail connections with Yeosu (about 1 hr), Suncheon (about 45 min) and Jeonju (about 30 min). Buses to Namwon from Seoul depart from Seoul Central City Bus Terminal (3 hrs 40 min). From Daejeon, buses to Namwon depart from Dongbu Intercity Bus Terminal (2 hrs 50 min). Buses from Jeonju take about 1 hour.

GWANGJU & JEOLLANAM-DO

HIGHLIGHTS

- Experience Namdo cuisine and learn what Korean food is all about

- Learn about Korea's struggle for democracy in Gwangju, a growing East Asian cultural center

- Let your camera lens roam over at the picturesque green tea plantations of Boseong

- Roam around Korea's scenic and culturally rich southern coast, including the towns of Haenam, Jindo & Gangjin

- Relax for a day or two in the pleasant port town of Yeosu, the host city of the 2012 Expo

- Spiritually recharge at Jogyesan Provincial Park, home to the spectacular Buddhist temples of Songgwangsa & Seonamsa

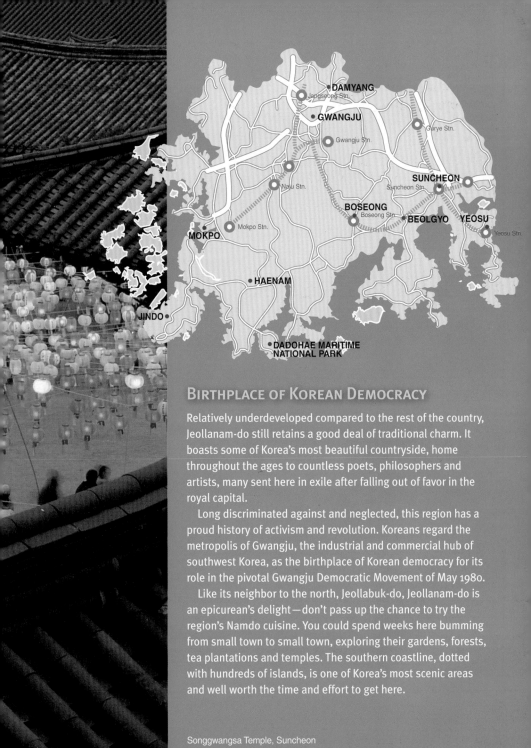

DAMYANG
Jangseong Stn.
GWANGJU
Gwangju Stn.
Gurye Stn.
SUNCHEON
Naju Stn.
Suncheon Stn.
BOSEONG
Boseong Stn.
BEOLGYO   YEOSU
MOKPO   Mokpo Stn.
Yeosu Stn.
HAENAM
JINDO
DADOHAE MARITIME
NATIONAL PARK

BIRTHPLACE OF KOREAN DEMOCRACY

Relatively underdeveloped compared to the rest of the country,
Jeollanam-do still retains a good deal of traditional charm. It
boasts some of Korea's most beautiful countryside, home
throughout the ages to countless poets, philosophers and
artists, many sent here in exile after falling out of favor in the
royal capital.

Long discriminated against and neglected, this region has a
proud history of activism and revolution. Koreans regard the
metropolis of Gwangju, the industrial and commercial hub of
southwest Korea, as the birthplace of Korean democracy for its
role in the pivotal Gwangju Democratic Movement of May 1980.

Like its neighbor to the north, Jeollabuk-do, Jeollanam-do is
an epicurean's delight — don't pass up the chance to try the
region's Namdo cuisine. You could spend weeks here bumming
from small town to small town, exploring their gardens, forests,
tea plantations and temples. The southern coastline, dotted
with hundreds of islands, is one of Korea's most scenic areas
and well worth the time and effort to get here.

Songgwangsa Temple, Suncheon

Monument to the Gwangju Democratization Movement, May 18 National Cemetery

GWANGJU 광주

With a population of more than 1.4 million, Gwangju is Korea's sixth largest city and the commercial and industrial hub of the southwest. It's best known in Korea for the important role the city played in the country's democratization movement during the past century. In recent years, the city has made efforts to reshape itself into an Asian cultural center, hosting the biannual Gwangju Biennale, Asia's first contemporary art biennale.

Gwangju has its fair share of apartment blocks and urban grittiness, but things are definitely on an upwards trajectory and, overall, the city is a relaxed and friendly place with great food, decent nightlife and a fascinating history. If the concrete jungle gets too much, just head to the hills of nearby Mt. Mudeungsan for a retreat. The city also makes a wonderful base from which to explore the rest of the beautiful province of Jeollanam-do.

History

Gwangju has a history that goes back to antiquity, taking its current name, which translates as "City of Light," in 940. Still, until the late 19th century, it was a relatively unimportant town compared to other cities in the region, namely Jeonju and Naju. From the turn of the 20th century, however, the city began to grow rapidly. In 1896, it was designated the provincial capital of Jeollanam-do, and during the Japanese colonial era (1910–1945), it became a major regional transportation hub and market, especially after the railway came to town in 1930. The city also became a major station for American missionaries—their schools, homes, churches and cemetery can still be found in the Yangnim-dong district 양림동 지역.

While the city grew under the Japanese, ruthless Japanese exploitation of the Jeolla-do region and discrimination against Korean students led to a huge student demonstration in 1929. Student activism would become a defining feature of the city for much of the 20th century.

With the defeat of Imperial Japan in the Pacific War in 1945, Korea regained its independence, but the new Korean state inherited an unenviable set of problems, including ideological conflict, national division and regional tensions. The people of the Jeolla-do provinces, who had long felt ignored by a succession of Korean dynasties, suffered again from perceived discrimination by the new Korean government, especially under the military dictatorships of Park Chung-hee and Chun Doo-hwan, both of whom hailed from the rival Gyeongsang-do region. This discontent came to a dramatic head in May of 1980, when pro-democracy demonstrators who were angered by Chun Doo-hwan's coup and the senseless violence inflicted upon the city's residents by Chun's troops enforcing martial law there, rose up. They seized control of Gwangju for several days until Korean army troops, laying siege to the city, were able to retake it (see p 446).

The brutality inflicted on the city in May 1980, the subsequent arrest of local hero and democracy activist Kim Dae-jung, and seven more years of dictatorship by yet another former general left deep scars on the city, which grew increasingly bitter and resentful towards the government and, by extension, its American allies. Pro-democracy political and labor activism, some of it decidedly left-wing and anti-American, became a defining characteristic of Gwangju life for much of the 80s and 90s. Korea's transformation to a multi-party democracy in 1987, liberalizing reforms throughout the 90s and, finally, the election of Kim Dae-jung as President of the Republic of Korea in 1998 did much to soothe the city's wounds. Just as importantly, the new atmosphere of freedom and retrospection allowed Gwangju residents to discuss freely for the first time the abuses they had suffered. As Koreans gained a better appreciation of the city's past, Gwangju itself embraced its history as Korea's bastion of democracy.

The Jeolla-do region has long been famous for producing many of Korea's finest artists, poets, musicians and writers, and Gwangju has tried to capitalize on this by transforming itself into an Asian cultural hub. The opening of the landmark Asia Cultural Complex 국립아시아문화전당, is set for completion in 2014 but the city already has a vibrant arts and culture scene, with a number of major galleries and exhibit halls like the Gwangju Biennale Exhibition Hall and Kunsthalle Gwangju.

Administratively, Gwangju is a metropolitan city, meaning it functions as its own province, and is not, technically speaking, a part of the province of Jeollanam-do, despite the fact that the Jeollanam-do Provincial Office was, until recently, located in the city.

Layout

Gwangju has a good deal of urban sprawl, and the city now spreads out on both sides of Yeongsangang River 영산강, with a tributary of the river, Gwangjucheon Stream 광주천, flowing through the heart of town. The old city, including the former provincial hall and the lively commercial and entertainment district of

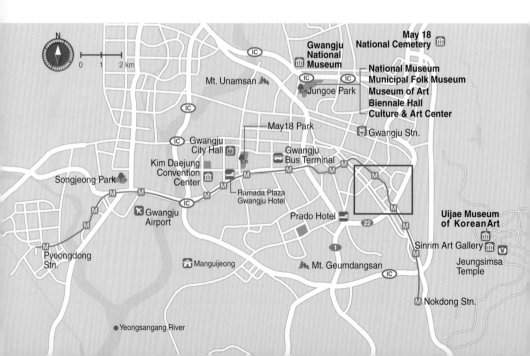

Chungjang-ro 충장로, is in the east of town, where most of the city's historic sites are concentrated.

Gwangju has a single subway line, running east–west and connecting the old downtown and Chosun University 조선대학교 to Gwangju Airport 광주국제공항 in the west. This makes getting across town fairly easy. What is a bit inconvenient, though, is that both Gwangju Station and U-Square (Gwangju's massive bus terminal/shopping center/cultural space) — both quite a distance from each other — are several kilometers from the old downtown, and neither is connected to the subway, which means you'll need to take a local bus or taxi to get from the station (or terminal) to where you want to go.

Mt. Mudeungsan overlooks the city to the east, and is just a short local bus ride away. The May 18 National Cemetery is several kilometers outside of town to the northeast.

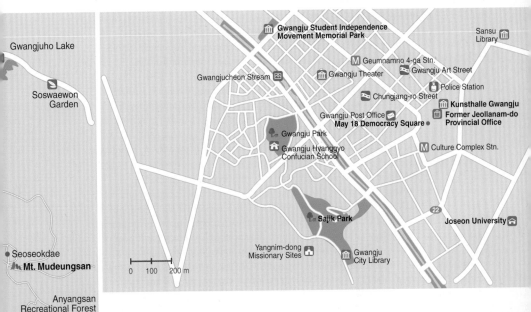

Former Jeollanam-do Provincial Office 옛전남도청 & May 18 Democracy Square 5.18민주광장

The former Jeollanam-do Provincial Office, completed in 1930, is a rare example of a major colonial-era public building designed by a Korean architect, Kim Sun-ha (1901–1966). Originally a two-story structure, the exterior of the Provincial Office is brick and granite; the red brick was painted white after Korea regained its independence in 1945.

Former Jeollanam-do Provincial Office, site of much of the drama and tragedy of the Gwangju Democratization Movement

GWANGJU DEMOCRATIZATION MOVEMENT

History and Culture

The Gwangju Democratization Movement—or, as it is mostly called in Korean, *O Il Pal* ("Five One Eight," or May 18) was one of the most galvanizing moments in Korea's modern history. For nine days in May of 1980, students and ordinary citizens faced down a military dictatorship in the hope of bringing democracy to their country. In the end, they were brutally cut down by their own army, but their bravery inspired a whole generation of pro-democracy activists who would succeed in bringing democracy to Korea in 1987.

On Oct 26, 1979, Korean president Park Chung-hee was assassinated, ushering in a period of political instability. A former general who had come to power in a coup in 1961, Park had ruled Korea with an iron fist for 18 years. While his rule had brought considerable economic development to Korea, his death had sparked hope that the country might transition to democratic rule. These hopes were dashed on Dec 12, 1979, when mutinous troops led by Gen. Chun Doo-hwan launched a bloody coup, seizing control of the government.

Chun's coup outraged pro-democracy forces, who demanded that Chun end martial law, which had been declared following Park's assassination, and step down. In response to growing protests, Chun responded on May 17 by intensifying martial law over the entire country, closing down universities (to prevent student protests) and banning political activity. To enforce martial law, he dispatched paratroopers to cities across Korea, including Gwangju, which historically had been a hotbed of discontent. Arriving in the city, the troops took up positions at Jeollanam-do Provincial Office and other points around the city.

On May 18, things began to unravel. Defying martial law, students at Chonnam National University gathered at the front gate of their school, where they clashed with paratroopers. Several students were beaten severely. The protests spread to downtown, with thousands of demonstrators gathering in front of Jeollanam-do Provincial Office. Again, paratroopers responded with brutal, seemingly uncontrolled violence, clubbing bloody protester and non-protester alike. The violence only served to anger Gwangju's citizenry, who gathered in increasing numbers in front of the provincial office. On May 20, 150,000 gathered to protest and, that night, local drivers, led by taxi drivers, launched an auto parade to the

The office, and the square in front of it (actually, a traffic roundabout) are best known as one of the most important sites of the 1980 Gwangju Uprising. It was at this office that masses of Koreans gathered to protest the declaration of martial law, and where, on May 21, paratroopers opened fire on demonstrators, the climax of violence that turned the demonstrations into a full-scale revolt. It was also here that the uprising came to an end, when at 7 am on May 27, government troops retook the provincial office, bringing the uprising to an end.

While the main building is a protected historical structure, the rest of the complex is being redeveloped into the Asia Cultural Complex, a massive, state-of-the-art arts and culture space that, the city hopes, will be the crown jewel in its efforts to transform itself into an Asian cultural mecca. Not everyone has welcomed this, however, and a coalition of Gwangju Uprising survivors, victims' families and conservationists have protested to preserve

provincial office in support of the demonstrators.

Things came to a head the next day, when paratroops fired into the crowd gathered in front of the provincial office. Enraged, students and residents raided the armories of local police stations. Forming militia groups, the demonstrators trained their newly acquired guns on the paratroopers, forcing them to withdraw from the city. Victorious, the protesters took control of the provincial office.

Taking up positions outside of the city, the paratroopers put it under siege as they awaited reinforcements. In the liberated city, local citizens and students formed committees to maintain order, communities cooperated to feed and nurse the demonstrators, and negotiations were held with government troops. Meanwhile, Chun moved the Korean Army's 20th Infantry Division to Gwangju, where it prepared to retake the city. Finally, in the pre-dawn hours of May 27, government troops moved into the city and reseized Jeollanam-do Provincial Office, where student militia made a desperate last stand. The uprising was over. According to Gwangju Metropolitan Government, 163 people were killed in the uprising, 166 went missing, 101 died after the uprising from wounds suffered in the violence, 3,139 were injured, and 1,589 were arrested or detained. Some, however, say the actual death toll was much higher.

The Gwangju movement, and the brutality with which it was put down, critically damaged the legitimacy of the Chun Doo-hwan government. It also inspired others to keep up the fight. In 1987, Chun again faced massive pro-democracy protests, this time in the capital, Seoul. Rather than deploy the army again, however, he chose to step down, and Korea held democratic elections. In 1995, Chun was put on trial for, amongst other charges, his role in suppressing the Gwangju movement, and sentenced to life in prison. In 1997, he was pardoned at the advice of incoming President Kim Dae-jung, a long-time democracy activist from the Gwangju area who himself had been sentenced to death after the uprising by Chun's government.

the site, which they regard as sacred ground, in its original state.

As of the writing of this book, the entire complex was hidden behind a decidedly colorful barrier (with paintings by young local artists) while construction was ongoing. In short time, the area may look very, very different.

🚇 Culture Complex Station

Kunsthalle Gwangju 쿤스트할레광주

Located right next to May 18 Democracy Square, this unique art space—easily recognized, as it is constructed of container crates stacked one upon the other—views itself as a "social sculpture," and seeks to bring artists, visitors and staff together. The programs here tend to be youthful and quirky: be sure to check out the opening and closing parties.

🕐 11 am to 8 pm, closed Mondays. 🚇 Culture Complex Station ✆ 062-236 0730~3 🖥 www.kunsthalle-gwangju.com

Sajik Park 사직공원

Gwangju's first civic park, this pleasant piece of hillside urban greenery was once the site of an altar where, during the Joseon Dynasty, sacrifices were offered for peace and prosperity. In the 1990s, the shrine was restored and the rites revived. There's also a three-story tower from the top of which great views of the city can be had.

🚌 From Culture Complex Station, take Geumnan Bus No. 55, get off at the Namdo Ilbo stop 남도일보 정거장, and walk to the park from there.

Missionary cemetery, Yangnim-dong

Yangnim-dong Missionary Sites
양림동 선교사 유적지

American missionaries of the American Southern Presbyterian Mission set up shop on Gwangju's Yangnim ("Willow Forest") Hill in 1904, establishing schools, hospitals and, of course, churches on the hillside. Much of what they built still remains. Sites to check out include the beautiful Owen Memorial Hall 오웬기념관 (1914), on the grounds of the Christian College of Nursing; the charming Wilson House 윌슨기념관 (1920s) on a lovely wooded section of the campus of Honam Theological University and Seminary 호남신학대학교; Bell Memorial Chapel 유진벨선교사 기념교회 (1921) and the former Gwangju Speer Girls High School 수피아여자고등학교 (1910s); and the missionary graveyard at the top of the hill. The graveyard is a somberly beautiful place—note that many of the graves are young children, an indication of the difficult circumstances that Korea's early missionary community faced. Yangnim-dong is a short walk from Sajik Park and, like the park, offers good views of the city from the top of the hill.

Bell Memorial Chapel

Yangnim Presbyterian Church, which seems to borrow from the style of the old colonial era church.

Chungjang-ro 충장로

If people watching is what you like to do, head to Chungjang-ro, the energetic commercial heart of Gwangju. At what is basically Gwangju's version of Seoul's Myeong-dong, you'll find tons of shops,

 TIPS

PLAY BALL!

The Kia Tigers, based in Gwangju, are the New York Yankees of Korea, having won ten Korean Baseball Organization (KBO) championships since the league was formed in 1982. The team went through a slump in the 2000s, but rebounded by winning the 2009 Korean Series. If you'd like to see a game, the Tigers play at Gwangju Mudeung Baseball Stadium 광주무등야구장—just hop on Bus No. 18 from U-Square.

restaurants, cafés, shopping malls and other elements of modern urban civilization—everything you'll need after a couple of days in the countryside. At night, this is also where you'll find Gwangju's most happening bars. 🚇 Exit 3, Culture Complex Station

Gwangjucheon Stream 광주천

Recognizing a potential tourism and leisure resource when it sees it, Gwangju Metropolitan City has pumped a good deal of money into cleaning and sprucing up Gwangjucheon Stream, which flows through the heart of the city. It's now a very pleasant place to go for an evening stroll or ride your bike, especially in summer. The section between Gwangju Bridge 광주대교 and Namgwanggyo Bridge 남광교 is particularly nice, especially at night when the uniquely designed bridges are lit up.

Gwangju Art Street 광주 예술의 거리

If Chungjang-ro is Gwangju's Myeong-dong, then Gwangju Art Street is its Insa-dong—more or less. On the street behind Jungang Elementary School 중앙초등학교, you'll find small galleries, art supply stores and antique shops. The wall-side murals lend added charm. There's an art flea market here every Saturday, when the road is blocked to traffic. Aficionados of olden architecture will want to check out Jungang Elementary School itself. The school was founded in 1907; the imposing, red brick buildings were constructed in the 1930s.

🚇 Exit 4, Culture Complex Station or Exit 4, Geumnamno 4-ga Station

Red apricot blossoms, Junghoe Park

Jungoe Park Culture Belt
중외공원 문화벨트

A nice slice of greenery in the northern part of town, Jungoe Park is where you'll find some of Gwangju's cultural spaces, including Gwangju Biennale Exhibition Hall, Gwangju Museum of Art, Gwangju Culture and Art Center, and Gwangju Municipal Folk Museum. Even if you're not especially into art, the park's a nice place to stroll about with its walking paths, ponds, cafés and outdoor exhibits. It's also got a small theme park that kids will enjoy.

Gwangju Biennale Exhibition Hall
광주비엔날레 전시관

Held every other year since 1995, the Gwangju Biennale is Asia's oldest biennial of contemporary art. It's a grand, two-month affair bringing in Asia's top contemporary artists. The exhibits are usually accompanied by concerts, dancing and other cultural events. The next Gwangju Biennale is scheduled for autumn of 2012 (Sep 7 to Nov 11), and will feature six young Asian women curators as artistic directors.

Since 2004, the Biennale has been accompanied in off-years by the Gwangju Design Biennale, an exploration of the relationship between design and culture. One of the artistic directors of the 2011 Design Biennale was Chinese architect, artist and dissident Ai WeiWei.

🕓 Closed except for during Biennale exhibits ✆ 062-608-4114 🖰 www.gb.or.kr 🚍 Sangmu Bus No. 64 from U-Square (30 min)

Gwangju National Museum
국립광주박물관

Not actually in Jungoe Park but a short walk north of it, Gwangju National Museum is home to Gwangju's best collection of historical artifacts and traditional art from Jeollanam-do. It has an especially rich collection of Buddhist art, pottery from the Goryeo and Joseon dynasties, and Joseon Dynasty paintings. The highlight of the collection, however, is the Shinan Ocean Floor Relic Hall, a collection of over 20,000 works of Chinese Song and Yuan Dynasty pottery and other artifacts raised from the wreck, discovered in 1976, of a Chinese trading ship that sank off the southwestern tip of Korea in 1323. 🕓 9 am to 6 pm (9 pm on Saturdays, March to Dec, 7 pm on Sundays). Closed Mondays 🚍 Free (admission charged for special exhibits) ✆ 062-570-7000 🖰 http://gwangju.museum.go.kr 🚍 Yongjeon Bus No. 84 from U-Square Bus (40 min)

Gwangju Museum of Art
광주시립미술관

Opened in 1992, the grand Gwangju Museum of Art houses a wide range of traditional and contemporary art. Particularly interesting is the eponymously named Ha Jung-woong Collection, consisting of 1,865 works donated by Mr. Ha, a second-generation Korean-Japanese businessman. Most of the donated works are by Korean-Japanese artists but you'll also find some by famous Western artists such as Picasso, Rouault, Chagall, Warhol and Ben Shahn.
🕓 9 am to 6 pm (9 pm on Wednesdays). Closed Mondays. 🚍 500 won (extra charge for special exhibits) ✆ 062-510-0700 🖰 www.artmuse.gwangju.go.kr 🚍 Sangmu Bus No. 64 from U-Square

Gwangju Culture & Art Center
광주문화예술회관

Gwangju Culture & Art Center is Jeollanam-do's preeminent performing arts center, with regular shows by local and overseas artists. Of

1. Gwangju National Museum 2. Gwangju Museum of Art
3. Gwangju Biennale Exhibition Hall 4. May 18 National Cemetery

particular note are its monthly performances by local traditional music groups—inquire at the center for specific dates.

ⓒ 062-613-8367 🖐 www.gjart.net (KR)
🚌 Pungam Bus No. 16 from U-Square Bus (10 min)

Gwangju Municipal Folk Museum
광주시립민속박물관

Through its many artifacts and miniature displays, Gwangju Municipal Folk Museum teaches visitors about the distinctive regional culture of southwestern Korea. Be sure to check out its collections of old photographs of Gwangju—oh my, how things have changed!

🕘 9 am to 6 pm, closed Mondays 🎫 500 won
ⓒ 062-613-5337 🚌 Yongjeon Bus No. 84 from U-Square Bus (40 min)

May 18 National Cemetery
5.18 국립묘지

The May 18 National Cemetery is the final place of rest for those who were killed during the Gwangju Uprising of May 1980. This is sacred ground for the Korean democracy movement, and the mood, while peaceful, is appropriately somber. Those who were killed, injured or detained during the uprising are eligible to be buried here—to date, there are 634 graves. The cemetery was opened in 1997 to honor the victims and provide a proper burial; after the uprising, many of the dead were quickly buried without ceremony. There are several monuments in the cemetery, the most eye-catching of which is the 4 m tall Memorial Tower, under which you'll find an incense burner where you can light a stick to honor the dead. To the right is a hall where the portraits of the dead are enshrined. Near the entrance, there's a memorial hall where you can learn more about the Gwangju Uprising—the photographs are moving, albeit occasionally very graphic. Every May 18, the cemetery holds memorial events attended by many Korean political notables, including the President himself.

🕘 8 am to 6 pm 🚌 From U-Square, take Bus No. 518 (no, the bus number is not a coincidence) and get off at the cemetery (1 hr). ⓒ 062-266-5187 🖐 http://518.mpva.go.kr

Mudeungsan Provincial Park
무등산도립공원

Mudeungsan Provincial Park

Gwangju's guardian mountain, Mt. Mudeungsan 무등산 (1,186 m) embraces the city from the east like a caring mother. This is where Gwangju's denizens go to commune with nature. Despite its height, it's an easy hike for all, and you'll be rewarded with up-close views of the funky, pillar-like volcanic rock outcrops near the peak. There's some grassy meadow around the peak, making it a nice place to relax. Mt. Mudeungsan is an absolute must in spring, when its fields of bright pink royal azaleas erupt along its slopes.

The mountain is well criss-crossed with trails, and the gentle slope lends itself to leisurely exploration. Beginning at Jeungsimsa Temple 증심사, the most popular gateway into the park, you could hike the main ridge, hit the peak, and descend the backside of the mountain to Mudeungsan Provincial Park Office in six hours.

🚌 Take Bus Cheomdan 9 from U-Square or Gwangju Station (50 min). ✆ 062-635-1187
🖱 www.mudeungsan.gwangju.co.kr

Uijae Museum of Korean Art 의재미술관

On the way to Jeungsimsa, be sure to stop at the lovely Uijae Museum of Korean Art, a small, but masterfully designed space dedicated to the work of Korean traditional landscape painter "Uijae" Heo Baek-ryeon (1891–1977), who lived the last 30 years of his life in a pretty Western-Japanese-style-home behind the museum. In addition to being a painter, Heo was also something of

Fields of pampas grass on Mt. Mudeungsan, Gwangju's guardian peak

an agricultural innovator, and by his old home you'll also find an old tea factory, teahouse and other pieces of Heo's legacy. Next to Jeungsimsa, you'll also find a small green tea field that Heo ran and cultivated with his own two hands. Visit this place in autumn when the trees turn color and a cup of tea at Munhyangjeong—Heo's old tea factory—warms the soul.

🕐 **Summer:** 10 am to 6 pm, **Winter:** 10 am to 5:30 pm. Closed Mondays 💷 2,000 won ☎ 062-222-3040 🌐 www.ujam.org (KR)

WHAT TO EAT

Almost by definition, everything's good here (the same applies to the rest of the Jeollanam-do). You're in Namdo ("South Province") cuisine country, where the food is fresh, plentiful, tasty and cheap. If you're a foodie and your wallet's up to it, head to Myeongseonheon 명선헌 (062-228-2942), a secluded Korean restaurant in an old garden residence up on Mt. Mudeungsan. Run by master kimchi maker Choi In-soon, this place specializes in *hanjeongsik* (Korean banquet cuisine), and take it from us—you haven't had *hanjeongsik* until you've had it Jeollanam-do-style. The menu starts at 40,000 won. Expect about 30 dishes to be put on the table. Another good place to try good Namdo *hanjeongsik* is Chodang Hanjeongsik 초당 한정식 (062-373-5515), which combines good food with graceful presentation. Meals go for 25,000–75,000 won. Especially charming is Songjukheon 송죽헌 (062-222-4234), a renovated *hanok* hidden in alley near Culture Complex Station run by a guy who's been preparing Namdo *hanjeongsik* for 20 years. The menu starts at 50,000 won. If you're hiking Mt. Mudeungsan—or even if you're not—there are a lot of pleasant Korean restaurants at the foot of the mountain in front of Jeungsimsa Temple.

Gwangju's best nightlife can be found in and around Chungjangno, the city's commercial district.

WHERE TO STAY

The plushest digs in town are at Ramada Plaza Gwangju Hotel 라마다플라자광주호텔 (062-717-7000), with five-star accommodation beginning at 198,000 won a night. The hotel is located in the newer part of the city, west of town, however, and not particularly close to anything. Also pleasant but out of the way is Hotel Midas 마이다스관광호텔 (062-973-5000), with rooms beginning from 66,000 won. Closer to the old downtown is Prado Hotel 프라도호텔 (062-654-9999), with good rooms starting at 140,000 won a night. In the heart of the old downtown is Gwangju Green Hotel 광주그린호텔 (062-252-1000), with rooms starting from 140,000 won. As usual, you can find plenty of budget accommodations around Gwangju Station and U-Square, with the nicer ones around the latter.

TRANSPORT INFO

🚆 Gwangju is well connected to the rest of the country by rail and road. It even has an airport. The fastest way to get to Gwangju from Seoul is via KTX from Yongsan Station (just under 3 hrs). The slower but cheaper Mugunghwa trains take about 4 hours 30 minutes. Note that some of the KTX trains to Gwangju stop not at Gwangju Station, but at Gwangju-Songjeong Station 광주 송정역, in the far west of town. From there, you're going to need to take a bus, subway or taxi into town. The KTX to Seoul from Gwangju also stops in Daejeon (Seodaejeon Station), Cheonan and Iksan. Trains to Busan take about six hours, and depart or arrive from Gwangju's Seogwangju 서광주, Hyocheon 효천 or Gwangju-Songjeong stations (i.e., NOT Gwangju Station). 🚌 Gwangju's bus traffic is handled by its fantastic U-Square bus terminal, with its shopping mall, restaurants, cafes and movie theater. U-Square also makes Gwangju the perfect jumping-off point for exploring the rest of Jeollanam-do. From Seoul, express buses to Gwangju depart from Seoul's Central City Bus Terminal (3 hrs 30 min). Express buses to and from Busan also take 3 hours 30 minutes (much quicker than the train). Daegu is 3 hours 30 minutes away by bus, too. ✈ If you really can't wait to get to Gwangju from Seoul, there are three flights a day from Gimpo to Gwangju International Airport (50 min).

DAMYANG 담양

Some 40 minutes outside the southwestern city of Gwangju is Damyang, one of Korea's most entrancing locations. An area renowned throughout Korea for its romantic bamboo forests, traditional gardens and proud literary history, Damyang is relatively untouched by foreign travelers, in large part due to its isolation. Thanks to the KTX express train service to Gwangju, however, visitors now have an easier time accessing this charming locale of outstanding scenery, great food and rich culture.

Siga Cultural Zone 시가문화유적지

Damyang's most scenic stretch follows the road that passes along Gwangjuho Lake 광주호. This densely wooded area on the backside of Mt. Mudeungsan (1,186 m), with some of the largest bamboo groves in the nation, is known as the Siga Cultural Zone—a reference to its important contributions to Korean classical literature. It's a naturebound wonderland of misty forests, briskly running streams and

handsome Joseon-era (1392–1910) pavilions.

For much of the Joseon period, the area was a place of exile for scholar officials who had found themselves on the losing side of one of the era's frequent factional disputes. In the deep bamboo forests, far from the conflict and corruption of the royal capital of Hanyang (Seoul), they found solace from the world. Their political careers prematurely terminated, these men

Soswaewon Garden is one of Korea's most spectacular traditional gardens and a masterpiece of Korean landscaping

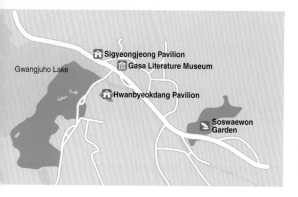

works of poetry by masters such as "Songgang" Jeong Cheol and Song Sun.

The museum also has a theater that plays a short film introducing the history of the area. However, few of the exhibits have English-language explanations; but it's also worthwhile to stroll around the museum grounds and appreciate the aesthetic quality of the works

⊙ 9 am to 6 pm ⊜ 2,000 won ⓒ 061-380-2701 ⓦ www.gasa.go.kr ⓑ Take Bus No. 2-1 from U-Square and get off at the musum (1 hr 15 min).

of learning focused their talents on literature and arts. And in this manner, Damyang became the birthplace of the *gasa*.

Gasa is a form of lyrical poetry that was particularly popular during the mid-Joseon era. Unlike the shorter *sijo* poems, they were longer works that often told tales of reclusion, love and exile, topics that should come as no surprise given the political circumstances of many of their early masters.

The poet-dissidents who called Damyang home built gardens and pavilions in the bamboo forests and atop scenic hilltops. In an oasis of beauty and learning, they would pass their days writing poetry and contemplating a better world free from corruption, avarice and vice.

Gasa Literature Museum 한국가사문학관

The place to learn more about Damyang's *gasa* poets is the Gasa Literature Museum, a large and superbly designed structure located just past Gwangjuho Lake (if you've started from Gwangju). The setting itself is magnificent, with the museum surrounded by wooded hillsides. In front of the museum is a courtyard with koi pond, a traditional pavilion and a tea shop. Inside the museum, you'll find some 1,300 articles left behind from Damyang's *gasa* golden age, including

Sigyeongjeong Pavilion 식영정

Immediately to the left of Gasa Literature Museum, high atop a forested hillock, is Sigyeongjeong Pavilion, one of Damyang's many scenic pavilions. The structure was built during the mid-16th century by Kim Seong-won for his teacher and father-in-law, "Seokcheon" Im Eong-nyeong. In 1972, it was designated a historical property by the province of Jeollanam-do.

Sigyeongjeong Pavilion was a favorite spot of Damyang's poets: Im Eong-ryeong, Kim Seong-won, Jeong Cheol and Go Gyeong-myeong were so fond of visiting, in fact, that they would become known as the "Four Hermits of the Sigyeongjeong Pavilion." From the pavilion, they each selected 20 scenic spots about which to write *gasa* verses. Jeong Cheol later used 80 verses that were composed to write the "Song of Mt. Seongsan," one of the era's greatest works of *gasa* poetry.

Hwanbyeokdang Pavilion 환벽당

Across from the museum and Sigyeongjeong Pavilion is a bridge leading over a stream feeding into Gwangjuho Lake. Cross the bridge, head left and just past a green hillock you'll come to a mossy stone and clay wall. Follow this romantic old wall past a small village and you'll come to

Man-made and nature converge at Soswaewon.

Soswaewon means "pure, refreshing garden."

Hwanbyeokdang Pavilion. Built in the mid-16th century by "Sachon" Kim Yun-jae, the name of the pavilion means "a place surrounded by green trees and water." Come, and you'll understand why.

Today, the pavilion sits stoically atop a lush green hill. Below, enclosed by the compound's clay and stone walls, is a wild grass field that was once the site of a private residence. You'll often find local residents and tourists relaxing on its fine wooden floor, taking in the surrounding scenery or simply enjoying a midday nap.

Soswaewon Garden 소쇄원

A 15 minute walk from Hwanbyeokdang is Soswaewon Garden, quite possibly the crown jewel of mid-Joseon era garden design. Joseon scholar-official Yang San-bo built this little piece of paradise in the mid-

16th century. Yang was typical of the personalities associated with this area of Damyang. He was a student of Jo Gwang-jo, a revered reformist Confucian scholar and official. In 1519, Jo and five other officials fell victim to a purge, and he was exiled to Neungju (now part of nearby Hwasun-gun), where he was executed. Yang, just 17 at the time, was so shocked by the injustice of it all that he abandoned the path to civil service. He returned to his hometown of Damyang and built Soswaewon Garden, where he could retreat from the brutal and corrupt outside world and devote himself to the study of neo-Confucianism.

The path to Soswaewon Garden is lined by thick bamboo groves that create a surreal atmosphere, especially in misty weather. The garden itself is representative of the harmony of the artificial with nature, a characteristic of Korean garden design; structures conform to nature, not the other way around. A waterfall plunges into a pool, which in turn feeds a rushing stream that cuts through the bamboo forest. Above the pool sits a pavilion while above the waterfall, a log bridge links the two sides of the garden. A gate pierces a garden wall to allow a stream to pass undisturbed.

At one time, the garden contained some 21 plant species and 10 man-made structures. Now, only few of the buildings remain but bamboo, pine, zelkova and

Beautiful stone wall of Soswaewon

maple trees grow everywhere. Soswaewon is beautiful all year round, presenting a different face for each season. In winter, the buildings are heated in the traditional Korean manner, so you can sit back in rustic comfort on a heated floor as you contemplate the fallen snow on the granite stones and roof tiles before you.

🕐 9 am to 6 pm 🎫 1,000 won ☎ 061-382-1071 🖥 www.soswaewon.co.kr 🚌 From Gwangju's U-Square, take Bus No. 225 and get off at Soswaewon, although you may wish to get off at Gasa Literature Museum and spend the rest of the day walking.

Jungnokwon Bamboo Garden 죽녹원

For even more bamboo-based scenery, head to Jungnokwon, a lovely bamboo garden/forest planted by the county of Damyang and used as a local leisure spot. At 2.2 km², it's a pretty spacious place with walking paths that crisscross the forest. It's all very

Jungnokwon Bamboo Garden is a lovely place to stroll.

picturesque, with plenty of romantic walks under fantastic canopies of bamboo. So pretty is it, in fact, that it's occasionally used for advertisements.

🎫 2,000 won 🕐 9 am to 7 pm ☎ 061-380-3244 🚌 The forest is about a 15 minute walk from downtown Damyang. Bus No. 311 from Gwangju's U-Square drops you off right at the forest itself (30 min).

WHAT TO EAT

Damyang is famous for two dishes, *tteok galbi* 떡갈비 and *daetongbap* 대통밥. *Tteok galbi* is minced patties of beef and pork, grilled on charcoal. You can find this at restaurants across Korea but Damyang is where it all started. *Daetongbap*, meanwhile, is rice steamed in a bamboo stem. Deogingwan 덕인관 (061-381-7781) is Damyang's most popular *tteok galbi* restaurant, and also offers *daetongbap*. Dul Pool 들풀 (061-381-7370) is another good *tteok galbi* restaurant, located just north of Gwangjuho Lake.

UNJUSA 운주사 & SSANGBONGSA 쌍봉사 TEMPLES

About an hour and a half outside of Gwangju, in the small rural county of Hwasun화순, are two of Korea's most unusual Buddhist temples. Unjusa Temple, with its bizarrely crafted pagodas and Buddhas, captivates visitors with its air of mystery, while Ssangbongsa—while not nearly as quirky as Unjusa, is nonetheless worth a visit for its rare wooden pagoda and its exquisite stone stupa from the 9th century.

Unjusa Temple 운주사

Unjusa is, putting it mildly, atypical for a Korean Buddhist temple. Basically, it's a narrow valley littered with unusual stone pagodas and Buddha statues. The site is sometimes called Cheonbul Cheontap 천불천탑 ("1,000 Buddhas and 1,000 Pagodas"), and was referred to as such in a Korean geographical text from 1481. For all we know, it may very well have had said numbers of pagodas and Buddhas, but over five centuries and four excavations (1984–1991) by Chonnam National University later, only 91 stone Buddhas and 21 pagodas remain.

Nobody has a definitive answer for when

The many unusual stone pagodas of mysterious Unjusa Temple.

Stone Buddhas, Unjusa Temple (left), Reclining Buddha, Unjusa Temple (right)

the temple was built, or why, heightening the already considerably aura of mystery hanging over the valley. Legend has it that it was founded in the 9th century by the great late-Silla Zen master and feng-shui theorist Doseon Guksa, who called down a thousand Taoist fairies one evening to build 1,000 stone pagodas and 1,000 Buddha statues so that he could open up a newer and better world. (Note: another version of this story cites a geomantic reason, namely, to balance out the Korean Peninsula—which is flatter in the west and more mountainous in the east—lest it capsize. Still another said he likened the S-shape valley to a boat, and felt it needed a sail and a skipper.) The catch, however, was that the fairies needed to do so before the sun rose the next morning. They almost did it, too, and were working on raising the last two Buddha statues when some mischievous monks let out a rooster sound, and the fairies all returned to heaven, leaving two Buddhas lying on one of the hilltops. You can see these two lying Buddhas, or *wabul*, for yourself—there's a path to the massive, 12.73 m lying Buddha and its 10.3 m partner atop the western hill.

Supernatural stone masons aside, there is no evidence that Doseon Guksa was involved in the temple's founding, however, and evaluations of the pagodas and statues indicates they were carved in the later Goryeo Dynasty. Some speculate that pagodas in the valley were placed to reproduce the constellations in the sky—and indeed, also on the western hill, not far from the laying Buddhas, are a collection of seven round stones placed in the shape of the Big Dipper. Other suggest that the site was simply a training ground for stone masons.

Several of the pagodas and Buddha statues have been designated important cultural properties by the government, including an impressive nine-story pagoda and a unique five-story pagoda with circular stories called, for obvious reasons, the "pancake pagoda." Many of the statues and towers, though, are rather simple and crude, and some of the Buddha statues look like they've just walked off a science fiction film set.

At the far end of the valley, there's a small collection of recently built wooden buildings where the temple's small community of bhikkhunis (Buddhist nuns) live and pray. Behind those is a path leading to Gongsabawi, a large rock at the top of the hill overlooking the valley. That's where you'll get the best views of the place.

🕐 8 am to 6 pm 💵 2,500 won 📞 061-374-0660
🚌 Take Buses No. 318 or 218 (make sure it says Unjusa!) from Gwangju's Gwangcheon Terminal, right across from U-Square (1 hr 30 min).

Ssangbongsa Temple 쌍봉사

If you're in Hwasun, it's also worth stopping by Ssangbongsa Temple. It's not a big temple, but its remote location and human scale give it a sense of warmth and serenity many other temples lack. It's also a very pretty place, largely thanks to its three-story wooden pagoda, a rarity in Korea, where all but a handful of wooden pagodas burned down long ago. Sadly, this wooden pagoda, which actually serves as the temple's main hall, is a reconstruction of the original, which was accidentally burned down in 1984. Still, it cuts a fine, almost exotic profile.

The temple's crown jewel, however, is hidden away on the hill just behind the precinct. There you'll find a stunning, eight-sided stone stupa, erected in the 9th century to hold the cremated remains of the Zen master Cheolgam Seonsa, the founder of Ssangbongsa. The stupa is richly decorated with carvings of lotuses, guardian deities, angels and other scriptural entities, and is in such good condition the inscriptions look as if they were made yesterday. You could spend hours looking at it and wouldn't get old.

ℂ 061-373-9041 🚌 Take buses No. 218-1 from Gwangju's Gwangcheon Terminal 광천터미널, right across from U-Square (1 hr 30 min). Or, if you're at Unjusa Temple, take a bus back to Hwasun Bus Terminal, and from there take Bus No. 218-1 to Ssangbongsa.

A rare wood pagoda at Ssangbongsa Temple

GANGJIN 강진

This quiet rural town on the Gangjin Bay doesn't get that many tourists, which is a shame, really, because it's a charming little part of the country with a rich and colorful past. Between the 10th and 14th centuries, Gangjin was Korea's foremost ceramics-producing region, its kilns producing the beautiful blue-green celadon for which Korea was famous throughout the Far East. Even today, the town's master craftsmen continue to produce some of Korea's highest quality ceramics. "Dasan" Jeong Yak-yong, one the greatest intellectuals in Korean history, spent 18 years in exile in the town, leaving behind a fascinating legacy. Hendrick Hamel, the 17th century Dutch sailor who spent 13 years in Korea after he was shipwrecked on Korean shores, lived seven years in Gangjin, an experience he documented in detail in his journal, providing the West with its first introduction to Korea.

Gangjin Celadon Museum 강진청자박물관

Located in the hamlet of Daegu-myeon 대구면, the historical heart of Gangjn's ceramics industry, Gangjin Celadon Museum houses a large collection of rare Goryeo celadon items. Granted, most of the really superb examples of celadon are found at the National Museum of Korea (Seoul, see p126), Gansong Museum (Seoul, see p98) or Hoam Art Museum (Yongin, Gyeonggi-do, see p209), or at overseas museums like the Louvre, but you'll find some beautiful

Celebrating Gangjin's celadon heritage at Gangjin Celedon Festival.

TIPS

GANGJIN CELEDON FESTIVAL

A good time to experience Gangjin's celadon heritage is during the Gangjin Celadon Festival 강진청자축제, held every summer. Held in Daegu-myeon in and around Gangjin Celadon Museum. Lots of fun events, including pottery-making programs, exhibits of ceramics by respected masters, and cultural performances. See www.gangjinfes. or.kr for more information.

GORYEO CELADON

History and Culture

The captivating jade blue color of celadon, or *cheongja* as it is called in Korea, is thanks to the iron in the clay and the iron oxide, manganese oxide and quartz in the glaze, and to the conditions of the kiln in which it is baked. Celadon was baked in reducing atmosphere kilns, in which oxygen levels are kept low, producing the unique color in the clay. The technique began in Song Dynasty China (960–1279), but really came into its own Korea during the Goryeo Dynasty (935–1392), where it became the dominant form of ceramics in Korea. Goryeo celadon reached its sublime heights in the 12th and 13th centuries, when craftsman stopped emulating Chinese models and adopted more indigenously Korean styles. At roughly the same time, the Goryeo celadon industry consolidated in southwestern Korean, particularly in and around Gangjin, where the royal court kilns were located. This was largely thanks to good quality clay, wood and water that could be found in the region, but also due to southwest Korea's well-developed maritime transportation links. Some 80% of the celadon items designated National Treasures by the Korean government were born in the kilns of Gangjin.

Goryeo artisans became especially skilled at an inlaid technique called *sanggam*, in which they would engrave designs—common motifs are flowers, trees, birds or clouds—on semi-dry clay, and then fill in the engravings with white or black clay slip. The glaze was then applied and the piece baked.

Craftsmen produced a variety of items out of celadon, including vases, bowls, incense holders and bottles. Celadon items could be both charmingly simple and spellbindingly ornate. Korean aristocrats and Buddhist temples tended to be the biggest consumers, but the reputation of Goryeo celadon transcended Korea's borders to China and Japan, too, where collectors held Goryeo celadon in very high regard.

The Mongol invasions of the 14th century, however, sparked a decline in celadon production. The fall of the Buddhist Goryeo Dynasty in 1392 and its replacement by the the Confucian Joseon Dynasty saw celadon give way to buncheong—blue-green stoneware for the masses—and later Joseon white porcelain, the subtle colorings and simple designs of which better suited the Confucian sensibilities of the new ruling elite.

In recent years, Korean artisans have striven to revive Korea's celadon tradition. In Gangjin area, there are 16 active kilns.

items here nonetheless, including 65 completely intact pieces and over 400 fragments on display.

The museum is located on the site of an old kiln, excavations of which you can see during your visit. The Gangjin area is home to 188 such kiln sites, more than half of all discovered kiln sites in Korea. The museum also houses a workshop where artisans produce new works and reproductions (in 2010, a vase made here was given to Pope Benedict XVI as a gift), as well as a shop where you can pick up an item or two. The museum also conducts hands-on programs in which you make your own celadon. Near the museum, Gangjin's local government is creating a "celadon village" where, they hope, artisans from around Korea will settle to pursue their craft.

🕘 9 am to 6 pm 🎫 2,000 won ✆ 061-430-3718 🚌 From Gangjin Bus Terminal, take a local bus for Maryang and get off at Gangjin Celadon Museum (30 min).

Dasan Chodang 다산초당

Hidden in the woods on the western slope of Mt. Mandeoksan 만덕산, Dasan Chodang was where late Joseon Dynasty intellectual and scholar Jeong Yak-yong lived in exile from 1801 to 1818. Jeong, a Confucian modernizer and early Catholic convert who is regarded as one of the greatest minds in Korean history, was exiled to Gangjin after he found himself on the wrong side of one

of the many factional disputes that plagued the late Joseon Dynasty.

Dasan Chodang is a typical example of simple, rustic Confucian charm. Shaded by trees, it's a simple wooden cottage, next to which there's a small pond, a water well, and a stone upon which Jeong used to sit and drink tea, a habit he picked up from his neighbors on the mountain, the Buddhist

Dasan Chodang (left), Gangjin O'sulloc Tea Plantation

JEONG YAK-YONG & GREEN TEA

History and Culture

Scholar, official and philosopher Jeong Yak-yong (1762–1836) is regarded by many to be the greatest thinker of the later Joseon Dynasty. Better known by his pen name of Dasan ("Tea Mountain"), a sobriquet he took during his exile at Dasan Chodang, he strove to incorporate modern scientific and social ideas into Joseon's dominant Neo-Confucian ideology to make it more relevant to life in 18th century Korea. His efforts were not always appreciated by conservative officials, however, and so he spent much of his life in exile, far from the centers of power.

Jeong was born in what is now Namyangju, Gyeonggi-do, the youngest of four brothers. Jeong and his brothers showed considerable academic talent, and with the coming to power in 1776 of visionary, reform-minded King Jeongjo, the stars of the brothers Jeong were on the rise.

Jeong was an adherent of *silhak*, or "Practical Learning," a movement, beginning in the 17th century, to reinterpret Neo-Confucianism to address contemporary problems. This involved adopting into Confucianism new technologies and ideas, some coming from the West through China, where Jesuit missionaries had been employed at the Ming court since the 16th century. It also involved refocusing Confucianism on real-world problems such as poverty and defense. Jeong's embrace of new ideas, and his concern for worldly issues, can be seen most dramatically at Suwon's Hwaseong Fortress, the construction of which he oversaw. The fortress, now designated a UNESCO World Heritage Site, was built using modern construction techniques and according to sound strategic principles.

Among the many new ideas that entered Korea was Roman Catholicism, and Jeong and his brothers were among the very first converts. King Jeongjo tacitly tolerated Catholics, but when he died, the situation changed drastically. With the new king too young to rule, his step grandmother, the Queen Regent Jeongsun, took power. A factional foe of reformers like Jeong, the queen regent launched a bloody purge of her enemies, citing the "perverse" new faith as a reason. Likely renouncing his faith, Jeong narrowly escaped with his life but was exiled to remote Gangjin. One of his brothers refused to renounce his faith and was beheaded.

Jeong spent 18 years in Gangjin, residing in a small, thatched-roof cottage on the side of Mt. Mandeoksan, overlooking Gangjin Bay. There he taught local students, chatted with the monks of nearby Baengnyeonsa Temple, and wrote, penning about 500 works during the exile. In 1819, King Sunjo, now in his majority, pardoned Jeong, allowing him to return to his hometown, which he did. Jeong maintained a low profile until his death in 1836.

One pastime Jeong embraced with gusto during his time in Gangjin was drinking tea, a habit he picked up from Ven. Hyejang, a Buddhist monk at nearby Baengnyeonsa Temple. In the Joseon Dynasty, tea drinking was associated with Buddhism, and hence scorned by the Confucian elite. Jeong, however, felt a good cup of tea went a long way in soothing the pain caused by injustice in a corrupt world. Jeong later befriended another Buddhist monk, the Ven. Choui (1786–1866), who often visited Jeong at Dasan Chodang. After learning about tea from Jeong, Choui spent much of the rest of his life drinking and writing about tea, and is widely credited with reviving Korea's unique tea culture.

monks of Baengnyeonsa Temple 백련사. It's a wonderful spot to relax and enjoy simple pleasures like the sea breeze or the sound of running water. The original cottage had a thatched roof; the current one, a 1959 reconstruction, has a tiled roof. The cottage signboard was penned by Kim Jeong-hui (1786–1856), one of Korea's greatest calligraphers. There's also a stone with Jeong's writing carved into it.

The tranquility up here and the tea must have suited Jeong—with the help of his students, whom he taught here, he wrote about 500 works during his time at Dasan Chodang. In between writing, teaching and drinking tea, he also raised carp in the pond. He was apparently quite fond of them, too—in letters sent to his students after he was released from exile and returned north, he made it a point to ask about them.

In addition to the cottage, there's also another small building that was used as a dormitory by Jeong's students; on the way up, you'll pass a pavilion with a pleasant view of Gangjin Bay 강진만. In the village below, there's a small museum that provides an overview of Jeong's life. There's a hiking trail from Dasan Chodang to Baengnyeongsa Temple, too.

🚌 From Gangjin Bus Terminal, take a bus to Mangho or Songhak and get off at Dasan Chodang (20 min).

Hamel Memorial Hall 하멜기념관

Besides tea and Dasan, Gangjin's other claim to fame is that for seven years it was the home of 17th century Dutch sailor and diarist Hendrick Hamel, whose journal account of his life in Korea provided the West with its first impressions of the country.

Shipwrecked on the island of Jeju-do in 1653, Hamel and 35 of his shipmates spent several years in Jeju and Seoul as involuntary guests of the state before being sent in exile to Gangjin in 1656 after some

Baengnyeonsa Temple, where scholar Jeong Yak-yong picked up his tea habit

HENDRICK HAMEL'S KOREAN ADVENTURE

History and Culture

In July 1653, as it was sailing from Dutch Batavia (present-day Jakarta) to the Dutch trading post in Nagasaki , the Dutch East India Company trading ship De Sperwer ("The Sparrowhawk") was caught in a typhoon and smashed into rocks off the coast of the Korean island of Jejudo. Some 36 survivors washed up ashore on Jeju, including a young bookkeeper from the Dutch city of Gorkum named Hendrick Hamel. For Hamel, it was the beginning of a 13 year adventure in Korea, a nation virtually unknown to the Western world.

It didn't take long for the presence of the scraggly Dutchman to come to the attention of the islanders. They were taken into custody by the authorities and questioned by the governor of Jeju-do, with the assistance of Jan Jansz Weltevree, a Dutch privateer who was shipwrecked in Korea in 1627. Weltevree, who had taken the Korean name Park Yeon, had gone completely native—according to Hamel, it took him a month to remember how to speak Dutch properly—and was an adviser to the Korean court, in large part thanks to his skill in producing much needed cannon for the Korean army. The Dutch asked asked the governor to be allowed to sail to Nagasaki, where the Dutch trading post of Deshima was located. The governor treated the men with kindness, feeding them well and allowing them some freedom of movement. He held parties to keep the men's spirits up as they awaited a decision from the king on whether the Dutch could leave. Weltevree, however, told the men that Korea generally did not let foreigners go once they'd arrived on Korean shores. You could check in, but you couldn't check out.

The old governor was replaced by a new one, one much less friendly to the Dutchmen. When some of them tried to escape, they were brutally beaten, and the rest of the Dutchmen placed in confinement for ten months. Finally, in May 1954, they were transported from Jeju to Seoul for a meeting with King Hyojong. At Changdeokgung Palace, the king, assisted by Weltevree, interrogated the men. The men pleaded that they be sent to Nagasaki, but Hyojong said no, Korea was not in the custom of granting permission to foreigners to leave, and that the Dutchmen should resign themselves to living the rest of their lives in Korea. The king—preparing for a retaliatory strike against the Manchu (see p37) and perhaps sensing the men and their knowledge could be of some use in that endeavor—took a liking to them, and enlisted them into the royal bodyguard, where they would build muskets for the Korean army.

The Dutchmen initially proved a curiosity in the capital, provoking stares, crowds and wild rumors. Eventually, however, the men adjusted, learning Korean, dressing in Korean style, and buying homes. In 1655, however, two of the Dutchmen—going against clear instructions—attempted to petition a Qing envoy to allow them to go home. The Koreans, who had worked very hard to keep knowledge of the Dutchmen's presence from the Qing, were forced to bribe the envoy not to tell the emperor. Embarrassed and angry, they imprisoned the two men (they would die in prison), and sentenced the rest to a severe beating. King Hyojong, who himself had spent his youth in China as a hostage of the Qing, annulled the sentence, arguing that the men were not in Korea on their own accord. Ignoring pressure from court officials who wanted the Dutchmen killed, the king instead sent them to live in exile in Gangjin, where they could make no trouble for the court.

Hamel and his shipmates spent seven years in Gangjin, at the fortress of Byeongyeongseong where they were ordered to maintain the governor's lawn. For the most part, the men got by well, making ends meet by doing odd jobs, cutting firewood and begging, the latter being particularly rewarding, wrote Hamel, as the locals—and the Buddhist monks of nearby temples in particular—were especially curious to hear stories about Holland and its people. One of the governors was especially kind to them, providing them with a decent house and a vegetable garden. In 1661, however, a prolonged famine caused by droughts struck Korea, and in 1663, the governor, no longer able to support the Dutchmen, asked the king that they be transferred to other cities that might be better able to care for them.

The Dutchmen were broken into smaller groups and sent to nearby towns. Hamel and 11 others were sent to the coastal town of Yeosu, where they were set to work for the governor. One of the governors took particular pity on the men—when one of the Dutchmen told him they did not try to escape because they had no boat, he told them, rather mischievously, that the coastal fishing villages had plenty of boats that could get them Japan. When this governor was replaced by a series of unpleasant, slave-driving governors, eight of the Dutchmen, including Hamel, purchased a boat from a local fisherman, rigged it, and sailed for Japan, reaching Nagasaki after a nine-day voyage. Hamel and his mates' great Korean adventure was over. It was 1666. After negotiations with the Japanese, the Koreans released the remaining Dutchmen in Korea, save for one, whom the Koreans had declared dead, but who in reality may have chosen to stay behind with his Korean wife and children.

Back in the Netherlands, Hamel published his journals, providing Europe with its first images of Korea and its people. In addition to documenting the events of his stay, Hamel also went into great detail about Korea's culture, politics, economy and military, providing scholars with a detailed look at conditions in 17th century Korea. Hamel died in his hometown in 1692. It would be over a century before Westerners would begin appearing on Korean shores again. To read an English translation of Hamel's journal by Kookmin University professor HennySavenije, visit www.henny-savenije.pe.kr.

of the Dutchmen tried to escape. The Dutchmen lived at Byeongyeongseong Fortress병영성, a walled military compound that served as the army headquarters for southwest Korea. There they got by doing odd jobs, begging and swapping tales of far-off lands for money and food. In 1663, the Dutchmen were broken up and sent to other towns; three years later, Hamel and seven others escaped to the Dutch trading post in Nagasaki, Japan. Hamel returned to the Netherlands, where in 1668 he published his journal of the adventure.

The old stone walls of Byeongyeongseong Fortress have largely been rebuilt, with plans in the works to restore the place fully. There's also a small museum with displays about Hamel and artifacts from Korea and the Netherlands of the 17th century. Nearby, there's also a lovely old stone bridge from the 18th century, and a stately ginkgo tree, about 800 years old, under which it is said Hamel and the other homesick Dutchmen would sit, pining for home. There's also a village with a very charming and very old stone wall road of the kind Hamel must have seen during his stay.

🕐 9 am to 6 pm (Mar–Oct), 9 am to 5 pm (Nov–Feb) 🎟 Free 🚌 Take a bus from Gangjin to Byeongyeong.

As is the case throughout Jeollanam-do, you'll find plenty of good places to eat.One good place near the Hamel Memorial Hall is Suingwan 수인관 (061-432-1027), a 50-year-old eatery known for its *dwaeji bulgogi baekban* 돼지불고기백반 (20,000 won), marinated pork, rice and lots of yummy side dishes.

WHAT TO EAT

For *namdojeongsik* (rice, soup and more side dishes than you can count), one place you'll want to try is Myeongdong Sikdang 명동식당 (061-433-2147), near Gangjin Bus Terminal. Jeongsik for one is 25,000 won, while for two costs 60,000 won. Another one you'll want to try is Heungjin Sikdang 흥진식당 (061-434-3031), where you'll find out what a table with 40 side dishes on it (30,000 won) looks like.

There's some motel and inn-like accommodation in downtown Gangjin, including Prince Tourist Motel 프린스관광호텔 (061-433-7300), near Gangjin Bus Terminal, where rooms go for 40,000 won a night. There's not as much choice here as you'd find elsewhere, though. The nicest place around is Wolchulsan Spa Hotel 월출산온천관광호텔 (061-473-6311), on the Yeongam 영암 side of Mt. Wolchulsan (see p469). This is a five-star place with a spa using spring water from 600m underground. Rooms go for 96,800 won a night.

WHERE TO STAY

Outside of Gangjin Town, though, there are some very pleasant *minbak* (homestay) options. In front of Dasan Chodang, for instance, there's the wonderful Dasan Myeongga 다산명가 (061-433-5555), an atmospheric *hanok minbak* in a nice wooded patch. Rooms go for 70,000 won a night. Also lovely is Dahyang Sochuk 다향소축민박(061-432-0360), another *hanok minbak* in front of DasanChodang, where the owner brews his own bamboo liquor. Rooms here begin at 60,000 won. There are some other nice *minbak* in the village in front of Dasan Chodang, too. On the south slopes of Mt. Wolchulsan is another beautiful *hanok minbak*, Gayeong Minbak 가영민박 (061-432-5232). Rooms are 30,000 won a night, and the scenery is lovely. An interesting accommodation in Gangjin is the Amisan Hotel 아미산호텔 (061-433-2136), a converted rural schoolhouse not far from Dasan Chodang. Rooms are 40,000 won a night.

From Seoul, buses to Gangjin depart from Central City Bus Terminal (4 hrs 50 min).Gangjin is well-connected by bus to the rest of Jeollanam-do, including Gwangju, Haenam, Boseong and Suncheon. From Gwangju, buses for Gangjin depart from U Square (1 hr 50 min).

TRANSPORT INFO

WOLCHULSAN NATIONAL PARK 월출산국립공원

At 56 km², Wolchulsan National Park is Korea's smallest national park, and Mt. Wolchulsan ("Rising Moon Mountain") itself is not especially high at 810m, but don't let that fool you—this is a beast of a mountain. While most of the mountains of southwest Korea tend to be rounded and gentle, Mt. Wolchulsan is steep, craggy and cliffy, bringing to mind Mt. Seoraksan in Gangwon-do. As the mountain's name would suggest, the sunsets and moon rises here are spectacular. The park is also home to a surprisingly large collection of cultural heritage sites, including ancient temples and dramatic rock carvings, so even if you've got no stomach for heights, the park is still worth a visit.

Hiking Mt. Wolchulsan

There are several possible hikes on Mt. Wolchulsan, but the most popular one follows the main ridge from Cheonhwangsa Temple 천황사 in the east to Dogapsa Temple in the west. It's a 9 km hike, and should take you at least nine hours. This is a pretty tough trail at times, with plenty of steep climbs, stairs, and, most thrilling of all, the "Cloud Bridge," a 52 m-long orange suspension bridge over a 120 m chasm between two rock peaks—whatever you do, don't look down! In fact, you don't have to take the bridge—there's an alternate route via the Baram Waterfall—but the bridge saves you time, and the views are, well, dramatic.

The rocky peaks of Mt. Wolchulsan, a tough hike despite its modest height

The Cloud Bridge of Mt. Wolchulsan spans a 120 m chasm. Don't look down!

You'll be seeing plenty of rock formations and cliffs along the way. Cheonwangbong, the highest peak, is in fact a big rock on which 300 people could sit. On the next peak, Gujeongbong, there are some interesting water pools that never seem to run dry, leading some to believe a dragon once lived there (in Korean folklore, dragons are associated with water). On the way down to Dogapsa Temple, you'll also pass a pleasant field of pampas grass, which is particularly nice in autumn. You'll also pass an old stone pagoda and, more importantly, a wondrously detailed cliff carving of the Maitreya Buddha (National Treasure No. 144), believed to have been carved either in the late Silla or early Goryeo era.

🚌 Free ✆ 061-473-5210 🚍 From Gangjin, you should first take an intercity bus to the town of Yeongam (1 hr). From Yeongam Bus Terminal, take a bus to Cheonhwangsa Temple (15 min).

Dogapsa Temple

Dogapsa Temple 도갑사

Dogapsa Temple was founded in 880 by the late Silla Zen master and feng shui theorist Doseon Guksa, who in fact was born on the slopes of Mt. Wolchulsan. By adopting Chinese geomantic theories to Korea's unique topographic and climatic conditions, Doseon is considered the father of Korean feng shui (*pungsu jiri* in Korean), and it wouldn't be an exaggeration to say that many Korean temples, shrines and even cities—including Seoul—are where they are because of his ideas.

Most of Dogapsa was burnt down during the Korean War, but it's still home to one National Treasure, the beautifully rustic Haetalmun Gate 해탈문 ("Gate of Liberation," or "Gate of Losing Suffering"), built in 1473 and designated National Treasure No. 50. It's also home to several other important heritage properties, including an 11th century stone sitting Buddha, an early Goryeo five-story pagoda, and a 17th century stone monument to Doseon Guksa. There's a small museum with relics of Doseon Guksa on display, too.

🚌 2,000 won ✆ 061-473-5122 🚍 Most visit this temple as the end of the Mt. Wolchulsan trail, but if you want to visit the temple directly, you need to take the Dogapsa-bound bus from Yeongam Bus Terminal.

Muwisa Temple 무위사

Tucked away on the Gangjin side of the mountain, this small temple doesn't get many visitors, which is a blessing, really, as it makes the place a hidden gem. Founded in 875 by Doseon Guksa, the temple is best known for its main hall, the Geungnakjeon ("Nirvana Hall"), a masterpiece of early Joseon Dynasty architecture, and the beautiful collection of 29 murals that it once housed and which are now preserved in a separate hall.

Built in 1430, during the reign of King Sejong, the Geungnakjeon Hall (National Treasure No 13) is a simple, gable-roofed building that shares similarities with the wooden architecture of the preceding Goryeo Dynasty, such as the main halls of Buseoksa Temple and Sudeoksa Temple.

The Geungnakjeon used to house 29 wall murals painted in 1476, not long after the hall was completed. Now, only one remains in the hall, the beautiful mural of the Buddhist triad in back of the main Buddha images. The rest have been moved to a separate hall for preservation.

The most beautiful of the paintings is the "Water—Moon Avalokitasvara," depicting the meeting, as told in the Avatamsaka Sutra, between the young Sudhana and Avalokitesvara, the Bodhisattva of Mercy, atop Mount Potalaka, the mythical abode of Avalokitesvara. In Korean Buddhist art, Avalokitesvara is usually painted as a woman, but in this painting it is a man, bare-chested, mustached and wearing the white robe of a monk. The young Sudhana, too, has been replaced with an old Buddhist nun.

According to legend, soon after the Geungnakjeon Hall was completed, an old monk came to the temple and offered to paint the murals, with one condition—that nobody look inside the hall for 100 days. On the 99th day, however, the abbot of the

Muwisa Temple is home to some spectacular 15th century artwork.

temple took a peek inside, and saw a bird flying around with a paint brush in its mouth, working on the mural. Startled, the bird flew off before it could paint the pupils into the eyes of the Avalokitesvara, leaving the painting incomplete.

📞 061-432-4974 🚌 Take a bus to Muwisa from Gangjin Intercity Bus Terminal (25 min).

GANGJIN O'SULLOC TEA PLANTATION & MUWIDAWON TEAHOUSE

On the southern slopes of Mt. Wolchulsan, not far from Muwisa Temple, are some very picturesque tea fields owned by Korean green tea giant O'sulloc. The tea of Mt. Wolchulsan has been praised by no less an authority than the great late Joseon Dynasty scholar and tea aficionado "Dasan" Jeong Yak-yong, who called Wolchulsan tea his "second favorite."

At Muwisa itself, you can have a cup of Wolchulsan tea at Muwidawon, the temple's teahouse. The teahouse was recently rebuilt—the old one was so well-regarded that monks from nearby temples would make it a point to go there—but it's still quite nice and, in addition to serving tea, it also sells packaged tea and locally produced ceramics.

Fishing boats, Mokpo

MOKPO 목포

As they say, Mokpo is a port (*"Mokponeun hangguda"*)—and an enchanting one at that. Called an "outdoor museum of Korean contemporary history," the city's old town, with its exotic foreign architecture, well-planned streets and relaxed atmosphere, has all the romantic—if a bit dilapidated—charm of a historic port. Add to the mix a picturesque location between the sea and the rugged peaks of Mt. Yudalsan, the hearty flavors for which southwestern Korea is famous, and easy accessibility via the KTX high-speed train, and you have all the makings of a wonderful weekend getaway.

History

Prior to its opening as a treaty port in 1897, Mokpo was little more than a provincial fishing village. By 1930, it had become one of Korea's most important commercial and industrial centers, a major port of export for Korean rice and cotton headed for Japan. In fact, colonial Mokpo was really two cities, divided by colonial policies of discrimination—a Japanese town south of Mt. Yudalsan with rows of neatly ordered Japanese-style homes along paved roads, grand colonial offices with their neoclassical façades and elegant steamships in the harbor; and a Korean town to the north of Mt. Yudalsan.

Liberation from colonial rule and post-war development have drastically altered Mokpo's socio-economic landscape, yet the old Japanese town south of Mt. Yudalsan still maintains a sleepy atmosphere of postcolonial malaise. Along its well-planned

streets are countless Japanese-style tile-roofed homes, red brick warehouses, Western-style colonial offices and other reminders of the colonial past, some in better repair than others. The best way to enjoy the old town is simply to stroll along its streets, seeing the sites and soaking in the atmosphere.

Mokpo Cultural Center 목포문화원

On the lower slopes of Mt. Yudalsan 유달산, overlooking the old Japanese town, is Mokpo Cultural Center, a beautiful Renaissance-style red brick building with some Japanese motifs thrown in for good measure. Built in 1900 as the Japanese consulate, it became Mokpo's town hall in 1914 after Japan's annexation of Korea. After Liberation in 1945, it was used as Mokpo City Hall and a public library, before being converted into a cultural research center in 1990. Mokpo Cultural Center is one of the best preserved pieces of colonial architecture in Korea. Next to the building is an old granite archive building and an old WWII-era air defense tunnel built to provide protection from American bombers.

🕐 9 am to 6pm. Closed weekends. 🕿 061-244-0044 🖐 www.mokpoculture.or.kr 🚶 Walk 15 minutes from Mokpo Station in the direction of Mt. Yudalsan.

Mokpo Modern History Museum
목포근대역사관

Located a short walk from Mokpo Cultural Center, the imposing Mokpo Modern History Museum—originally the Mokpo branch of the Oriental Development Company—is a granite edifice built in neoclassical style in 1923. The Oriental Development Company—Japan's answer to the British East India Company—was concerned with land acquisition and promoting Japanese settlement in Korea.

A few years back, the building was in dreadfully poor shape and in danger of being torn down. Fortunately, conservationists won the day, and the structure was renovated for use as a museum. The first floor displays many old photographs of colonial-era Mokpo while the second highlights Japanese atrocities from the era.

🕐 9 am to 6 pm. Closed Mondays.
🕿 061-270-8728

Mokpo Cultural Center

Mokpo Modern History Museum

House Full of Happiness

House Full of Happiness 행복이가득한집

Just across the street from Mokpo Modern History Museum is a beautiful two-story Japanese traditional home renovated into a café. The café, originally the residence for the head of the Mokpo branch of the Oriental Development Company, is an atmospheric blend of eras and cultures. The history of the place is accentuated by its beautiful Japanese garden. It's a great place to have a cup of coffee (6,600 won) or a beer—in fact, it's a highlight of the trip. Indoor and outdoor seating are available.

⏲ 11:30 am to 9 pm ℭ 061-247-5887

Lee Hun-dong Garden 이훈동 정원

One of the most enchanting sites in the old colonial city is Lee Hun-dong Garden, the largest garden in southwestern Korea and one of Korea's few remaining colonial-era Japanese gardens. Built in the 1930s by Uchitani Manhei, a wealthy rice and cotton trader who was reportedly the richest man in Mokpo, the garden was purchased by Korean lawmaker Park Gi-bae and later by businessman Lee Hun-dong. Located on the lower slopes of Mt. Yudalsan, the garden is home to over 100 species of plants from Korea, Japan and China. Japanese-style stone lanterns and ponds accentuate the beauty. If the garden gate is closed, ring the buzzer for someone to let you in.

Lee Hun-dong Garden

Mokpo Central Church (left), Yangdong Presbyterian Church

Mokpo Central Church 목포중앙교회

Located just to the north of the old Japanese town, Mokpo Central Church is an odd-looking Christian house of worship, and for good reason—built in the 1930s, it was originally Higashi Honganji Temple, a Japanese Buddhist temple. The building is constructed of wood and stone in traditional Japanese style, and the only thing to tip you off to its current use is the large cross that's been affixed to its entrance. With the construction of a new church in another part of the city, the old building is being restored for use as a museum.

Christian Monuments

While Japanese made up the bulk of Mokpo's foreign population in the colonial era, they were not alone. In the old Korean town, Western missionaries set up shop, building churches, schools and Western-style homes. Remnants of that period include Yangdong Presbyterian Church 양동교회, built by American missionaries in 1910, and an old missionaries' home on the campus of Jeongmyeong Girls' High School 정명여자고등학교. The granite used in their construction was taken from Mt. Yudalsan.

Mt. Yudalsan 유달산

Mokpo's most dominant topographical feature is Mt. Yudalsan (228 m), a rocky peak that offers wonderful views of the surrounding city, sea and islands. It's also a strategic place to take in the sunset.

The mountain has steps and walking paths linking a series of scenic pavilions from which to take in the views—it takes

View of Mokpo from Mt. Yudalsan

Statue of Yi Sun-sin, Mt. Yudalsan (left), Sunset from Nakjodae Pavilion

about 30 minutes to get to the highest peak. Along the path is a statue of Admiral Yi Sun-sin and an old cannon used in the old days to signal noon. In spring, the mountain comes alive in color when forsythias and cherry blossoms bloom. To celebrate the mountain's spring colors, Mokpo hosts Mt.

Yudalsan Spring Festival in April.

On the lower slopes of Mt. Yudalsan overlooking the sea to the west is a small Korean pavilion called Nakjodae 낙조대. This is an ideal place to watch the sunset over the islands off the coast of Mokpo.

WHAT TO EAT

As you'd imagine, Mokpo is noted for its seafood. There's a large seafood market near the waterfront—it's an interesting place to walk around and take in the sights. Note the sea skates: served raw and fermented (*hongeohoe* 홍어회), they are a regional delicacy. Mokpo's most famous dish, however, is octopus. Octopus in Mokpo comes in two forms—*saebal nakji* 세발낙지 (thin-legged octopus) and *ppeol nakji* 뻘낙지 (small octopus caught on tidal flats). They are most often eaten live, sometimes wrapped on a stick or chopped up into little squirming bits—be sure to chew well. They can also be consumed in soups, stews and *bibimbap*. Sinan Ppeol Nakji 신안뻘낙지 (061-243-8181) in Honam-dong is worth a try. The area around Bukhang 북항 ("North Port") has a Raw Fish Center where you'll find tons of *hoe* (sliced raw fish) places.

WHERE TO STAY

There are a number of places to stay around the old city, including Joseon Beach Motel 조선비치모텔 (061-242-0485~6), Good Day Motel 굿데이모텔 (061-245-2929) and Seaside Motel 스카이모텔 (061-285-2333) in Haean-dong 해안동 (near the Passenger Ferry Terminal 목포여객선터미널). Most of these will cost 40,000–45,000 won a night. There are also quite a few hotels near Bukhang Port Jukgyo-dong 죽교동, including the first-class Shinan Beach Hotel 신안비치호텔 (061-243-3399), which will cost you 100,000 won a night and up.

TRANSPORT INFO

🚉 The easiest way to get to Mokpo from Seoul is by KTX from Yongsan Station (3 hrs). Once you're in Mokpo, take a taxi to Jungang-dong, in the heart of the old city. Mokpo has rail links to Gwangju, Iksan and Daejeon, too. 🚌 Buses to Mokpo from Seoul depart from Central City Express Bus Terminal (4 hrs). Mokpo's bus terminal is a bit to the west of the historic waterfront area, so you'll need to take a taxi or a local bus. From Gwangju, buses take just 90 min. ⛴ Mokpo is also home to a very large and very busy ferry terminal. Mokpo is the favored point of departure for travelers going to Jejudo by sea. There are daily ferries for Jeju (3 hrs 10 min–4 hrs 50 min) and well as to the islands of Dadohae Maritime National Park.

Children explore the mudflats of Haenam's Ttangkkeut Village,
the southernmost point of the Korean mainland.

HAENAM 해남 & JINDO 진도

If you're looking to get away, it's hard to get much further than Haenam and Jindo Island. Located on the far southwest corner of the Korean Peninsula, Haenam and Jindo form the heart of what is often referred to as Namdo—the area of southwestern Korea famous for its fine seaside scenery, rich traditional culture and, above all else, excellent food. Not so long ago, getting to this remote area of the country was an adventure in and of itself, but thanks to the opening of the KTX express train to Mokpo, it is now possible to enjoy the wonderful region as a weekend trip from Seoul.

To get to Haenam, take the KTX from Seoul's Yongsan Station to Mokpo. From Mokpo, Haenam is an hour away by bus. From Haenam, there are frequent buses to Jindo Island. If you want to stop by Jindo Bridge, catch a bus from downtown Haenam to the tourist area of Usuyeong 우수영.

Haenam 해남

Haenam is a rural community that is known mostly for its location—it is here that the mainland of the Korean Peninsula reaches its southwestern point. The downtown area—Haenam-eup—is a typical countryside town with little to hold your interest other than a few hotels, a bus terminal and vibrant country market. South of the town, however, are the spectacular Buddhist temples of Daeheungsa and Mihwangsa (the latter being one of the most recommended sites of the region), a Joseon-era village now home to a museum for legendary Korean poet and scholar "Gosan" Yun Seon-do, and the popular tourist destination of Ttangkkeut Village, literally "Land's End Village."

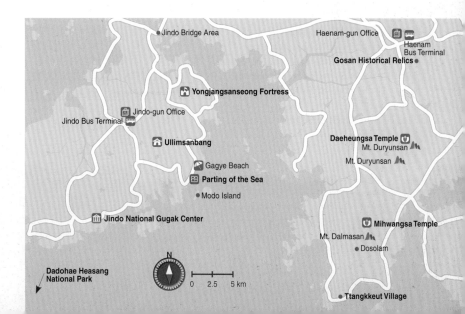

Old home of Yun Seon-do

Old Home of Yun Seon-do
고산윤선도 유적지

Not far from the downtown area, in the small village of Yeondong-ri 연동리, is a complex dedicated to perhaps Haenam's most famous historical resident, "Gosan" Yun Seon-do. Gosan was a famed 17th century poet and scholar who spent much of his life in exile in this remote part of the country—it is here that he composed his epic poem "The Fisherman's Calendar," now required reading for Korean students. The complex contains a museum where you can find examples of works by Gosan and his descendants (including the famed 18th century painter Yun Doo-seo), a number of shrines, and the ancestral home of the Haenam Yun clan, which is still owned and occupied by members of the family.

Daeheungsa Temple 대흥사

Hidden deep within the ancient forests of Mt. Duryunsan 두륜산, is the important Buddhist monastery of Daeheungsa Temple. Depending on which legend you believe, the temple was founded either in the fifth or sixth century, and has been rebuilt numerous times since then. During the Japanese Invasion of 1592, legendary warrior monk Seosan used the temple as the headquarters of his monk army fighting against the invaders.

The monastery complex itself is quite large and approached by a very nice walk (or shuttle bus ride) through some of Korea's oldest forests. There are a number of architecturally important structures, including the Main Hall with its amazingly crooked wooden pillars. The main courtyard is off to the left, separated from the rest of the complex by a beautiful stream. To the rear of the monastery is a Confucian shrine dedicated to Seosan.

Mt. Duryunsan, at 703 meters, makes for an especially pleasant hike, especially when the primitive forest turns color. If you don't want to hike it, there's a cable car (once Korea's longest) which takes you to one of the lower peaks. On a clear day, the peak offers clear views of the sea.

🎫 3,000 won ✆ 061-534-5502 🖰 www.daeheungsa.co.kr (KR) 🚌 Take a bus from Haenam Terminal (25 min).

Mt. Dalmasan provides a spectacular backdrop to Mihwangsa Temple.

Dosolam Hermitage, Mt. Dalmasan (left), Fishing boat near Ttangkkeut Village

Mihwangsa Temple 미황사

About 30 minutes south of Daeheungsa on the road to Ttangkkeut Village is another Buddhist temple, Mihwangsa. While smaller than Daeheungsa, Mihwangsa makes up for its smaller size with an absolutely breathtaking backdrop, set against the craggy peaks of Mt. Dalmasan 달마산, named for Bodhidharma, the Indian monk and transmitter of the Zen tradition.

Mihwangsa sits atop a series of terraces—from the rear terraces, you can gaze upon the sea. The Main Hall has been designated National Treasure No. 947, and is noted for its intricate interior artwork. A short walk from the temple is a garden of stone monuments to notable monks, many of which have been intricately carved.

Mt. Dalmasan is a recommended climb but its series of rocks greatly adds to its difficulty. One of the highlights is the Buddhist hermitage of Dosolam 도솔암, perched on cliff with an awe-inspiring view of the surrounding peaks.

ⓒ 061-533-5521 🚌 Take a bus from Haenam Terminal (50 min). 🖰 www.mihwangsa.com

Ttangkkeut Village 땅끝 마을

Once a small backwater fishing village, Ttangkkeut Village ("Land's End Village") has in recent years become a major tourist destination owing to its location, which marks the southwesternmost point of the Korean Peninsula. Here, you'll find a number of motels, seafood restaurants, shops selling the village's famous seaweed, and the ferry to Bogildo 보길도, a noted off-shore island. The best views can be had from the observation platform atop a hill overlooking the harbor—there's a monorail that goes to the top (3,000 won one way, 4,000 won round trip). Be sure to arrive in time for the sunset. 🚌 Take a bus from Haenam Terminal (30 min).

Jindo Island 진도

Just across the narrow and notoriously turbulent Myeongnyang Strait is the island community of Jindo. Korea's third largest island (after Jejudo and Geojedo), Jindo is noted for its beautiful maritime scenery, local firewater and rich traditional culture.

Jindo National Gugak Center 국립남도음악원

Jindo is one of the bastions of Korean traditional performing arts, with a number of noted folk songs such as "Jindo Arirang" and shaman rituals. The music of Jindo tends to reflect the humble and difficult existence of island living. To sample Jindo's traditional culture, stop by the impressive Jindo National Gugak Center, one of Korea's most important centers of traditional music and dance. The complex sits at the base of the mountain and overlooks the sea—one of the most finely situated performing arts venues in the country. ⓒ 061-540-4031 🚌 From Jindo Bus Terminal, take a bus for Tamnip 탑립/Ganggye 강계 and get off at Gwiseong 귀성. From there, walk about 500 m (1 hr 40 min).

Jindo's 'Parting of the Sea' is sometimes called 'Moses' Miracle.'

Parting of the Sea 진도 신비의 바닷길

The biggest event of the year in Jindo is the Jindo Moses' Miracle, when low tide exposes a narrow, 2.8 km land bridge linking Jindo with nearby Modo Island 모도. This happens just a few times a year, but when it does, it's festival time—thousands upon thousands of tourists descend upon the site to witness the miracle. Nearby are a number of popular beaches which are packed in summer.

📁 From Jindo Bus Terminal, take a bus for Hoedong-ri 회동리 and get off at the festival venue.

Jindo Bridge Area 진도대교

One of Jindo's most spectacular scenes is the impressive Jindo Bridge, linking Haenam and Jindo. The twin spans, completed in 1984 and 2005, cut an impressive figure against the aquamarine waters and the surrounding verdant hills. When gripped by frequent fog, it's not unlike San Francisco's Golden Gate Bridge. There is an observation point atop a hill on the Jindo side. The bridge spans the Myeongnyang Strait, known for its fierce currents. The strait was the scene of the 1597 Battle of Myeongnyang, one of the greatest victories of Korean hero Admiral Yi Sun-sin.

📁 From Jindo Bus Terminal, take a bus for Nokjin 녹진/ Usuyeong 우수영 and get off at Nokjin.

Yongjangsanseong Fortress 용장산성

Not far from the bridge are the remains of Yongjangsanseong Fortress, which served as one of the headquarters in the anti-Mongolian resistance during the Mongol invasion of Korea of the 13th century. Some of the walls remain, and there's a museum detailing the history of the fortress and the Mongol invasion.

📁 From Jindo Bus Terminal, take a bus for Byeokpa 벽파/ Yeondong 연동 (50 min).

GREAT BATTLE OF MYEONGNYANG FESTIVAL

The Great Battle of Myeongnyang Festival 명량대첩축제 celebrates the miraculous triumph at the 1597 Battle of Myeongnyang, when war hero Admiral Yi Sun-sin led 13 Korean ships to victory over an enemy Japanese fleet of 333 ships. The four day festival, held in October in the area around the Myeongnyang Strait (also known as the Uldol Strait), is highlighted by a spectacular reenactment of the battle. In addition, the festival features parades, folk singing and dancing, and commemorative ceremonies. www.mldc.kr (KR)

The scenic Jindo Bridge spans the Myeongnyang Strait.

Ullimsanbang 운림산방

In the interior of the island is the former studio of the famous 19th century painter Sochi. The surrounding mountains and forests make a perfect backdrop, and the pond in front of the studio has been used in film shoots. You can easily see how such scenery might inspire artistic genius. Interestingly, the studio is still owned by Sochi's descendants.

🚌 From Jindo Bus Terminal, take a bus for Sacheon-ri 사천리 (30 min).

WHAT TO EAT

The Korean southwest is famous for, above all else, its food. Namdo cooking comes fresh, plentiful and comparatively cheap. Eating well will not be a concern. For the adventurous, one of the regional specialties is fermented skate, or *hongeohoe* 홍어회. This is not for the fainthearted—the flesh of the fermented skate is high in ammonia, with a scent that's guaranteed to clean out your sinuses. If you're in Ttangkkeut Village, try Jonggajip Hanjeongsik 종가집한정식, where some Namdo-style *hanjeongsik* for two will cost you 60,000 won. If you visit Daeheungsa Temple, a good choice for lunch is the Jeonju Sikdang 전주식당 (061-532-7696) which is famous for its mushroom dishes and *sanchae jeongsik* 산채정식 ("mountain vegetable banquet"), which is a bit pricey at 60,000 won for four, but absolutely delicious and will leave you so stuffed you may not have to eat for the rest of the day.

WHERE TO STAY

You'll find standard Korean motel accommodation in Haenam, Jindo and the Haenam tourist spot of Usuyeong, near the Jindo Bridge. You'll also find accommodation at Ttangkkeut Village and Jindo's beach areas. One place of accommodation worth recommending is the Yuseongwan 유선관 (061-534-2959), located right below Daeheungsa Temple. Formerly a guesthouse used by the temple, the Korean hanok inn—itself a century old—has a lovely garden and overlooks a running mountain stream. The site was used for the shooting of the famous Korean film *Sopyonje*. Staying here will run you about 40,000–80,000 won, depending on the room. Breakfast costs 7,000 won. Another great place to stay—this one on the other side of Mt. Duryunsan—is Seora Dawon 설아다원 (061-533-3083), a hanok bed & breakfast that sits on an organic green tea farm. Rooms begin at 100,000 won a night.

DADOHAE MARITIME NATIONAL PARK 다도해 해상국립공원

Korea's largest national park, Dodohae Maritime National Park spans 2,321 km²
over seven coastal areas along the South and West seas, with no fewer than 1,596
islands. There's some really spectacular scenery here—cliffs plunging into the
ocean, sandy beaches, verdant islands dotting the horizon on an endless surface of
shimmering blue. You can appreciate it from the mainland if you like, or if you've
got the time, hop on a boat and head to one of the many scenic islands and
experience a Korea far different from the hustle and bustle of Seoul.

Layout Dadohae Maritime National Park can be broken down into seven coastal and
island districts, spread out along Korea's southwestern tip (see the map on
p486). This includes parts of the cities and counties of Sinan, Jindo, Goheung, Wando
and Yeosu. Most of the islands are small, the major exception being Jindo, which is
Korea's third largest island. The park is divided into several districts (described in this
section), each best experienced as a separate trip.

The fantastically rocky coast of Hongdo Island

Hairpin turns, Heuksando

Heuksando 흑산도

Heuksando ("Black Mountain Island") is one of the larger islands of the park, and home to over 3,000 people. Not so long ago, tourists regarded it as mostly a stopover along the way to scenic Hongdo island, but nowadays, more and more people are coming to appreciate the island's own set of charms, including its lovely coastal ring road, its unusual coastal rock formations and, last but not least, its fermented skate, one of Jeollanam-do's signature dishes.

The most popular tourist activity here is to take a bus or taxi around the circular coastal road. A taxi obviously gives you the option of stopping to take in the various scenic and historical spots along the way—expect to spend about 60,000 to 80,000 won for three hours. You can take a local bus, too (fare: 1,000 won), but when you disembark, be prepared to wait for the next bus. The coastal road—opened in 2010 after 27 years of construction—offers some spectacular views. One stretch in particular consists of a steep climb of twelve hairpin turns, at the top of which there's an observatory. Sections of the road are also lined with murals documenting the island's culture and history.

Interestingly enough, Heuksando was also the place of exile for Jeong Yak-jeon, the elder brother of famed Joseon scholar Jeong Yak-yong (see p464). Like his more famous brother, Jeong was a scholar, official and an early convert to Roman Catholicism, the latter for which he was banished from Seoul in 1801. He spent almost the entirety of the last fifteen years of his life on Heuksando, mixing with the local fishermen, opening up a school, studying measures to improve their lives and, most famously, undertaking a comprehensive study of the island's marine life.

🚢 There are four ferries a day from Mokpo Coastal Ferry Terminal to Heuksando (1 hr 50 min), departing at 7:50 am, 8:10 am, 1 pm and 4 pm. Return boats to Mokpo depart at 9 am (or 11 am), 3:30 pm, 4:10 pm. (061-243-2111). Fare: 34,300 won

🛏 There's a good deal of accommodation in Yeri. If you need a hotel-type accomodations, try the Heuksan Beach Hotel 흑산비치호텔 (061-246-0090~2), with rooms starting at 140,000 won (peak season: Jul 29–Aug 7). Most of what you'll find available, though, are *minbak* (homestay).

WHAT TO EAT

As for food, you're looking at fish—Heuksando cannot support agriculture so residents make their living from the sea. The island's most famous product is *hongeo* or skate, and you'll find plenty of *hongeo* restaurants/wholesalers along Yeri's waterfront, including Hongeo House #15 15번홍어집 (061-275-5033). Expect to pay about 40,000 won for a plate of *heongoehoe* 홍어회 (raw, fermented skate).

HONGEO 홍어

If there is one dish Jeollanam-do is famous for, it's *hongeo* or skate. This is usually eaten raw and fermented, with a slice of skate placed with a slice of steamed pork on a slice of kimchi, a dish called a *hongeo samhap* 홍어삼합 ("combination of three"). It's an ubiquitous dish in southwest Korea, especially during festivities—as a friend of this writer from Gwangju once put it, "Down here, it's not a party unless there's *hongeo*." It frequently makes an appearance in Namdo *jeongsik*, the full-course meals that are the epitome of Jeolla-do cooking.

Hongeo is, to put it very mildly, an acquired taste. Skates are related to sharks, and like sharks, they urinate through their skin. When the flesh is left to ferment, the urine turns to ammonium. This gives the meat a very distinctive, sharp ammonium taste. Actually, it's the smell rather than the taste that gets you. It'll clean your sinuses out and first-time eaters often gag. If you can't get used to it, don't feel too bad—truth be told, many if not most Koreans from other regions of the country can't stand it, either. Indeed, its Icelandic equivalent, hákarl (made from Greenlandic shark rather than skate), once made celebrity chef Gordon Ramsay vomit. But if you do get used to it, you'll soon find yourself craving the dish's pungent flavor and the unforgettable sting to the tongue.

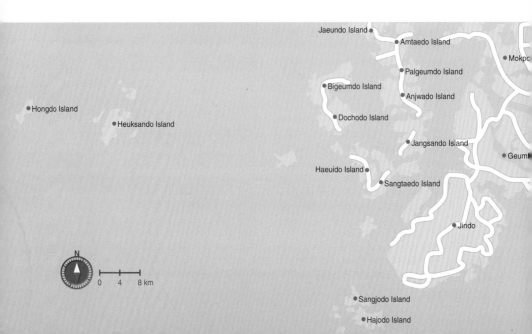

Jaeundo Island

Amtaedo Island

Mokpo

Palgeumdo Island

Bigeumdo Island

Anjwado Island

Hongdo Island

Dochodo Island

Heuksando Island

Jangsando Island

Geum

Haeuido Island

Sangtaedo Island

Jindo

N

0   4   8 km

Sangjodo Island

Hajodo Island

Hongdo Island

Hongdo 홍도

Hongdo or "Red Island" (so named because the island takes on a reddish hue at sunset thanks to its soil rich in quartzite) is essentially one big nature preserve, home to 270 varieties of evergreens and 170 animal species. The scenery here is quite spectacular; the island's coastline is lined with cliffs and 33 beautifully eerie rock formations, the most famous being Nammun, a dramatic rock gate.

Because of the island's designation as a natural monument, most of it is off-limits to tourists. If you're looking for views, though, there's an observatory a short walk above the port of Hongdohang 홍도항, where boats will drop you off. Most visitors take in the island's scenic sites by tour boat, which you can join at Hongdohang. Boat tours take about two hours, 30 minutes to go around the island, and charge 22,000 won a person.

Note: You needn't to stay on the island, but if you'd like to anyway, you'll find some accommodation and restaurants in Ilgu Village 일구마을.

🚪 There's a 1,000 won fee to enter Hongdo.

🚢 There are two ferries a day from Mokpo Coastal Ferry Terminal 목포여객선터미널 to Hongdo (2 hr 30 min; fare: 38,000 won), departing at 7:50 am and 1 pm. These ferries also stop in Heuksando. Return boats to Mokpo depart at 10:30 am and 3:40 pm.

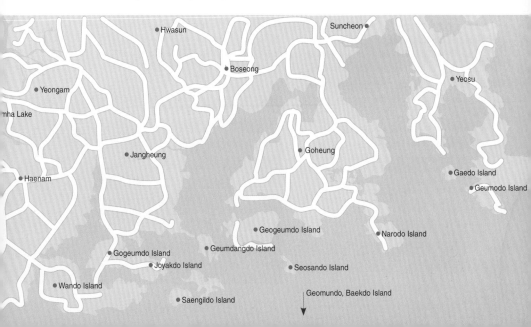

Famed heart-shaped beach of Bigeumdo Island

Bigeumdo-Dochodo District
비금도 도초도 지역

This district is comprised of the islands of Bigeumdo and Dochodo, which are connected to each other by bridge, and to the mainland by ferry. Bigeumdo is known largely for its beaches, including a unique heart-shaped beach that's popular with couples. It's also home to the massive Daedong Salt Farm 대동염전, where sea salt using wind and sunlight has been produced since 1948. Additionally, there's a pleasant little village called Naechon 내촌, where there are some charmingly rustic alleyways lined with old stone walls of the type that used to grace many Korean villages. The island of Dochodo has beaches, too, although there are plans afoot to turn the island into a big zoo.

🚢 Three ferries a day to Bigeumdo's port of Gasan from Mokpo Coastal Ferry Terminal (7 am, 1 pm and 3 pm). The trip takes 2 hours, 20 minutes. There're also four fast boats to the port of Sudaehang at 7:50 am, 8:10 am, 1 pm and 4 pm (50 min).
Boats from Bigeumdo (Gasan) to Mokpo depart at 7: 00 am, 10 am and 4 pm. Fast boats from Sudae 수대 to Mokpo depart at 10 am, noon, 4:20 pm and 5:20 pm. Fast boat: 17,600 won; slow boat: 8,000 won

Jodo District 조도 지역

This district consists largely of a thick cluster of islands off the coast of Jindo called Jodo or "Bird Islands," because, it's said, from the coast they look like a flock of birds floating on the ocean. There are 119 islands in the group, 35 of which are inhabited. If you're a lighthouse fan, there's a 101-year-old lighthouse at the end of the biggest island of the group (Hajodo 하조도), reached via a hiking trail from the main port.

🚢 There are eight ferries a day from Jindo's Paengmokhang Port 팽목항 to Hajodo Island (35 min), and eight back.

Jodo Island

Wando District 완도 지역

This district consists of the islands off Wando 완도, the most important being the island of Bogildo 보길도. Like most of the islands of Dadohae Maritime National Park, Bogildo has its natural charms and beaches, including the beautiful Yesong-ri Beach 예송리해수욕장, a 1 km crescent of blue pebble beach wedged between a mountain and the sea.

A must-see in Bogildo is Yun Seon-do Historical Site 윤선도유적지, comprised largely of Seyeonjeong Garden 세연정, one of the most beautiful examples of Korean traditional gardening in the country. The garden was created by "Gosan" Yun Seon-do (1587–1671), a Joseon Dynasty official, scholar and, most importantly, poet. Like many of the great intellectuals of the Joseon Dynasty, Yun spent much of his life exiled to remote parts of the country. In 1637, upon learning that King Injo had surrendered to the invading Manchus (see p36), Yun exiled himself to Jejudo out of despair. Along the way, his boat ran into a typhoon so he stopped in Bogildo to let the storm pass. He liked the island so much that he decided to stay for 13 years. He built a home and a garden, and put pen to paper, penning his greatest poetry.

Seyeonjeong Garden is a textbook example of a Korean garden: the landscape is left as natural-looking as possible, with enhancements here and there for greater visual impact. Overlooking the pond is a wooden pavilion where Yun once sat, taking in the surroundings with a bit of music and wine, perhaps conjuring some artistic inspiration in the process.

🚢 You can either take the ferry from Haenam's Ttangkkeut Village (see p479) or Wando's port of Hwaheungpohang 화흥포항. The former will take about 50 minutes, and is the more popular of the two. From Bogildo's harbor, there are buses and taxis that'll take you where you want to go.

🛏 Near Yesong-ri Beach 예송리해수욕장, there are a number of *minbak* (homestay) and pension facilities, including Hanbang Hwangto Hanok Pension 한방황토 한옥펜션 (061-553-6370), a nice *hanok*-style pension house where rooms go for 60,000 won a night on weekends (50,000 won on weekdays) during off-peak months.

Lovely Seyeonjeong Garden, a beautiful garden created by exiled Joseon Dynasty scholar Yun Seon-do

Geumodo Island

Narodo District 나로도 지역

Narodo is a decent-sized island now linked by bridge to the town of Goheung 고흥 on the mainland. There's a pretty good beach at Wuju Beach 우주해수욕장, but the island is now best known as the home of Korea's space port, Naro Space Center and Space Science Museum 나로우주센터 우주과학관 (3,000 won admission; hours: 10 am to 5:30 pm, closed Mondays), where you can see an assortment of indoor and outdoor exhibits dedicated to space science. As of the writing of this book, there have been two launches from Naro Space Center, completed in 2009, although on both attempts, the rockets failed to put their packages into orbit.

📱 Take a bus from Goheung Terminal to Narodo Bus Terminal (40 min). From Narodo Bus Terminal, take a local bus to Naro Space Center (20 min).

Geumodo District 금오도 지역

In the eastern extreme of the park is the Geumodo District, which centers on Geumodo Island, an island much beloved by weekend anglers for its rich schools of *gamseongdom* 감성돔, or black porgy. According to a 1872 map, you could see Japan's Tsushima from its highest point— hyperbolic at best, but feel free to hike up and test it. The best part of this section of the park is not the island itself, but the Buddhist hermitage of Hyangiram 향일암 on the mainland (see p505).

📱 Ferries to Geumodo depart from Yeosu Ferry Terminal.

Geomundo-Baekdo District 거문도 백도 지역

This district consists of the island of Geumundo (historically Port Hamilton) and the Baekdo archipelago. See "Geumondo" on p490.

Narodo Space Center

BOSEONG 보성

When spring arrives, few places in Korea are as spectacular and ravishing to the eye as Boseong. This is a land of rolling hills covered with verdant green tea fields that cover the hillsides like an emerald blanket. In the fields, workers busy picking the year's harvests mingle with couples and families strolling about the perfectly manicured rows of tea bushes. If you're lucky, the early morning mist will still be hanging in the hillsides, providing a romantic setting second to none. But Boseong is more than just fairy tale walks amidst tea fields. Not far from the tea fields, in the small railroad hamlet of Beolgyo, visitors can learn about the tragic cauldron of colonialism, polarization and war in which was born modern Korea.

Daehan Dawon Plantation 대한다원

When Koreans think of Boseong, they think of green tea. Green tea has a long history in Korea. The drink arrived in the 9th century, when a Korean envoy brought back tea seeds from Tang China. The seeds were planted on the slopes of Mt. Jirisan 지리산 near Ssanggyesa Temple 쌍계사, where they took root and prospered.

The plantations in Boseong, however, are of much more recent vintage. In the 1930s, colonists from green tea-obsessed Japan

The beautiful rolling hills of Daehan Dawon Plantation, one of Korea's most scenic locations

Taebaek Mountain Range
Literature Museum

Mt. Jesuksan

Beolgyo

Borimsa Temple

Boseong Bus Terminal

Boseong County Office
Boseong Tourist Motel

Mt. Obongsan

Daehan Dawon Tea Plantation

Udo Island

Mt. Jeamsan

Jeamsan Recreational Forest

Daewonsa Temple
Jangheung County Office

Yulpo Haesu Nokchatang

Boseong Dabeach Condo

Yulpo Beach

N

0   1.5   3 km

took notice of the hillsides of the coastal town, blessed with soil, humidity and day-night temperature differences perfect for tea cultivation. In 1939, they established the first commercial tea plantation in the area.

In 1945, with Japan's defeat in World War II, Korea's Japanese overlords went home and Boseong's lone tea plantation fell into disuse. In 1957, however, a Korean businessman purchased the old tea fields and established Daehan Dawon Tea Plantation. Soon, more tea plantations were established nearby, stretching all the way to the coast. Boseong's tea industry flourished, and today the town accounts for some 40 percent of Korea's green tea production.

The place everyone goes to is the aforementioned Daehan Dawon Tea Plantation. This is the oldest, largest and most beautiful of the area's tea gardens. The plantation bills itself as a "watercolor-like tea field," and this is no exaggeration. Spread out over some 561 hectares of hillside, the fields are a pleasant mix of

rows of green tea and beautiful forests. Before you get to the tea fields, however, you must walk along a wooden path lined by a running brook and towering Japanese cedar trees. This walkway, shaded by a canopy of green not unlike the vaulted roofs of the great cathedrals of Europe, is just as famous as the green tea plantation itself. You might even spy the occasional squirrel or chipmunk scurrying about the woods.

The green tea fields are criss-crossed with walking paths and flights of stairs. There are viewing galleries strategically placed throughout—you'll have no trouble finding them. In spring, the fields release the strong scent of green tea—the aroma is truly enchanting, and when the trees begin flowering, it's as if you've entered paradise.

Entry to Daehan Dawon Tea Plantation is 2,000 won. Below the fields, there is a wooded pond where you can enjoy green tea ice cream or just a cup of tea. The plantation also has restaurants (specializing in green tea food products), shops and other visitor facilities. If you're looking to purchase tea by bulk, this might be a good place to do it.

Besides Daehan Dawon Tea Plantation, there are several large plantations that continue all the way to the port village of Yulpo 율포. In fact, just five minutes up the road is Botjae Tea Plantation 봇재다원, which offers visitors magnificent views of terraced hillsides stretching all the way to the sea. In the plain below, Daehan Dawon's second plantation 대한다원 제2농장 is also worth a visit. 🍽 2,000 won ⏰ 9 am to 8 pm ☎ 061-852-4540 💻 www.dhdawon.com 🚌 There are frequent buses to Daehan Dawon Tea Plantation from Boseong Bus Terminal.

Yulpo Beach 율포해수욕장 & Yulpo Haesu Nokchatang 율포해수녹차탕

If walking amidst hillside green tea fields, drinking copious amounts of green tea and dining on green tea-flavored food still leaves you wanting, you can always take a relaxing bath in the stuff. After you've spent an hour or two at Daehan Dawon Tea Plantation, get on the same bus that took you there and take it to the beach village of Yulpo. Yulpo Beach is a pleasant enough place to stretch your legs—its sunrises are especially nice. The real reason to come here, however, is to relax in

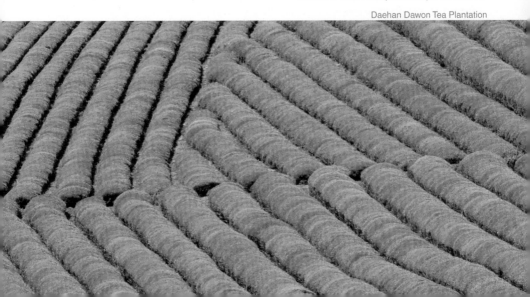

Daehan Dawon Tea Plantation

Yulpo Beach

Yulpo Haesu Nokchatang ("Yupo Sea Water Green Tea Spa"), a spa that specializes in baths of seawater and green tea.

While bathing in seawater mixed with green tea leaves might seem like an odd way to conclude an afternoon—and indeed, the smell takes a second to get used to—it's an incredibly rejuvenating experience. If taking a dip in a pool of green tea isn't your thing, there are also plain seawater and freshwater baths, too. Basic entrance to the spa is 3,500 won.

WHERE TO
STAY

If you like good food, you've come to the right place. The province of Jeollanam-do is famous for having some of the best food in the country. In Boseong, the specialty dish is *nokdon samgyeopsal* 녹돈삼겹살, grilled pork made from pigs fed green tea leaves. This, however, is only one of the many dishes into which Boseong restaurateurs have managed to inject green tea. In Beolgyo, the town specialty is *ggomak* 꼬막, the ark shell clam. These are picked out of the mud flats of the South Sea shore and served with vegetables and hot sauce.

WHAT TO
EAT

In downtown Boseong (a pleasant if fairly non-descript place), there are a number of motels and inns. Boseong Tourist Motel 보성관광모텔 (061-853-7474), close to the bus terminal—at 50,000 won a night (with Internet), is perfectly adequate. The beach town of Yulpo also has a large number of *minbak* (homestay) facilities available, too, and a very well-appointed condo, Boseong Dabeach Condo 보성다비치콘도 (061-850-1114), which accommodate four persons (rooms begin 180,000 won during the high season). During high season, you may want to book well in advance. Give the people at Boseong-gun's Tourism & Culture Division a call at 061-850-5224 for assistance.

TRANSPORT
INFO

Buses to Boseong depart from Seoul's Central City Bus Terminal. The trip takes about five hours. You can also take a five hour train ride from Seoul's Yongsan Station to Suncheon, and take an hour-long bus ride to Boseong from there (buses to Boseong depart from Suncheon Intercity Bus Terminal). There are frequent buses to Beolgyo from Boseong Bus Terminal.

Off the Beaten Track

Beolgyo 벌교 — Remains of a Tortured Past

About 45 minutes by bus east of downtown Boseong, on the road to Suncheon, is the village of Beolgyo, made famous as the setting for Korean novelist Jo Jung-rae's multi-volume magnum opus, *The Taebaek Mountains* (later made into a 1994 film by renowned director Im Kwon-taek).

The history of Boseong, so graphically depicted in the novel, is a microcosm of the history of the painful birth of the Republic of Korea. During the Japanese colonial period, the village was developed as a transportation hub connecting the interior with coastal ports. Colonial administrators also engaged in divisive land reclamation projects that widened the gap between the town's wealthy landlords and its poor peasantry. Liberation from colonial rule in 1945 changed little—badly needed land reform was not enacted and the landlords grew even wealthier.

Tensions hit a peak in 1948 when communist-led elements of the South Korean army mutinied and took control of nearby Yeosu and Suncheon. The mutineers spread out from Suncheon to take over nearby towns, including Beolgyo. Rightists and landlords who hadn't fled were executed. The mutiny collapsed, however, and rightist forces retook Beolgyo. Leftists (and suspected leftists) were rounded up and executed; those who managed to escape formed guerrilla bands in the surrounding mountains and launched raids into the village at night. An atmosphere of terror and violence held sway straight up to the Korean War.

Many of the sites described by Jo in his novel (or seen in Im's film) can still be found in Beolgyo. If you read Korean, Boseong Train Station carries maps of the relevant sites. They include Namdo Inn 남도여관, a Japanese black-shingled inn where counterinsurgency forces lodged; a Japanese bank used as a financial collective; Sohwa Bridge 소화다리, a colonial-era bridge under which rightists and leftists traded executions in the lead-up to the Korean War; a beautiful Joseon-era stone arch bridge (National Treasure No. 304); and perhaps best of all, Hyeon Buja Jip 현부자집, a beautiful landlord's home that, with its incorporation of Japanese influences, is perhaps a perfect representation of the times. From the second floor of its Japanese-style front gate, you can sit and look out over the reclaimed lands—built with Korean labor and farmed by Korean tenant farmers—that were at the heart of the tragedy that would come. Next to the Hyeon Buja Jip is a new museum dedicated to Jo Jung-rae and *The Taebaek Mountains*.

🚌 Buses to Beolgyo depart from Suncheon or Boseong bus terminals.

SUNCHEON 순천

The city of Suncheon, located along Korea's southwestern coast in the province of Jeollanam-do, is a bustling community of 250,000 people and a major commercial and educational center of the region. Known for its outstanding food and natural beauty, the town is home to Mt. Jogyesan 조계산, one of Korea's holiest peaks, on the slopes of which sit two of Korea's most exquisite Buddhist monasteries, Songgwangsa and Seonamsa. Not far from the temples is Naganeupseong Folk Village, Korea's best preserved Joseon-era walled town with its extensive collection of traditional thatched roof homes. Further down the road from there is the small hamlet of Beolgyo (see previous page), where visitors with a bit of background information can learn about and experience some of Korea's painful recent past.

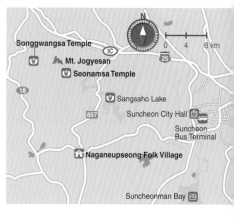

Registered with the Ramsar Convention, the tidal flats of Suncheonman Bay Ecological Park are an ecological treasure trove.

Paper lanterns, Songgwangsa Temple

Songgwangsa Temple 송광사

At the southern tip of Sobaeksan Mountains 소백산맥, the mountainous spine that cuts southwesterly across the southern half of the Korean Peninsula, is the 844 m peak of Mt. Jogyesan. One of Korea's most spiritually important mountains, it should come as no surprise that it's home to two of Korea's most important temples, Songgwangsa and Seonamsa.

The forests on the west side of Mt. Jogyesan embrace the massive Buddhist monastery complex of Songgwangsa or "Spreading Pine Temple." The monastery was most likely founded as a small temple during the latter part of the Silla Dynasty. In the Goryeo Dynasty, National Master Jinul established in 1200 a center for the study of Zen meditation and scriptural learning. This became one of the most important centers of what would eventually become Korea's dominant Buddhist denomination, the Jogye Order. In the roughly 180 years between its founding by Jinul and the founding of the anti-Buddhist Joseon dynasty, the monastery produced no less than 16 monks of the rank of National Master.

Since then, the temple has seen its ups and downs. Much of the precinct was reduced to ashes during the Korean War but a massive reconstruction project in 1988 restored the monastery to its former glory. Moreover, despite the calamities that have befallen the temple, not everything was lost—Songgwangsa Temple possesses many registered cultural properties, including three National Treasures and several Treasure-level properties.

Just before the main temple complex, cross over a picturesque covered bridge. Samcheonggyo Bridge 삼청교, built in 1707, is widely considered the temple's most beautiful attraction, and is featured in many paintings, drawings and photographs. The water beneath symbolically cleanses you as you pass over the bridge into the "other world" that is Songgwangsa Temple. The monastery is a huge complex centered on a broad courtyard. The massive Main Hall is built to hold the temple's large monk community and laypersons participating in the various Buddhist ceremonies.

Songgwangsa in not your usual temple. It is one of the "Three Treasures" of Korean Buddhism, the other two being Haeinsa Temple (near Daegu, see p546) and Tongdosa Temple (near Busan, see p597). It represents the Buddhist Sangha, or community of monks and laypeople. As such, it is home to a large community of Buddhist monks, and young monks from all over Korea come here to train. You'll even spot a foreign monk or two, since the monastery is home to an International Zen Center.

Evening may be the best time to be on hand. As the sun begins to set, the monks assemble for the evening *yebul*, a chanted homage to the Buddha and recitation of scripture (the Heart Sutra, to be specific). The chanting is proceeded by the playing of the temple drum and the ringing of the temple bell. Combined with the sounds of the mountain, far away from the hustle and bustle of civilization, it's an otherworldly experience that should not be missed.

🎫 3,000 won ⓒ 061-755-0107 🖱 www. songgangsa.org 🚌 Take Bus No. 111 from Suncheon Bus Terminal (1 hr 20 min).

Seonamsa Temple 선암사

Don't make the mistake of believing Songgwangsa is the only monastery on the mountain. On the east side of the peak is the ancient temple Seonamsa, or "Zen Rock Temple." From Songgwangsa Temple, it's a four or five hour hike to Seonamsa Temple, depending on whether you choose to bag the peak (recommended if you have the time) or take a lower path that cuts through a couple of passes. Whichever one you choose, be sure to bring water—there are no springs along the paths, although if you take the lower route, there is a barley rice restaurant

History and Culture

KOREAN BUDDHISM

One of Korea's traditional faiths, Buddhism still enjoys a healthy following—as of 2005, 22.5% of the population professed to be Buddhist, making it the country's second largest religion behind Christianity (29.2%). Korea's endless mountains are dotted with Buddhist temples and monasteries, and Buddhism has had a great impact on Korean philosophy, literature and arts.

Buddhism originated in India some 2,400 years ago, and came to the Korean peninsula via China in the fourth century. It first reached the Korean kingdoms of Goguryeo and Baekje (see p33) in 372 and 384, respectively. The new faith was warmly received in both kingdoms. It got a considerably colder reception in Silla, where it first arrived in the fifth century. According to legend, the turning point took place in 527, when a Buddhist court official by the name of Ichadon was martyred—when he was beheaded, it's said milk poured from his neck rather than blood. Under King Chinhung (r. 540-576), Buddhism was made the state religion in Silla.

When Silla unified Korea in 668, the peninsula experienced a golden age of peace and stability. Enjoying state patronage, Buddhism flourished in this environment. Countless Buddhist temples, such as Gyeongju's grand Bulguksa, were built throughout the country. Several of Korea's greatest Buddhist theologians—including the monks Wonhyo and Uisang—were active in this era, too. Towards the end of Silla, the practice of *Seon*— better known in the West as Zen—began to take root.

Buddhism continued to flourish under the Goryeo kingdom (918-1392), where it was the state religion. During this period, there was a movement toward reconciling scholastic Buddhism—with its emphasis on learning the Buddhist sutras—and Zen, which along the way where you can stop to eat or purchase a refreshing beverage.

Seonamsa's monks belong to the smaller Taego Order of Korean Buddhism, which broke away from the larger Jogye Order in 1970. Unlike the monks of the Jogye Order, monks of the Taego order may marry.

Seonamsa Temple is a large complex, although it seems considerably less spread out than Songgwangsa Temple and, as a result, exudes a friendlier, cozier feel. Unlike Songgwangsa, Seonamsa was not burnt down during the Korean War, so many of its buildings date back at least a century and are appropriately faded. The temple seeks not to dazzle but to harmonize with its natural surroundings, and it does to remarkable effect.

Path to Seonamsa Temple

emphasized enlightenment through meditation.

Unfortunately, however, state patronage also led to corruption and, by the end of the Goryeo era, Confucian scholars were attacking the vice and greed of Buddhist temples, which often controlled considerable land and wealth. When the Confucians took control of the country and established the Joseon kingdom (1392-1910), they placed difficult new conditions on Buddhism. They limited the number of temples, restricted who could join the monkhood and, most notably, drove temples into the mountains. Buddhist monks were barred from cities. The situation improved somewhat from the 16th century, however, thanks to the active participation of Buddhist monks as warriors in the Imjin War (1592-1598) against the Japanese.

In modern times, Buddhism has had to hold its own against the rising popularity of Christianity and a general trend towards secularism and materialism resulting from Korea's industrialization and modernization. Overall, it hasn't done too poorly—nearly half of Koreans who consider themselves religious are Buddhists. Moreover, even non-Buddhists generally recognize the rich heritage the religion has left Korea.

Like Christianity, Korean Buddhism is broken into several sects, the most prominent being the Jogye Order, which merges *Gyo* (scholastic Buddhism) and *Seon* (Zen). In keeping with Korean tradition, its monks are celibate. The order controls most of Korea's major Buddhist temples, including its headquarters, Jogyesa, in downtown Seoul.

Naganeupseong Folk Village

Seonamsa is certainly one of the most photogenic temples in Korea. The walk to the temple takes you through a thick forest and passes a running stream. Along the way, you'll come to two stately stone arch bridges. The second and larger of the two, Seungseongyo Bridge 승선교, is considered Korea's finest stone arch bridge and has been designated a National Treasure. Dating from 1713, the bridge is the subject and setting for many paintings, photographs and films. Other structures you'll want to check out are the front gate, Main Hall, stone pagodas in the main courtyard (designated Treasures), the exquisite Wontongjeon Hall 원통전, and an early 20th century outhouse—yes, an outhouse—that is both architecturally fascinating and functional (but be careful—it's a long drop if you fall in).

🏛 1,500 won ⓒ 061-754-5247 ⓦ www. seonamsa.net (KR) 🚌 Take Bus No. 1 from Suncheon Bus Terminal (50 min).

Naganeupseong Folk Village 낙안읍성

Not far from Seonamsa Temple is Naganeupseong Folk Village, Korea's best-preserved Joseon-era walled town. In the old days, most Korean towns were fortified to provide protection during those rough and ready times. In the case of the village of Nagan-eup, earthen walls were erected around the town in 1397 to protect it from marauding Japanese pirates. The earthworks were replaced with sturdier stone fortifications in 1424. Those walls still stand today (aided by restoration work in 1983); inside, more than 100 traditionally built homes and buildings beckon visitors looking for a sense of old Korea. The view from the top of the wall as you gaze over a sea of thatched roofs, the Nagan plain and the surrounding hillsides, is not to be missed.

Like Hahoe Village in Andong, most of the houses of this folk village are occupied—as of 2010, the community was home to 120 families. Many, however, have been converted into homestay facilities (*minbak*) and/or restaurants, and there is a slightly touristy feel about the place, although by no means oppressively so.

🕐 9 am to 6 pm (9 am to 5 pm in Dec to Jan) 🏛 2,000 won ⓒ 061-749-3347 ⓦ www.nagan. or.kr 🚌 Take Bus No. 61, 68 from Suncheon Bus Terminal (40 min).

Suncheonman Bay Ecological Park 순천만자연생태공원

One of the world's five largest coastal wetlands, Suncheonman Bay Ecological Park, consists of 39.8 km of nearly pristine coastline and 22.6 km² of mud flats, populated by vast fields of reeds (210 hectares worth), wetland plants, 25 species of rare bird (including the Black-faced Spoonbill, Nordmann's Greenshank, Spoonbill Sandpiper, and Relict Gull) and other forms of aquatic life. It is one of Korea's most beautiful ecological sites, and in 2006 was added to the Ramsar Convention on Wetlands. If you're in southern Korea, it really is a must-visit, especially in autumn when the reeds turn golden as they bloom, and winter, when large flocks of migratory birds descend upon the bay. The sunsets here are truly inspiring, as is early morning when the fog and mist create an enchanting landscape.

The park is equipped with walking paths that take you through the reed fields and strategically placed observatories providing bird's-eye views of the natural majesty below. The best view of all is from Yongsan Observatory 용산전망대, with views of the "S Line" of Dongcheon Stream 동천 as it gently meanders through the mud flats to the bay. Also eye-catching is the population of *Suaeda japonica*, a marsh weed that turns a vibrant red in autumn.

In addition to the ecological splendor, the park has a museum and information hall where you learn more about the place. There are also tour boats operating mornings only that take you down Dongcheon Stream into the bay—these depart from a dock near the museum, and cost 4,000 won (no cruises on Mondays).

⊙ 9 am to sunset 💰 1,000 won ✆ 061-749-3006~7 🌐 www.suncheonbay.go.kr 🚍 Take Bus No. 66 or 67 at Suncheon Bus Terminal.

WHAT TO EAT

As is the case in the rest of the province, Suncheon is a great place to eat. One of the better—and cheaper—places to fill up is Heungdeok Sikdang 흥덕식당 (061-744-9208), which serves a good *baekban* 백반 (rice, soup and side dishes) for 7,000 won. For something a bit more substantial, try Geumbin Hoegwan 금빈회관 (061-744-5554), which does a fine *tteokgalbi jeongsik* 떡갈비정식 (fried meat patty with lots of side dishes) for 12,000 won (*dwaeji* or pork) or 30,000 won (*hanu* or Korean beef) per person. It can found behind Suncheon City Hall, not far from Suncheon Bus Terminal. If you have money to burn and like to eat, Daewon Sikdang 대원식당 (061-744-3582), also near Suncheon Bus Terminal, does a wonderful Jeollado-style *jeongsik* for 80,000 won (lunch) or 100,000 won (dinner)—meals are for four people; be prepared to do some serious eating. If you're visiting Songgwangsa Temple, there are plenty of fine eateries at the tourist village in front of the temple. Around Suncheonman Bay, a number of restaurants specialize in a local favorite, *jjangttungeotang* 짱뚱어탕, a spicy, rich soup made from boiled mud hopper. Solo diners can usually get a bowl for 10,000 won but if you're with friends, try the *jjangttungeo jeongol* 짱뚱어전골, a heartier stew serving for two for 30,000 won.

WHERE TO STAY

If you're staying downtown, the usual places—i.e., near Suncheon Station and Suncheon Bus Terminal—have lots of cheap and mid-range places to stay for 40,000–80,000 won a night. If you're looking for something more upscale, try EcoGrad Hotel Suncheon 에코그라드호텔 (061-811-0000), west of Suncheon Station. A lovely 18-story building, it's a Suncheon landmark and comes complete with a stylish and very relaxing Roman bath. Rooms begin at 220,000 won a night. For something more Korean in atmosphere, on the road to Suncheonman Bay there's a Korean-style *hanok*, Haeryongseong Gotaek 순천만해룡성고택 (061-744-1760), which has been renovated for use as a guesthouse. Rooms sleeping up to 10 go for 100,000 won a night during the low season. Also on the road to Suncheonman Bay is another *hanok* pension, Galdaebat Sarangchae 갈대밭 사랑채 (010-8490-6626). The rooms here have beds. They can also pick you up from Suncheon Station or Suncheon Bus Terminal if you give them a ring after 9 pm). Rooms go for 80,000 won on a weekend. Near Naganeupseong Fortress and Beolgyo, there's Han Sang-hun Gaok 한상훈가옥 (061-857-5064), a lovely old Korean *hanok* home that was moved to its current location from Seoul, where it was in danger of being town down to make way for road construction. The interior has been renovated, but in a way that preserves the essence and spirit of the *hanok*. At 150,000 won a night, it's somewhat pricey but highly recommended. To get there, you'll probably want to take a cab from Beolgyo or Naganeupseong Fortress.

The sunrises from Hyangiram Hermitage are worth the effort.

YEOSU 여수

Yeosu has always been a favorite for those game to explore Korea in greater depth. Take in the view from Jasan Park and you'll know why. Spread out before you is a breathtaking landscape. Here, the rugged mountains slope down to the emerald waters of the South Sea. Further out, jade islands dot the coastline. Along the hillside, rows of houses sit precariously while ships steam in and out of the fine natural harbor. Positively idyllic (and not a bad place to spend a weekend), Yeosu is undoubtedly one of the country's underrated destinations.

Blessed with one of the finest natural environments in Korea, Yeosu is a pungent stew of rustic, small-town Korean charm and salty port-town atmosphere, served with a slice of history and delectable Jeolla-do cuisine. If you're into ecological tourism, the town's countless islands and the pristine wetlands of the nearby Suncheonman Bay offer countless opportunities. For view seekers, the city's hills and mountains afford splendid vistas of the port and its surrounding coastline, while the Buddhist hermitage of Hyangiram—with its dramatic location perched high atop granite cliffs overlooking the sea—is arguably the finest location in Korea to take in the sunset. Less adventurous types can simply kick back or perhaps take a stroll along one of the city's fine beaches, breathing deep the wonderful seaside atmosphere.

Layout

Yeosu is located on the Yeosu Peninsula 여수반도, which juts down from the city of Suncheon on Korea's South Sea coast. In addition to the mountainous peninsula, which is connected to the mainland by a narrow isthmus, Yeosu is blessed with some 317 islands, many of which are included in Dadohae Maritime National Park and Hallyeo Maritime National Park 한려해상국립공원.

Yeosu actually has two downtowns, the legacy of the 1998 merging of the cities of Yeosu and Yeocheon 여천. For tourists, the old Yeosu downtown (and more specifically, the Central Rotary), located on a natural harbor at the southern end of the peninsula, is one of the most interesting—it's here that you'll find the train station, ferry terminal and most of the fine views (the intercity bus terminal, however, is a bit outside downtown).

Most of downtown Yeosu is accessible by foot or taxi. Some locations, like Hyangiram Hermitage, require local bus rides, while the islands, logically enough, require boat trips. With its fine harbor and strategic location guarding the waterways of southern Korea, Yeosu has served throughout the ages as a port and naval base. During the Imjin War of 1592–1598, the port served as the first naval headquarters of the legendary Admiral Yi Sun-sin; Korea's revolutionary "turtle ships," the world's first ironclad warships, were built here.

Today, Yeosu is home to 293,000 residents and has become a major industrial and logistical center—the city boasts a large fishing fleet, cargo ships from all over the world call in regularly, and just nearby looms Gwangyang Steel Works 광양제철소, one of the

Yeosu Bus Terminal · Seokcheonsa Temple
Mt. Goraksan
Yeosu Stn.
Mt. Mangmasan
17
Mt. Ganggunsan
Yeosuhang Port
Odongdo Island
Jinnamgwan Hall
Jasan Park
Mt. Gubongsan
Yeosu Passenger
Ferry Terminal
Namsan Park
Dolsan Bridge · Dolsan Park
N
Dolsando Island
Geomundo, Baekdo Island
0 500 m 1 km
Hyangiram
Hermitage

world's largest—perhaps the largest—and most modern steel mills in the world. Despite this, Yeosu differs from the massive industrial ports of Busan and Masan in that it has managed to preserve its provincial atmosphere. Like a small fishing village, things in Yeosu are friendlier and much more relaxed.

Jinnamgwan Hall 진남관

The first spot you'll want to check out is the massive Jinnamgwan Hall, located in the heart of downtown Yeosu overlooking the harbor. Designated National Treaure No. 304, Jinnamgwan Hall is the largest single-story wood building in Korea. The massive structure—supported by 68 imposing pillars—was built in 1598 and used as a state guesthouse and naval headquarters; it was from this site during the Imjin War that Admiral Yi engineered several of his victories over the invading Japanese. Noted previous guests included Hendrick Hamel, the 17th century Dutch sailor whose journal provided the West with its first descriptions of the so-called Hermit Kingdom. As you'd expect from a former naval headquarters, the hall provides a good view of the harbor, including the landmark Dolsan Bridge.

From Yeosu Intercity Bus Terminal, take Bus No. 24, 35, 73, 84, 88 or 102 and get off at Jinnamgwan Hall. From Yeosu Station, it's a short taxi or local bus ride away.

Dolsan Bridge 돌산대교
& Odongdo Island 오동도

The Dolsan Bridge, which links the mainland with Dolsando Island 돌산도, is Korea's largest cable-stayed bridge. It's also one of the country's most picturesque

Jinnamgwan Hall, Admiral Yi Sun-sin's wartime headquarters

spans, especially at night when it's lit up in rotating schemes of 50 different colors. Good views of the bridge and of Yeosuhang Port 여수항 can be had from either end of the bridge (or, for that matter, the bridge itself), although the recommended photo spot is Dolsan Park 돌산공원 on Dolsando Island, especially at sundown.

Odongdo is a small island connected to the mainland by a long breakwater. The island actually marks the entry to Hallyeo Maritime National Park, and is famous for its camellia trees, which produce beautiful red blossoms in spring. Strolling amidst the island's thick forests makes for a pleasant way to spend an afternoon. Wedged between the hills and the sea, Yeosu has a number of scenic spots. The hilltop Jasan Park 자산공원 is the city's most popular photo spot, providing awesome views of the harbor and nearby islands, including Odongdo. The park comes complete with a statue of Admiral Yi Sun-sin, as well.

Another nice spot to take in the city is Seokcheonsa 석천사, a Buddhist temple in the hillside overlooking downtown. The prime viewing spot is a short hike from the temple, past some public outdoor exercise equipment and near an old grave site.

🚌 Dolsan Bridge: Take Bus No. 102, 111, 113 or 999 from Yeosu Intercity Bus Terminal. Odongdo & Jasan Park: Take Bus No. 102, 111, 113 or 999 from Yeosu Intercity Bus Terminal. Seokcheonsa: Take Bus No. 333 from Yeosu Station and get off at Jungang Girls High School 중앙여자고등학교 and hike to the temple from there. From Yeosu Intercity Bus Terminal, take Bus No. 113 and get off at Jungang Girls High School.

Hyangiram Hermitage 향일암

Aside from Odongdo Island, Hyangiram Hermitage is probably Yeosu's most popular tourist attraction. Perched high above the crashing waves of the South Sea, the temple—founded by the great Silla monk Wonhyo, in 644—offers some of the best sunrises and sunsets in all of Korea.

Dolsan Bridge

The hermitage was recently reconstructed after a fire in 2009.

The hike to the temple takes you up a steep flight of steps and through some narrow rock gorges—to witness the sunrise, you'll be walking a bit in the dark, which can be a bit spooky. The hermitage itself is built into the rocky face of Mt. Geumsan 금오산, and offers spectacular views of the sea

Odongdo Island

Hyangiram Hermitage, recently restored after a 2009 fire

and coastline, with the best perspectives from Gwaneumjeon Hall 관음전, the highest hall in the complex.

If you go for the sunrise, there will likely be some chanting going on at the hermitage when you arrive, imparting a remarkably spiritual ambience to the experience.

🚌 Take a bus from Yeosu Bus Terminal (1 hr).

Geomundo 거문도 & Baekdo 백도

Off the coast of Yeosu lie some 317 islands, many of which are part of Korea's national park system. This is an extremely scenic part of the country, so if time permits, you'd be a fool not to take a boat out and enjoy some of it. The ferry terminal is where you'll want to begin.

Geomundo island (a two-and-half hour boat trip from the mainland) is, inarguably,

BEACHES GALORE

It's not Hawaii but Yeosu's got beaches aplenty. Just north of Yeosu Station is Korea's only "black sand" beach, Manseongni Beach 만성리해수욕장. The black sand is said to alleviate a number of ailments: bury yourself up to the neck as beachcombers are likely to do in the summers.

Other smaller beaches include Jangdeung Beach 장등해변, Sado Beach 사도해변, Bangjukpo Beach 방죽포해변 and Ando Beach 안도해변. There are more, of course, if you're willing to do a little exploring.

one of the most interesting islands in Korea. Aside from its beautiful natural scenery, the island has a fascinating history, including a

EXPO 2012 YEOSU KOREA

History and Culture

Yeosu is not only a charming place to visit in its own right: it's also the host city of International Exposition Yeosu Korea 2012 (Expo 2012 Yeosu Korea). Taking place at a newly built venue site overlooking Hallyeo Marine National Park and Odongdo Island, Expo 2012 Yeosu Korea promises to be an opportunity to experience a bit of the future today. The theme of the Expo 2012 is "The Living Ocean and Coast"; accordingly, the focus will be on boosting the world's understanding and appreciation of the Earth's oceans and coasts. Visitors will see and experience cutting-edge maritime science and technology from all over the globe, learn about the miracles of our oceans and coastlines, and marvel at the venue itself, a showcase of seaside architecture. (May 12 to Aug 12, http://eng.expo2012.kr)

영국군묘지
←100M

Path to British graves, Geomundo Island (left), Lighthouse, Geomundo Island

brief period under British occupation (when it was known as Port Hamilton). In 1885, the Royal Navy—seeking to ward off Russia—seized the island as a naval base. The British would leave just two years later, but they left behind the graves of nine British sailors and marines, of which the markers for two still remain.

The island is also home to a beautiful old lighthouse (one of Korea's first), built in 1905. It's a bit of a hike to get to, though, so bring comfortable shoes.

Another popular island destination is Baekdo, a collection of 39 uninhabited islands not far from Geomundo island. While one cannot land on the islands—they are a protected ecological environment—they still make for beautiful viewing from a cruise ship from Geomundo island, with their dramatic rock formations plunging into the sea.

🚢 Ferries to Geomundo depart from Yeosu Ferry Terminal, and take about 2 hours, 30 minutes. Ferries depart at 7:40 am and 1 pm. To get to the ferry terminal, take Bus No. 999 from Yeosu Station and get off at Jungang Market 중앙시장 or Bus No. 88 from Yeosu Intercity Bus Terminal and get off at Gyodong Daeseong Drugstore 교동대성약국.

WHAT TO EAT

Yeosu is a major fishing port, so it should surprise no one that fish is the local specialty. You'll be overwhelmed by fish restaurants all over the waterfront area—if the place is full of people, it usually means you should eat there, too. Other local dishes include *dolsangat kimchi* 돌산잣김치 (Dolsan mustard leaf kimchi) and, on Geomundo Island, largehead hairtail or cutlassfish (*galchi* 갈치 in Korean).

WHERE TO STAY

Yeosu is chockfull of low to mid-ranged motels, so finding a place to stay for 30,000 to 50,000 won a night shouldn't present much of a problem—Motel Sky 스카이모텔 (061-662-7784), located near the Central Rotary, comes recommended. If you'd like to stay somewhere a bit classier, there are a number of tourist hotels in town, including Yeosu Beach Tourist Hotel 여수비치관광호텔 (061-663-2011), Yeosu Tourist Hotel 여수관광호텔 (061-662-3131), Chambord Tourist Hotel 샹보르관광호텔 (061-662-6111) and Bellagio Tourist Hotel 벨라지오관광호텔 (061-686-7977). If you're feeling flush, a night in Bellagio's Presidential Suite will set you back 320,000 won.

TRANSPORT INFO

Unless you live nearby or are flying into Yeosu Airport (there are flights to Yeosu from Gimpo Airport), it's quite a trek to Yeosu. There are frequent trains to Yeosu from Seoul's Yongsan Station—the trip, however, takes five hours from Seoul (KTX: 3 hr 40 min). Likewise, you can take a bus to Yeosu from Seoul's Central City Bus Terminal; either way, it's a long trip—about five and half hours.

DAEGU &
GYEONGSANGBUK-DO

HIGHLIGHTS

- Spend at least a couple of days in Gyeongju, an outdoor museum of ancient Korean history

- Hang out in Andong & Hahoe Village, where Joseon Dynasty Confucianism lives on

- Get your urban culture fix in the fast-paced metropolis of Daegu

- Head to Haeinsa Temple to marvel at its UNESCO-registered wood blocks of the Buddhist canon, carved in the 13th century

- Spend the Buddha's Birthday at Mungyeong's Bongamsa Temple, an ancient Zen monastery open just once a year

- Soak your aches and pains away in one of Uljin's famous hot springs

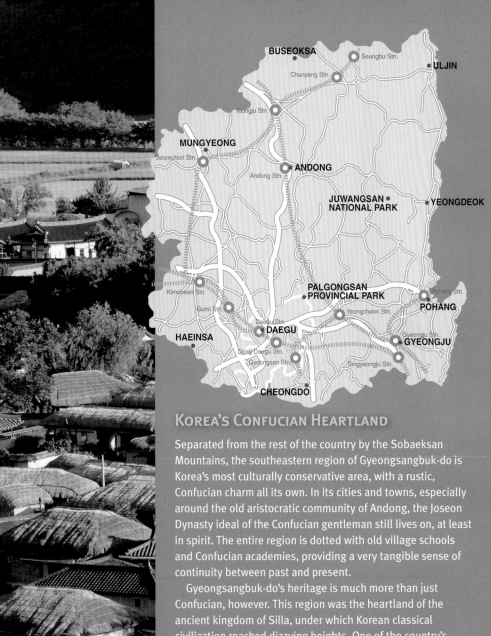

BUSEOKSA

Seungbu Stn.

Chunyang Stn.

ULJIN

Yeongju Stn.

MUNGYEONG

Jeomchon Stn.

ANDONG

Andong Stn.

JUWANGSAN
NATIONAL PARK

YEONGDEOK

PALGONGSAN
PROVINCIAL PARK

Pohang Stn.

Kimcheon Stn.

Gumi Stn.

Yeongcheon Stn.

POHANG

Daegu Stn.

DAEGU

Gyeongju Stn.

GYEONGJU

HAEINSA

Dong-Daegu Stn.

Gyeongsan Stn.

Singyeongju Stn.

CHEONGDO

KOREA'S CONFUCIAN HEARTLAND

Separated from the rest of the country by the Sobaeksan Mountains, the southeastern region of Gyeongsangbuk-do is Korea's most culturally conservative area, with a rustic, Confucian charm all its own. In its cities and towns, especially around the old aristocratic community of Andong, the Joseon Dynasty ideal of the Confucian gentleman still lives on, at least in spirit. The entire region is dotted with old village schools and Confucian academies, providing a very tangible sense of continuity between past and present.

Gyeongsangbuk-do's heritage is much more than just Confucian, however. This region was the heartland of the ancient kingdom of Silla, under which Korean classical civilization reached dizzying heights. One of the country's most visited tourist destinations, the old Silla capital of Gyeongju is a virtual outdoor museum of Korean history — you could spend months exploring the place. In fact, the same could be said for the province as a whole, one of the most heritage-rich in the entire country.

Andong Hahoe Village

Beautiful Gyesan-dong Cathedral, built in 1902

DAEGU 대구

Home to more than 2.5 million souls, Daegu is the political, commercial and industrial heart of the surrounding province of Gyeongsangbuk-do. For much of Korea's modern history, it was also the most politically powerful city in the country; the city and its environs have produced three of Korea's presidents, including long-serving strongman Park Chung-hee.

To many Koreans, Daegu is synonymous with extreme weather, conservative politics, women renowned for their beauty, and excellent apples. For travelers, it's a great transportation hub, with good rail and road connections to destinations throughout the region. In fact, it's the primary gate to two UNESCO World Heritage Sites, the marvelous Buddhist monastery of Haeinsa Temple and the ancient Silla Kingdom capital of Gyeongju, a virtual outdoor museum of classical Korean civilization.

What many travelers overlook, however, is that the city has its own particular charms, including a fascinating Korean medicine market, old American missionary homes, historic Catholic holy sites and a bustling nightlife. Overlooking the city is the sacred mountain of Palgongsan, with its many Buddhist temples and shrines, while just outside of town in the rural suburb of Dalseong, you'll find some delightful reminders of Korea's Confucian past, including a Confucian school, a Confucian shrine and a 19th century clan village.

History

Daegu took its current name in AD 757, and was an important town in the Silla Dynasty. It really came into its own as a city in the Joseon Dynasty, when in 1601 it was made the administrative capital of the province of Gyeongsang-do, which includes today's Gyeongsangbuk-do and Gyeongsangnam-do. Daegu became a large walled city, and was a major transportation junction on the old Dongnae (today's Busan)–Seoul road, with arterial connections to the important fortress towns of Jinju and Gyeongju. It was in the Joseon Dynasty that the city's famous Eastern medicine market also developed.

In 1896, the province of Gyeongsang-do was divided into two, and Daegu became the capital of the new province of Gyeongsangbuk-do. At the turn of the 20th century, Japanese merchants and American missionaries began setting up in the city, especially after the opening of the Seoul–Busan railway in 1905 with a stop in Daegu. During the Japanese colonial era, the city's modernization picked up steam, with modern schools and hospitals established, but at great cost to the city's historical and cultural heritage. Significantly, the city's historic walls were torn down without a trace.

Korea regained its independence from Japan in 1945, but this was soon followed by national division and the Korean War. Daegu was just one of a handful of cities, most notably Busan, that were not captured by the North Koreans at the start of the war, and it briefly served as the South Korean capital. The area around it, however, saw some of the most brutal fighting of the war as UN and South Korean forces established the so-called

Busan Perimeter just to the west and north of the city. In August 1950, the North Koreans launched a concerted effort to break through the perimeter and take the city, but were stopped by the Americans and South Koreans in a mountain valley just north of city in the Battle of the Bowling Alley.

After the war, Daegu started to flourish. A succession of three Korean presidents, Park Chung-hee, Chun Doo-hwan and Roh Tae-woo, hailed from Gyeongsangbuk-do (Roh from Daegu itself), and the city became a hub within a major industrial belt that included the surrounding cities of Pohang (steel), Gumi (electronics), Ulsan (automobiles and shipbuilding), and Busan (heavy industries and port facilities). Daegu itself became the center of Korea's textile industry, an important engine of the country's early growth. This legacy, along with the region's famous cultural conservatism, explains why today the city is considered a bastion of Korea's conservative political parties. Since the 1990s, Daegu's economy has taken something of a hit due to the decline of Korea's textile industry in the face of competition from China. In response, the city has poured considerable effort in promoting its fashion industry. In 2011, its international profile received a boost when it hosted the 13th IAAF World Championships in Athletics.

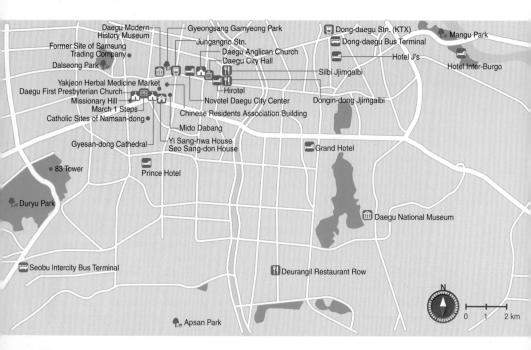

Daegu Duryu Park

Layout

Daegu sits in a basin, with peaks of 1,000 m or more to the north (Mt. Palgongsan 팔공산) and to the south (Mt. Biseulsan 비슬산). In fact, right in the south of town is Mt. Apsan 앞산, a 600 m peak that serves as an urban park (much like Mt. Namsan does for Seoul). This unique topography is largely responsible for the city's notorious weather—the basin traps hot air in summer, and cold air in winter. The city is largely oval-shaped, with Mt. Apsan to the south and the Geumhogang River 금호강, a tributary of the Nakdonggang River, flowing to the north and west. The old city—where most of the interesting sites are located—is smack-dab in the middle of it all, around Daegu Station.

Most KTX trains from Seoul and Busan arrive at Dongdaegu Station which is located in the east of town (along with nearby Daegu Express Bus Terminal), which means you'll need to take a subway to get downtown. There are two subway lines in Daegu: Line 1 goes northeast to southwest, while Line 2 goes east to west. A third line, a monorail, is under construction and is scheduled for completion in 2014. Just to the southwest of town is the county of Dalseong 달성군. Administratively speaking, it has been part of Daegu Metropolitan City since 1995, but in reality, it's a piece of rural, old-time Korea, and about as far removed atmosphere-wise from Daegu's concrete jungle as you can get.

83 Tower 83타워
& Daegu Duryu Park 대구두류공원

Daegu's most visible landmark is 83 Tower (formerly Woobang Tower), a 202 meter tower where you can get the best views of the city. At the top, there's a revolving restaurant serving surf & turf and the Sky Lounge wine bar/café, along with an observation deck. Admission for the deck is 5,000 won, although you get just as good views from the Sky Lounge, which is at the very top floor anyway. There's also an ice rink on the bottom floor—5,000 won admission, with rentals available.

The tower is surrounded by a wooded, grassy park, an amusement park called E-World 이월드, baseball and football stadiums, an outdoor concert hall, and a

SkyJump!

If you suffer from thrill-seeking behavior, you're definitely going to want to give 83 Tower's SkyJump a try...Think BASE jumping but, like bungee jumping, attached to a wire thong that will guide you safely to your landing target at the bottom of the tower. You start your descent from a platform on the 77th floor, and for the first 129 meters of the drop, you'll be falling at 75 km per hour. After that, you'll gradually slow down until you touch bottom. There's no more exhilarating—or insane—way to see the city.

There are only four cities in the world with SkyJumps—Auckland (where it began, in 2001), Macao, Daegu (starting in 2006), and Las Vegas. Cost is 40,000 won, including a souvenir photo.

snow sledding slope in winter. It's also home to Daegu Culture and Arts Center 대구문화예술회관 and Seongdangmot Pond 성당못, which makes for a very pleasant stroll.

🕐 10 am to 10 pm (restaurant and lounge are open until 11 pm) 🚇 Seongdangmot Station, Subway Line 1 or Duryu Station, Subway Line 2. Either way requires about a 20 minute walk.
📞 053-625-1949 🖥 www.eworld.kr

Daegu Apsan Park 대구앞산공원

What Mt. Namsan is to Seoul, Mt. Apsan is to Daegu. This mountain park, which tops off at around 660 m, is criss-crossed with hiking trails and contains mineral springs, sports fields, a traditional archery range, horse stable, memorial towers and other leisure and culture facilities. You get great

Panoramic view of Daegu and drawing of new observation point in Apsan Park

Daegu National Museum (left), Yeongnam Jeilgwan Gate

views of the city from the top. There are some Buddhist temples hidden in the valleys, too. If you don't feel like hiking to the top, there's a scenic cable car—6,000 won round trip.

🚌 Take Bus No. 410 from Exit 3 of Anjirang Station, Daegu Subway Line 1.

Daegu National Museum 국립대구박물관

This pleasant museum was opened in 1994 to collect, conserve and study the cultural heritage of Daegu and the western and northern parts of Gyeongsangbuk-do—in other words, the entire province, except for Gyeongju (which has its own excellent national museum). It has a collection of 30,000 artifacts, including three beautiful gilt bronze Buddhist statues from the Unified Silla Era (National Treasures No. 182, 132 and 184), unearthed from a hillside in the town of Gumi during construction work in 1976.

🕐 9 am to 6 pm (7 pm on weekends and holidays). Closed Mondays. 🚌 Free (admission for special exhibits) 🚌 From Daegu Express Bus Terminal (near Dongdaegu Station), take Bus No. 514 or 814. From Daegu Station, take Bus No. 349 or 524. 📞 053-768-6051 🌐 http://daegu. museum.go.kr

Mangu Park 망우공원

This park in the eastern part of town, on the bank of the Geumhogang River 금호강, is dedicated to the famed Korean general Gwak Jae-woo, one of Korea's greatest military leaders during the Japanese invasions of 1592–1598. There is the picturesque reconstruction of Yeongnam Jeilgwan 영남제일관, the old south gate of Daegu's much missed city walls, which were pulled down by the Japanese in 1907. The grand two-story gate you see was built in 1980, and it's nowhere near its original location, but it still gives you a sense of what the old city walls must have looked like way back when. Also in the park is Joyanghoegwan 조양회관, a pretty two-story brick building from 1922 where independence leaders lectured local youth to boost national consciousness while Korea languished under Japanese rule. It is now a independence movement history hall.

🚌 Take Bus Ganseon No. 651 from Daegu Station, or Bus Bukgu No. 3 from Dongdaegu Station, and get off at Dongchon Yuwonji 동천유원지.

Old Daegu Historic Walks

In recent years, Daegu has taken a renewed interest in its early modern history. It's best to start your tour at Gyeongsang Gamyeong Park near Exit 4, Jungangno Station, Line 1. Most of these sites are located between the station and Dalseong Park to the west. You can find signs written in English and Korean pointing history walkers in the right direction throughout. You can also see the "Downtown Modern Culture Tour" map at the KTO homepage (english.visitkorea.or.kr).

Gyeongsang Gamyeong Park 경상감영공원 The pleasant little park near Jungangno Station 중앙로역, Daegu Subway Line 1, was the site of the old governor's complex during the Joseon Dynasty when Daegu was the provincial capital of Gyeongsang-do. Much of the old government complex has been lost but there are still two handsome wooden halls around, including the old governor's residence and an office.

Daegu Modern History Museum 대구근대역사관 Built in 1932 as a Japanese bank, this stately colonial-style structure has recently been converted into a museum dedicated to Daegu's 20th century history.
⊕ 9 am to 7 pm. Closed Mondays.

Chinese Residents Association Building 대구 화교협회 Daegu does have a Chinatown, albeit a small one. On the grounds of the Chinese Elementary School, you can find the Chinese Residents Association Building, a beautiful red brick building from 1929. Interestingly, it's said the bricks were baked in Pyongyang and its wood taken from the forests of the Geumgangsan Mountains.

Mido Dabang (Teahouse) 미도다방 It's not really that old, but this Korean-style coffee house is a throwback to yesteryear, and is popular with local granddads. Order a coffee along with a plate of Korean snacks and soak in the atmosphere.

Yakjeon Herbal Medicine Market 대구약령시장 Probably Daegu's best known tourist spot,

the 350-year-old Yakjeon Herbal Medicine Market used to be one of the biggest herbal medicine markets in Asia, supplying not just Korea, but China, Manchuria, Japan and Russia. Southeastern Korea's mountains and the Nakdonggang River Valley were natural treasure troves of medicinal herbs, and Daegu was the place to sell them. During the Joseon Dynasty, it used to be said if you couldn't find the medicine you were looking for in Seoul, you should go to Daegu. Traditionally, the market met twice a year—in the second and tenth months of the lunar calender. In the 20th century, however, it took on its current incarnation, an alleyway lined one end to the other with herbal medicine shops. These can be fascinating places to explore—you'll come across all sorts of exotic remedies including, of course, the wonder root ginseng. The aromas generated by the

Yangyeongsi Herb Medicine Festival

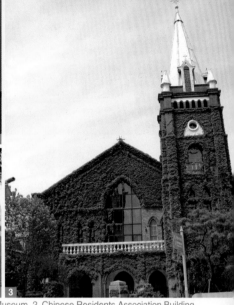

1. Daegu Modern History Museum 2. Chinese Residents Association Building
3. Daegu First Presbyterian Church

medicine brewing process can be quite intoxicating. There are about 50 herbal medicine stores, 25 herbal clinics and 20 ginseng shops. Next to Daegu First Presbyterian Church, there's a museum, the Yangnyeongsi Oriental Medicine Cultural Center 약령시한의학문화관, with exhibits about the history of herbal medicine and Daegu's market. Smaller, but more interesting, is the Petite Joong-Ang Family Museum 작은중앙가족박물관 (070-8977-6606), run by a family who has been practicing herbal medicine for three generations. In addition to the family's old herbalist equipment, they also do free herbal medicine consultations, provide visitors with herbal tea and can provide explanations in English. Every May, the market hosts the Daegu Yangyeongsi Herb Medicine Festival 대구약령시한방문화축제, with cultural festivals, herbal tea samplings, free check-ups, body-type analysis and more.

Former Site of Samsung Trading Company 옛삼성상회터 On this little patch of Daegu in 1938, local businessman Lee Byung-chull founded Samsung Trading Company, a small company that traded in groceries and manufactured noodles. Seven decades later, Samsung Group runs a multinational corporate empire that includes the world's largest electronics manufacturer and the second largest shipbuilder. The old Samsung Trading Company house was torn down in 1997, but Samsung Group recently spared some loose change to build a small commemorative park in its honor, with a model of the old office/warehouse, some bamboo trees and a few plaques (in Korean and English) recounting the founding of the firm.

Daegu First Presbyterian Church 대구제일교회 American missionaries set up shop in Daegu quite early. In 1893, Rev. William M. Baird appeared in Daegu's Yakjeon Herbal Medicine Market, handing out pamphlets on the street. This was the beginning of Daegu First Presbyterian Church. Originally a *hanok* church, it was rebuilt in mixed Korean-Western style in 1907, and again in 1933 as the current Gothic brick structure. The steeple was added in 1937. In addition to founding the

1,2. Gyesan-dong Cathedral 3. Switzer House, Cheongna Hall
4. Catholic Cemetery, Namsan-dong 5. Missionary Cemetery, Cheongna Hall

church, Presbyterian missionaries founded Daegu's first Western hospital and school, taking an important role in the city's modernization.

Gyesan-dong Cathedral 계산동성당 When Gyesan-dong Cathedral was completed in 1902, it became Daegu's first Western-style building and the first Western-style Catholic church in the Yeongnam region. It was designed by Father Achille Paul Robert of the Paris Overseas Missions Society to replace a thatched-roof Korean-style church that had burned down. Chinese stonemasons who'd helped build Myeong-dong Cathedral in Seoul were entrusted with its construction. Of particular note are the beautiful twin spires that were added in 1918, and the beautiful rose window with its intricate flower design. As the central church of the Diocese of Daegu, it has played a central role in the development of Catholicism in the Korean southeast.

Cheongna Hill 청라언덕 On the hill across from Gyesan-dong Cathedral is the new Daegu First Presbyterian Church, a massive dual-spired church that almost seems to

have been built to compete with its Catholic neighbor. Behind the church, however, are three lovely American missionary homes that were built around 1910. The brick bungalows were built atop a breezy hill with views of the city, complete with gardens, lawns and veranda. One of the homes, the Switzer House, has a pretty Korean-style roof. The foundation stones of the homes come from Daegu's old city walls, which were pulled down in 1907. The homes are now used as museums to the missionaries' early medical efforts. Near the bungalows is a small garden cemetery where several of the missionaries and their children are buried. Also nearby is Dongsan Medical Center 동산의료원, founded by Presbyterian medical missionary Dr. Woodbridge O. Johnson in 1899. The facade of a 1931 reconstruction still remains.

March 1 Steps 3.1운동 계단 Leading up to the missionary homes is an old flight of steps where students—trying to avoid detection by the Japanese police—moved into position before the mass independence protests of March 1, 1919.

Yi Sang-hwa House 이상화 고택 This Korean *hanok* was the home of famed Daegu poet Yi Sang-hwa from 1939 to 1943, when he died at the age of 42. Yi's poetry reflected nationalist despair at life under Japanese colonial rule. His home was almost demolished, but was preserved as a museum after a campaign collected a million signatures.

Seo Sang-don House 서상돈 고택 Just next to Yi Sang-hwa House is Seo Sang-don House, another lovely *hanok* home. Seo was a wealthy Daegu man who in 1907 started the National Debt Repayment Movement, a collection campaign that aimed to repay Korea's debt to Japan and preserve the nation's independence.

Catholic Sites of Namsan-dong 남산동 가톨릭타운 In Namsan-dong, around Catholic University of Daegu, you'll find what is sometimes called "Catholic Town," complete with an old Catholic seminary, the bishop's office, convent and shrine to Our Lady of Lourdes. St. Justin's Catholic Seminary 성유스티노신학교기념관 was built in 1914 on orders from the first Bishop of Daegu, Msg. Florian-Jean-Baptiste Démange. Its design was entrusted to Father Victor Louis Poisnel, the man responsible for Jeondong Cathedral, Gupo-dong Catholic Church and some of Myeongdong Cathedral. Unfortunately, most of St. Justin's Seminary has disappeared; all that remains is the beautiful chapel. Nearby is the St. Paul of Chartres Convent 샬트르성바오로수녀원, run by the Sisters of St. Paul of Chartres. It's a beautiful complex full of gardens and early 20th century buildings. You can't just go in—it is, after all, a convent—but if you ask nicely, the nuns might let you in to see the convent museum, full of interesting displays from its past. Also still around is a grotto shrine to the Virgin Mother 성모당 built in 1918, modeled on the Grotto to Our Lady of Lourdes, and a cemetery for Catholic clergy, containing the graves of some of Daegu's first Catholic missionaries.

🚇 Short walk from Exit 3, Seomun Market Station, Line 2

1. Yi Sang-hwa House 2. Seo Sang-don House 3. St. Justin's Catholic Seminary
4, 5. Interior of St. Justin's Catholic Seminary 6. Grotto shrine to Virgin Mother

TIPS

WHAT TO EAT

While Daegu and Gyeongsangbuk-do are not generally known for their food, Daegu does have a couple of signature dishes.

Dongin-dong Jjimgalbi 동인동 찜갈비 is a local favorite that will knock your socks off. Steamed beef ribs are placed in a nickel bowl and cooked with red pepper sauce and garlic. This is a bowl of lovely meat that is both tender and spicy, emphasis on the spicy. The leftover sauce is then mixed with rice. It originated as

Dongin-dong Jjimgalbi

a dish to drink with, and is still best enjoyed with a glass of *soju*. You can find a whole alley of *jjimgalbi* restaurants in Dongin-dong (not far from Daegu City Hall)—the alley has been there since the 1960s, and everyone around there knows where it is. Expect to pay 14,000 won for imported beef or 25,000 won for Korean *hanu* beef.

Another Daegu specialty is fried chicken gizzards or *dak ttongjip*. For these, there's an alley in the Pyeonghwa Market 평화시장 by Dongdaegu Station 동대구역. A big plate should

Dak Ttongjip Alley

cost 10,000 won—you can usually get a mixed plate of gizzards seasoned in soy sauce (*ganjang dak ttongjip* 간장닭똥집) and gizzards covered in a tangy sauce (*yangnyeom dak ttongjip* 양념닭똥집). To get there, it's best to take a cab and tell the driver where you're going.

Likely Daegu's most famous dish is *makchang-gui* 막창구이— the fourth compartment of the cow's stomach is sliced up, seasoned and cooked on a metal grill over a charcoal fire. You dab the meat in a bean paste sauce, add a slice of garlic, wrap it in a lettuce leaf and consume. It's cheap and it's good, if a bit chewy. A related dish is *gopchang* 곱창, where the small intestine of a cow or pig is used. Like *jjimgalbi*, it's a dish best enjoyed with liquid accompaniment. For this dish, you want to head to either Bukhyeon Ogeori Makchang Golmok 북현오거리막창골목 ("Bukheon Intersection Makchang Alley") or to the *gopchang* alley near Anjirang Station 안지랑역, Daegu Subway Line 1. Expect to pay about 8,000 won per person.

If none of this appeals to you, you'll find more restaurants—Korean, Chinese, Japanese, Western— than you can count along "Deurangil Restaurant Row" 들안길먹거리타운 near Suseong Resort 수성리조트.

Gopchang

At night, a particularly happening area of town is so-called Rodeo Street 로데오거리 in Samdeok-dong 삼덕 동, a short walk from Exit 10, Banwoldang Station, Line 2. This area is popular with locals and Koreans alike. The Deurangil area is packed with bars and clubs, too.

WHERE TO STAY

Daegu is a big town so there's lots of accommodation available. The spiffiest place in the city is Novotel Daegu City Center 노보텔대구시티센터 (053-664-1101), with a great location and everything you'd expect from the Novotel brand. Rooms start at 306,000 won a night. Equally upscale is Hotel Inter-Burgo 호텔인터불고 (053-602-7114) near Mangu Park, with rooms starting at 330,000 won a night.

A bit cheaper but with a nicer location closer to downtown is Prince Hotel 프린스호텔 (053-628-1001), where rooms begin at 145,000 won. By Dongdaegu Station, the most upscale hotel is Hotel J's 제이스호텔 (053-756-6601), a business hotel with rooms beginning at 170,000 won a night.

A good value stay downtown is Hirotel 히로텔 (053-421-8988), with clean, simple rooms at 40,000 won a night on weekends. Near Daegu Station, a decent budget place to stay is Grand Hotel 그랜드호텔 (053-424-4114), with rooms starting at 45,000 won. Most of your budget accommodation can be found around Daegu Station, Dongdaegu Station and the various bus terminals. Keep in mind that there are also accommodation options near Mt. Palgongsan and Dalseong.

TRANSPORT INFO

Daegu sits on the Seoul—Busan line, and is well-serviced by both regular trains and KTX. Be advised, though, that the main KTX station for Daegu is Dongdaegu Station in the east of town. From Seoul, KTX trains depart from Seoul Station (2 hrs). From Busan, the city is just an hour away by KTX (high-speed rail). Saemaeul (express) and Mugunghwa (non-express) trains from Seoul Station take about 3 hours, 30 minutes.

Daegu has five—count 'em, five—intercity bus terminals. Fortunately, most of the time you'll only need to use Daegu Express Bus Terminal, but a couple of destinations require the smaller ones.

- **Daegu Express Bus Terminal:** Daegu's express bus terminal is almost right next to Dongdaegu Station. Travel times as follows: Seoul (3 hrs 30 min), Busan (1 hr 10 min), Daejeon (2 hrs), Gwangju (3 hrs 30 min), Ulsan (1 hr 40 min), Gyeongju (1 hr), Andong (1 hr 40 min)

- **Dongbu Intercity Bus Terminal:** Not far from the express terminal, Dongbu Intercity Bus Terminal is where you'd go for destinations east and northeast like Gyeongju, Pohang, Ulsan, Cheongdo, Samcheok and Donghae.

- **Bukbu Intercity Bus Terminal:** Located in the northwest part of town, this terminal takes you to destinations (mostly) to the northwest, like Andong, Gumi, Gimcheon, Mungyeong and Yeongju.

- **Seobu Intercity Bus Terminal:** The main reason you'd want to come here is to catch the bus to Haeinsa Temple or the old fortress town of Jinju. This terminal is in the west of town.

- **Nambu Intercity Bus Terminal:** This terminal serves destinations south of Daegu like Cheongdo, Miryang and Busan.

Inheung Village 인흥마을

Off the Beaten Track

While technically part of Daegu Metropolitan City, the rural district of Dalseong is a relaxing piece of old Korea. Particularly worth seeing in Dalseong 달성 is Inheung Village, a Joseon Dynasty village founded in the 18th century by Mun Gyeong-ho, the wealthy descendant of the man who introduced cotton from China in the 15th century. As were many villages of the Joseon Dynasty, it is a clan village, which is to say, its residents mostly belong to a single clan, in this case, the Nampyeong Mun clan. While not as large or famous as other clan villages such as Andong's Hahoe Village (see p554) or Gyeongju's Yangdong Village (see p535), its rustic old wooden homes and clay walls with surrounding paddies and orchards make for a great retreat from Daegu. One hall of particular note is Insumungo Library 인수문고, where a collection of about 10,000 old and rare books may be found.

The only catch here is that the village is still an actual village, and in order to make tourists descending upon local residents tolerable, you now need to make a reservation to visit. Call 053-631-8686—visiting hours are 10 am to 6 pm—and you might also be able to score an English-speaking guide.

🚇 From Exit 1, Daegok Station, Line 1, take Dalseong Bus 1 and get off at Bolli 1-ri 본리1리 (16 min)

PALGONGSAN PROVINCIAL PARK 팔공산도립공원

Daegu's guardian mountain to the north, Mt. Palgongsan (1,192 m) is a high, broad massif that covers chunks of the towns of Chilgok 칠곡, Gunwi 군위 and Yeongcheon 영천. Since the days of Silla, Buddhists have regarded it as a sacred peak, and in its forests and valleys are several major Buddhist temples, monasteries and Buddhist rock carvings, including Donghwasa, Pagyesa, Eunhaesa and Geojoam.

Mt. Palgongsan is big, but not especially steep, so it's an easy hike for the most part. The main problem is distance—the main ridgeline, from Gasansanseong Fortress in the east to Gwanbong Peak 관봉 in the west, is 26.9 km, and takes about 13 hours to hike. The park is divided into several sections, so it's probably best to simply pick one and explore.

TIPS

SKYLINE CABLE CAR

If you're not feeling up for the full hike, there's a cable car at the base of the mountain, near the Donghwasa entrance to the park. It will bring you to an elevation of about 820 m. From there you can either bag the peak or simply enjoy the views. Fare: 7,000 won round trip, 4,000 won one-way.

The slopes of Mt. Palgongsan are home to many temples and Buddhist rock carvings.

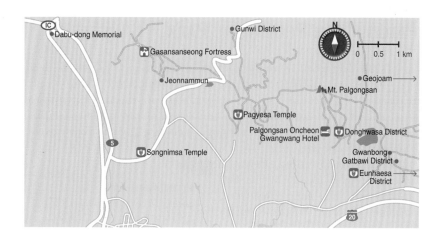

Donghwasa Temple Area 동화사지역

This is one of the mountain's most popular districts to visit. The biggest attraction here is the Buddhist monastery of Donghwasa, founded in AD 493. Most of the current buildings date from an 18th century reconstruction. The temple and its several hermitages are home to a large collection of heritage sites, including six treasures, most notably the beautiful Daeungjeon 대웅전 (Main Hall), completed in 1732. Be sure to check out the lovely latticework on the doors. Also hard to miss is the 17 m tall statue of the Medicine Buddha, dedicated in 1992 as a prayer for Korean reunification.

2,500 won 🚌 Take Bus No. 105 from Daegu Station and get off at Donghwasa (1 hr).

Donghwasa Temple, one of the biggest temples in the Daegu area

EATING & SLEEPING

At the foot of the mountain, particularly around the entrances of Donghwasa and Pagyesa temples, are more restaurants, motels and inns than you can count. Most of the accommodation is reasonably priced but if you were looking for something a bit more upscale, try Palgongsan Spa Tourist Hotel 팔공산온천관공호텔 (053-985-8080), with rooms going for 90,000 won a night.

Gatbawi Area 갓바위지역

This district in the eastern part of the park is highlighted by Gatbawi, a 9th century carving of the Buddha atop a high ridge at 850 m. The statue is unique for the odd flat rock that sits atop its head in a manner similar to the hats (*gat*) worn by Korean genlemen of yesteryear. You'll find tons of Koreans up here in the early morning hours of New Year's Day to welcome the first sunrise of the year. Another particularly busy day is the day of the university entrance exam, when it seems every school child's mother in Daegu is up here praying for their offspring's success.

🚩 Gatbawi is about an hour's hike from Donghwasa Temple. See Donghwasa Temple Area for more details.

Eunhaesa Temple Area 은해사지역

Eunhaesa Temple is a major Buddhist temple, located in the western valleys of Mt. Palgongsan. It was founded in 809 and moved to its current location in 1546. In addition to being a monastery, it's also an important learning center, home to a Buddhist university. The main precinct is lovely enough, but what is truly spectacular about this temple is two of its hermitages, Baekheungam and Geojoam.

💴 2,000 won 🚩 First take a bus from Daegu's Dongbu Intercity Bus Terminal to the city of Yeongcheon (45 min). From there, take a bus to Eunhaesa Temple (45 min).

Baekheungam Hermitage 백흥암 Two beautiful examples of Korean Buddhist architecture and art are Baekheungam and Geojoam, hermitages attached to Eunhaesa Temple. Baekheungam is a 3 km walk up Mt. Palgongsan from the temple. Much of the current hermitage dates from an 18th century reconstruction, and is a picture of

Crafted in the 9th century, the rock-carved Buddha of Gatbawi is a popular destination on New Year's and university entrance exam day.

Gate, Eunhaesa Temple (left), Gunwi Buddhist Triad

rustic Korean beauty in its stone and clay walls, simple, unpainted wooden halls and natural wood lines. Its Geungnakjeon 극락전 (Nirvana Hall) is a masterpiece of Joseon Dynasty architecture with its well preserved eave painting and, most spectacularly, its intricately carved wooden altar. The Buddhist nuns who use this place as a meditation center like to keep things quiet, however, so visitors are allowed only twice a year—the springtime Buddhist's Birthday and summertime Baekjungnal 백중날 ("Day of the Servants"), an old holiday when commoners used to gather in temples for games and good food.

Geojoam Hermitage 거조암 Geojoam, on the other hand, is open to visitors all year round, but is 4 km away from Eunhaesa Temple and has a different entrance route, so it is another trip altogether. Geojoam might be a hermitage subordinate to Eunhaesa today but it is, in fact, older than its parent temple, and for most of its history was its own temple. Its crown jewel is its graceful Yeongsanjeon 영산전 ("Arhat Hall"), built in 1375 and one of only a handful of surviving wooden buildings from the Goryeo Dynasty. Typical for wood buildings of the period, it is a simple, gabled structure with unadorned brown-yellow walls; it is said to have been built by a master carpenter sent from Ming Dynasty China. The temple houses 526 clay statues

of the arhat, the disciples of the Buddha. Examine the faces, expressions and poses of the statues, and you'll see that each one is different. The statues are believed to date from the mid-Goryeo Dynasty.

🚌 From Yeongcheon Bus Terminal, take Bus No. 251 and get off at Sinwon-ri. The hermitage is a 200m walk from there.

Gunwi Buddhist Triad Grotto Area
군위삼존석굴지역

The star attraction here is Gunwi Buddhist Triad Grotto 군위삼존석굴 (National Treasure No. 109), often called the "Second Seokguram Grotto." While it's nowhere near as spectacular as its more famous cousin in Gyeongju, it's nonetheless worth seeing. It's also a century older. Here, you'll find a beautiful sitting stone Amitabha Buddha flanked by stone statues of the Bodhisattva of Power and the Bodhisattva of Compassion, sitting in a round, natural cave in a cliff. The cave, 4.25 m wide and 4.3 m high, is 20 m up the cliff, but there are stairs leading to the entrance. Compared to other parts of Mt. Palgongsan, this section sees relatively few tourists.

🚌 First, take a bus to the town of Gunwi from Daegu's Bukbu Intercity Bus Terminal. From Gunwi Bus Terminal, take a local bus to Mt. Palgongsan.

Gasansanseong Fortress 가산산성
Guarding the northern passes to Daegu, Gasansanseong Fortress on Mt. Gasan 가산

The walls of Gasansanseong Fortress still bear the scars of the Korean War.

(901 m) is about 10 km west of Mt. Palgongsan but is often regarded as part of the park. The impressive stone fortresses were built over the course of a century beginning in 1640, not long after the invasions of Korea by the Japanese and Manchus. The walls would eventually see combat, but sadly, that was in 1950 when the fortress was the site of bitter fighting between North Korean and South Korean/American troops—the walls still bear the scars of the battle. The fortress also sports a unique three-wall structure of outer, middle and inner walls for extra protection.

Hikes begin at Jinnammun 진남문, the south gate of the fortress, and end at Hangmyeong-dong 학명동. If you bag the peak of Mt. Gasan, it's a 10 km hike, but the views of Daegu are wonderful. If you skip the peak and hike to Gasan Bawi 가산바위 ("Gasan Rock") via the East Gate, it's just a 5 km hike. On the way down, you can also check out Songnimsa Temple 송림사, with its rare brick pagoda from the Unified Silla Era.

At Daegu's Bukbu Bus Terminal, get on Bus No. 427 to Dongmyeong and get off at Giseong-ri (about 1 hr).

Dabu-dong Memorial 다부동전적기념관

In the valley west of Gasansanseong Fortress is the large memorial complex in the village of Dabu-dong. Celebrating the combined South Korea-US victory in the Battle of Dabu-dong (called by Americans the "Battle of the Bowling Alley"), the memorial is at the foot of Mt. Yuhaksan 유학산, a towering 800 m peak where some of the battle's most brutal fighting took place.

If time permits, you'll want to combine a visit to the memorial with a hike along Mt. Yuhaksan. The scene of some of the most bitter combat of the Korean War, the peak is considered a "Korean War pilgrimage site" and is one, starkly so: to this day, bones are still recovered from the hillsides.

Technically, you can start hiking from the memorial, but most people begin their hike from Yuhaksan Rest Stop, a 10,000–15,000 won taxi ride away. From the rest stop, hike up to Dobongsa Temple 도봉사, and hike to the peak from there, approximately a two hour hike.

From Daegu, buses to Dabu-dong depart from Bukbu Intercity Bus Terminal.

Dabu-dong Memorial

The 7th century Cheomseongdae Observatory, Asia's oldest astrological observatory.

GYEONGJU 경주

It's early evening at the ancient stone observatory of Cheomseongdae, during that wondrous time of the day called "magic hour," when the light of sky become diffused and here, turns a beautiful, deep purple. To the west, the faint orange glow of a just-set sun haloes the distant mountains; a bit closer, a cluster of rounded mounds, Gyeongju's distinctive royal tombs, rise up from a grass field. Above, the evening stars glow amidst a sea of violet unobscured by the lights of the city.

The small southeastern city of Gyeongju is the ancient capital of the great Korean kingdom of Silla (57 BC–AD 935) and boasts of one of Korea's richest scenic and cultural landscapes. It is home to no fewer than three UNESCO World Heritage Sites: the magnificent Buddhist monastery of Bulguksa and its sublime Seokguram Grotto, the countless Silla relics of Gyeonggju National Park, and the picturesque Joseon-era community of Yangdong Village. To properly appreciate the place, you need weeks (if not months), but even a weekend visit is well worth the time and effort—especially in spring when flowers bloom and the town is ablaze in brilliant shades of yellow and pink.

Layout

Gyeongju sits in a wide river basin surrounded by low, rugged hills that separate the urban area from the Korean interior to the west and the sea to the east. The downtown area is not especially big or difficult to navigate: the train station is to the east, the city bus terminals (and a good selection of the more affordable lodging) are to the west, and most of the town's historic remains are to the south. You could cover most of the distances on foot, but if that's not your style, Gyeongju is one of Korea's most bicycle-friendly cities, with many pleasant bike paths and plenty of shops willing to rent you a bike for 10,000 won a day. Some sites, like Bulguksa Temple 불국사, are a bit further afield and will require the use of local buses. The city bus terminal is a short walk from the intra-city bus terminal on the west side of town, although you might be able to catch local buses to your destination elsewhere, too—it's best to inquire at the tourist information centers at Gyeongju Station and the intra-city bus terminal.

Cheomseongdae Observatory 첨성대

Cheomseongdae is a Gyeongju landmark, the 7th century stone tower, Asia's oldest surviving astrological observatory. Lit up at night, the site provides a beautiful view of the heavens, even today. A short walk from there is the Banwolseong 반월성 ("Half Moon Fortress"), a crescent-shaped set of earthworks that marks the site of the old Silla royal palace. In spring, the old palace site is shaded by beautiful cherry blossoms, while the surrounding fields are covered in bright yellow rape flowers. ⏰ 9 am to 10 pm (summer), 9 am to 9 pm (winter) 💵 500 won

Anapji Pond 안압지

A few minutes walk east of Cheomseongdae brings you to Anapji, a gorgeous pleasure pond that was once a favorite relaxation spot of Silla kings. When lit up in the early evening, the pond and its surrounding pavilions make for one of

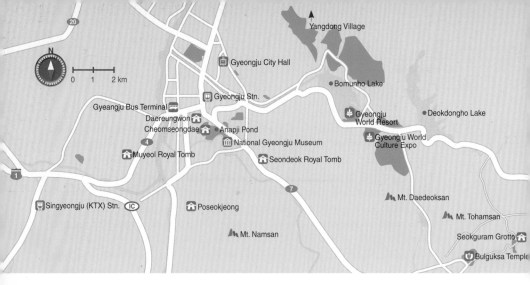

Yangdong Village

Gyeongju City Hall

Bomunho Lake

Gyeongju Stn.

Gyeangju Bus Terminal

Daereungwon
Cheomseongdae

Anapji Pond

Gyeongju
World Resort

Deokdongho Lake

Gyeongju World
Culture Expo

Muyeol Royal Tomb

National Gyeongju Museum

Seondeok Royal Tomb

Mt. Daedeoksan

Singyeongju (KTX) Stn.

Poseokjeong

Mt. Tohamsan

Seokguram Grotto

Mt. Namsan

Bulguksa Temple

Korea's most photogenic night scenes. King Munmu of Silla ordered the pond's construction in 674; when it was restored in the 1970s and 80s, an archeological treasure trove was unearthed, offering great insight into life in the Silla era.

⏱ 9 am to 10 pm 🪙 1,000 won

Daereungwon 대릉원

The most conspicuous of Gyeongju's relics are the burial mounds (tumuli) found all over town. Gyeongju and its environs are home to more than 200 tumuli, but the best place to see them is Daereungwon (Tumuli Park), a pleasant park of 23 tombs. The highlight of the park is the famed Cheonmachong 천마총 ("Horse of Heaven Tomb"), the tomb of an unknown 5th century Silla king that yielded over 10,000 artifacts when it was excavated in 1974. Many of these artifacts are now on display at Gyeongju National Museum 경주국립박물관.

⏱ 9 am to 10 pm 🪙 1,500 won

Formerly a royal pleasure garden, Anapji Pond is one of Korea's most scenic spots.

Bulguksa Temple (left), Seokguram Grotto

Gyeongju National Museum 국립경주박물관

Widely regarded as Korea's finest museum save for the National Museum of Korea in Seoul, Gyeongju National Museum is home to an expansive and priceless collections of art and artifacts from the Silla Kingdom, including 30,000 artifacts excavated from Anapji Pond alone. To explore this place properly, set aside several hours. Be sure to stop by the belfry to check out the Divine Bell of King Seongdeok 성덕대왕신종, a giant bronze temple bell crafted in the 8th century.

🕘 9 am to 6 pm (extended hours on weekends). Closed Mondays 💷 Regular exhibits are free. Some special exhibits may charge admission.
📞 054-740-7500 🌐 http://gyeongju.museum.go.kr

Bomun Lake 보문호

To the east of downtown Gyeongju is Bomun Lake, a massively popular resort area full of upper-end hotels, amusement parks and other merriment facilities. It's especially beautiful in spring when its famous cherry blossoms bloom. If you are staying in the area, the lake is a nice area for a stroll, and there are places offering bikes and quad bikes for rent.

🚌 Take Bus No. 10 or 18 from across from Gyeongju Intercity Bus Terminal.

Bulguksa Temple 불국사
& Seokguram Grotto 석굴암

The jewels of Korean antiquity are a short bus ride east of town on the slopes of the holy mountain Mt. Tohamsan 토함산. Here you can find the splendid Buddhist monastery of Bulguksa and the bewitching Seokguram Grotto. The grotto, in particular, is considered one of Korea's finest cultural achievements, and visitors should try to see it at least once.

Bulguksa was originally completed in 774; its name, which means "Temple of the Buddhist Country," reflects Silla's belief that the kingdom was an earthly Buddhist paradise. It's a large complex of stone works and wooden halls and cloisters, built upon a masterful series of stone and earth terraces. The temple has seen a number of calamities over its history (its current state of good repair is largely thanks to a major restoration carried out in the 1960s and 70s), but its masonry is mostly original. Bulguksa is home to six National Treasures, including the beloved stone pagodas in the main courtyard, the beautiful stone staircases leading to the main precincts, and two Silla-era bronze Buddhas.

Above Bulguksa, commanding a view of the East Sea, is the Seokguram Grotto. The "grotto" is really an artificial space built of granite consisting of an entrance, antechamber, and rotunda topped with a domed ceiling. The grotto houses a Buddhist pantheon, the highlight of which is the sublime sitting Buddha, carved of granite and 3.5 meters in height. At sunrise, the morning rays light up the statue, highlighting the entrancing smile on the lips of the meditating Buddha.

Buddhist grottos such as this one first began in India. Their appearance in Korea is indicative of Silla's role as the eastern terminus of the legendary Silk Road. Seokguram itself exhibits a number of foreign influences, including even Hellenistic elements.

🕐 7:30 am to 6 pm 🎫 4,000 won 🚌 **Bulguksa Temple:** Take Bus No. 10 or 11 from Gyeongju Intercity Bus Terminal, Express Bus Terminal or Gyeongju Station and get off at Bulguksa (takes about 40 minutes). From the bus stop, it's a 10 minute walk to the temple. **Seokguram:** Take Bus No. 12 from Bulguksa to Seokguram (departs hourly). You can also walk from Bulguksa to Seokguram: the hike takes about an hour.

Mt. Namsan 남산

One of the more rewarding ways to pass your time in Gyeongju is to head to Mt. Namsan ("South Mountain"), a 494 meter peak covered in many relics and remains of Silla's Buddhist culture. The mountain is quite broad and crisscrossed with hiking paths, some of which take you through ravines and along ridges full of Buddhist statues, cliff reliefs and stone pagodas. Highlights include a 7 m tall Buddhist relief on a cliff overlooking the Gyeongju basin and a set of seven stone reliefs at Chilburam Hermitage 칠불암. The views of

Gyeongju alone make the hike worthwhile. To explore Mt. Namsan properly, you really should set aside a full day. It's easy to get lost so be sure to pick up a map of Mt. Namsan at one of the several tourist information centers in town.

At the western foot of Mt. Namsan is Poseokjeong 포석정, an artificial stone stream that was once part of a royal pleasure garden. Kings and their retainers would play drinking games here, floating on the stream cups of wine upon the stream to be consumed if participants were unable to compose lines of poetry before the cup reached them. More soberingly, the penultimate monarch of Silla, King Gyeongae, was killed at Poseokjeong as rebel forces sacked Gyeongju in 927, nearly marking the end of the once great kingdom.

🚌 Take Bus No. 500 to the Samneung Tombs, where the hiking path up the mountain begins.

Underwater Tomb of King Munmu 문무왕 수중릉 & Gameunsaji Temple Site 감은사지

If you've got the time, take the bus from Gyeongju to the East Sea coast to see the Underwater Tomb of King Munmu and Gameunsaji Temple Site. Located on some rocks just off the coast, the tomb is said to be where King Munmu (661–681), the

Rock-carved Buddha on Mt. Namsan, a virtual outdoor museum of Korean history

greatest of Silla's kings, had his ashes buried in an urn beneath a submerged piece of granite in hopes of becoming a sea dragon to protect Silla's coast from Japanese raiders. Nearby is the former site of Gameunsa Temple; while the temple burned down long ago, its splendid stone pagodas—two symmetrical giants that cut a dramatic figure against the surrounding pastoral landscape—still stand as they have since the 7th century.

🚌 From Gyeongju Intercity Bus Terminal, take Bus No. 150 and get off at Gameunsaji (1 hr). After seeing the temple site, walk to Bonggil Beach 봉길해수욕장 where the tomb is located.

Girimsa 기림사 & Golgulsa 골굴사 Temples

The monastery of Girimsa, hidden in the mountains east of Gyeongju, makes for a nice daytrip. Founded in 643, the temple is home to some outstanding pieces of Buddhist art, including a mesmerizing gilt image of the Bodhisattva of Mercy with 1,000 arms and 1,000 eyes.

On the road to Girimsa is another Buddhist temple, Golgulsa, which is most famous for Seonmudo, a martial art practiced by its monks as a form of meditation. The monks conduct Seonmudo demonstrations at 11 am and 3 pm every day (except Monday), and templestay programs—including Seonmudo lessons—are available.

🚌 Take Bus No. 100 or 150 from Gyeongju Intercity Bus Terminal (1 hr). If Girimsa is your destination, get off at Yangbuk-myeon Eoil-ri 양북면 어일리 and take a cab to the temple (fare: 6,000 won). If you want to go to Golgulsa, get off at Andong Intersection 안동삼거리 and walk about 15 minutes to the temple. 🖱 www.golgulsa.com

Yangdong Village 양동마을

Korea's newest UNESCO World Heritage site, Yangdong Village is no kitsch folk village of "traditional" homes recently built and cobbled together to give a taste of old Korea. It is located deep in the countryside northeast of Gyeongju, with buses dropping you off a good 30 minute walk from the village itself. Taking pride in its isolation, this has helped keep it as one of Korea's largest and best-preserved Joseon-era communities. Delightfully picturesque, it is a case study in Confucian aesthetics and Korean reverence for nature, with simple, rustic tile-roof and thatched-roof homes lining the hillsides and valleys in perfect harmony with the natural topography.

Yangdong Village was formed in the 15th century by two aristocratic Korean clans, the Yeogang Lee and Wolseong Son families. The village grew and prospered throughout the Joseon era (1392–1910),

Yangdong Village, a beautifully preserved Joseon Dynasty clan village

producing a number of great Confucian scholars, most notably "Hoejae" Lee Eon-jeok (1491–1553), one of the so-called "Five Great Sages of the East." Many of the homes have, in recent years, been converted into restaurants and guesthouses, but several are still occupied by members of the Lee and Son clans, and clan members who live elsewhere return regularly for annual ancestral rites ceremonies.

The village has over 160 homes—many more than 200 years old, and a couple over 500 years old—spread out along several valleys and ridgelines in accordance with feng shui principles. From overhead, it resembles the Chinese character "勿." It is often compared to its better known cousin, Andong's Hahoe Village (see p554), together with which it was registered as a UNESCO World Heritage Site. Both are clan villages formed by illustrious families in the Joseon era, and while there are similarities, the differences are also noteworthy. Topography is an obvious one: while Hahoe Village is a typical oxbow village, Yangdong Village is built along the hillsides, the roof lines blending with the undulating terrain. The houses are smaller and more humble, reflecting the rustically charming modesty of Korean Confucianist scholar life.

By examining the village landscape, one can gather a bit about the hierarchical social order of Joseon society. Tile roof homes—those belonging to Korea's

HISTORY OF SILLA

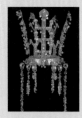

Relative to its rival kingdoms of Goguryeo and Baekje, the kingdom of Silla developed late: it was still little more than a tribal federation as late as third century AD, by which time Baekje had become a centralized kingdom and Goguryeo a regional power. Silla soon solidified and grew to challenge Goguryeo and Baekje for supremacy on the Korean Peninsula, conquering Baekje in 660 and Goguryeo in 668 to unify nearly the entire Korean Peninsula. United Silla ushered in a golden age of Korean classical civilization, a period that would leave an indelible imprint on the development of Korean culture.

EARLY SILLA

According to legend, Gyeongju was founded by King Park Hyeokgeose in 57BC. The kingdom began as a collection of clans around the city of Gyeongju, which became the capital. Leadership rotated between three clans—Kim, Park and Seok—names that are now amongst the most popular family names in Korea. Isolated from the rest of Korea by rugged mountains to the north and west, Silla developed in a relatively independent fashion, its society and culture remaining true to its indigenous and tribal roots. Silla grew in influence and solidified as a state. Under King Naemul (r. 356–402), it became a hereditary monarchy and adopted many administrative and cultural aspects from China. Under King Beopheung (r. 514–540), the kingdom adopted Buddhism as the state religion. By the end of the sixth century, Silla had conquered and absorbed the Gaya Confederation, a minor alliance of kingdoms around the Nakdonggang River valley between Silla and Baekje.

yangban aristocracy—are found higher on the hillsides. Below them are thatched roof homes that once housed the tenant farmers of *yangban* who owned the farmland in the valleys below. Household servants—technically slaves—lived within the *yangban* compounds themselves.

All of Yangdong Village is designated a cultural property (and, of course, a UNESCO World Heritage Site), but 24 of the village's assets are separately designated as heritage properties, including one national treasure and four other offical treasures. The large manor houses are the most spectacular, especially Hyangdan 향단 (Treasure No. 412), a stately mansion built atop a hill overlooking the entrance of the village. Built in 1543 for the mother of Lee Eon-jeok upon his appointment as governor of the province of Gyeongsang-do, it originally had 99 rooms—only the king could live in a bigger home—but many were irretrievably lost during the Korean War.

At another beautiful compound, the Gwangajeong 관가정, is best experienced from the inside. Gaze out the windows: in the distance, the white clouds float over the green hills against a blue sky; in the foreground, just beyond the wood and paper sliding panels, a lone tree stands in the garden. One can easily imagine oneself as a *seonbi* scholar, passing the day sitting here, book in hand, enjoying the autumn breeze and captivating scenery.

WARS OF UNIFICATION

Under King Jinheung (r. 540-576), Silla strengthened its military forces, creating the legendary *hwarang* ("Flower Youth"), an elite band of warriors steeped in Buddhist and Taoist teachings. Breaking an alliance with Baekje, Jinheung allied with the kingdom of Goguryeo to drive Baekje from the strategic Hangang River valley, absorbing the territory for Silla itself. In the seventh century, Silla fought a dramatic series of wars against both Baekje and Goguryeo to unify the Korean Peninsula with the aid of Tang China, with whom it had formed an alliance. With an army led by the brilliant general Kim Yu-shin, Silla had conquered Baekje and Goguryeo but now its former ally, Tang China, was making moves to turn Korea into a Chinese colony. For six years, Silla waged war on the Tang until, in 676, the Chinese finally decided to withdraw from Korea. Most of the Korean Peninsula was now under Silla rule, save for those areas north of the Daedonggang River that became part of the newly established kingdom of Balhae, founded by a former Goguryeo general.

Unifed Silla experienced a blossoming of culture and art. The capital of Gyeongju became a city of palaces, temples and gardens. The grand Buddhist temple of Hwangnyongsa, crowned by a nine-story wooden pagoda, was famous even in China. Buddhism flowered thanks to royal patronage and brisk exchange with Tang China, to

 which Korea sent many monks for study. Many of Silla's most famous sites today, including Cheomseongdae, Bulguksa Temple and Seokguram Grotto, were erected in this period. Politically, the power of the king grew while the influence of Silla's noble clans decreased; Confucian bureaucratic techniques were even introduced from China.

Gyeongju: *Ssambap*—rice and meat wrapped in lettuce leaves—is a local specialty. You can find a number of *ssambap* restaurants at the south entrance of Daereungwon, including Guro Sambap 구로쌈밥 (054-749-0600). *Ssambap jeongsik* goes for 10,000 won. If you're in a party of two or more, Dosol Maeul 도솔마을 (054-748-9232) is worth a try. Specializing in traditional Korean meals (*jeongsik*), the restaurant is in an old hanok, mixing taste with atmosphere. You'll love its mountains of side dishes. The restaurant is located to the south of Daereungwon; it's best to ask directions or take a cab—everybody knows it. One unique Gyeongju treat is Gyeongju *ppang* ("Gyeongju bread"), a small, tasty pastry filled with red bean paste. It's hard to walk five minutes in the touristed areas of Gyeongju without passing a shop selling boxes of them. Try Hwangnamppang 황남빵 (054-749-7000) just north of Daereungwon—they invented the treat in 1935. A box of 20 goes for 14,000 won. Another local dish treat is *chalborippang* 찰보리빵, small pancakes made from barley.

Yangdong Village: A number of the traditional homes in Yangdong Village now function as restaurants. One of the most famous of these is Uhyangdaok 우향다옥 (054-762-8096), an old *yangban* home that specializes in *jeongsik* 정식: soup, rice and plenty of side dishes. The home also serves as a guesthouse. Yangdong Village is also famous for *cheongju* 청주, a clear Korean rice wine likened to Japanese sake.

WHAT TO EAT

Gyeongju: Bomun Lake is home to many luxury hotels, including the Gyeongju Hilton 경주힐튼호텔 (054-745-7788), Hotel Hyundai 호텔현대 (054-748-2233), and Commodore Hotel 코모도호텔 (054-745-7701), just to name a few. The amenities are first rate, but they come at a price of 200,000 won a night or more for the top ones. If you're flush, look no further than Millennium Palace Resort & Spa: Ragung 신라밀레니엄파크 라궁 (054-778-2100), a sumptuous *hanok* hotel near Bomun Lake. If the beautiful Korean traditional architecture, upscale Korean cuisine and charming Korean interiors aren't enough, the private outdoor hot tubs attached to each room should do the trick. Prices begin at 300,000 won a night. There are some lovely *hanok* guesthouses in Gyeongju, too. If you don't mind staying way out of town, Dongnakdang 독락당 is a gorgeous 16th century residence near the beautiful Oksan Seowon Confucian Academy 옥산서원. Rooms begin at 40,000 won a night. Out past Bomun Lake is the sublime Jongojeong 종오정, an 18th century scholar's home on a big lotus pond. Rooms here begin at 120,000 won on a weekend. See www.gjgotaek.kr or call 054-774-1950 for more information on these *hanok* stays and others. A very popular *hanok* guesthouse with international backpackers is Sa Rang Chae 사랑채 (054-773-4868, www.kjstay.com), a friendly place run by an English-speaking couple with double rooms with a bathroom for 30,000 won a night (breakfast included). There are plenty of reasonably priced motels and inns just behind Gyeongju Intercity Bus Terminal.

Yangdong Village: Some of the homes also serve as guesthouses, including Uhyangdaok 우향다옥—call ahead to the village information center at 054-779-6105 (Korean).

WHERE TO STAY

Gyeongju: The quickest way to Gyeongju from Seoul is to take the KTX from Seoul Station direct to Singyeongju Station (2 hrs 10 min). Unfortunately, Singyeongju Station is about 40 minutes outside of town by bus. If you don't mind spending six hours on the train, there are two trains from Cheongnyangni Station that stop at Gyeongju Station, smack in the middle of downtown. They depart Cheongnyangni at 8:10 am and 9 pm. Buses to Gyeongju depart from Seoul Express Bus Terminal (4 hrs). From Daegu, buses to Gyeongju depart from Daegu Express Bus Terminal (1 hr). From Busan, buses to Gyeongju depart from Busan Bus Terminal (50 min). From Ulsan, buses depart from Ulsan Intercity Bus Terminal (1 hr).

Yangdong Village: From Gyeongju, take Bus No. 200, 201–212, 208, 212 or 217 to Yangdong Village (about 40 minutes). The easiest place to do this is from Gyeongju Station, but you can also catch one from a short walk from Gyeongju Express Bus Terminal (ask the tourist info booth at the terminal). Be warned: the bus drops you off about 2 km short of the village, so be prepared to stretch your legs.

TRANSPORT INFO

POHANG 포항

For first-time visitors, Pohang can be a pleasant surprise. The "Pittsburgh of Korea," the thriving industrial port is more than just a steel mill and home to one of the country's most storied soccer clubs. It's also a city of much charm and scenic beauty, especially along its lovely East Sea coast where visitors can take in Korea's earliest sunrises. Even the industrial grit can be beautiful, creating awe-inspiring, almost science fiction-like cityscapes that leave a lasting impression.

Layout

Pohang is a fairly large city of over 500,000 that wraps around Yeongilman Bay 영일만 on the southeastern coast of Korea. The downtown area surrounds the port on the inner part of the bay, straddling the mouth of the Hyeongsangang River 형산강. The southern part of the bay is protected by a small peninsula that juts out into the East Sea, forming Homigot Cape 호미곶, mainland Korea's easternmost point. The downtown area is where you'll find most of your accommodations, the best restaurants, transportation in/out of the city and, not to forget, the massive Pohang Iron and Steel Company (POSCO). The eastern coast, especially along Homigot Cape, has some especially lovely scenery, while the inland areas are fairly mountainous and home to two beautiful Buddhist temples, Oeosa Temple 오어사 to the south and Bogyeongsa Temple 보경사 to the north.

'Hand of Coexistence,' Homigot Sunrise Plaza

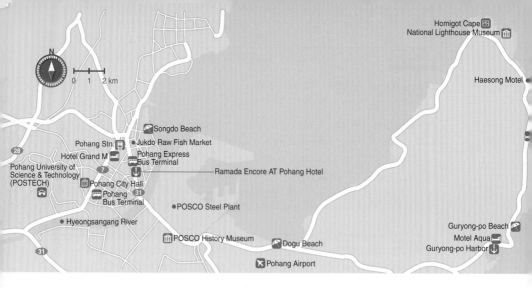

0 1 2 km

Homigot Cape
National Lighthouse Museum

Haesong Motel

Songdo Beach

Jukdo Raw Fish Market

Pohang Stn.

Pohang Express
Bus Terminal

Hotel Grand M

28

Pohang University of
Science & Technology
(POSTECH)

Pohang City Hall

Ramada Encore AT Pohang Hotel

Pohang
Bus Terminal

31

POSCO Steel Plant

Hyeongsangang River

Guryong-po Beach

Motel Aqua

Guryong-po Harbor

POSCO History Museum

Dogu Beach

31

Pohang Airport

POSCO Steel Plant 포항제철소

Admittedly, one might not visit Pohang to see a steel plant alone, but POSCO is a place worth seeing. Built in four phases between 1970 and 1981, POSCO's Pohang integrated steel plant is one of the world's largest producers of steel, and a city unto itself. It is smokestacks, pipes, furnaces and plant facilities for as far as the eye can see. At night, the complex is lit up, with additional lighting provided by flames billowing out of smokestacks—think "Blade Runner" without the Vangelis soundtrack (although an iPod could probably provide that, too). You can see it from the other side of the bay as well—it's all rather awe-inspiring.

POSCO is an impressive monument to the "Can Do" spirit upon which Korea's miraculous post-war economic development was based. When the Korean government initially proposed the construction of the mill in the late 1960s, the World Bank and other Western donors refused to help finance it, considering it overambitious and doomed to failure. Korea's leaders pressed ahead anyway and today, POSCO owns massive integrated steel mills in Pohang and Gwangyang 광양 (the latter being the world's

largest) and is the world's third biggest producer of steel. Its growth also transformed a formerly sleepy fishing village into a symbol of Korean industrial might.

If you're in a group, you may be able to arrange a formal tour of the complex (call 054-220-1114). The best views, however, can be had from the riverside park opposite the mill, where you can sit at night with a cold beer and watch the lights reflect off the water. Outside the complex, however, is the POSCO Museum, a beautifully appointed

POSCO, one of the world's largest steel plants

facility that presents you the history and development of the Korean steel industry.

▣ Take Bus No. 130 from Pohang Intercity Bus Terminal to Sinheung Mansion and walk to the riverside park.

Jukdo Raw Fish Market 죽도어시장

Jagalchi Market in Busan might get all the fame but for the best raw fish in Korea, travelers in the know head to Jukdo Raw Fish Market, near Pohang Harbor. Here you'll find the freshest raw fish in Korea at remarkably reasonable prices. Go at dawn to see the daily fish auctions take place as local restaurants compete to get their hands on the freshest catches.

▣ Take Bus No. 100 from Pohang Intercity Bus Terminal and get off at the market.

Guryongpo 구룡포

To get an idea of what Pohang must have looked like before POSCO, head to the fishing village of Guryongpo, a 30 minute bus ride from downtown Pohang. Guryongpo—its name means "Nine Dragon Port"—is a major east coast fishing center, and has a salty East Coast fishing port charm. There's a fairly popular beach nearby, so the town is blessed with a goodly amount of seafood restaurants and places to stay.

Behind the waterfront main drag of Guryongpo is an alleyway of Japanese-style homes, formerly used by Japanese settlers who came to the town in the colonial era to exploit the region's fishing industry. City authorities have designated the alleyway a protected zone. With their wood panel walls, distinctive Japanese-style windows and doors, and straight woodlines, the ramshackle houses possess an exotic feel. Of particular note is the stairway leading to Guryongpo Park 구룡포공원; lined by Japanese stone markers, it once led to a Shinto shrine (removed March 2008) located in the park.

▣ Take Bus No. 200 from Pohang Intercity Bus Terminal and get off at Guryongpo Beach (1 hr).

Guryongpo

Homigot Cape 호미곶

If the Korean Peninsula is a tiger clawing at the Asian mainland, Homigot Cape is its tail. The country's easternmost point (not counting Ulleungdo and Dokdo), the cape is the place to come to see the earliest sunrises—on New Year's Day, it's flooded with tourists who come to take in the first sunrise of the year.

Almost ten years ago, there was nothing but a few seafood restaurants, a cheap hotel and a very impressive lighthouse. The lighthouse is still there, but it's been joined by the recently opened National Lighthouse Museum 국립등대박물관, a great many more hotels and restaurants, and Homigot Sunrise Plaza 호미곶 해맞이광장, a park/cultural facility dedicated to the cape's most notable natural resource—the sunrise. This is not to say it's been "ruined," but it certainly has changed.

If you're a lighthouse lover—and who isn't?—you'll definitely want to check out the National Lighthouse Museum, where you'll find everything you've wanted to know about lighthouses but were afraid to ask. The real star of the show, however, is Homigot Lighthouse, one of Korea's oldest, largest and most beautiful lighthouses. Designed by a French architect, the graceful lighthouse was completed in 1908—check out the intricate details on the doors and windows.

Homigot Sunrise Plaza 호미곶해맞이광장, on

Homigot Sunrise Plaza (left), Homigot Lighthouse

the other hand, is of much more recent vintage, having been built to usher in the first sunrise of the new millennium. It's dominated by the "Hands of Coexistence," two giant iron hands, one rising from the land, the other rising dramatically from the waves just off the beach. The work of Korean artist Kim Seung-guk, the two hands were meant to represent the spirit of peace and coexistence in the 21st century. Events since 2000 have put a damper on that spirit, but the hand rising from the sea provides a rather nice resting spot for local seagulls that find respite on the tip of each digit.

🚌 Take Bus No. 200 from Pohang Intercity Bus Terminal and get off at Guryongpo. From there, transfer to bus 203 and get off at Homigot.

Oeosa Temple 오어사

Worth checking out is the Buddhist temple of Oeosa, just outside of town on the road to Gyeongju. The temple sits lakeside, a rarity for Korean Buddhist temples, due to modern-day dam construction on a local river. The temple, while not big, is quite scenic, and there's a nice, short hike to a hermitage perched on a nearby cliff. The temple's name translates as "My Fish Temple." According to legend, the great Silla monks Wonhyo and Hyegong once engaged in a rather unusual contest here. They went to the river, where each of them pulled out a fish, swallowed it whole, and then evacuated their bowels into the river. One of the fishes came out dead, but one of them came out alive, proof that the mystical powers of one of the monks was stronger. Each of the monks claimed the live fish as his own, hence the temple's name.

🚌 Take Bus No. 107 from Pohang Intercity Bus Terminal and get off at Daegak-ri (50 min). From there, it's a nearly 2 km hike to the temple.

TRANSPORT INFO

There are infrequent trains to Pohang that leave directly from Seoul Station so you're better off taking the KTX to Dongdaegu, then switching to a local train to Pohang (or, even better, taking the limousine bus to Pohang that frequently departs from the back of Dongdaegu Station. If pressed for time, you can also fly to Pohang from Gimpo Airport.

WHERE TO STAY

There are tons of motels around Pohang Intercity Bus Terminal—most charge 30,000–40,000 won for very acceptable accommodation. The swankiest places in town are Hotel Grand M 호텔 그랜드엠 (054-275-2000) and Ramada Encore AT Pohang Hotel 라마다앙코르 포항호텔 (054-282-2700), both of which run around 100,000 won a night. If you'd like to stay in Guryongpo, try Motel Aqua 아쿠아모텔 (054-284-6900), which offers lovely views of the harbor. If it's the sunrise from Homigot Cape you're after, there's Haesujang Motel 해수장모텔 (054-284-8044), Haesong Motel 해송모텔 (054-284-8245) and a number of minbak (homestays) available.

CHEONGDO 청도

This small town south of Daegu is most renowned for its spring bullfighting festival, a lively event that attracts Koreans from around the country, not to mention a good number of expats and foreign particpants and spectators. Also in the vicinity is Unmunsa Temple, home to the largest Buddhist nunnery in Korea.

Cheongdo Bullfighting Festival
청도소싸움축제

The highlight of Cheongdo's year is the Cheongdo Bullfighting Festival, held every spring. Unlike the Spanish version, this is not a bull vs. man event, it's bull-on-bull. The bulls—names painted prominently on their flanks—go horn to horn with one another for several minutes (usually) until one decides he's had enough and quits. The game is a legacy of Korea's agrarian past, when villages would pit their prize bulls against one another in a bit of friendly competition. Bulls will get bloodied, but not dead—Koreans are far too attached to their bulls, which were usually a farmer's most valuable asset.

In recent years, the bullfighting has been supplemented by rodeo shows featuring teams from overseas, as well as a team representing US troops in Korea.

During non-festival periods, bullfights are held every Saturday and Sunday. Ten fights are held a day, beginning at 11 am. To promote interest in the sport, betting is allowed.

⏰ April 🎫 4,000 won 🚌 Take a local bus for Punggak 풍각 from the stop across the street from Cheongdo Station and get off at Chilseong Samgeori (15–20 min) 🌐 www.청도소싸움.kr (KR)

Unlike Spanish bullfighting, Korean bullfighting is bull-on-bull

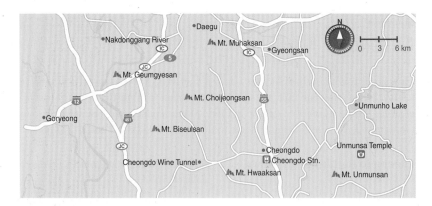

Cheongdo Wine Tunnel 청도와인터널

In 2006, Chung Do Persimmon Wine Co. turned an abandoned, century-old railway tunnel into a wine cellar to age its flavorful wines made from locally grown persimmons. The stone and brick tunnel, completed in 1896 for the Seoul–Busan railroad, has a Victorian elegance, and is surrounded by persimmon orchards—come here in autumn when the cobalt skies and bright orange persimmons create an amazingly colorful landscape. In addition to being a wine cellar, the tunnel also has a wine market and café where you can sample the various wines. They hold concerts on occasion, too, especially at Christmas.

🕐 9:30 am to 8 pm 🎫 Free ✆ 054-371-1100 🖱 www.gamwine.com 🚉 First, take a train from Daegu Station to Cheondo (20 min). Across from Cheongdo Station, you'll find Cheongdo Bus Terminal. From there, take a bus bound for Songgeum-ri 송금리 and get off at either Songgeum Church 송금교회 or the Wine Tunnel 와인터널.

A disused railroad tunnel, Cheongdo Wine Tunnel is now used to store tasty persimmon wine.

Unmunsa Temple 운문사

Home to about 260 nuns, Unmunsa Temple is Korea's largest Buddhist nunnery and serves as a university for Buddhist nuns. The nuns here run a tight ship, and the groundkeeping here is really quite nice—check out the ancient weeping red pine in the courtyard. Surrounded by the lush forests of Mt. Unmunsan, the precinct is a pleasantly tranquil environment, except when it's overrun by visitors on autumn weekends.

🪙 2,000 won ☎ 054-372-8800 🚌 Buses to Unmunsa depart from Daegu's Nambu Bus Terminal (1 hr 20 min).

Lovely Unmunsa Temple is home to about 260 Buddhist nuns.

HAEINSA TEMPLE 해인사

Some visitors to Korea may believe (quite wrongly) that once you've seen one Korean Buddhist temple, you've seen them all. Some temples are truly unique, however. Haeinsa Temple is one of them.

Located deep in the mountains of Hapcheon-gun County 합천군 in southeast Korea—emphasis on the word "deep"—Haeinsa Temple is one of Korea's three largest Buddhist monasteries or one of the "Three Jewels," as Korean Buddhists prefer to call them. A UNSECO World Heritage Site, the compound is home to the Tripitaka Koreana—Palman Daejanggyeong in Korean—a 13th century collection of woodblock carvings of Buddhist scriptures and the oldest and most complete edition of Buddhist canon in Chinese characters. For centuries, the monastery has been the scholastic center of Korean Buddhism, preserving the tradition of scriptural studies through the generations.

Like most major temples in Korea, Haeinsa offers adventurous visitors an opportunity to experience temple life through "templestay" programs that provide the opportunity to rediscover beauty, both inside and out.

Haeinsa Temple 해인사

Haeinsa Temple is a one hour, 30 minute bus ride from Daegu through beautiful countryside. From where the bus drops you off, it's a five-six km hike along a scenic mountain stream until you reach the temple. The path, named Haeinsa Sorigil 해인사 소리길 ("Haeinsa Temple Sound Path"), puts you in the right frame of mind. Just before you reach the monastery compound itself, you'll pass through several gates. The first of these gates, Iljumun 일주문, signifies that you are about to enter the world of Buddha.

Haeinsa Temple, which means "Temple of Reflection on a Smooth Sea," takes its name from a passage in the Avatamsaka Sutra, which compares the wisdom of the Buddha to a calm sea. When the mind—like the sea—is freed from the waves of worldly desire, it will perfectly reflect existence as it truly is.

Haeinsa is, as Korean Buddhist temples go, a massive complex, and a truly remarkable feat of landscaping, architecture and engineering. Some of the complex is off-limits to visitors—Haeinsa is, after all, a functioning Buddhist monastery with a large community of Buddhist monks. The central courtyard of the temple is dominated

by the imposing Daejeokgwangjeon 대적광전, the main Dharma Hall which, in contrast to most other Korean temples, is dedicated to the Vairocana Buddha, the universal aspect of the historical Buddha who lived in India in 400 BC, and a symbol of the doctrine of emptiness.

The complex is gorgeously terraced, with higher terraces offering superb views of the temple and surrounding mountains. It's remarkably calming to stare out at the sea of curved Korean tile roofs, their lines harmonizing seamlessly with the verdant undulating hills beyond.

One rarely hopes for rain while on the road, but Haeinsa is one place where the experience is actually enhanced by a little precipitation. Here, when it rains, the mist hangs in the surrounding hills and forests, giving the monastery a romantic and other-worldly aspect.

⏱ 8:30 am to 6 pm (summer), 8:30 am to 5 pm (winter) 💴 3,000 won ☎ 055-934-3000 🖱 www.haeinsa.or.kr 🚌 From Daegu Seobu Bus Terminal 대구서부버스터미널 take the direct bus to Haeinsa Temple—there are frequent departures throughout the day (1 hr 30 min).

TEMPLESTAY

One of the most popular—and rewarding—programs for foreign residents and visitors to Korea is a stay at a Buddhist temple.

These (usually) overnight programs, run by the Jogye Order of Korean Buddhism, give you unique insight into the life of a Buddhist monk. They also give you an opportunity, if only for a short time, to escape the daily grind and appreciate the beauty of living.

Haeinsa is one of many temples that opens its door to templestay guests. Typically, you will eat with the monks, participate in Zen meditation, engage in traditional crafts, and participate in morning and evening Buddhist chanting and bowing ceremonies known as *yebul*, or Homage to the Buddha. You really need to be an early riser for this—the morning *yebul* takes place before sunrise, usually about 4 am.

For more information on the templestay program, call 02-2011-1972. Programs usually cost about 50,000–80,000 won.

Mt. Gayasan National Park
가야산국립공원

Haeinsa Temple sits on the southwest slope of Mt. Gayasan 가야산 (1,433 m), a beautiful, craggy peak that makes for a lovely hike if you've got five or so hours to kill. From the peak, there are breathtaking views of nearby mountains, including massive Mt. Jirisan 지리산 and Mt. Deogyusan 덕유산. In the early morning, the sea of clouds below the peak (weather permitting) makes for an inspiring vista.

The most popular hiking trail begins from the entrance to Haeinsa Temple. Just past the temple's Iljumun Gate is the start of the hiking path. Most of the path is quite gentle, but the upper reaches, including the peak, are quite rocky cliffy and require a good deal of care. From the peak, you can descend the way you came or via the beautiful Baegundae Valley 백운대계곡. All together, it should take you about five hours.

PALMAN DAEJANGGYEONG 팔만대장경

In the temple's rear courtyard, located above the Daejeokgwangjeon (quite unusual for a Korean Buddhist temple, where tradition places the main Dharma Hall highest), is the astounding Janggyeong Panjeon 장경판전, the four halls preserving the Tripitaka Koreana and a miracle of medieval Korean science and engineering.

Work on the first edition of the Tripitaka Koreana began in 1011 as a national prayer for the Buddha's protection from invading Manchurian nomads. This copy, completed in 1087, was sadly destroyed in 1232 when another invading army—the Mongols—invaded Korea. Once again seeking the Buddha's help, the Korean court ordered another copy produced. The result, completed in 1251, was the most complete collection of Buddhist texts anywhere in the Far East. In 1398, it was moved to its current location in Haeinsa; the halls in which it is now stored are believed to date to the late 15th century.

Woodblocks, naturally, are subject to the elements, and particularly tricky to preserve. Yet Janggyeong Panjeon—which has miraculously managed to survive several disasters that destroyed the rest of the temple complex—has done a perfect job in preserving this most important Korean cultural treasure. Its builders utilized nature and creative architectural techniques to create a space where humidity is kept at ideal levels for preserving the woodblocks. Its location prevents damp winds from the south and cold winds from the north. Its slatted windows—which are sized differently in the north and south halls—ventilate the halls, while its materials absorb excess humidity in the hot summer and retain humidity during the dry winter. The blocks themselves were made from sturdy birch from southern Korea. The wood was soaked in sea water for two years, cut into blocks and then boiled in salt water. Afterwards, they were left exposed to the wind for three years, carved and then covered in lacquer to protect against insects.

Not even modern technology has bested the Janggyeong Panjeon—when the woodblocks were moved to a newly built modern storage facility in 1970, they developed mildew, and were promptly returned to their original storage location.

While you're in the hall, be sure to gaze out the oval-shaped entrance to the southern hall—it's the Korean sense of aesthetics at its best.

ANDONG 안동

To see the "real Korea," one must head to Andong. Gyeongju and Jeju Island may draw the tourist set, but the provincial town of Andong—located deep in the province of Gyeongsangbuk-do—is like going back in time. Here, at the center of Korea's Confucian heartland, the old ways coexist and, in some instances, trump the 21st century. Andong is a treasure trove of artifacts from the genteel days of the Joseon era, including magnificent Confucian academies and rustic riverside villages that have changed little over the centuries. But make no mistake— Andong is no tourist trap; it's a living, breathing village and home to a people fiercely proud of their heritage and way of life.

Andong bills itself as Korea's "spiritual cultural capital," and there's no denying that the Confucian way of life still runs strong. Confucianism has had a profound effect on Korean culture and still informs a good many of the social mores of modern Korea. Nowhere is this more apparent than in Andong. The locals may have traded in their *hanbok* for Western clothing, and youngsters may attend modern schools, but they maintain the dignity and grace of their aristocratic ancestors.

Andong's unique cultural charm is due to its close association with Korea's *yangban* culture. Part scholar, part government official, part landowner, the

Dosan Seowon, a stately Confucian academy founded in the 16th century

yangban formed the elite of Joseon era society, armed with knowledge of Chinese classics and the intricate system of ritual and etiquette demanded by Joseon's guiding neo-Confucian ideology. Andong was home to many influential yangban families, and one of the Joseon era's two greatest Confucian scholars, Yi Hwang, lived and taught here. Among its secluded valleys, great Confucian academies were built, producing many of the Joseon era's greatest minds.

Today, Andong is a pleasant provincial town and major regional educational center. The yangban system may be gone, but in the hearts and minds of Andong, aristocracy lives on. In 1999, Queen Elizabeth II celebrated her 73rd birthday here. While the downtown has little to keep your attention, the countryside is a cornucopia of Joseon-era culture. Key destinations include the major Confucian academy of Dosan Seowon to the north, the exquisite Buddhist temple of Bongjeong-sa to the northwest, and the Joseon-era hamlet of Hahoe Village and magnificent Byeongsan Seowon Confucian academy to the west.

Dosan Seowon Confucian Academy 도산서원

It wouldn't be a stretch to call Andong the Cambridge of Joseon-era Korea. The rugged mountains of the northern region of Gyeongsangbuk-do were virtually dotted with seowon, private Confucian academies established by leading scholars and influential yangban families. From the 15th century when these schools first appeared, to their closure by the regent Heungseon

Daewongun in 1871, the seowon was a backbone of rural gentry society.

Dosan Seowon, about 30 minutes by bus from downtown Andong, is both the largest and most famous of Korea's seowon. Founded in 1574 by the students of Yi Hwang some four years after their mentor's death, Dosan Seowon is a masterpiece of Korean Confucian architecture. The complex consists of numerous classrooms, dormitories, shrines,

Old testing place, Dosan Seowon (left), Bongjeongsa Temple

pavilions, courtyards and the very spot where *seowon* students sat for the critical civil service examinations. It's best to set aside at least a half-day to wander through the maze of stone walls and tile roofs and imagine *yangban* life at its prime.

🚇 1,500 won 🚏 From Andong Bus Terminal, take Bus No. 67 to Dosan Seowon.

Bongjeongsa Temple 봉정사

Andong isn't generally associated with Buddhist culture, but in Bongjeongsa sits one of Korea's most beautiful Buddhist temples. Since it's off-the-beaten path, Bongjeongsa, unlike other crowded temples, can be enjoyed in real peace and serenity.

Bongjeongsa was founded in 672 by National Preceptor Uisang, one of Korea's greatest Buddhist monks. Legend has it that a paper crane he let loose from the nearby monastery of Buseoksa (see p561) landed on this spot. Thanks to its isolation, the temple was spared the ravages of war and civil unrest, and today represents one of the most splendid displays of traditional Korean architecture.

From the parking lot, it's a pleasant walk up to the temple complex. Just before Iljumun Gate, which separates the secular and spiritual worlds, there's a small Korean

pavilion overlooking a waterfall that was built in 1665 by students of Yi Hwang. The temple itself sits atop a series of terraces and, passing an impressive two-storey pavilion, the main courtyard comes into view. The Daeungjeon 대웅전 (Treasure No. 55) or Main Hall, and its stunning original murals, are breathtaking. To your left is the Hwaeom Gangdang 화엄강당 (Treasure No. 448), a study hall dating from 1588, and overlooking the terraces is Manseru Pavilion 만세루, which houses the temple's ceremonial musical instruments.

Behind Hwaeom Gangdang is another courtyard featuring Geungnakjeon 극락전 ("Nirvana Hall"), Korea's oldest wooden building, dating back to 1363 and designated National Treasure No. 15. It's a simple earth-yellow hall with slatted windows and no door, and is one of only a handful of Goryeo-era wood buildings still in existence. In front of the hall is a small stone pagoda (dating from the Goryeo era) and the small Gogeumdang Hall 고금당, built in 1616 and designated Treasure No. 449.

A short distance from the main courtyard is a small detached hermitage called Yeongsanam 영산암 that's simply not to be missed. Built in the 19th century, this locale is as close to Nirvana as you're likely to get. A few weathered old buildings, exquisitely painted interiors, a breezy open courtyard, some gnarled old trees, a small perfect stone lantern—it's the epitome of Korean traditional design. So enchanting is the atmosphere that it was featured as the film set for the 1989 Buddhist classic, *Why Has Bodhi-Dharma Left For The East?*

🏛 1,500 won. 🚌 The bus to Bongjeongsa leaves from Andong Elementary School's front entrance 안동초등학교정문 (40 min).

Hahoe Village 하회마을

Andong's most famous tourist attraction is, undoubtedly, Hahoe Village. This small hamlet, about 30 minutes by bus from downtown Andong, sits on a bend of Hwacheon Stream 화천, a tributary of the mighty Nakdonggang River. Since the 16th century, it's been solely a one-clan village, home of the influential Pungsan Ryu family, including Ryu Seong-nyong, the great prime minister during the Imjin War (1592–1598), and members of his family live here to this day.

This idyllic village, surrounded by the meandering Hwacheon Stream and backed by dramatic cliffs, is quite the tourist draw card, with all the trappings. That being said, it's still a must-visit site—wandering

Hahoe Mask Dance Drama

around its romantic clay-walled alleys, or sipping a bowl of *dongdongju* 동동주 rice wine on the wooden porch of a century-old home, is an unforgettable way to spend an afternoon. Despite the abundance of traditional Korean homes, some of which are designated treasures, this is most certainly not a "folk village" (even if many of the residences have been converted into restaurants and homestay facilities), but a real community dating back some 500 years. A bird's-eye view of the village from Buyongdae 부용대, a cliff across the river from the village, is unforgettable.

The village is also famous for the *Hahoe Byeolsin-Gut Tal-Nori* or Hahoe Mask Dance Drama. The Hahoe Mask Dance, dating back to the Joseon era, is a six-act

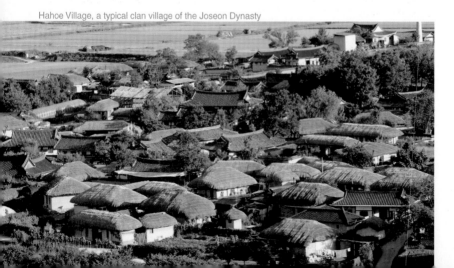

Hahoe Village, a typical clan village of the Joseon Dynasty

satire of hierarchical Joseon society—lecherous monks, pedantic scholars, crude commoners—combining shamanist ritual and popular entertainment. From March to November, there are regular performances of the Mask Dance at Hahoe Village (3 pm Saturday and Sunday at from May to October, and 3 pm Sunday at in March, April and November). The highly popular Andong International Mask Dance Festival takes place here in autumn.

🍜 2,000 won 🚌 Take a bus to Hahoe Village from Andong Bus Terminal (30 min).

Byeongsan Seowon 병산서원

Not far Hahoe Village is Byeongsan Seowon, another of Andong's Confucian academies. While not as large or famous as Dosan Seowon, Byeongsan Seowon lacks nothing in terms of aesthetic beauty. Moved to its current location in 1572 by Prime Minister Ryu Seong-nyong to train students, this *seowon* is set against dramatic cliffs, the graceful lines of the school buildings and a natural backdrop said to resemble a folding screen.

Entry into Byeongsan Seowon is free but it's a bit difficult to get to. Buses are infrequent; by taxi, a trip to Buyongdae cliff, Byeongsan Seowon and Hahoe Village can be had for about 40,000 won, and is well worth it.

WHAT TO EAT

Gyeongsangbuk-do isn't generally known for its food, but Andong is noted for its unique cuisine. Perhaps most famous is Andong steamed chicken or *Andong jjimdak* 안동찜닭—chunks of chicken with potatoes and glass noodles in a sweet and spicy dark sauce. The best place to score this is an alley of restaurants in Andong's downtown market. A whole chicken will run you about 15,000 won but it's enough to feed a party of three or four. More regional specialties are Andong salted mackerel (*gan godeungeo* 간고등어) and *heotjesabap* 헛제사밥 or "fake ancestral rites food," steamed and fried foods served on brassware commonly used during the *jesa* or ancestral rites. Like "true" ancestral rites food, no red pepper is added. Andong *soju*, meanwhile, is one of Korea's most famous traditional firewaters—at 45% alcohol it's got quite a kick. It comes in beautiful ceramic bottles, and gets better with age. Another local beverage is Andong *sikhye* or fermented rice nectar. While you're there, Hahoe Village is also a good place to eat. Highly recommended is Hadong Gotaek 하동고택 (054-853-3776), a century-old home that now serves as a restaurant/inn, with excellent food and an atmosphere that can't be beat.

WHERE TO STAY

Like many other provincial towns, downtown Andong is full of cheap inns and motels but luxury accommodation is lacking. The swankiest place in town is Andong Park Tourist Hotel 안동 파크관광호텔 (054-859-1500), across from Andong Train Station, where suites are available for 87,000 won. The most culturally rewarding option is a homestay or *minbak*, in Hahoe Village. Usually costing 50,000 won or so, it's best to reserve a room early, especially in the autumn high season. The Korean homepage of Hahoe Village (http://hahoe.or.kr/) has a list of places and phone numbers in Korean. The nicest place is lovely Bukchondaek 북촌댁 (010-2228-1786, www.bukchondaek.com), a 200-year-old house where rooms begin at 200,000 won a night. Another upscale option is RakKoJae Hahoe Maeul 락고재 하회마을 (010-8555-1407 1407, http://rkj.co.kr), a beautiful collection of thatched roof homes where rooms begin at 160,000 won a night.

TRANSPORT INFO

Andong can be reached via train or bus. Frequent buses to Andong leave from Dong Seoul Terminal and take about 3 hours. If rail is more your style, trains to Andong depart from Seoul's Cheongnyangni Station eight times a day. The trip takes four hours.

KOREAN CONFUCIANISM

History and Culture

It's often said that Korea is the world's most Confucian nation. Given the impact the philosophical system has had on Korean culture and society, it's a claim that's hard to dispute.

Confucianism—or *yugyo* in Korean—is a system of ethics and philosophy based on the moral, religious and political teachings of the Chinese philosopher Kong Zi (551–479 BC), better known in the West by his Latinized name, Confucius. At its heart, Confucianism is a highly humanistic system that seeks to develop benevolence through the development of personal character. Great emphasis is placed on learning, interpersonal relationships, respect for your elders, tradition and relations between rulers and the ruled.

Andong's Byeongsan Seowon, one of the many Confucian academies built throughout Korea during the Joseon Dynasty

Confucianism has been part of the Korean cultural landscape going back to at least the Three Kingdoms period. Until the Joseon Dynasty, however, Confucianism's impact was limited largely to the administrative sphere, while the state religion of Buddhism had a much greater cultural and social impact.

This changed in 1392, when Gen. Yi Seong-gye launched a coup and, with the support of Confucian officials, founded the Joseon Dynasty. Under its Confucian élites, the new dynasty revolutionized Korea—Buddhism was sidelined, and all aspects of society were reorganized along Confucian lines. Joseon's rulers favored a school of thought known as Neo-Confucianism, a form of Confucianism that borrowed spiritual and metaphysical elements of Taosim and Buddhism. On the throne sat an absolute king assisted by a court of scholar-officials schooled in Confucian learning. At the top of the social ladder was a class of scholar elites known as *yangban* who, at least in theory, owed their position to their mastery of the Confucian classics. Great emphasis was placed on rites and ceremonies, especially rites to honor ancestors. In the arts, the more ostentatiously ornate designs favored by previous dynasties were replaced by simpler, more rustic motifs.

Korean Confucianism underwent a Golden Age in the 16th century with the appearance of its two greatest scholars, "Toegye" Yi Hwang (1501–1570) and "Yulgok" Yi I (1536–1584). Yi Hwang, who was born and educated in Andong, spent 40 years of his life in public service, and used much of the rest to pen countless essays and commentaries on Neo-Confucian philosophy. More on Yi I, meanwhile, can be found on p259. Confucianism underwent a second Golden Age in the 17th and 18th centuries during the *silhak* movement (see p203).

Confucianism's role as a ruling ideology ended with the collapse of the Joseon Dynasty in 1910. Today, very few Koreans would identify themselves as Confucianist, but Confucianism's impact on Korean culture and society is still very much in evidence. Koreans' famous thirst for education is a Confucian legacy, as is the culture of test-taking in Korean schools. Age, seniority and rank are very important in Korean society, especially at the workplace. Once regarded as an impediment to Korean development, scholars now praise the Confucian work ethic and educational spirit as key to the nation's phenomenal economic growth over the last century.

Yecheon 예천

Off the Beaten Track

One town over to the west of Andong is Yecheon, another old *yangban* village. A pleasant enough piece of rural Korea it may be, but the real reason you'd want to come here is to check out the scenic riverbend village of Hoeryongpo or sip some milky rice wine at Samgang Jumak.

Hoeryongpo 회룡포

Like its more famous cousin, Andong's Hahoe Village (and the less famous Museom Village in Yeongju), Hoeryongpo is a beautiful riverbend village of the kind found along the meandering Nakdonggang River 낙동강 and its tributaries. The river, village, fields, mountains and sky harmonize to form a charming vista. Unlike Hahoe Village, though, it's not overrun by tourists and tourist facilities. In recent years, Yecheon has been working hard to attract tourists, so on a weekend, you'll find a good many visitors (but nowhere near the amount you'll find in Andong). If you're looking for something "pristine," this might fit the bill.

There's not a whole lot to see in the village itself—also in contrast to ultra-elite Hahoe Village, Hoeryongpo was and still is a small community of humble farmers who grow rice, red peppers and watermelon.

That said, it has a beautiful sandy beach, and access to the village is limited to the so-called "Ppyongppyong Bridge 뿅뿅다리," made of scaffolding metal. The scenery is really quite beautiful, and extremely peaceful—nothing but the sound of the crystal clear river and cool autumn breeze.

▣ From Yecheon Bus Terminal, take a bus to the smaller town of Yonggung 용궁 (20 min), then take a taxi to Jangansa Temple 장안사 (5 min), and from there follow the path to the observation point.

Samgang Jumak 삼강주막

Samgang Jumak—built about 100 years ago on the bank of the confluence of the Nakdonggang River and Naeseongcheon and Geumcheon streams—was run by Yoo Yok-yeon for about 70 years until she passed away at the age of 90 in 2005. A *jumak* is a traditional Korean pub/inn—during the Joseon Dynasty, such places of hospitality could be found all over Korea, particularly on major travel routes for *yangban* going to the royal capital to take the civil service exam. With Korea's modernization, however, *jumak* disappeared; Yoo's was pretty much the only one left.

After her death, however, the venerable institution was left empty and fell into a sad state of disrepair until the county stepped in. Operated now by Yecheon-gun, it's back doing what it used to do—serving *makgeolli*, *dongdongju* and Korean pub food. The tree behind the pub, incidentally, is about 200 years old.

▣ From Yecheon Station, take a local bus to Samgang 삼강. The bus passes through the towns of Pungyang and Yeongsun, and takes about 40 minutes. If you're visiting Hoeryongpo, however, it may be easier just to take a cab from Yonggung.

MUNGYEONG 문경

Located in the foothills of Sobaeksan Mountains in the province of Gyeongsangbuk-do, the town of Mungyeong is a most underrated scenic destination. What it lacks in name recognition, it makes up for in small-town charm, history and pristine mountain scenery. Koreans know it mostly for the beautiful Mungyeong Saejae Pass, a historic thoroughfare that once linked southeast Korea with the capital area, but there's much more to the town, including one of Korea's most intriguing Buddhist temples and some of the best hiking destinations you've never heard of.

Mungyeong Saejae Pass 문경새재

Mungyeong's biggest drawing card is the fabled Saejae Pass, historically one of the few passes through the Sobaeksan Mountains, which separate the central Chungcheong provinces from the southeastern Yeongnam region (i.e., the Gyeongsang-do provinces). It is for this reason that the town has long been called the "Gateway to Yeongnam." The area around the pass is now Mungyeong Saejae Provincial Park 문경새재도립공원.

The Saejae, literally "Bird Pass," is a narrow passageway flanked on both sides by towering peaks. Besides its obvious economic and social importance, the pass was also a pivotal strategic point for the defense of the capital region. At no time was this better illustrated than in the opening stages of the Imjin War (1592–1598), when the Korean commander Gen. Sin Lip inexplicably left the pass undefended, allowing two Japanese columns to converge on him on the plains

Mungyeong Saejae Pass, the old road linking the Korean southeast with the central region around Seoul

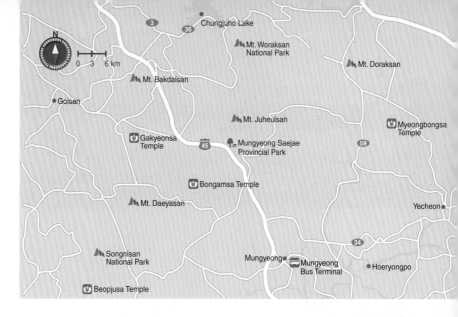

of Chungju, where he and his defenders were slaughtered to the last man.

After the Imjin War, Korea's rulers were determined not to repeat the mistake and built a series of fortifications to defend the pass. The three fortress walls remain to this day, with later restoration work having returned them to their former glory. It's a 3.4 km walk from the first fortress wall to the third—the path takes you past imposing fortress gates, green forests, cool mountain streams and dramatic stone peaks.

The pass is bounded on one side by majestic Mt. Juheulsan 주흘산 at 1,106 m and the other by Mt. Joryeongsan 조령산 at 1,024 m. Mt. Juheulsan is by far the easier and more popular hike—the trail takes you past the Buddhist temple of Hyeguksa 혜국사, and the peak offers outstanding views of the surrounding peaks and countryside. The hike takes about five hours. Joryeongsan can be hiked in four hours. The rocky peak of Bubong 부봉 can also be hiked.

Mungyeong Saejae Provincial Park is also home to a large film set used by the Korean TV producer KBS. The set also serves as a folk village, with the order of the day being a Goryeo-era palace and residential architecture. The set is, in fact, one of the largest of its kind in the world.

🚍 From Jeomchon City Bus Terminal 점촌버스터미널, take Bus No. 100 (50 min).

Bongamsa Temple 봉암사

Founded in the late ninth century, the Buddhist monastery of Bongamsa is, simply put, magical. In this remote valley deep in the mountains of the central Korean town of Mungyeong, pristine nature, scenic beauty and spiritual energy converge to produce a hidden wonderland that is both entrancing and otherworldly. It's a charm enhanced and protected by the temple's

Second Gate, Mungyeong Saejae

A true hidden gem, Bongamsa Temple is open to the public only once a year.

special status: designated by Korea's Jogye Order of Korean Buddhism as a special meditation center and training members of the order, it is closed to the public for 364 days a year. Only on the Buddha's Birthday does it open its gates, making a visit a once-in-a-year experience.

A short walk from the temple brings you to a most idyllic spot, the pristine valley stream of Baegundae 백운대. Here is one and everything: trees, stone, water and the occasional sound of the moktak, a Buddhist wood block. The monks use Baegundae as a relaxation and mediation spot. Little wonder why, either—the tranquility of the stream, surrounded as it is by thick forests, is absolutely sublime. Some of the granite slabs, rocks and boulders sport carvings of Chinese characters. One rock face features a

relief of a Bodhisattva, carved in the late Goryeo era (918–1392). All of this serves to complement the natural beauty of the valley.

A final note: Bongamsa is open but just once a year—we cannot stress this enough. Visit on any day other than Buddha's Birthday and you will be turned away at the gate, no questions asked. Don't plan on hiking Mt. Huiyangsan from the Mungyeong side, either—the monks have closed off the paths (you can, however, hike it from the Goesan 괴산 side).

In Jeomchon, head to the city bus terminal and take a bus to Bongamsa. Buses depart from Jeomchon at 7:40, 9:40, 1:40, 5:40 and 7:10 pm. The trip takes about 30 minutes, but on the Buddha's Birthday, traffic spikes considerably and the bus drops you off on the main road—it's another 20 minute walk to the temple. Shuttle buses are in operation, though.

You'll find plenty of restaurants in front of Mungyeong Saejae Provincial Park. One particularly nice place is Somunnan Sikdang 소문난식당 (054-572-2255), which does a local specialty called *mukjobap* 묵조밥 (6,000 won), millet rice with acorn jelly.

WHAT TO EAT

There are plenty of cheap inns and motels in front of Jeomchon Station, Jeomcheon Intercity Bus Terminal and Mungyeong Saejae. The nicest places, however, are around Mungyeong Oncheon 문경온천 (054-571-2002), the hot springs resort a few kilometers south of Mungyeong Saejae. Mungyeongsaejae Youth Hostel 문경새재유스호스텔 (054-571-5533, www.saejae-yh.co.kr) is conveniently located in front of Mungyeong Saejae Provincial Park, and has rooms beginning at 14,000 won.

WHERE TO STAY

Buses to Mungyeong leave from Seoul's Dongseoul Bus Terminal. The trip takes about two hours. Mungyeong's intercity bus terminal is located in Jeomchon 점촌, Mungyeong's new "downtown" area. The city bus terminal is a short taxi ride from the intercity terminal—it's here that you can find buses to other locales in the city.

TRANSPORT INFO

BUSEOKSA TEMPLE 부석사

If asked about the single greatest piece of architecture existing in Korea today, one would, without hesitation, answer Buseoksa Temple. Simply put, Buseoksa ("Temple of the Floating Rock") is a perfect architectural expression of Buddhism, each terrace and angle shedding new light on the nature of existence itself.

Buseoksa Temple is located on the southern slope of Mt. Bonghwasan 봉화산, with a commanding view of the surrounding Sobaeksan Mountains separating the provinces of Gyeongsangbuk-do and Gangwon-do. It was founded in 676 AD by Uisang, one of Korea's greatest Buddhist scholars and a progenitor of the Hwaeom (Avatamsaka) sect in Korea.

According to legend, a young woman by the name of Shan-miao fell in love with the monk while he was studying in China. When Uisang returned to Korea, Shan-miao threw herself into the sea, where she transformed into a protective dragon. When villagers refused to clear the spot selected for Buseoksa by Uisang, the she-dragon persuaded the stubborn locals to relocate by threatening to crush them with a boulder. The rock, which seems to float in the air, is still there, and it is from this legend that the temple takes its name.

The temple has had remarkably good fortune. In 1916, while repairs on the

The Buddhist temple of Buseoksa may be Korea's most stunning.

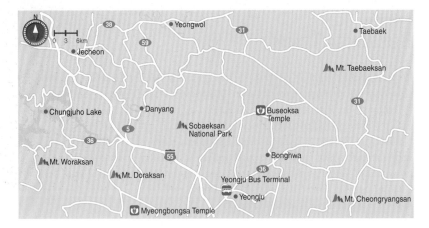

central Muryangsujeon Hall 무량수전 were being conducted, records were discovered indicating it was last reconstructed in 1376, making it the second oldest surviving wooden building in Korea, and one of only a handful of wooden structures dating from the Goryeo era. Further up on the mountain is another small hall, the Josadang 조사당, also built in the late Goryeo era.

108 Steps

Any visit to Buseoksa begins with the hike to the temple itself. The path to the complex is preceded by a series of 108 stone steps that pass through a succession of gates. The number 108 is significant: according to Buddhism, mankind is afflicted with 108 defilements—gluttony, quarrelsomeness and lecherousness being among them. The steps, accordingly, are divided into nine blocks, symbolically representing the nine degrees of rebirth of Pure Land Buddhism. Accordingly, as you ascend the steps, you symbolically shed the 108 defilements and pass through the nine degrees of rebirth until you finally enter Nirvana.

Nirvana Land

Just before you reach the main courtyard, you pass under a wooden gateway/pavilion known as Anyangmun 안양문 or "Nirvana Gate." As you pass through, Nirvana—

108 Steps, Buseoksa Temple

Sunset over Mt. Sobaeksan, Buseoksa Temple

represented by Muryangsujeon Hall—gradually comes into view. Once you arrive, a most spectacular view greets you—the countless peaks of the Sobaeksan Mountains.

At the heart of this Nirvana world is Muryangsujeon Hall, National Treasure No. 18. The hall, with its simple adornment, presents an effortless refined dignity. It is noble yet inviting, an architectural expression of Pure Land Buddhism, an embodiment of its concept of Western Paradise. Appropriately, enshrined in the western end of the hall is a magnificent clay statue of Amitabha Buddha, the Buddha of the Western Paradise. It is the oldest clay statue in Korea and National Treasure No. 45.

In front of Muryangsujeon Hall is a handsome stone lantern dating from the Unified Silla period. With its finely carved lotus leaf pedestal and Bodhisattva reliefs, it is a masterpiece of Silla art. The lantern is designated National Treasure No. 17.

WHAT TO EAT

Yeongju 영주 is famous for its ginseng and its apple harvest in autumn—you should be able to purchase apples along the path to the temple. If you'd prefer to reach Nirvana a bit early, stalls along the way sell—by the cup—milky Korean rice wine or *dongdongju*, with added ginseng. Like most major Buddhist temples, there's a number of good restaurants near the temple parking lot. Buseoksa Sikdang 부석사식당 (054-633-3317) does a really good *gangodeungeo jeongsik* 간고등어정식 (about 10,000 won a person)—rice, soup and plenty of side dishes along with salted mackerel, a regional specialty. You can also try *insam mukbap* 인삼묵밥, a mixed rice dish with ginseng and acorn jelly, for 6,000 won a person.

WHERE TO STAY

Rich Hotel 리치호텔 (054-638-7070) near Yeongju Station is adequate for 40,000 won a night. There are a couple of cheaper but dingier options near Yeongju Station as well.

TRANSPORT INFO

Buseoksa Temple is best approached via the provincial city of Yeongju in Gyeongsangbuk-do. You can reach Yeongju via bus from Seoul's Dong Seoul Terminal or Express Bus Terminal (2 hrs 30 min). Or take a train from Seoul's Cheongnyangni Station (3 hrs 30 min), the scenery being particularly nice in autumn.

From Yeongju, there are frequent city buses to Buseoksa—it's probably easiest to catch the one that leaves from the bus stop opposite Yeongju Intercity Bus Terminal. If you've arrived by train, taking a taxi from Yeongju Station to Yeongju City Bus Terminal is best.

ULJIN 울진

One of the nicer spots to spend a winter weekend is the small east coast town of Uljin-gun, in the province of Gyeongsangbuk-do. A small fishing community some five hours away from Seoul by bus, this is about as far removed from the madding crowds of Seoul and Busan as one can get in the Republic of Korea. It has a quaint provincial feel that is as relaxing and reinvigorating as it is disarmingly charming. From the beautiful vistas of the East Sea, backed by the majestic peaks of the Taebaeksan Mountain Range, to soaking in both the water and splendid scenery of the outdoor bath of Deokgu Spa, Uljin provides plenty of ways to recharge both the mind and spirit.

Crab Kingdom

The northern part of Uljin is dominated by the minor transportation hub of Bugu 부구 and the small fishing village of Jukbyeon 죽변. About a 20 minute bus ride from Uljin Bus Terminal, Jukbyeon is a major center for Korea's trade in snow crabs, called *daege* 대게. Uljin—and much of the rest of the East Sea coast—lives on the back of this sweet and succulent crustacean that thrives in the cold waters of the North Pacific Ocean.

Jukbyeon is a place you want to visit in the morning. Head by the waterfront at around 9 am to see the daily crab market,

Port of Jukbyeon

Uljin takes its crabs seriously.

where fishermen and restaurateurs haggle over the morning's catch. This is a full sensory experience—the port area is surrounded, unsurprisingly, by a ton of restaurants specializing in—you guessed it—crab. Winter is a good time for seafood, and nothing quite beats a delicious steamed crab on a windy winter day on the East Sea coast. Crab prices vary from day to day depending on the catch, but most of the time, one crab will run you anywhere from 7,000 won to 30,000 won.

Also nearby, sitting atop a hill overlooking the harbor, is the Jukbyeon Lighthouse, a beautiful white structure built in 1910 and once the film set for the KBS TV drama *Into the Storm*. The setting, a lovely house perched on a cliff overlooking the East Sea, is a very romantic spot for both couples or singles looking for a quiet place to reflect.

Hupo 후포 & the East Sea Pavilions

About a 45 minute bus ride south of Uljin Bus Terminal is the port of Hupo, where there is a weekly passenger ferry to the island of Ulleungdo (daily in summer months). This harbor, located in the extreme south of Uljin almost on the border with Yeongdeok-gun, has a major seafood market (if you missed the crabs in Jukbyeon 죽변, you can get them here) that attracts visitors from all over the province. Superb views of the port can be had from the Hupo Lighthouse, a handsome hilltop building built in 1968.

The bus ride to Hupo is a relaxing experience in itself. The route passes by the beautiful Giseong Mangyang 기성망양해수욕장 and Gusan beaches 구산해수욕장, some of the finest on Korea's east coast. Along Giseong Mangyang Beach, you can see sport fishermen sitting atop craggy rocks battered by the whitecaps of the winter sea. At the

Port of Hupo

Mangyangjeong Pavilion provides beautiful views of the East Sea.

sandy Gusan Beach, sit and watch as the tide rolls in, staring out upon the distant horizon—an opportunity rarely afforded in mountainous Korea.

Along the coast between Uljin and Hupo are several beautiful Korean pavilions that overlook the East Sea. The Mangyang-jeong Pavilion 망양정, a few minutes south of downtown Uljin, provides a panoramic view of the East Sea and is an outstanding spot from which to enjoy the sunrise. So beautiful the view is, in fact, that is considered one of the eight most beautiful scenes of the Gwandong region (the northern East Sea region, centering on Gangwon-do). Further south toward Hupo, in the small community of Pyeonghae-eup, is Wolsongjeong Pavilion. This pavilion, too, was counted among the Gwandong region's eight most beautiful scenes, surrounded by a beautiful virgin forest and providing a lovely view of the East Sea.

Bulyeong Valley 불영계곡 & Bulyeongsa Temple 불영사

A small Buddhist nunnery at the foot of Mt. Cheonchuksan 천축산, Bulyeongsa is a pleasant enough place, especially when trees turn color in autumn. The reflecting pool—actually a lotus pond in summer—is especially photogenic. In fact, the temple

takes its name, which means "Temple of the Buddha's Reflection," from the pond, in which the reflection of a Buddha-shaped rock from the ridge of one of the surrounding peaks may be seen.

What makes the visit to Bulyeongsa most rewarding, however, is the ride to it. The temple sits at the bottom of Bulyeong Valley, a twisting river gorge cutting its way through the Taebaeksan Mountain Range to the East Sea. The road twists and turns along with it, providing great views, if a bit of a queasy stomach. The road—National Road No. 36, linking Uljin with the town of Bonghwa—was constructed in the 1980s by Korean Army engineers.

🚌 Take a bus from Uljin Bus Terminal to Bulyeongsa Temple (30 min).

Bulyeongsa Temple, at the bottom of the Bulyeongsa Valley

Hot Springs

As spiritually revitalizing that strolls along the winter beach may be, the flesh may need more—this is where Uljin's famous hot springs come in. The town is home to not just one but two major spa resorts. Baegam Spa 백암온천, founded by the Japanese in 1913, is Korea's only radioactive sulfur spa. Nestled on the slopes of Mt. Baegamsan 백암산 (1,004 m), this spa has tons of places to stay and soak in the water, which is rich in potassium chloride, sodium hydroxide and magnesium hydroxide, and is said to be good for various nervous disorders, arthritis, arteriosclerosis, stomach disorders and many other ailments. It's also good for soothing muscles fatigued from the daily grind.

The newer Deokgu Spaworld 덕구스파월드, on the other hand, is Korea's only natural open-air spa. If you're accustomed to playing with macaque monkeys in natural Japanese hot springs, you may be disappointed, but it's a world apart from your neighborhood bathhouse. Surrounded by beautiful mountains that become a

Deokgu Spaworld

winter wonderland after a heavy snow, Deokgu Spa is *the* place to come to soak and enjoy the beautiful outdoors at the same time. You'd be hard-pressed to find a more relaxingly blissful way to pass a winter afternoon.

Admission to Hanwha Resort Baegam Hot Springs (6 am to 9 pm; 10 pm on weekends) is 9,000 won. Deokgu Spaworld 덕구 스파월드 (6 am to 10 pm), a massive spa complex that takes care of all your hot water needs, costs 7,000 won for the baths only, but 25,000 won (peak season) will get you into the baths, other spa pools including the outdoor pool. Buses to the Baegam and Deokgu spring areas depart from Uljin Bus Terminal. You can also find direct buses to/ from Seoul's Dong Seoul Bus Terminal.

WHAT TO EAT

Uljin is best known for its snow crab, and the best places to dine are the ports of Jukbyeon and Hupo, where you'll find plenty of seafood restaurants, including a big seafood center (shaped like a boat) in Hupo. The town holds a crab festival in late February–early March, so this is the best time to go if eating is your objective.

WHERE TO STAY

The best places to stay in Uljin are the hot spring districts, although these can book up in late summer and winter peak seasons. Western-style rooms at Backam Springs Hotel 백암스프링스호텔 (054-787-3007, www.springshotel.co.kr [KR]) begin at 55,000 won a night during peak season. Baegam Oncheon Hotel Phoenix 백암온천호텔 피닉스 (054-787-3006, baekam-hotspa. co.kr) is a pleasant place to stay with Western-style rooms beginning at 65,000 won in peak season. If you've got a family, try Hanwha Resort-Baegam Spa 한화호텔앤드리조트 백암온천 (054-787-7001), where Western rooms for five go for 237,999 won in the peak season (rates come down considerably off-peak). Twin rooms at Hotel Deokgu 호텔덕구온천, part of Deokgu Spaworld, start at 150,000 won during peak season.

TRANSPORT INFO

From Seoul, buses to Uljin depart from Dong Seoul Bus Terminal (5 hrs). From Daegu, buses to Uljin depart from Dongbu Bus Terminal (4 hrs 40 min).

JUWANGSAN NATIONAL PARK 주왕산국립공원

The rugged agricultural town of Cheongsong 청송 is, well, off the beaten path. Trains don't run here. Buses from Seoul are infrequent, and travel time is long thanks to the high, verdant mountains that dominate this region of southeastern Korea. It is famous for its apples—which are about as big as an infant's head—and, more notoriously, for its prison, reputedly the most heavily guarded in Korea.

It is also famous for its autumn scenery, some of the most spectacular in all Korea. On your average autumn Saturday or Sunday, Mt. Juwangsan National Park is overrun with hikers who come to see the park's stunning foliage, fantastic rock formations and enchanting waterfalls. The mysterious Jusanji Pond, meanwhile, mesmerizes visitors with the surreal imagery of snarled trees rising from the misty lake, like claws grasping at the early morning sky. If you're willing to make the rugged four and a half hour bus trek, you couldn't ask for a better autumn weekend getaway from Seoul.

Hikers enjoying the autumn foliage of Daejeonsa Temple and Mt. Juwangsan

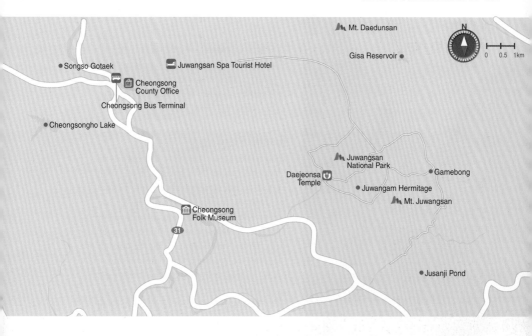

Mt. Juwangsan 주왕산

Even if you're not the mountain-hiking type, Mt. Juwangsan is well worth your time. While peak-baggers are free to challenge the mountain's granite summits, most visitors opt for a leisurely stroll up the Jubang Valley 주방계곡, which cuts a path through the middle of the park. Along the way, you're treated to a breathtaking display of sheer canyons and crystal-clear streams that have carved a variety of pools and waterfalls from the smooth granite. Above your head, craggy rock formations, cliffs and peaks add to the natural splendor.

To enjoy Mt. Juwangsan at its very best, however, you have to visit in autumn. When the foliage is at its zenith, the mountainsides become a brilliant display of bright crimson and gold. Throw in the other colors—the aquamarine pools, silver rock walls, and the gaudy but functional attire of a good portion of the hiking population—and you can suffer from

 TIPS

MORNING CLOUDS

If you can get up early, visit the park at daybreak, when the clouds and fog accumulate at the base of the rocky peaks.

APPLE DONGDONGJU

Many of the restaurants in front of Daejeonsa sell *dongdongju* 동동주—a variation of the favorite Korean rice beer *makgeolli*—infused with apple, jujube and Korean bellflower root (*deodeok* 더덕).

Hiking path, Mt. Juwangsan

sensory overload.

The main trail takes you past a couple of spots of historical interest, too. At the entrance to Jubang Valley trail is the ancient Buddhist temple of Daejeonsa 대전사, famous for its stupendous setting, the rock peaks of Mt. Juwangsan forming a folding screen-esque backdrop. Also of interest is Juwangam 주왕암, a small hermitage where, it is said, Juwang—a nobleman from Tang China and the mountain's namesake—hid following a failed uprising against the Chinese emperor.

3,200 won There are frequent local buses a day, several each hour, from downtown Cheongsong to Juwangsan (20 min)

HIKING COURSE

Daejeonsa Temple ——→ 1st Waterfall (and Juwangam Hermitage) ——→ 2nd Waterfall ——→ 3rd Waterfall ——→ Return to Daejeonsa. (approx. 4 hrs)

Jusanji Pond 주산지

Jusanji Pond is the very definition of "hidden treasure." Or, at least, it was. Not even a decade ago, hardly anyone besides locals knew it even existed. Then Korean auteur Kim Ki-duk came to town to shoot his 2003 art house classic, *Spring, Summer, Fall, Winter...and Spring*. Using the pond as the film's main setting, Kim put it on tourist maps, although luckily, Cheongsong's (and the pond's!) general isolation prevent it from being overrun by visitors. Among photographers and nature connoisseurs, it is considered one of Korea's most picturesque sites.

Technically speaking, Jusanji Pond is an agricultural reservoir, first constructed between 1720 and 1721. Located within the confines of Mt. Juwangsan National Park, the pond is ringed by dense forests and hillsides that enhance an atmosphere of otherworldliness. The banks are lined with gnarled willow trees, the roots of which are submerged beneath the pond's surface when water levels are high enough (as they are in spring and the summer rainy season). In the early morning hours, when fog covers the pond surface, the view is beyond surreal.

The best time to go is just prior to sunrise. This might require a relatively expensive 20 minute taxi ride, but if you've made it this far, you might as well splurge.

To get to Jusanji Pond by bus, take a local bus from Cheongsong to Ijeon-ri. From there, take the trail to the pond—it's just over 1 km.

An 18th century reservoir, Jusanji Pond is a must-visit in the morning when the lake is covered in fog.

WHERE TO STAY

Downtown Cheongsong and Mt. Juwangsan National Park are home to several inns and motels. Mt. Juwangsan Spa Tourist Hotel 주왕산온천관광호텔 (054-874-7000) is the nicest, if somewhat pricey (standard rooms go for 80,000 won). The village in front of Daejeonsa Temple has many homestay facilities (*minbak*). The best option may be Songso Gotaek 송소고택 (054-873-0234, www.songso.co.kr), a beautiful 130-year-old *hanok*-style villa once home to an aristocrat. Rooms start at 50,000 won a night for two, but be sure to call first. Breakfast costs 6,000 won.

WHAT TO EAT

There are tons of restaurants serving standard Korean fare in front of Daejeonsa Temple, and this is probably where you'll eat. As a general rule, choose one that is busy but if a particular place strikes your fancy, it's probably OK.

TRANSPORT INFO

Cheongsong is best experienced as a two-day trip. Buses to Cheongsong depart from Seoul's Dong Seoul Terminal at 6:20, 8:40, 10:20, 11:40 am, 3 and 4:30 pm. Return buses depart at 8:50, 10:57 am, 1:25, 2:40, 4:15 and 5:29 pm (4 hrs). There are also direct buses from Dong Seoul Terminal to Juwangsan National Park, which depart at the same time.

ULLEUNGDO 울릉도

Located some 130 km from the mainland, the East Sea island of Ulleungdo—labeled "Dagelet Island" in early Western maps—is one of Korea's most unique destinations. An extinct volcanic cone rising sharply from the sea, the remote island possesses a natural allure all its own, be it the dramatic coastal cliffs plunging straight into the sea, tiny fishing villages wedged in hidden coves, the exotic volcanic topography of the island itself, or the beautiful nearby islets of Dokdo, Korea's easternmost point. A weekend here is well worth the time and effort, but prepare to stay a day or two longer than planned if the weather turns bad and transport to the mainland is suspended.

Ulleungdo is home to about 10,000 people, about half of whom are engaged in the fishing industry. The island is especially well-known for its squid, and at night, the surrounding seas are dotted with the lights of the squid boat fleet.

History

In ancient times, Ulleungdo was actually an independent state named Usanguk until Silla general Lee Sabu conquered the island in AD 512. Legend has it Lee affixed wooden lions to the prows of his ships, threatening to unleash the beasts on the locals unless they submitted. Throughout the medieval period, Ulleungdo was subject to frequent raids by Japanese and Manchurian pirates. In 1407, the Japanese lord of Tsushima Island even petitioned King Taejong of the Joseon Dynasty for control of the island, a petition that was refused. Frustrated with the constant pirate

Dodonghang Port, seen from Manghyangbong Peak

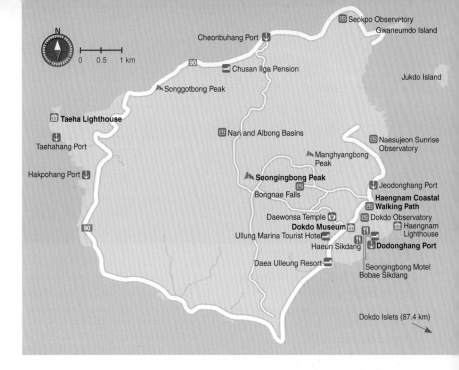

raids, King Taejong in 1416 ordered Ulleungdo depopulated and its population was relocated to the mainland where it could better be protected. The ban on people wasn't perfect, however, and Korean and Japanese fishermen occasionally clashed in the waters off Dokdo until Japan's shogun banned Japanese from sailing to the island in 1696.

In 1787, a French maritime expedition led by Jean-François de Galaup, Comte de Lapérouse, "discovered" the island; the Frenchmen named it "Dagelet Island" after Joseph Lepaute Dagelet, the expedition's astronomer. In 1884, King Gojong ordered the island resettled, but with the outbreak of the Russo-Japanese War in 1904, Imperial Japan occupied the strategic island to build telegraph towers and other military facilities. Imperial Japan would also exploit the island's rich forestry and fishery resources.

In modern times, Ulleungdo has developed into a major fishing center and a growing tourism destination. The islets of Dokdo, located 87 km east of Ulleungdo, have also been subject to sovereignty claims by Japan and accordingly are a subject of diplomatic friction between Seoul and Tokyo.

Layout

The island is roughly circular and about 10 km wide and 72.56 km² in area. It is the very tip of a giant undersea volcanic cone, with steep slopes culminating at Seonginbong Peak (984 m), the island's highest. There's very little flat land, and the bulk of the population lives in small villages along the coast. The exceptions are the Nari and Albong basins 나리–알봉 분지, two small, inland plains formed by a caldera in the north of the island. The coastal areas are quite weatherbeaten, characterized by jagged cliffs and rock formations. It's an almost prehistoric landscape.

Transportation around Ulleungdo is either on foot (quite possible, as the island is not that big) or via a stunning coastal road that rings the island.

Haengnam Coastal Walking Path makes for a wonderful stroll from Dodonghang Port.

Dodonghang Port 도동항 & Haengnam Coastal Walking Path 행남해안산책로

Hidden in a cliff-lined nook, Dodonghang Port has been likened to a pirate cove and, seen from the incoming ferry, the comparison appears apt. The port is the administrative capital of the island and its largest settlement, and it is here you'll find the best selection of accommodations and restaurants. It is also the gateway to the island, where ferries from the mainland arrive and return ferries depart.

The port and its town are scenic enough, wedged into a steep, narrow valley. For a truly inspiring hike, however, follow the hiking path that begins on the left side of the port (if you're facing the sea). Called the Haengnam Coastal Walking Path, the narrow 3.6 km trail (hiking time: 1 hr 20 min) follows the coastal cliffs to Haengnam Lighthouse 행남등대, providing stunning views of both the sea and the island's natural majesty—some of the junipers in the cliffs are 2,000 years old. The path is even lit up at night. Don't miss it!

Dokdo Museum 독도박물관

A 15 minute walk from the harbor—keep heading up, swing a left at the gym and follow the road to the end—brings you to the Dokdo Museum, an exhibit space full of maps, old documents, photographs, films and other materials from Korea, Japan and elsewhere proving Korea's historical ownership of the nearby Dokdo Islets.

The museum is in a small park with an unusual mineral spring with water containing iron carbonate—it tastes like a fizzy drink, and rice cooked in the water turns blue. There's a small Buddhist temple nearby and the terminal for the cable car up Manghyangbong Peak.

🕐 9 am to 6 pm ✆ 054-790-6432~3 🖰 www.dokdomuseum.go.kr

Dokdo Observatory 독도전망대

Atop Manghyangbong Peak 망향봉 is the Dokdo Observatory, a vantage point offering views—weather permitting—of the Dokdo Islets 92 km to the east. Don't get your hopes up, though—normally, this is possible only 50 days a year. Even if you don't glimpse Dokdo, the views of the sea are wonderful, and the sunrises are awesome. The observatory is attached by steps and paths to another observation point where it is said the first settlers came to sooth their sadness.

🚡 Access to the observatory is via a cable car (round trip: 7,500 won) that brings you to Manghyangbong Peak—operation begins 30 minutes prior to sunrise, and ends at 8 pm.

Dodonghang Port (left), Squid boat at night

Seonginbong Peak 성인봉

The highest point on the island is Seonginbong Peak (983.6 m). It's a steep climb considering you start at nearly sea level, but the effort is compensated by the beautiful views over the entire island. The lower slopes of the mountain are covered in verdant primeval forests.

Most hikers begin the trek from Dobong 도봉 (the path begins by Daewonsa Temple 대원사), bag the peak and descend via the Bongnae Waterfall 봉래폭포 to Jeodong 저동, a small port near Dodong. The 9 km hike takes about four hours. If you have a bit more time, however, try descending to the port of Cheonbudong 천부동 on the north side of the island via the Nari Basin, a caldera formed by the partial collapse of the volcanic cone. It is the biggest piece of flat land on the island, and villagers here cultivate medicinal herbs in its rich volcanic soil. You'll also find in the village a few preserved shingle-roof homes of the type lived in by the island's first settlers and not unlike those found in the slash-and-burn mountain towns of Gangwon-do. There's a road from the basin to Cheonbudong, where you can catch a bus back to Dodong.

Songgotbong Peak, seen from port of Cheonbudong

Dokdo Islets are both beautiful and nationalistically significant.

North Shore

The northern coast of Ulleungdo is not quite as rugged as the south, but it has some picturesque sites, most notably the massive rock peak of Songgotbong 송곳봉 behind the port of Cheonbu 천부항. Taking a bus along the coastal ring road is a good way to see it all, but it's also worth stopping by the Seokpo Observatory 석포전망대 at the northernmost end of the island. From Seokpo, you could always head back to Cheonbu to grab a cup of coffee before heading back to Dodong. There's also a rugged hiking path linking Seokpo to the Naesujeon Sunrise Observatory 내수전 일출전망대 on the east shore of the island.

🚌 Take a bus from Dodong to Jugam (1 hr 10 min) and take a taxi or walk from there to the observatory.

Taeha Lighthouse 태하등대

The best view on Ulleungdo, however, might be at Taeha Lighthouse, at the far west end of the island. Indeed, this might be one of the best vistas in all of Korea as you gaze over the rugged, uniquely beautiful north coast of the island. There are some ancient juniper trees up here, too. If you've got a camera—or even if you don't—it's a must see. The sunsets here are especially nice.

🚡 The lighthouse is approached by a specially built tourist monorail (round trip: 4,000 won). ⏰ 6 am to 7 pm (Apr–Oct), 8 am to 6 pm (Nov–Mar) 🚌 Take the bus to Taeha from Dodong.

Dokdo Islets 독도

The spectacularly beautiful Dokdo Islets are not only Korea's easternmost point and one of the country's most scenic spots, but also a symbol of Korean nationalism thanks to Japan's continued claim on them. In the West, they are sometimes referred to as the Liancourt Rocks, after the French whaling ship that "discovered" them in 1849.

The islets are essentially two giant volcanic rocks thrust up from the ocean floor several million years ago. Jagged cliffs dotted by caves make up most of their coastlines. The islets are home to a rich diversity of flora and fauna, especially birds.

Legally speaking, two Korean fishermen are registered as permanent residents of Dokdo. The real human presence, however, is the special detachment of the Korean Coast Guard that is deployed to the islets to protect them from would-be aggressors.

There are tourist ferries from Ulleungdo to Dokdo, but the schedule is quite irregular—best to call 1330 to see if there are boats going out. The trip to Dokdo takes between 2 hours, 10 minutes and four hours depending on the boat, and tourists are allowed only 20 minutes at the pier constructed on the easternmost islet. Still, the views from the boat are magnificent.

Squid drying on a beach of Ulleungdo

WHAT TO EAT

Fish and squid. Almost half the islanders are fishermen, with many working the squid boats, and this is reflected in the island's cuisine. One local specialty is *honghapbap* 홍합밥, or steamed rice with mussels. Bobae Sikdang 보배식당 (054-791-2683) near Ulleung Tourism Information Center is a good place to score this. Another good restaurant to try is Haeun Sikdang 해운식당 (054-791-0002), which does *honghapbap*, traditional Korean favorites like *bibimbap*, and another local specialty, *ojingeo naejangtang* 오징어내장탕, a stew made from vegetables and squid tripe. One Ulleungdo specialty you're likely to run across is *hobakyeot* 호박엿, a taffy made from pumpkin, of which many are grown on the island.

WHERE TO STAY

There are motels, inns and *minbak* (homestay) facilities in Dodong, but you may wish to book a place early during the summer vacation season. The plushest place in town is Ullung Marina Tourist Hotel 울릉마리나관광호텔 (054-791-0020~4, www.ullungmarina.co.kr [KR]), with Western-style rooms starting at 80,000 won a night. If you've got a group together, try Daea Ulleung Resort 울릉대아리조트 (054-791-8800, www.daearesort.com [KR]), with rooms for four beginning at 170,000 won. Seonginbong Motel 성인봉모텔 (054-791-2677, www.uld-sunginmotel.com [KR]) is good value with Western-style rooms beginning at 65,000 won a night. If you want to stay on the north shore, Chusan Ilga Pension 추산일가펜션 (054-791-7788, www.chusanilga.com [KR]) is a pension-style B&B right under Songgotbong Peak. The rooms are in traditional shingle-roof homes, and while basic rooms are nice at 90,000 won during the July–August peak season, the "special rooms" for 150,000 won a night sit right on the coastal cliffs—the views are magnificent.

TRANSPORT INFO

Fast catamarans to Ulleungdo depart from the port of Mukho 묵호항 in Donghae 동해 (see p267, departure: 9 am, 10 am, 2 hrs 20 min–3 hrs) and Pohang 포항 (see p539, departure 10 am, 3 hrs). From Ulleungdo, ferries to Mukho depart at 5:30 pm, while ferries to Pohang depart at 3 pm. Boats leave daily, but the weather out here can be finicky, and there are frequent cancellations due to storms, wind and high waves. Even when the weather is good, the waters of the East Sea can be choppy, making for an exhilarating (or nausea-inspiring) ride.

BUSAN, ULSAN & GYEONGSANGNAM-DO

HIGHLIGHTS

- Experience the pulsating energy, spectacular scenery & seafood offerings of Busan, Korea's second largest city

- Take in the sights along Hallyeohaesang National Park, including the lovely island of Geoje-do

- Explore the mountainous wilds of Jirisan National Park

- Appreciate the tranquility at Upo, Korea's largest inland wetland

- Enjoy a good cup of green tea in Hadong

- Experience Korea's industrial might in Ulsan

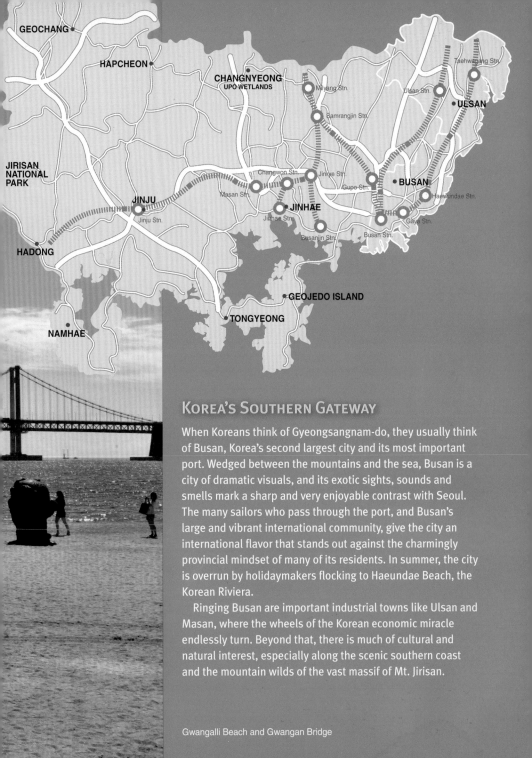

GEOCHANG

HAPCHEON

CHANGNYEONG
UPO WETLANDS

Milyang Stn.

Taehwagang Stn.

Ulsan Stn.

ULSAN

Samrangjin Stn.

JIRISAN
NATIONAL
PARK

Changwon Stn.   Jinye Stn.

Masan Stn.   Gupo Stn.

BUSAN

Haeundae Stn.

JINJU
Jinju Stn.

JINHAE
Jinhae Stn.

Busanjin Stn.   Busan Stn.

Gaya Stn.

HADONG

GEOJEDO ISLAND

NAMHAE

TONGYEONG

KOREA'S SOUTHERN GATEWAY

When Koreans think of Gyeongsangnam-do, they usually think of Busan, Korea's second largest city and its most important port. Wedged between the mountains and the sea, Busan is a city of dramatic visuals, and its exotic sights, sounds and smells mark a sharp and very enjoyable contrast with Seoul. The many sailors who pass through the port, and Busan's large and vibrant international community, give the city an international flavor that stands out against the charmingly provincial mindset of many of its residents. In summer, the city is overrun by holidaymakers flocking to Haeundae Beach, the Korean Riviera.

Ringing Busan are important industrial towns like Ulsan and Masan, where the wheels of the Korean economic miracle endlessly turn. Beyond that, there is much of cultural and natural interest, especially along the scenic southern coast and the mountain wilds of the vast massif of Mt. Jirisan.

Gwangalli Beach and Gwangan Bridge

Busan's spectacular nighttime scenery.

BUSAN 부산

With a metropolitan area of nearly 4.4 million people, Busan is Korea's second largest city, largest port and the commercial, industrial, cultural and educational nexus of southeast Korea. It is to Seoul what Osaka is to Tokyo (or Liverpool to London, or Naples to Rome). Compared with Seoul's esprit de corps of cosmopolitan sophistication, Busan is a rougher, tougher place of salt air, thick regional accents, haphazardly planned neighborhoods, second-city angst and a parochial outlook locals liken to that of a big village. Added to the mix is a bit of industrial seaport grit, complete with Russian sailors on shore leave.

Does this mean you should give Busan a pass? Absolutely not—Busan's grit, urban entropy and salt-of-the-earth denizens give the city a wholly unique charm. Its energetic and free-wheeling ways are infectious. Moreover, few cities enjoy as breathtaking a location as Busan, wedged into a narrow strip of land between the mountains and the sea; some neighborhoods climb the steep valleys almost like Brazilian favelas. You could explore ancient mountainside temples in the morning, lounge the afternoon away on the Korean Riviera, and spent the evening sampling some of the best nightlife in the country—and never even leave the city limits. For visitors in October, you might even bump into a star or two in town to attend the Busan International Film Festival, Asia's biggest celebration of cinema.

History

Prior to the late 19th century, what is now Busan (spelled "Pusan" prior to 2000) was nothing more than a small fishing village and military outpost. In the Japanese invasion of 1592, the Korean fortress of Dongnae—in what is now Busan's district of Dongnae-gu 동래구—was the site of the first battle of the seven-year war. Prior to and following the Japanese invasion, it was also the site of a small Japanese settlement and trading post through which Japan conducted most of its commercial activity with Korea for centuries.

Things began to change greatly for Busan in 1876. Under pressure from Japan, Korea signed the Treaty of Ganghwa, thereby opening three ports to international trade: Incheon, Wonsan and Busan. As the closest port to Japan, Busan became Japan's primary gate into and out of Korea. With dreams of building an empire on the Asian mainland, the Japanese invested heavily in the city's infrastructure, developing its port facilities and equipping the town with a sewage system and even a tram. The city's growth and importance was greatly enhanced by the opening of the Seoul–Busan railway line in 1905. In 1925, the Japanese colonial government transferred the provincial capital of Gyeongsangnam-do from Jinju to Busan. Urbanization and Japanese exploitation created tensions and resentment, however, expressed in acts of resistance like a massive strike by dockworkers in 1921 and a textile workers' strike in 1922.

In 1945, Korea regained its independence, but the newly freed nation was soon wracked by political instability and division. Finally, on June 25, 1950, North Korea invaded the South, kicking off the Korean War. When the North quickly seized most of

Yachts near Haeundae

the South, the South Koreans and their (mostly) American allies set up a defensive perimeter around the city of Busan where they made their last stand. The "Pusan Perimeter" held, giving the allies the time they needed to build up their forces and turn the war around. Busan was one of only a handful of cities to avoid capture during the war, and served as the temporary capital of South Korea for much of the conflict.

While Busan avoided physical capture, the war still stretched the city's resources to near-breaking point as refugees flooded in from all over the country. Prior to the war, Busan's population was 470,000. In 1951, at the height of the war, it had ballooned to 840,000. In 1955, it was over 1 million. The city became a virtual refugee camp, and a dangerous one at that. In 1953, a massive fire ripped through Gukje Market and the refugee shantytown around it, leaving 30,000 homeless.

After the war, Busan assumed a major role in Korea's industrialization. The city and surrounding region became Korea's industrial heartland, home to textile mills, steel refineries, auto factories, heavy machinery plants and shipbuilders. When Korea shifted to export-led growth in the 1960s, Busan's port became the gateway through which Korean-made industrial goods passed en route to overseas markets. The 1970 opening of the Gyeongbu Expressway, linking Busan and Seoul, proved an additional boon to the city; it remains the country's most heavily travelled highway.

Busan also played a major role in Korea's democratization. In 1979, large-scale protests in the city helped bring down the dictatorship of Park Chung-hee. Busan was the hometown of long-time democracy activist and opposition politician Kim Young-sam, who was elected president in 1992, becoming the first civilian to hold the office since 1960.

In recent years, the city has worked hard to boost its international profile. Since 1996, it has hosted the Busan International Film Festival, one of the world's most prominent. It also played host to the 2002 Asian Games and 2005 APEC summit, as well as several matches of the 2002 FIFA World Cup. The city has grown increasingly affluent, too, especially in the Haeundae area, a beachside district of high-rise condos and luxury hotels. And things are looking up—and we do mean up: the city is currently constructing three skyscrapers of 100 floors or more,

Nurimaru APEC House and Gwangan Bridge from Dongbaekseom

including the landmark 110-story Busan Lotte World Tower, to be completed in 2015.

Layout

Busan is wedged in between mountains to the north, the estuary of the Nakdonggang River to the west, and the sea to the south and east. The old downtown is located mostly along the waterfront in the district of Dong-gu. In the east of town is the district of Haeundae, with the best (and most crowded!) beach in Korea, and a truly spectacular skyline of luxury condos. The north is mostly residential, but it's also home to Mt. Geumjeongsan, where you'll find some interesting Joseon Era fortress walls and the beautiful Buddhist monastery of Beomeosa. The west, like the north, is mostly residential sprawl, mixed in with industrial zones, a big new port and Gimhae International Airport.

While most of the bigger mountains lie to the north, even the built-up downtown area is punctuated by steep hills, which often serve to separate one neighborhood from the next. The unique topography can make getting around a bit time-consuming—roads either go around, over or through the mountains. The city does have a four-line subway system, though, which makes traveling much easier.

Port of Busan, as seen from Busan Tower

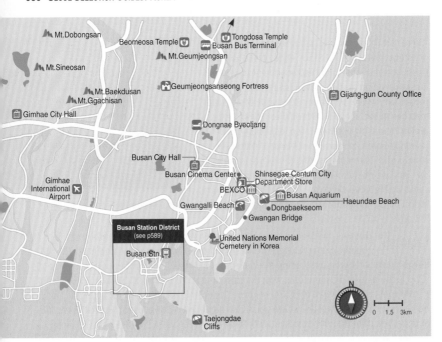

Jagalchi Market, Korea's best known fish market

Busan Station District

Busan's old downtown, Nampo-dong is an energetic district of bustling (and odorous!) markets, colorful alleys, great street food and restaurants, not to mention hilltop parks with terrific views. There's a lot of history here, too. This is a fun place to wander about and explore, taking in the exotic sites, sounds and aromas. Most of what you'll want to see is within easy walking distance of Busan Subway Line 1's Jagalchi, Nampo or Jungang stations—see map on p730.

Jagalchi Market 자갈치시장

One of Busan's must-see sites, this sprawling mass of man and fish is one of Asia's largest seafood markets. The market area stretches along the waterfront from Yeongdo Bridge 영도대교 in the east to the landmark Jagalchi Market building and beyond in the west. A part of the market specializing in dried fish near Yeongdo Bridge is a piece of old Busan—it's a narrow alley lined with small shops, many of them built in Japanese style during the colonial era. While not part of the market itself, there's an especially atmospheric alley right next to Yeongdo Bridge—the ramshackle homes used to a be an enclave of fortune tellers, where countless refugees came to seek solace during the dark days of the Korean War.

Jagalchi Market proper, meanwhile, is a piece of modern Busan, housed in a distinctive, seven-story building. This is THE place to go for raw fish. It's an electric, noisy and, well, smelly place where the energy is infectious. The first floor is where you'll find merchants selling fresh fish, shellfish and other slimy creatures of the sea, much of it still very much alive in tanks. Get here at dawn to witness the daily auction of the day's catch, fresh off the boat. The second floor is mostly raw fish restaurants—select a fish and get it gutted, skinned and sliced to perfection, right on the spot and enjoy leftovers in a hearty seafood stew to end the meal. There's also a roof garden on the 7th floor with great views of the harbor.

Around Jagalchi Market, you'll find still more alleyways of seafood shops and restaurants, including the multi-story Sindonga Seafood Market 신동아시장, home to some 186 raw fish restaurants. Even better, lots of street stalls—or *pojangmacha* 포장마차—set up shop near Jagalchi Market at night. These are great places to enjoy some raw or grilled fish and a shot of *soju* while savoring the local atmosphere. A specialty of these stalls is *kkomjangeo* 꼼장어—charcoal roasted hagfish, marinated in a spicy sauce. After you've finished the meat, you can fry some rice in the leftover sauce. Admittedly, the hagfish—a slimy eel-like fish—is not the most pleasant thing to look at, but it is the only currently living animal with a skull but no vertebrae, which has to count for something.

🚇 Jagalchi Station, Busan Subway Line 1.

JAGALCHI AJIMAE

History and Culture

The Jagalchi Market takes its name for the gravel (Korean: *jagal*) surface on which the market was first established. The people of Busan have made their living from the sea for centuries, but the Jagalchi Market came into its own right after the Korean War, when Busan was flooded by refugees. In order to support their families, womenfolk went to work in the fish market near Yeongdo Bridge. As Busan grew, so did the market until it became the national landmark it is today.

To this day, most of the merchants at the Jagalchi Fish Market are middle-aged women called "Jagalchi Ajimae" ("Jagalchi Aunties"). You can tell them by their

rubber gowns, gloves and boots, visor caps, scarves, perms and thick Busan accents. These are tough, salt-of-the-earth types, but their friendliness and warmth are a big part of the market's charm. When you step inside the market, you can here them call, in their thick accents, "Oiso! Boiso! Saiso!" ("Come! See! Buy!").

Yeongdo Bridge 영도대교

When it was built in 1934, Yeongdo Bridge was one of the most advanced in Asia. Connecting the port with the island of Yeongdo, it was originally a drawbridge, but the span was last raised in 1966. For much of Busan's history, it was the city's best-known landmark. During the Korean War, when families were separated as they fled south, they would tell their relatives, "Let's meet at the Yeongdo Bridge." In 2011, work began on restoring the bridge, bascule and all. The project should be completed by 2013.

BIFF Square BIFF 광장

The Busan International Film Festival (BIFF) Square is Busan's movie theater district, and has been for 80 years. True, this place has receded in recent years with the opening of large multiplex theaters throughout the city, but thanks to its history, its liveliness, and its proximity to the sea and other major Busan sites like the Jagalchi Fish Market and Yongdusan Park, it has an atmosphere all its own. There are tons of great shops, restaurants and food stalls in the area, too.

Fans of Korean cinema will want to check out Star Street, where you'll find handprints of big-name Korean and international actors and directors. This neighborhood really comes alive during the Busan International Film Festival, when temporary ticket booths open here so you can purchase admission to the films you want to see (films are shown in theaters across Busan, including Haeundae and Nampo-dong).

Yongdusan Park 용두산공원 & Busan Tower 부산타워

Yongdusan ("Dragon Head Mountain") is a hill overlooking Busan Harbor. During the colonial era, the hill was the center of the Japanese residential district. The Japanese turned it into a park, complete with Shinto shrine; the shrine was destroyed after Korea regained its independence in 1945, though, and replaced with suitably nationalist symbols like a statue of legendary 16th century admiral Yi Sun-sin. The area still has an old-time feel about it, though. The park's most visible feature is Busan Tower, which tops out at 120 m. The views of the harbor and city are, needless to say, gorgeous. Even if you don't go up the tower, the views from the park are worth the trip.

🕐 **Busan Tower**: 9 am to 10 pm (Oct–Mar), 8:30 am to 10 pm (Apr–Sep) 🎟 **Busan Tower**: 4,000 won

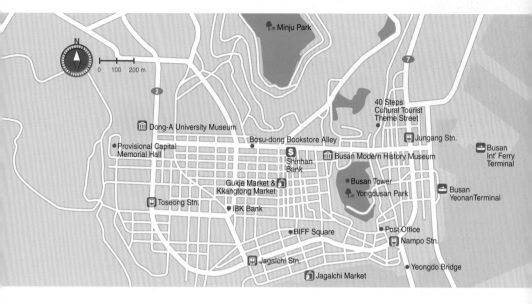

Gukje Market 국제시장
& Kkangtong Market 깡통시장

Gukje ("International") Market is the biggest and best known of Busan's outdoor wholesale markets. Its history goes back to 1945, when Japanese colonists in Korea and Manchuria, forced to return to Japan after Tokyo's defeat in the Pacific War, gathered in what is now Gukje Market to sell off their worldly possessions before getting on the boat home. The market really took off during the Korean War when Busan—and the market area in particular—was flooded with refugees from elsewhere in Korea. Tons of black market goods from US military bases magically found their way into the market, which till the 70s was the place in Korea to find hard-to-get imported cosmetics, clothing and other foreign luxuries.

They say you can find anything at Gukje Market (and the smaller satellite markets around) which is probably a bit of an exaggeration, but you'll find a dizzying variety of goods. If you're looking for

Korean handicrafts, this is a good place to find them. The atmosphere and business practices are similar to that of Seoul's Namdaemun Market, which is to say

GUKJE MARKET STREET FOOD

There's one street in the Gukje Market—everyone knows where it is, so just ask—where there's a row of outdoor food stalls selling some of the best street food in Korea. The specialty is Chungmu *gimbap*—a simple dish of rice rolled in small pieces of dried seaweed, accompanied by radish kimchi and spicy squid slices. You'll find a lot of other delectables here, too, including *bibimdangmyeon* (glass noodles mixed with vegetables and a tangy sauce), *yubu jeongol* (deep-fried bean curd and dumpling stew), and old standbys like *tteokbokki* and *sundae*. Busan is particularly renowned for its *odeng* (Japanese: *oden*), processed fish cakes stewed in a savory broth—these really hit the spot in winter.

The cliffs of Taejongdae are Busan's most popular sunrise spot.

there's a lot of energy in the air, you'll find a lot of good deals, but product quality can vary—caveat emptor.

Connected to the Gukje Market is the Kkangtong ("Can") Market, where you'll find shops selling imported canned goods, booze and foodstuffs. In the old days, these shops were largely stocked with black market goods smuggled from US military bases, but today you'll find a good many foodstuffs and brands from Japan.

Bosu-dong Bookstore Alley 보수동책방골목
Another piece of old Busan can be found at the very charming Bosu-dong Bookstore Alley, a collection of 50 bookshops just past Gukje Market in the direction of Daecheong-ro 대청로. Most of the shops here trade in used books—the merchandise is largely in Korean but if you explore, you'll find magazine back issues and used books in a variety of foreign languages. The bookshop alley has been around since 1950 when the first shop was founded by a refugee couple from North Korea who sold used magazines and books from nearby US military bases—and is one of Korea's few remaining used book markets. Even if you can't read a thing, it's a nice place to wander or sit in a café sipping a cup of coffee.

40 Steps Cultural Tourist Theme Street 추억의40계단
Just outside Exit 13 of Jungang-dong Station 중앙동역, Busan Subway Line 1, this flight of steps was where Korean War refugees built shantytowns, set up markets and looked for missing family members. To honor its history, a number of sculptures have been erected in the area, including a young girl carrying water from a well, a man playing the accordion, a merchant making puffed rice (*ppeongtwigi* 뻥튀기) and other representative figures from the district's wartime and post-wartime past. At the top of the steps is a small memorial hall with photos and exhibits depicting the neighborhood's colonial, Liberation and wartime history.

⊙ 10 am to 6 pm (5 pm on weekends). Closed Mondays 🎫 free ✆ 051-600-4041

Taejongdae 태종대
Located at the southern tip of Yeongdo Island 영도, these rock cliffs offer some of the best sunrises in Busan, if not Korea. Most folk head to the lighthouse where the rocks are pretty dramatic. There's also an observatory from which it's said you can see Japan's Tsushima Island on a clear day. Along the cliffs, you'll find some raw fish stands set up by local entrepreneurs which are quite popular with local tourists.

The best way to see this park is by one of the 40 minute cruises (cost: 10,000 won) departing from a dock near the entrance of the park to Korea Maritime University that will take you along the cliffs. Otherwise, you can just take the walking paths around.

🚌 From Busan Station, take Bus No. 88 or 101 and get off at Taejongdae Park (30 min ride).

Historic Busan

Provisional Capital Memorial Hall
임시수도기념관

For most of the Korean War, Busan served as the provisional capital of the Republic of Korea (a.k.a. South Korea) due to the capture of Seoul by the North Koreans and, after its recapture, its distance from the front lines. During that time, Korean President Syngman Rhee lived in a lovely red brick home built by the Japanese in 1926 as the residence of the colonial governor. The home has been restored to its prior state when Rhee resided here, with artifacts, exhibits and videos depicting Rhee's career, his time in Busan and the history of the Korean War. It has a beautiful garden in back, too.

🕘 9 am to 6 pm. Closed Mondays. 🎟 Free
🚇 Exit 2 of Toseong Station, Busan Subway Line 1. From there, walk straight until you get to Dong-A University. Right before the university, there's an alleyway on the left going up. Take that alley and go straight until you reach the Memorial Hall. Note: The whole area near Toseong Station has been turned into a "Provisional Capital Memorial Street," complete with street art.

Dong-A University Museum
동아대학교박물관

Just a short walk from the Provisional Capital Memorial Hall, this grand red brick building on the campus of Dong-A University was built in 1925 as the Gyeongsangnam-do Provincial Hall. During the Korean War, it was used as the

Provisional Capital Building. In 2009, it was renovated into a museum with a fine collection of historical artifacts, including 11 designated treasures.
🕘 9:30 am to 5 pm. Closed Sundays. 🎟 Free

Busan Modern History Museum
부산근대역사관

This quasi-art deco building just north of Yongdusan Park was built in 1929 as the Busan branch of the Oriental Development Company, Japan's answer to the British East India Company. The Americans took it over in 1949 to use as their USIS Cultural Center in Busan, but turned it over to the Koreans in 1999. In 2003, Busan reopened the renovated building as a museum dedicated to Korea's modern history. It holds about 200 artifacts dating from the 1876 opening of Busan to today. It's worth popping in just to see the old photographs of the city. 🕘 9 am to 6 pm. Closed Mondays 🎟 Free 📞 051-253-3845

United Nations Memorial Cemetery in Korea 유엔기념공원

This beautifully landscaped park is the final resting place of 2,300 troops from 11 nations who fell during the Korean War. Britons account for the largest number but you'll also find a lot of Turks, Canadians and Australians buried here. The cemetery is the only "UN memorial cemetery" in the world, so designated by the UN General

Provisional Capital Memorial Hall (left) Dong-A University Museum

UN Cemetery (left), Dongnae Byeoljang

Assembly in 1955. In addition to the graves, you'll find a number of lovely gardens and memorials. Definitely worth the visit.

⏱ 9 am to 5 pm (winter), 9 am to 6 pm (summer) 🎫 Free 🚌 Take Bus No. 134 from Busan Station and get off at UN Memorial Cemetery. You can also take the subway to Daeyeon Station, Line 2 and take a short cab ride.

Dongnae Byeoljang 동래별장

This beautiful mixed Japanese-style villa and garden was built by a wealthy Japanese as a spa-side retreat in the early 1940s. After Korea's liberation from colonial rule, it was used as a *yojeong*—an expensive, secluded restaurant where politicians and businessmen could discuss matters over a glass of wine. It is now a restaurant open to the public and a lovely place to have a meal or drink yourelf.

🚇 Exit 1, Oncheonjang Station, Line 1. 📞 051-552-0157 🌐 www.dnbj.com

Haeundae District

With its magnificent stretch of beach, and a strip of luxury apartments, condos and hotels, along with a plethora of bars and clubs, Haeundae is sometimes lauded as the "Korean Riviera." Well, it's not Nice but it's still Korea's most popular summertime holiday destination—attested by the throngs of holidaymakers lining the sand, it is truly a sight to behold.

In 2009, Haeundae set a world record with the opening of Shinsegae Centum City, the world's single largest department store. In addition to fun in the sun, Haeundae is also the main venue of the Busan International Film Festival.

Gwangalli Beach 광안리해수욕장
& Gwangan Bridge 광안대교

A 1.4 km long stretch of fine white sand, Gwangalli Beach can be nearly as crowded as the more famous Haeundae Beach. Lined with bars, clubs and restaurants, this place has some of the best nightlife in the city, especially in summer when it and nearby Haeundae are overrun by young holidaymakers. It's as close as you'll get to Fort Lauderdale at spring break in Korea.

The views from the bridge are vastly improved by the presence of the Gwangan Bridge (a.k.a. Diamond Bridge), the picturesque suspension bridge that spans the bay. To further accentuate the mise-en-scène, the bridge is lit up in alternating colors at night. For some truly spectacular nighttime scenery, be here for the Busan International Fireworks Festival in October.

🚇 Exit 3 or 5, Gwangan Station, Busan Subway Line 2.

Haeundae Beach 해운대 해수욕장

This 1.5 km long, 30 to 50 m wide stretch of coarse white sand, backed up by the shining towers of Busan's recent affluence, is widely considered Korea's finest beach.

That it probably is, but it's also Korea's most crowded, at least at the height of the summer vacation period (July–August), when approximately a million tourists descend upon it. With the number of beach umbrellas that get planted here, it's amazing any sunlight hits the sand at all. On Aug 2, 2008, the beach set a Guinness World Record with 7,937 beach umbrellas set up in a single day.

Haeundae ("Sea and Clouds Rock") initially got its name from Choe Chi-won, a Silla scholar and poet whose pen name was Haeun. He was reportedly quite taken with the beach, and carved his pen name on a nearby rock. What Choe never got to see is modern Haeundae's stunning night scenery—when lit up at night, the beach and its surroundings are electric.

In addition to the sand, what makes Haeundae so popular is its facilities. Just behind the beach is a wall of restaurants, bars, nightclubs and hotels, making this a one-stop shopping center for all your summer fun needs. There are festivals that go on throughout the year, too, including the Haeundae Sand Festival (a must for fans of sand sculpture), the Busan Sea Festival and yes, even a winter Polar Bear festival—held every first week of January, when the brave welcome the new year with a dip in the zero degree water. 🚇 Walk 600 m from Exit 3 or 5 of Haeundae Station, Line 2

Busan Aquarium 부산 아쿠아리움

Korea's best aquarium outside of Seoul, Busan Aquarium is home to 35,000 species of fish and other aquatic life. The best part of the aquarium is the lowest level, which is a 80 m (simulated) seabed tunnel.

💰 18,000 won 🕐 9 am to 9 pm (Jul 17–Aug 22), 10 am to 7 pm (Mon–Thur), 9 am to 9 pm (Fri, Sat, Sun)

Gwangalli Beach, a popular evening entertainment spot

Haeundae Beach

Dongbaekseom 동백섬

Despite the name ("Camellia Island"), Dongbaekseom is no longer an island but a wooded peninsula with great views and, yes, plenty of camellia trees. There's a coastal hiking path well worth the walk, especially in the evening, with the best views from near Nurimaru APEC House, the venue of the 2005 APEC Summit. The views of Haeundae Beach and Gwangan Bridge are amazing. 🚇 10 minute walk from Dongbaek Station, Line 2

Busan Cinema Center 영화의 전당

Opened on Oct 6, 2011, the landmark Busan Cinema Center serves as the primary venue of the Busan International Film Festival. Designed by renowned Austrian architecture house Coop Himmelblau, the US$150 million center is visually stunning, featuring the world's largest free cantilever, as big as an American football field. It hosts a 1,000 seat theater, three smaller theaters, and a 4,000-seat outdoor theater. Undeniably a bold piece of architecture, this could do for Busan what Frank Gehry's Guggenheim Museum did for Bilbao.

Shinsegae Centum City Department Store 신세계센텀시티백화점

Named by the Guinness Book of World Records the largest department store in the world with 293,905 square meters of floor space, Shinsegae Centum City Department Store is a retail and entertainment city under one very big roof. It's got a movie multiplex, spa, ice rink, a driving range, restaurants and more shops than anyone can count—you could literally spend days here, frolicking in retail splendor. 🚇 Centum City Station, Line 2

BUSAN INTERNATIONAL FILM FESTIVAL (BIFF)

Held every autumn since 1996, the Busan International Film Festival (formerly the Pusan International Film Festival) is one of Asia's top film festivals. Over 196,000 moviegoers attended the 2011 festival, which featured 307 films from 70 nations and 11,268 invited guests and press members.

Beomeosa Temple (left), Geumjeongsan

North Busan District

Beomeosa Temple 범어사

Once you've had enough of Busan's urban grind, head into the hills north of the city for a bit of Zen-style rest and relaxation.

Nestled on the forested slopes of Mt. Geumjeongsan, Beomeosa Temple ("Heaven Fish Temple") was founded by the great Silla monk and temple builder Uisang in 678. Its colorful name is derived from the legend of its founding: it was said that at the top of Mt. Geumjeongsan, there was a well where the water, which never ran dry, was golden colored. In this well lived a golden fish. The fish would ride the multicolored clouds to play on the slopes below, where the temple now stands. It is from this that we get the name, "Temple of the Fish from Heaven."

Some consider Beomeosa one of the "three great temples" of southeastern Korea (along with Tongdosa and Haeinsa) although, truth be told, there are far larger temples in the region—though that shouldn't detract from the monastery's charms. Like most Korean temples, it was burnt down during the Japanese invasions of the 16th century, but there are some splendid examples of late Joseon Dynasty architecture here. Of particular note is its unusual, low-slung Iljumun 일주문 ("Gate of Non-Duality"), with granite pillars almost as high as the gate itself. The interior artwork of the halls, including the 17th century Daeungjeon (Main Hall), also merit some attention. Once you've visited the temple, you can follow it with a hike up Mt. Geumjeongsan.

From Exit 5 or 7, Beomeosa Station, Line 1, walk about five minutes to Samsin bus stop. From there, take Bus No. 90 to Beomeosa Ticket Booth.

Geumjeongsan 금정산 & Geumjeongsanseong Fortress 금정산성

Overlooking Busan, Mt. Geumjeongsan (801.5 m) is Busan's guardian mountain. It provides plenty of gentle hikes with great views of the city, but is best known for the fortress that rings it. Geumjeongsanseong Fortress was formerly one of the most important military outposts in this part of the country—one of the first battles of the Japanese invasion of 1592 was waged beneath its walls. The current stone walls date from 1703 as part of a national effort to bolster the kingdom's defenses against another potential invasion from Japan, although many stretches were restored during the 1970s. It takes about an hour and half to walk from Beomeosa to the tourist village in the fortress via the northern gate, and more or less the same time going back.

Tongdosa Temple 통도사

Along with Haeinsa Temple and Songgwangsa Temple, Tongdosa Temple is regarded as one of the "Three Jewels" of Korean Buddhism. While Haeinsa represents the dharma and Songgwangsa the sangha (the Buddhist community), Tongdosa—located in the Busan suburb of Yangsan—represents the Buddha himself. Indeed, the temple houses several relics of the historic Buddha, including a robe, begging bowl and a piece of his skull. The temple is one of Korea's largest, and it is a veritable treasure trove of cultural and historical artifacts.

Tongdosa was founded in 646 by the Silla monk Jajang upon his return from Tang China, bringing with him some relics of the Buddha. Compared to other Korean Buddhist temples, it has held up surprisingly well over the centuries—even during the Japanese invasions of the late 16th century, when most temples were reduced to ash, Tongdosa's main hall managed to survive unharmed. The temple has no fewer than 65 buildings—many built in the Joseon Dynasty—and houses more than 800 designated cultural properties. The buildings here have a warm, aged feel, with beautifully faded paintwork and centuries-old murals.

On the 19th century Geungnakjeon (Nirvana Hall) is a particularly lovely (and faded) mural of the the Dragon Boat bringing the deceased to Paradise.

Tongdosa is, broadly speaking, divided into three courtyards, each one surrounded by a variety of halls. The innermost courtyard is also the most holy, home to the Geumgang Gyedan 금강계단 ("Diamond Altar"), a stone altar and stupa where the Buddha's relics are housed, and the spectacular 17th century Daeungjeon (main hall), which quite unusually houses no Buddha image as it overlooks the "real" Buddha in the Geumgang Gyedan. Don't make a beeline for it, though—the best way to appreciate this place is to go slowly, exploring as you proceed deeper and deeper into the precinct.

The path to the temple follows a stream and crosses over a couple of picturesque bridges, while verdant Mt. Yeongchuksan 영축산 (1,081 m) forms an impressive backdrop to the monastery. On the grounds of the temple is a small museum (hours: 9 am to 6 pm, closed Tuesdays) with displays of some of the temple's treasures.

🎫 3,000 won. The museum has a separate admission of 2,000 won. 🚌 From Busan, take a bus for Sinpyeong from the Dongbu Intercity Bus Terminal (near Nopodong Station, Line 1) and get off at Tongdosa. The entrance to the temple is a short walk from the bus stop. ☎ 055-382-7182

One of Korean Buddhism's 'Three Jewels,' Tongdosa Temple represents the Buddha himself.

WHAT TO EAT

Seafood tops the list of Busan's culinary highlights. A must-experience is Jagalchi Market, Korea's best-known fish market. Most of the raw fish joints are on the second floor. Expect to pay about 30,000 won for raw fish for two. If you like street food, the street stalls of the Gukje Market in Nampo-dong is a great place to score cheap, tasty eats. Be sure to try the *eomuk* 어묵 or *odeng* 오뎅 (boiled fish cakes), a Busan specialty.

The districts of Gwangalli and Haeundae are overrun with places to eat. At the northern end of Gwangalli, you'll find Millak Town Raw Fish Center 민락회센터, another good place to score seafood in its uncooked form. Haeundae has a number of Asian and fusion restaurants of note. Of great comfort to Western travelers is Wolfhound Irish Pub & Restaurant 아이리쉬펍 울프하운드 (051-746-7913) near Haeundae Station.

A Busan favorite (and a favorite of this writer) is *dwaeji gukbap* 돼지국밥 (usually 5,000 won)—rice in a rich pork soup. You'll find places serving this all over the city, although a particularly well-known place is Ssangdungi Dwaeji Gukbap 쌍둥이 돼지국밥 (051-628-7020) near Daeyeon Station (not far from the UN Cemetery).

Texas Street is a good place to find Russian food—give Amby's Restaurant a try (051-467-6206). Another good option is Samarkand 사마르칸트 (051-466-4734), which serves home-made Russian and Uzbek fare.

Busan has more nightlife options than anyone can hope to count. One major nightlife area is the Gwangan Beach, Kyungsung University and Pukyoung National University distict. These bars tend towards a younger crowd. Your upper-end clubs—including hotel nightclubs—are in the Haeundae district. Finally, the commercial area around Seomyeon Station, Line 1 or 2, is home to a thriving bar and club scene. Texas Street, too, has a couple of colorful bars.

WHERE TO STAY

Busan has the second biggest selection of accommodations behind Seoul. Most of the upscale places are along Haeundae Beach. This is where you'll find luxury establishments like the Westin Chosun Beach, Novotel Busan Ambassador and Paradise Hotel. You'll find some cheaper options here, too, including Rord Beach Hotel 로드비치호텔 (051-747-9911), Milky Way Motel 은하수모텔 (051-747-0935), Star Motel 스타모텔 (051-746-9129) and Theme 21 Motel 테마21모텔 (051-747-9021). Most of these cheaper places go for 50,000–80,000 won a night.

You can find some decent budget hotels near Gwangalli Beach, too. A bit more upscale is Hotel Homers 호메로스호텔 (051-750-8000), with doubles beginning at 264,000 won a night.

The areas around Busan Central Bus Terminal, Busan Seobu Intercity Bus Terminal and Busan Station have tons of budget motels and *yeogwan*.

TRANSPORT INFO

🚆 Most visitors get to Busan by train from Seoul. KTX express trains to Busan depart from Seoul Station (2 hrs 40 min). From Dongdaegu Station, it takes just an hour.

🚌 Bus has two major bus terminals. Busan Central Bus Terminal, near Exit 3 of Nopo Station, Line 1, is where most intercity buses to and from Busan arrive and depart. Here you'll find buses to Seoul's Dong Seoul Terminal (4 hrs 20 min), Daegu (1 hr 10 min), Daejeon (3 hrs 10 min), Gwangju (3 hrs 30 min) and elsewhere. Busan Seobu Intercity Bus Terminal, near Exit 5 of Sasang Station, Line 2, is dedicated to routes due west of Busan, including Geoje (1 hr), Jinhae (1 hr), Jinju (1 hr 30 min), Hadong (2 hrs 20 min), Namwon (3 hrs) and Gwangju (3 hrs 30 min).

✈ Busan also has an international airport. Gimhae International Airport, just west of Busan, is in fact one of Korea's busiest airports with frequent flights to Seoul's Gimpo Airport and Jeju. Gimhae also has frequent flights to Tokyo Narita, Osaka, Beijing and Hong Kong.

⛴ Finally, there's the ferry. Busan has Korea's busiest ferry terminal, with ferry service to several Japanese cities, including Fukuoka (2 hrs 55 min), Shimonoseki (8 hrs 30 min), Izuhara (2 hrs 40 min), Hitakatsu (1 hr) and Osaka (16 hrs 30 min).

ULSAN 울산

Take Detroit during its heyday, put it together with Newcastle during its heyday, and you've got Ulsan. Little more than a sleepy fishing and whaling village just 50 years ago, this thriving port city of 1.1 million people is an industrial giant, home to the world's largest auto plant, its largest shipyard and one of its largest oil refineries. This is where the Korean economic miracle became a reality.

As you might expect, Ulsan used to be a pretty gritty place, and it's still very industrial. The city has been using some of its newfound prosperity to do a bit of beautifying, though, so now you'll find a good many urban parks, especially along the Taehwagang River. The real charms of the city, however, can be found along the coast and in the high peaks overlooking the city.

Layout Ulsan is built on the estuary of the Taehwagang River, which bisects the city as it meanders east to west. Most of the metropolitan area is actually quite mountainous and sparely populated, with the urban area restricted to the estuary flats and the narrow valley linking Ulsan with Gyeongju to the north. The coastal areas are rocky and quite scenic. To the west of the city are the grand Yeongnam Alps, a picturesque mountain range capped by Mt. Sinbulsan (1,159 m), famous for its golden field of pampas grass in autumn.

Ulsan's SK Oil Refinery, one of the largest such facilities in the world

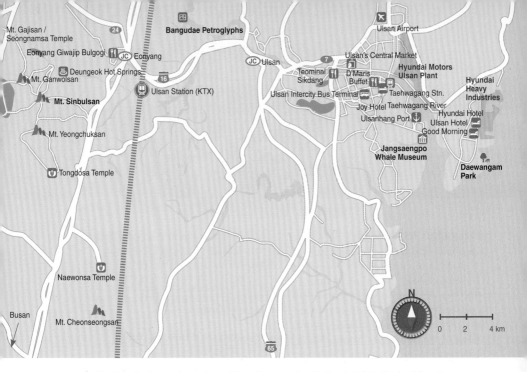

Ulsan is designated a metropolitan city, meaning that, administratively, it functions as its own province. Alone amongst metropolitan cities, however, it does not have a subway, meaning you'll need to take buses to get from place to place.

As far as facilities go, Taehwagang Station (formerly Ulsan Station) is located in the east of town, about a 20 minute walk from the city core. Ulsan Station, the new KTX station, is located way out of town in the satellite town of Eonyang 언양, a 30 minute bus ride away. The express and intercity bus terminals, meanwhile, are conveniently located in the heart of downtown Ulsan.

The beautiful highland pampas grass fields of Mt. Sinbulsan

Daegokcheon Stream, Bangudae (left), Petroglyphs, Bangudae. Etched between the Neolithic Age and the Bronze Age, they indicate Koreans have been whaling for quite some time.

Bangudae Petroglyphs 반구대암각화

One of Korea's more unique historical sites can be found on the cliffs overlooking Daegokcheon 대곡천, a tributary of Taehwagang River 태화강. Here you'll find over 200 prehistoric rock engravings depicting local wildlife and hunting scenes. Some of the scenes even depict whaling, indicating that the industry has been a time-honored Ulsan tradition. Discovered by a Dongguk University research team in 1971, the petroglyphs are believed to have been etched between the Neolithic Age and the Bronze Age, although there's currently no way to know for certain.

The petroglyphs have been designated a national treasure, but preservation has been an ongoing concern. In the 1960s, prior to the discovery of the engravings, a dam was built on the river, and now the cliffs are submerged eight months of the year. Experts now worry about the condition of the artwork, which is on UNESCO's list of tentative World Heritage sites.

As spectacular as the petroglyphs are, actually seeing them is not without its hassles. Firstly, the images can be seen only between October to February, when water levels are low and engravings rise above the waves. Secondly, since the river blocks direct access to the cliffs; you have to take in the engravings from the far side of the river. Fortunately, there are binoculars set up to help visitors get a closer view, and there's also a replica set up to give you a better understanding of what you're looking at.

🚌 Take Bus No. 513, 515, 516, 313, 314 or 317 from Ulsan Intercity Bus Terminal to Eonyang, and from there transfer to Bus No. 361, 365, 369 or 373 bound for Dudong 두동 or Duseo 두서, and get off at Bangudae.

Jangsaengpo Whale Museum
장생포고래박물관

Prior to the 1986 international ban on whaling, Ulsan was the center of Korea's whaling industry and had been for millennia judging from the prehistoric cliff engravings at Bangudae. Jangsaengpo Whale Museum contains artifacts and displays, including whale skeletons, recalling this history. It's not an especially big place, but worth a look if you've got an interest in whales or whaling. There's an old whaling boat displayed in front of the museum for you to explore, too.

Around the museum you'll find restaurants

Whale artwork at Jasaengpo

Whale-watching (left), Hyundai Motors Ulsan Plant

specializing in whale meat, most commonly minke whale. Unlike in Japan, whaling is illegal in Korea, but if fishermen accidentally catch a whale while trying to catch other fish, they can keep it. Whale meat is prepared in a number of ways, including boiled, raw, frozen and cured in salt. To get a platter of whale meat will run you between 70,000 won (good for one to two people) and 100,000 (good for three to four).

Every Saturday and Sunday (weather permitting) between April and October, you can also take a whale watching tour. The boat departs from a dock near the museum at 9:30 am and returns at 12:30 pm. Get to the dock an hour before departure, and bring your ID. Cost: 20,000 won.

🍴 2,000 won ⏰ 9:30 am to 6 pm (admission ends 1 hour before closing). Closed Mondays. ✆ 052-256-6301~2 🌐 www.whalemuseum.go.kr (KR) 🚌 From in front of Ulsan Express Bus Terminal, take Bus No. 246 and get off at Haegun Budae Ap stop 해군부대앞 정류소 (2 min). The museum is a short walk from there.

Hyundai Heavy Industries 현대중공업

When Korea—with little capital and even less experience building oceangoing vessels—decided to enter the global shipbuilding industry in the 1970s, international experts thought the nation had gone insane. Today, Korea is the world's largest shipbuilder by far. The country's massive shipyards produce the lion's share of the world's big ships, including oil tankers, container ships and LNG/LPG carriers.

Hyundai Heavy Industries got the Korean shipbuilding industry underway in 1972 when it began work on its Ulsan shipyard. Hyundai is now the world's biggest shipbuilder, and its Ulsan facility the world's largest shipyard. It's truly a site to behold—the 7.2 million m^2 of industrial might stretching 4 km along the coast with nine large dry docks and seven Goliath cranes. Manning the yard is a workforce of about 25,000 workers.

You can join free tours of the facility, but you need to make a reservation three days in advance—see http://english.hhi.co.kr/contact/tour_application.asp or call 052-202-2235 for details.

🚌 Take Bus No. 401, 1114, 1401 from Ulsan Intercity Bus Terminal and get off at Hyundai Heavy Industries (30 min).

Hyundai Motor Ulsan Plant
현대자동차울산공장

Once you've seen Hyundai's shipyard, check out its car factory, the world's largest. Here an army of 34,000 produces an average of 5,600 cars a day. The plant has its own fire station, hospital and massive port where Hyundai cars are loaded onto ships bound for markets all around the world. It truly is a city unto itself. Tours are available, but you should call in advance (052-280-2232~5).

🚌 Take Bus No. 401 or 1104 from Ulsan Intercity Bus Terminal to Hyundai Motor Ulsan Plant.

Scenic Daewangam Park has its historical monuments, too.

Daewangam Park 대왕암공원

Not far from Hyundai Heavy Industries is a lovely seaside park of pleasant walking paths, weather beaten pines, craggy rock and green-blue sea. It's a nice place to feel the ocean breeze and smell the salt air.

The highlight of the park is a small rock island connected to the mainland by a picturesque foot bridge. It is said this is the burial place of King Munmu of Silla (r. 661–681), the great monarch who united Korea under Silla rule. When Munmu died, he asked to be cremated and have his ashes scattered in the sea, where he would turn into a dragon and protect the kingdom from foreign invasion. There's a similar rock just up the coast in Gyeongju with which it shares this legend. Also in the park is a stately old lighthouse built in 1906 to replace a wooden one built by the Japanese the year before for the Russo-Japanese War.

🚍 From Ulsan Intercity Bus Terminal, take Bus No. 401, 1114, or 1401 and get off at Ulgideungdae Observatory 울기등대.

Mt. Sinbulsan 신불산
& the Yeongnam Alps 영남알프스

The western reaches of Ulsan are dominated by the so-called Yeongnam Alps, a range of majestic mountains with seven peaks of 1,000 m or more which covers parts of the cities and towns of Ulsan, Miryang 밀양 and Cheongdo 청도. The most popular peak to hike is Mt. Sinbulsan (1,159 m), a gentle mountain most famous for its giant highland fields of pampas grass, the golden reeds of which bloom in October–November.

Most hikers do Mt. Sinbulsan in combination with some of the other peaks on the ridge like Mt. Yeongchuksan 영축산 (1,081 m) and Mt. Ganwolsan 간월산 (1,069 m). Depending on how you go about attacking the peak, the hike could take you anywhere between four and nine hours. If you include Mt. Yeongchuksan in your hike, you can if you like descend to the great Buddhist monastery of Tongdosa 통도사 (see p597), which is at the foot of the mountain.

If you're looking for a rewarding multi-day hike, though, you can walk the entirety of the Yeongnam Alps, including the highest peak in the range, Mt. Gajisan 가지산 (1,240 m), a rugged mountain famous for its beautiful valleys and brilliant colonies of royal azaleas that bloom in spring. Not only is this hike scenically rewarding; it is culturally fascinating, too, thanks to region's many important Buddhist temples

Paragliding from Mt. Sinbulsan

like Tongdosa, Seongnamsa 석남사 (at the base of Mt. Gajisan) and Unmunsa 운문사 (see p545). If you're going to do this hike, you should consult the website Yeongnam Alps Mountain Tour Guide (www. yeongnamalps.kr), an excellent online resource with plenty of English-language information on trails and sights.

▤ From Ulsan Intercity Bus Terminal, take Bus No. 1703, 1713 or 1723 and get off in Eonyang. In Eonyang, transfer to Bus No. 323 and get off at the Deungeok Hot Springs 등억온천.

WHAT TO EAT

Ulsan's best known specialty is whale—you'll find plenty of restaurants serving this dish up near Jangsaengpo Whale Museum. If whale is not your red meat of choice, though, the satellite town of Eonyang is famous for its fresh Korean beef, or *hanu*. Give Eonyang Giwajip Bulgogi 언양 기와집 불고기 (052-262-4884) and its namesake dish a try for 17,000 won. The restaurant, an old *hanok* near the intersection one block in front of Eonyang Elementary School 언양초등학교, is lovely in and of itself. There are many other places doing *bulgogi* in Eonyang, so look around if this place is too busy.

Downtown, you can score really good, really reasonably priced Korean *hanjeongsik* (rice, soup and plenty of side dishes, 6,000 won) at Teominal Sikdang 터미날식당 (052-275-8808) just south of Taehwa Rotary 태화로타리. North of the river, in Ulsan's Central Market 울산중앙시장, you'll find an alley of restaurants specializing in *ggomjangeo* 꼼장어, or inshore hagfish. Sometimes called the "slime eel," the "fish" (it has a skull but no backbone, making its classification a matter of scientific controversy) is indeed eel-shaped and very, very slimy, but bathe it in a tangy sauce and grill it up, and it makes for great eating, especially over a bottle of *soju*.

Ulsan's old downtown, otherwise known as *sinae* 시내, has a lively bar scene, as does the newer downtown area of Samsan-dong 삼산동.

WHERE TO STAY

At the top end, the Hyundai Hotel 현대호텔 (052-251-2233, http://www.hyundaihotel.com/ ulsan_en/index.jsp) near Hyundai Heavy Industries has everything you'd expect in a luxury hotel. Rooms start at 220,000 won a night. Lotte Hotel (052-960-1000, www.lottehotelulsan. com) is conveniently located near the bus terminals and the happening downtown area. Rooms here go for 363,000 won a night. Not nearly as expensive but good value is Ulsan Hotel Good Morning 울산 굿모닝호텔 (052-209-9000, www.ulsangoodmorninghotel.com), also near Hyundai Heavy Industries, with rooms beginning at 169,400 won. Budget travelers will probably want to look around Taehwagang Train Station for affordable lodging options. Joy Hotel 조이호텔 (052-257-6827), right across the street from the station, is popular with travelers, with rooms beginning at 50,000 won on weekends.

TRANSPORT INFO

🚄 The easiest way to get to Ulsan is by KTX express train. KTX trains to Ulsan depart from Seoul Station (2 hrs 15 min). From Busan Station it takes just 20 minutes, and from Daegu's Dongdaegu Station about 30 minutes. Ulsan Station, built for the KTX, is located in Eonyang, about 20 minutes by bus from downtown Ulsan. Taehwagang Station in downtown Ulsan is serviced by Saemaeul and Mugunghwa trains connecting Busan's Bujeon Station and Daegu's Dongdaegu Station. From Busan, it takes about 1 hour 15 minutes. 🚌 Ulsan's Intercity and Express bus terminals are located in the heart of downtown, near the landmark Lotte Wheel 롯 데백화점 공중관람차. From Seoul, Ulsan-bound buses depart from Seoul Express Bus Terminal (4 hrs 30 min). From Daegu, buses to Ulsan depart from Daegu Express Bus Terminal (1 hr 40 min). Coming from the south, buses from Busan Bus Terminal take just one hour. ✈ Ulsan does have an airport for domestic flights. There are pretty frequent flights to and from Seoul's Gimpo International Airport (55 min) and two flights a day to and from Jeju (1 hr 10 min). The airport is just north of town, about 20 minutes by bus from downtown.

JINHAE 진해

Jinhae is a pleasant little port town about 40 minutes by bus from Busan. The Japanese developed the town as a naval base during the colonial period, and a navy town it remains today—it's home to Commander-in-Chief Republic of Korea Fleet (CINCROKFLT) and the Republic of Korea Naval Academy. Compared to other major ports on the South Sea coast such as Busan and Masan, Jinhae is quite small with a laidback feel. In spring it comes alive with its famous cherry blossom festival 진주벚꽃축제, but fall is also a nice time to come, when the leaves start falling and the town is embraced by a romantic, almost exotic charm.

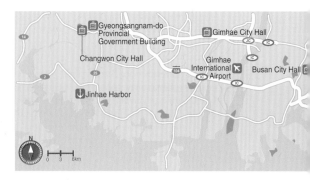

Jinhae's famous cherry blossoms

Jinhae Post Office 진해우체국

On the Jungwon Rotary 중원로타리—the old "downtown" before the City Hall moved elsewhere—is the old Jinhae Post Office, one of the most beautiful and best preserved examples of colonial era architecture in Korea. The post office, a one story wood building, was constructed in 1912 by the Japanese. Built in a Russian style, it is crowned with a copper-plated roof (restored in the 1980s; the Japanese had replaced the original copper with zinc plating during World War II); it has turned a beautiful emerald color that matches the doors, windows and cute Japanese-style bulletin board. Actually, the Russian style of the building suggests that the building may have initially housed the old Russian

consulate. At any rate, the building is a good example of the development of Western architecture in early 20th century Japan, transposed to its imperial ambitions in Korea.

Black & White Teahouse 흑백다방

On the other side of the rotary is a two-story wood building that holds one of Jinhae's hidden treasures, the Black & White Teahouse (Heukbaek Dabang). The Black & White Teahouse was one of Korea's few remaining "old-style" teahouses of the kind popular during more rustic times. Painter Yu Taeng-nyeol opened the place in 1955—the black and white interior was painted by Yu himself. Many of Gyeongsangnam-do's artists, including painter Lee Jung-seop and composer Yun I-sang, visited the teahouse to compose poetry and hold exhibits and performances. There's a lot of history in this place, which exudes nothing but charm. Sadly, it no longer functions as a teahouse, but it does hold small concerts in the evenings of every first and third Saturday. Call 055-542-2257 for more information.

JINHAE GUNHANGJE 진해군항제

History and Culture

This is Korea's most famous cherry blossom festival, so if you're into the beautiful whitish pink flower, this is the event for you. It has been held annually since 1963 to commemorate the patriotic spirit of Admiral Yi Sun-sin and has since developed into one of Korea's leading spring festivals. Locals and tourists can enjoy the beautiful sight of cherry blossoms in full bloom, as well as take part in joyful cultural art events or snoop around markets full of products from all parts of Korea. It's also a good chance to visit the Korea Naval Academy. The festival draws upwards of a million tourists to Jinhae yearly.

TONGYEONG 통영

Few cities in Korea can match the natural beauty of Tongyeong. A port city on Korea's scenic southern coast, it is an intoxicating blend of rustic small-town charm, port city cosmopolitanism and stunning seaside scenery. Often praised as the "Naples of the Orient" (minus the ominous volcano), the city also boasts an unusually prominent place in the history of the Korean arts, having been home to several respected artists, poets, writers and composers. It's the perfect place to spend the weekend, recharging batteries exhausted by the big city grind.

History Tongyeong has a long and fascinating history, especially for those with an interest in Korean naval warfare. It was in the waters just off Tongyeong that the Battle of Hansan Island, one of the most important battles of the seven-year Imjin War (1592–1598), was fought. On Aug 14, 1592, a Korean fleet of 54 vessels under the command of legendary Korean hero Admiral Yi Sun-sin did battle against a Japanese fleet of 73 warships. By the end of the day, 47 Japanese warships were resting at the bottom of the South Sea, 12 had been captured and Japanese warlord Toyotomi Hideyoshi's war plans lay in tatters.

After the battle, a massive naval command complex was constructed on the peninsula.

Port of Tongyeong, the 'Naples of the Orient'

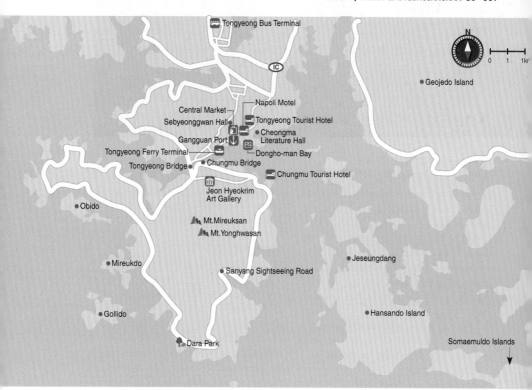

This complex, with command over the naval forces of Chungcheong, Jeolla and Gyeongsang provinces, was called Samdosugun Tongjesayeong (literally, "Command Post of the Navys of Three Provinces"), and it is from this that "Tongyeong" got its name.

Layout

Tongyeong is located on the small but very mountainous peninsula jutting out from Goseong-gun 고성군, Gyeongsangnam-do. The downtown area nestles between hillsides and a narrow bay that cuts almost entirely through the peninsula at its midsection from the east. In fact, the bay is only connected to the sea west of the peninsula through the Tongyeong Canal, which was built by the Japanese in 1932. This has turned the southern part of the peninsula into a virtual island, with the two halves connected by the picturesque Tongyeong and Chungmu bridges, creating a downtown bisected. To the east, the peninsula is also connected to Geoje Island by Geoje Bridge and the New Geoje Bridge. Tongyeong also has some 150 islands, only 41 of which are inhabited. The islands are part of Hallyeo Maritime National Park 한려해상공원, a scenic stretch of sea and coast that includes the islands and waterways between Yeosu, Jeollanam-do and Tongyeong. The most popular of these islands can be reached via passenger ships and tour boats that depart from the downtown waterfront area.

Tongyeong Canal and Tongyeong Bridge

Tongyeong Bridge 통영대교
& Chungmu Bridge 충무교

Blessed as it is with a beautiful harbor and superb natural surroundings, Tongyeong is an excellent spot for sightseeing. One of the more romantic things to do is stroll along the Tongyeong Canal 통영운하 at night. The Chungmu and Tongyeong bridges are lit up in blue and green light, and the colorful reflections off the canal waters are truly beautiful. The scenery is particularly breathtaking at dusk, when the sky behind the surrounding hillsides turns orange just before the deep purple of the nighttime sky sets in.

Sebyeonggwan Hall 세병관

There are more than a few reminders of the city's importance in Korea's naval history. On a hillside overlooking the harbor is Tongjesayeong, the former command post for Korean naval forces in the Gyeongsang, Jeolla and Chungcheong provinces. Much of the compound has been recently restored but the magnificent Sebyeonggwan Hall—designated

National Treasure No. 293—is original. The massive, open-sided meeting hall was built in 1603 and has managed to survive the ravages of time. It's a must-see for anyone interested in Korean traditional architecture.

Gangguan Port 강구안

Of more recent manufacture is a replica of a *geobukseon* 거북선 ("turtleship") moored in Gangguan Port. Built in Seoul and sailed to Tongyeong in late 2005, the vessel is a perfect replica of the revolutionary warship so ably used by Admiral Yi Sun-sin. Although a point of contention, turtleships are considered by many to be the world's first iron-clad vessels. The neighborhood around Gangguan Port, coincidently, has been designated a "cultural plaza" by the city. The area is full of restaurants, especially those specializing in Chungmu *gimbap* 충무김밥, and is a particularly pleasant place to stroll around. The Jungang Market 중앙시장, with lots of live fish for sale, is located nearby.

Sebyeonggwan Hall (left), replica of a *geobukseon* at Gangguan Port

Mireukdo 미륵도

Most visitors to Tongyeong make it a point to visit the city's scenic offshore islands. Choosing which one can be problematic, especially if you're on a tight schedule. But if you'd just like to see the islands without actually setting foot on them, climb Mt. Mireuksan 미륵산 on Mireukdo (just south of the downtown area) or take a bus (or car, if you've got one) along the beautiful Sanyang Ring Road 산양관광도로 to Dara Park 달아공원, where you're afforded stunning views of the South Sea and its islands. The view from Dara Park is particularly recommended at sunset, when the sky is flooded with color.

Worth a visit is the Jeon Hyuck Lim Museum 전혁림미술관 (055-645-7349). Painter Jeon Hyuck Lim was a pioneer in Korean color field abstraction. Except for a brief time in Busan, he lived his entire life in Tongyeong, far removed (by choice) from the painter circles in Seoul. His distinctly designed three-story museum comes equipped with a coffee shop and outdoor tables with fine views, so be sure to stop by.

TIPS

TONGYEONG INTERNATIONAL MUSIC FESTIVAL

The Tongyeong International Music Festival (055-645-2137, www.isangyuncompetition.org) is one of Korea's biggest music celebrations. Held each spring and fall, the festival draws some of the biggest names in music around the world—featuring several genres, including classical and jazz. The festival is held to honor composer Yun I-sang (1917–1995), who was born in Tongyeong but lived much of his life in exile in Germany.

Hansando Island 한산도

Hansando Island, the largest of Tongyeong's islands, is probably the most popular to visit thanks to its pine tree-lined paths and the Jeseungdang Shrine 제승당. The Jeseungdang, lovingly restored in 1976, was the command post of Admiral Yi Sun-sin during the Imjin War. Surrounded by beautiful red pines and blessed with spectacular views of the sea, it's said the

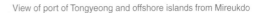

View of port of Tongyeong and offshore islands from Mireukdo

shrine compound is straight out of a traditional Korean painting. Entry into the shrine costs 1,000 won.

🎫 Getting to Hansando is a simple affair. There are hourly ferries to Hansando from Tongyeong Ferry Terminal. Ferry fare is 4,100 won.

Somaemuldo Island 소매물도

Another popular island destination is Somaemuldo, along with nearby Deungdaeseom 등대섬 (Lighthouse Islet). Somaemuldo is home to some 50 residents; it used to have its own elementary school, too, before it closed in 1996. The major reason you'd want to come here, however, is to check out the view of Deungdaeseom. Topped by a lighthouse (built in 1917), Deungdaeseom is absolutely breathtaking with its weather-battered cliffs rising straight out from the sea. At low tide, a land bridge connects Deungdaeseom and

Somaemuldo Island

Somaemuldo, allowing you to walk between the two.

⛴ There are three ferries a day to Somaemuldo from Tongyeong Ferry Terminal. A round-trip ticket will run you 13,200 won.

WHAT TO EAT

The dish most popularly associated with Tongyeong is Chungmu *gimbap* (Chungmu being the city's former name, taken from the honorific name of Admiral Yi Sun-sin). This is a simple dish of rice rolled in small pieces of dried seaweed, accompanied by radish kimchi and spicy squid slices. Originally a quick meal for fishermen on the waves, Chungmu *gimbap* has gone national as a cheap and tasty way to fill your belly. The best place to score this local delicacy is across from Tongyeong Ferry Terminal—there's a whole row of restaurants specializing in it. One serving will run you 3,500 won. Being a port, the city also has a plethora of raw fish restaurants.

WHERE TO STAY

You shouldn't have much of a problem finding places to stay. There are a ton of Korean inns or *yeogwan*, around the Tongyeong Intercity Bus Terminal. If you'd like to go a bit more upscale, the best places in town are Tongyeong Tourist Hotel 통영관광호텔 (055-644-4411), Chungmu Tourist Hotel 충무관광호텔 (055-645-2091) and Chungmu Beach Hotel 충무비치호텔 (055-642-8181). A cheaper option with a nice view of Gangguan Port is Napoli Motel 나폴리모텔 (055-646-0202). A night here is 40,000 won and the view out the window is outstanding—especially at night. Some rooms come equipped with high-speed Internet.

TRANSPORT INFO

Intercity buses run between Seoul's Nambu and Express bus terminals and Tongyeong. This is not a short trip at a little over 4 hours (assuming the traffic's good). Fare is between 20,000 and 30,800 won. If buses aren't your thing, you could train it to Busan and take the considerably shorter bus trip from there to Tongyeong—the direct bus from Busan's Seobu Bus Terminal costs 9,800 won and the ride takes about two hours.

YI SUN-SIN & THE IMJIN WAR

In Korea's long history, there are few heroes as beloved as Yi Sun-sin (1545–1598), the 16th century admiral lauded as the Lord Nelson of Korea. Showing promise in the military arts from a young age, Yi earned his first battlefield victories with a successful campaign against Manchurian Jurchen raiders in 1580s. It was during the brutal Imjin War of 1592-1598, however, that his brilliance was put on full display.

By the 1590s, the Japanese warlord Hideyoshi Toyotomi had unified Japan and had set his sights on something far grander—the conquest of China. To do this, of course, he first needed passage through Korea. A Japanese request to allow Japanese troops passage through Korea was rejected by the Korean court, who were allies of Ming China. So Japan decided to invade Korea instead.

The massive Japanese invasion force that landed near Busan in May 1592 was a competently-led professional force containing many battle-hardened veterans of Japan's century of civil war. They were armed with arquebuses, early guns introduced to Japan by the Portuguese and mass-produced by Japanese gunsmiths. They made short work of the overwhelmed Korean defenders as they rushed up the peninsula.

If the Japanese had a weakness, though, it was that their army was dependent on bases in Japan for supplies and troops. Admiral Yi exploited this weakness to brilliant effect. In a series of naval battles against the Japanese in the waters off Korea's southern coast, Yi shattered several larger Japanese fleets with few losses of his own. In one

battle, Yi's fleet of 13 ships annihilated a Japanese fleet of 333 warships.

In September 1598, a dying Hideyoshi ordered the withdrawal of his army from Korea. In December, Yi fought his final battle against the Japanese, leading an allied Korean-Chinese fleet against a Japanese fleet preparing to withdraw Japanese troops back to Japan. Again, the Japanese were soundly defeated, but this time, Korean victory came at a terrible price—as the Koreans were pursuing the fleeing Japanese, a Japanese arquebusier shot Admiral Yi in the chest. He died a few minutes later, but not before ordering his death be kept a secret from his men.

TURTLE SHIP

Adding to Yi's brilliance was an innovative new piece of naval technology, the turtle ship, or *geobukseon*. These large, heavily armored ships—designed by Yi himself—may not have been "ironclad," as was until recently claimed, but they did have fully covered decks designed to deflect enemy fire. Their decks were also covered with iron spikes to deter would-be boarding parties—a crucial defense, since boarding enemy ships to engage in hand-to-hand combat was a popular naval tactic of the age. They were armed with 11 cannons—Japanese ships, by contrast, rarely carried cannons—and smoke emitted from their bows helped hide their movements. While it's open to question just how important the ships were in Yi's victories, they nevertheless have come to symbolize the admiral's ingenuity.

Geojedo Island 거제도

Korea's second largest island, Geoje-do is a popular weekend getaway destination for Busan residents. The island marks the eastern end of Hallyeo Maritime National Park, a maritime park that comprises much of Korea's southeastern coastline. Some of the scenery here is spectacular, especially the craggy cliffs and islets of beautiful Geoje Haegeumgang. In addition to being a tourist destination, Geojedo is also home to shipyards of Daewoo Shipbuilding and Marine Engineering and Samsung Heavy Industries, two of the world's largest shipbuilders.

Busan-Geoje Fixed Link 거가대교

Opened in December of 2010, this 8 km scenic stretch of bridge and tunnel directly links Busan with Geojedo, reducing what used to be a long drive or ferry ride to a mere 50 minute drive. An engineering marvel—its tunnel is one of the longest and deepest in the world—the link is also quite picturesque in its own right.

Former POW Camp 포로수용소유적공원

During the Korean War, Geojedo was the site of the largest UN prisoner of war camp. Some 170,000 North Korean and Chinese POWs were housed here during the course of the war. Conditions in the camp were difficult, in no small part because the prisoners themselves were often in a state of near-civil war between anti-communists who

Opened in 2010, the Busan-Geoje Fixed Link has made Geojedo much easier to visit.

The dramatic coast of Geoje Haegeumgang is Geoje's top scenic spot.

were pressed into the communist armies and communist loyalists. One uprising in 1952 led to the capture of the camp's American commander. The camp has largely been restored and now serves as a museum.

⏱ 9 am to 5 pm (Nov–Feb), 9 am to 6 pm (Mar–Oct) 💴 3,000 won ☎ 055-639-8125~7 🚌 The camp is a 5 minute taxi ride from Gohyeon Bus Terminal 고현버스터미널 in Gohyeon, Geoje-do's biggest town.

Geoje Haegeumgang 거제해금강

This stunning piece of coastline in the southeastern corner of the island, designated National Scenic Site No. 2, is Geojedo's biggest draw. It's a dramatic landscape of jagged cliffs plunging into the deep green sea. The sunrises and sunsets here are quite inspiring, especially at Ilwolbong Rock 일월봉, a well-known scenic spot popular with landscape photographers.

The best way to see Haegeumgang is by tour boat—you'll find the dock at Galgot-ri 갈곶리. There are a number of tours available but the most popular one (16,000 won)

takes you around the more famous scenic spots before heading to the nearby island garden of Oedo 외도, where you'll have 90 minutes to explore before the boat heads back to port. The highlight of the trip is Sipjagul ("Cross") Cave 십자굴, whose craggy rock walls tower over the cruise boats as they enter the narrow cavern.

💴 1,600 won (park fee for Hallyeo Maritime National Park)

Oedo Botania 외도보타니아

Admittedly, some exaggeration was employed in the name, but Oedo is still a very pleasant place, albeit an odd one. Essentially, the island is one big Mediterranean-style botanical garden, complete with Roman columns, marble ladies and a Versailles-inspired zig-zag camellia hedge. Covered with rare flowers and plants from all over the world, it's certainly one of the country's loveliest gardens—just not what you'd expect just off the southern coast of Korea.

Oedo Botania, a privately owned island covered with spectacular gardens

The island has an interesting history: in 1969, local fisherman Lee Chan-ho was fishing in nearby waters when he ran into a storm. He took shelter on the island and apparently liked it so much that, over the next three years, he and his wife bought the entire island. For 30 years, the couple turned the island into their secret garden paradise before opening it up to the general public in 1995. Lee passed away in 2003 but his wife, Choe Ho-suk, still runs the place.

⏰ 7:30 am to 5:30 pm (summer season), 8 am to 5 pm (winter season). Visits are limited to just 90 minutes. 💰 8,000 won ℂ 070-7715-3330 🚢 To get to Oedo, take a tour boat from Haegeumgang. If you're in Okpo (home of Daewoo Shipbuilding), there are ferries to Oedo from nearby Jangseungpo Harbor.

What to Eat

Geoje's port areas are full of seafood restaurants. For something a bit less fishy, Cheonhwawon 천화원 (055-681-2408) in Jangseungpo 장승포 has been doing good Chinese food since 1951. A local specialty of Geoje and Tongyeong is *meongge bibimbap* 멍게비빔밥 (12,000 won), a bowl of rice mixed with vegetables and sea squirt. Give Baengmanseok 백만석 (055-638-3300) in front of the old POW camp a try—the sea squirt has a delightful sweet taste, and the rice is a lovely yellow hue.

Where to Stay

Samsung Hotel Geoje 삼성거제호텔 (055-631-2114) near Samsung Heavy Industries 삼성중공업 is a lovely place with great views of either the sea or the Samsung shipyard. Samsung likes to put foreign engineers, ship owners and other dignitaries up in here, so if you like hanging with people in the nautical profession, give it a try. Rooms begin at 260,000 won a night.

One of the nicest places to stay is the architecturally splendid Tropical Dream Resort 트로피칼드림리조트 (055-681-5550) on the south coast of the island in Hallyeo Haesang National Park. Not only is the hotel itself a work of art, but rooms have individual whirlpool with views of the ocean. Off-peak, rooms begin at 180,000 won.

A decent budget option is Geojedo Sky Motel 스카이모텔 (055-682-4040~2) in Jangseungpo. It's got views of the harbor, and is attached to a sauna. Rooms begin at 40,000 won a night. In Gohyeon, there are cheap motels just behind Gohyeon Bus Station, including the friendly Oh-de-yang Motel 오대양모텔 (055-638-1239).

Transport Info

There are frequent buses to Gohyeon from Busan's Seobu Bus Terminal. Thanks to the new bridge, what was at one time a long trip is now just 1 hour. There are also frequent buses from Seoul's Nambu Bus Terminal to Gohyeon (5 hrs).

JINJU 진주

Jinju is pleasant old community nestled in a bend on the Namgang River, a tributary of the Nakdonggang River. Historically, the city was a strategically important fortress town—during the Japanese invasions of 1592–1598, it was the target of two major sieges. The city's old fortress walls, overlooking the river as they have for centuries, still stand and are well worth the visit, especially during the autumn Jinju Namgang Lantern Festival 진주남강유등축제, when the river and the night sky are lit brightly by the light of hundreds of lanterns.

Jinjuseong Fortress 진주성

Guarding a strategic bend in the Namgang River 남강, the walls of Jinjuseong Fortress trace their history back to the Three Kingdoms Era. The original earthworks were replaced by more solid stone walls in the late 14th century. The fortress was important in defending Korea's southeastern coastal regions from the predations of Japanese pirates, a serious nuisance in medieval Korea.

To most Koreans, however, the fortress is most famous for the role it played in the devastating Japanese invasions of 1592–1598. The Japanese laid siege to the strategically vital fortress, which defended the routes to Korea's agriculturally rich Jeolla provinces, not just once, but twice.

Namgang River and Jinjuseong Fortress' Chokseongnu Pavilion

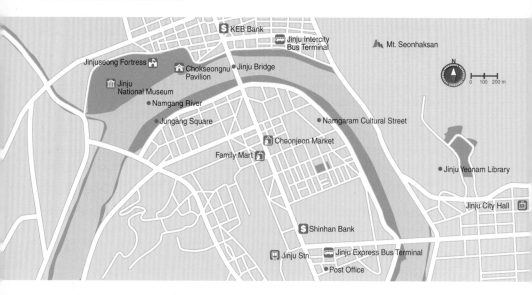

The first siege in 1592 ended in a brilliant Korean victory, when a force of 3,800 Korean irregulars led by the guerrilla leader Gwak Jae-u held the fortress against a heavily armed Japanese force nearly 10 times their number. The next year, the Japanese launched a second siege. The Koreans, again outnumbered and outgunned, held out for 11 days, but in the end, the fortress fell and the defenders were massacred to a man. The Koreans did exact their revenge, however, when during the Japanese victory celebration, a Korean *gisaeng* by the name of Nongae managed to kill one of the Japanese generals.

The fortress is now a very pleasant riverside park—the walls provide lovely views of the river. Within the walls, which

Jinju Namgang Lantern Festival

NONGAE

When the Japanese finally took Jinju Fortress after an 11 day siege, the victorious generals celebrated their conquest with a party that evening at the Chokseongnu Pavilion. For entertainment, they invited the local *gisaeng* (singing and dancing girls). With the Japanese ebullient from their victory, the wine flowed freely. One of the *gisaeng*, a young woman from southwest Korea named Nongae, approached one of the Japanese generals. She lured him over to a rock overlooking the beautiful Namgang River. She embraced the general, but instead of surrendering herself to him, she held him tight and leaped into the water below, drowning them both. There is a shrine dedicated to Nongae not far from the Chokseongnu Pavilion. The rock from which she leapt is just below the pavilion.

underwent a major restoration in the 1970s, there are a number of pavilions, shrines and historical monuments, including a shrine to Nongae and the Chokseongnu Pavilion, where the Korean commanders fell in the closing moments of the second siege of Jinju.

🕐 9 am to 6 pm 🎫 1,000 won 🚌 From Jinju Express Bus Terminal, take Bus No. 15, 25, 37 or 38 and get off after crossing the Jinju Bridge. From Jinju Intercity Bus Terminal, the fortress is a 10 minute walk.

Jinju National Museum 국립진주박물관

The beautifully designed Jinju National Museum, located within the fortress walls, is dedicated to the history of the Japanese invasions of 1592–1598. Military history buffs will love it—some 200 artifacts from the war are on display, including old weapons and uniforms.

🕐 9 am to 7 pm (9 am to 9 pm on Saturdays, Apr–Oct) 🎫 Free, but special exhibits may charge admission ☎ 055-742-5951 🌐 http://jinju.museum.go.kr

WHAT TO EAT

Like the city of Jeonju, the city of Jinju is also famous for its *bibimbap*. The local variety, however, is served with raw beef on top. The best place to try this delicacy is Cheonhwang Sikdang 천황식당 (055-741-2646) which has been doing the dish for three generations. The old home lends a bit of character, too. The *bibimbap* here costs 12,000 won.

Another local specialty to try is *minmul jangeogui* 민물장어구이 (broiled freshwater eel, 28,000 won a serving) at Yujeong Jangeo 유정장어 (055-746-9235) overlooking the Namgang River near Jinjuseong Fortress.

WHERE TO STAY

You'll find the usual assortment of places to stay near the bus terminal. A good one to try is Lotte Motel 롯데모텔 (055-741-4886) with rooms beginning at 35,000 won a night.

TRANSPORT INFO

There are frequent express buses to Jinju from Busan Bus Terminal (2 hrs). There are even more buses from Seoul's Express Bus Terminal (3 hrs 50 min), including overnight buses.

JIRISAN NATIONAL PARK 지리산국립공원

Korea's oldest national park, Jirisan National Park is also one of its largest, spread over 440 km² in three provinces. The centerpiece of the park is Mt. Jirisan 지리산, a majestic massif that rises to a height of 1,915 m, making it the tallest peak on the South Korean mainland. Its name means "Mountain of the Odd and the Wise" which is to say, a stay here would turn a foolish man wise.

The park is a treasure trove of both natural and cultural treasures. Mt. Jirisan's thick forests and deep valleys host 4,989 species of flora and fauna, including most famously the Asiatic black bear, of which there are about 20 roaming the wooded hillsides. A sacred peak, the mountain is home to several major Korean Buddhist temples, including the august precinct of Hwaeomsa Temple, home to no fewer than four national treasures, and Ssanggyesa Temple (see p628), a lovely monastery famous for its role in bringing tea to Korea.

Layout

Jirisan National Park is a big place. The massif itself is 320 km in circumference, and along its main ridge alone there are about 10 high peaks and 85 smaller peaks. Unlike Mt. Seoraksan, with its jagged peaks and dramatic, granite cliffs, Mt. Jirisan is a gentler, broader landscape of curved ridge lines, high plateaus and verdant forests. It's the perfect place for multi-day hikes.

The main ridge line runs 25.5 km in a generally east–west line from Nogodan Altar

Sunrise from Cheonwangbong Peak (1,915 m), the highest peak of the South Korean mainland

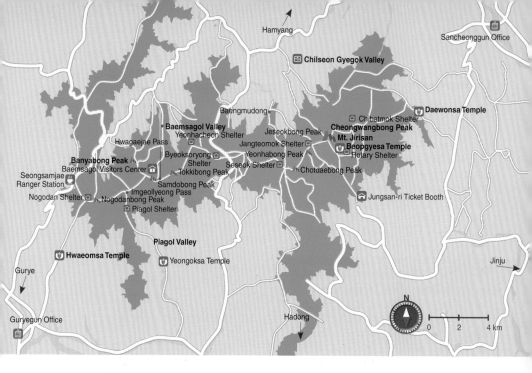

(1,507 m) to Cheonwangbong Peak (1,915 m), with 16 peaks over 1,500 m in height. It is possible to hike the entire ridge—in fact, many do—but when you add in ascending and descending, it comes to about 50–60 km, making it a three-day, two night trek. Of course, there's no need to do the whole ridge, and many of the park's most popular hikes take between six and nine hours. From the main ridge of Mt. Jirisan flow many smaller ridges, between which are countless valleys. Some of these valleys are worth exploring on their own. Three of the park's better known valleys are Piagol, Baemsagol and Chilseon Gyeok. Recently, the authorities have even crafted some *dulle-gil*, scenic walking paths connecting the villages on the lower slopes.

Your base town will depend on which part of the park you are hiking. If you're coming from the east, Jinju (see p615) is the most frequently used based town, although some hikes are best approached through the town of Hamyang 함양. Many of the more popular hikes in the western half of the park, however, are approached through the small town of Gurye in Jeollanam-do, although the Baemsagol Valley is best approached through Namwon (see p434) in Jeollabuk-do.

Cheongwangbong Peak Course

천왕봉 코스　　　　　(Duration: 8 to 9 hrs)

If bagging Cheongwangbong Peak 천왕봉 (1,915 m) is your sole objective, the most direct route begins at Jungsan-ri 중산리, a tiny village about halfway up the southeast side of the mountain. From Jungsan-ri, follow the path to the Jungsan-ri Ticket Booth 중산리매표소, and from there proceed to Beopgyesa Temple 법계사 (3.4 km), which at 1,450 m is one of the highest Buddhist temples in Korea, a fact that has earned it the appellation, "First Temple Under the Sky." Most of the temple was rebuilt after the Korean War, but its beautiful three-story stone pagoda, erected atop a natural bolder during the Goryeo Dynasty (918–1392), still remains. You'll also find a rather curious historical oddity here, too: a big metal spike that was removed from a nearby peak in 2006. The spike is said to have been driven into the peak by the Japanese to cut off the flow of energy to Beopgyesa, a temple that, it was rumored, would lead to the destruction of Japan if allowed to flourish.

From Beopgyesa, it's another 2 km hike

TIPS

10 SCENIC VIEWS OF MT. JIRISAN

1. Sunrise from Cheonwangbong Peak
2. The "sea of clouds" below Nogodanbong Peak (best seen in the early morning)
3. Sunset from Banyabong Peak
4. The full moon rising above Byeoksoryeong Pass
5. The sunset through the mountain haze around Yeonhabong Peak
6. The Buril Waterfall behind Ssangyesa Temple
7. The autumn foliage of Piagol Valley
8. The royal azaleas in the big highland field around Seseok Shelter (May–June).
9. Chilseon Gyegok Valley
10. The Seomjingang River as it meanders towards the sea

to Cheonwangbong Peak. Ideally, you'd want to time this for sunrise, which from the peak is spectacular. From the peak, you could hike down the way you came, or you could follow the ridge to Jeseokbong Peak 제석봉 (1,808 m) and Jangteomok Shelter 장터목대피소, and from there descend to

Clouds below Cheonwangbong Peak

Dalgung Valley (left), Piagol Valley

Baengmudong 백무동, on the northern side of the mountain. From Baengmudong, you can take a bus to the town of Hamyang, and from there, there are buses to other cities near and far.

📑 From Jinju Bus Terminal, take one of the hourly buses to Jungsan-ri. If you are approaching from Baengmudong, however, you need to take a bus from the small town of Hamyang. From Seoul, buses to Hamyang depart from Dong Seoul Terminal (3 hrs 40 min).

Banyabong Peak Course

반야봉 코스　　　　　　(Duration: 6 hrs)

This hike begins at Seongsamjae Ranger Station 성삼재휴게소 and rises sharply to the main ridge line at Nogodanbong Peak 노고단봉 (1,507 m), a great rounded peak that marks the western end of Mt. Jirisan's main ridge. It's a large highland grassland topped by a stone altar, at which rites were held for the goddess of the mountain. It should take about an hour to reach the peak. At sunrise, the spectacle of the clouds hanging in the valleys below is worth the early wakeup time. Along the path to Nogodan you'll pass some old stone ruins. An old hill station used by American missionaries in the early 20th century, complex was destroyed during the Korean War and never rebuilt.

From Nogodan, follow the main ridge

line for about two and a half hours until you reach the peak of Banyabong 반야봉, or "Prajñ Peak" (1,734 m), which takes its name from the Buddhist term for wisdom. The sunset from here is considered one of Mt. Jirisan's 10 most beautiful sights. Backtrack from Banyabong Peak to the Imgeollyeong Pass 임걸령, and from there descend via Piagol Valley to Yeongoksa Temple 연곡사.

📑 There are eight buses a day from Gurye to Seongsamjae/Nogodan (1 hr).

Piagol Valley Course

피아골 코스　　　　　(Duration: 5 to 8 hrs)

Meaning "Valley of Blood," Piagol Valley 피아골계곡 takes its macabre name from its bright autumn foliage. In autumn, the maples here turn a brilliant crimson; so beautiful is it that the foliage is often featured in promotional literature. The path follows a lovely mountain stream with some picturesque waterfalls. The best time to come here is usually October or November, depending on the weather.

While you're here, be sure to check out the stupa garden of Yeongoksa Temple. There you'll find several brilliantly carved stupas from the Unified Silla Era, when Yeongoksa was a major Zen center. The

TIPS

GURYE 구례

Gurye is a pleasant but quiet farming town best known as a base camp for exploring Jirisan National Park. It's got shops, restaurants and motels, as well as convenient road and rail links to Suncheon, Gwangju, Seoul and other cities.

A particularly scenic part of town, at least in spring, is Sansuyu Village 산수유마을, a tiny hamlet on the foothills of Mt. Jirisan. In late March–early April, the village's many dogwood trees blossom, producing a beautiful landscape of yellow. After strolling about the village, you can relax a bit at the nearby hot spring baths, too.

From Seoul, buses to Gurye depart from Seoul's Nambu Bus Terminal (3 hrs). From Gwangju, buses to Gurye depart from U Square (1 hr 30 min). Buses from Suncheon take just 30 minutes. From Busan, buses depart from Busan Seobu Intercity Bus Terminal (3 hrs).

Baemsagol Valley Course

뱀사골 코스 (Duration: 8 hrs)

Baemsagol 뱀사골 is a 9 km valley leading from Baemsagol Visitors Center 뱀사골안내소 to Hwagaejae Pass 화개재, on the main ridge line of the mountain. Like Piagol Valley, it boasts of some fine autumn foliage, when the landscape is awash in brilliant shades of red and yellow. It's a popular summer retreat, too, thanks to the thick forests and cool mountain streams.

The valley's name means "Valley Where the Snake Died," and takes its name from a local legend. Long ago, there used to be a temple here from which, every August, a monk would head up to the valley to Sinseon Rock, where he would spend the night praying. If he did this, it was said, he would turn into an immortal in Heaven. A skeptical high monk who'd heard about this visited the temple to observe this rite. Suspicious, he asked the monk selected for the rite to wear a poisoned robe. Clad in the poisoned robe, the monk hiked up the valley to pray. In the morning, the high monk hiked to Sinseon Rock, where he

so-called East Stupa and North Stupa are especially sublime—the carvings are so well-preserved, they'll move you to tears.

Most hikes here go from Yeongoksa to Piagol Shelter 피아골대피소 and/or Imgeollyeong Pass, but if you're up to it, you could continue from Imgeollyeong Pass to Samdobong Peak 삼도봉 and descend via the Baemsagol Valley (roughly eight hours).

From Gurye, board a bus for Yeongoksa Temple or Piagol Valley (1 hr).

Baemsagol Valley

SHELTERS

There are eight shelters on Mt. Jirisan's main ridge. The Nogodan, Byeoksoryong, Seseok and Jangteomok shelters—located roughly equidistant to one another along the ridge—are quite large, with shops selling snacks (like instant noodles) and other basic supplies. The others are rather spartan. With the exception of the simple Piagol and Chibatmok shelters, you need to reserve a space. Piagol and Chibatmok lodges are 5,000 won a night; the rest are 7,000 won (8,000 won peak season).

Jangteomok Shelter 장터목대피소	(010-2883-1750)
Chibatmok Shelter 치밭목대피소	(No phone)
Byeoksoryong Shelter 벽소령대피소	(011-1767-1426)
Seseok Shelter 세석대피소	(010-3346-1601)
Rotary Shelter 로타리대피소	(010-2851-1401)
Yeonhacheon Shelter 연하천대피소	(010-6536-1586)
Nogodan Shelter 노고단대피소	(061-783-1507)
Piagol Shelter 피아골대피소	(061-783-1928)

found both the monk, who was dead, and the carcass of a great snake. The temple had in fact been conducting annual sacrifices to the monstrous serpent.

Baemsagol Valley has some sad modern history, too. During the Korean War, it and Piagol Valley were major hideouts for communist partisans fighting South Korean and UN forces. Accordingly, it was subject to intense and often brutal counterinsurgency operations that left homes, villages and temples destroyed and many dead. Near the entrance to the trail is a small museum/memorial to this history, with old photographs and captured weaponry. ▣ From Namwon, take one of the hourly buses for Baemsagol.

Hiking the Entire Ridge

지리산 종주코스 (Duration: 3 days 2 nights)
These hikes usually begin at Hwaeomsa Temple in the west and end at Daewonsa Temple in the east (or vice versa). It's a serious hike for serious hikers, requiring at least two nights sleeping on the mountain. Fortunately, there are a number of lodges and shelters along the way where you can bed down.

Hwaeomsa Temple 화엄사

If you can visit only one temple on Mt. Jirisan, make it Hwaeomsa Temple. Founded in 544 AD in the kingdom of Baekje by an Indian monk, the monastery came into its own in 634 when it was expanded by the great Silla monk Uisang, who founded in Korea the Hwaeom ("Avatamsaka") school of Buddhism, from which the temple takes its name. The

POINTS OF CAUTION

The long hike along Mt. Jirisan's main ridge is no joke. Even experienced hikers find it a tough slog. Here are some points of caution to make your hike safer and more enjoyable.

1. Be wary of localized heavy rain, especially during the summer monsoon season. In fact, when rain is expected, hikers may be barred from the mountain.

2. After heavy showers, look out for flash floods, especially in the valley streams.

3. Be extra careful of lightning during thunderstorms. If a thunderstorm approaches, get inside. If this is not possible, at least try to get off the ridge line. The key is staying off and away from the nearest high point. Stay away from water and metal, too. If your skin begins to tingle or your hair stands on end, a lightning strike may be imminent. Crouch on the balls of your feet, placing your hands on your knees and your head down. You want to get as low to the ground without your hands or knees touching the ground. Whatever you do, don't lie down!

4. Know your limits. Push yourself too hard, and you could get hurt.

5. Go prepared. Make sure you've got proper footwear, sleeping equipment, a flashlight, cooking equipment, food and water, and a detailed map.

Hwaeom school bases its philosophy on the Avataṃsaka Sūtra, or Flower Garland Sutra, and stresses the universal oneness of all things.

The monastery is a cornucopia of Korean national treasures. The most impressive among these is the grand, two-story Gakhwangjeon Hall 각황전, built in 1643 and one of the biggest Buddhist halls in Korea. On its altar are Buddhist triad and four bodhisattva. Particularly beautiful are

the graceful pillars that hold up the ceiling—the curve of the original wood was left as is, to great visual effect.

Also spectacular are the great stone lantern in front of the Gakhwangjeon, carved in the Unified Silla Era, and the very unusual Unified Silla-era pagoda 4사자3층석탑 held aloft by four stone lions. These are just the tip of a very deep architectural and artistic iceberg, however—be sure to take your time exploring.

Hwaeomsa Temple

After you're done with the main temple itself, stroll about 10 minutes beyond to Gucheungam Hermitage 구층암 and check out pillars on one of the buildings—two gnarled quince tree trunks. ℂ 061-782-7600 ⊕ www.hwaeomsa.org (KR) ▤ From Guyre, take a bus for Hwaeomsa Temple (20 min).

Daewonsa Temple

Daewonsa Temple 대원사

Daewonsa Temple was founded in 548 AD, but 20th century history was not especially kind to it—it was completely destroyed in a massive fire in 1914, and destroyed again during the Yeosu–Suncheon Mutiny of 1948, when government forces burned it to prevent its use by communist rebels. The current monastery dates from a post-Korean War reconstruction and, while not especially old, it's still a pleasant place. For many visitors, it is the eastern starting point of a trek up Mt. Jirisan.

ℂ 055-972-8068 ⊕ www.daewonsa.net
▤ From Jinju, take one of the hourly buses to Daewonsa Temple.

Chilseon Gyegok Valley 칠선계곡   *Off the Beaten Track*

The longest valley in Jirisan National Park is the Chilseon Gyegok ("Seven Fairies Valley"), a 16 km stretch of rushing water, deep primeval forests and very rugged terrain leading from the village of Chuseong-ri 추성리 to Cheonwangbong Peak. The path is punctuated by seven waterfalls and 33 ponds. The deeper you go into the valley, the harder it gets—the valley has claimed so many lives, in fact, that it has earned the rather sobering title "The Valley of Death," and in winter, Korean teams preparing to scale the Himalayas come here to practice their ice-climbing skills.

Accordingly, it is open just four months of the year—May, June, September and October—and even then, you need to get permission to hike (only 40 people a day) by reserving a spot in advance. Call 055-960-5114 for reservation details.

▤ From Hamyang, take a bus to Chuseong 추성.

HADONG 하동

At the foothills of Mt. Jirisan 지리산, far from the madding rush of modern Korean urban life, lies the rustic rural community of Hadong. Bordered on the west by the broad, meandering Seomjingang River 섬진강, to the south by the South Sea and to the north by towering peaks over 1,500 meters high, Hadong is the birthplace of Korea's green tea culture and prized by tea connoisseurs for the best tea leaves in the land. Easy to reach it's not, but if you're looking to get away from it all and relax in a scenic environment that nourishes body and spirit, Hadong is the place.

Downtown Hadong

Interestingly enough, Hadong-eup used to be a major port. In the days before Hyundai, the Gyeongbu Expressway and KTX, rivers were major transportation arteries carrying people and goods across the country. Seomjingang River, the long, wide and slow-moving navigable river forming the border between Gyeongsang and Jeolla provinces, was a major regional transportation route, and Hadong, sitting on a commanding bend on the river near its mouth, was the gateway. The old port area, Hadongpogu 하동포구, is located outside the downtown area, just past Hadong Stadium.

Hadong-eup 하동읍, the downtown, has a

The tranquil Seomjingang River, a wonderful nature walk spot

very rural bus terminal, a couple of low to mid-priced motels and *yeogwan*-level inns, some restaurants, a market, and several thousand inquisitive but very friendly residents.

Hwagae Market 화개장터

To really understand what Hadong's about, hop on the first bus to the old market town of Hwagae, located at the mouth of the dramatically beautiful Hwagae Valley 화개계곡. This is the heart of Hadong's green tea country and the birthplace of Korea's green tea culture.

Hwagae is a 30 to 40 minute bus ride upstream from Hadong-eup. Located on the river at a strategic meeting point between Hadong, Gyeongsangnam-do and Gurye, Jeollanam-do, Hwagae used to be home to one of the five busiest markets in pre-independence Korea. Sea products from coastal towns would be brought upstream to the Hwagae Market, held every five days, where they would be traded for rice and barley from Jeolla-do towns like Namwon and Hamyang, and forest vegetables such as potatoes, brackens, and the highly prized and nutritious *codonopsis*

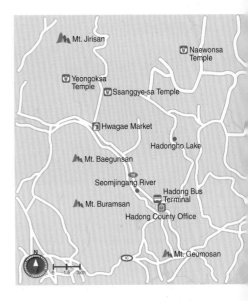

lanceolata or bonnet bellflower roots (*deodeok*), produced by the slash-and-burn farmers of the Jirisan Mountains.

There isn't much left of the old marketplace today, however. The spot is marked, but replacing the old traditional market is a tourist-oriented one where visitors can pick up local specialty goods,

Hwagae Market

Wild green tea of Hadong (left), Hwagae Market

including green tea and green tea products. The marketplace is also a good spot to pick up something to eat—there are a number of eateries around, so if you're hungry, sit down and have a bite.

Hwagae is probably the best place in Hadong to spend the night. There are a number of pleasant *yeogwan* in Hwagae and along the Hwagae Valley, and further up the valley near Ssanggyesa Temple and the surrounding tea plantations, there are a number of homestay or *minbak* facilities offering comfortable accommodation amidst much more pleasant surroundings. Hwagae might be smaller than Hadong-eup, but scenically, it's in a different world—it straddles a low gorge where the Seomjingang River meets a crystal clear stream flowing down Mt. Jirisan. Spanning Seomjingang River is the picturesque Namdo Bridge 남도대교. The 6 km road linking Hwagae and Ssanggyesa Temple is lined with cherry blossoms that are absolutely spectacular in spring. The steep hillsides that form the walls of the valley, meanwhile, are dense with small farms producing what Hadong is best known for—wild green tea.

🚌 Buses to Hwagae depart from Hadong Bus Terminal.

Ssanggyesa Temple 쌍계사

At the end of the valley on the lower slopes of Mt. Jirisan and surrounded by thick forest, is the gorgeous Buddhist temple complex of Ssanggyesa (055-883-1901). Though it was founded in 722, most of the temple's structures date back to its 17th century reconstruction. Its name means "Double Stream Temple," taken from the two streams that flow alongside it.

The walk up to the temple along a forested path will take you over stone bridges crossing sparklingly clear streams—be sure to keep your ears as well as your eyes open. The artwork contained in the temple complex and the mansonry of the temple itself is absolutely breathtaking. Don't forget to spend a couple of minutes appreciating the Stele for Buddhist Priest Jingamseonsa in front of the temple's main hall. Designated National Treasure No. 47, this is your chance to check out 9th century Korean calligraphy.

From Ssangyesa Temple, there are hiking paths up the slopes of Mt. Jirisan. Many visitors make the 2.5 km hike to the Buril Falls 불일폭포, an impressive cascade 60 m high.

🚌 There are direct buses to Ssanggyesa from Hadong Bus Terminal.

Ssanggyesa Temple is reportedly the birthplace of Korea's tea culture.

Seomjingang River 섬진강 and Maehwa Village 매화마을

The Seomjingang River, on which Hadong sits, is a relatively undeveloped stretch of water that makes for some very pleasant country walks. One particularly lovely spot on the river is Maehwa ("Apricot") Village, so called because it's covered each year in flowering apricot trees. When the white flowers blossom in spring (usually March), the village transforms into an almost dream-like landscape. Well worth the visit.

🚏 Maehwa Village is in the limits of neighboring city Gwangyang. From GS Seomjin Gas Station GS 섬진주유소 (100 m from Hadong Bus Terminal), take bus No. 35-2 and get off at Maehwa Village.

Springtime in Maehwa Village

TRANSPORT INFO Buses to Hadong depart six times daily from Seoul's Nambu Bus Terminal, the first at 9:10 am. The trip takes about 4 hours and 30 minutes and costs 25,000 won (23,300 won to Hwagae). You could also fly to Jinju from Gimpo Airport (three flights daily) — the flight takes about one hour, and then it's another hour bus ride to Hadong. Likewise, you can ride the KTX to Busan (3 hrs) and take a 2 hour bus ride from there.

'IF YOU WANT A GOOD CUP OF TEA, COME TO HADONG'

For the past decade, Korea has been in the throes of a healthy lifestyle craze, as the ubiquitous use of the term "well-being" surely attests. Green tea has been a big part of the health food boom—between 2001 and 2003, Korea's green tea production more than doubled, and green tea is now being used in everything from soap and cosmetics to *bibimbap* rice dishes. Compared to green tea-crazy Japan, Korean green tea consumption is still rather modest, but it's come a long way.

Korea's warm, wet southern regions produce the bulk of the country's green tea. Three regions in particular are noted for their tea—Boseong-gun (in Jeollanam-do), Jeju-do and Hadong-gun. Boseong, of course, is famous throughout Korea for its picture-perfect green tea fields that cover the rolling hills like a verdant blanket—its plantations are often used in Korean films and dramas. Jeju Island actually produces much of the mass-produced green tea consumed by Koreans. But Hadong is where it all started: in 828, Kim Dae-ryeom, a Silla envoy in Tang China, brought back to Korea green tea seeds, which he planted on the mountain slopes of Ssanggyesa Temple. From that single tea field, green tea spread throughout the Hwagae Valley, which until the early 20th century was Korea's premier green tea cultivation area.

Today, the Hwagae Valley is literally covered with these picturesque green tea fields. Unlike the gentle, rolling green tea fields of Boseong, however, Hadong's green tea fields line the narrow valleys that climb up between steep mountainsides. The fields have a charmingly rustic and altogether Korean feel—they are roughly hewn, with patches growing here and there in irregular shapes. They sharply contrast with the Japanese-built plantations of Boseong, with their perfectly lined rows betraying their imperial roots. Unlike other green tea areas, Hadong's tea is produced entirely by hand. This has given Hadong a reputation among tea connoisseurs for producing the finest tea in the land. Explained Jo Mun-hwan, who runs "well-being" events for Hadong County, "It's said that if you want to see pretty tea fields, you go to Boseong. But if you want to drink a good cup of tea, you come to Hadong."

At the Hadong Tea Culture Center (055-880-2955), located at the floor of the beautiful valley not far from Ssanggyesa Temple, you can learn all about Hadong tea. Exhibits will take you through the entire process, from picking to drying to drinking. Hands-on programs are also conducted, and of course there is the tea room, where you can sample the county's tea and learn about local tea culture from knowledgeable experts. Further up along the valley are small tea plantations, often with their own stores and tea

shops. There are also several *minbak* homestay facilities that are a good option for those staying the night. Hadong Golmangtae (055-882-2237) costs 60,000 won on weekends (80,000 won from Jul 15 to Aug 20) for a double room—and is blessed with a splendid view of the valley.

UPO 우포

Upo Wetland is the largest natural inland wetland in Korea. It was registered with the Ramsar Convention in March 1998 and designated an Ecological Conservation Area by the Ministry of Environment in 1997. Spanning almost nine square kilometers with two square kilometers of surface water, Upo Wetland has some of Korea's richest biodiversity, and is also home to a number of the country's endangered species.

According to a 1997 survey when Upo was first declared protected, the area was home to a number of endangered or threatened species including 168 plants, 62 birds, 12 mammals, and seven reptile species. There is even an Upo Crested Ibis (a white bird with a red head and long black and red beak) Restoration Center at the park. In 2003, two of the birds were brought from China to the center to restore the population; there are now seven of them on the premises.

Since the wetland's designation as an ecological conservation area, more and more visitors have been coming to the area. Migratory birds such as the Eurasian spoonbill, whooper swan, mallard, egret, heron and common kingfisher flock to Upo, especially in autumn.

The wetlands of Upo are more than beautiful, they also host a rich ecosystem.

The wetlands are also rich in flora like pampas grass, cattails, water chestnuts and lotuses, as well as the famed prickly water lily, which resembles a floating cactus. In and around the water are bullfrogs, bass, bluegill and beetles. There is enough outdoor life to make any nature lover dizzy.

Autumn is one of the best times of year to visit the park because of the bird migration. So pack a lunch, grab your backpack, camera and binoculars, and head to Upo to experience one of Korea's greatest nature shows.

Getting Around the Park

There are trails running for about 15 km around the wetlands. The main trail, called the Upo Natural Trail, takes three to four hours to walk. The best way to see the wetlands, though, is by bike. At the entrance, next to the Ecology Center, is a bike rental shop. It's open 10 am to 5:30 pm, with rentals costing 3,000 won for two hours and 5,000 won for four hours. Closed Mondays. Tandem bikes are also available. For something a little slower, try the "Oxcart Experience" and enjoy the views as you are pulled around on a cart.

FOR FAMILIES

Take your children to the hands-on exhibits at Upo Wetland Ecology Center 우포늪생태관. There is also a small botanical garden—open from 9 am to 6 pm. 1,000 won for children and 2,000 won for adults. Closed Mondays.

WHAT TO EAT

There are a few restaurants just outside the bus station and near the entrance to the park. Also recommended is to pack a lunch and have a picnic in the park. Be sure to grab a couple of bottles of home-brewed *makgeolli* at the park's gift shop.

WHERE TO STAY

If you'd like to stay near the wetland, try Upo Minbak 우포민박 (055-532-6202), a homestay facility near the park entrance. Otherwise, there are a number of reasonably priced inns and motels in Changnyeong.

TRANSPORT INFO

From Seoul, there are five buses a day to Changnyeong (4 hrs 20 min).
From Busan, there are 19 buses a day from Sasang Bus Terminal (1 hr 10 min.). From Yeongsin Bus Terminal in Changnyeong, take a bus to the wetlands or travel by taxi (about 10,000 won).

JEJU-DO

HIGHLIGHTS

- Hike the extinct volcano of Mt. Hallasan, South Korea's highest peak

- Explore Ollegil walking paths, taking in the splendid scenery as you go

- Visit the south coast and frolic at leisure-oriented Jungmun Resort

- Head to Seongsan Ilchulbong at dawn to watch the spectacular sunrise

- Gaze at the primal wonder of Sangumburi Crater, a 1 km deep volcanic crater

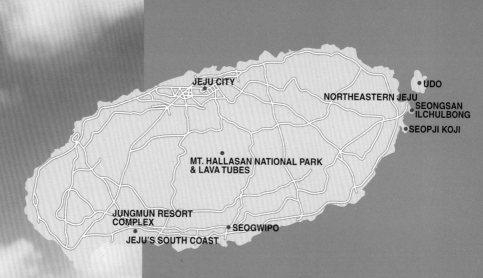

JEJU CITY

UDO

NORTHEASTERN JEJU

SEONGSAN ILCHULBONG

SEOPJI KOJI

MT. HALLASAN NATIONAL PARK & LAVA TUBES

JUNGMUN RESORT COMPLEX

SEOGWIPO

JEJU'S SOUTH COAST

MARADO ISLAND

ISLAND OF NATURAL WONDER

Dubbed "Korea's Hawaii," the volcanic island of Jejudo—administratively speaking, Jeju Special Self-Governing Province—is one of Korea's most popular tourist destinations, largely thanks to its beautiful scenery and unique island culture. Located some 85 km off the southwestern tip of Korea, Jejudo was once its own nation and does, indeed, have a history all its own, distinct customs and lifestyles, and a local dialect so different from standard Korean as to make it virtually unintelligible to mainlanders. The island's exotic charms make it a favored honeymoon destination for Koreans and, recently, Japanese and Chinese tourists looking for a nice getaway.

Jejudo is the smallest of Korea's provinces, but that shouldn't indicate a lack of things to do. Dominated by the massive dome of the extinct volcano of Mt. Hallasan (1,950 m), South Korea's highest peak, the island is a place of immense natural beauty, with verdant meadows dotted by volcanic cones, mysterious caves and lava tubes, dramatic coastlines and thick forests. The weather here is considerably warmer than that of the mainland, giving Jejudo a distinctive ecology. To give hikers a better appreciation for the island's natural beauty, 19 well-marked walking trails or Olle-gil, have been marked out in scenic spots along the coast. Other than hiking, the island lends itself to other outdoor activities including scuba diving, golf, horseback riding, surfing, windsurfing, and even paragliding.

Dol hareubang, or "grandfather rock," is a symbol of Jejudo.

Yongduam Rock is a good place to see Jejudo's famous women divers at work.

JEJU CITY 제주시

Home to just over 400,000 people, the city of Jeju is the island's largest town and the provincial capital. Area-wise, it's a big place—since 2005, when the city proper merged with the surrounding counties, the city has comprised the entire northern half of the island. The actual urban center, however, is considerably smaller—there's an older downtown that surrounds the seaport, and some newer development southwest of the city.

The city of Jeju is not especially different from other Korean cities its size, although its seaside location and Mt. Hallasan, which looms just behind it, lend it a unique charm. For the traveler, the city is mostly a transportation hub and a place to bed down for the night. That said, it has a couple of things worth checking out, most notably Yongduam Rock, the city's best-known tourist attraction.

Yongduam Rock 용두암

A jagged piece of volcanic rock that juts out from the sea, Yongduam ("Dragon Head Rock") is said to resemble a dragon writhing in pain. According to legend, the rock was, in fact, a dragon who wished to soar to heaven. To do this, he stole a precious pearl from the mountain god of Mt. Hallasan. He almost got away with it, but just as he was making his way to the sea, he was discovered by the mountain god and shot with an arrow. In agony, the dragon fell into the sea and turned into stone, with only its head remaining above the waves.

The winds and seas here can be pretty intense, making for a dramatic scene when the seas are up as the waves batter the rock. The sunsets here are especially lovely. The area around the rock has been turned into a park, complete with walking paths, bridges and other amenities. As this is a major tourist attraction, there are a good many cafés and restaurants nearby. Yongduam is also a good place to see Jejudo's famous women divers or *haenyeo*, in action.

🚌 From Jeju Bus Terminal, take a bus for Hagwi 하귀 and get off at Yongmun Rotary 용문로타리. From there, walk five minutes to the seaside, and you'll find the walking path to the rock. Likewise, it's just as easy to take a cab from the airport or Jeju Bus Terminal—it'll be just over basic fare.

Jeju National Museum 국립제주박물관

Opened in 2001, Jeju National Museum has a decent collection of artifacts and artwork from around the island. Special attention is given to the ancient Tamna Kingdom, when Jeju was an independent country, and the Goryeo era.

🕘 9 am to 6 pm 🎟 Free 🚌 Best to take a taxi—the museum is on the eastern outskirts of town. ✆ 064-720-8000

Jeju Love Land 제주러브랜드

One of Korea's most surreal tourist destinations, Jeju Love Land is a sculpture theme park dedicated to sex. Opened in 2004, the park is home to about 140 statues and other sculptures, most engaging in some sort of sexual activity—think pop art meets Penthouse Forum. The most impressive work on display is "Desire," a gigantic and very anatomically correct sculpture of a woman in the throes of a self-administered orgasm. Most of the displays, in addition to being erotic, also

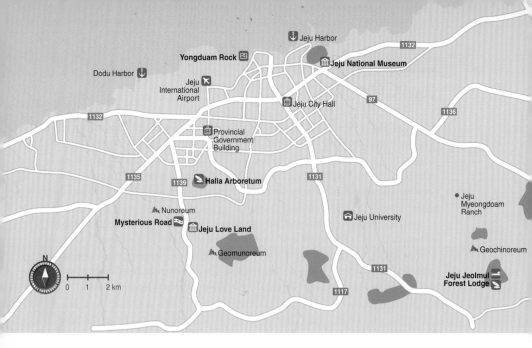

display a great sense of humor. Lest you think this is low culture, many of the works here were crafted by graduates of Hongik University, Korea's best known art school. Obviously, this is not a place for children—entry is limited to age 18 or over.

🕐 9 am to midnight (admission ends 11 pm) 💷 9,000 won 🚌 From Jeju Bus Terminal, take a bus for Chuksanjinheungwon and get off at Mysterious Road. 📞 064-712-6988

Mysterious Road 도깨비도로

Also known as Dokkaebi Road 도깨비도로 ("Goblin Road"), this road on which Jeju Love Land is located, might look like it's climbing, but in fact it is descending—what you see is an optical illusion due to the surrounding terrain. If you're driving, try putting your car in neutral and watch it seemingly roll uphill! Better experienced than read about.

🚌 From Jeju Bus Terminal, take a bus for chuksanjinheungwon and get off at Mysterious Road.

Halla Arboretum 한라수목원

Just south of the newer part of town, Halla Arboretum is a wonderful piece of greenery where you'll find 909 kinds of native and subtropical plants. It's a pleasant place to walk about, especially if you've got some time to kill. 🕐 9 am to 6 pm 💷 Free 🚌 From Jeju Bus Terminal, take a bus for Jeju Agriculture High School and get off at the last stop (30 min). The arboretum is a five minute walk from there. 📞 064-710-7575

NORTHEASTERN JEJU 제주도 북동부

The northeastern region of Jejudo is home to some of the most spectacular sites on the island, if not the entire country, most notably the UNESCO-recognized Geomunoreum lava tube system and the magnificent Seongsan Ilchulbong ("Sunrise Peak"), a volcanic tuff cone that rises dramatically out of the sea. If you have time to explore only one part of the island, make this it. In addition to the lava tubes and Seongsan Ilchulbong, you'll also want to check out the island of Udo, just off the eastern coast of Jejudo; the newly opened Haenyeo Museum, which offers insight into a unique aspect of Jejudo culture; and the immersive Gimnyeong Maze Park, a hedge maze maintained since 1987 by an expatriate American professor. If lying around on the beach is your sort of thing, there are a couple of decent spots in the area, too.

Geomunoreum Lava Tube System
거문오름용암동굴

According to UNESCO, the Geomunoreum lava tube system is the finest, best-preserved system of lava tubes anywhere in the world. There are five tubes in the system; the longest of these, Manjanggul Cave 만장굴, is over 13 km long. These impressive tubes must be experienced to be believed—channels of black volcanic rock decorated by fantastical lava pillars and stalactites, the tunnels form a universe all their own.

The tube system begins at Geomunoreum (456.6 m), one of the many parasitic cones (*oreum*) that rise up from the island, and runs in a northeasterly direction until it

The volcanic landscape of Jejudo. The island has about 360 *oreum*, or parasitic volcanic cones.

reaches the coast. It was formed during an eruption some 200,000–300,000 years ago: as lava flowed to the surface, it formed channels, much as a river does. When exposed to the air, the surface of the lava began to cool, turning into an insulating crust of rock. Underneath this crust, the lava continued to flow, cutting into the rock beneath, much as a river forms canyons. Eventually, the channels drained out, forming the amazing arch-ceiling tubes we see today.

The unique volcanic environment in which the tubes were formed produced a landscape completely unlike those of the limestone caves of the mainland. Inside you'll find lava stalactites, caused by superheated air remelting the ceiling's rock; impressive lava pillars, formed when lava dripped from a hole in the ceiling; and a variety of other lava rock formations. The sides of the wall are marked by tell-tale flowlines, indicating the depth of previous lava flows. Only one of

Jejudo's lava tubes are a protected UNESCO World Heritage Site.

the five caves, Manjanggul, is actual open to the public, although Gimnyeongsagul 김녕 사굴 is often visited thanks to its colorful local legend.

Manjanggul Cave 만장굴

The Manjanggul Cave is, by far, the most visited of the tubes, although only the first 1 km of the 13,422 m tube is open to the public. Unlike many lava tubes which can get pretty cramped, this one is truly cavernous, with a width of up to 18 m and a height that reaches 23 m. The highlight here is the magnificent, nearly 8 m high lava pillar with elephant foot-like "lava toes." Also notable is Geobukbawi ("Turtle Rock") 거북바위, a "lava raft" (a rock that floated on the lava flow until it solidified into place) shaped like, well, a turtle. The cave is also home to Korea's largest colony of bats. The open areas should take about 40 minutes to explore. Wear sensible footwear; high-heels are banned.

⊕ 9 am to 6 pm (summer); 9 am to 5:30 pm (winter) 🗐 2,000 won 🚍 Take a Donghoeseon bus from Jeju Bus Terminal and get off at Manjanggul Cave parking lot (1 hr 20 min). From the parking lot, there are shuttle buses to the entrance of the cave. ℂ 064-783-4818

Gimnyeongsagul Cave 김녕사굴

Located 2 km north of Manjanggul, this 700 m cave earned its name ("Snake Cave of Gimnyeong") because it is a single, S-shaped tube, not unlike the shape of a snake. Adding to the snake metaphor, the entrance is wide, much like the head of a snake, but past the entrance the tube grows progressively narrower. The floor of the tube is largely covered in sand blown in from the beach.

Gimnyeongsagul Cave is regarded along with Manjanggul Cave as the most important of the system. Unfortunately, due to fear of falling rock and to preserve the natural environment, you can't actually

Gimnyeongsagul Cave

enter the cave but some do make the visit (usually as part of a visit to Manjanggul) intrigued by the legend of virginal sacrifice associated with the cave (see next page).

Gimnyeong Maze Park 김녕미로공원

Conveniently located between Manjanggul and Gimnyeongsagul caves, Gimnyeong Maze Park is an intriguing hedge maze designed by the globally renowned maze designer Adrian Fisher. The garden was founded in 1987 by Frederic H. Dustin, an American professor at Jeju National University who has lived in Korea continuously since 1958 and on Jejudo since 1971.

Gimnyeong Maze is no ordinary maze. Shaped like Jejudo itself, the design incorporates a number of traditional and historical symbols, including a pony's head (symbolizing the Mongols, who invaded the island in 1276, bringing with them the horses for which the island is now famous), a snake and a ship (symbolizing the "De Sperwer," the Dutch trading vessel that was wrecked on Jejudo in 1653, depositing on the island Hendrick Hamel (see p466), one of the first Westerners to write about Korea). There are some elevated walkways

SNAKES, VIRGINS AND CAVES

History and Culture

In the days of old, it was said that a giant and ill-tempered serpent lived in Gimnyeongsagul Cave. This serpent would cause bad harvests, bring typhoons and other calamities, and generally make life unpleasant for the locals unless it was placated yearly with a sacrifice of food and, most painfully, a young virgin of 15 or 16 years of age. So every year, villagers would toss a young virgin into Gimnyeongsagul Cave, whom the serpent would eat alive.

In the 10th year of King Jungjong (r. 1506–1544), a man named Seo Lin was dispatched as a judge to Jeju-do. When he heard of the sacrifices, he was outraged. Assembling a few dozen soldiers, he went to Gimnyeongsagul Cave. At the entrance of the cave, they placed food, as if they were preparing the annual rite. The serpent emerged from the cave, but this time, instead of a pretty young virgin, what it got was cold steel as Seo dispatched the beast with his sword.

Later, a stone monument was erected to pay tribute to Seo at the mouth of the cave.

Traditionally, the people of Jeju have many legends and folk beliefs connected to snakes, which are plentiful on the island. In fact, some regard the legend of Seo Lin and the serpent of Gimnyeongsagul Cave as an allegory for the repression of shamanism and other folk beliefs by the neo-Confucianists of the central government during the early Joseon Dynasty.

and observation points from which to view the whole maze, although the best way to experience it is from inside as you make your way through the labyrinth. While there are maps available, just wandering about and getting lost is most fun.

🕐 8:30 am to 7:50 pm 💳 3,300 won
📞 064-782-9266 🖥 www.jejumaze.com
📖 See "Manjanggul Cave" on previous page.

Gimnyeong Maze Park

Seongsan Ilchulbong 성산일출봉

Seongsan Ilchulbong ("Sunrise Peak") is one of Korea's most breathtaking sights. Registered by UNESCO in 2007, Seongsan Ilchulbong is what volcanologists call an archetypal tuff cone, a steep volcanic cone with a wide, flat-floored crater composed of cemented volcanic ash. Tuff cones form from small but explosive eruptions in which magma meets water and are most often found, not surprisingly, at water's edge or just off the coast. Seongsan Ilchulbong was formed by an underwater eruption some 40,000 to 120,000 years ago. The cone is attached to the mainland by a thin isthmus; over the millennia, the sea has eroded the cone almost down to the base, producing a dramatic cliff that plunge almost straight down into the blue sea. As the name would suggest, it's truly a sight to behold at sunrise.

The bowl-shaped crater has a diameter of 570 m; the rim tops out at 179 m, while

Seongsan Ilchulbong, a dramatic tuff cone that plunges straight into the sea.

the floor bottoms out at 89 m. The crater floor is covered by a beautifully verdant grass field. The isthmus linking the crater to the mainland is covered in rapeseed flowers in spring, when it turns a brilliant yellow. The isthmus, incidentally, is also the best place to photograph the crater, especially at sunrise. Another good vantage point is the nearby beach of Seopjikoji.

Hikes up the crater's landside slope begin from the parking lot and end up the crater's lip. Visitors are prohibited from hiking the rim or entering the crater, which is a protected area. To get to the top, where there's an observation deck, plan on about 50 minutes round trip.

🕐 Open 1 hour before sunrise to 8 pm (winter), 1 hour before sunrise to 9 pm (summer)
💳 2,000 won 🚌 From Jeju Bus Terminal, take a bus to Seongsan and get off at Seongsan-ri Ipgu (2 hours). You could also take a bus from Seogwipo Bus Terminal to Seongsan (2 hrs 30 min). 📞 064-710-7923

Seopjikoji 섭지코지

Just south of Seongsan Ilchulbong is another hilly protrusion into the sea. This protrusion, called Seopjikoji, is an especially pleasant piece of coastline with rocky ocean cliffs and open meadows of grass and rapeseed flowers—interrupted by not a single tree. Seopjikoji also offers fine views of Seongsan Ilchulbong.

🚌 Take a cab or bus from Seongsan Ilchulbong. If you are going from Jeju Bus Terminal, take a bus from Ilju Road and get off at Sinyang-ri 신양리 (1 hr 30 min).

Seopjikoji

Udo 우도

Udo or "Cow Island" got its name because, on approach, it is said to resemble a cow laying down. The head of the cow is a volcanic tuff cone, Udobong 우도봉, formed by an underwater eruption during the Pleistocene era. The rest of the island is a flat and very fertile lava plateau. Settlers from the main island, attracted by the rich volcanic soil, received permission from the government to begin moving to Udo from 1843. The locals are a tightly knit community, mostly born and raised on the island for generations. Many engage in agriculture, growing sweet potatoes, barley, garlic and peanuts (for which the island is famous), as well as herding and fishing. Korea's best known community of *haenyeo* (women divers) also operate from below the island's cliffs.

Nowadays, the islanders are joined by boatloads of tourists who come to the island to take in its sights and enjoy the pleasant island atmosphere. Like many places in Korea, it has its obligatory "eight scenic sights," which you can find on maps and tourist literature on the island. One of the ones you'll definitely want to see is Seobin Baeksa 서빈백사, a lovely white coral sand beach with emerald blue water, producing what is, for Korea, a very exotic, almost Caribbean-like landscape. Another sight you'll want to take in is Huhaeseokbyeok Cliffs 후해석벽, dramatic black lava cliffs that are best seen from a tour boat.

Another one of the eight sights worth checking out is Haesikdonggul Cave 해식동굴. At noon, when the sun reflects off the water, which in turn reflects on the ceiling of the cave, an illusion makes it appear as if the moon is rising at midday.

Atop Udobong are two lighthouses including old Udo Lighthouse, built in 1906 by the Japanese after their victory in the Russo-Japanese War. While it's not big, it is one of the oldest lighthouses in Korea.

🪙 1,500 won (park fee), 500 won tax at the terminal. 🚢 Ferries to Udo depart from the port of Seongsan 성산항, an hour's trip from either Jeju Bus Terminal or Seogwipo Bus Terminal. Ferries depart every hour, and take just 15 minutes to complete the trip.

Just off the eastern coast, the island of Udo is a nice day trip.

TIPS

RIDING ABOUT UDO

The best way to enjoy Udo is to rent a bike, scooter or ATV (rentals available near the dock by Udo Harbor) and ride about the island, taking in the rustic charm as you navigate the roads lined by locals' volcanic stone fences. It's particularly pretty in spring when the rapeseed fields blossom, turning the island into a riot of yellow and green.

In 2001, the entire island was designated as a maritime park, meaning there is a 1,500 won fee to enter the island.

- **Bike rentals:** 2,000 won (1 hr), 5,000 won (3 hrs), 10,000 won (1 day)
- **Scooter rentals:** 15,000 won (1 hr), 20,000 won (2 hrs), 35,000 won (1 day)
- **ATV rentals:** 30,000 won (1 hr), 40,000 won (2 hrs)

Seongeup Folk Village 성읍민속마을

At the foot of Mt. Hallasan is Seongeup Folk Village, a beautifully maintained Joseon Dynasty walled town with many beautiful homes, old administrative offices and shrines built in Jeju-do's unique indigenous style.

The administrative capital of a large swath of Jeju-do from 1423 until 1941, the village is ringed by protective walls, access through which is controlled by several gates, the south gate being the most important. Inside the walls are an old official inn, and old official office, the town's old Confucian school and many historic private residences. Even the trees are old. The village is typical of the Jeju-do of old—the thatched roofs of the homes are tied down with straw rope to protect against the island's notoriously strong winds. The walls are made from stone and mud instead of wood and mud. The alleyways are curvy to block the wind, and lined with walls made of volcanic black stone. In front of the gates, we can also find some of Jeju-do's iconic *dol hareubang* statues.

🚌 At Seogwipo Bus Terminal, take the Dongilju bus 동일주 버스 and get off at Pyoseon-ri local office 표선리 사무소. From there, walk straight, turn left at the intersection, and go straight until you get to the bus stop. From there, hop on the Beonnyeong-ro bus 번영로 버스 and get off at Seupeup 1-ri.

Haenyeo Museum 해녀박물관

Opened in 2006, the Haenyeo Museum is a smartly designed exhibit space in the pleasant little seaside village of Hado-ri 하도리 dedicated to the lives of Jejudo's women divers. This is a good place learn a bit about the history and culture of the *haenyeo* through photos, artifacts and other memorabilia.

🕐 9 am to 6 pm (Mar–Oct), 9 am to 5 pm (Nov–Feb) 💳 1,200 won 🚌 From Jeju Bus Terminal, take a bus for Sehwa 세화 or Seongsan and get off at the museum in Hado-ri 하도리 (60 min). ✆ 064-782-9898

Sangumburi Crater 산굼부리 분화구

About 40 minutes inland from Jeju City is one of Jejudo's largest parasitic craters, the spectacular Sangumburi Crater. Some 650 m wide and 100 m deep, Sangumburi is unique among Jeju's craters in that it is a maar crater—it was formed when underground magma met groundwater, producing a great explosion of steam that produced what can only be described as a massive hole in the ground and the floor collapsed. No rock or magma was emitted during the eruption, just gas. It must have been quite the sight.

You can walk up to the lip of the crater—the views of both the aforementioned hole in the ground and the surrounding Jejudo scenery are awesome. Unfortunately, since the crater is a protected area, you cannot circumnavigate it or descend into it. Over 400 species of plants and animals, including deer, live in the crater. In fall, the area is covered in beautiful, golden reeds and is truly a sight to behold.

🕐 8:30 am to 6:30 pm (summer), 8:30 to 5:30 pm (winter) 💳 3,000 won 🚌 From Jeju Bus Terminal, take the bus for Beonnyeong-ro and get off at Sangumburi (30–40 min). 🌐 www.sangumburi.net (KR)

HAENYEO: KOREA'S MERMAIDS

Jeju-do's diving women or *haenyeo* are a local cultural icon and a symbol of the country's distinctive culture. We don't know when, exactly, Jeju's women first took to the sea, but one governor in 1105 banned women from diving in the nude, and another governor in the 17th century banned men and women from diving together.

Under the influence of Neo-Confucianism, Korea developed into a very patriarchal society, but not on Jejudo, where women were often the chief breadwinners of the family. So valued women were, in fact, that a local saying goes, "Have a baby girl and we will throw a pork barbecue party; have a baby boy and we will kick his ass." In fact, in many coastal villages, what developed was the polar opposite of what developed on the mainland, with women earning money by diving for shellfish and other bounty of the sea, and men staying home to care of the children.

Haenyeo begin learning their trade from the time they are girls. It takes great skill to be a *haenyeo*—the women should be able to free dive (i.e., dive without oxygen tanks) to depths of 20 meters and hold their breath for several minutes. Divers go out with little gear—just a wetsuit, face mask, weights, iron pick to dredge shell fish, nets into which to place the catch, and a buoy to alert the surface to their location. For added safety against sharks and accidents, *haenyeo* almost always work in groups. The reliance on the old ways—particularly the refusal to use oxygen tanks—is a piece of collective wisdom that prevents overfishing and keeps seafood stocks plentiful. Favored catches are conch, abalone, octopus and sea cucumber, not to mention seaweed.

The life of the *haenyeo* is not an easy one, however, and Korea's current-day prosperity has lured many of Jeju's daughters away from diving. Accordingly, the number of women divers has dropped dramatically in recent years. In the 1970s, there were 15,000 *haenyeo* in Jeju; today, there are about 5,000, most of whom are elderly.

DOL HAREUBANG

Dol hareubang, or "Grandfather Rock," is a true Jeju icon. Carved of volcanic stone, the phallic statues with the bulging but pupil-less eyes and impish grins used to be placed in

front of town gates to ward off evil, much in the same way the ubiquitous *jangseung* was used on the mainland. There are still 45 original *dol hareubang* from the 18th century, mostly in Jeju City, Seongeup Folk Village and Daejeong-eup 대정읍 in southern Jeju. Besides these, you'll find countless replicas all over the island, and small stone replicas are commonly sold as souvenirs.

JEJU-DO'S SOUTH COAST 제주도 남부

Seogwipo's convenient bus and boat connections make it easy to explore Jejudo's beautiful southern coast where there are numerous attractions—natural (albeit, ticketed) and others more touristic—for the visitor.

Seogwipo 서귀포

With over 155,000 people, Seogwipo is Jejudo's other major city, and the commercial hub of the southern half of the island. Much of what was said about Jeju City can be said about Seogwipo—as an exercise in urban planning and architecture, it's neither particularly desirable nor unpleasant, but it's a perfect base from which to explore southern

Jejudo. There are many heralded sites, namely the scenic Cheonjiyeon and Jeongbang Falls.

Cheonjiyeon Falls 천지연 폭포

This beautiful waterfall, and the lovely pool that it forms, is to be found on the river just west of town. Its name translates as "Pond Where Heaven and Earth Meet" and, according to legend, seven nymphs descended from Heaven on a step of clouds

Jungmun Resort Complex and Jejudo's southern coast are Korea's answer to Hawaii.

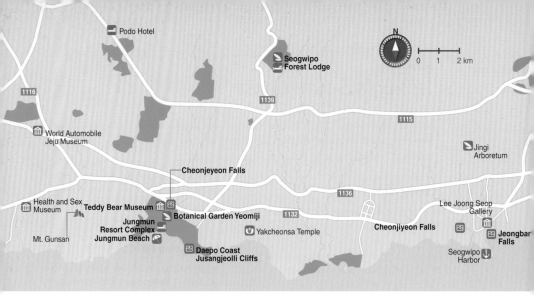

to bathe in the cool, clean waters. Nowadays you're unlikely to find any nymphs, but you will find the next best thing in the pool—a large school of marbled eel. Designated by the Korean government as a natural monument, the waterfall itself is 22 m high, the water cascading from a cliff made of volcanic rock into a pool that reaches a depth of 20 m. The valley around the falls is also thickly wooded with a variety of subtropical and temperate-zone trees, and the falls are lit up at night, making it a good place to come for an evening stroll.

🕐 7 am to 11 pm (admission ends at 10:10 pm) 🎫 2,000 won ☎ 064-733-1528 🚌 From Seogwipo Bus Terminal, take Bus No. 1 to the last stop (10 min).

Jeongbang Falls 정방폭포

One of Jejudo's most popular tourist attractions, especially with the honeymooner crowd, Jeongbang Falls has the distinction of being Asia's only waterfall that empties directly into the ocean. Indeed, it's a geological phenomenon seen in very few places in the world (the best known example globally being Dunn's River Falls in Jamaica). The water here falls 23m from a sheer volcanic cliff into the sea below; between the visuals and the sound, it makes for a dramatic sight, even with throngs of tourists around you.

🕐 8 am to 7 pm (6 pm in winter) 🎫 2,000 won 🚌 From Seogwipo Bus Terminal, take a bus for Bomok 보목 and get off at the KAL Hotel (5 min): the waterfall is right there. Otherwise, just take a taxi. ☎ 064-760-6341

Jeongbang Falls is Asia's only waterfall that empties directly into the sea.

Botanical Garden Yeomiji (left), Teddy Bear Museum

Jungmun Resort Complex
중문관광단지

The sprawling Jungmun Resort Complex is Jeju's one-stop center for all your leisure, vacation and convention needs: several luxury hotels, a marine theme park, popular beach areas, a botanical garden, shopping center, two casinos, museums, shopping centers, a ton of restaurants, a convention center, sea fishing programs, scuba and diving opportunities, and golf courses. Throw in Cheonjeyeon Falls, Daepo Coast Jusangjeolli Cliffs, and the Mt. Hallasan scenery and seaside into the mix, and you have everything you need for a very pleasant, entertaining stay.

✆ Give the Jungmun Resort Complex Tourist Information Center a ring at 064-739-1330 or visit them on the north side of the complex.
🚌 Airport Limousine No. 600 will take you there (50 min). Likewise, you can take buses bound for the resort from Jeju Bus Terminal (50 min) or Seogwipo Bus Terminal (50 min).

Botanical Garden Yeomiji 여미지식물원

Even if you're not into tourist resorts, Jungmun has some things worth checking out. Botanical Garden Yeomiji 여미지식물원 has both an indoor garden that is home to 2,000 rare, tropical and subtropical plants underneath a futuristic greenhouse and an outdoor garden with traditional Korean, Japanese, Italian and French sub-sections. Views from the 38m high observatory shouldn't be missed.

💰 3,500 won ✆ 064-735-1100

Teddy Bear Museum 테디베어뮤지엄

If you've got kids (or even if you don't), the Jeju Teddy Bear Museum 테디베어뮤지엄 is worth a visit. The world's largest museum dedicated to the teddy bear in all its cute and cuddly incarnations.

💰 6,000 won ✆ 064-738-7600

Other Museums

The World Automobile Jeju Museum 세계자동차제주박물관 (064-792-3000, 8,000 won), opened in 2008 by a mainland businessman with a passion for cars, has about 70 classic cars, including a rare 1928 Hillman Straight 8 and the iconic Mercedes-Benz 300SL. There's a Ripley's "Believe It or Not!" Museum 믿거나말거나박물관 (064-738-3003, 8,000 won) near the entrance of the complex. And if Jeju Love Land and the nearby World Eros Museum aren't enough, there's also the Health and Sex Museum 건강과성박물관 (064-792-5700, 3,500 won, minors not allowed), with more exhibits of the very adult-oriented kind.

Museum of African Art near Jusangjeolli Cliffs

The spectacular Cheonjeyeon Falls

Jungmun Beach 중문해수욕장

Along with Haeundae, Daecheon and Gyeongpodae, Jungmun Beach is one of Korea's most popular, in no small part thanks to its inclusion in the Jungmun Resort Complex. As the surfers would attest, it's probably got the best waves in Jejudo. The waves are so good, in fact, that you'll probably want to keep an eye on your kids—the Pacific swells can get pretty powerful. This 560 m stretch of white sand is as close to Hawaii as you'll get in Korea; not only the waves and tropical vegetation, including palm trees, but resort conveniences with comcomitant high prices and hordes of tourists, both domestic and international, in the summer months. Thanks to the waves, Jungmun Beach is Korea's top surfing, parasailing and

windsurfing destination. If you'd like to learn the art of surfing, one recommended instructor is Kim Hee-cheol (010-7275-2725), who runs a surfing school with instruction available in English—day classes are 60,000 won, including suit and board rental.

Cheonjeyeon Falls 천제연폭포

Cheonjiyeon and Jeongbang falls may be more famous but Cheonjeyeon Falls are likely the most spectacular falls on the island. It's actually a system of three falls, although the first, which drops into a pool dramatically lined by basalt column cliffs, often runs dry in seasons other than summer. The second of the falls cascades some 30 m, and is the most impressive of the system. A picturesque arch bridge spans the gorge, Victoria Falls Bridge-style, providing beautiful views of the surroundings. The gorge is surrounded by thick warm-temperate forests that are home to some rare plants, including ferns and elaeocarpus trees.

🕐 8 am to 6:30 pm (Mar–Oct). 9 am to 5:30 pm (Nov–Feb) 💳 2,500 won 🚌 Take a bus from Seogwipo Bus Terminal towards Jungmun and get off at Cheonjeyeon. Or take Airport Limousine Bus No. 600 and get off at the International Convention Center at Yeomiji Botanical Garden. Both routes take about 50 minutes.

Daepo Coast Jusangjeolli Cliffs
대포해안주상절리대

This fantastic stretch of coastline near the massive Jungmun Resort complex is Jeju-do's answer to Northern Ireland's Giant's Causeway. The spectacular black cliffs were formed by a phenomenon known as columnar jointing—lava, when it cools rapidly, contracts and cracks, often into polygonal columns. The results can be spectacular, with rows of polygonal columns that appear more man-made than natural. While the most famous example of this geological formation is Giant's Causeway, some American visitors may better recognize the phenomenon from the landmark Devil's Tower in Wyoming.

The basalt columns of the Daepo Coast, some as high as 30 to 40 m, jut out into the sea, making for quite a dramatic scene, especially at sunset and at high tide when the waves crash into the pillars.

⊙ 8 am to 7 pm (6 pm, Nov to Feb) 🎫 2,000 won 🚌 From Seogwipo, take Airport Limousine Bus No. 600 and get off at the International Convention Center (50 min). You could also take Airport Limousine Bus No. 600 from Jeju Bus Terminal (60 min).

The Daepo Coast's Jusangjeolli Cliffs were formed by quickly cooling lava.

Itami Jun's Wind, Water & Stone

Off the Beaten Track

Inland from Jungmun Resort Complex is another upscale resort/residential area in the making, centered on the architecturally inspired Podo Hotel 포도호텔. In front of the hotel's golf courses is a new development of mostly vacation homes named Biotopia. On the outskirts of this development can be found three small museums by the late Japanese-Korean architect Itami Jun (1937–2011). If you have the time, do try to stop by these beautiful Zen-like meditation spaces, each one dedicated to one of Jeju's three symbols: wind, water and stone. The Water Museum is particularly inspiring, with its minimalist concrete spaces, its open roof and masterful use of water, light and reflections.

Hallasan National Park

South Korea's highest peak at 1,950 m, the grand cone of Mt. Hallasan is more than just Jejudo's highlight—it is Jejudo, or as the locals put is, "Jejudo is Hallasan, Hallasan is Jejudo." The mountain is a gigantic shield volcano, one formed entirely of lava flows, characterized by their enormous size but relatively low profiles. Mauna Kea, which forms the big island of Hawaii, is also a shield volcano, lending more credence to the oft-cited comparison between the two islands.

Mt. Hallasan began forming in the Pliocene epoch; it is no longer active, with the last recorded eruptions in 1002 and 1007 (powerful earthquakes were recorded in 1455 and 1670, however). It is crowned by a 400 meter-wide caldera, Baengnokdam 백록담 ("Lake Where the White Deer Drinks") which, depending on the time of year, is partially filled by a shallow crater lake. The mountain also has over 360 smaller parasitic cones, or *oreum*, found throughout the island—these parasitic cones are a defining piece of Jeju-do's landscape.

Crater lake of Baengnokdam atop Mt. Hallasan

Seasonal views of Mt. Hallasan

Mt. Hallasan is beautiful any time of year, but spring—when its vast colonies of royal azaleas blossom—is the best season to visit. If you can deal with the cold and the snow, winter is a good time to hike the mountain—its snow-encrusted trees, or "snow flowers," produce a magical, almost surreal landscape. During heavy snowfalls, however, some roads are hazardous or closed to traffic.

Hiking Mt. Hallasan

Hiking Mt. Hallasan is one of the most popular activities for visitors to the island, and well worth the time and effort. Thanks to its broad flanks, the hikes here are not especially difficult despite the height of the peak. There are several well-marked and well-traveled hiking paths up the mountain, almost all under 10 km. Still, you should probably set aside a whole day for this, with hikes generally taking eight to nine hours return. Be warned, too, that the winds can get very strong, and the weather is fickle at best. Dress accordingly.

From the Jeju City side, the best course—but the most strenuous—is Gwaneumsa Trail 관음사탐방로 (8.7 km, nine hours round trip), which begins at the Buddhist temple

of Gwaneumsa 관음사 (Jejudo's oldest Buddhist temple) and climbs to Baengnokdam. You can descend the same way you went up, but most choose to descend along the Seongpanak Trail 성판악탐방로, which skirts the Sara Oreum 사라오름 (1,324 m), an impressive cone with its own crater lake that can be reached by another 40 minute side hike. While Seongpanak Trail (9.6 km, eight hours round trip) is the easiest and most popular trail to ascend the peak, it's also by far the most crowded.

Be aware that if you want to reach the peak, you need to start off early—they won't let you on the peak if you don't make it to certain ranger stations by certain times. In the case of Gwaneumsa Trail, you need to reach Samgakbong Shelter, not far

Gwaneumsa Trail

Eoseunsaengak Trail

Seongpanak Trail

Uitseoreum Shelter

Samgakbong Shelter

Sara Oreum

Sajebi Hill

Baekrokdam

Jindalaebat Shelter

Pyeonggue Shelter

Myeongsil Trail

Donnaeko Trail

from the peak itself, by 1 pm during the summer months (or even earlier during spring and fall) if you wish to reach the summit. You're encouraged to check out the park's website at www.hallasan.go.kr for precise times and more info. There are several other popular trails, but they do not reach Baengnokdam. They do present some beautiful views of the opposite side of the peak, however.

🚌 To get to the start of Gwaneumsa Trail, take a bus to Gwaneumsa from Jeju Bus Terminal or Jeju International Airport. Both take about 20 minutes. Buses to Gwaneumsa from Seogwipo take a bit longer at 30 minutes.
To get to the head of Seongpanak Trail, take a bus from either Jeju or Seogwipo bus terminals for Seongpanak Ipgu 성판악입구 (30 min).

Despite its subtropical setting, Mt. Hallasan sees a lot of snow in winter.

Wild deer on the slopes of Mt. Hallasan

Off the Beaten Track

Jeju Olle Trails 제주올레길

The best way to explore Jeju-do is on foot. In 2007, former journalist Suh Myung-sook—inspired by Spain's legendary Camino de Santiago pilgrimage route—began work on plotting and restoring Jeju-do's old walking paths. The walking paths—called *Olle-gil*, taking their name from the old Jeju word for the paths that connected homes to the main road—take hikers through scenic pastoral and coastal landscapes in hopes of giving them "peace, happiness and healing." They proved a tremendous success, and there are now over 300 km of these paths ringing almost the entire island.

There are 19 trails in all (plus several optional paths), each trail between 15 km and 20 km long. Look to spend about five to eight hours on each trail. The trails are not especially taxing physically, but be sure to bring plenty of water in summer. Walking or hiking shoes are recommended, although in summer, sandals might help on the sandy beach routes. Be sure to check out Jeju Olle Trails' website (www.jejuolle.org) for details on each course.

1 Siheung Elementary School 시흥초등학교 to Gwangchigi Beach 광치기해변 (15 km, 5–6 hrs) This path takes hikers past several *oreum* (small volcanic cones) and ends at Gwangchigi Beach, with excellent views of Seongsan Ilchulbong. **1-1** Udo Island (16.1 km, 4–5 hrs) See 'Udo Island' **2** Gwangchigi Beach to Onpyeong Port 온평항 (17.2 km, 5–6 hrs) The highlight here is the view from Daesusanbong Peak 대수산봉, with panoromic views of Seongsan Ilchulbong and the rest of the east coast. **3** Onpyeong Port to Dangke Port 당케포구 (22 km, 6–7 hrs) A nice mix of forest, pastoral and seaside scenery. You also pass the Kim Young Gap Gallery 김영갑갤러리 (admission: 3,000 won), dedicated to the work of a photographer who spent much of his life photographing the island's nature. **4** Pyoseon 표선 to Namwon Port 남원포구 (23 km, 6–7 hrs) The first half of this hike is lovely coastal scenery, but the second involves *oreum* and highland walking. **5** Namwon Port to Soesokkak 쇠소깍 (15 km, 5–6 hrs) The cliffs of Keuneong Promenade 큰엉산책로 make for one of Korea's most beautiful coastal walks. The cliff-lined Soesokkak Estuary, with its blue-green water, is quite picturesque, too. **6** Soesokkak to Oedolgae Rock 외돌개 (14.4 km, 5 hrs) More coastal scenery, leading through Seogwipo. Hikers pass the Cheonjiyeon Falls, too. While at Soesokkak, spend 50 minutes and explore the estuary by *teu*, a traditional raft pulled along by rope connected to the side of the river. **7** Oedolgae Rock to Wolpyeong Port 월평포구 (15.1 km, 4–5 hrs) This scenic stretch passes along some lovely, rocky coastline. A point of interest is Hwanguji Beach 황우지해안 (right at the beginning), where there's a cliff

Olle Trail Map

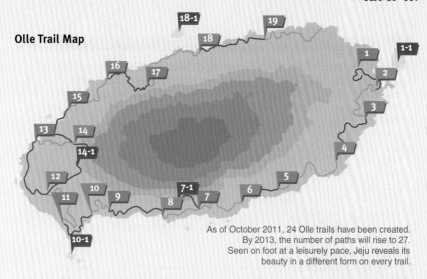

As of October 2011, 24 Olle trails have been created. By 2013, the number of paths will rise to 27. Seen on foot at a leisurely pace, Jeju reveals its beauty in a different form on every trail.

with 12 caves dug by the Japanese military to fortify the island during World War II. **7-1 World Cup Stadium** 월드컵경기장 **to Oedolgae Rock** (15.6 km, 4–5 hrs) This course involves some inland walking along rice paddies and villages along with some stretches along high grassy plains with views of Mt. Hallasan. **8 Wolpyeong** 월평 **to Daepyeong Port** 대평포구 (17.6 km, 5–6 hrs) A beautiful stretch of coast, including Jeju's famous Jusang Jeolli Cliffs. **9 Daepyeong Port to Hwasun Beach** 화순해수욕장 (8.8 km, 3–4 hrs) A relatively strenuous course that takes you along high cliffs and into the Andeok Valley 안덕계곡. You pass some cows along the way, too. **10 Hwasun Beach** 화순해수욕장 **to Moseulpo** 모슬 포 (14 km, 4–5 hrs) This spectacular stretch takes you along wild volcanic cliffs, past the dramatic volcanic plug of Mt. Sanbangsan 산방산 and up the tuff cone of Mt. Songaksan 송악산. During World War II, the area around Moseulpo was highly fortified; along the way, you'll pass man-made caves, bunkers and even an old Japanese airfield. **10-1 Gapado Island** 가파도 (5 km, 1 hr) Gapado is a flat volcanic island just off the southern coast with pretty fields of barley. There are three ferries a day from the port of Moseulpo (20 min). **11 Hamo Beach** 하모해수욕장 **to Mureung 2-ri** 무릉2리 (20 km, 6–7 hrs) The scenery from the top of Moseulpo Peak, with views of Mt. Sanbangsan, Mt. Songaksan and Gapado, make this hike worth it. **12 Mureung 2-ri to Yongsu Port** 용수포구 (17.6 km, 5–6 hrs) Jeju City's first *Olle-gil* skirts the western coast of Jejudo. The area around Jagunae port 자구내포구 is particularly nice. **13 Yongsu to Jeoji** 저지 (15.3 km, 4–5 hrs) This path is almost entirely inland, taking you through forests and up the Jeoji Oreum 저지오름. **14 Jeoji to Hallim** 한림 (19.3 km, 6–7 hrs) Course 14 mixes inland walking with coastal walking. Check out the wild cactus around the port of Wollyeong 월령포구. **14-1 Jeoji to Mureung** (17.5 km, 5–6 hrs) Another inland course, this path takes you through the beautiful O'-sulloc green tea plantation (check out O'-sulloc Tea Museum) and the old growth of Gotjawal Forest. **15 Hallim Port** 한림포구 **to Gonae Port** 고내포구 (19 km, 6–7 hrs) More inland walking through fields, farms, villages and old stone walls. **16 Gonae Port to Gwangnyeong** 광녕 (17.8 km, 5–6 hrs) This nice, easy walk is a good mixture of coastal and rural scenery. **17 Gwangnyeong to Sanjicheon** 산지천 (18.4 km, 6 hrs) The path here takes you through some pleasant countryside and into downtown Jeju City. Be sure to see Yongduam Rock along the way. **18 Sanjicheon to Jocheon** 조천 (18.8 km, 6 hrs) Some lovely coastline along this walk, as well as great views of Jeju City. **18-1 Chujado Island** 추자도 (17.7 km, 6–8 hrs) Chujado is actually several islands, some linked together by bridges. This is a demanding trail more akin to mountain hiking than walking. Ferries to Chujado depart from Jeju City. **19 Jocheon to Gimnyeong Olle** 김녕올레 (18.8 km, 6–8 hrs) This is largely coastal walking, with a highlight being beautiful Hamdeok Beach 함덕해수욕장. To learn about a particularly tragic piece of Korean history, check out the memorial to Jeju April 3 Incident.

WHAT TO EAT

Due to its topography, Jejudo doesn't produce much rice. What it does have in abundance, however, is seafood. *Jeonbokjuk* 전복죽, a porridge made from abalone once served to the kings of Joseon, is an island specialty. You'll also find plenty of places serving abalone grilled with butter, an absolutely delightful meal. *Okdom gui* 옥돔구이, or grilled tilefish, is a local favorite, as is *haemul ttukbaegi* 해물뚝배기, a hot pot made from various seafoods. Raw fish restaurants abound throughout the island. Another specialty of the island is pork taken from the famous local black pigs 흑돼지. In the old days, these pigs were fed a diet of human excrement — outhouses, in fact, were built right over the pigsty. This is no longer the case, but the pigs still make for some mighty fine eating. The meat is first smoked over burning hay before being grilled, giving the pork a distinctive flavor. Thanks to its subtropical setting, Jejudo produces some of Korea's best citrus fruit. Ones you're likely to see in abundance are the *gamgyul* 감귤 (tangerines) and *hallabong* 한라봉, a sweet hybrid tangerine easily recognized by the distinctive protuberance at the stem. You can find these fruits all over the mainland, too.

Jeju City

Near Yongduam is Yongdamgol 용담골 (064-752-2344), a local institution specializing in *jeonbok* (abalone) cuisine. The *jeonbokjuk* (abalone porridge) will run you about 10,000 won but if you want something a bit more, try the *jeonbok samhap* 전복삼합 (35,000 won) — grilled abalone with butter, served with sliced pork eaten with seaweed and kimchi. Also well-known is Yubin Sikdang 유빈식당 (064-753-5218) near the Ramada Plaza Hotel. They do all things abalone, including *jeonbokjuk* (10,000 won), *jeonbok gui* 전복구이 (grilled abalone, 60,000 won) and *jeonbok hoe* 전복회 (raw, sliced abalone, 60,000 won). In the new part of town south of Jeju Airport is Heukdonga 흑돈가 (064-747-0088), where you can enjoy some quality *heukdwaeji saenggui* 흑돼지 생구이 (grilled black pig pork belly) for 14,000 won a serving. For something a bit simpler, Samdae Guksuhoegwan 삼대국수회관 (064-759-6644), in front of Jeju Folklore and Natural History Museum, does a lovely *gogiguksu* 고기국수 (5,000 won), a noodle soup served with slices of pork.

Seogwipo City

Not far from Seogwipo Bus Terminal is Yongi Sikdang 용이식당 (064-732-7892), which looks humble but does a mean *duruchigi* 두루치기 (6,000 won), pork grilled with vegetables on tin foil. Absolutely delightful, and be sure to order the *bokkeumbap* 볶음밥 (fried rice) afterwards. In fact, the entire alley — called Arangjoeul Geori 아랑조을 거리 by the locals but named Cheon-ji Ro 천지로 in English — is lined by about 60 restaurants (including the Yongi Sikdang) serving all sorts of Jeju specialties. On the waterfront, not far from Cheonjiyeon Falls, is Jeju Halmang Ttukbaegi 제주할망뚝배기 (064-733-9934), which does a very nice *jeonbok ttukbaegi* 전복뚝배기 (10,000 won), a hot pot with abalone, mussels and other seafoods. Another place that has been doing good *jeonbok ttukbaegi* for close to 30 years is Sambo Sikdang 삼보식당 (064-762-3620), also not far from Cheonjiyeon Falls. The port of Daepohang has a whole "town" of raw fish restaurants. Keun Gaetmul Hoetjip 큰갯물횟집 (064-738-1625) is expensive — look to drop about 150,000–200,000 won here — but the fish is fresh, the surroundings are immaculate, the presentation artistic and the views gorgeous. Much more humble is Hwanggeumeojang 황금어장 (064-738-4418), a very popular place in the Arcade Market that does take-away raw fish. A kilo of fish will cost you 35,000 won. For something a bit different, try Gamgyul Jjinppang 감귤찐빵 (064-733-2900) near the tourist information center just south of Cheonjiyeon Falls. They do cheap steamed buns flavored with Jeju's famous tangerines. Red bean and tangerine jam fillings available.

WHERE TO STAY

Jeju City

Because of Jeju-do's status as a major tourist destination, you'll be tripping over accommodations. You'll find plenty of *minbak* and B&Bs along almost the entire coast, and lots of hotels and motels in urban Jeju City. Be warned, though, that in the summer vacation season many of the choice accommodations may be booked out. Starting at the high end, the Ramada Plaza Jeju 라마다프라자 제주호텔 (064-729-8100, www.ramadajeju.co.kr), designed like an ocean liner, sits on the water in downtown Jeju. Doubles with a view of the ocean begin at 352,000 won a night. To the west of the airport is the beautiful Resort & Spa Olle 올레리조트 (064-799-7770), with rooms beginning at 320,000 won a night (peak season). Rooms have pulpwood interiors and private jacuzzis. In downtown Jeju City is Jeju KAL Hotel 제주칼호텔 (064-724-2001, english.kalhotel.co.kr) with twin rooms beginning at 220,000 won. Also downtown is Daemyung Resort 대명리조트 제주 (064-782-8311), with family rooms beginning at 320,000 won. Nice, but not bank-breaking, is Hotel Marina 제주마리나관광호텔 (064-746-6161) with doubles going for 99,000 won a night. At the budget end, Neulsong Parktel 늘송파크텔 (064-749-3303) has nice, clean rooms in a downtown location for 40,000 won. Backpackers like Yeha Guesthouse 예하게스트하우스 (064-724-5506, www.yehaguesthouse.com) by Jeju Intercity Bus Terminal. Dormitory rooms start at 22,000 won (private rooms for two at 80,000 won) in peak season.

Seogwipo City

One of the most spectacular places to stay in Korea is the architecturally magnificent Phoenix Island Resort 휘닉스아일랜드 (064-731-7000~5, www.phoenixisland.co.kr) near Seopjikoji, with condo-style accommodation for 450,000 won a night. The resort, with great views of Seongsan Ilchulbong, features work by renowned Japanese architect Ando Tadao and Swiss master Mario Botta. Highlights include Ando's Genius Loci meditation center; Botta's Agora Club House, a glass pyramid seemingly built of light; and Ando's Glass House, a glass and stone masterpiece that seems to float over the sea. Mint, a restaurant in the Glass House, is a good place to have a meal or a cup of coffee. Also spectacular is late architect Itami Jun's Podo Hotel 핀크스 포도호텔 (064-793-7000, www.thepinx.co.kr/podohotel), which blends East and West in an sublime exercise in ecological architecture. Rooms begin at 300,000 won. The hotel also sits amidst one of Korea's best golf courses. The best known of Jeju's luxury hotels are located in the Jungmun Resort Complex, including Lotte Hotel Jeju 롯데호텔제주 (064-731-1000, www.lottehoteljeju.com), Hyatt Regency Jeju 하얏트리젠시 제주 (064-733-1234, www.hyattjeju.com) and The Shilla Jeju 호텔신라제주 (064-735-5114, www.shilla.net). Look to drop about 400,000 won a night at any of these places. You'll find plenty of mid-ranged and affordable accommodation, especially pensions and *minbak*, both in Seogwipo itself and scenic spots like Seongsan Ilchulbong. Seongsan Ilchulbong Guesthouse 성산일출봉게스트하우스 (064-784-6434) has dormitory rooms beginning at 15,000 won, and the views from the upper floor can't be beat. Also near Seongsan Ilchulbong is Sunrise Castle, with rooms for two for 120,000 won. Near Cheonjiyeon Falls is the BENIKEA Hotel Jeju Crystal 호텔크리스탈 (064-732-8311), with doubles for 150,000 won. Also near Cheonjiyeon Falls is Jeju Hiking Inn 제주하이킹INN (064-763-2380, hikinginn.com), a backpacker-friendly inn with double beds for 30,000 won. They also provide bike rentals, and the views of Seogwipo Harbor from the rooftop picnic area are quite nice.

FACTS FOR VISITORS

ESSENTIAL INFO

INFO RESOURCES

Korea Tourism Organization (KTO)

 Korea's national tourism agency, Korea Tourism Organization (KTO), does an excellent job of providing information about tourist sites, accommodation, transportation and just about anything else you'd need to know while traveling in Korea. The KTO headquarters (02-729-9600) is located on the Cheonggyecheon Stream, a short walk from Exit 2 of Eulji-ro 1-ga Station, Line 2 or Exit 5 of Jonggak Station, Line 1. Perhaps more useful, however, is its informative website at http://english. visitkorea.or.kr.

The KTO also has a number of overseas offices that will be all too happy to dispense information to visitors. See the list below for contact info.

Seoul Tourism Promotion Division

Seoul Metropolitan Government also provides a wealth of information to tourists visiting the city. Visit http://english.visitseoul.net.

KTO OVERSEAS OFFICES

North America
(Toll Free in US 1-800-868-7567)
Los Angeles 1-323-634-0280
New York 1-201-585-0909
Toronto 1-416-348-9056/7

Europe
Frankfurt 49-69-233226
Paris 33-1-4538-7123
London 44-20-7321-2535

Russia
Moscow 7-495-735-4240
Vladivostock 7-4232-49-1163

Oceania & Asia
Sydney 61-2-9252-4147/8
Kuala Lumpur 60-3-2143-9000
Jakarta 62-21-5785-3030

Singapore 65-6533-0441/2
Bangkok 66-2-354-2080/2082
Hanoi 84-4-3831-5180
Taipei 886-2-2720-8281
New Dehli 91-124-492-1200
Dubai 971-4-331-2288

China
Beijing 86-10-6585-8213/4
Shanghai 86-21-5169-7933
Guangzhou 86-20-3893-1639
Shenyang 86-24-2281-4155
Hong Kong 852-2523-8065

Japan
Tokyo 81-3-3597-1717
Osaka 81-6-6266-0847/0828
Fukuoka 81-92-471-7174/5
Nagoya 81-52-223-3211/2

TRAVEL APPS

The Korea Tourism Organization has joined the mobile revolution with two very useful apps, Visit Korea and MediApp Korea (iPhone, Android). The Visit Korea app offers tons of useful travel information conveniently based on GPS location, as well as a direct link to the 24-hour "1330" KTO information and interpretation center. Mediapp Korea, meanwhile, targets medical tourism visitors, providing a wealth of information about medical services in Korea, including facility locations (via Google Maps), contact information, specialties and costs.

If you're sticking around Seoul only, you can download the iTour Seoul app (iPhone, Android) for detailed travel information on the city, including the lowdown on sightseeing, restaurants, hotels and transportation. Visit the Apple App Store or Android Market to download the free apps.

Local Travel Agents

If you're tired of doing things on your own and would like something a bit more organized, there are plenty of English-speaking tourism agencies happy to assist you. Here are just a few:

Aju Incentive Tours
02-786-0028, www.ajutours.co.kr
Bridge Travel
02-754-2252, www.bridge-tour.com
Grace Travel
02-332-8946, www.triptokorea.com
DiscoverKorea Jejueco
064-738-7706, www.discoverkorea.co.kr
Cosmojin Tour Consulting
02-318-0345, www.cosmojin.com
Exodus DMC
031-907-8044, www.koreabound.com
GOnSEE
02-6243-7071, www.gonseekorea.com
Holiday Planners Co., LTD
02-336-3532, www.holidayplanners.co.kr
Plaza 21 Plus Travel Inc.
02-364-4171, www.plaza21travel.com

KOREAHAS & Good Morning Tours
02-757-1232, www.koreahas.com
Korea Business Travel Co., Ltd.
02-739-8111, www.kbs-travel.com
Plaza 21 Travel Service, Inc.
02-364-1670, www.koreatourplaza.com
US Tour and Travel
02-720-1515, www.ustravel.kr
Xanadu Travel Service Co.,Ltd.
02-795-7771, www.xanadu.co.kr
TOUR ROAD
031-244-6003, www.tourod.com

IMMIGRATION & CUSTOMS

Visas

All foreign visitors to Korea need a valid passport and a visa obtained prior to arrival. Some 99 countries (including the US, Canada, the UK, Australia and many Western European nations) have visa waiver agreements with Korea or are given visa waiver status for national interest reasons—for citizens of these nations, tourist visas are automatically given upon arrival at the airport. (See http://english. visitkorea.or.kr for further information) Depending on the nation, these visas may last for 30, 60, 90 or—in the case of Canada—180 days.

To extend your visa, you need to visit your local Immigration Office (for location, call the Immigration Contact Center at 1345) at least a day before your visa expires and fill out an application—you'll need a recent passport-sized color photo and the application fee. Visa extensions are usually for 90 days. All visas are single entry only. For a multiple entry visa, you need to apply at your local Immigration Office. This can also be taken care of at the Immigration Office of Incheon International Airport prior to your outbound flight.

Work Visas

If you'd like to work in Korea—teaching English, for example—you need a work visa. These must be obtained from an embassy or consulate outside of Korea. Work visas are usually valid for one year. To get one, you need to have an endorsement from your potential employer in Korea. Be warned—if you engage in money-making activities without a proper work visa, you can be fined and/or deported. Moreover, work visas are usually good only for your specific place of employment—to change jobs, you need to leave the country and get a new visa.

* Ministry of Foreign Affairs and Trade: www. mofat.go.kr * Korea Immigration Service: www.immigration.go.kr

Customs
Duty-Free Articles

• Visitor goods you will take with you when you leave Korea (do declare the quantity of the goods, though)
• Goods you declared upon leaving Korea and are bringing back
• One bottle of alcohol (not over a liter) and 200 cigarettes (or 50 cigars or 250 grams of tobacco)
• Two ounces of perfume

Restricted Articles

• Guns, firearms, knives and explosives
• Drugs (narcotics and psychotropic substances)
• Quarantine-required goods (food, animal material, plant material, etc.)
• Articles controlled by the CITES convention

Prohibited Articles

• Books, publications, drawings and paintings, films, phonographic materials, video work and other items of similar nature that may either disturb the constitutional order or be harmful to public security or traditional custom
• Goods that may reveal confidential information on the government or that may be used for intelligence activities
• Coins, currency, bank notes, debenture and/or other negotiable instrument counterfeited, forged or imitated

Foreign Currency

If you are carrying in foreign or Korean currency worth over US$10,000, you must declare it to a Customs official. If you are departing Korea with over US$10,000 in local or foreign currency, you must obtain permission from a bank or customs (not including the amount you carried in). For a full rundown on Korea's customs regulations, visit the website of the Korea Customs Service (http://english.customs.go.kr)

Basic Korean Culture

While Korea has modernized rapidly in the past couple of decades, Confucian ideals remain embedded in society. Koreans place a great deal of emphasis on showing respect based on social and age hierarchies and adhere to many unstated social rules in their daily interactions.

Koreans tend to judge people based on their appearance. People dressed neatly and with greater care are treated with more respect than those dressed sloppily.

Etiquette

• **GREETINGS**: Bow or nod slightly to show respect when greeting somebody.

• **SHOES**: In private homes, temples, Korean style restaurants, and guesthouses, take off your shoes and leave them by the entrance.

• **GIFTS**: When invited to visit someone's home, always bring a small gift. Gifts can be flowers, fruit, dessert, a bottle of alcohol, tea or a token from your home country. Your host may initially protest the gift to avoid appearing greedy, but you should insist that they accept it. Present and receive gifts using both hands. If you must use one hand, however, be sure to use your right one.

• **TIPPING**: There is no tipping in Korea, including taxis and restaurants.

• **DINING**: Never pick up your eating utensils before your elders. After finishing your meal, return your spoon and chopsticks to their original setting. Do not rise from your seat unless your elders have finished their meals. After finishing your meal, be sure to compliment the chef or host.

• **DRINKING**: Always pour drinks for your elders using two hands, or with one hand supporting the wrist of the other. When receiving a drink from an elder, use two hands. If drinking with elders, turn your glass and body away from your elders as you drink.

Language

Koreans, of course, speak Korean, a language sometimes placed—somewhat controversially—in the Altaic language family along with Turkish and Mongolian. It is characterized by a subject-object-verb sentence structure, and parts of speech are identified by suffixes. While the language itself is in no way, shape or form related to Chinese, much of its vocabulary—particularly nouns—has been borrowed from Chinese, the result of centuries of cultural influence from Korea's giant neighbor to the West.

English is widely studied in Korea, but relatively few Koreans are proficient in the language. That being said, you may still be able to communicate in basic English if you're in a fix, especially at public places like train stations, etc.

Korean is considered a difficult language to learn for speakers of Western languages like English. Few Koreans expect tourists to be fluent in the language, but a few basic phrases will go along way. See the "Basic Korean" (p710) for help.

Religion

Korea has been, by and large, a fairly tolerant place in terms of religion, with Buddhism, Christianity (including Catholicism and Protestantism), shamanism and other smaller faiths existing side-by-side in relative harmony with little in the way of sectarian strife. Roughly half the population identifies itself as religious—that half, in turn, splits about 50-50 between Christians and Buddhists. Over the last several decades, Protestant Christianity has been especially vibrant—Korea is home to several of the world's largest churches. Buddhism, too, has witnessed a revival in recent years with heightened interest and confidence in Korean traditional culture. Few people identify themselves as shamanists, per se, but shamanism and shamanistic practices influence larger Korean faiths, including Buddhism and Christianity.

Ultimately, however, it's Confucianism that has provided the philosophical underpinnings of Korean society—it's said, in fact, that Korea is the most Confucian country in the world. Even in Korea's increasingly cosmopolitan and modernized society, Confucian ideals and principles still have a tremendous influence (regardless of the professed faith of the individual), particularly in family and personal relations. Traditional Korean rites and practices such as regular ancestral remembrance rites (*jesa*) are derived from Confucianism as well.

LOCAL INFO

Business Hours
• Banks: 9 am to 4 pm, Mon to Fri.
• Government offices and organizations: 9 am to 6 pm, Mon to Fri.
• Post Offices: 9 am to 6 pm (Mon to Fri) and 9 am to 1 pm (Sat).
• Foreign diplomatic missions: differ from country to country.
• Department stores: 10:30 am to 8 pm. They are usually closed one Monday a month.

Korean Holidays

Koreans might be some of the hardest-working people on the planet, but at least one can't accuse the nation of skimping on public holidays. Major Korean holidays include:

Spring
• **Independence Declaration Day** (March 1): This holiday marks the beginning of the March 1, 1919 Independence Movement (see p74), a nationwide uprising against Japanese colonial rule. Like Liberation Day, it's marked by lots of flying flags and an address by the President.

• **Buddha's Birthday** (8th day of the 4th lunar month): This spring Buddhist holiday is celebrated at Buddhist temples across Korea with beautiful paper lotus lanterns. In Seoul, it is preceded by several days by the Lotus Lantern Festival (see p727), one of the city's best-loved festivals.

• **Children's Day** (May 5): Yep, children get their own day. Needless to say, theme parks are packed on this day.

• **Memorial Day** (June 6): This holiday celebrates those Koreans who fell in war or fighting for the nation's independence.

Summer
• **Liberation Day** (Aug 15): Marks the end of Japanese colonialism in Korea with Japan's surrender in the Pacific War.

Autumn
• **Chuseok** (15th day of the 8th lunar month): The second of Korea's two major holidays, Chuseok is Korea's autumn harvest celebration. Like Seollal, it is accompanied by a long holiday during which Koreans return to their ancestral hometowns. The representative dish for

Chuseok is *songpyeon* (a rice cake steamed on pine needles)—you'll be consuming these until you're sick of them.

• **National Foundation Day** (Oct 3): Known in Korea as Gaecheonjeol, this celebrates the mythical foundation of Korea by Dangun (see p32) in 2333 BC. Originally celebrated according to the lunar calendar, it is now celebrated according to the solar calendar.

Winter

• **Christmas** (Dec 25): Yes, Koreans—well, Christian ones, anyway—celebrate Christmas, although it's nowhere near the family holiday it is in the traditionally Christian West. Young people on this day meet friends and go on dates.

• **Seollal** (1st day of the 1st lunar month): The Lunar New Year, Seollal is one of Korea's two biggest celebrations. It is marked by a long holiday, and city dwellers flock to their ancestral hometowns for family gatherings. Seoul will become eerily quiet, although most tourist sites will remain open. If you're planning a trip to the countryside during the holiday, be sure to book your transportation way in advance, and if you're going by road, prepare for the worst traffic you've ever seen (this applies to the Chuseok holiday, too). It is traditional to eat a bowl of *tteokguk* (rice cake soup) on the morning of the New Year.

Legal Matters

It's always best to stay out of trouble, of course. Still, if legal trouble does befall you, you're going to need a lawyer. Your embassy can often provide a list of recommended lawyers. If you're the victim of a crime, the police are there to help, although language may be an issue. To their credit, police will eventually find a translator, but it can take some time, depending on the station.

* List of English-Speaking Lawyers: http://wiki.galbijim.com/English-speaking_lawyers_throughout_Korea * Ministry of Justice: www.moj.go.kr * Korean National Police Agency: www.police.go.kr

History and Culture

VALENTINE'S DAY, WHITE DAY, BLACK DAY, PEPERO DAY

Like much of the rest of the world, Korea celebrates Valentine's Day on Feb 14. However, unlike in other countries, women give chocolate to men. The favor is returned one month later on March 14, or White Day (an importation from Japan), when men give candy (but not chocolate) to women. On April 14, those who received nothing on Feb 14 or March 14—i.e., the unattached—mourn their solitude over a bowl of Chinese black *jajangmyeon* noodles for "Black Day." Finally, there is Pepero Day on Nov 11, when young couples exchange chocolate-dipped cookie sticks known as Pepero (produced by the company Lotte)—Pepero because they look similar to the four "1"s in Nov 11 (11/11).

Money and Banking

The Korean currency is the won. Bills come in 50,000 won, 10,000 won, 5,000 won and 1,000 won denominations, while coins come in 500 won, 100 won, 50 won and 10 won denominations. 100,000 won cheques are also used but Koreans are not big cheque users, and you'll find yourself frequently walking around with large wads of cash. For travelers from places such as the United States, this can be uncomfortable. ATM machines are a ubiquitous presence in Korea—for instance, they can be found in most major convenience store chains. Nowadays, most merchants accept foreign cards but some do not. If you have an account with Citibank, however, you can visit a local Citibank branch (www.citibank.co.kr, T. 02-3704-7100) for ATM or counter services. ATM hours vary, and often depend on your card.

Changing Money

Most banks will change money for you. US dollars are the most commonly converted currency, although you should find no trouble exchanging most common hard currencies. If you're having trouble converting the currency you're carrying, give Korea Exchange Bank (www.keb.co.kr/main/en) a try. Besides banks, most major hotels and, of course, the airport will change money for you, but the rates might not be as good. The Itaewon area (see p121) has a number of licensed currency exchangers, too.

Wire Transfers

Transferring money within Korea is fairly easy. If you have a local bank account, you can do this at almost any ATM as long as you have the bank account information of the recipient. If you don't have a local account, you can simply go to a bank and tell the teller you'd like to make a domestic transfer. Again, you'll need the bank account information of the recipient to do this.

To send money overseas, you'll need to make a wire transfer. No restrictions exist for transfers under US$1,000. Fees and transfer restrictions vary depending on the bank. In order to transfer money, you must bring your passport, employment contract, foreigner registration card, and receipts. Money may be remitted freely up to US$10,000; amounts exceeding US$10,000 must be reported to the tax office. Remittances greater than US$50,000 must be reported to the Bank of Korea. However, up to 100% of a foreigner's legally earned annual income may be remitted if individuals provide proof from their employer verifying the amount earned, such as pay stubs.

Western Union is another option for sending money to and from Korea. Visit www.westernunion.co.kr for more information.

Credit Cards

International credit cards are widely accepted in Seoul. Still, many places—especially smaller shops and restaurants—operate on a cash-only basis.

Korea Pass

Korea Pass is a pre-paid tourism card designed by the Ministry of Culture, Sports and Tourism and the Korea Tourism Organization. Coming in 50,000 won, 100,000 won, 300,000 won and 500,000 won denominations, the card can be used for transportation (except for trains), shopping, entertainment and sightseeing, and gets you discounts at some 300 tourist sites around Korea. It is particularly useful with Lotte-related shops and destinations. There are restrictions to its use, however—visit koreapass.or.kr for more details, including purchasing information.

Communication

Internet Cafés

Korea is one of the most wired countries in the world, and internet cafés (known locally as PC *bang* 피시방, meaning "PC room") are ubiquitous in Seoul. In every neighborhood of the city PC *bang* abound. Korean internet cafés are open 24 hours a day, and are generally dark rooms filled with lines of glossy-screened modern computers connected to high-speed internet. Patrons can surf the web, and send e-mails at a PC *bang;* most, however, don't have printers, so to print things out, you're better off going to somewhere like Kinkos. Most Koreans frequent these locations to play the latest computer games. Use of a computer at a PC *bang* generally runs you 500 to 1,000 won per hour. Headsets with attached microphones are available free of charge.

Pay Phones

Pay phones are available throughout the country but, given the ubiquity of cellphones, are rarely used. Phones are operated by coins or phone cards. On coin-operated phones, only domestic calls are possible. Card-operated phones accept phone cards, credit cards, and IC cards. Phone cards can be purchased in 2,000 won, 3,000 won, 5,000 won and 10,000 won denominations at newsstands and banks. The rate for local land-line calls is 70 won per three minutes, and the cost for calls to mobile phones is 100 won per minute. When making international calls from a pay phone, the number of the service provider must be entered before the country code. Pre-paid phone cards offer the best prices on overseas calls and can be purchased at convenience stores or online shopping malls. For more information, visit www.cardstation.net.

- To call Korea from abroad, press the international call code + Korea's country code (82) + area code (*sans* the first zero) + phone number.
- To call abroad from Korea, press the international call code* + country code + area code (*sans* the first zero) + phone number.   *001, 002 or 00700

Cellphones

Korea's cellphone network operates on a specialized CDMA system. Unlocked GSM phones will not function in Korea, and it is not possible to simply replace a phone's SIM card to access service. Three service providers allow cellphone rentals: SK Telecom, KTF and LG Telecom. Cellphones can be rented at the airport or at major hotels.

The most convenient option for short-term visitors is to rent a cellphone at the airport. KTF operates two phone rental booths in Incheon International Airport that allow foreigners to rent a phone for 3,000 won a day. Service on these phones costs 100 won per 10 seconds plus VAT for outgoing domestic calls. The cost of international calls depends on the call destination, and all incoming calls are free.

KTF rental phone booths can be found on both the arrivals (between Gate 10 and 11 on the first floor; open 24 hours) and departures level (third floor, open 6 am to 10 pm) of the airport. Have your passport and a credit card or 800,000 won deposit ready. You can estimate the total cost of your cell phone rental service on the KTF website at http://roaming.kt.com/eng/index.asp, or call 2190-0901 for English service.

There are also websites that offer phone rental and service with optional insurance and free shipping. One such company is Sroaming (www.sroaming.com), which offers cell phones, smartphones (Android) and pocket Wi-Fi for rent. Smartphones cost 6,400 won a day (online reservation special rate, exclusive 10% VAT), including an unlimited data plan. Reserve your phone online and you can pick it up at the Sroaming Center on the 1st floor of Incheon International Airport.

Post

Post offices in Korea are recognizable by a red and white sign that says "Korea Post" and has with a flying-bird emblem. There is a local post office in every neighborhood of Seoul, as well as mailboxes on the street. Although postal codes are not in common use, they are required when sending any piece of mail within or outside of Korea.

Domestic postage for standard size letters runs between 220 and 270 won. Non-standard mail is 340 won for the first 50 g and an additional 120 won for every additional 50 g. International postage varies according to the destination. Airmail letters to North America, Europe, the Middle East, Australia and New Zealand cost 580 won. Parcel post to the United States of a 2 kg package costs 27,700 won by airmail and 12,000 won by surface mail. The weight limit for parcel post is 20 kg, which costs 182,500 won by airmail and 48,000 won by surface mail.

Addresses in Korea follow the opposite order of addresses in Western countries and appear as follows:

> Country + City + Postal Code District Office (gu) + Street + Building/Unit Number + Name of Recipient

However, even if letters are addressed in the Western format, they will generally reach their recipient. Mail is delivered Monday through Saturday in most areas.

Most post offices in Seoul remain open from 9 am to 6 pm Monday through Friday. Seoul Central Post Office and a few other large branches are open 9 am to 8 pm Monday through Saturday.

For more information on rates, fees, zip codes and branch locations, visit www.koreapost.go.kr or call 1588-1300. Other options for sending post and larger shipments:

DHL Korea www.dhl.co.kr
FedEx www.fedex.com/kr_english
UPS www.ups.com
Hanjin Shipping www.hanjin.co.kr
EMS www.epost.go.kr
Korea Express www.korex.co.kr

Newspapers and Magazines

The primary English-language newspapers distributed in Korea are *The Korea Times* (1,000 won; www.koreatimes.co.kr) and *The Korea Herald* (1,000 won; www.koreaherald.com). These newspapers are issued daily Monday through Saturday, although the Friday Korea Times and the Saturday Korea Herald include a weekend update section with listings and articles on Seoul events, restaurants, and performances.

The other newspaper offerings are translated from Korean into English. Major Korean-language dailies like the *Chosun Ilbo* (http://english.chosun.com), *Donga Ilbo* (http://english.donga.com), *The Kyunghyang Shinmun* (http://english.khan.co.kr) and *Hankyoreh* (http://english.hani.co.kr) have online English editions.

The Joongang Daily accompanies *The International Herald Tribune* as its Korean news partner. Many of its articles are translated directly from Korean to English. *The Joongang Daily* also includes a comprehensive weekend preview and calendar.

Koreana (www.koreana.or.kr) is a quarterly academic magazine that analyzes a particular theme in depth each issue, with the intent of raising awareness of Korea's cultural heritage overseas. The content of this publication can be read in its entirety online in English and several other foreign languages.

SEOUL, a monthly travel and culture magazine, presents a diverse array of information and resources on the happenings and cultural hotspots of Seoul.

10 is another monthly entertainment and culture guide to Korea. It offers an extensive listing of local events, as well as feature articles about different aspects of Korean society. *Groove* is another English-language magazine that makes for a good read.

Television & Radio

Korea has three major terrestrial TV broadcasting companies: **KBS, MBC,** and **SBS** (joined recently by several stations owned by local newspapers). These companies are all Korean-language TV networks, although if foreign movies are shown dubbed in Korean, most TVs have a button that reverts the sound to the original language. **EBS** is Korea's educational channel.

AFN Korea is an English-language TV station operated by the US military that offers American programs, sports and films. **Arirang** is a Korean government-funded channel that broadcasts programs in both Korean and English. This channel is only available with cable or satellite subscriptions. On that note, Seoul offers a vast array of cable and satellite channels with a subscription. Many American shows are available on cable. A cable subscription provides numerous options for foreign news, films, sports, religious programming, documentaries and talk shows. On radio, **TBS eFM** (101.3MHz) does music and English-language programming almost around the clock.

Blogs

In the age of the Internet, it seems everyone's got a blog, including a good many English-speaking expatriates in Korea. Good ones to check out for information on things to see and do in the city include:

• **Chris in South Korea** (www. chrisinsouthkorea.com): Written by Chris Backe, an English teacher in Korea, this travel blog is chock-full of great travel and tourism information from around Korea.

• **The QiRanger Adventures** (www. qiranger.com): Steve Miller's outstanding vlog (video blog) is an absolute must-visit for anyone coming to Korea.

• **Seoul Sub→urban** (www.seoulsuburban. com): Charlie Usher's and Elizabeth Groeschen's team effort explores the city of Seoul, one subway station at a time.

• **Hermit Hideaways** (www. hermithideaways.com): Seoul-based photographer Gregory Curley beautifully captures the subtle charms of Korea.

• **Eat Your Kimchi** (www.eatyourkimchi. com): Run by a very enthusiastic Canadian married couple in Korea, this vlog is the place to go for info on K-pop, Korean food and life in Korea.

• **ZenKimchi** (www.zenkimchi.com): Run by long-time Korea hand and foodie Joe McPherson, this blog is one of the best sites on the planet for info on Korean dining. Another great site to check out for food and dining info is **Seoul Eats** (www. seouleats.com).

• **The Marmot's Hole** (www.rjkoehler.com): This writer's personal blog deals mostly with political, social and media matters, but does on occasion feature travel-related photo essays.

• Two non-blog websites worth checking out are **Galbijim** (wiki.galbijim.com), the definitive wiki on everything Korean, and **Korea4expats.com** (www.korea4expats. com), which has a ton of info about visiting, living and working in Korea.

Medical Services

Pharmacies

Pharmacies are ubiquitous in Seoul. Just look for 약국 (*yakguk*—"pharmacy") or 약 (*yak*—"medicine") in the window. Korean pharmacies stock both over-the-counter and prescription medications. Pharmacists in Korea, while not able to distribute prescription medications freely, give excellent recommendations for medications based on the described symptoms. If you have trouble communicating with your pharmacist, it may help to write your symptoms on a piece of paper. Another option is to call the Korean tourist helpline at 1330 for an interpreter.

Foreigner Medical Facilities

Korea has first-rate medical facilities, although communication can be an issue. This is less of a problem in major cities, where you can even find hospitals and clinics that specialize in services for international patients, with doctors and nurses who speak English, Japanese, Chinese and other foreign languages. Even in smaller towns, though, doctors can often speak enough English to communicate in an emergency.

For international visitors, Seoul is the best place to get sick. Seoul's medical facilities have opened more international clinics to meet the needs of the city's continuously growing expatriate population. Seoul Global Center (SGC) manages a **24-hour Medical Referral Service** (MRS) for the city's foreign residents. The entire English-speaking staff is medically trained and provides foreigners with information and advice on Korea's medical services. The MRS team routinely visits medical facilities serving foreigners and gathers feedback from foreigners who have used the services. The MRS can be reached during regular business hours (8 am to 8 pm) at 010-4769-8212 or 010-8750-8212, or by e-mailing medicalreferral@seoul.go.kr. In the case of emergencies, the MRS can be used during the hours of 8 pm to 8 am at the same contacts.

English is spoken in many medical facilities in Seoul, but it is still recommended that foreigners use the international clinics at Seoul's largest hospitals. These facilities include Asan Medical Center, Severance Hospital, Samsung Medical Center, and Seoul Medical Center. These four public hospitals offer medical consultations and treatments to foreign residents of Seoul with the assistance of volunteer interpreters.

The international clinics of these four facilities are generally open between the hours of 9 am and 4:30 pm on weekdays, and all require advance appointments. Severance Hospital is also open on Saturdays from 9:30 am to 12 pm.

SEOUL

Asan Medical Center
1688-7575, www.amc.seoul.kr
Samsung Medical Center
1599-3114, www.samsunghospital.com
Seoul Medical Center
02-2276-7000, www.seoulmc.or.kr
Severance Hospital
(International Health Care Center)
Sinchon: 02-2228-5810, Gangnam: 02-2019-3690, www.yuhs.or.kr/en

BUSAN

Inje University Busan Paik Hospital
051-890-6114, www.paik.ac.kr/en
Pusan National Unversity Hospital
051-890-6114, www.pnuh.co.kr/english/english_index.html

DAEGU

Keimyung University Dongsan Hospital
053-768-7467, http://global.dsmc.or.kr
Kyungpook National University Hospital
053-420-5525, http://knuh.knu.ac.kr

DAEJEON

Eulji University Hospital
042-611-3000,
www.emc.ac.kr/international
Sun General Hospital
042-220-8000,
http://eng.sunhospital.com
Konyang Univerity International Health Care Center
042-600-9999,
www.kyuh.co.kr/eng/eng_01.htm

GWANGJU

Chonnam University Hospital
062-220-6902, www.cnuh.com/english
Chosun University Hospital
062-232-5723, http://hosp.chosun.ac.kr

Medical Tourism

Korea has an excellent medical system, and the authorities have been keen to promote the country as a medical tourism destination. Indeed, Korea has much to recommend in this regard—high-quality medical care in Korea costs only a fraction of what it would cost in the United States and Japan, and care is of a much higher standard what you'd find in China and Russia.

Rightly or wrongly, Korea has developed a reputation for plastic surgery, and you'll find plenty of places—especially in the Gangnam area of Seoul—providing cosmetic procedures to local and international patients alike. Dentistry, too, is much cheaper than in Japan or the United States.

Special visas are granted to visitors coming to Korea for medical treatment—these are granted for stays of three months to a year. It's highly recommended that you bring a diagnosis and referral from your home country. The website of the Korea Tourism Organization (visitkorea.or.kr) has a section on medical tourism with more details and links.

There's a Medical Tourist Information Center on the first floor of Incheon International Airport where you can get brochures and other usual pieces of information.

Emergency Information

Emergency, Fire, Ambulance: 119
Medical Emergency: 1339
Police: 112
Seoul Metropolitan Police Foreign Affairs: 700-6200 (1566-0112)
If English-speaking staff are not available, call the 24-hour tourist information and help line: **1330**.

Travel Hotline 1330

The Korea Tourism Organization's 1330 call center provides 24/7 tourist information in Korean, English, Japanese and Chinese. Service is free—all callers are charged with the cost of a local phone call. The center is an especially useful service if you're in a pinch. It also handles calls for immigration inquiries and medical emergencies, forwarding calls to the Ministry of Justice, emergency services and other relevant bodies. From a landline in Korea, just dial 1330. From a mobile phone, you'll need to add the local area code (ex. 02-1330 for Seoul).

Dasan Center 120

Seoul Metropolitan City operates a call center that dispenses up-to-date tourism information in English, Japanese and Chinese. To use the service, just dial 120 (or 02-120 from a cell phone) and press "9" for foreign language services. Business hours are 9 am to 6 pm, Monday to Friday.

Foreign Embassies in Seoul

Australia: 02-2003-0100, www.southkorea.embassy.gov.au, 19th Flr., Kyobo Bldg, Jongno 1-ga, Jongno-gu

Canada: 02-3783-6000, www.korea.gc.ca, 16-1, Jeong-dong, Jung-gu

China: 02-738-1038, www.chinaemb.or.kr, 54, Hyoja-dong, Jongno-gu

France: 02-3149-4300, www.ambafrance-kr.org, 30 Hap-dong, Seodaemun-gu

Germany: 02-748-4114, www.seoul.diplo.de, 308-5 Dongbinggo-dong, Yongsan-gu

Ireland: 02-774-6455, www.irelandhouse-korea.com, 13th Flr., Leema Bldg, 146-1, Susong-dong, Jongno-gu

Japan: 02-2170-5200, www.kr.emb-japan.go.jp, 18-11 Junghak-dong, Jongno-gu

Netherlands: 02-311-8600, http://southkorea.nlembassy.org 10th Flr., Jeong-dong Building, 15-5 Jeong-dong, Jung-gu

New Zealand: 02-3701-7700, www.nzembassy.com/korea, 8th Flr., Jeong-dong Building, Jeong-dong, Jung-gu

Philippines: 02-796-7387, www.philembassy-seoul.com, 5-1 Itaewon 1-dong, Yongsan-gu

Russia: 02-318-2116, http://seoul.rusembassy.org, 34-16 Jeong-dong, Jung-gu

Singapore: 02-744-2464, www.mfa.gov.sg/seoul, 28th Flr., Seoul Finance Center, 84 Taepyeongno 1-ga, Jung-gu

Taiwan: 02-399-2767, www.taiwanembassy.org/kr, Visa Office, 6th Flr., Gwanghwamun Bldg, Jongno-gu

UK: 02-3210-5500, http://ukinrok.fco.gov.uk, 4 Jeong-dong, Jung-gu

USA: 02-397-4114, http://seoul.usembassy.gov, 32 Sejongno, Jongno-gu

Foreign Consulates Outside of Seoul

Japan, China, Russia and several other nations maintain consulates in Busan, Korea's second largest city. Oddly enough, given the close relations between the two nations, the United States does not have a consulate in Busan, but it does have an American Presence Post.

Japan: 051-465-5101, 1147-11 Joryang-dong, Dong-gu, Busan

China: 051-743-7985, 1418 U-dong, Haeundae-gu, Busan

Russia: 051-441-1104, 10th floor, Korea Exchange Bank Bld., 89-1 4-ga, Jungang-dong, Jung-gu, Busan

Australia: 051-742-3989, Room 802 Samwhan Officetel, 830-295, Bumil 2-dong, Dong-gu, Busan

Canada: 051-204-5581, Dongsung Chemical Co. Ltd., 472 Sinbyeong-dong, Saha-gu, Busan

BOOKS ON KOREA

There are tons of good books about Korea out there, but for starters you might wish to try:

• *Korea's Place in the Sun*: Although Bruce Cumings is sometimes criticized as a "revisionist scholar," particularly about North Korea and the Korean War, his book *Korea's Place in the Sun* remains one of the best introductions to Korea ever written.

• *The Two Koreas*: Written by former journalist Don Oberdorfer, *The Two Koreas* examines the divergent paths of North and South Korea, with plenty of anecdotes and interesting history.

• *The Koreans: Who They Are, What They Want, Where Their Future Lies*: Long-time Korea resident and journalist Mike Breen introduces the truth about Koreans to a largely ignorant world.

• *Korea Old and New: A History*: Produced by several prominent Korea scholars, including Harvard University Korean history professor Carter Eckert, this is one of the most widely used texts on Korean history.

• *Korea and Her Neighbors*: An 1898 account of Korea by English female traveler and adventurist Isabella Bird, this wonderful—if Orientalist—read looks at pre-modern Korea during one of the most eventful periods in the nation's history.

• *The Dawn of Modern Korea*: While Andrei Lankov is best known as one of the world's most respected experts on North Korea, his *The Dawn of Modern Korea* is a fascinating look at the development of modern South Korea, with tons of fascinating historical tidbits.

• *Korea Film Director Series*: The Korean Film Council's series of 18 books is chock full of interviews, film reviews and essays on some of Korea's greatest film directors.

TIPS

BUYING BOOKS

Most of these books can be found in the English section of Kyobo Bookstore (located in Gwanghwamun and Gangnam, 02-1544-1900) or, at Seoul Selection Bookshop (located in Gwanghwamun, 02-734-9565; online purchases can be made at www.seoulselection.com). The homepage of the Korea Tourism Organization (english.visitkorea.or.kr) also has a list of recommended books.

• *Spirit of Korean Cultural Roots*: With 25 volumes so far, this bilingual series produced by Ewha Womans University Press examines the evolution of Korean culture.

• *Korean Culture Series*: This Korea Foundation series on Korean traditional culture is expertly written and a good resource for those looking for a deeper understanding.

• *Korea Bug*: A collection of fascinating interviews from J. Scott Burgeson's zine *Bug*, this book is full of irreverent observations on both Korean and expat culture.

• *Pop Goes Korea*: Korean pop culture expert Mark Russell examines the rise of Korean film, music and Internet culture.

• *Korea Essentials Series:* This co-operative project between Korea Foundation and Seoul Selection aims to furnish international readers with basic understanding of the arts and culture of Korea.

• *Baekdudaegan Trail:* This trusty guide is a must if you intend to hike the Baekdudaegan, Korea's mountainous spine and the local equivalent of the Appalachian Trail.

• *Moon Tides: The Women Divers of Jeju Island:* Author and photojournalist Brenda Paik Sunoo's lovely work documents in text and photos the lives of the *haenyeo*, Jeju-do's remarkable diving women.

GETTING TO/FROM KOREA

Airport

Although Korea operates eight international airports, only one services destinations outside of Asia: Incheon International Airport (T. 1577-2600 or www.airport.kr/eng). Located 52 km west of downtown Seoul, Incheon International Airport (code: ICN or IIA) is seated on reclaimed tidal lands between two islands on the Yellow Sea.

Korea also has three other "international airports" that serve destinations in Asia. Gimhae International Airport, just outside Korea's second city of Busan, has regular flights to cities in China (including Hong Kong), Japan, Southeast Asia and Russia's Vladivostok. Gimpo International Airport,

about 40 minutes from Seoul, used to be Korea's primary international airport prior to the opening of Incheon Airport in 2001. It still handles regular shuttle flights to Japan's Haneda and Kansai airports, as well as to Shanghai and Beijing. As a major tourist destination, Jeju International Airport has regular flights to China, Taiwan and Japan.

LIMOUSINE BUS: Limousine buses offer the most efficient, low-cost means of transport to and from Incheon International Airport. They run between the airport and most areas of Seoul and major Gyeonggi-do area. Information and ticket stands are located just outside airport exits 2, 4, 9 and 13 on the ground floor (baggage claim level). Each bus has a clearly marked post on the curb, which

shows a map of its route. Most buses begin service from Seoul between 4 and 6 am and the last buses to the city depart the airport anywhere between 7 and 11 pm. A detailed schedule of routes and departure times is available on the Incheon Airport website. Limousine bus tickets range from 9,000 to 15,000 won to Seoul.

Airport Limousine Company recently opened late-night bus services for those traveling at red-eye hours. These buses offer infrequent service to the main areas of Seoul and can be found at platform 5A.

AIRPORT TRAIN: Another option is to take the airport express train (A'REX) from Seoul Station (downtown Seoul) or Gimpo International Airport, which can be reached via the Seoul Metro subway. There are two trains available. The A'REX commuter train will take you from Seoul Station to Incheon Airport (and vice versa) with five stops in between in 53 minutes for 3,850 won fair, and runs every twelve minutes. The express train, meanwhile, runs direct from Seoul Station to Incheon Airport, taking just 43 minutes, and departs every 30 minutes. Tickets to the express train cost 13,800 won, however.

If you're taking the express train from Seoul Station to Incheon International Airport for an international flight with Korean Air, Asiana or Jeju Air, you can check in your luggage and complete immigration procedures at the so-called Korail Airport Railroad Seoul Station & Terminal (KARST), located in the basement of Seoul Station. If you're going from Incheon Airport to Seoul, the A'REX station is in the basement of the airport terminal. A'REX operating hours are 5:30 am to 11:38 pm. For more info, visit www.arex.or.kr.

TAXI: Private taxis are the fastest mode of transportation to and from the airport. A taxi costs approximately 44,000 won from the Seoul City Hall area and takes about one hour to reach the airport. From Gangnam, it should cost around 55,000 won and take 75 minutes. In addition to the fare, the passenger is responsible for a 7,700 won toll. The fare increases by 20% between the hours of midnight and 4 am. Deluxe taxis are also available, offering a more luxurious ride for approximately double the price. For those departing from the airport, taxi stands are located on the arrivals level (1F) between platforms 5C and 8C.

Ferries

An alternate mode of transport to Korea from Japan, China or Russia is via sea.

JAPAN: From Busan, there is daily ferry service to destinations throughout southern Japan, including Osaka, Shimonoseki and Fukuoka. Boats to Osaka depart in the afternoon and take 16 hours, 30 minutes, arriving in Japan the next morning. High-speed hydrofoils to Fukuoka, however, take just three hours. There are also boats to the nearby Japanese island of Tsushima—boats to Hitakatsu depart Monday and Friday and take just an hour, while boats to Izuhara depart Wednesday, Saturday, Sunday and every other Thursday and take two hours, 40 minutes.

CHINA: Ferries to destinations throughout northeast China depart from Incheon, Korea's primary West Sea port. Incheon has two international ferry terminals: Terminal 1 has boats to Dandong, Yingkou, Qinhuangdao, Yantai and Shi Dao, while Terminal 2 has boats to Lianyungang, Weihai, Qingdao and Tianjin. Ferries typically leave two or three times a week, and take anywhere from half a day to 25 hours, depending on the destination.

RUSSIA: The East Coast ports of Sokcho and Donghae have international passenger terminals with ferries to the Russian Far East ports of Zarubino and Vladivostok. See the "Sokcho" and "Donghae" sections for more information. Special tickets are available for joint Korea-China travel or Korea-Japan travel that provide the bearer with discounts on train services in both countries of travel and ferry transport between the two. These tickets are valid for between one week and 20 days from the first date of travel. For more information, visit http://english.visitkorea.or.kr and see Getting To Korea section.

GETTING AROUND KOREA

Domestic Flights

Korea's not that big, but those so inclined can travel by air. Korea's domestic flight network is operated by Korean Air (1588-2001, http://koreanair.com) and Asiana Airlines (1588-8000, http://flyasiana.com), linking 15 major cities. Domestic flight one-way fares generally range from 58,000 to 85,000 won.

Trains

The Korea Railroad Corporation (KORAIL) provides access to all areas of Korea with an extensive, fast and reliable railway system. There are three major railway line categories in Korea. First, the KTX, or Korea Train Express, is a bullet train that runs from Seoul to Busan, Gwangju and Mokpo. This high-speed train runs at 300 km/h, cutting the time to Busan just under three hours (two and a half hours to Gwangju and two hours and 58 minutes to Mokpo). The second fastest service is the Saemaeul train, which only stops in major cities. Next, there is the Mugunghwa train, which offers comfortable and relatively fast service with more frequent stops. Finally, the Tongil Express stops at every station and offers the cheapest fares.

Train tickets can be purchased up to one month in advance at a train station or with a travel agent. Trains tend to be full on weekends and holidays, and it is advisable to reserve tickets in advance. This is particularly the case on the Chuseok and

KTX ROUTE

Haengsin
Seoul
Yongsan
Yeongdeungpo
Gwangmyeong
Suwon

Cheonan-Asan

Osong

Seodaejeon Daejeon
Nonsan Gyeryong
Iksan
Jeonju
Gimje
Jeongeup
Namwon
Gokseong
Jangseong Guryegu
Gwangjusongjeong Gwangju
Naju
Suncheon
Yeocheon
Yeosuexpo
Mokpo

Gimcheon(Gumi)
Dongdaegu
Singyeongju
Miryang Ulsan
Jinyeong
Changwon
Masan Gupo
Changwonjungang Busan

Lunar New Year holidays (see "Korean Holidays" on p668), when tickets can sell out weeks or even months in advance. Information about train timetables and ticket prices is available at the Korea Railroad Corporation (T. 1544-7788 or www.korail.com).

TIPS

KR Pass

Overseas visitors can buy a special KR Pass, which must be purchased overseas at a ticket office, through a travel agent, or on the Korean National Railroad website (www.korail.com). The KR Pass can be used an unlimited number of times during its period of validity to obtain a registered ticket, regardless of travel class. KR Passes are valid for 3 to 10 days and come as normal adult and children passes, saver passes or youth passes.

Express and Inter-City Buses

Korea's excellent highway and inter-city road system makes the bus a quick and convenient option for getting around the country. Unlike trains, buses service virtually every town in Korea, and it is not necessary to purchase tickets in advance, unless traveling during a major holiday or weekend. Korean coach buses are (usually) clean and comfortable, and almost always depart on time. Bus fares tend to be quite reasonable, too.

Broadly speaking, there are two kinds of coach bus service in Korea, express (*gosok* 고속버스) and intercity (*sioe* 시외버스) buses. Express buses run on Korea's network of highways. True to their name, they don't usually make stops in cities beside their final destination, although on longer trips, they may stop at a highway rest-stop to allow passengers an opportunity to have a snack, use the bathroom or stretch their legs. Express buses frequently come in two flavors, regular (*ilban* 일반) and luxury (*udeung* 우등): the latter have wider seats, but fares are slightly higher.

Intercity buses, meanwhile, are used on non-highway roads. Normal (*ilban* 일반) intercity buses will make a number of stops between the city of departure and their final destination. Direct (*jikhaeng* 직행) intercity buses, meanwhile, go straight to the final destination. If you're traveling long distances, take the direct bus. Intercity buses are not quite as comfortable as the express buses, but they are frequently cheaper, depart more frequently, and in some cases, especially for smaller towns, may be the only means of getting from point A to point B.

Cities frequently have two bus terminals: an express bus terminal (*gosok teomineol* 고속터미널) for express buses, and an intercity bus terminal (*sioe teomineol* 시외터미널) for intercity buses. Many cities, however, have general bus terminals from which express and intercity buses depart. Larger cities, meanwhile, often have multiple express and/or intercity bus terminals servicing destinations in different parts of the country. Seoul, for instance, has no fewer than seven major bus terminals, including Seoul Express Bus Terminal, servicing destinations in southeast Korea, and Central Terminal, and express bus terminal servicing destinations in southwest Korea.

City Buses

Within a city, especially one without a subway, people get around on city buses, or *sinae beoseu* 시내버스 (called *gunnae beoseu* 군내버스 in smaller towns). In big cities like Seoul, city buses can get quite crowded, especially during rush hour.

Each city operates its own unique bus numbering system. Fares are quite low—usually about 1,000 won. In big cities, you can usually pay by credit card or transportation cards sold by individual municipalities, but in the countryside, you're going to need cash. Have small bills available, preferably 1,000 won bills.

Car Rental

With their high traffic density and frenetic driving patterns, Seoul and other major Korean cities can be a tough place for international drivers. Besides, Korean cities have excellent public transportation systems, so you probably won't want to drive anyway. For excursions outside of Seoul, however, a car can be handy. Korean navigation services are generally excellent: as long as you have an address, you can find where you want to go. Navigation systems can be rented cheaply when you rent a car. Fuel prices are high: as of the writing of this

book, they were at 1,900-2,200 won a liter for gasoline, and 1,700-1,900 won a liter for diesel.

Rental cars can be hired for about 62,000 won to 460,000 won a day, depending on the model. To rent a car, you need meet the following qualifications:

- Over one year of driving experience
- An international driver's license
- Over 21 years of age
- A valid passport
- Pay by credit card

Car rental services include:

KT Kumho Rent-a-car: T. 1588-1230 or 82-2-797-8000 for international reservations. You can get a quote and make a reservation online at http://www.ktkumhorent.com/eng/main/main.jsp.

Avis Rental Cars: T. 1544-1600 or 82-2-862-2847 for international reservations. http://www.ajrentacar.co.kr/eng/index.jsp Both are available at Incheon International Airport; numerous other options are available in Seoul and elsewhere.

TIPS

DRIVER'S LICENSE

If you're a short-term visitor to Korea, you can drive on an international driver's license. It's probably best you obtain your international driver's license in your home country. Citizens of several countries, including the United States, Canada and Japan, can exchange their foreign licenses for Korean ones. If you're staying longer and don't want to turn in your foreign license, you can apply for a local Korean license—you need to pass a rigorous written test (in English), pass a driving test and attend a safety class. (Driver's License Examination Office: http://dl.koroad.or.kr/english/index.jsp)

Subway

Seoul has one of the world's most extensive and heavily used subway systems, with nine lines and a number of connected communter train systems that integrate the entirety of the city as well as suburbs and cities as far away as Cheonan and Chuncheon. The major metropolises of Busan, Daegu, Gwangju and Daejeon also have subway systems. These local systems are much more limited in scale—in the case of Gwangju and Daejeon, just one line—but can be very useful for getting across town quickly and cheaply. All subway maps are labeled in both Korean and English, and announcements of the station arrival on the train are delivered in English as well.

Subway fares can be paid in cash or with a transportation card. Tickets can be purchased from automated ticket-dispensing machines located at all stations—instructions are given in Korean and English. Fares vary depending on the distance. A subway fare of 1,000 won (900 won with a transportation card) takes you up to 10 km, and each additional 5 km tacks on an additional 100 won. The average ride within Seoul costs between 900 and 1,500 won. Please note that if you purchase a one-trip ticket, your fare will also include a 500 won deposit fee, which you can retrieve when you turn in your used ticket at a deposit machine upon reaching your destination. See the end of the book for a subway map.

Taxis

Taxis are relatively affordable, offering a speedy and comfortable means of transport around the city. There are two types of taxis: *ilban* and *mobeom*.

Ilban taxis 일반택시 are regular taxis and come in silver, white and, in Seoul, orange. Those with white caps are privately owned taxis, while those with blue caps are company-owned vehicles. Standard fare for *ilban* taxis is 2,400 won for the first 2 km and 100 won for every additional 144 m. In heavy traffic, 100 won is added every 35 seconds. Fares are increased by 20% between the hours of midnight and 4 am.

Mobeom taxis 모범택시 are luxury taxis, identifiable as black cars with yellow caps. These taxis offer a more comfortable ride at an inflated price. Basic fare in a *mobeom* taxi is 4,500 won for the first 3 km, and increases by 200 won every 164 m. You are not likely to find these cabs outside of major cities.

Another option is the call taxi, which is sometimes useful when you're out late or in an area not frequented by taxis. In Seoul, you can get an English-speaking "international taxi" at 02-1644-2255, but these are 20% more expensive than ordinary cabs. If you're out and would like to call a taxi, the place you're at will most likely know a number to call. Taxis (but not international taxis) charge an extra 1,000 won when they are called.

Many taxis offer a free interpretation service via phone, but it is a good idea to have your destination written down in Korean to show your driver (For basic Korean expressions, see p710). Tipping is not expected.

ACCOMMODATIONS

Korea does not lack for places to stay. In major cities like Seoul and Busan, you'll find a wide range of places to lay your head down for the night, from palatial top-floor suites to rustic *hanok* guesthouses. Your selection is limited only by your budget.

In smaller provincial cities, the selection is a bit more limited, but not intolerably so. Most medium-sized towns have at least one three-star-level hotel, and plenty of comfortable motel and inn-like accommodations. You can find pleasant bed & breakfasts in scenic coastal and mountain areas, too.

As a rule of thumb, the more popular the destination, the bigger the selection of accommodations. Popular hotels can get booked out quickly, especially on weekends and holidays, so it's a good idea to reserve a room or, at the very least, call ahead to confirm if there are vacancies.

Hotels

Since the 1990s, when Korea's IT sector began to take off and Seoul rose to become one of Asia's busiest financial hubs, Korea's hotel industry has developed by leaps and bounds. This is most evident in Seoul, where you'll find Korea's greatest collection of high-end luxury hotels and accommodations.

Korea does not use the traditional "five star" system to classify its hotels. Instead, it classifies hotels as (in descending order of poshness) super deluxe, deluxe, first class, second class and third class. At deluxe and super deluxe hotels, count on there being a fitness center, sauna, restaurants (Korean, Western, Japanese and Chinese), bar, café, business center and other facilities. High-end hotels also have multilingual staff, but even medium-range hotels can usually be

counted on having at least a few English-speakers on hand to handle international guests.

Most hotels offer guests a choice between Western-style rooms with beds (often identified by English classifications like single, double and twin) and Korean-style rooms (usually called *ondolbang*) in which guests sleep on a comforter spread out on the heated floor. Korean-style rooms are usually a bit cheaper than Western-style ones. At super deluxe hotels, expect double rooms to go for 200,000 won to 400,000 won a night, not including service and facility charges. At the opposite end of the spectrum, rooms at third class hotels can go for as low as 30,000 won, but expect something more in the 70,000–80,000 won range. Rates usually include breakfast. High-end hotels also offer a variety of plush suites for more discriminating (and better healed) guests.

Super-deluxe hotels—often big international chains—are mostly limited to major cities and a few major tourist destinations like Jejudo and Gyeongju. Almost every city and large town has at least a third-class hotel, though.

TIPS

BENIKEA

BENIKEA (Best Night in Korea) is a cooperative group of mostly deluxe hotels that provide comfortable and quality accommodations. About 50 hotels in the program, supported by the Korea Tourism Organization, provide high-quality services at reasonable rates. You can find BENIKEA hotels in major cities and popular tourist destinations around the country.

Motels / Inns

For the budget traveler, the best options are motels and Korean-style inns. These are usually congregated around bus terminals, train stations and sometimes major nighttime entertainment zones.

Motels offer clean, comfortable rooms for 30,000–50,000 won a night. Like hotels, you can usually chose between Western-style and Korean-style rooms. Nowadays, motel rooms can be quite nice, with flatscreen TVs, high-speed Internet and mini-refrigerators. Motels can sometimes be identified quite easily by their loud, almost gaudy exteriors. The 2004 World Cup witnessed a spate of motel construction, with whole "villages" of motels erected in host cities.

Korean-style inns, or *yeogwan*, tend to be older than motels and are not quite as nice, but most are still quite comfortable, and many in fact are now repackaging themselves as motels. Like motels, they are often found around bus terminals and train stations. Rooms usually include a TV, Internet, a small refrigerator and a private bath.

Be aware that in most motels and inns, you are expected to take off your shoes before entering your room, regardless of whether it is Korean-style or Western-style. Also be aware that neither motels nor inns provide meals.

TIPS

GOODSTAY

The Korea Tourism Organization gives out the Goodstay logo quality establishments with reliable and affordable accommodations. So far, about 345 establishments nation-wide have received the Goodstay seal of approval. These hotels are especially good for backpackers and business travelers. See the homepage of the Korea Tourism Organization (english.visitkorea.or.kr) for a list of Goodstay establishments.

Hanok Guesthouses

All visitors to Korea should spend at least one night in a *hanok* for a taste of traditional Korean living. A *hanok* is a Korean traditional home, an architectural expression of the Korean way of life. Made from simple, natural ingredients like stone, wood, paper and clay, *hanok* provide cozy, comfortable and above all refined accommodation with a characteristically Korean elegance. While many *hanok* guesthouses are recently built, others are venerable homes with generations of history and cultural treasures in their own right.

A *hanok* has two kinds of rooms: an *ondolbang* (floor-heated space) and a *marubang* (with an unheated, wood-panel floor). Guests are often given the *ondolbang* while the *marubang* are used communally, but this arrangement differs from place to place. *Hanok* often have beautiful courtyard gardens, and indeed, the simple joy of sitting in a *hanok* looking into the garden is sometimes the highlight of a trip to Korea. Traditionally, *hanok* lacked indoor plumbing and the calls of nature were usually answered in an outhouse. Some of the more historic *hanok* guesthouses still follow this tradition, but these days, many have private indoor bathrooms and showers. You may wish to check first if this is a concern, however.

You can find *hanok* guesthouses all over the country, but the largest concentration can be found in Seoul's Bukchon neighborhood and the historic cities of Andong, Gyeongju and Jeonju. Rates differ widely—most charge between 50,000 won to 80,000 won a night, but some of the nicer ones charge 200,000 won a night and up. Many provide breakfast, and some include dinner (you may have to pay extra, though).

PEAK SEASON & WEEKENDS

Accommodation rates can fluctuate dramatically depending on whether it's peak or non-peak season. In Korea, peak season usually falls in the periods of April-May, July-August and October-November, although this may differ from destination to destination. Depending on the establishment, rates may fall 50% or more in off-peak months.

Pensions

In scenic parts of Korea, especially coastal areas and mountain districts, you'll find plenty of so-called "pensions" (from the Italian, *pensione*), which are essentially bed & breakfast establishments. These are especially popular with couples and families looking to get away for a couple of days.

Pensions come in many shapes and sizes. Typically, however, they are privately-owned homes with often beautifully decorated rooms with private baths. Others would best be described as small cabins. Many pensions have barbecue facilities for guest use; sometimes, the owners will host barbecue parties (for a cost).

Expect to pay 50,000 won to 80,000 won a night, but some of the nicer places charge much, much more. Rates also fluctuate greatly depending on whether it's peak or off-peak season.

Youth Hostels

There are currently 52 hostels in Korea. Like hostels everywhere, they provide basic but comfortable accommodations at budget rates. Generally, rooms are dormitory-style, but private and family rooms may be available, too. Hostels usually have communal bathrooms, showers and lounges, the last of which are often good places to meet fellow travelers from around the world.

Rates can be as low as 10,000 won a night. If you have a Hostelling International Card, you can get discounts of 20–30%. If you'd like to pick up an Hostelling International Card in Korea, you can buy one from the Korea Youth Hostels Association Office (02-725-3031, www. kyha.or.kr) near Exit 6, Gyeongbokgung Station, Line 3 for 30,000 won.

Minbak (homestay)

For an opportunity to experience authentic Korean culture directly, opt for a homestay—known in Korean as *minbak*. *Minbak* are more of an option for those traveling in the Korean countryside than in the city. Although less private than a hotel,

> **TIPS**
>
> **KOREASTAY**
>
>
>
> Koreastay is a Korea Tourism Organization (KTO) certified homestay program that provides international visitors with a special opportunity to experience Korean culture and lifestyle by living with a Korean family for a desired amount of time. Koreastay hosts are carefully selected after undergoing strict assessment of such criteria as residential environment, guestroom & cleanliness, mindset, service and convenience. For more details, call 02-729-9460 or email to koreastay@knto.or.kr.

> **TIPS**
>
> **SLEEPING IN A JJIMJILBANG**
>
> Many Korean sauna/spas, or *jjimjilbang* (which are open 24 hours), have communal sleeping quarters for nighttime visitors. Don't expect much in the way of creature comforts—there's usually a mat, a pillow and nothing else—but they are a cheap accommodation option (usually between 10,000 and 15,000 won).

minbak allow you to indulge in Korean food and observe Korean customs and family relations firsthand. In some remote areas, *minbak* may in fact be your only lodging option.

Another advantage of *minbak* is the relatively low cost. Most cost only 30,000 won to 50,000 won, and you may be able to arrange deals in regards to rates and meals.

Templestay

Many Korean Buddhist temples offer "templestay" programs for visitors wishing to experience Korean Buddhist temple life. This is not as much an accommodation option as it is a cultural experience program. It's usually a multi-day program involving chanting, Zen meditation, Buddhist vegetarian meals, chores and other activities. Rates differ from temple to temple and depending on your length of stay. See eng.templestay.com for more information.

Apartment Rental

Serviced apartments are an increasingly common option as the numbers of foreign businesspeople increase. These apartments are extremely modern and include all the amenities of a high-class hotel, but with the comfort of a home. Long-term visitors may choose to rent an apartment, although this may be difficult given the sometimes complex Korean rental system.

Korean food is one of the country's greatest draws. Korean cuisine is made from all-natural ingredients and covers a wide range of tastes and styles. Many Korean dishes are not only tasty, but are also recognized for carrying tangible health benefits.

The foundation for creating delicious Korean dishes is in the use of spices and seasonings, as well as fermentation. The staple Korean ingredients are *gochu*, or red hot peppers, used as a crushed powder and also a fermented red pepper paste called *gochujang*; *doenjang*, a fermented soybean paste with evidence of cancer-preventing properties; *ganjang*, or soy sauce, made through a similar soybean fermentation process with *doenjang*; as well as onions, garlic, scallions, ginger and sesame oil.

Korean restaurants are plentiful throughout the country and generally reasonably priced. There is no tipping at Korean restaurants.

Korean Banquet Cuisine
Hanjeongsik

Hanjeongsik—often referred to as Korean Table d'hote—is the most lavish of Korean meals, consisting of rice, soup and a dizzying array of tasty side dishes, brought out in stages. How many side dishes—and which side dishes—varies widely (there are currently about 1,500 side dishes in use throughout the country), depending on region, season, restaurant, and price. Traditionally speaking, however, side dishes have varied from three to twelve, depending on social class. The dishes are prepared and arranged by taste and color, which reflect

KIMCHI

Kimchi, fermented cabbage seasoned with plentiful garlic and crushed red pepper, is considered the most representative food of the Korean peninsula. It is generally consumed with every meal. There are over 200 types of *kimchi*, depending on the fermentation process and weather. *Kimchi* is considered one of the world's healthiest foods, full of vitamins A, B and C, but most importantly, plentiful in healthy bacteria called lactobacilli, which are found in fermented foods like yogurt. Lactobacilli aid in digestion and prevent yeast infections; the compounds found in the fermented cabbage are even reported to inhibit the growth of cancer.

the Asian philosophies of *ying* and *yang* and the five primary elements. The Bukchon area and Seoul have a number of restaurants specializing in *hanjeongsik*, but be warned—some meals can cost up to 100,000 won per person.

Royal Cuisine

The *surasang* was the dining setting for the king and queen and included only unique ingredients of the finest quality, imported from every province of the country as tribute to the king. Ingredients used in the *surasang* had to pass a quality control test by the royal chefs, and the recipes and cooking methods in the palace were known only to the exclusive palace chefs.

Luckily for modern citizens, anyone can

enjoy the tastes of royal cuisine in a restaurant. Unlike a standard Korean meal, where all side dishes are often served simultaneously with the main meal, a royal cuisine meal is supposed to come out in different courses and include a set of 12 side dishes.

Temple Cuisine

Korean temple cuisine, a creation of Buddhist monastics, is very simple and excludes any foods thought to be potentially harmful to monks' health or mental discipline. Temple food avoids tastes that are too spicy or salty, as it is believed that these strong flavors carry with them the threat of overexciting emotions and thus interfering with Buddhist discipline. Temple

food does not include meat or fish out of compassion for living beings, and necessary proteins and fats are therefore obtained from grains, beans and soy, nuts, and vegetable proteins. Ideal for vegetarians.

Selecting a Place to Eat

Budget

PRICE RANGE: 2,000–6,000 won
• Snack foods: Outdoor food stalls (*pojangmacha* 포장마차), outdoor markets, *gimbap* chains, *tteokbokki* chains, etc.
• Menu: *gimbap, ramyeon, tteokbokki, sundae, twigim* (see p699), *guksu* (see p695)

PRICE RANGE: 6,000–12,000 won
• General restaurants, usually places with names ending in *sikdang* 식당 or *jip* 집
• Menu: *jjigae* (see p694), *bokkeum, deopbap, tang*. Family-style *baekban* ometimes available, too.

PRICE RANGE: 20,000 won and up
• Gourmet Restaurants specializing in *hanjeongsik*, palace and temple cuisine; meat or seafood specialized restaurants
• Menu: *samgyeopsal, dwaeji galbi, sogalbi* (see p696), steamed meats (*jjim*) and stews (*tang*) (see p694); seafood restaurants like raw fish restaurants (*hoetjip*) and seafood buffets.

Spot the Restaurant!

1. ASK AROUND: The best way to learn where the good eats are at is to ask a local resident. Of course, opinions differ, and language can be an issue, but if you're searching for hidden culinary gems, this is how you do it.
2. GO WHERE THE PEOPLE ARE: If a restaurant is packed, it's usually a sign they do something well. The opposite is sometimes but not always true.

3. KNOW YOUR NEIGHBORHOOD: Individual towns, neighborhoods or streets are frequently known for particular dishes. Seoul's Sindang-dong neighborhood, for instance, is known for its alley of *tteokbokki* (spicy pan-fried rice cakes), while the southwest town of Jeonju is famous for its *bibimbap* (rice mixed with vegetables).
4. TEST OF TIME: Korean restaurants go in and out of business all the time. Restaurants that have survived for 20 to 30 years are virtual national treasures.
5. GO ONLINE: If you read Korean, you'll find tons of websites dedicated to dining. If you don't, two expatriate-run blogs, Zenkimchi (www.zenkimchi.com) and Seoul Eats (www.seouleats.com) offer plenty of advice on food and eateries.

Ordering Tips

Sitting

While many restaurants have tables and chairs like their Western counterparts, others require you to sit on the floor. You'll usually find cushions to sit on under or near the tables.

Ordering

In most Korean restaurants, the waiter/waitress/owner will take your order shortly after you arrive. Sometimes, however, you might have to get his or her attention, first—a simple "*jeogiyo*" (Hey, over there!) will suffice. Some places have electronic buzzers that call over staff, too.

Table Settings

Korean dishes are usually placed on the table all at once, although sometimes, the side dishes will be served just prior to the main dishes. Traditionally, three, five, seven, nine or 12 side dishes are served, depending on the size of the meal. The rice and soup are usually placed just in front of the diner, with the rice on the left and soup on the right. The chopsticks and spoon are placed just to the right of the soup.

In meals with multiple diners, the side dishes, stews and meats are placed between the diners and are consumed communally.

Tipping

Tipping is not customary in Korea and rarely if ever practiced. In some high-end restaurants like hotel restaurants, service charges are added to your bill.

Korean Table Manners

1. Seating is important. Let elders sit nearest the door.
2. Don't begin eating until your elders have begun. Also, try not to finish before them.
3. Don't hold your chopsticks and spoon with one hand. Also, use the spoon only for your rice and soup.
4. Don't pick around in the dishes.
5. Eat only what's within reach. Don't reach across the table.
6. Don't stick your chopsticks into your rice bowl and leave them standing—this resembles the incense sticks places in a burner during a funeral, or how food is offered to the spirits during an ancestral rites ceremony.
7. Eat and chew quietly. And keep your mouth shut.
8. Traditionally, meals were taken silently. This is much less the case now, but at the same time, don't feel compelled to make polite table conversation, either.
9. When passing and accepting drinks, dishes, etc., be sure to use two hands, especially if you're giving or taking something to/from an elder.
10. Don't pour your own drinks—let someone pour for you. Always be sure to

pour for your elders when their cups run dry, and be sure to pour with two hands or with your left hand supporting your right. When drinking alcohol with elders, it is considered polite to turn your head to the side as you sip from your cup.
11. Don't blow your nose at the table. In fact, Koreans generally avoid blowing their noses in public.
12. Unlike the West, picking your teeth is acceptable—in fact, you'll often find toothpicks at the table. Just cover your mouth with your other hand when you do so.

Vegetarian Cuisine

For the vegetarian, Korea is not an especially accommodating place, but you'll still find ways to survive. Korean temple cuisine is vegetarian, and a number of dishes—like tofu dishes—may or may not be vegetarian, depending on the restaurant. Telling the proprietor when you order that you're a vegetarian ("Jeoneun chaesikjuuija imnida 저는 채식주의자입니다") when you order might help, but not always. Also be aware that certain seemingly vegetarian dishes—even kimchi!—use animal products like fish sauce.

Local Cuisines

Seoul/Gyeonggi-do

Seoul enjoys a rich and varied cuisine, in no small part thanks to its status as Korea's capital. Seoul cuisine tends to be milder in flavor than that of other regions. At the haute cuisine end of things is **Korean palace cuisine**, featuring lovingly prepared dishes made from the rarest of ingredients. Much more affordable is *seolleongtang* 설렁탕, a rich, milky soup made with brisket. Gyeonggi-do, meanwhile, has long been one of Korea's major breadbaskets. The area around Icheon, in particular, used to produce the rice served to the kings of the

Joseon Dynasty. The city of Suwon, meanwhile, is famous for its *galbi* 갈비, or grilled beef ribs.

Chungcheong-do

Being primarily agricultural regions, the provinces of Chungcheongnam-do and Chungcheongbuk-do produce a wide range of food products. The towns of Buyeo and Gongju, in particular, have well-developed local cuisines thanks to their history as capitals of the Baekje Kingdom. *Dolssambap* 돌쌈밥 (rice in a stone pot, which is eaten wrapped in lettuce with other vegetables and condiments) is popularly eaten in the two towns. One dish of particular note is *yeonipbap* 연잎밥, rice wrapped in a lotus leaf, a specialty of Buyeo.

Gangwon-do

The rugged mountain region of Gangwon-do doesn't produce a lot of rice, but what it does produce is a lot of buckwheat, potatoes, corn and acorns, all of which feature prominently in the local cuisine. Cold buckwheat noodles, or *makguksu* 막국수, is a regional specialty, especially in the Chuncheon region. *Gamjajeon* 감자전 (potato pancakes) and *dotorimuk* 도토리묵 (acorn jelly) are also popular. The city of Chuncheon is also famous for *dalk galbi* 닭갈비, or pan-fried chicken served with vegetables and a tangy sauce. The coastal regions of Gangwon-do produce a lot of seafood, with squid being a specialty. Try the *ojingeo sundae* 오징어순대: squid stuffed with noodles and other ingredients.

Jeolla-do

Korea's southwest is widely regarded as having the best cuisine in the country. Here, the food comes plentiful, rich, and (relatively) cheap. The Honam Plain of Jeollabuk-do is Korea's breadbasket,

producing an endless supply of high-quality rice. The city of Jeonju is home to one of Korea's best-known (and best-loved) dishes, **Jeonju Bibimbap** 전주비빔밥. The southern coast of Jeollanam-do, meanwhile, is home to so-called Namdo cuisine, an incredibly rich and varied cuisine using the many high-quality agricultural and seafood products of the region's valleys and seas. Dishes are well-seasoned with locally-produced pastes and sauces. Expect a lot of tasty side dishes to be served with whatever you order. One particular specialty of the Namdo area is raw fermented skate, or *hongeohoe* 홍어회. This is very much an acquired taste, but one enjoyed almost universally by the locals of Jeollanam-do.

Gyeongsang-do

Truth be told, southeast Korea is not especially known for its food—dishes tend to be saltier than they are elsewhere. Still, there's plenty this region does well, especially seafood, hauled in from the rich fishing grounds of the East Sea—visit Busan's Jagalchi Market to experience what we're talking about. The city of Andong, too, stands apart with a unique cuisine that includes a variety of unusual dishes, including *jjimdak* 찜닭 (steamed chicken), Andong soju and *heotjesabap* 헛제사밥 (a meal modeled on the food served during ancestral rites).

Jeju-do

Jeju is an island, so it should come as no surprise that seafood like fish, shellfish and seaweed are an important part of local cusine. Raw fish is common. Due to topographical conditions, rice is less plentiful on the island than it is on the mainland, so millet, buckwheat and barley feature much more prominently.

STEWS

• **Kimchi Jjigae** 김치찌개: A tasty *kimchi* stew made with older *kimchi* and slices of pork. This extremely spicy dish is loved by Koreans but can be a bit of a shock for foreign visitors unaccustomed to its sharp, spicy flavor. Eating it with rice will soften the intensity of the spiciness and make it a bit easier to consume.

• **Doenjang Jjigae** 된장찌개: Another fermented favorite, *doenjang jjigae* is a fermented soybean-paste stew that is considered one of Korea's representative dishes. It often contains dried anchovies and clams, and the special ingredient of *doenjang* is widely touted as having anti-cancer properties.

• **Cheonggukjang** 청국장: Somewhat similar to *doenjang jjigae*, but the soybeans are fermented for only two or three days rather than three months. The result is a rich, nutritious stew that's absolutely delicious if you can get past the smell, which has sometimes been likened to a rotting corpse.

• **Budae Jjigae** 부대찌개: Literally, "Army Base Stew," this spicy dish is made from sausages, Spam, beans, instant noodles and rice cakes, among other variations. It dates back to the era after the Korean War, when the ingredients entered Korea via US military bases.

• **Sundubu Jjigae** 순두부찌개: Handmade soft tofu, stewed in a spicy soup of vegetables and red pepper. A raw egg is often placed in the boiling stew. It's a filling and nutritious dish that has been catching on overseas as well.

• **Gamjatang** 감자탕: An extremely popular stew, *gamjatang* is a spicy dish created by boiling a pork spine with potatoes and other vegetables. It is most popular during the cold winter months.

• **Samgyetang** 삼계탕: Made by boiling a whole chicken with ginseng, jujubes and garlic, this soup is believed to restore people's energy on hot summer days. It is chock-full of quality, healthy ingredients with noted health benefits.

• **Seolleongtang** 설렁탕: If spicy dishes aren't your thing, this might do the trick. Seasoned only with salt and spring onions, the soup is made from ox bones that have been boiled for an entire day.

• **Kkori Gomtang** 꼬리곰탕: Another hearty stew, this one is made from ox tail bones boiled for hours and beef brisket. If you'd like a break from the spicy dishes, give this dish a try.

• **Jeongol** 전골: *Jeongol* differs from *jjigae* in that while the latter is prepared primarily from one ingredient, the former is made from a variety. Historically, *jeongol* was eaten by the upper classes, while *jjigae* was eaten by the lower cases. Common *jeongol* dishes include:

* **Sinseollo** 신선로: A rich meat, mushroom and vegetable stew, served in a large silver bowl with a hole in the center where hot embers were placed to heat the dish. The dish is a staple of Korean palace cuisine.

* **Beoseot Jeongol** 버섯전골: Mushroom stew

* **Soegogi Jeongol** 쇠고기전골: Beef stew

* **Nakji Jeongol** 낙지전골: Octopus stew

Kimchi Jjigae

Doenjang Jjigae

Samgyetang

Seolleongtang

- **Haejangguk** 해장국**:** This rich stew is commonly referred to as a "hangover stew," as it is often eaten in the wee morning hours after a night of hardcore drinking. The broth is prepared by boiling ox bones over a long period of time, while the soup itself contains bean sprouts, radish, scallions and cabbage. There are several varieties of *haejangguk*, including *kongnamulguk* (heavy on the bean sprouts), *ugeojiguk* (made with dried Chinese cabbage leaves) and *seonjiguk*.

  * **Seonji Haejangguk** 선지해장국**:** A soup made from cabbage, beef broth and other vegetables, it is particularly good to chase a hangover. Some might be turned off by the big globs of coagulated ox blood, though.

- **Chueotang** 추어탕**:** This spicy dish—a specialty of southern Korea—is prepared by boiling a mudfish whole—bones and entrails included. The result is a rich stew that is both filling and nutritious.

NOODLES

- **Kalguksu** 칼국수**:** The name of this soup literally means "knife-cut noodles." *Kalguksu* consists of handmade knife-cut wheat noodles served in a broth made with anchovies, shellfish and kelp.

- **Sujebi** 수제비**:** This dish is similar to *Kalguksu*, with the primary difference being that while the latter is made with thick wheat noodles, the former is prepared with big wheat flakes. It is a dish particularly enjoyed on rainy days.

- **Janchi Guksu** 잔치국수**:** This noodle dish is literally translated as "Banquet Noodles," as it was traditionally eaten at weddings, birthdays and other festivities (the noodle represents longevity). The thin wheat noodles are prepared in a light broth with green onions and a sauce of soy, sesame oil and chili powder.

- **Mul Naengmyeon** 물냉면**:** This icy noodle soup is a refreshing favorite, with thin buckwheat noodles in a sweet and sour meat broth. Served with sliced vegetables, sesame seeds and a boiled egg.

- **Bibim Naengmyeon** 비빔냉면**:** Like its cousin above, this dish consists of iced buckwheat noodles, but served with a spicy red pepper sauce.

- **Kongguksu** 콩국수**:** One of Korea's most unique dishes, this summer specialty consists of wheat noodles in a cold, thick broth made from soybeans.

- **Makguksu** 막국수**:** Another cold noodle dish, this specialty of the mountain town of Chuncheon is similar to *naengmyeon*, but the noodles use more buckwheat, while the dish itself makes more plentiful use of cold vegetables.

- **Ramyeon** 라면**:** Better known in the West as ramen, instant noodles are ubiquitous in Korea—you'll find stacks of them in just about any shop. Korea's *ramyeon* dishes, however, tend to be a good deal spicier than their Japanese (and Western) counterparts. The spicy Sin Ramyeon is a particularly popular brand.

Haejangguk

Kalguksu

Janchi Guksu

Makguksu

GRILLED MEATS

• **Galbi** 갈비: One of the most popular Korean foods among foreigners, *galbi* is a dish of barbecued, marinated beef ribs. Each restaurant's methods of marinating its *galbi* ribs differs, but this is a dependably delicious dish. Served either on the bone or deboned (*galbi sal*), the meat is cooked on a fire in front of the diner and eaten wrapped in a lettuce leaf. You can usually get either beef or pork ribs, although the former is considerably more expensive.

• **Bulgogi** 불고기: Another popular dish among the foreign population, *bulgogi* is another type of barbecued and marinated meat, though thinly sliced in this dish. Generally garnished with sesame seeds and green onions.

• **Dakgalbi** 닭갈비: A specialty of the city of Chuncheon, this popular dish consists of chunks of chicken pan fried in red pepper paste with vegetables, sweet potato and rice cakes. If you like spicy food, you'll love this. After the chicken is consumed, rice is fried up in the remaining sauce.

• **Jjimdak** 찜닭: A specialty of the Andong region in southeastern Korea, *jjim dak* ("steamed chicken") is, as the name would suggest, pieces of steamed chicken, served in a sweet sauce with vegetables and cellophane noodles.

• **Samgyeopsal** 삼겹살: Made from unmarinated and unseasoned grilled pork belly, these slices of meat are grilled directly on the diners' table, then dipped in a mixed sauce of sesame oil, ground pepper and salt, and wrapped in a fresh lettuce leaf or sesame leaf with a slice of garlic and mixed *gochujang* (red pepper) and *doenjang* (fermented soy bean) paste.

• **Jokbal** 족발: Marinated pig's feet, deboned and sliced into thin strips and served on a platter. Usually eaten wrapped in a lettuce leaf, often with a condiment of fermented shrimp. Try washing it down with a shot of *soju*. The Jangchung-dong neighborhood of Seoul is famous for its many *jokbal* restaurants. (see p108)

• **Bossam** 보쌈: Steamed pork, wrapped in a leaf of lettuce and topped with sweet *kimchi* and a thick paste of fermented soybean and red pepper.

SEAFOOD

• **Maeuntang** 매운탕: Literally "spicy stew," *maeuntang* is a fish—which fish depends on the restaurant—boiled in a soup prepared with red pepper paste, chili powder and vegetables. This is often served after a dish of sashimi, with the unused parts of the fish boiled up in the soup. Makes a great accompaniment to *soju*.

• **Haemultang** 해물탕: As the Korean name (meaning "seafood stew") would suggest, *haemultang* is a spicy stew made from various seafood products, including but not limited to crab, shrimp and shellfish.

• **Haemuljjim** 해물찜: Steamed seafood, including squid, shrimp, clams and mussels. Usually quite spicy.

• **Agujjim** 아구찜: A form of *haemuljjim* made from bean sprouts and steamed anglerfish, this specialty of southeastern

Bulgogi   Jjimdak   Samgyeopsal   Nakji Bokkeum

Korea is actually quite nice, even if the fish itself has to be the ugliest sea creature on God's green earth.

• **Nakji Bokkeum** 낙지볶음**:** Commonly known as one of Korea's spiciest dishes, *nakji bokkeum* is prepared from tiny octopuses, chopped up and pan-fried with a red pepper paste sauce. After consumption, the leftovers are used to prepare a spicy fried rice.

• **Sannakji** 산낙지**:** Tiny octopuses, sliced up and eaten while the parts are still wiggling about. Be sure to chew well—the octopus parts will fight back, and this can present a choking hazard.

• **Hoe** 회**:** Known better in the West by its Japanese name of sashimi, *hoe* is slices of raw fish, served with a dipping sauce of soy sauce and *wasabi* paste. Red pepper paste mixed with vinegar is often used as a dipping sauce, too. Best enjoyed with a shot of *cheongha*, a rice wine similar to Japanese sake.

• **Chobap** 초밥**:** Referred to as sushi in Japan and the United States, *chobap* is vinegar rice usually topped with a slice of raw fish. A cheaper, non-fish variant is *yubu chobap*: vinegar rice in a pouch of fried tofu.

• **Saengseon Gui** 생선구이**:** Grilled fish. Popular fishes to grill include mackerel and cutlass fish.

• **Jangeo Gui** 장어구이**:** Grilled marinated eel. This dish is eaten primarily in summer, when it is believed to provide the extra energy boost needed to overcome heat exhaustion.

• **Hongeohoe** 홍어회**:** Slices of raw, fermented skate. No, we're not making it up—it's particularly popular in southwestern Korea, and you can find it at seafood restaurants in Seoul. High in ammonia, the meat will clean out your sinuses quick—it's sort of like eating sashimi in a latrine.

RICE DISHES

• **Bibimbap** 비빔밥**:** This simple yet healthy concoction is another representative Korean dish. It is a mixture that includes rice, an assortment of vegetables, meat, an egg, and red pepper paste. Varients include *sanchae bibimbap*, prepared with wild mountain vegetables; *dolsot bibimbap*, which comes in a stone hotpot; and *yangpun bibimbap*, served for two in a large bowl.

• **Sotbap** 솥밥**:** *Sotbap* is a stone hotpot of rice, usually served with steamed chestnut, jujube, ginkgo nuts and mushrooms. The rice is eaten with soy sauce. After eating the rice, you pour hot water into the hotpot, which turns the leftover rice stuck to the pot into a soup called *nurungji*.

• **Ssambap** 쌈밥**:** Steamed rice, meat and side dishes, served in a wrap of lettuce and leaf vegetables.

• **Boribap** 보리밥**:** A throwback to Korea's less prosperous days, rice and barley are mixed together with vegetables for a hardy meal.

• **Juk** 죽**:** Rice porridge, *juk* comes in many varieties, including *jeonbokjuk* (abalone porridge), *jatjuk* (pine nut porridge), *hobakjuk* (pumkin porridge), *patjuk* (red

Saengseon Gui

Hongeohoe

Bibimbap

Patjuk

TIPS

BON JUK

This popular chain of *juk* restaurants provides big, filling bowls of porridge of a variety of kinds. You can get *juk* cheaper at markets, but if you want a good bowl of *juk*, Bon Juk is highly recommended.

bean porridge), *saeujuk* (shrimp porridge) and *yachaejuk* (vegetable porridge).

OTHERS

• **Japchae** 잡채: Cellophane noodles, stir fried in sesame oil and served with a variety of vegetables, including sliced carrots, onions and peppers. This dish is commonly found at parties and tends to be popular with foreigners. Chinese restaurants often serve it on a bed of rice as a dish called *japchae-bap*.

• **Gejang** 게장: Fresh, raw crab, marinated in soy sauce or red pepper sauce. This is something of an acquired taste, mostly thanks to the consistency, but is quite nice once you've gotten used to it.

• **Tteokguk** 떡국: This rich soup of boiled slices of rice cake is a New Year's Day treat, when it is believed to bring good fortune in the coming year. A popular variant is *tteok manduguk*, in which large *mandu* (Korean meat dumplings) are added.

• **Mandu** 만두: *Mandu*, or Korean dumplings, are a popular cheap meal. Variants include *jjin mandu* (steamed dumplings) and *gun mandu* (fried dumplings). Several different fillings are used, including kimchi and meat.

• **Bindaetteok** 빈대떡: A savory Korean pancake made from ground mung beans. A good place to score these is at Gwangjang Market (see p105).

• **Pajeon** 파전: Another form of Korean pancake, *pajeon* is made from egg, flour and green onions. A variant is *haemul pajeon*, in which seafood like sliced squid is added to the recipe.

• **Dubu Kimchi** 두부김치: As the name would indicate, this dish consists of slices of *dubu* (tofu) and *kimchi*. It is a popular side dish when drinking.

KOREAN CHINESE FOOD

Just as Chinese food transformed itself when it was brought to the United States to suit American tastes, so it changed to suit Korean tastes when it was brought here. Chinese food in Korea is based primarily on the cuisine of China's Shandong region, the place of origin of the bulk of Korea's ethnic Chinese population.

• **Jjajangmyeon** 짜장면: The most popular of Chinese dishes in Korea, *jjajangmyeon* is noodles covered in a sweet black bean sauce. Based on the Northern Chinese dish of *zha jiang mian*, this dish was reportedly invented by Incheon's Chinese population.

• **Jjamppong** 짬뽕: A spicy seafood and noodle soup, this dish is based on *champon*, a Chinese dish invented in Meiji-era Nagasaki, Japan, for Chinese students.

Gejang

Tteokguk

Pajeon

Dubu Kimchi

CHINATOWN FOOD

Some of the best Chinese restaurants in Seoul can be found in the small Chinatown in Myeong-dong (see p86). If you're in Incheon, of course, you can score outstanding Chinese fare in the city's famous Chinatown (see p172).

- **Bokkeumbap** 볶음밥: Fried rice, often topped with a fried egg.

- **Tangsuyuk** 탕수육: Sweet and sour pork, not altogether different from what you'd get in Chinese restaurants in the West.

STREET FOODS

Seoul is a haven of delicious street foods, purchased from street snack stalls called *pojangmacha*. Street food, all selections under 3,000 won each, is conveniently found in virtually any location in Seoul that has a great deal of foot traffic.

- **Gimbap** 김밥: *Gimbap* is a favorite fast food of Korean schoolchildren and probably one of Korea's most popular dishes. It can be likened to a sushi roll—a seaweed roll filled with rice and slices of fried egg, ham, cucumber, picked radish and other varieties as desired. You can find it everywhere—at convenience stores, Korean "fast food" shops and often streetside stalls. It's served at almost every Korean picnic.

- **Tteokbokki** 떡볶이: *Tteokbokki* is a *pojangmacha* staple—a bright red, spicy rice cake dish broiled in a *gochujang* (red pepper) seasoning with vegetables and *odeng* (Japanese-style fish cakes).

- **Odeng** 오뎅: Japanese fish cakes, usually served on a stick. Great tummy warmer in the winter.

- **Sundae** 순대: This Korean-style sausage is stuffed with a mix of viscid rice, ox or pig's blood and potato noodles. This is really quite good, although the additional slices of pork liver and kidneys might put some off. The neighborhood of Sillim-dong (in front of Seoul National University) is famous for its many *sundae* restaurants.

- **Twigim** 튀김: *Twigim* are assorted fried foods, including hard-boiled eggs, sliced vegetables, squid, potato slices, shrimp and more. These delicious items are difficult to resist, especially when the vendor serves them piping hot out of the fryer.

- **Gunmandu** 군만두: Fried dumplings are another popular selection off the *pojangmacha*. They come in a range of meat-filled and vegetarian options.

- **Dak-kkochi** 닭꼬치: Chicken kebabs, served with a hot sauce.

GIMBAP CHEONGUK

Literally, "Gimbap Paradise," this popular chain of restaurants serves up several kinds of *gimbap* along with other simple Korean fare. Great for a cheap meal.

GIM-TTEOK-SOON

Some food stalls sell a set of *gimbap*, *tteokbokki* and *sundae*. This is a good way to sample the three pillars of Korean street cuisine.

Jjajangmyeon

Gimbap

Tteokbokki

Twigim

- **Hotteok** 호떡: Sino-Korean pancakes filled with a honey sauce. The good ones are baked without oil.

- **Bungeo-bbang** 붕어빵: Carp-shaped fried bread filled with sweet red bean paste, *bungeo-bbang* is a quick, sweet street snack.

- **Toast** 토스트: Yes, the standard piece of toast, although this one is pan fried in butter and served with a fried egg. The Seokbong Toast franchise can be found throughout Seoul.

- **Ppeongtwigi** 뻥튀기: These popped rice disks are a popular snack among those watching their calorie intake. A Korean equivalent to low-fat popcorn.

- **Beondegi** 번데기: These are boiled, seasoned silkworm pupae, often served in a paper cup and consumed as a snack. Definitely an acquired taste. This is often cited as Korea's most "bizarre" food, mostly because it is in full public view at streetside food vendors everywhere.

DESSERTS

- **Hangwa** 한과: Korean confections that come in all shapes, sizes and colors. A popular kind is *yakgwa*, a small fried honey cake. *Hangwa* are commonly served with Korean traditional teas.

- **Yaksik** 약식: Translated as "medicinal food," *yaksik* is steamed glutinous rice mixed with chestnuts, jujubes and pine nuts and sweetened with honey.

- **Tteok** 떡: Made from steamed rice flour, *tteok*—Korean rice cakes—are a staple of Korean dessert cuisine. There are hundreds

of kinds of *tteok*, some of which are consumed on holidays and special days. Some of the more popular forms of *tteok* include:

* **Injeolmi** 인절미: Soft clumps of pounded rice cake covered in mugwort or red bean powder.
* **Sirutteok** 시루떡: Steamed rice cakes that also come in a wide variety of shapes and colors. A common form is the rainbow-colored *mujigae tteok*, usually served at a baby's first birthday.
* **Jeolpyeon** 절편: Made from steamed rice powder that has been pounded and cut into shape, *jeolpyeon* are pressed with intricate designs.
* **Kkultteok** 꿀떡: Rice cakes with honey inside.
* **Songpyeon** 송편: These half-moon shaped rice cakes filled with nuts or honey are steamed on a bed of pine needles. You'll eat a ton of them on the Chuseok holiday.

DRINKS

- **Soju** 소주: *Soju* is the most popular alcoholic beverage in Korea. A clear liquor, it is made by distilling fermented rice or sweet potatoes. It is extremely cheap, and therefore ubiquitous in the restaurants and grocery stores of Korea.

- **Makgeolli** 막걸리: *Makgeolli* has the longest history of all Korea's liquors and is frequently referred to as the "liquor of the common people" because of its popularity among farmers. This liquor, made from fermented sweet rice, has the appearance of milk and a low alcohol content.

Yaksik   Songpyeon   Makgeolli   Bungeo-bbang

- **Insamju** 인삼주: A liquor made with *insam* (Korean ginseng), *insamju* is believed to have special medicinal properties. Sometimes sold with a ginseng root visible through the glass bottle, this alcohol makes a popular souvenir.

- **Maesilju** 매실주: This liquor is created from plums and is available in grocery stores, although it is commonly made at home. *Maesilju* has a low alcohol content.

- **Sikhye** 식혜: *Sikhye* is a unique Korean dessert drink created from malt and rice. This sweet drink is said to aid with digestion.

TRADITIONAL TEA

- **Boricha** 보리차: Barley tea
- **Oksusucha** 옥수수차: Corn tea
- **Gyeolmyeongjacha** 결명자차: *Senna tora* tea
- **Dunggeullecha** 둥글레차: Solomon's Seal tea
- **Hyeonmi Nokcha** 현미녹차: Green tea blended with roasted rice
- **Saenggangcha**: Ginger tea
- **Daechucha**: Jujube tea
- **Yujacha**: Yuja (yuzu) tea
- **Ssanghwacha**: Herbal medicine tea
- **Omijacha**: "Five flavor" tea
- **Sujeonggwa**: Spicy persimmon punch

TIPS

LOCAL FOLK LIQUORS AND SPIRITS

While *soju*, *makgeolli* and beer might be the potent potables of choice for the masses, Korea does produce a wide range of higher-quality folk liquors and spirits. While most are regional in character, they can often be found outside their home provinces, too, especially in Seoul.

- **Gyeongju Gyodong Beopju:** Brewed for generations by the Choi family of Gyeongju, this clear, slightly yellow firewater is about 16% alcohol. It has a sweet taste with a full aroma. Price: 32,000 to 35,000 won.

- **Jeonju Leegangju:** Made from pear, ginger, cinnamon, honey and rice, this liquor has an alcohol content of around 22 to 25%. Price: 16,000 to 220,000 won.

- **Andong Soju:** Brewed forever by the Cho family of Andong, this is one of Korea's most famous traditional alcohols. With an alcohol content of 45%, it's got a bit of a kick, and indeed, has been used as a folk medicine. Price: 20,000 to 50,000 won.

- **Munbaeju:** If it was good enough for the South-North Korean Summit of 2000, it's good enough for you. Be careful, though—it has an alcohol content of 40%. Price: 30,000 to 100,000 won.

- **Hansan Sogokju:** Once enjoyed by the Baekje royal family, this specialty of Chungcheongnam-do is famous for its taste and medicinal properties. It's also rather mild with an alcohol content of 18%. Price: 10,000 to 140,000 won.

- **Gochang Bokbunjaju:** A sweet liquor made from raspberries, this drink is said to have anti-aging and anti-cancer effects. Price: 20,000 to 50,000 won.

Insamju

Sujeonggwa

Omija Punch

Ssanghwacha

DOG MEAT AND BOYANGSIK

As you've no doubt heard—either from late-night talk show comedians or concerned friends and family—Koreans eat dog meat. Well, *some* Koreans eat dog meat—many others see it as a national embarrassment. Since the 1988 Olympics, when dog meat restaurants were banned from using the term *bosintang* (the common name for dog meat soup) out of fear it would make Korea look bad in the eyes of foreigners, dog meat has been a source of heated controversy. Even foreigners have jumped into the fray—French actress and animal rights activist Brigitte Bardot, for instance, attempted to use Korea's hosting of the 2002 World Cup to launch a campaign against dog meat, generating a fierce nationalist counterattack by Korean defenders of the delicacy.

Dog meat—sometimes procured from dogs specially raised for human consumption—is most often consumed in a soup called *bosintang* and a heavier stew called *bosinjeongol*. Consumers—usually but not exclusively men—cite its energizing effect in summer and its supposed effect on the male libido. Both the soup and stew make for a rich, hardy meal—the meat is stewed with a generous amount of perilla leaves, onions, garlic and pepper. If you're able to get past the cultural taboo you may or may not have against eating dog, it's really quite delicious.

Interestingly enough, dog meat represents something of an odd legal gray area—it's not legally recognized, but it's not expressly forbidden, either. Supportive politicians have for some time tried to correct this situation by officially legalizing it, but this has run into resistance from animal rights activists and politicians afraid of creating a national embarrassment. Interestingly enough, the ownership of dogs as pets has skyrocketed in recent years, too—nowadays, it seems like everyone has one.

A funny byproduct of the 1988 ban on the use of the term *bosintang* was the proliferation of new names for the dish. Some of these are still in use, including *sacheoltang* ("All Season Soup") and *yeongyangtang* ("Nutritious Soup").

Dog meat is only one of many foods Koreans consume to boost their stamina during the—sorry for this—dog days of summer. Other energy-boosting dishes include *samgyetang* (chicken and ginseng soup), *otdak* (chicken and lacquer sap stew), *jangeogui* (broiled eel) and *chueotang* (mudfish soup). All these are quite delicious and worth trying, although a word of caution is warranted about the *otdak*—the lacquer sap causes allergic skin rashes and itching in some people. These high-protein dishes are referred to in Korean as *boyangsik*, or "vitalizing food."

RECOMMENDED DOG MEAT RESTAURANT

If you're really in the mood for the meat of the dog, Ssarijip near Buam-dong (see p101) is one of Seoul's best places to try *bosintang*. Located in a Korean-style *hanok* home with a wonderful courtyard, the restaurant is packed in the summer, but is still a relaxing place to have a meal. A bowl of *bosintang* will cost you 15,000 won, but a heavier stew, or *jeongol*, is worth the money at 28,000 won. Hours: 11 am to 9:30 pm. (02-379-9911)

SHOPPING

Koreans love to shop. Korea's post-war economic boom sparked a consumer culture second-to-none, especially in big cities like Seoul, where you'll find grand department stores, cavernous shopping malls, high-end luxury shops, traditional outdoor markets, supermarkets, hole-in-the-wall shops and a myriad of other places eager to relieve you of your excess currency.

Perhaps unsurprisingly, Seoul is—by far—the best place to shop, with Korea's biggest collection of department stores and widest selection of goods, although Busan certain earns a special mention as home of the world's largest department store, the gargantuan Shinsegae Centum City. Korean retail culture accommodates shoppers of all budgets, from the jetsetter to the backpacker, so if spending money is what you seek, the opportunities are endless.

THINGS TO BUY

Antiques: If you've got the money and means to bring it home, you can purchase very nice antique furniture and art. Insa-dong and Itaewon in Seoul have a number of good antique shops.

Pottery: Korea has been producing high-quality ceramics for centuries. When Queen Elizabeth II visited Korea in 1999, she purchased pottery in Seoul's Insa-dong. The ceramics villages of Icheon just outside of Seoul and the medieval ceramics center of Gangjin in southwest Korea are excellent places to score high-quality ceramic wares.

Clothing and Fashion: For quality clothing at budget prices, few places beat Korea. In particular, the sprawling Dongdaemun Market in Seoul is a budget fashion shopper's paradise, home to countless young designers and manufacturers hawking their wares at bargain prices. Those looking more upscale brands should explore Seoul's Apgujeong-dong neighborhood, the Beverly Hills of Korea.

Fabrics: If you're a clothing producer, or just like fabric, Dongdaemun is the place to go.

Shoes: Shoes—all leather goods—tend to be cheaper in Korea than they are elsewhere. Give Myeong-dong and Itaewon in Seoul a try.

Cosmetics: Korean women love their cosmetics. Accordingly, you'll find cosmetic shops almost everywhere. Seoul's Myeong-dong is an especially good place to go cosmetics shopping.

Ginseng and Herbal Medicines: Korea is one of the world's largest exporters of ginseng, the magic root sought after in much of Asia for its rejuvenatory effects. The Gyeongdong Market in Seoul and Daegu Medicine Market are certainly good places to try, but real ginseng aficionados should go to the small market town

of Geumsan in Chungcheongnam-do, the ginseng capital of Korea.

Tea: Health fanatics will want to buy Korean green tea, produced on plantations in the southern part of the country and on Jejudo Island. Korea also produces a number of other traditional teas, including ginseng tea. You can find Korean tea products in almost any supermarket (or even in small hole-in-the-walls), or you could go straight to the source and visit the tea plantations of Boseong, Hadong or Jeju.

Traditional Liquor: Korea produces a number of fine traditional tipples, including *soju*, *baekseju*, *yakju* and more. Korea's best-known handcrafted booze is Andong soju (45% proof), produced in the lovely southeastern town of Andong, but you can find locally produced specialty beverages in virtually every region of Korea.

Seaweed: A favorite of Japanese travelers, you can buy *gim* (dried seaweed) or which you buy cheaper in Korea than in most other places. Seoul's Namdaemun Market and, of course, Busan's sprawling seafood district around Jagalchi Market are good places to purchase *gim*, although you can find it in just about any supermarket.

Electronics: Koreans love their gadgets, and Korea produces some of the world's highest quality consumer electronics. Seoul is the best place for electronics shopping: the places to pick up gadgets are the better structured but pricier Techno Mart, and the bustling and cheaper Yongsan Electronics Market.

SHOPS AND MARKETS

Duty-Free Shops

Naturally, Seoul has the most duty-free shops, although Busan has a couple, and Jeju has one (at the Lotte Hotel in Jungmun Resort). Popular duty-free shops include the ones at Shilla Hotel and Lotte's two major hotels in Seoul, the one at the Sheraton Wakerhill Hotel, Dongwha Duty Free in Gwanghwamun and AK Duty Free at Incheon International Airport, Gimpo Airport and COEX. If you're in Busan, try Paradise Hotel's Duty Free and Lotte Duty Free in Haeundae.

Department Stores

Seoul has the largest number of department stores in Korea, but Busan also has some major department stores, including the massive Shinsegae Centum City, designated the world's largest department store by the Guinness Book of World Records. Popular Korean department chains include Lotte, Shinsegae, Hyundai and Galleria. Galleria in Seoul's Apgujeong-dong is particularly well-known for its luxury brands.

Shopping Malls

Seoul is home to several large malls or shopping centers, including the enormous COEX Mall (www.coex.co.kr), one of the largest shopping malls in Asia; Lotte World, a virtual city onto itself; the giant fashion shopping centers of Dongdaemun Market; Yongsan Station's I'Park Mall; and the recently opened Times Square Mall in Yeongdeungpo. COEX, in particular, is a site to behold, with its countless shops and restaurants, movie theaters, kimchi museum and aquarium. These are places you could spend all day, and many do.

In addition to these urban malls, there are two outlet malls in the suburbs around Seoul. Yeoju Premium Outlet, just south of Seoul, is an American-style outlet mall with big discounts on major luxury brand goods. After opening in 2007, this mall has done so well that a second outlet mall, Paju Premium Outlet, was opened just north of Seoul in 2011. The Paju outlet focuses more on casual brands, but still has its fair share of high-end brands, too. Being suburban outlet malls, these malls are usually frequented by those with their own cars, although public transportation is also available: see www.premiumoutlets.co.kr (Korean/English/Japanese/Chinese) for transportation information. Lotte recently opened its own outlet next to Paju Premium Outlet

Luxury Boutiques

The Apgujeong-dong area of Seoul is full of luxury boutiques, particularly along the notoriously posh "Rodeo Drive," where you'll find Prada, Gucci, Dolce & Gabbana, Hugo Boss, Armani, Louis

Dongdaemun Market at night

Vuitton, Jimmy Choo and all your other favorite luxury brands.

A variation on a theme is the so-called "multi-shop," of which you'll find several in Apgujeong-dong, too. These chic, artistically designed shops house multiple luxury brands under one roof.

Outdoor Markets

Every town, regardless of how small, has a market. Depending on the town, these can be colorful, lively places where you'll find merchants—often older women—hawking all sorts of foodstuffs, clothing, sundries and other goods. Traditionally, markets were held every five days, and some towns and localities still keep to this schedule. In many other places, however, outdoor markets are held every day, or something close to it.

In the bigger outdoor markets, you can find almost anything under the sun. This is especially so at Seoul's sprawling Namdaemun Market, the largest and most famous outdoor market in Korea. Some larger outdoor markets are more specialized. A typical example would be Dongdaemun Market in Seoul, a massive shopping center specializing in fashion and textiles.

Outdoor markets usually have the lowest prices, but product quality can be iffy—be sure to examine what you want to buy well before handing over your money. Don't expect refunds, either. Unlike at department stores, haggling is not only permitted at an outdoor market, it's almost required (see TIPS on p695). Even in outdoor markets, however, there are merchants who run fixed-price establishments. Be sure to bring Korean currency, too—most merchants in outdoor markets don't take credit cards.

Markets are often home to or surrounded by cheap Korean traditional restaurants and food stalls, so they make good places to eat on the cheap, too.

Supermarkets

Over the last decade, large-scale supermarket chains like E-Mart, Costco, Home Plus and Lotte Mart have become a part of Korean daily life, much to the chagrin of merchants at outdoor markets and local mom-and-pop grocery stores. You can find branches of these chains in all large and medium-sized Korean cities. If you're buying in bulk, these are convenient and (relatively) cheap places to shop for groceries, although Costco requires a low yearly fee. Nowadays, you'll also find a wide-range of foreign food products that are hard to find elsewhere, including wines and cheeses.

Convenience Stores & Hole-in-the-Wall Shops

No town, no matter how small, is without a convenience store or, at the very least, a family-run hole-in-the-wall shop. These shops are convenient places for the traveler to stock up on sundries, including beverages, bread, noodles and other basic life-sustaining supplies.

Korea is home to several foreign and domestic convenience store chains, including 7-Eleven, Buy the Way,

FamilyMart and GS 25. Many convenience stores have counters where you can eat food purchased at the shop, such as *gimbap* (rice rolls), *samgak gimbap* ("triangle *gimbap*," triangular rice balls wrapped in seaweed), and instant noodles. Accordingly, if you're on the road and need someplace to fill up quickly and cheaply, a convenience store is a good bet.

Family-run hole-in-the-wall shops are, likewise, good places to buy milk, soda, instant coffee, cigarettes and other groceries. Almost all neighborhoods have them, and some even offer discounts to or run tabs for regular customers. They are often slightly cheaper than convenience stores but, unlike convenience stores, many hole-in-the-wall shops don't accept credit cards.

TAXES AND REFUNDS OF VAT

Foreign visitors can get a partial refund on the 10% VAT from Global Refund (02-776-2170 or www.globalrefund.com) and Korea Refund (02-537-1755). If you spend more than 30,000 or 50,000 won at a participating retailer, you can show your passport and request a special sales receipt, which can be redeemed for a refund when departing the country at Incheon International Airport. Just go to a Customs Declaration Desk (located near check-in counters D and J) prior to checking in your luggage, so that the customs officer can verify the items that you purchased in order to stamp your receipt. After passing through immigration, show the stamped receipts to the appropriate refund desk located next to the duty-free shops to receive a won refund in the form of cash or cheque. Refunds generally range from 5% to 7%.

BASIC KOREAN

As in any foreign country, any and all efforts to speak the local language—Korean, in this case—are highly appreciated and may sometimes be necessary.

Hangeul is a phonetic writing system created in 1446 by the revered King Sejong the Great (see next page). The alphabet is comprised of 14 consonants and 10 vowels, and each consonant mimics the placement of the tongue and lips when the sound is created.

The Romanization of *hangeul* varies depending on which system is used, although the Korean government released the Revised Romanization system in 2000 as the official Korean language Romanization system. Revised Romanization does not include any non-alphabetic symbols, which simplifies and standardizes Romanization of Korean.

Koreans place a great deal of emphasis on respect and social hierarchy, and the Korean language reflects this. Korean includes different levels of speech, depending on the relationship between the speaker and listener, their level of familiarity with one another, the setting, and the age difference. The phrases listed on the following pages use the honorific from of speech.

Statue of King Sejong the Great, Deoksugung Palace

KING SEJONG THE GREAT & THE HANGEUL ALPHABET

Ask a Korean who Korea's greatest king was, and he or she is almost certain to answer "King Sejong the Great." This remarkable 15th century monarch—one of only two Korean kings to earn the appellation "the Great"—was one of the most enlightened rulers of his age, a scholar-king whose interests extended far beyond politics into science and culture.

King Sejong, who ruled from 1418 to 1450, was the fourth king of the Joseon era. The third son of the energetic King Taejong, he proved an excellent student and managed to win his father's favor. He was fortunate enough, too, to have elder brothers who, far from feeling threatened, actually conspired to have him put on the throne—both got themselves banished from the court, with one becoming a wandering traveler while the other became a Buddhist monk.

Upon assuming the throne, Sejong put his leadership skills to immediate work, launching military campaigns against Japanese pirates to the south and Manchurian raiders to the north. A tremendous patron of the sciences, he oversaw the development of a number of key publications and technologies, including agricultural handbooks, weather instruments (including the world's first rain gauge) and a water clock.

King Sejong's greatest accomplishment, however, was overseeing the creation of Korea's ingenious indigenous writing system, the *hangeul* alphabet. Prior to the creation of the alphabet, Chinese characters were used for written communication, which limited literacy to only a small, educated elite. Since Korean is completely different from Chinese in terms of its grammar, this also posed difficulties in properly putting the language to paper. To rectify this, the king put together a committee to create a scientific but easy-to-learn alphabet that could better express the sounds of the Korean language. The result, promulgated in 1446, was a 28-letter alphabet—consonants were designed to reflect the position of the lips, tongue and throat during pronunciation, while the vowels reflected Korea's traditional *yin-yang* cosmology. Originally called Hunminjeongeum ("Proper Sounds for the Instruction of the People"), the alphabet is today known—at least in South Korea—as *hangeul*, or "Korean letters."

Conservative aristocrats were not immediately impressed. Yet, as time passed, the use of the alphabet flourished, and in 1894, it was adopted for use in official documents. In 1896, the first *hangeul* newspaper was published. The current alphabet and spelling rules were largely finalized in 1933, although North and South Korea would carry out separate smaller reforms: the latest South Korean spelling reform was promulgated in 1988.

Today's *hangeul* alphabet has 24 letters—14 consonants and 10 vowels. When it was first promulgated in 1446, the accompanying explanatory guide said a smart man could learn it in a morning, while even a dumb man could pick it up in 10 days. This is probably about right—the alphabet is so simple, you can pick it up with relatively little effort. And for travelers, it IS worth putting in the time to learn—you'll be able to recognize place names, menu items and other pieces of helpful information.

USEFUL EXPRESSIONS

Greetings

Hello.	Annyeong hasimnikka? / Annyeong haseyo. 안녕하십니까? / 안녕하세요.
Goodbye.	Annyeonghi gaseyo (if the listener is leaving) / Annyeonghi gyeseyo (if the listener is staying). 안녕히 가세요 / 안녕히 계세요.
What's your name?	Ireumi moeyo? 이름이 뭐에요?
My name is...	Je ireumeun ...imnida. 제 이름은 ... 입니다.
Where are you from?	Eodieseo osheosseumnikka? 어디에서 오셨습니까?
I'm from...	Jeoneun _____-eseo wasseoyo. 저는 ____에서 왔어요.
Nice to meet you.	Mannaseo bangapseumnida. 만나서 반갑습니다.

Basic Terms

Yes.	Ne/Ye.	네/예.
No.	Ahniyo.	아니요.
Please... (always attached to the end of a request)	...Haejuseyo.	... 해주세요.
Thank you.	Gamsa hamnida.	감사합니다.
You're welcome.	Cheonmaneyo.	천만에요.
Excuse me.	Sillye hamnida.	실례합니다.
Sorry.	Jwoesong hamnida.	죄송합니다.

How to Ask for Directions

Excuse me.	Sillye hamnida.	실례합니다.
Where is...?	...eodie isseoyo?	...어디에 있어요?
I'm looking for a...	...reul/eul chatgo isseoyo.	...를/을 찾고있어요.

Question Words

Who?	Nugu seyo?	누구세요?
What is this?	Igeo moyeyo?	이게 뭐예요?
When?	Eonjeyo?	언제요?
Where?	Eodieyo?	어디에요?
How?	Eotteokeyo?	어떻게요?

How much is this?
Igeo eolma eyo?
이거 얼마에요?

Please lower the price.
Jogeum kkakka juseyo.
조금 깎아주세요.

That's too expensive.
Neomu bissayo.
너무 비싸요.

Please give me one.
Hana juseyo.
하나주세요.

Please give me a different one.
Dareun geo hana juseyo.
다른 거 하나 주세요.

Do you have any other colors?
Dareun saekkal iseu seyo?
다른 색깔 있으세요?

Please give me a larger size.
Deo keun saijeu juseyo.
더 큰 사이즈 주세요.

Please give me a smaller size.
Deo jageun saijeu juseyo.
더 작은 사이즈 주세요.

Please give me a receipt.
Yeongsujeung juseyo.
영수증 주세요.

Numbers and Shopping

Two numerical systems are used in Korea—Sino-Korean, or numbers based on Chinese characters, and native Korean. The two number systems are used in different situations. For example, Sino-Korean numerals are used when counting money, while native Korean numbers are used for telling a person's age.

	Sino-Korean		Native Korean	
0	영/공	yeong / gong	–	–
1	일	il	하나	hana
2	이	i	둘	dul
3	삼	sam	셋	set
4	사	sa	넷	net
5	오	o	다섯	daseot
6	육	yuk	여섯	yeoseot
7	칠	chil	일곱	ilgop
8	팔	pal	여덟	yeodeol
9	구	gu	아홉	ahop
10	십	sip	열	yeol
11	십일	sibil	열 하나	yeol hana
12	십이	sibi	열 둘	yeol dul
13	십삼	sipsam	열 셋	yeol set
14	십사	sipsa	열 넷	yeol net
15	십오	sibo	열 다섯	yeol daseot
16	십육	simnyuk	열 여섯	yeol yeoseot
17	십칠	sipchil	열 일곱	yeol ilgop
18	십팔	sippal	열 여덟	yeol yeodeol
19	십구	sipgu	열 아홉	yeol ahop
20	이십	isip	스물	seumul
30	삼십	samsip	서른	seoreun
40	사십	sasip	마흔	maheun
50	오십	osip	쉰	swin
60	육십	yuksip	예순	yesun
70	칠십	chilsip	일흔	ilheun
80	팔십	palsip	여든	yeodeun
90	구십	gusip	아흔	aheun
100	백	baek	온	on
1,000	천	cheon	즈믄	jeumeun
10,000	만	man	드먼	deumeon
100,000,000	억	eok	잘	jal

Accommodations

I'm looking for a ....

... chatgo isseoyo. ... 찾고 있어요.

- guesthouse / yeogwan 여관
- hotel / hotel 호텔
- youth hostel / yuseu hoseutel 유스호스텔

Do you have any rooms available?

jigeum bang isseoyo?   지금 방 있어요?

I'd like a...

...juseyo. ... 주세요.

- bed / chimdae 침대
- shared room / gachi sseuneun bang 같이 쓰는 방
- Western-style room / chimdae bang 침대 방
- Korean-style room / ondol bang 온돌 방
- room with a bathroom / yoksil inneun bang 욕실 있는 방

How much is it...?

... eolmayeyo?   ... 얼마예요?

- per night / harut bam 하룻밤
- per person / han saram 한 사람

Days of the Week

• Sunday	iryoil	일요일	• Monday	weoryoil	월요일
• Tuesday	hwayoil	화요일	• Wednesday	suyoil	수요일
• Thursday	mogyoil	목요일	• Friday	geumyoil	금요일
• Saturday	toyoil	토요일			

Directions

• North	bukjjok	북쪽	• South	namjjok	남쪽
• East	dongjjok	동쪽	• West	seojjok	서쪽
• Left	woenjjok	왼쪽	• Right	oreunjjok	오른쪽

When Driving or Giving Directions

- Go straight   jikjin   직진
- Turn left   jwahoejeon   좌회전
- Turn right   uhoejeon   우회전

Transportation

Please take me to...

...e gajuseyo.   ...에 가주세요.

How can I get to...?

...e eotteokke gayo?   ...에 어떻게 가요?

What time does the ... leave/arrive?

... eonje tteonayo/dochakhaeyo?

... 언제 떠나요/도착해요?

- airport bus   gonghang beoseu   공항 버스
- ferry boat   yeogaekseon   여객선
- bus   beoseu   버스
- city bus   sinae beoseu   시내 버스
- train   gicha   기차
- subway   jihacheol   지하철
- airplane   bihaenggi   비행기

I want to go to...

...e gago sipseumnida.   ...에 가고 싶습니다.

- the first / cheot 첫
- the last / majimak 마지막
- bus stop / beoseu jeongnyujang 버스정류장
- subway station / jihacheol yeok 지하철역
- train station / gicha yeok 기차역
- ticket vending machine / pyo japangi 표 자판기
- timetable / siganpyo 시간표

Food

- breakfast achim 아침
- dinner jeonyeok 저녁
- eat meogeoyo 먹어요
- lunch jeomsim 점심
- snack gansik 간식
- drink masyeoyo 마셔요

Can you recommend a...?

..chucheon hae jusillaeyo? ...추천 해 주실래요?

- bar/pub sul jip 술 집
- café kkape/keopisyop 까페/커피숍
- restaurant sikdang 식당

Ordering Food

I would like ___, please.
_____ juseyo. _____ 주세요.

Please give me more water.
Mul deo juseyo. 물 더 주세요.

Please ring up the bill.
Gyesan hae juseyo. 계산 해주세요.

Emergencies

Help! Dowa juseyo! 도와주세요!

I'm lost. Gireul ireosseoyo. 길을 잃었어요.

Leave me alone! Jom naebeoryeo duseyo! 좀 내버려 두세요!

Call...! ...bulleo juseyo! ...불러 주세요!

- a doctor / uisa 의사
- the police / gyeongchal 경찰
- an ambulance / gugeupcha 구급차

LANGUAGE PROGRAMS

Opportunities for learning Korean are numerous in the country. The most rigorous programs are offered by universities, which have 5-day-a-week programs with a policy requiring attendance in order to advance to the next level. Programs of varying intensities exist, however, including evening classes and weekend classes.

University Classes

University classes are the most intensive and usually the most effective, but are also the most rigorous and time-consuming. Sogang University is recognized for its strong emphasis on spoken Korean. The Yonsei, Seoul National University, and Ewha Womans University programs are well-known and extremely popular. They tend to emphasize written Korean, but build a strong base for learning the Korean language.

- **Sogang University:** Korean Language Education Center
  ℂ 02-705-8088 🖱 http://klec.sogang.ac.kr
- **Yonsei University:** Korean Language Institute
  ℂ 02-2123-8550 🖱 www.yskli.com
- **Seoul National University:** Korean Language Education Center
  ℂ 02-880-5483 🖱 http://lei.snu.ac.kr
- **Ewha Womans University:** Ewha Language Center
  ℂ 02-3277-3682~3 🖱 http://elc.ewha.ac.kr

Private Language Academies

Private academies are also available for learning Korean. Language academies are significantly cheaper than university programs, and tend to be much more flexible. However, the quality of instruction varies widely between academies, so be sure to observe a class before enrolling.

Free Language Programs

Free Korean language classes are available from a few civic organizations and volunteer groups, particularly for people in the migrant worker population.

- **Korea Foundation Cultural Center:** Classes are offered once a week on either Monday, Wednesday or Friday from 4 to 6 pm or 7 to 9 pm.
  ℂ 02-2046-8500 🖱 www.kfcenter.or.kr
- **Seoul Global Center:** Classes meet twice a week.
  ℂ 02-2075-4130 🖱 http://global.seoul.go.kr

PERFORMING ARTS

KOREAN PERFORMING ARTS

Music

Like most societies, Korea has a long musical tradition, best represented by so-called *gugak* ("national music"). In recent years, however, it's popular music of Western forms such as rock, pop and hip-hop that is dominating the airways. And not just Korea's airways, mind you— Korean pop music is gaining a huge following worldwide.

Gugak

Gugak ("National Music"), or Korean traditional music, is quite diverse and includes both vocal and instrumental music. Some forms of *gugak* are derived from Chinese musical forms, while others are native Korean forms.

Broadly speaking, Korean traditional music can be divided into court music, chamber music and folk music. *Aak* (court music) was the music that accompanied the important royal rites of the Joseon era. This is rarely performed today except by specialized organs such as the National Gugak Center or at rare events like the Jongmyo Jerye. *Jeongak* (chamber music) was the music that accompanied aristocratic banquets and parties. Folk music, meanwhile, consisted of folk songs and other musical forms for the masses.

With the introduction of Western musical forms, Korean traditional music has suffered from a general lack of interest, but has nevertheless survived. Korean traditional musicians have also been experimenting, breaking from set musical forms to create new works. Some musicians, meanwhile, are merging Korean and Western form to create "fusion" music.

Korean Traditional Musical Instruments

- **Gayageum**: A 12-string zither, frequently used as both a solo instrument and as accompaniment for vocal pieces.
- **Geomungo**: A 6-string zither.
- **Daegeum**: A bamboo transverse flute with a beautiful, breathy tone.
- **Piri**: A double-reed wind instrument that sounds similar to an oboe.
- **Haegeum**: A Korean fiddle with silk strings.

Pansori

Thanks in large part to director Im Kwon-taek's 1993 classic film *Sopyonje*, the Korean art of lyrical storytelling known as *pansori* has become one of Korea's best known traditional performing arts.

Often compared to the blues tradition of the United States, *pansori* is an extremely soulful way of singing. It involves a single vocalist accompanied by a drummer. The singer carries a folding fan to punctuate movements and announce scene changes. The *pansori* repertoire initially consisted of

12 tales, but only five remain today. The five include some of Korea's best loved folk tales, including the beautiful love story of Chunhyang and the moving tale of filial piety, Simcheong.

It's said that to be a real *pansori* master, you need to first embody the feeling of *han*, a sense of bitterness and loss that many Koreans will tell you is a uniquely Korean emotion. By all means, watch *Sopyonje* to get a better understanding of both *pansori* and *han*.

Pop Music

Korean pop music's history goes back to the 1930s, when Korean singers began performing Japanese musical forms—so-called "trot" music, similar to Japanese *enka* music, has its roots in this period. After independence, US pop music began infiltrating the country through the many US military bases around the country. Some of the early names in Korean pop, for instance, learned their craft in the clubs in front of US bases.

Since the 1990s, the most popular forms of music in Korea have included rap, pop, R&B, hip-hop and rock. In recent years, boy and girl bands have grown popular. A couple of big names are:

• **Rain**: Born Jeong Ji-hoon, Rain has been dazzling crowds with his smooth dancing and R&B tunes. He's also moved into acting, appearing in Hollywood films such as *Speed Racer* and *Ninja Assassin*.

• **BoA**: This female singer, influenced by American hip-hop and R&B, is actually even more popular in Japan than she is in Korea. Trained for stardom from a young age, she has used her language skills—she speaks Korean, Japanese, English and some Chinese—to good use in winning fans throughout Asia. She has recently attempted to break into the US music industry with her

debut English album, BoA.

• **Girls' Generation**: Also known as SNSD (an abbreviation of their Korean name, Sonyeo Sidae), Girls' Generation is a nine-member dance-pop girl band that, as of the writing of this book, might be the hottest group in Korea—according to Gallup Korea, they've been the most popular singers in Korea for three years straight. They're getting noticed overseas, too, with a recent appearance on the "David Letterman Show" in the United States. They're omnipresent in advertisements and commercials, too.

• **Super Junior**: At one time 13 members strong, boy band Super Junior has been the best selling K-pop group for three years straight. What's more, their success in areas outside of music, including acting, have inspired ambitious music producers to train their artists in a variety of arts, too.

• **Wonder Girls**: All five members of this highly popular girl group were selected through auditions. Huge commercial successes in Korea, they've managed to get on the radar in the United States, too, where their 2009 dance-pop hit "Nobody" became the first song by a Korean artist to make the Billboard chart.

• **2PM**: This six-member boy band has legions of fans in both Korea and overseas, especially Japan, where their single "Take Off" reached No. 1 in the charts. Their dance acts are particularly impressive.

- **Big Bang:** Five-member boy group Big Bang is known just as much for its flamboyant fashion taste as its music. They've been wildly successful both in Korea and Japan, and even managed to win Best Worldwide Act at the 2011 MTV Europe Music Awards.

- **2NE1:** The four members of girl group 2NE1 have an edgier, "punkier" look. If you like hip-hop and goth, this is your group. Initially linked to "Big Bang," to whom they are sometimes likened.

Dance

Koreans are a dancing people. Dance was traditionally used in both palace ceremonies and by the common people as a way of satirizing the nation's social elites. It also featured prominently in shaman ceremonies. Nowadays, it's mostly done for fun, although Korea has also produced a number of noted ballerinas, choreographers and modern dancers. Most notably, Korean crews have featured prominently in the world of B-boying, better known to those who grew up in the 1980s as breakdancing.

Traditional Dance

- **Court Dance:** Korean court dances, traditionally performed at state functions in the Joseon era, were divided into two forms, Chinese-derived dances and natively developed ones. The dances were often

KOREAN TRADITIONAL DANCES

Seungmu: ("Monk Dance"): Reportedly developed by Buddhist monks, this dance was further developed by Korea's *gisaeng*, or female entertainers. Performed in long, flowing robes, it is considered one of the most beautiful Korean dances.

Taepyeongmu ("Great Peace Dance"): The origin of this dance for peace is unknown, but it was developed into a folk dance in the early 20th century. It is performed by dancers wearing attire similar to that of Korea's kings and queens.

Talchum ("Mask Dance"): As the name would suggest, this dance was performed while wearing masks. The masks represent different social figures—corrupt aristocrats, lecherous monks, etc. These dances were performed by commoners to lampoon Korea's high-handed aristocracy. The Andong International Mask Dance Festival, held in the southeastern city of Andong every autumn, is probably the best time to see this form of dance.

Ganggangsullae: Traditionally performed by a circle of *hanbok*-clad women for the Chuseok holiday, this dance was offered as a prayer for a good harvest.

Buchaechum: ("Fan Dance"): Despite being a relatively modern creation, this dance—a development of earlier shaman and court dances—is one of the more commonly performed dances at traditional folk dance shows. The dancers use their fans to create images of flowers, butterflies and more.

performed by large numbers of specially trained dancers. Since the end of the monarchy, these dances have rarely been performed, although specialized organs like the National Gugak Center keep the tradition alive.

• **Folk Dances**: Korean folk dances, traditionally performed by farmers, Buddhist monks, shamans and other non-royal types, were performed for various social and religious functions. Some, like the *talchum* ("mask dance"), also served as means of expression, ways for the masses to criticize the corruption and absurdities of

the Joseon Dynasty's political and social elites.

* Places to see Korean traditional dance include the National Gugak Center (see p153) and Chongdong Theater (see p76).

Modern Dance

Western dance forms first came to Korea during the colonial period. Today, modern dance and ballet have healthy followings in Korea, while Korean dancers like Stuttgart Ballet principal dancer Kang Sue Jin bring their talents to a global audience.

• **B-Boy**: While its roots may be found in the streets and clubs of the South Bronx of the 1970s, B-boying a.k.a. Breakdancing has developed a huge following in Korea. Performed by small groups, or crews, this acrobatic form of dancing can be quite exhilarating to watch. In recent years, Korean B-boy crews have done exceptionally well in international competitions. B-boy is an important element in a number of Korean non-verbal performances, too, including "B-boy Korea," "Sachoom," "Battle B-boy," "Ballerina Who Loves B-Boy" and more.

MUSEUMS & GALLERIES

Seoul has a bewildering variety of museums large and small, public and private. They range from the mammoth National Museum of Korea, probably the largest museum in Asia, to smaller, quirkier gems tucked away in unexpected places. Galleries, meanwhile, are also to be found in abundance, exhibiting all forms of art in buildings that are often architectural specimens themselves. Here are just a few of the city's many museums and galleries.

HISTORY MUSEUMS

If there's one thing that Korea has a lot of, it's history. From the arrival of the nation's earliest mythical progenitor in 2333 BC to the kaleidoscopic sequence of upheavals in the 19th and 20th centuries, at least one museum in Seoul will have events covered.

National Museum of Korea

The largest storehouse of artifacts representing Korean history and culture, the National Museum of Korea relocated to a new facility in 2005. This new site makes the National Museum the sixth largest museum in the world in terms of floor space and the largest in Asia. The museum's collection includes approximately 150,000 artifacts, 5,000 pieces of which comprise the permanent exhibit. There are six permanent exhibition galleries: Pre-history

and Ancient History, Medieval and Early Modern History, Calligraphy and Painting, Donated Works, Sculpture and Crafts, Asian Arts and Outdoor Exhibitions. Guided tours of the museum are available multiple times daily in Korean, English, Chinese, Japanese and sign language.

⊕ 9 am to 6 pm (Tue, Thur, Fri), 9 am to 9 pm (Wed, Sat), 9 am to 7 pm (Sun, holidays) ⊟ Free; special exhibitions ticketed separately. 🚇 Ichon Station, Line 4 or Jungang Line, Exit 2 ✆ 02-2077-9045~7 🖰 www.museum.go.kr

National Palace Museum of Korea

Occupying the buildings on the grounds of the Gyeongbokgung Palace that formerly held the National Museum of Korea, this museum's large collection of royal artifacts from the Joseon era offers a fascinating glimpse into the lives of the country's monarchs and their courts.

⊕ 9 am to 6 pm (weekdays), 9 am to 7 pm (weekends) Ticket sales stop one hour to closing. Closed Mondays ⊟ As of the writing of this book, free. However, the museum plans to introduce ticketing at a yet-to-be-decided date. 🚇 Gyeongbokgung Station, Line 3, Exit 5; Gwanghwamun Station, Line 5, Exit 1 ✆ 02-3701-7500 🖰 www.gogung.go.kr

National Folk Museum of Korea

The place to go for those interested in the evolution of the lives of Korean people since prehistoric times. You can often catch folk performances here, too.

🕐 9 am to 6 pm (Mar–Oct), 9 am to 5 pm (Nov–Feb), 9 am to 7 pm (Sat, Sun, holidays). Ticket sales stop one hour to closing. Closed Tuesdays 🎫 As of the writing of this book, free. However, the museum plans to introduce ticketing at an as yet-to-be-decided date. 🚇 Gyeongbokgung Station, Line 3, Exit 5; Anguk Station, Line 3, Exit 1 ☎ 02-3074-3114 🌐 www.nfm.go.kr

The War Memorial of Korea

A huge complex of indoor and outdoor exhibition halls, offering a better understanding of the conflict that left such huge scars on the Korean peninsula in the early 1950s.

🕐 9 am to 6 pm. Ticket sales stop one hour to closing. Closed Mondays 🎫 Free 🚇 Samgakji Station, Line 4 or 6, Exit 12 ☎ 02-709-3139 🌐 www.warmemo.or.kr

Seoul Museum of History

The place to go for those who want to know the stories that lie behind and beneath today's metropolis.

🕐 Weekdays 9 am to 9 pm; Weekends & holidays 9 am to 7 pm (Mar–Oct), 9 am to 6 pm (Nov–Feb) 🎫 Free 🚇 Gwanghwamun Station, Line 5, Exit 7 ☎ 02-724-0274 🌐 http://museum.seoul.kr

Seodaemun Prison History Hall

Constructed during the Japanese occupation of Korea, Seodaemun Prison was used to imprison, torture and execute Korean nationalist patriots. The prison is generally well preserved and is a moving monument documenting the history of the Korean independence movement and the exemplary individuals who made incredible sacrifices in the name of Korean nationalism.

🕐 9:30 am to 6 pm (Mar–Oct), 9:30 am to 5 pm (Nov–Feb). Closed Mondays 🎫 Adults 1,500 won, Children 500 won 🚇 Dongnimmun Station, Line 3, Exits 4 & 5 ☎ 02-360-8582

Independence Hall of Korea

Located about an hour outside of town in the city of Cheonan, Independence Hall aims to educate visitors about the history of the Korean independence movement during the Japanese colonial period. Its exhibits focus on enriching understanding of the patriotism of Koreans throughout history, particularly during the Japanese occupation. Independence Hall also includes a Reunification Monument, a Patriots Memorial and a Circle Vision Theater with a 360-degree screen.

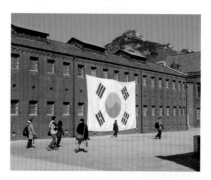

⊙ 9:30 am to 6 pm (Mar–Oct), 9:30 am to 5 pm (Nov–Feb). Ticket sales stop one hour to closing. Closed Mondays 🖃 Free 🖾 From Cheonan Express Bus Terminal, take Bus No. 400 to Independence Hall (about 30 minutes); From Cheonan Train Station, take Bus No. 400 to Independence Hall (about 20 minutes). ✆ 041-560-0114 🖐 www.independence.or.kr

ART MUSEUMS & GALLERIES

Seoul is a city with a vibrant arts culture. Besides a number of nationally sponsored museums, the city is replete with boutique galleries and art collections.

Seoul Museum of Art

Housed in the former Korean Supreme Court Building, SeMA is a contemporary art museum that functions as an important cultural space in the city of Seoul. This museum makes a concerted effort to combine pieces that exemplify current trends in Korean contemporary art with the work of foreign artists who represent the modern art trends abroad.

⊙ Weekdays 10 am to 8 pm; Weekends and holidays 10 am to 7 pm (Mar–Oct), 10 am to 6 pm (Nov–Feb). Closed Mondays 🖃 Free 🖾 City Hall Station, Line 1, Exit 1 or Line 2, Exit 11 or 12 ✆ 02-2124-8800 🖐 http://seoulmoa.seoul.go.kr

National Museum of Contemporary Art, Korea

The National Museum of Contemporary Art showcases both Korean and international contemporary modern art, with the aim of educating citizens and cultivating a culturally rich atmosphere in Seoul. Established in 1969, the museum rapidly expanded to accommodate increasing interest and moved to its present location in 1986. Visitors can trace the development of modern Korean art, particularly in the genres of painting, sculpture and crafts.

⊙ Weekdays 10 am to 6 pm (Mar–Oct), 10 am to 5 pm (Nov–Feb); Weekends 10 am to 9 pm (Mar–Oct), 10 am to 8 pm (Nov–Feb). Closed Mondays 🖃 Permanent Exhibition Free; Special Exhibitions 3,000 won. 4th Saturday of each month free. 🖾 Seoul Grand Park Station, Line 4, Exit 4. Take shuttle bus (arrives every 20-30 min). ✆ 02-2188-6000 🖐 www.moca.go.kr

National Museum of Contemporary Art— Deoksugung

The National Museum of Contemporary Art was once housed in this space at Deoksugung before the collection expanded and was relocated to Gwacheon. After the move, this space was transformed into the National Museum of Art, serving as an annex space. Many special exhibitions are hosted here.

⊙ 10 am to 9 pm. Closed Mondays 🖃 Depends on exhibition 🖾 City Hall Station, Line 1, Exit 2 or Line 2, Exit 12, or a 20-minute walk from Exit 1, 2 or 3 ✆ 02-2022-0600

Seoul Calligraphy Art Museum—Seoul Arts Center

The world's only museum dedicated to calligraphy alone, offering education in calligraphy and traditional paintings, as well as exhibitions.

⊕ 11 am to 8 pm (Mar–Oct), 11 am to 7 pm (Nov–Feb) 🎫 Depends on exhibition 🚇 Nambu Bus Terminal Station, Line 3, Exit 5. Walk for 5-10 minutes. ✆ 02-580-1651 🖰 www.sac.or.kr

Gana Art Center

An architectural gem of a gallery situated in the beautiful mountainside neighborhood of Pyeongchang-dong.

⊕ 10 am to 7 pm 🎫 3,000 won 🚇 Take green bus 1020 or 1711 from Exit 3, Gyeongbokgung Station, Line 3 ✆ 02-720-1020 🖰 www.ganaart.com

Insa-dong

Insa-dong, the traditional arts and crafts center of Seoul, is home to many small art

galleries. Art galleries began to settle in the area in the 1970s and now number around 70. Galleries display the work of both professional traditional artists, whose creations are considered intangible cultural assets, and amateur artists. All works can be purchased for personal collections.

CERAMICS

Koreans have been producing cermaics since the neolithic age. The golden age of Korean ceramics, however, were the Goryeo (918-1392) and Joseon (1392-1910) eras, when Korean pottery grew famous throughout Asia. Goryeo artisans were particularly renowned for their jade-colored celadon (*cheongja*) masterpieces, while Joseon potters were known for their white porcelain (*baekja*). So well-respected were Korean ceramic  artisans that they were highly valued war booty—during the Japanese invasions of the late 16th century, Korean potters were often dragged away to Japan, where they contributed significantly to Japan's ceramics industry—so much so, in fact, that in Japan, the invasions are sometimes referred to as the "Pottery War."

Korean pottery, naturally enough, has been influenced by religious and cultural trends within society—Joseon ceramics, for instance, are white and simply adorned, a reflection of the rustic simplicity favored by the era's Confucian elites. Even today, Korean potters favor a simple, naturalistic aesthetic you can see at the many pottery shops of Insa-dong.

Korean traditional wood-burning kilns can still be found aplenty in countryside towns just outside of Seoul like Icheon (see p212), Gwangju and Yeoju. The pottery villages of Icheon, in particular, are good places to pick up quality ceramics at reasonable prices.

Bukchon

The Bukchon area, a neighborhood of traditional Korean residential homes, has a culturally rich and authentic atmosphere making it an ideal site for art galleries. This unique area is home to a number of traditional and contemporary art galleries, most of them art boutiques.

Hakgojae Gallery

A gallery by the western wall of the Gyeongbokgung Palace that works on the principle of creating the new by understanding the old. The building itself is divided between traditional and modern styles.
⊙ Weekdays 9:30 am to 7 pm, Weekends 10 am to 6pm (Mar to Nov); Mon to Sat 10 am to 6 pm (Dec to Feb). Closed Mondays ▣ Free ▣ Anguk Station, Line 3, Exit 1 ✆ 02-720-1524 ⚲ www.hakgojae.com

Museum of Korean Embroidery

This small museum provides a glimpse into the world of the feminine craft of traditional Korean embroidery. On display are approximately 3,000 items, from patchwork wrapping cloths and boxes to screens, shoes and thimbles. While there are no English descriptions posted within the exhibit, illustrated books on Korean embroidery are available for purchase.
⊙ 10 am to 4 pm. Closed Weekends & public holidays ▣ Free ▣ Hakdong Station, Line 7, Exit 10 ✆ 02-515-5114 ⚲ www.bojagii.com

---

KOREAN PAINTING

Traditionally, Korean painting has been influenced greatly by Chinese artistic forms and Buddhism. In a country as scenically beautiful as Korea, perhaps it's no surprise that landscape paintings were a particular favorite of Korean painters, especially so-called *sansuhwa*, or "Mountains and Water Paintings." Buddhist temples, meanwhile, are home to countless treasures of Buddhist iconography, including brilliantly colored hanging screens and wall murals. In the 18th century, great painters like Kim Hong-do and Sin Yun-bok focused their brushes on depicting the daily lives of Koreans, both aristocrats and commoners, often to great comedic effect. Separate from the highly rarefied paintings preferred by the upper class, the common folk have traditionally enjoyed so-called folk paintings. Folk paintings were typically produced by unknown artists for practical purposes, including simple decoration and to ward off evil spirits. These paintings often use animals such as the tiger, mountain spirits or Confucian symbols as popular motifs. In the modern era, Korean painters have by and large moved away from Eastern painting styles and adopted Western styles, although some continue to plug away at Korean styles or combine the two.

A folk painting from Gahoe Museum (see p69)

FESTIVALS

SEOUL

In recent years, Seoul has grown increasingly keen on hosting festivals, both as a means of building community spirit and, of course, to bring in the tourists. Two highlights of the year are the Hi Seoul Festival, when the entire downtown area becomes one big street party, and the Lotus Lantern Festival, a popular Buddhist celebration and parade most famous for its beautiful floats and lanterns. The regions around Seoul, too, have their own interesting festivals that may interest the visitor.

Hi Seoul Festival Spring

The Hi Seoul Festival, held annually in spring, is one of the biggest bashes of Seoul's social calendar. First convened in 2003, the weeklong festival—organized by the Seoul Foundation for Arts and Culture—aims to bring Seoul's residents together to celebrate the city's culture and history and build a stronger sense of community. The festival program includes cultural performances, parades, charity events, international food festivals and more, although the specifics depend on the festival theme, which changes annually. Most of the festival events are held in the old downtown area, particularly at Seoul Plaza in front of Seoul City Hall.
🖬 Free ⓒ 02-3290-7000 ♨ www.hiseoulfest.org

Unhyeongung Festival April & October

On the third or fourth Saturdays of April and October, the wedding ceremony between King Gojong (see p37) and Queen Myeongseong (see p53) is reenacted in this festival, held twice each year on the spot where the marriage actually took place.
🏠 Unhyeongung Palace 🚇 Anguk Station, Line 3, Exit 4 ⓒ 02-766-9090
♨ www.unhyeongung.or.kr

Lotus Lantern Festival May

One of the most highly anticipated celebrations of the year because of its cultural authenticity, this annual celebration takes place around the time of Buddha's birthday, which falls on the 8th day of the 4th lunar month. At the festival, visitors can

create their own lotus lanterns, watch Buddhist performances, experience Buddhist culture and view exhibits of traditional lanterns. The culminating event of the festival occurs on the Sunday evening before Buddha's birthday, when a massive lotus lantern parade of over 100,000 lanterns takes place on Jongno Street running from Dongdaemun Stadium to Jogyesa Temple. The beautiful sight of thousands of paper lanterns winding down the street to Jogyesa Temple is not to be missed.

⊙ Week of Buddha's Birthday (8th day of 4th lunar month) 🎫 Free 🚇 Jonggak Station, Line 1, Exit 2; Anguk Station, Line 3, Exit 6 ✆ 02-2011-1744

Insa Korean Art and Culture Festival May or June

Going strong for two decades, the Insa Korean Art and Culture Festival celebrates Insa-dong's heritage as a center of the Korean traditional arts and crafts. There are street performances, historical reenactments, singing, dancing and more.

🏠 Insa-dong 🚇 Jonggak Station, Line 1, Exit 3

Dano Festival Late May or Early June

In traditional Korea, Dano—held on the fifth day of the fifth lunar month—was one of the most important holidays. In the modern era, its importance has waned, but nobody's told Namsangol Hanok Village this. Participants can try Korean traditional wrestling, wash their hair with water infused with iris, swing on a Korean traditional swing and experience other Dano traditions.

🏠 Namsangol Hanok Village 🚇 Chungmuro Station, Line 3 or 4, Exit 3 or 4

Seoul Fringe Festival August

Like its progenitor, the Edinburgh Fringe Festival, the Seoul Fringe Festival is a celebration of non-mainstream and mostly youth-oriented arts, including theater, painting, music and street performances. Not surprisingly, it's held in the Hongik University area, the heart of Seoul's indie culture. Artistic troupes from all over Asia attend.

🏠 Hongik University Area 🚇 Hongik University Station, Line 2, Exit 9 ✆ 02-325-8150 🖱 www.seoulfringe.net

Chungmuro Film Festival Aug–Sept

An outdoor international film festival, the Chungmuro Film Festival features classic works and current trends in the modern film industry. The festival, which draws about 700,000 visitors a year, includes outdoor film screenings, a domestic film competition, a master class, and seminars and workshops.

🏠 Film theaters in the Chungmu-ro area. 🚇 Chungmuro Station, Line 3 or 4. ✆ 02-2236-6231-4 🖱 www.chiffs.kr

Seoul Drum Festival September

This highly anticipated percussion festival features a series of performances by Korean and international drum artists. Visitors are introduced to traditional Korean percussion music as well as the percussion ensembles of various international artists.

🏠 Ttukseom Seoul Forest. 🚇 Seoul Plaza, City Hall Station, Line 1 or 2, Exit 5 ✆ 02-3290-7000 🖱 www.seouldrum.go.kr

Seoul International Dance Festival October

Seoul International Dance Festival, also known as SIDance, began in 1998 with the purpose of promoting Korean dance in the international arena. This notable festival features Korea's leading contemporary dance performers, as well as an array of invited international modern dance groups and collaborative performances.

🏠 Performing art venues throughout Seoul ✆ 02-3216-1185 🖱 www.sidance.org

Seoul Herbal Medicine Festival October

Held at the sprawling Jegi-dong Herbal Medicine Market, this is a great opportunity for visitors to learn about Korea's herbal medicine heritage. Herbalists perform free medical examinations, and expensive herbal medicines can often be purchased at affordable prices.
🏠 Jegi-dong Herbal Medicine Market
🚇 Jegi-dong Station, Line 1

Seoul Performing Arts Festival Oct–Nov

This annual performing arts festival showcases the latest theater, dance and fusion pieces in the contemporary performing arts world. Performers hail from all over the world, and the festival includes some collaborative pieces between Korean artists and international artists. This festival, the largest performing arts festival in Korea, always proves itself to be at the cutting edge of modern performing arts.
🏠 Daehangno Theater District 🚇 Daehangno Station, Line 4, Exit 1 or 4. ✆ 02-3673-2561 🖰 www.spaf.or.kr

OUTSIDE SEOUL

Boryeong Mud Festival July

An annual event since 1997, the Boryeong Mud Festival is an enormously popular gathering that draws about two million visitors each year. For ten days, visitors come to Daecheon Beach to enjoy about 200 tons of mud. Activities include a giant mud pool, a mud photography contest, mud body painting, mud *ssireum* (Korean wrestling), mud soccer, and the Super Mud Slide—a 44-m-long, 12-m-high inflatable slide. Additionally, visitors can enjoy street parades and performances and meet celebrity guests. The event is sponsored by

a cosmetics company that creates its products out of Boryeong mud, which contains a healthy level of infrared rays that revitalize the skin.
🏠 Daecheon Beach, Chungcheongbuk-do
🚇 Trains for Boryeong Station leave from Yongsan Station. Trip takes about 2 hours, 40 minutes ✆ 041- 930-3882 🖰 www.mudfestival.or.kr

Puchon International Fantastic Film Festival July

This unique independent film festival distinguishes itself from traditional film festivals by focusing on works of a more imaginative and futuristic bent. Films featured in this festival come from the genres of fantasy, science fiction, horror, thriller and adventure, as well as animation.
🏠 Bucheon 🚇 Songnae Station, Line 1. Exit the station in the North Square direction, from where you can take a shuttle bus or embark on a 15-minute walk to Boksagol Cultural Center ✆ 032-327-6313 🖰 www.pifan.com

Jisan Valley Rock Festival July

From nowhere in 2008 to hosting big hitters such as Weezer and Oasis (2009), Muse and Vampire Weekend (2010) and Radiohead (2012), Jisan Valley Rock

Festival has claimed the crown of Korea's biggest rock event, with a location and line-ups that have propelled Korea to being a real contender in the Asian summer rock festival circuit.

🏠 Jisan Forest Resort, Icheon 🚇 Take Bus No. 103 from Yongin Bus Terminal and get off at Jisan Forest Resort. ☏ 1566-2226 🌐 valleyrockfestival.mnet.com

Pentaport Rock Festival
Last Weekend of July

The Pentaport Rock Festival is one of the largest live music events in Korea. It features many genres of music, but particularly focuses on rock and electronic styles. The festival aims to cultivate an open environment for collective music appreciation and environmental consciousness.

🏠 Songdo, Incheon 🎫 88,000/ 132,000/ 165,000 won for 1-, 2-, 3-day tickets 🚇 Dongmak Station, Incheon Subway. Take a shuttle bus to venue. 🌐 www.pentaportrock.com

Andong International Maskdance Festival
September

The *talchum*, or masked dance, genre is one of Korea's most distinctive and socially fascinating traditions. Not simply dances but danced dramas, these performances often contain bitterly satirical social messages and frequently functioned as a means of venting the common people's wrath at the figures who maintained the social system: apostate Buddhist monks, corrupt and decadent noblemen, and shamans. Andong International Maskdance Festival (maskdance.com), held in Hahoe Village every autumn, features not only Korea's beautiful *talchum*, but other forms of masked dance from all over the world as well.

🏠 Hahoe Village, Andong 🚇 Take Bus No. 46 from Andong Intercity Bus Terminal to Hahoe Village ☏ 054-841-6397~8 🌐 maskdance.com

Korean Traditional Performing Arts Festival September

The Korean Traditional Performing Arts Festival showcases Korea's numerous traditional performing arts in different genres, including *madanggeuk* (outdoor theater), shadow theater, dance musicals, *minyo* (traditional Korean folk song) musicals, percussion music and mime. Many of Korea's greatest cultural figures, considered intangible cultural assets, participate in this festival.

🏠 National Museum of Korea 🚇 Ichon Station, Line 4 and Jungang Line, Exit 2 ☏ 02-580-3265 🌐 www.openpan.com

Chungju World Martial Arts Festival
Late Sept or Early Oct

Hosted by the city of Chungju, the home of the ancient Korean martial art of *taekkyeon*, this festival celebrates martial arts. It includes demonstrations of different martial arts from around the world, boasting participation from over 30 international martial arts groups annually.

🏠 Chungju, Chungcheongbuk-do 🚇 Buses leave for Chungju from Seoul's Dong Seoul Terminal. Trip takes about 1 hour, 40 minutes. ☏ 043-850-7981 🌐 www.martialarts.or.kr

Busan International Film Festival October

One of the most influential film festivals in all of Asia, the Busan International Film Festival focuses primarily on Asian films. However, works are screened from all over the world, allowing visitors to gain a comprehensive understanding of international trends in the film industry. Films are screened simultaneously in multiple theaters, as well as on a giant outdoor screen in Suyeongman Bay.

🚇 It takes three hours to get from Seoul to Busan by KTX express train. Frequent trains to Busan depart from Seoul Station. ☏ 051-747-3010 🌐 www.biff.kr

ACTIVITIES

SPAS & SAUNAS

In Korea, saunas are a popular nighttime destination. In fact, Korean-style saunas are growing increasingly popular outside of Korea, too, especially in the United States, where Koreatown saunas are gaining the attention of neighboring communities.

Like bathhouses everywhere, Korean saunas have shower facilities, hot and cold baths, and saunas (very often several types of sauna). Major sauna/spa facilities—called *jjimjilbang* in Korean—have much more, including unisex lounge facilities, TV rooms, restaurants and massage services. Most have a sleeping room, too—in fact, if you're looking for a place to bed down for the night on the cheap, saunas are a good option.

The Jjimjilbang Experience

All *jjimjilbang* complexes contain a bath section where guests get thoroughly soaked and scrubbed. The Korean concept of getting thoroughly washed goes beyond cleaning the surface of the skin—it involves taking off the surface of the skin. This is usually accomplished with the use of small, rough cloths that rub away the outer layers of dead skin cells, leaving the victim glowing red for a while. These cloths usually come in bright green, yellow or red colors and can be bought very cheaply at the entrance to most bathhouses and steam

rooms. Ask for an "*itaeri tawol*" if you can't already see them. Scrubbing each other's backs is considered a good way of expressing friendship between friends or between fathers and sons.

There are plenty of showers around the baths themselves. The unbreakable rule is that bathers wash themselves thoroughly in the shower, from head to foot, before getting into the baths.

Washing in the baths is just the beginning of a proper *jjimjilbang* experience. From here onwards, customers don the comfortable, loose-fitting cotton clothes they were issued at the entrance and settle down for any number of hours in rooms of varying degrees of heat and humidity. Sexual segregation ends at the exit of the baths, allowing whole families, couples or groups of friends to enjoy each other's company. Warm lounges, steamy saunas, massage rooms, PC rooms and sometimes DVD rooms are just some of the elements that make up a typical *jjimjilbang* complex. But it is the opportunity for socializing in a self-contained, comfortable space, free from outside concerns, that gives *jjimjilbang* their enduring appeal.

Recommended Spas

Dragon Hill Spa p128: Seven floors of spa goodness await you at this massive complex next to Yongsan Station. The main hall sports a Chinese design motif, but the rest of the place is an assortment of different

Dragon Hill Spa

8,000 won (day), 10,000 won (night), 10,000 won (weekends) 🚇 Leave Exit 3 of Jangji Station, Line 8 and walk 700 m ☎ 02-404-2700

Sports Club Seoul Leisure p155: Also located in Songpa-gu, this is a massive complex with a health club, screen golf range, swimming pool and squash court...in addition to a well-equipped sauna and bathhouse and several kinds of Korean-style steam rooms. 8,000 won (day), 10,000 won (night) 🚇 Exit 1 of Bangi Station, Line 5 ☎ 02-404-7000

Oh Happyday Sports Center D1, p152: Seven above-ground floors (eight all together) of splish-splashy fun in the district of Gwangjin-gu in eastern Seoul. Make use of the wide variety of Korean kiln saunas, Western-style saunas, hot and cool pools and other facilities. Golf fans will love the rooftop screen golf simulator. 8,000 won (day), 10,000 won (night). 1,000 won deposit for robe rental ☎ 02-452-5656

saunas (including a charcoal sauna), baths, whirlpools, lounge facilities, pools and more. Check out the heated outdoor pool while you're here. The spa tends to be quite popular with foreigners. 10,000 won (5 am to 8 pm), 12,000 won (8 pm to 5 am) ☎ 02-797-0002

Itaewonland F3, p123: Located in the heart of foreigner-friendly Itaewon, this five-story spa has six kinds of steam rooms and kiln saunas (including an ice room), bathing rooms, DVD rooms, massage rooms, a karaoke room and sleeping facilities. 6,000 won (day), 8,000 won (night) ☎ 02-749-4122~3

Central Spa A3, p152: Located in Central City (near Express Bus Terminal), this sauna has all the facilities you'd expect in a spa—including a charcoal sauna—with the added bonus of being located in a big shopping mall. 10,000 won (5 am to 9 pm), 13,000 won (9 pm to 5 am) 🚇 Exit 7 of Express Bus Terminal Station, Line 3 or Exit 4 of Line 7 ☎ 02-6282-3400

Spa in Garden 5 p155: This smartly designed spa in the Songpa-gu district of Seoul (near Lotte World) is big and very well-appointed with state-of-the-art facilities. If you like your spas with a big helping of style, this is the place to go.

KARAOKE

Karaoke is a popular nocturnal pastime in Korea, where karaoke clubs are called *noraebang* ("singing rooms"). Unlike karaoke clubs in the West, however, Korean *noraebang* consist mostly of private rooms where friends gather to sing, dance and drink till the wee hours. If you go out for a night in the town with Korean friends, chances are high you will end up in such an establishment before morning's light. Most *noraebang* play both Korean and Western standards; those in Seoul's developing ethnic neighborhoods like Dongdaemun have music in other languages as well.

Be advised that in addition to *noraebang*, there are more upscale forms of karaoke clubs, too. *Dallanjujeom*, for instance, employ hostesses who sing, dance and chat with customers. Really, really upscale *dallanjujeom* are called room salons—if you're independently wealthy or playing with a corporate expense account, these places can be great fun, but an evening can easily cost in the thousands of US dollars.

Noraebang can be found aplenty in all entertainment areas. Costs differ, but a basic *noraebang* usually costs about 12,000 to 20,000 won an hour.

INTERNET CAFÉS

You'd think in a country where almost every household has a computer and broadband Internet access that there wouldn't be much of a need for Internet cafés.

But you'd be wrong. Seoul is home to countless *PC bang*, or Korean-style Internet cafés. Like their counterparts in the West, the *PC bang* will have rows of computers for costumers to use. Most *PC bang* have vending machines or refrigerators from which you can purchases cans of coffee or soft drinks (or simple snacks like instant noodles). *PC bang* usually have cards at the front desk with an ID number to imput to start up your computer. Hourly rates input are cheap: usually 1,000 won.

Where the *PC bang* differs from the Western Internet café is its raison d'être—whereas the Internet café is used primarily to check email and surf the web, the *PC bang* is dedicated to one thing—gaming. Walk into a *PC bang*, and you'll find dozens of people absorbed in online games. Younger Koreans tend to enjoy RTS (real-time simulation) games like Starcraft and World of Warcraft or first-person shooters like Counter-Strike, while older Koreans tend towards online games of *baduk* (Japanese: *go*) and Go Stop (a card game using Japanese *hanafuda* cards, called *hwatu* in Korean). Many gamers spend hours at a *PC bang*, while some even spend the entire day or, on rare occasions, even more.

Korean gaming culture is strongly influenced by Confucian norms, which is to say, Koreans game as a group. The *PC bang* plays an important role in this regard—it allows groups of friends to gather in one spot to enjoy gaming together, barking out commands, jeering and encouraging one another as they go. This contrasts with the Western gamer, who tends toward the "lone wolf" approach to gaming.

Of course, if all you want to do is check your email or chat with your friends back home, you can do that at a *PC bang*, too. Video chatting is quite popular in Korea, and most *PC bang* have computers set up for it.

KOREA'S "BANG" CULTURE
History and Culture

The term *bang* means "room" in Korean, and you'll see it used for a lot of establishments about town. Besides the *noraebang*, PC *bang* and *jjimjilbang*, other *bang* include:

- *Bidiobang:* "Video rooms," where you can watch videos.
- *DVD bang:* Like a *bidiobang*, with DVDs.
- *Manhwabang:* "Comic rooms," where you can read comic books.

ZEN PRACTICE

Seoul International Zen Center
90-Day Intensive Meditation Retreat Program

Affiliated with Hwagyesa, a Buddhist temple located on a ridge of Bukhansan Mountain, Seoul International Zen Center offers a 90-day intensive meditation retreat program each summer and winter. Participants examine Buddha's teachings and the concept of enlightenment in this intensive study. Interested individuals can also opt for a shorter program, with a minimum stay of one week. The Seoul Zen Center also offers free Sunday meditation classes.

⊕ Sat noon to Sun 10 am ⑤ 40,000 won (day); 350,000-450,000 won (month) ⓔ Suyu Station, Line 4. Take taxi to Hwagyesa ⓒ 02-900-4326 ⬙ http://seoulzen.org

Most other Buddhist temples offer one- to two-day temple experience programs, including Jogyesa (the headquarters of the Jogye Buddhist Order), Naksan Myogaksa (a temple embedded in a natural environment and the headquarters of the Kwan-Um Order of Korean Buddhism) and Bongeunsa (an expansive temple located next to COEX Mall).

Seoul International Zen Center

Ahnkook Zen Center

Located in Seoul's beautiful Bukchon neighborhood, Ahnkook Zen Center offers foreigners classes (in English) every Saturday from 2:30 to 4 pm. The classes are taught by foreign lecturers who majored in Korean Buddhism, with a focus on the scriptures of Korean Buddhism and Korean Buddhism culture.

⑤ Free ⓔ Anguk Station, Line 3, Exit 2. From there, walk north toward the Gahoe Museum. ⓒ 02-732-0772 ⬙ www.ahnkookzen.org

Jogyesa Temple

Jogyesa Temple offers a variety of programs. The basic program includes a tea ceremony, meditation and a guided tour of the temple. The experience program offers a meal at the temple and a program explaining the traditional dishes and dining etiquette of Korean monks. The participation program teaches Buddhist painting and lotus-lantern-making.

⑤ 10,000 won per program. Reservations should be made one week in advance. ⓔ Jonggak Station, Line 1, Exit 2; Anguk Station, Line 3, Exit 6. ⓒ 02-732-5115 ⬙ www.jogyesa.kr

Naksan Myogaksa

Myogaksa's program includes striking the *beomjong* (temple bell), singing Buddhist songs, dining in the traditional Buddhist manner with traditional Buddhist dishes, constructing lotus lanterns and conversing with monks.

⑤ One-day program: 20,000 won, two-day program: 30,000 won; Temple experience participants must bring their own toiletries and personal items. Temple experience uniforms are provided. ⓔ Dongmyo Station, Line 1 or 6, Exit 2 ⓒ 02-763-3109 ⬙ www.myogaksa.net

Lotus Lantern International Meditation Center

Located not far from Jeondeungsa Temple on the Ganghwado Island, this international meditation center is home to foreign monks and nuns and open to lay people who wish to experience Korean Buddhism. It conducts two-night and three-night programs every weekend (except the last weekend of the month). Instruction is in English.

💰 50,000-70,000 won 🚌 Take the bus to Onsu-ri from Sinchon Bus Terminal (Exit 7, Sinchon Station, Line 2). When you get off at Onsu-ri, take a taxi to the Lotus Lantern International Meditation Center (Yeondeung Gukje Seonwon). ☎ 032-937-7032~3 🖐 www.lotuslantern.net

KOREAN TRADITIONAL MEDICINE

Korea has a long and time-honored medical tradition with a history as long as that of the Korean people itself—the Korean foundation myth, after all, involves a she-bear eating the medicinal herb mugwort. Korean traditional medicine shares many of the same practices as Chinese traditional medicine, although many of Korea's medicinal herbs are unique to Korea.

Korean medicine is holistic, which is to say, it sees body and mind as an interconnected whole. While acute illnesses and injuries might be better off treated by a modern (i.e. Western) physician, chronic disorders such as arthritis, obesity and fatigue often respond well to Korean medicine. Its holistic approach also promotes wellness and prevents the onset of illness.

Korean Traditional Medical Practices

Korean traditional medicine doctors, or *hanuisa*, prescribe treatment after diagnosing the patient. Diagnosis is given following a patient physical status and analysis of his or her lifestyle. Korean medicine also makes use of *sasang uihak*, a medical typology in which individuals are characterized by four body types based on *yin-yang* theory; certain body types are more susceptible to certain illnesses than others. Common treatments include:

Herbal Medicine

Korean medicine makes use of a wide variety of medicinal herbs (the Korea Pharmacopoeia lists 395 medicinal herbs in current use), often used in combination with one another for heightened medical effect. Herb preparation varies widely, too: some herbs are dried, for instance, while others are

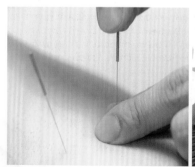

boiled to create liquid remedies. Most are taken orally, although creams and oils are also made.

Acupuncture

According to Korean traditional medical theory, there are 365 acupuncture points on the human body. When stimulated (using acupuncture needles made of gold, silver or platinum), these point can enhance the flow of energy throughout the body, promoting organ function and curing illnesses. Which points are stimulated depends on the disorder the doctor is attempting to treat.

Moxibustion

In this technique, a stick of burning mugwort is placed on the skin, usually above an ill or injured part, to warm the area and promote blood and energy flow.

Cupping

Similarly, the use of heated glass cups that stick to the skin of the back stimulates energy flow points, promotes circulation and has a detoxifying effect. This technique leaves you with telltale red circles on your back (these go away in a few days, though).

Recommended Korean Medicine Centers

Jaseng Hospital of Oriental Medicine : This well-known hospital specializes in non-surgical treatments for spinal disorders, blending Korean and Western treatment methods. Its international clinic has specialists who speak English, German, Japanese and Chinese. ⊙ 9 am to 6 pm. Closed Tuesdays 🚇 There is hospital shuttle bus service from Exit 2 of Apgujeong Station, Line 3 ☎ 02-3218-2105 🖥 www.jaseng.net

Oriental Medical Hospital, Kyung Hee University: Founded in 1971, Kyung Hee University's Oriental Medicine Hospital is one of the largest East Asian medical centers in the world, with 300 beds and 99 doctors in eight departments.
⊙ 9 am to 5 pm (weekdays), 9 am to noon (Sat). Closed Sundays 🚇 Hoegi Station, Line 1. Walk 10 minutes or take a local (green) bus from the station to Kyung Hee University ☎ 02-958-8114 🖥 www.khuoh.or.kr

Amicare : Located in Apgujeong-dong, this small Korean traditional medicine hospital is run by Kim So-hyung, a former Miss Korea. It is particularly known for its healthy diet treatments.
⊙ 10 am to 9 pm (Mon), 10 am to 10 pm (Tue, Thu), 10 am to 7 pm (Fri), 10 am to 4 pm (Sat). Closed Wednesdays and Sundays 🚇 Exit 3, Apgujeong Station, Line 3. Walk 400 meters and it's on the left. ☎ 02-544-6500 🖥 www. n-clinic.com

Jahayun Clinic : Located in Sinsa-dong, not far from Apgujeong-dong, Jahayun Clinic specializes in treatments for nervous disorders using herbal medicines. It also provides Korean traditional medicine treatments for dieting, skincare, gynecological health and infertility.
⊙ 9:30 am to 6:30 pm (Mon, Fri) 9:30 am to 8 pm (Tue, Thu) 2 pm to 6:30 pm (Wed) 9:30 am to 4 pm (Sat) 🚇 Exit 3 of Gangnam-gu Office Station, Line 7. Walk 10 minutes to Hakdong Junction. You will see the Cine City building diagonally opposite. Jahayun is on the second floor of the KMD Building, just next door to Cine City. ☎ 02-3448-7575 🖥 www.jahayun.com

Choonwondang : First founded in 1847, this Korean traditional medicine practitioner's has a Korean traditional medicine museum and conducts exhibits and educational programs.
⊙ 9 am to 6 pm (Mon–Fri), 9 am to 12:30 pm (Sat). Closed Sundays 🚇 Leave Exit 5 of Jongno 3-ga Station, Line 5 and walk 100m in the direction of Tapgol Park. Swing a left at Mr. Choi's Suit Shop and walk about 90m. ☎ 02-766-0000 🖥 www.choonwondang.co.kr

COOKING

There are many programs in which foreigners can learn to cook Korean dishes. Prices at each institute differ, but they generally range from about 40,000 won to 100,000 won.

Institute of Traditional Korean Food

At this institute, participants learn to make traditional Korean drinks, rice cakes, and a few dishes of royal cuisine.
💷 50,000 to 70,000 won, depending on class 🚇 Jongno 3-ga, Lines 1, 3 and 5, Exit 6
☎ 02-741-5411 🖱 www.kfr.or.kr

Son's Home

The Son family hosts guests to learn about Korean cooking in the comfort of their home, where many generations of Sons have lived. Visitors learn to make *kimchi*, set up a traditional tea table, and play traditional Korean instruments.
💷 60,000 to 70,000 won, depending on the class 🚇 Yeoksam Station, Line 2, Exit 3
☎ 02-562-6829 🖱 www.sons-home.com

Yoo's Family

This cultural program, hosted by the Yoo family, teaches visitors how to make *kimchi*, *jeon* and *tteokbokki*.
💷 20,000 to 60,000 won, depending on the class 🚇 Anguk Station, Line 3, Exit 4
☎ 02-3673-0323 🖱 www.yoosfamily.com

VOLUNTEERING

In a city of this size, there are plenty of organizations to which visitors can donate their time and talents. Most volunteer organizations use native English speakers for proofreading, editing and/or teaching English.

Willing Workers on Organic Farms (WWOOF)

Since 1996, WWOOF Korea has been connecting foreign visitors with organic farms in Korea, where volunteers can work four to six hours a day in exchange for room and board and the opportunity to experience rural Korean culture. WWOOF

experiences usually last between one week and several months, although individual arrangements must be made with the owners of the particular farm. WWOOF Korea is a member of WWOOF International.

☎ 02-723-4510 🖰 www.wwoofkorea.co.kr

Korea International Volunteer Organization

Although this organization primarily works on providing aid to populations in need in developing countries, KVO volunteers also support facilities for local homeless elderly persons and orphans. The organization also runs an environmental protection program, which includes leading environmental education field trips for students.

☎ 02-471-1004 🖰 www.kvo.or.kr

HOPE (Helping Others Prosper through English)

A relatively new nonprofit organization started by a group of Canadian teachers, this group's objective is to provide free, accessible English education to those underprivileged students in Korea who do not have the resources to enroll in expensive academies like their wealthier classmates. Because English language skills have become an essential part of enjoying a bright future in Korea, HOPE helps less privileged students stay on par with their peers. Currently, HOPE volunteers at a couple of community centers and an orphanage.

☎ 010-2414-5683 (volunteer director) 🖰 www.alwayshope.or.kr

Planting Love

While not actually a volunteer opportunity, per se, Planting Love—a Catholic charity group run by the Sisters of Charity of Seton Hall—operates a rehabilitation center in the southwestern city of Gwangju and a school for the visually impaired in Chungju. They can always use a donation—see www. plantinglove.com for more information.

INDEX

SEOUL SUBWAY MAP

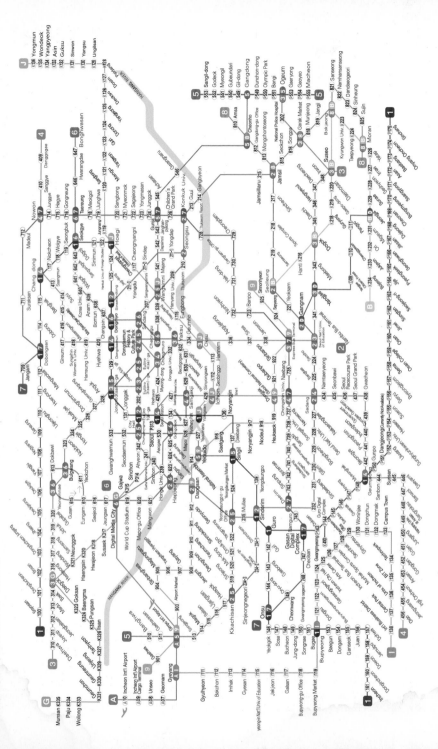

Central Seoul Subway Map

BUSAN SUBWAY MAP

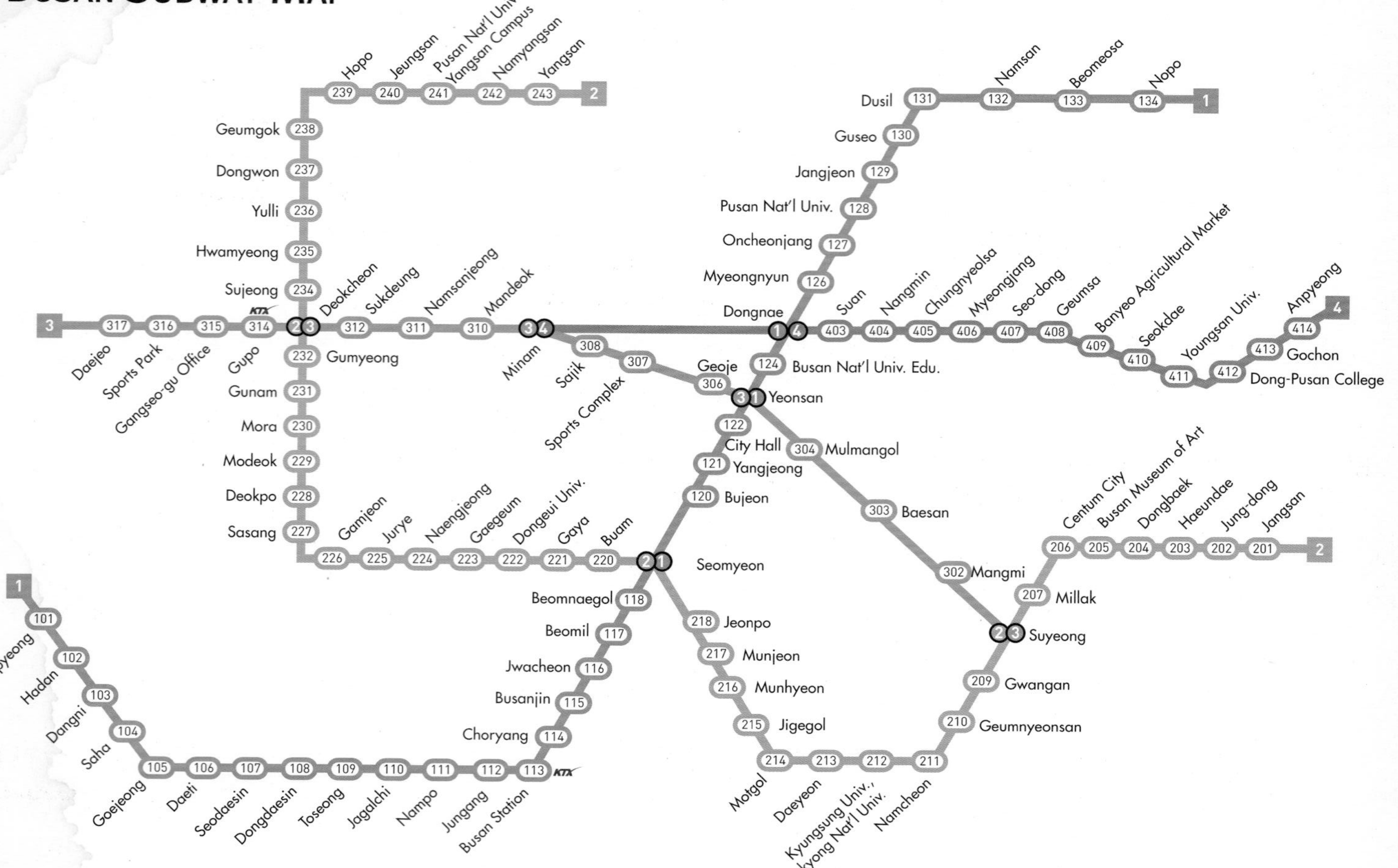

Line 1
- 101 Sinpyeong
- 102 Hadan
- 103 Danggri
- 104 Saha
- 105 Goejeong
- 106 Daeti
- 107 Seodaesin
- 108 Dongdaesin
- 109 Toseong
- 110 Jagalchi
- 111 Nampo
- 112 Jungang
- 113 Busan Station
- 114 Choryang
- 115 Busanjin
- 116 Jwacheon
- 117 Beomil
- 118 Beomnaegol
- 119 Seomyeon
- 120 Bujeon
- 121 Yangjeong
- 122 City Hall
- 123 Yeonsan
- 124 Busan Nat'l Univ. Edu.
- 125 Dongnae
- 126 Myeongnyun
- 127 Oncheonjang
- 128 Pusan Nat'l Univ.
- 129 Jangjeon
- 130 Guseo
- 131 Dusil
- 132 Namsan
- 133 Beomeosa
- 134 Nopo

Line 2
- 201 Jangsan
- 202 Jung-dong
- 203 Haeundae
- 204 Dongbaek
- 205 Busan Museum of Art
- 206 Centum City
- 207 Millak
- 208 Suyeong
- 209 Gwangan
- 210 Geumnyeonsan
- 211 Namcheon
- 212 Kyungsung Univ.·Pukyong Nat'l Univ
- 213 Daeyeon
- 214 Mothgol
- 215 Jigegol
- 216 Munhyeon
- 217 Munjeon
- 218 Jeonpo
- 219 Seomyeon
- 220 Buam
- 221 Gaya
- 222 Dongeui Univ.
- 223 Gaegeum
- 224 Naengjeong
- 225 Jurye
- 226 Gamjeon
- 227 Sasang
- 228 Deokpo
- 229 Modeok
- 230 Mora
- 231 Gunam
- 232 Gumyeong
- 233 Deokcheon
- 234 Sujeong
- 235 Hwamyeong
- 236 Yulli
- 237 Dongwon
- 238 Geumgok
- 239 Hopo
- 240 Jeungsan
- 241 Busan Nat'l Univ. Yangsan Campus
- 242 Namyangsan
- 243 Yangsan

Line 3
- 301 Suyeong
- 302 Mangmi
- 303 Baesan
- 304 Mulmangol
- 305 Yeonsan
- 306 Geoje
- 307 Sports Complex
- 308 Sajik
- 309 Minam
- 310 Mandeok
- 311 Namsanjeong
- 312 Sukdeung
- 313 Deokcheon
- 314 Gupo
- 315 Gangseo-gu Office
- 316 Sports Park
- 317 Daejeo

Line 4
- 403 Dongnae
- 404 Suan
- 405 Nangmin
- 406 Chungnyeolsa
- 407 Myeongjang
- 408 Seo-dong
- 409 Geumsa
- 410 Banyeo Agricultural Market
- 411 Seokdae
- 412 Youngson Univ.
- 413 Dong-Pusan College
- 414 Gochon
- Anpyeong

Daegu Subway Map

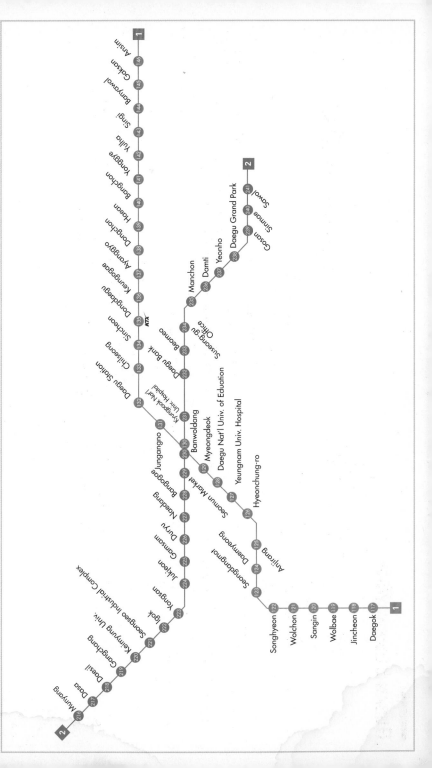

DAEJEON SUBWAY MAP

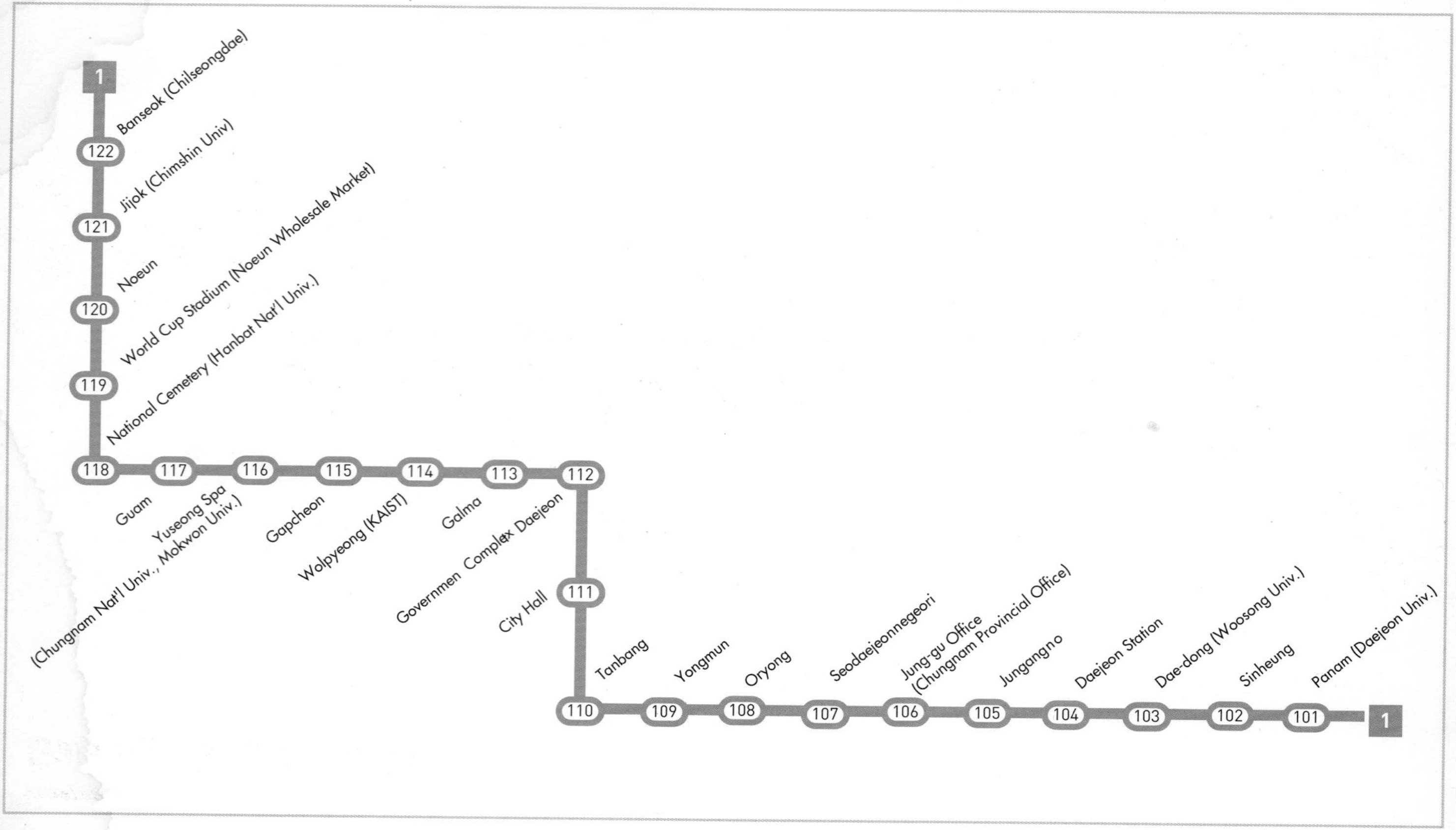

1

101 Panam (Daejeon Univ.)
102 Sinheung
103 Dae-dong (Woosong Univ.)
104 Daejeon Station
105 Jungangno
106 Jung-gu Office (Chungnam Provincial Office)
107 Seodaejeonnegeori
108 Oryong
109 Yongmun
110 Tanbang
111 City Hall
112 Government Complex Daejeon
113 Galma
114 Wolpyeong (KAIST)
115 Gapcheon
116 Yuseong Spa (Mokwon Univ.)
117 Guam (Chungnam Nat'l Univ., Mokwon Univ.)
118 National Cemetery (Hanbat Nat'l Univ.)
119 World Cup Stadium (Noeun Wholesale Market)
120 Noeun
121 Jijok (Chimshin Univ.)
122 Banseok (Chilseonggdae)

1

GWANGJU SUBWAY MAP

1

100 Nok-dong
101 Sotae
102 Hak-dong · Jeungsimsa Temple
103 Nam Gwangju
104 Culture Complex (former. South Jeolla Provincial Office)
105 Geumnamno 4-ga
106 Geumnamno 5-ga
107 Yangdong Market
108 Dolgogae
109 Nongseong
110 Hwajeong
111 Ssangchon
112 Uncheon (Honam Univ.)
113 Sangmu
114 Kimdaejung Convention Center (Mareuk)
115 Airport
116 Songjeong Park
117 Songjeong-ri
118 Dosan
119 Pyeong-dong

1

Acknowledgement

It might be my name on the cover, but putting a book together is very much a team effort. Especially so with a guidebook like this. Editor Lee Jin-hyuk and designer Jung Hyun-young deserve special thanks for spending much longer hours putting this book together than anyone rightfully should. This book is just as much their work as it is mine. Thanks should also go to the rest of Seoul Selection's staff for taking the time to confirm phone numbers and times and, worst of all, put together the index. Thanks go out, too, to Helen Lee for copy-editing this book, which at 700-plus pages was no easy task. And of course, a word of thanks go to Ben Jackson for the proof-reading.

Of course, I'd be remiss if I didn't express appreciation to my publisher and my boss Kim Hyung-geun, who not only provides me with gainful employment as a magazine editor, but also gave me yet another opportunity to realize a longstanding goal of mine.

Most importantly, I'd like to thank my wife, Solongo, for her love and encouragement, and express my heartfelt apologies for the countless hours away at the office and on the road.

History Disclaimer

History is a subject that lends itself easy to controversy and disputes, and Korean history is no different. In doing the research for this book, I spent more hours wading through books, magazines, brochures, homepages, blogs, online encyclopedias and wikis—in English and Korean—than I care to count. I tried to be balanced and, more to the point, non-controversial in the historical accounts given in this book, which is, after all, a tourist guidebook, not a university history text. Still, accounts differ, so don't take what you read here as the final word. If you really want to expand your knowledge of Korean history, some English-language resources you may wish to consider are:

Books
- *New History of Korea* by Lee Hyun-hee, et. al. (Jimoondang)
- *Korea Old and New: A History* by Carter Eckert, Ki-baik Lee et. al. (Harvard University Press)
- *Korea's Place in the Sun: A Modern History* by Bruce Cumings (W. W. Norton & Company)

Websites
- Korea.net (www.korea.net)
- Korean History Project (www.koreanhistoryproject.org)

Credits

Publisher	Kim Hyung-geun
Writer	Robert Koehler
Assisting Writers	Peter DeMarco (Upo section), Ben Jackson, Jacqueline Kim
Editor	Lee Jin-hyuk
Assisting Editors	Ko Yeon-kyung, Park Shin-hyung
	Jang Woo-jung, Kim Eugene, Park Hye-young
Copy-Editor	Lee Hyun-ju
Proofreader	Ben Jackson
Designer	Jung Hyun-young
Assisting Designers	Min So-young, Shin Eun-ji, Lee Bok-hyun
Cartographers	Jung Hyun-young, Park Min-cheol
Photographers	Robert Koehler, Ryu Seung-hoo